AND DATA COMMUNICATIONS TECHNOLOGY

WIRELESS COMMUNICATIONS AND NETWORKS

A comprehensive, state-of-the art survey. Covers fundamental wireless communications topics, including antennas and propagation, signal encoding techniques, spread spectrum, and error correction techniques. Examines satellite, cellular, wireless local loop networks and wireless LANs, including Bluetooth and 802.11. Covers Mobile IP and WAP. ISBN 0-13-040864-6

CRYPTOGRAPHY AND NETWORK SECURITY, THIRD EDITION

A tutorial and survey on network security technology. Each of the basic building blocks of network security, including conventional and public-key cryptography, authentication, and digital signatures, are covered. The book covers important network security tools and applications, including S/MIME, IP Security, Kerberos, SSL/TLS, SET, and X509v3. In addition, methods for countering hackers and viruses are explored. **Second edition received the TAA award for the best Computer Science and Engineering Textbook of 1999.** ISBN 0-13-091429-0

NETWORK SECURITY ESSENTIALS, SECOND EDITION

A tutorial and survey on network security technology. The book covers important network security tools and applications, including S/MIME, IP Security, Kerberos, SSL/TLS, SET, and X509v3. In addition, methods for countering hackers and viruses are explored. ISBN 0-13-035128-8

LOCAL AND METROPOLITAN AREA NETWORKS, SIXTH EDITION

An in-depth presentation of the technology and architecture of local and metropolitan area networks. Covers topology, transmission media, medium access control, standards, internetworking, and network management. Provides an up-to-date coverage of LAN/MAN systems, including Fast Ethernet, Fibre Channel, and wireless LANs, plus LAN QoS. **Received the 2001 TAA award for long-term excellence in a Computer Science Textbook.** ISBN 0-13-012939-9

ISDN AND BROADBAND ISDN, WITH FRAME RELAY AND ATM: FOURTH EDITION

An in-depth presentation of the technology and architecture of integrated services digital networks (ISDN). Covers the integrated digital network (IDN), xDSL, ISDN services and architecture, signaling system no. 7 (SS7) and provides detailed coverage of the ITU-T protocol standards. Also provides detailed coverage of protocols and congestion control strategies for both frame relay and ATM. ISBN 0-13-973744-8

W9-BUL-485

OPERATING SYSTEMS
INTERNALS AND DESIGN PRINCIPLES
FIFTH EDITION

William Stallings

PEARSON
Prentice
Hall

Upper Saddle River, New Jersey 07458

Library of Congress Cataloging-in-Publication Data

Stallings, William.
    Operating systems : internals and design principles / William Stallings. — 5th ed.
      p. cm.
    Includes bibliographical references and index.
    ISBN 0–13–147954–7
    1. Operating systems (Computers) I. Title

QA76.76.O63S733 2004
005.4′3 — dc22

2004053108

Vice President and Editorial Director, ECS: *Marcia J. Horton*
Publisher: *Alan Apt*
Associate Editor: *Toni D. Holm*
Editorial Assistant: *Patrick Lindner*
Vice President and Director of Production and Manufacturing, ESM: *David W. Riccardi*
Executive Managing Editor: *Vince O'Brien*
Managing Editor: *Camille Trentacoste*
Production Editor: *Rose Keman*
Cover Photos: *Suzanne Behnke*

Director of Creative Services: *Paul Belfanti*
Creative Director: *Carole Anson*
Art Director: *Maureen Eide*
Cover Designer: *Suzanne Behnke*
Managing Editor, AV Management and Production: *Patricia Burns*
Art Editor: *Gregory Dulles*
Manufacturing Manager: *Trudy Pisciotti*
Manufacturing Buyer: *Lynda Castillo*
Marketing Manager: *Pamela Hersperger*
Marketing Assistant: *Barrie Reinhold*

© 2005, 2001, 1998, 1995, 1992 Pearson Education, Inc.
Pearson Prentice Hall
Pearson Education, Inc.
Upper Saddle River, NJ 07458

Pearson Prentice Hall® is a trademark of Pearson Education, Inc.

The author and publisher of this book have used their best efforts in preparing this book. These efforts include the development, research, and testing of the theories and programs to determine their effectiveness. The author and publisher make no warranty of any kind, expressed or implied, with regard to these programs or the documentation contained in this book. The author and publisher shall not be liable in any event for incidental or consequential damages in connection with, or arising out of, the furnishing, performance, or use of these programs.

Printed in the United States of America
10 9 8 7 6 5 4 3 2 1

ISBN: 0-13-147954-7

Pearson Education Ltd., *London*
Pearson Education Australia Pty. Ltd., *Sydney*
Pearson Education Singapore, Pte. Ltd.
Pearson Education North Asia Ltd., *Hong Kong*
Pearson Education Canada, Inc., *Toronto*
Pearson Educacíon de Mexico, S.A. de C.V.
Pearson Education—Japan, *Tokyo*
Pearson Education Malaysia, Pte. Ltd.
Pearson Education Inc., *Upper Saddle River, New Jersey*

As always,
for my loving and brilliant wife A.
and her constant companion Geoffroi

WEB SITE FOR *OPERATING SYSTEMS: INTERNALS AND DESIGN PRINCIPLES*, FIFTH EDITION

The Web site at WilliamStallings.com/OS/OS5e.html provides support for instructors and students using the book. It includes the following elements.

Course Support Materials

The course support materials include

- Copies of figures from the book in PDF format.
- Copies of tables from the book in PDF format.
- A set of PowerPoint slides for use as lecture aids.
- Lecture notes in HTML that can serve as a useful study aid.
- **Computer Science Student Resource Site**: contains a number of links and documents that students may find useful in their ongoing computer science education. The site includes a review of basic, relevant mathematics; advice on research, writing, and doing homework problems; links to computer science research resources, such as report repositories and bibliographies; and other useful links.
- An errata sheet for the book, updated at most monthly.

Supplemental Documents

The supplemental documents include

- A PDF copy of all the algorithms in the book in an easy-to-read Pascal-like pseudocode.
- All of the Windows, UNIX, and Linux material from the book reproduced in three PDF documents for easy reference.
- A number of documents that expand on the treatment in the book. Topics include complexity of algorithms, Internet standards, and Sockets.

OS Courses

The OS5e Web site includes links to Web sites for courses taught using the book. These sites can provide useful ideas about scheduling and topic ordering, as well as a number of useful handouts and other materials.

Useful Web Sites

The OS5e Web site includes links to relevant Web sites. The links cover a broad spectrum of topics and will enable students to explore timely issues in greater depth.

Internet Mailing List

An Internet mailing list is maintained so that instructors using this book can exchange information, suggestions, and questions with each other and the author. Subscription information is provided at the book's Web site.

Operating System Projects

The Web site includes links to the Nachos and BACI web sites. These are two software packages that serve as frameworks for project implementation. Each site includes downloadable software and background information. See Appendix C for more information.

CONTENTS

PREFACE

OBJECTIVES

This book is about the concepts, structure, and mechanisms of operating systems. Its purpose is to present, as clearly and completely as possible, the nature and characteristics of modern-day operating systems.

This task is challenging for several reasons. First, there is a tremendous range and variety of computer systems for which operating systems are designed. These include single-user workstations and personal computers, medium-sized shared systems, large mainframe and supercomputers, and specialized machines such as real-time systems. The variety is not just in the capacity and speed of machines, but in applications and system support requirements. Second, the rapid pace of change that has always characterized computer systems continues with no letup. A number of key areas in operating system design are of recent origin, and research into these and other new areas continues.

In spite of this variety and pace of change, certain fundamental concepts apply consistently throughout. To be sure, the application of these concepts depends on the current state of technology and the particular application requirements. The intent of this book is to provide a thorough discussion of the fundamentals of operating system design and to relate these to contemporary design issues and to current directions in the development of operating systems.

EXAMPLE SYSTEMS

This text is intended to acquaint the reader with the design principles and implementation issues of contemporary operating systems. Accordingly, a purely conceptual or theoretical treatment would be inadequate. To illustrate the concepts and to tie them to real-world design choices that must be made, three operating systems have been chosen as running examples:

- **Windows XP and Windows 2003:** A multitasking operating system for personal computers, workstations, and servers. As a new operating system, it incorporates in a clean fashion many of the latest developments in operating system technology. In addition, Windows is one of the first important commercial operating systems to rely heavily on object-oriented design principles. This book covers the technology used in the most recent versions of Windows, XP for workstations and PCs, and 2003 for servers.
- **UNIX:** A multiuser operating system, originally intended for minicomputers, but implemented on a wide range of machines from powerful microcomputers to supercomputers. Two flavors of UNIX are included. UNIX SVR4 is a widely used system that incorporates many state-of-the-art features. Solaris is the most widely used commercial version of UNIX. Solaris includes multithreading and other features not found in SVR4 and most other UNIX variants.
- **Linux:** An open-source version of UNIX that is now widely used.

These systems were chosen because of their relevance and representativeness. The discussion of the example systems is distributed throughout the text rather than assembled as a single chapter or appendix. Thus, during the discussion of concurrency, the concurrency mechanisms of each example system are described, and the motivation for the individual design choices is discussed. With this approach, the design concepts discussed in a given chapter are immediately reinforced with real-world examples.

INTENDED AUDIENCE

The book is intended for both an academic and a professional audience. As a textbook, it is intended as a one-semester undergraduate course in operating systems for computer science, computer engineering, and electrical engineering majors. It covers the topics recommended in *Computer Curricula 2001*, from the Joint Task Force on Computing Curricula of the IEEE Computer Society and the ACM, for the Undergraduate Program in Computer Science. The book also covers the topics recommended in the *Guidelines for Associate-Degree Curricula in Computer Science 2002*, also from the Joint Task Force on Computing Curricula of the IEEE Computer Society and the ACM. The book also serves as a basic reference volume and is suitable for self-study.

PLAN OF THE TEXT

The book is divided into six parts (see Chapter 0 for an overview):
- Background
- Processes
- Memory
- Scheduling
- Input/Output and files
- Distributed systems and Security

The book includes a number of pedagogic features, including the use of numerous figures and tables to clarify the discussion. Each chapter includes a list of key words, review questions, problems, suggestions for further reading, and pointers to relevant Web sites. In addition, a test bank is available to instructors.

INTERNET SERVICES FOR INSTRUCTORS AND STUDENTS

There is a Web site for this book that provides support for students and instructors. The site includes links to other relevant sites, transparency masters of figures and tables in the book in PDF (Adobe Acrobat) format, PowerPoint slides and sign-up information for the book's Internet mailing list. The Web page is at WilliamStallings.com/OS/OS5e.html. See the section, "Web Site for Operating Systems: Internals and Design Principles," preceding this Preface, for more information. An Internet mailing list has been set up so that instructors using this book can exchange information, suggestions, and questions with each other and with the author. As soon as typos or other errors are discovered, an errata list for this book will be available at WilliamStallings.com. Finally, I maintain the Computer Science Student Resource Site at WilliamStallings.com/StudentSupport.html.

OPERATING SYSTEM PROJECTS

For many instructors, an important component of an OS course is a project or set of projects by which the student gets hands-on experience to reinforce concepts from the text. This book provides an unparalleled degree of support for including a projects component in the course. In the body of the text, two major programming projects are defined. The Instructor's Web site offers on-line references that can be used by students to tackle these projects in a step-by-step fashion. Information is provided on three software packages that serve as frameworks for project implementation: OSP and Nachos for developing components of an OS, and BACI for studying concurrency mechanisms. In addition, the Instructor's Web site includes a series of small programming projects, each intended to take a week or two, that cover a broad range of topics and that can be implemented in any suitable language on any platform, as well as research projects and reading/report assignments. See the appendices for details.

WHAT'S NEW IN THE FIFTH EDITION

In the four years since the fourth edition of this book was published, the field has seen continued innovations and improvements. In this new edition, I try to capture these changes while maintaining a broad and comprehensive coverage of the entire field. To begin the process of revision, the fourth edition of this book was extensively reviewed by a number of professors who teach the subject and by professionals working in the field. The result is that, in many places, the narrative has been clarified and tightened, and illustrations have been improved. Also, a number of new "field-tested" problems have been added.

Beyond these refinements to improve pedagogy and user friendliness, the technical content of the book has been updated throughout, to reflect the ongoing changes in this exciting field. The case study for Linux has been significantly expanded and is based on the most recent version, Linux 2.6. The Windows case study has been updated to reflect Windows XP and Windows Server 2003. The material on concurrency has been expanded and revised for greater clarity. Some of the concurrency material has been moved to a new appendix, and a new section on race conditions has been added. The scheduling treatment now includes a discussion of priority inversion. There is a new chapter on networking, including a discussion of the Sockets API. The treatment of object-oriented design has been expanded.

ACKNOWLEDGMENTS

This new edition has benefited from review by a number of people, who gave generously of their time and expertise. These include Stephen Murrell (University of Miami), David Krumme (Tufts University), Duncan Buell (University of South Carolina), Amit Jain (Bosie State University), Fred Kuhns (Washington University, St. Louis), Mark McCullen (Michigan State University), Jayson Rock (University of Wisconsin- Madison), David Middleton (Arkansas Technological University), and Binhai Zhu (Montana State University), all of whom reviewed most or all of the book.

Thanks also to the many people who provided detailed reviews of one or more chapters: Javier Eraso Helguera, Andrew Cheese, Robert Kaiser, Bhavin Ghandi, Joshua Cope, Luca Venuti, Gregory Sharp, Marisa Gil, Balbir Singh, Mrugesh Gajjar, Bruce Janson, Mayan Moudgill, Pete Bixby, Sonja Tideman, Siddharth Choudhuri, Zhihui Zhang, Andrew Huo

Zhigang, Yibing Wang, Darío Álvarez, and Michael Tsai. I would also like to thank Tigran Aivazian, author of the Linux Kernel Internals document, which is part of the Linux Documentation Project, for the review of the material on Linux 2.6. Ching-Kuang Shene (Michigan Tech University) provided the examples used in the section on race conditions and reviewed the section.

In addition, Fernando Ariel Gont contributed a number of homework problems; he also provided detailed reviews of all of the chapters.

I would also like to thank Michael Kifer and Scott A. Smolka (SUNY–Stony Brook), for contributing Appendix D; Bill Bynum (College of William and Mary) and Tracy Camp (Colorado School of Mines) for contributing Appendix E; Steve Taylor (Worcester Polytechnic Institute) for contributing the programming projects and reading/report assignments in the instructor's manual; and Professor Tan N. Nguyen (George Mason University) for contributing the research projects in the instruction manual. Ian G. Graham (Griffith University) contributed the two programming projects in the textbook. Oskars Rieksts (Kutztown University) generously allowed me to make use of his lecture notes, quizzes, and projects.

Finally, I would like to thank the many people responsible for the publication of the book, all of whom did their usual excellent job. This includes the staff at Prentice Hall, particularly my editors Alan Apt and Toni Holm, their assistant Patrick Lindner, production manager Rose Kernan, and supplements manager Sarah Parker. Also, Jake Warde of Warde Publishers managed the reviews; and Patricia M. Daly did the copy editing.

CHAPTER 0

READER'S GUIDE

This book, with its accompanying Web site, covers a lot of material. Here we give the reader an overview.

0.1 OUTLINE OF THE BOOK

The book is organized in seven parts:

Part One. Background: Provides an overview of computer architecture and organization, with emphasis on topics that relate to operating system design, plus an overview of the OS topics in remainder of the book.

Part Two. Processes: Presents a detailed analysis of processes, multithreading, symmetric multiprocessing (SMP), and microkernels. This part also examines the key aspects of concurrency on a single system, with emphasis on issues of mutual exclusion and deadlock.

Part Three. Memory: Provides a comprehensive survey of techniques for memory management, including virtual memory.

Part Four. Scheduling: Provides a comparative discussion of various approaches to process scheduling. Thread scheduling, SMP scheduling, and real-time scheduling are also examined.

Part Five. Input/Output and Files: Examines the issues involved in OS control of the I/O function. Special attention is devoted to disk I/O, which is the key to system performance. Also provides an overview of file management.

Part Six. Distributed Systems and Security: Examines the major trends in the networking of computer systems, including TCP/IP, client/server computing, and clusters. Also describes some of the key design areas in the development of distributed operating systems. Chapter 16 provides a survey of threats and mechanisms for providing computer and network security.

This text is intended to acquaint you with the design principles and implementation issues of contemporary operating systems. Accordingly, a purely conceptual or theoretical treatment would be inadequate. To illustrate the concepts and to tie them to real-world design choices that must be made, two operating systems have been chosen as running examples:

- **Windows:** A multitasking operating system designed to run on a variety of PCs, workstations, and servers. It is one of the few recent commercial operating systems that have essentially been designed from scratch. As such, it is in a position to incorporate in a clean fashion the latest developments in operating system technology.
- **UNIX:** A multitasking operating system originally intended for minicomputers but implemented on a wide range of machines from powerful microcomputers to supercomputers. Included under this topic is Linux.

The discussion of the example systems is distributed throughout the text rather than assembled as a single chapter or appendix. Thus, during the discussion of concurrency, the concurrency mechanisms of each example system are described, and the motivation for the individual design choices is discussed. With this approach, the design concepts discussed in a given chapter are immediately reinforced with real-world examples.

0.2 TOPIC ORDERING

It would be natural for the reader to question the particular ordering of topics presented in this book. For example, the topic of scheduling (Chapters 9 and 10) is closely related to those of concurrency (Chapters 5 and 6) and the general topic of processes (Chapter 3) and might reasonably be covered immediately after those topics.

The difficulty is that the various topics are highly interrelated. For example, in discussing virtual memory, it is useful to refer to the scheduling issues related to a page fault. Of course, it is also useful to refer to some memory management issues when discussing scheduling decisions. This type of example can be repeated endlessly: A discussion of scheduling requires some understanding of I/O management and vice versa.

Figure 0.1 suggests some of the important interrelationships between topics. The bold lines indicate very strong relationships, from the point of view of design and implementation decisions. Based on this diagram, it makes sense to begin with a basic discussion of processes, which we do in Chapter 3. After that, the order is

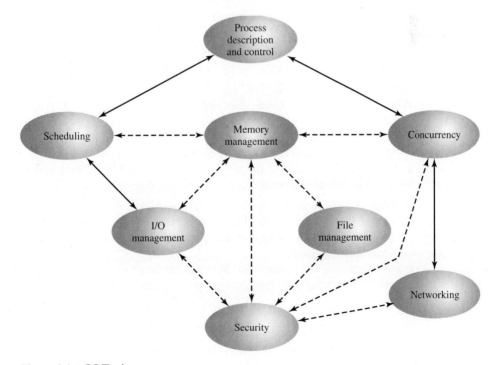

Figure 0.1 OS Topics

somewhat arbitrary. Many treatments of operating systems bunch all of the material on processes at the beginning and then deal with other topics. This is certainly valid. However, the central significance of memory management, which I believe is of equal importance to process management, has led to a decision to present this material prior to an in-depth look at scheduling.

The ideal solution is for the student, after completing chapters 1 through 3 in series, to read and absorb the following chapters in parallel: 4 followed by (optional) 5; 6 followed by 7; 8 followed by (optional) 9; 10. Finally, do the following chapters in any order: 11; 12 followed by 13; 14; 15. However, although the human brain may engage in parallel processing, the human student finds it impossible (and expensive) to work successfully with four copies of the same book simultaneously open to four different chapters. Given the necessity for a linear ordering, I think that the ordering used in this book is the most effective.

0.3 INTERNET AND WEB RESOURCES

There are a number of resources available on the Internet and the Web to support this book and to help one keep up with developments in this field.

Web Sites for This Book

A special Web page has been set up for this book at **WilliamStallings.com/ OS/OS5e.html**. See the two-page layout at the beginning of this book for a detailed description of that site. Of particular note are two documents available at the Web site for the student:

- **Pseudocode:** For those readers not comfortable with C, all of the algorithms are also reproduced in a Pascal-like pseudocode. This pseudocode language is intuitive and particularly easy to follow.

- **Windows, UNIX, and Linux descriptions:** As was mentioned, Windows and various flavors of UNIX are used as running case studies, with the discussion distributed throughout the text rather than assembled as a single chapter or appendix. Some readers would like to have all of this material in one place as a reference. Accordingly, all of the Windows and UNIX material from the book is reproduced in three documents at the Web site.

As soon as any typos or other errors are discovered, an errata list for this book will be available at the Web site. Please report any errors that you spot. Errata sheets for my other books, as well as discount ordering information for the books, are at **WilliamStallings.com.**

I also maintain the Computer Science Student Resource Site, at **William Stallings.com/StudentSupport.html**; the purpose of this site is to provide documents, information, and links for computer science students. Links are organized into four categories:

- **Math:** Includes a basic math refresher, a queuing analysis primer, a number system primer, and links to numerous math sites.

- **How-to:** Advice and guidance for solving homework problems, writing technical reports, and preparing technical presentations.
- **Research resources:** Links to important collections of papers, technical reports, and bibliographies.
- **Miscellaneous:** A variety of useful documents and links.

Other Web Sites

There are numerous Web sites that provide information related to the topics of this book. In subsequent chapters, pointers to specific Web sites can be found in the "Recommended Reading" section. Because the URL for a particular Web site may change, I have not included URLs in the book. For all of the Web sites listed in the book, the appropriate link can be found at this book's Web site.

USENET Newsgroups

A number of USENET newsgroups are devoted to some aspect of operating systems or to a particular operating system. As with virtually all USENET groups, there is a high noise-to-signal ratio, but it is worth experimenting to see if any meet your needs. The most relevant are as follows:

- **comp.os.research:** The best group to follow. This is a moderated newsgroup that deals with research topics.
- **comp.os.misc:** A general discussion of OS topics.
- **comp.unix.internals**
- **comp.os.linux.development.system**

PART ONE

Background

Part One provides a background and context for the remainder of this book. This part presents the fundamental concepts of computer architecture and operating system internals.

Chapter 1 Computer System Overview

An operating system mediates among application programs, utilities, and users, on the one hand, and the computer system hardware on the other. To appreciate the functionality of the operating system and the design issues involved, one must have some appreciation for computer organization and architecture. Chapter 1 provides a brief survey of the processor, memory, and I/O elements of a computer system.

Chapter 2 Operating System Overview

The topic of operating system (OS) design covers a huge territory, and it is easy to get lost in the details and lose the context of a discussion of a particular issue. Chapter 2 provides an overview to which the reader can return at any point in the book for context. We begin with a statement of the objectives and functions of an operating system. Then some historically important systems and OS functions are described. This discussion allows us to present some fundamental OS design principles in a simple environment so that the relationship among various OS functions is clear. The chapter next highlights important characteristics of modern operating systems. Throughout the book, as various topics are discussed, it is necessary to talk about both fundamental, well-established principles as well as more recent innovations in OS design. The discussion in this chapter alerts the reader to this blend of established and recent design approaches that must be addressed. Finally, we present an overview of Windows and UNIX; this discussion establishes the general architecture of these systems, providing context for the detailed discussions to follow.

COMPUTER SYSTEM OVERVIEW

An operating system exploits the hardware resources of one or more processors to provide a set of services to system users. The operating system also manages secondary memory and I/O (input/output) devices on behalf of its users. Accordingly, it is important to have some understanding of the underlying computer system hardware before we begin our examination of operating systems.

This chapter provides an overview of computer system hardware. In most areas, the survey is brief, as it is assumed that the reader is familiar with this subject. However, several areas are covered in some detail because of their importance to topics covered later in the book.

1.1 BASIC ELEMENTS

At a top level, a computer consists of processor, memory, and I/O components, with one or more modules of each type. These components are interconnected in some fashion to achieve the main function of the computer, which is to execute programs. Thus, there are four main structural elements:

- **Processor:** Controls the operation of the computer and performs its data processing functions. When there is only one processor, it is often referred to as the **central processing unit** (CPU).
- **Main memory:** Stores data and programs. This memory is typically volatile; that is, when the computer is shut down, the contents of the memory are lost. In contrast, the contents of disk memory are retained even when the computer system is shut down. Main memory is also referred to as *real memory* or *primary memory*.
- **I/O modules:** Move data between the computer and its external environment. The external environment consists of a variety of devices, including secondary memory devices (e.g., disks), communications equipment, and terminals.
- **System bus:** Provides for communication among processors, main memory, and I/O modules.

Figure 1.1 depicts these top-level components. One of the processor's functions is to exchange data with memory. For this purpose, it typically makes use of two internal (to the processor) registers: a memory address register (MAR), which specifies the address in memory for the next read or write; and a memory buffer register (MBR), which contains the data to be written into memory or which receives the data read from memory. Similarly, an I/O address register (I/OAR) specifies a particular I/O device. An I/O buffer register (I/OBR) is used for the exchange of data between an I/O module and the processor.

A memory module consists of a set of locations, defined by sequentially numbered addresses. Each location contains a bit pattern that can be interpreted as either an instruction or data. An I/O module transfers data from external devices to processor and memory, and vice versa. It contains internal buffers for temporarily holding data until they can be sent on.

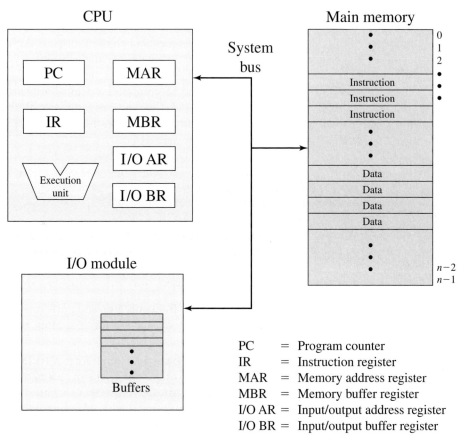

Figure 1.1   Computer Components: Top-Level View

1.2   PROCESSOR REGISTERS

A processor includes a set of registers that provide a type of memory that is faster and smaller than main memory. The registers in the processor serve two functions:

- **User-visible registers:** Enable the machine- or assembly-language programmer to minimize main memory references by optimizing register use. For high-level languages, an optimizing compiler will attempt to make intelligent choices of which variables to assign to registers and which to main memory locations. Some high-level languages, such as C, allow the programmer to suggest to the compiler which variables should be held in registers.

- **Control and status registers:** Used by the processor to control the operation of the processor and by privileged, operating system routines to control the execution of programs.

There is not a clean separation of registers into these two categories. For example, on some machines the program counter is user visible, but on many it is not. For purposes of the following discussion, however, it is convenient to use these categories.

User-Visible Registers

A user-visible register may be referenced by means of the machine language that the processor executes and is generally available to all programs, including application programs as well as system programs. Types of registers that are typically available are data, address, and condition code registers.

Data registers can be assigned to a variety of functions by the programmer. In some cases, they are general purpose in nature and can be used with any machine instruction that performs operations on data. Often, however, there are restrictions. For example, there may be dedicated registers for floating-point operations and others for integer operations.

Address registers contain main memory addresses of data and instructions, or they contain a portion of the address that is used in the calculation of the complete or effective address. These registers may themselves be general purpose, or may be devoted to a particular way, or mode, of addressing memory. Examples include the following:

- **Index register:** Indexed addressing is a common mode of addressing that involves adding an index to a base value to get the effective address.
- **Segment pointer:** With segmented addressing, memory is divided into segments, which are variable-length blocks of words.[1] A memory reference consists of a reference to a particular segment and an offset within the segment; this mode of addressing is important in our discussion of memory management in Chapter 7. In this mode of addressing, a register is used to hold the base address (starting location) of the segment. There may be multiple registers; for example, one for the operating system (i.e., when operating system code is executing on the processor) and one for the currently executing application.
- **Stack pointer:** If there is user-visible stack[2] addressing, then there is a dedicated register that points to the top of the stack. This allows the use of instructions that contain no address field, such as push and pop.

In some machines, a procedure or subroutine call will result in automatic saving of all user-visible registers, to be restored on return. The saving and restoring is performed by the processor as part of the execution of the call and return instructions. This allows each procedure to use these registers independently. On other machines, it is the responsibility of the programmer to save the contents of the relevant user-visible registers prior to a procedure call, by including instructions for this purpose in the program.

---

[1]There is no universal definition of the term *word*. In general, a **word** is an ordered set of bytes or bits that is the normal unit in which information may be stored, transmitted, or operated on within a given computer. Typically, if a processor has a fixed-length instruction set, then the instruction length equals the word length.

[2]A stack is located in main memory and is a sequential set of locations that are referenced similarly to a physical stack of papers, by putting on and taking away from the top. See Appendix 1B for a discussion of stack processing.

Thus, the saving and restoring functions may be performed in either hardware or software, depending on the processor.

Control and Status Registers

A variety of processor registers are employed to control the operation of the processor. On most machines, most of these are not visible to the user. Some of them may be accessible by machine instructions executed in what is referred to as a control or operating system mode.

Of course, different machines will have different register organizations and use different terminology. We provide here a reasonably complete list of register types, with a brief description. In addition to the MAR, MBR, I/OAR, and I/OBR registers mentioned earlier (Figure 1.1), the following are essential to instruction execution:

- **Program counter (PC):** Contains the address of the next instruction to be fetched.
- **Instruction register (IR):** Contains the instruction most recently fetched.

All processor designs also include a register or set of registers, often known as the program status word (PSW), that contains status information. The PSW typically contains condition codes plus other status information, such as an interrupt enable/disable bit and a supervisor/user mode bit.

Condition codes (also referred to as *flags*) are bits typically set by the processor hardware as the result of operations. For example, an arithmetic operation may produce a positive, negative, zero, or overflow result. In addition to the result itself being stored in a register or memory, a condition code is also set following the execution of the arithmetic instruction. The condition code may subsequently be tested as part of a conditional branch operation. Condition code bits are collected into one or more registers. Usually, they form part of a control register. Generally, machine instructions allow these bits to be read by implicit reference, but they cannot be altered by explicit reference because they are intended for feedback regarding the results of instruction execution.

In machines using multiple types of interrupts, a set of interrupt registers may be provided, with one pointer to each interrupt-handling routine. If a stack is used to implement certain functions (e.g., procedure call), then a system stack pointer is needed (see Appendix 1B). Memory management hardware, discussed in Chapter 7, requires dedicated registers. Finally, registers may be used in the control of I/O operations.

A number of factors go into the design of the control and status register organization. One key issue is operating system support. Certain types of control information are of specific utility to the operating system. If the processor designer has a functional understanding of the operating system to be used, then the register organization can be designed to provide hardware support for particular features such as memory protection and switching between user programs.

Another key design decision is the allocation of control information between registers and memory. It is common to dedicate the first (lowest) few hundred or thousand words of memory for control purposes. The designer must decide how much control information should be in more expensive, faster registers and how much in less expensive, slower main memory.

1.3 INSTRUCTION EXECUTION

A program to be executed by a processor consists of a set of instructions stored in memory. In its simplest form, instruction processing consists of two steps: The processor reads (*fetches*) instructions from memory one at a time and executes each instruction. Program execution consists of repeating the process of instruction fetch and instruction execution. The instruction execution may involve several operations and depends on the nature of the instruction.

The processing required for a single instruction is called an *instruction cycle*. Using the simplified two-step description, the instruction cycle is depicted in Figure 1.2. The two steps are referred to as the *fetch stage* and the *execute stage*. Program execution halts only if the machine is turned off, some sort of unrecoverable error occurs, or a program instruction that halts the processor is encountered.

Instruction Fetch and Execute

At the beginning of each instruction cycle, the processor fetches an instruction from memory. In a typical processor, the program counter (PC) holds the address of the next instruction to be fetched. Unless instructed otherwise, the processor always increments the PC after each instruction fetch so that it will fetch the next instruction in sequence (i.e., the instruction located at the next higher memory address). So, for example, consider a simplified computer in which each instruction occupies one 16-bit word of memory. Assume that the program counter is set to location 300. The processor will next fetch the instruction at location 300. On succeeding instruction cycles, it will fetch instructions from locations 301, 302, 303, and so on. This sequence may be altered, as explained subsequently.

The fetched instruction is loaded into a register in the processor known as the instruction register (IR). The instruction contains bits that specify the action the processor is to take. The processor interprets the instruction and performs the required action. In general, these actions fall into four categories:

- **Processor-memory:** Data may be transferred from processor to memory or from memory to processor.
- **Processor-I/O:** Data may be transferred to or from a peripheral device by transferring between the processor and an I/O module.

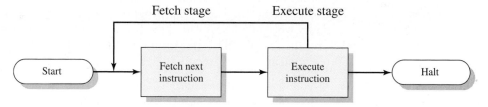

Figure 1.2 Basic Instruction Cycle

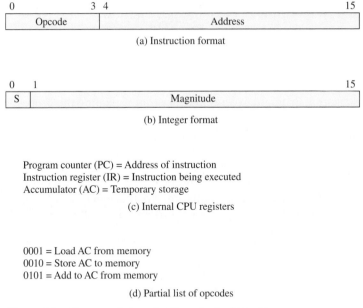

Figure 1.3   Characteristics of a Hypothetical Machine

- **Data processing:** The processor may perform some arithmetic or logic operation on data.
- **Control:** An instruction may specify that the sequence of execution be altered. For example, the processor may fetch an instruction from location 149, which specifies that the next instruction be from location 182. The processor sets the program counter to 182. Thus, on the next fetch stage, the instruction will be fetched from location 182 rather than 150.

An instruction's execution may involve a combination of these actions.

Consider a simple example using a hypothetical machine that includes the characteristics listed in Figure 1.3. The processor contains a single data register, called the accumulator (AC). Both instructions and data are 16 bits long, and memory is organized as a sequence of 16-bit words. The instruction format provides 4 bits for the opcode, allowing as many as $2^4 = 16$ different opcodes (represented by a single hexadecimal[3] digit). With the remaining 12 bits of the instruction format, up to $2^{12} = 4,096$ (4K) words of memory (denoted by three hexadecimal digits) can be directly addressed.

Figure 1.4 illustrates a partial program execution, showing the relevant portions of memory and processor registers. The program fragment shown adds the contents of the memory word at address 940 to the contents of the memory word at address 941 and stores the result in the latter location. Three instructions, which can be described as three fetch and three execute stages, are required:

---

[3]A basic refresher on number systems (decimal, binary, hexadecimal) can be found at the Computer Science Student Resource Site at **WilliamStallings.com/StudentSupport.html.**

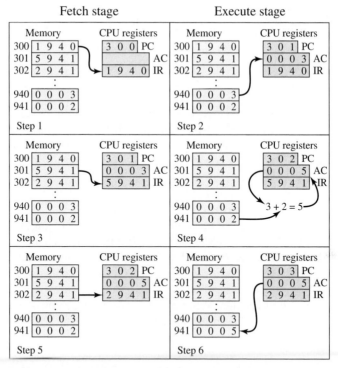

Figure 1.4 Example of Program Execution (contents of memory and registers in hexadecimal)

1. The PC contains 300, the address of the first instruction. This instruction (the value 1940 in hexadecimal) is loaded into the instruction register IR and the PC is incremented. Note that this process involves the use of a memory address register (MAR) and a memory buffer register (MBR). For simplicity, these intermediate registers are not shown.

2. The first 4 bits (first hexadecimal digit) in the IR indicate that the AC is to be loaded from memory. The remaining 12 bits (three hexadecimal digits) specify the address, which is 940.

3. The next instruction (5941) is fetched from location 301 and the PC is incremented.

4. The old contents of the AC and the contents of location 941 are added and the result is stored in the AC.

5. The next instruction (2941) is fetched from location 302 and the PC is incremented.

6. The contents of the AC are stored in location 941.

In this example, three instruction cycles, each consisting of a fetch stage and an execute stage, are needed to add the contents of location 940 to the contents of 941. With a more complex set of instructions, fewer instruction cycles would be needed. Most modern processors include instructions that contain more than one address. Thus the execution stage for a particular instruction may involve more than one reference to memory. Also, instead of memory references, an instruction may specify an I/O operation.

I/O Function

Data can be exchanged directly between an I/O module (e.g., a disk controller) and the processor. Just as the processor can initiate a read or write with memory, specifying the address of a memory location, the processor can also read data from or write data to an I/O module. In this latter case, the processor identifies a specific device that is controlled by a particular I/O module. Thus, an instruction sequence similar in form to that of Figure 1.4 could occur, with I/O instructions rather than memory-referencing instructions.

In some cases, it is desirable to allow I/O exchanges to occur directly with memory to relieve the processor of the I/O task. In such a case, the processor grants to an I/O module the authority to read from or write to memory, so that the I/O-memory transfer can occur without tying up the processor. During such a transfer, the I/O module issues read or write commands to memory, relieving the processor of responsibility for the exchange. This operation, known as direct memory access (DMA), is examined later in this chapter.

1.4 INTERRUPTS

Virtually all computers provide a mechanism by which other modules (I/O, memory) may interrupt the normal sequencing of the processor. Table 1.1 lists the most common classes of interrupts.

Interrupts are provided primarily as a way to improve processor utilization. For example, most I/O devices are much slower than the processor. Suppose that the processor is transferring data to a printer using the instruction cycle scheme of Figure 1.2. After each write operation, the processor must pause and remain idle until the printer catches up. The length of this pause may be on the order of many

Table 1.1 Classes of Interrupts

Program	Generated by some condition that occurs as a result of an instruction execution, such as arithmetic overflow, division by zero, attempt to execute an illegal machine instruction, and reference outside a user's allowed memory space.
Timer	Generated by a timer within the processor. This allows the operating system to perform certain functions on a regular basis.
I/O	Generated by an I/O controller, to signal normal completion of an operation or to signal a variety of error conditions.
Hardware failure	Generated by a failure, such as power failure or memory parity error.

thousands or even millions of instruction cycles. Clearly, this is a very wasteful use of the processor.

To give a specific example, consider a PC that operates at 1 GHz, which would allow roughly 10^9 instructions per second.[4] A typical hard disk has a rotational speed of 7200 revolutions per minute for a half-track rotation time of 4 ms, which is 4 million times slower than the processor.

Figure 1.5a illustrates this state of affairs. The user program performs a series of WRITE calls interleaved with processing. Code segments 1, 2, and 3 refer to sequences of instructions that do not involve I/O. The WRITE calls are to an I/O routine that is a system utility and that will perform the actual I/O operation. The I/O program consists of three sections:

- A sequence of instructions, labeled 4 in the figure, to prepare for the actual I/O operation. This may include copying the data to be output into a special buffer and preparing the parameters for a device command.
- The actual I/O command. Without the use of interrupts, once this command is issued, the program must wait for the I/O device to perform the requested function (or periodically check the status, or poll, the I/O device). The program might wait by simply repeatedly performing a test operation to determine if the I/O operation is done.
- A sequence of instructions, labeled 5 in the figure, to complete the operation. This may include setting a flag indicating the success or failure of the operation.

Because the I/O operation may take a relatively long time to complete, the I/O program is hung up waiting for the operation to complete; hence, the user program is stopped at the point of the WRITE call for some considerable period of time.

Interrupts and the Instruction Cycle

With interrupts, the processor can be engaged in executing other instructions while an I/O operation is in progress. Consider the flow of control in Figure 1.5b. As before, the user program reaches a point at which it makes a system call in the form of a WRITE call. The I/O program that is invoked in this case consists only of the preparation code and the actual I/O command. After these few instructions have been executed, control returns to the user program. Meanwhile, the external device is busy accepting data from computer memory and printing it. This I/O operation is conducted concurrently with the execution of instructions in the user program.

When the external device becomes ready to be serviced, that is, when it is ready to accept more data from the processor, the I/O module for that external

---

[4]A discussion of the uses of numerical prefixes, such as giga and tera, is contained in a supporting document at the Computer Science Student Resource Site at **WilliamStallings.com/StudentSupport.html.**

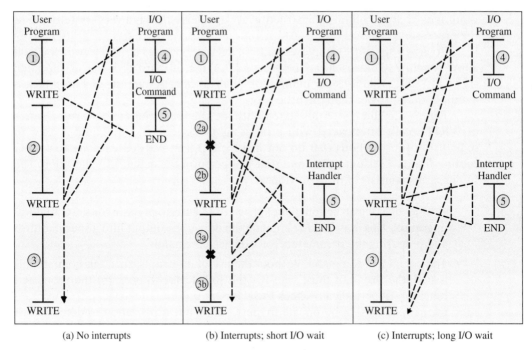

(a) No interrupts   (b) Interrupts; short I/O wait   (c) Interrupts; long I/O wait

Figure 1.5 Program Flow of Control Without and With Interrupts

device sends an *interrupt request* signal to the processor. The processor responds by suspending operation of the current program; branching off to a routine to service that particular I/O device, known as an interrupt handler; and resuming the original execution after the device is serviced. The points at which such interrupts occur are indicated by a **X** in Figure 1.5b. Note that an interrupt can occur at any point in the main program, not just at one specific instruction.

For the user program, an interrupt suspends the normal sequence of execution. When the interrupt processing is completed, execution resumes (Figure 1.6). Thus, the user program does not have to contain any special code to accommodate interrupts; the processor and the operating system are responsible for suspending the user program and then resuming it at the same point.

To accommodate interrupts, an *interrupt stage* is added to the instruction cycle, as shown in Figure 1.7 (compare Figure 1.2). In the interrupt stage, the processor checks to see if any interrupts have occurred, indicated by the presence of an interrupt signal. If no interrupts are pending, the processor proceeds to the fetch stage and fetches the next instruction of the current program. If an interrupt is pending, the processor suspends execution of the current program and executes an *interrupt-handler* routine. The interrupt-handler routine is generally part of the operating system. Typically, this routine determines the nature of the interrupt and performs whatever actions are needed. In the example we have been using, the handler determines which I/O module generated the interrupt and may branch to a program that will write more data out to that I/O module.

User program   Interrupt handler

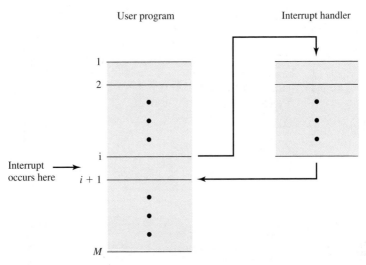

Figure 1.6   Transfer of Control via Interrupts

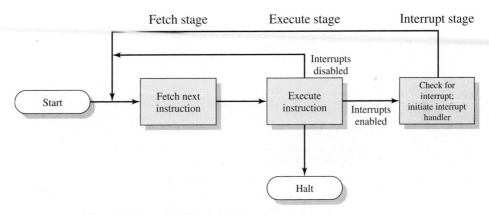

Figure 1.7   Instruction Cycle with Interrupts

When the interrupt-handler routine is completed, the processor can resume execution of the user program at the point of interruption.

It is clear that there is some overhead involved in this process. Extra instructions must be executed (in the interrupt handler) to determine the nature of the interrupt and to decide on the appropriate action. Nevertheless, because of the relatively large amount of time that would be wasted by simply waiting on an I/O operation, the processor can be employed much more efficiently with the use of interrupts.

To appreciate the gain in efficiency, consider Figure 1.8, which is a timing diagram based on the flow of control in Figures 1.5a and 1.5b. Figures 1.5b and 1.8 assume that the time required for the I/O operation is relatively short: less

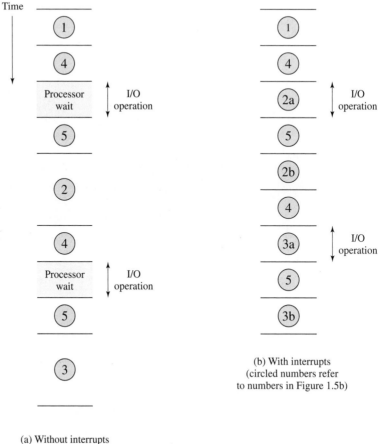

(a) Without interrupts
(circled numbers refer
to numbers in Figure 1.5a)

Figure 1.8   Program Timing: Short I/O Wait

than the time to complete the execution of instructions between write operations in the user program. The more typical case, especially for a slow device
such as a printer, is that the I/O operation will take much more time than executing a sequence of user instructions. Figure 1.5c indicates this state of affairs.
In this case, the user program reaches the second WRITE call before the I/O
operation spawned by the first call is complete. The result is that the user program is hung up at that point. When the preceding I/O operation is completed,
this new WRITE call may be processed, and a new I/O operation may be started.
Figure 1.9 shows the timing for this situation with and without the use of interrupts. We can see that there is still a gain in efficiency because part of the time
during which the I/O operation is underway overlaps with the execution of user
instructions.

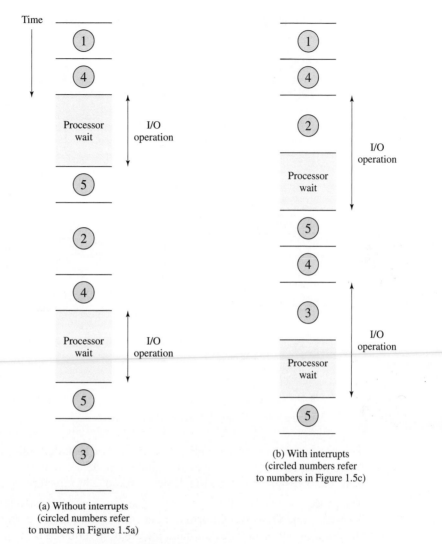

(a) Without interrupts
(circled numbers refer
to numbers in Figure 1.5a)

(b) With interrupts
(circled numbers refer
to numbers in Figure 1.5c)

Figure 1.9 Program Timing: Long I/O Wait

Interrupt Processing

The occurrence of an interrupt triggers a number of events, both in the processor hardware and in software. Figure 1.10 shows a typical sequence. When an I/O device completes an I/O operation, the following sequence of hardware events occurs:

1. The device issues an interrupt signal to the processor.
2. The processor finishes execution of the current instruction before responding to the interrupt, as indicated in Figure 1.7.

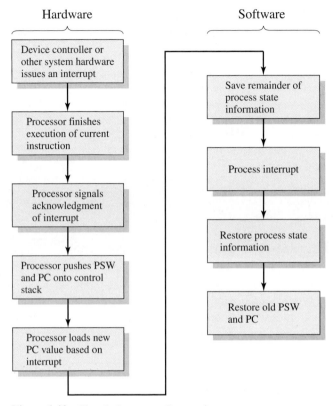

Figure 1.10 Simple Interrupt Processing

3. The processor tests for a pending interrupt a request, determines that there is one, and sends an acknowledgment signal to the device that issued the interrupt. The acknowledgment allows the device to remove its interrupt signal.

4. The processor now needs to prepare to transfer control to the interrupt routine. To begin, it needs to save information needed to resume the current program at the point of interrupt. The minimum information required is the program status word (PSW) and the location of the next instruction to be executed, which is contained in the program counter. These can be pushed onto the system control stack (see Appendix 1B).

5. The processor now loads the program counter with the entry location of the interrupt-handling routine that will respond to this interrupt. Depending on the computer architecture and operating system design, there may be a single program, one for each type of interrupt or one for each device and each type of interrupt. If there is more than one interrupt-handling routine, the processor must determine which one to invoke. This information may have been included in the original interrupt signal, or the processor may have to issue a request to the device that issued the interrupt to get a response that contains the needed information.

Once the program counter has been loaded, the processor proceeds to the next instruction cycle, which begins with an instruction fetch. Because the instruction fetch is determined by the contents of the program counter, the result is that control is transferred to the interrupt-handler program. The execution of this program results in the following operations:

6. At this point, the program counter and PSW relating to the interrupted program have been saved on the system stack. However, there is other information that is considered part of the state of the executing program. In particular, the contents of the processor registers need to be saved, because these registers may be used by the interrupt handler. So all of these values, plus any other state information, need to be saved. Typically, the interrupt handler will begin by saving the contents of all registers on the stack. Other state information that must be saved is discussed in Chapter 3. Figure 1.11a shows a simple example. In this case, a user program is interrupted after the instruction at location N. The contents of all of the registers plus the address of the next instruction $(N + 1)$, a total of M words, are pushed onto the control stack. The stack pointer is updated to point to the new top of stack, and the program counter is updated to point to the beginning of the interrupt service routine.

7. The interrupt handler may now proceed to process the interrupt. This will include an examination of status information relating to the I/O operation or other event that caused an interrupt. It may also involve sending additional commands or acknowledgments to the I/O device.

8. When interrupt processing is complete, the saved register values are retrieved from the stack and restored to the registers (e.g., see Figure 1.11b).

9. The final act is to restore the PSW and program counter values from the stack. As a result, the next instruction to be executed will be from the previously interrupted program.

It is important to save all of the state information about the interrupted program for later resumption. This is because the interrupt is not a routine called from the program. Rather, the interrupt can occur at any time and therefore at any point in the execution of a user program. Its occurrence is unpredictable.

Multiple Interrupts

The discussion so far has only discussed the occurrence of a single interrupt. Suppose, however, that multiple interrupts can occur. For example, a program may be receiving data from a communications line and printing results at the same time. The printer will generate an interrupt every time that it completes a print operation. The communication line controller will generate an interrupt every time a unit of data arrives. The unit could either be a single character or a block, depending on the nature of the communications discipline. In any case, it is possible for a communications interrupt to occur while a printer interrupt is being processed.

Two approaches can be taken to dealing with multiple interrupts. The first is to disable interrupts while an interrupt is being processed. A *disabled interrupt* simply means that the processor can and will ignore any new interrupt request signal. If an interrupt occurs during this time, it generally remains pending and will be checked by the processor after the processor has reenabled interrupts. Thus, when a user program is executing

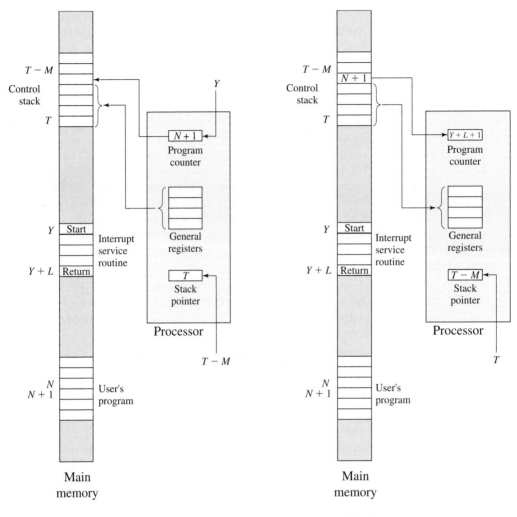

(a) Interrupt occurs after instruction
      at location N

(b) Return from interrupt

Figure 1.11   Changes in Memory and Registers for an Interrupt

and an interrupt occurs, interrupts are disabled immediately. After the interrupt-handler routine completes, interrupts are reenabled before resuming the user program, and the processor checks to see if additional interrupts have occurred. This approach is nice and simple, as interrupts are handled in strict sequential order (Figure 1.12a).

The drawback to the preceding approach is that it does not take into account relative priority or time-critical needs. For example, when input arrives from the communications line, it may need to be absorbed rapidly to make room for more input. If the first batch of input has not been processed before the second batch arrives, data may be lost because the buffer on the I/O device may fill and overflow.

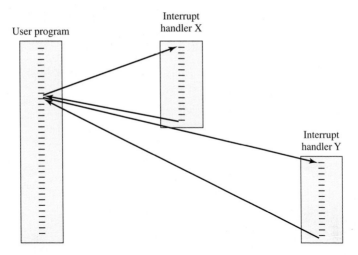

(a) Sequential interrupt processing

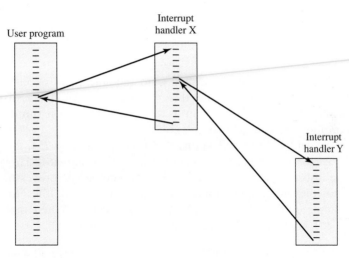

(b) Nested interrupt processing

Figure 1.12   Transfer of Control with Multiple Interrupts

A second approach is to define priorities for interrupts and to allow an inter-rupt of higher priority to cause a lower-priority interrupt handler to be interrupted (Figure 1.12b). As an example of this second approach, consider a system with three I/O devices: a printer, a disk, and a communications line, with increasing priorities of 2, 4, and 5, respectively. Figure 1.13, based on an example in [TANE97], illustrates a possible sequence. A user program begins at $t = 0$. At $t = 10$, a printer interrupt occurs; user information is placed on the system stack and execution continues at the printer interrupt service routine (ISR). While this routine is still executing, at $t = 15$ a communications interrupt occurs. Because the communications line has higher priority than the printer, the interrupt request is honored. The printer ISR

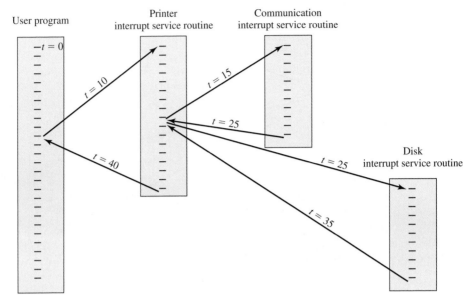

Figure 1.13   Example Time Sequence of Multiple Interrupts

is interrupted, its state is pushed onto the stack, and execution continues at the communications ISR. While this routine is executing, a disk interrupt occurs ($t = 20$). Because this interrupt is of lower priority, it is simply held, and the communications ISR runs to completion.

When the communications ISR is complete ($t = 25$), the previous processor state is restored, which is the execution of the printer ISR. However, before even a single instruction in that routine can be executed, the processor honors the higher-priority disk interrupt and transfers control to the disk ISR. Only when that routine is complete ($t = 35$) is the printer ISR resumed. When that routine completes ($t = 40$), control finally returns to the user program.

Multiprogramming

Even with the use of interrupts, a processor may not be used very efficiently. For example, refer to Figure 1.9b, which demonstrates better utilization of the processor. If the time required to complete an I/O operation is much greater than the user code between I/O calls (a common situation), then the processor will be idle much of the time. A solution to this problem is to allow multiple user programs to be active at the same time.

Suppose, for example, that the processor has two programs to execute. One is simply a program for reading data from memory and putting it out on an external device; the other is some application that involves a lot of calculation. The processor can begin the output program, issue a write command to the external device, and then proceed to begin execution of the other application. When the processor is dealing with a number of programs, the sequence with which programs are executed will depend on their relative priority as well as whether they are waiting for I/O.

When a program has been interrupted and control transfers to an interrupt handler, once the interrupt handler routine has completed, control may not immediately be returned to the user program that was in execution at the time. Instead, control may pass to some other pending program with a higher priority. Eventually, the user program that was interrupted will be resumed, when it has the highest priority. This concept of multiple programs taking turns in execution is known as multiprogramming and is discussed further in Chapter 2.

1.5   THE MEMORY HIERARCHY

The design constraints on a computer's memory can be summed up by three questions: How much? How fast? How expensive?

The question of how much is somewhat open ended. If the capacity is there, applications will likely be developed to use it. The question of how fast is, in a sense, easier to answer. To achieve greatest performance, the memory must be able to keep up with the processor. That is, as the processor is executing instructions, we would not want it to have to pause waiting for instructions or operands. The final question must also be considered. For a practical system, the cost of memory must be reasonable in relationship to other components.

As might be expected, there is a tradeoff among the three key characteristics of memory: namely, cost, capacity, and access time. At any given time, a variety of technologies are used to implement memory systems. Across this spectrum of technologies, the following relationships hold:

- Faster access time, greater cost per bit
- Greater capacity, smaller cost per bit
- Greater capacity, slower access speed

The dilemma facing the designer is clear. The designer would like to use memory technologies that provide for large-capacity memory, both because the capacity is needed and because the cost per bit is low. However, to meet performance requirements, the designer needs to use expensive, relatively lower-capacity memories with fast access times.

The way out of this dilemma is not to rely on a single memory component or technology but to employ a **memory hierarchy**. A typical hierarchy is illustrated in Figure 1.14. As one goes down the hierarchy, the following occur:

a. Decreasing cost per bit
b. Increasing capacity
c. Increasing access time
d. Decreasing frequency of access to the memory by the processor

Thus, smaller, more expensive, faster memories are supplemented by larger, cheaper, slower memories. The key to the success of this organization is the last item: decreasing frequency of access. We will examine this concept in greater detail

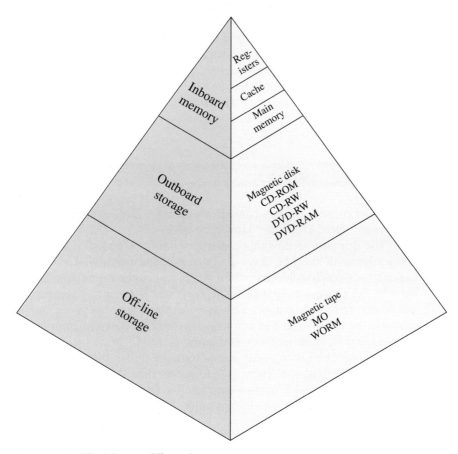

Figure 1.14   The Memory Hierarchy

later in this chapter, when we discuss the cache, and when we discuss virtual memory later in this book. A brief explanation is provided at this point.

Suppose that the processor has access to two levels of memory. Level 1 contains 1000 bytes and has an access time of 0.1 μs; level 2 contains 100,000 bytes and has an access time of 1 μs. Assume that if a byte to be accessed is in level 1, then the processor accesses it directly. If it is in level 2, then the byte is first transferred to level 1 and then accessed by the processor. For simplicity, we ignore the time required for the processor to determine whether the byte is in level 1 or level 2. Figure 1.15 shows the general shape of the curve that covers this situation. The figure shows the average access time to a two-level memory as a function of the **hit ratio** H, where H is defined as the fraction of all memory accesses that are found in the faster memory (e.g., the cache), T_1 is the access time to level 1, and T_2 is the access time to level 2.[5] As can be seen, for high percentages of level 1 access, the average total access time is much closer to that of level 1 than that of level 2.

_____

[5]If the accessed word is found in the faster memory, that is defined as a **hit**. A **miss** occurs if the accessed word is not found in the faster memory.

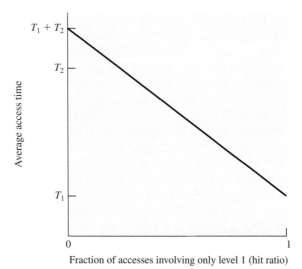

Figure 1.15   Performance of a Simple Two-Level
Memory

In our example, suppose 95% of the memory accesses are found in the cache ($H = 0.95$). Then the average time to access a byte can be expressed as

$$(0.95)(0.1 \ \mu s) + (0.05)(0.1 \ \mu s + 1 \ \mu s) = 0.095 + 0.055 = 0.15 \ \mu s$$

The result is close to the access time of the faster memory. So the strategy of using two memory levels works in principle, but only if conditions (a) through (d) apply. By employing a variety of technologies, a spectrum of memory systems exists that satisfies conditions (a) through (c). Fortunately, condition (d) is also generally valid.

The basis for the validity of condition (d) is a principle known as *locality of reference* [DENN68]. During the course of execution of a program, memory references by the processor, for both instructions and data, tend to cluster. Programs typically contain a number of iterative loops and subroutines. Once a loop or subroutine is entered, there are repeated references to a small set of instructions. Similarly, operations on tables and arrays involve access to a clustered set of data bytes. Over a long period of time, the clusters in use change, but over a short period of time, the processor is primarily working with fixed clusters of memory references.

Accordingly, it is possible to organize data across the hierarchy such that the percentage of accesses to each successively lower level is substantially less than that of the level above. Consider the two-level example already presented. Let level 2 memory contain all program instructions and data. The current clusters can be temporarily placed in level 1. From time to time, one of the clusters in level 1 will have to be swapped back to level 2 to make room for a new cluster coming in to level 1. On average, however, most references will be to instructions and data contained in level 1.

This principle can be applied across more than two levels of memory. The fastest, smallest, and most expensive type of memory consists of the registers internal to the processor. Typically, a processor will contain a few dozen such registers, although some machines contain hundreds of registers. Skipping down two levels, main memory is the principal internal memory system of the computer. Each location in main memory has a unique address, and most machine instructions refer to one or more main memory addresses. Main memory is usually extended with a higher-speed, smaller cache. The cache is not usually visible to the programmer or, indeed, to the processor. It is a device for staging the movement of data between main memory and processor registers to improve performance.

The three forms of memory just described are, typically, volatile and employ semiconductor technology. The use of three levels exploits the fact that semiconductor memory comes in a variety of types, which differ in speed and cost. Data are stored more permanently on external mass storage devices, of which the most common are hard disk and removable media, such as removable disk, tape, and optical storage. External, nonvolatile memory is also referred to as **secondary memory** or **auxiliary memory**. These are used to store program and data files and are usually visible to the programmer only in terms of files and records, as opposed to individual bytes or words. Disk is also used to provide an extension to main memory known as virtual memory, which is discussed in Chapter 8.

Additional levels can be effectively added to the hierarchy in software. For example, a portion of main memory can be used as a buffer to temporarily hold data that are to be read out to disk. Such a technique, sometimes referred to as a disk cache (examined in detail in Chapter 11), improves performance in two ways:

- Disk writes are clustered. Instead of many small transfers of data, we have a few large transfers of data. This improves disk performance and minimizes processor involvement.
- Some data destined for write-out may be referenced by a program before the next dump to disk. In that case, the data are retrieved rapidly from the software cache rather than slowly from the disk.

Appendix 1A examines the performance implications of multilevel memory structures.

1.6 CACHE MEMORY

Although cache memory is invisible to the operating system, it interacts with other memory-management hardware. Furthermore, many of the principles used in virtual memory schemes (discussed in Chapter 8) are also applied in cache memory.

Motivation

On all instruction cycles, the processor accesses memory at least once, to fetch the instruction, and often one or more additional times, to fetch operands and/or store results. The rate at which the processor can execute instructions is clearly limited by the memory cycle time (the time it takes to read one word from or write one word to memory). This limitation has in fact been a significant problem because of the persistent mismatch between processor and main memory speeds; over the years, processor speed has consistently increased more rapidly than memory access speed. We are faced with a tradeoff among speed, cost, and size. Ideally, the main memory

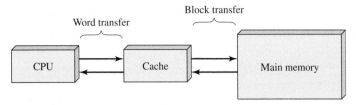

Figure 1.16   Cache and Main Memory

should be built with the same technology as that of the processor registers, giving memory cycle times comparable to processor cycle times. This has always been too expensive a strategy. The solution is to exploit the principle of locality by providing a small, fast memory between the processor and main memory, namely the cache.

Cache Principles

Cache memory is intended to provide memory access time approaching that of the fastest memories available and at the same time supports a large memory size that has the price of less expensive types of semiconductor memories. The concept is illustrated in Figure 1.16. There is a relatively large and slow main memory together with a smaller, faster cache memory. The cache contains a copy of a portion of main memory. When the processor attempts to read a byte of memory, a check is made to determine if the byte is in the cache. If so, the byte is delivered to the processor. If not, a block of main memory, consisting of some fixed number of bytes, is read into the cache and then the byte is delivered to the processor. Because of the phenomenon of locality of reference, when a block of data is fetched into the cache to satisfy a single memory reference, it is likely that many of the near-future memory references will be to other bytes in the block.

Figure 1.17 depicts the structure of a cache/main memory system. Main memory consists of up to 2^n addressable words, with each word having a unique n-bit address. For mapping purposes, this memory is considered to consist of a number of fixed-length **blocks** of K words each. That is, there are $M = 2^n/K$ blocks. Cache consists of C **slots** (also referred to as *lines*) of K words each, and the number of slots is considerably less than the number of main memory blocks $(C << M)$.[6] Some subset of the blocks of main memory resides in the slots of the cache. If a word in a block of memory that is not in the cache is read, that block is transferred to one of the slots of the cache. Because there are more blocks than slots, an individual slot cannot be uniquely and permanently dedicated to a particular block. Therefore, each slot includes a tag that identifies which particular block is currently being stored. The tag is usually some number of higher-order bits of the address and refers to all addresses that begin with that sequence of bits.

As a simple example, suppose that we have a 6-bit address and a 2-bit tag. The tag 01 refers to the block of locations with the following addresses: 010000, 010001, 010010, 010011, 010100, 010101, 010110, 010111, 011000, 011001, 011010, 011011, 011100, 011101, 011110, 011111.

---

[6]The symbol $<<$ means *much less than*. Similarly, the symbol $>>$ means *much greater than*.

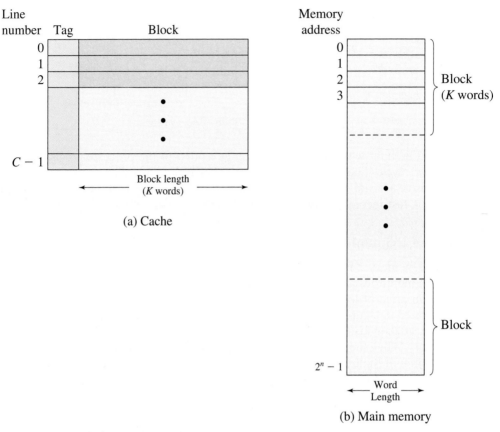

Figure 1.17   Cache/Main-Memory Structure

Figure 1.18 illustrates the read operation. The processor generates the address, RA, of a word to be read. If the word is contained in the cache, it is delivered to the processor. Otherwise, the block containing that word is loaded into the cache and the word is delivered to the processor.

Cache Design

A detailed discussion of cache design is beyond the scope of this book. Key elements are briefly summarized here. We will see that similar design issues must be addressed in dealing with virtual memory and disk cache design. They fall into the following categories:

- Cache size
- Block size
- Mapping function
- Replacement algorithm
- Write policy

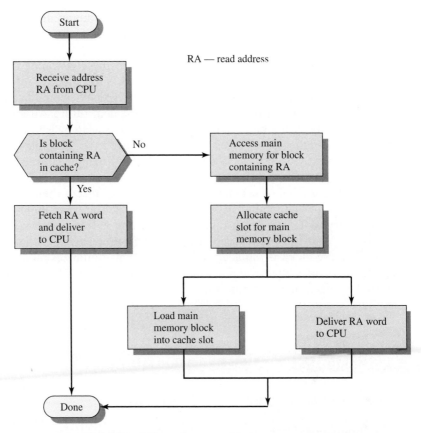

Figure 1.18   Cache Read Operation

We have already dealt with the issue of **cache size**. It turns out that reasonably small caches can have a significant impact on performance. Another size issue is that of **block size**: the unit of data exchanged between cache and main memory. As the block size increases from very small to larger sizes, the hit ratio will at first increase because of the principle of locality: the high probability that data in the vicinity of a referenced word are likely to be referenced in the near future. As the block size increases, more useful data are brought into the cache. The hit ratio will begin to decrease, however, as the block becomes even bigger and the probability of using the newly fetched data becomes less than the probability of reusing the data that have to be moved out of the cache to make room for the new block.

When a new block of data is read into the cache, the **mapping function** determines which cache location the block will occupy. Two constraints affect the design of the mapping function.

First, when one block is read in, another may have to be replaced. We would like to do this in such a way as to minimize the probability that we will replace a block that will be needed in the near future. The more flexible the mapping function, the more scope we have to design a replacement algorithm to maximize the hit ratio. Second, the more flexible the mapping function, the more complex is the circuitry required to search the cache to determine if a given block is in the cache.

The **replacement algorithm** chooses, within the constraints of the mapping function, which block to replace when a new block is to be loaded into the cache and the cache already has all slots filled with other blocks. We would like to replace the block that is least likely to be needed again in the near future. Although it is impossible to identify such a block, a reasonably effective strategy is to replace the block that has been in the cache longest with no reference to it. This policy is referred to as the least-recently-used (LRU) algorithm. Hardware mechanisms are needed to identify the least-recently-used block.

If the contents of a block in the cache are altered, then it is necessary to write it back to main memory before replacing it. The **write policy** dictates when the memory write operation takes place. At one extreme, the writing can occur every time that the block is updated. At the other extreme, the writing occurs only when the block is replaced. The latter policy minimizes memory write operations but leaves main memory in an obsolete state. This can interfere with multiple-processor operation and with direct memory access by I/O hardware modules.

1.7 I/O COMMUNICATION TECHNIQUES

Three techniques are possible for I/O operations:

- Programmed I/O
- Interrupt-driven I/O
- Direct memory access (DMA)

Programmed I/O

When the processor is executing a program and encounters an instruction relating to I/O, it executes that instruction by issuing a command to the appropriate I/O module. In the case of programmed I/O, the I/O module performs the requested action and then sets the appropriate bits in the I/O status register but takes no further action to alert the processor. In particular, it does not interrupt the processor. Thus, after the I/O instruction is invoked, the processor must take some active role in determining when the I/O instruction is completed. For this purpose, the processor periodically checks the status of the I/O module until it finds that the operation is complete.

With this technique, the processor is responsible for extracting data from main memory for output and storing data in main memory for input. I/O software is written in such a way that the processor executes instructions that give it direct control of the I/O operation, including sensing device status, sending a read or write

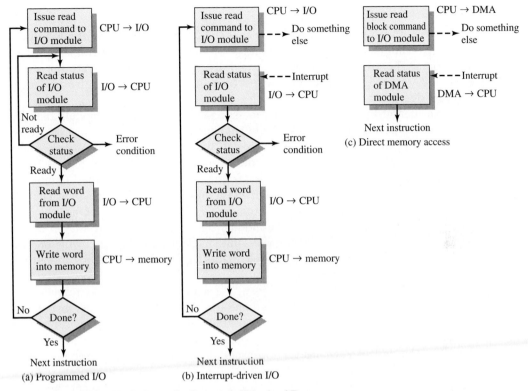

Figure 1.19   Three Techniques for Input of a Block of Data

command, and transferring the data. Thus, the instruction set includes I/O instructions in the following categories:

- **Control:** Used to activate an external device and tell it what to do. For example, a magnetic-tape unit may be instructed to rewind or to move forward one record.
- **Status:** Used to test various status conditions associated with an I/O module and its peripherals.
- **Transfer:** Used to read and/or write data between processor registers and external devices.

Figure 1.19a gives an example of the use of programmed I/O to read in a block of data from an external device (e.g., a record from tape) into memory. Data are read in one word (e.g., 16 bits) at a time. For each word that is read in, the processor must remain in a status-checking loop until it determines that the word is available in the I/O module's data register. This flowchart highlights the main disadvantage of this technique: It is a time-consuming process that keeps the processor busy needlessly.

Interrupt-Driven I/O

The problem with programmed I/O is that the processor has to wait a long time for the I/O module of concern to be ready for either reception or transmission of more data. The processor, while waiting, must repeatedly interrogate the status of the I/O module. As a result, the performance level of the entire system is severely degraded.

An alternative is for the processor to issue an I/O command to a module and then go on to do some other useful work. The I/O module will then interrupt the processor to request service when it is ready to exchange data with the processor. The processor then executes the data transfer, as before, and then resumes its former processing.

Let us consider how this works, first from the point of view of the I/O module. For input, the I/O module receives a READ command from the processor. The I/O module then proceeds to read data in from an associated peripheral. Once the data are in the module's data register, the module signals an interrupt to the processor over a control line. The module then waits until its data are requested by the processor. When the request is made, the module places its data on the data bus and is then ready for another I/O operation.

From the processor's point of view, the action for input is as follows. The processor issues a READ command. It then saves the context (e.g., program counter and processor registers) of the current program and goes off and does something else (e.g., the processor may be working on several different programs at the same time). At the end of each instruction cycle, the processor checks for interrupts (Figure 1.7). When the interrupt from the I/O module occurs, the processor saves the context of the program it is currently executing and begins to execute an interrupt-handling program that processes the interrupt. In this case, the processor reads the word of data from the I/O module and stores it in memory. It then restores the context of the program that had issued the I/O command (or some other program) and resumes execution.

Figure 1.19b shows the use of interrupt-driven I/O for reading in a block of data. Interrupt-driven I/O is more efficient than programmed I/O because it eliminates needless waiting. However, interrupt-driven I/O still consumes a lot of processor time, because every word of data that goes from memory to I/O module or from I/O module to memory must pass through the processor.

Almost invariably, there will be multiple I/O modules in a computer system, so mechanisms are needed to enable the processor to determine which device caused the interrupt and to decide, in the case of multiple interrupts, which one to handle first. In some systems, there are multiple interrupt lines, so that each I/O module signals on a different line. Each line will have a different priority. Alternatively, there can be a single interrupt line, but additional lines are used to hold a device address. Again, different devices are assigned different priorities.

Direct Memory Access

Interrupt-driven I/O, though more efficient than simple programmed I/O, still requires the active intervention of the processor to transfer data between memory and an I/O module, and any data transfer must traverse a path through the processor. Thus both of these forms of I/O suffer from two inherent drawbacks:

1. The I/O transfer rate is limited by the speed with which the processor can test and service a device.

2. The processor is tied up in managing an I/O transfer; a number of instructions must be executed for each I/O transfer.

When large volumes of data are to be moved, a more efficient technique is required: direct memory access (DMA). The DMA function can be performed by a separate module on the system bus or it can be incorporated into an I/O module. In either case, the technique works as follows. When the processor wishes to read or write a block of data, it issues a command to the DMA module, by sending to the DMA module the following information:

• Whether a read or write is requested
• The address of the I/O device involved
• The starting location in memory to read data from or write data to
• The number of words to be read or written

The processor then continues with other work. It has delegated this I/O operation to the DMA module, and that module will take care of it. The DMA module transfers the entire block of data, one word at a time, directly to or from memory without going through the processor. When the transfer is complete, the DMA module sends an interrupt signal to the processor. Thus the processor is involved only at the beginning and end of the transfer (Figure 1.19c).

The DMA module needs to take control of the bus to transfer data to and from memory. Because of this competition for bus usage, there may be times when the processor needs the bus and must wait for the DMA module. Note that this is not an interrupt; the processor does not save a context and do something else. Rather, the processor pauses for one bus cycle (the time it takes to transfer one word across the bus). The overall effect is to cause the processor to execute more slowly during a DMA transfer when processor access to the bus is required. Nevertheless, for a multiple-word I/O transfer, DMA is far more efficient than interrupt-driven or programmed I/O.

1.8 RECOMMENDED READINGS AND WEB SITES

[STAL03] covers the topics of this chapter in detail. In addition, there are many other texts on computer organization and architecture. Among the more worthwhile texts are the following. [PATT98] is a comprehensive survey; [HENN02], by the same authors, is a more advanced text that emphasizes quantitative aspects of design.

HENN02 Hennessy, J., and Patterson, D. *Computer Architecture: A Quantitative Approach.* San Mateo, CA: Morgan Kaufmann, 2002.

PATT98 Patterson, D., and Hennessy, J. *Computer Organization and Design: The Hardware/Software Interface.* San Mateo, CA: Morgan Kaufmann, 1998.

STAL03 Stallings, W. *Computer Organization and Architecture, 6th ed.* Upper Saddle River, NJ: Prentice Hall, 2003.

Recommended Web Sites:

- **WWW Computer Architecture Home Page:** A comprehensive index to information relevant to computer architecture researchers, including architecture groups and projects, technical organizations, literature, employment, and commercial information
- **CPU Info Center:** Information on specific processors, including technical papers, product information, and latest announcements

1.9   KEY TERMS, REVIEW QUESTIONS, AND PROBLEMS

Key Terms

address register	instruction cycle	reentrant procedure
cache memory	instruction register	register
cache slot	interrupt	secondary memory
central processing unit (CPU)	interrupt-driven I/O	segment pointer
condition code	I/O module	spatial locality
data register	locality	stack
direct memory access (DMA)	main memory	stack frame
hit ratio	multiprogramming	stack pointer
index register	processor	system bus
input/output (I/O)	program counter	temporal locality
instruction	programmed I/O	

Review Questions

1.1   List and briefly define the four main elements of a computer.

1.2   Define the two main categories of processor registers.

1.3   In general terms, what are the four distinct actions that a machine instruction can specify?

1.4   What is an interrupt?

1.5   How are multiple interrupts dealt with?

1.6   What characteristics distinguish the various elements of a memory hierarchy?

1.7   What is cache memory?

1.8   List and briefly define three techniques for I/O operations.

1.9   What is the distinction between spatial locality and temporal locality?

1.10 In general, what are the strategies for exploiting spatial locality and temporal locality?

Problems

1.1   Suppose the hypothetical machine of Figure 1.3 also has two I/O instructions:

        0011 = Load AC from I/O
        0111 = Store AC to I/O

In these cases, the 12-bit address identifies a particular external device. Show the program execution (using format of Figure 1.4) for the following program:

1. Load AC from device 5.
2. Add contents of memory location 940.
3. Store AC to device 6.

Assume that the next value retrieved from device 5 is 3 and that location 940 contains a value of 2.

1.2 The program execution of Figure 1.4 is described in the text using six steps. Expand this description to show the use of the MAR and MBR.

1.3 Consider a hypothetical 32-bit microprocessor having 32-bit instructions composed of two fields: The first byte contains the opcode and the remainder an immediate operand or an operand address.
   a. What is the maximum directly addressable memory capacity (in bytes)?
   b. Discuss the impact on the system speed if the microprocessor bus has
      1. a 32-bit local address bus and a 16-bit local data bus, or
      2. a 16-bit local address bus and a 16-bit local data bus.
   c. How many bits are needed for the program counter and the instruction register?

1.4 Consider a hypothetical microprocessor generating a 16-bit address (for example, assume that the program counter and the address registers are 16 bits wide) and having a 16-bit data bus.
   a. What is the maximum memory address space that the processor can access directly if it is connected to a "16-bit memory"?
   b. What is the maximum memory address space that the processor can access directly if it is connected to an "8-bit memory"?
   c. What architectural features will allow this microprocessor to access a separate "I/O space"?
   d. If an input and an output instruction can specify an 8-bit I/O port number, how many 8-bit I/O ports can the microprocessor support? How many 16-bit I/O ports? Explain.

1.5 Consider a 32-bit microprocessor, with a 16-bit external data bus, driven by an 8-MHz input clock. Assume that this microprocessor has a bus cycle whose minimum duration equals four input clock cycles. What is the maximum data transfer rate across the bus that this microprocessor can sustain in bytes/s? To increase its performance, would it be better to make its external data bus 32 bits or to double the external clock frequency supplied to the microprocessor? State any other assumptions you make and explain. *Hint:* Determine the number of bytes that can be transferred per bus cycle.

1.6 Consider a computer system that contains an I/O module controlling a simple keyboard/printer Teletype. The following registers are contained in the CPU and connected directly to the system bus:
   INPR: Input Register, 8 bits
   OUTR: Output Register, 8 bits
   FGI: Input Flag, 1 bit
   FGO: Output Flag, 1 bit
   IEN: Interrupt Enable, 1 bit
   Keystroke input from the Teletype and output to the printer are controlled by the I/O module. The Teletype is able to encode an alphanumeric symbol to an 8-bit word and decode an 8-bit word into an alphanumeric symbol. The Input flag is set when an 8-bit word enters the input register from the Teletype. The Output flag is set when a word is printed.
   a. Describe how the CPU, using the first four registers listed in this problem, can achieve I/O with the Teletype.
   b. Describe how the function can be performed more efficiently by also employing IEN.

1.7 In virtually all systems that include DMA modules, DMA access to main memory is given higher priority than processor access to main memory. Why?

1.8   A DMA module is transferring characters to main memory from an external device transmitting at 9600 bits per second (bps). The processor can fetch instructions at the rate of 1 million instructions per second. By how much will the processor be slowed down due to the DMA activity?

1.9   A computer consists of a CPU and an I/O device D connected to main memory M via a shared bus with a data bus width of one word. The CPU can execute a maximum of 10^6 instructions per second. An average instruction requires five machine cycles, three of which use the memory bus. A memory read or write operation uses one machine cycle. Suppose that the CPU is continuously executing "background" programs that require 95% of its instruction execution rate but not any I/O instructions. Assume that one processor cycle equals one bus cycle. Now suppose that very large blocks of data are to be transferred between M and D.
   a.   If programmed I/O is used and each one-word I/O transfer requires the CPU to execute two instructions, estimate the maximum I/O data transfer rate, in words per second, possible through D.
   b.   Estimate the same rate if DMA transfer is used.

1.10   Consider the following code:

```
for (i = 0; i < 20; i++)
    for (j = 0; j < 10; j++)
        a[i] = a[i] * j
```

   a.   Give one example of the spatial locality in the code.
   b.   Give one example of the temporal locality in the code.

1.11   Generalize Equations (1.1) and (1.2) in Appendix 1A to n-level memory hierarchies.

1.12   Consider a memory system with the following parameters:

$$T_c = 100 \text{ ns} \qquad C_c = 0.01 \text{ cents/bit}$$
$$T_m = 1{,}200 \text{ ns} \qquad C_m = 0.001 \text{ cents/bit}$$

   a.   What is the cost of 1 MByte of main memory?
   b.   What is the cost of 1 MByte of main memory using cache memory technology?
   c.   If the effective access time is 10% greater than the cache access time, what is the hit ratio H?

1.13   A computer has a cache, main memory, and a disk used for virtual memory. If a referenced word is in the cache, 20 ns are required to access it. If it is in main memory but not in the cache, 60 ns are needed to load it into the cache (this includes the time to originally check the cache), and then the reference is started again. If the word is not in main memory, 12 ms are required to fetch the word from disk, followed by 60 ns to copy it to the cache, and then the reference is started again. The cache hit ratio is 0.9 and the main-memory hit ratio is 0.6. What is the average time in ns required to access a referenced word on this system?

1.14   Suppose a stack is to be used by the processor to manage procedure calls and returns. Can the program counter be eliminated by using the top of the stack as a program counter?

APPENDIX 1A PERFORMANCE CHARACTERISTICS OF TWO-LEVEL MEMORIES

In this chapter, reference is made to a cache that acts as a buffer between main memory and processor, creating a two-level internal memory. This two-level architecture provides improved performance over a comparable one-level memory, by exploiting a property known as locality, which is explored in this appendix.

Table 1.2   Characteristics of Two-Level Memories

	Main Memory Cache	**Virtual Memory (Paging)**	**Disk Cache**
Typical access time ratios	5:1	10^6:1	10^6:1
Memory management system	Implemented by special hardware	Combination of hardware and system software	System software
Typical block size	4 to 128 bytes	64 to 4096 bytes	64 to 4096 bytes
Access of processor to second level	Direct access	Indirect access	Indirect access

The main memory cache mechanism is part of the computer architecture, implemented in hardware and typically invisible to the operating system. Accordingly, this mechanism is not pursued in this book. However, there are two other instances of a two-level memory approach that also exploit the property of locality and that are, at least partially, implemented in the operating system: virtual memory and the disk cache (Table 1.2). These two topics are explored in Chapters 8 and 11, respectively. In this appendix, we look at some of the performance characteristics of two-level memories that are common to all three approaches.

Locality

The basis for the performance advantage of a two-level memory is the principle of locality, referred to in Section 1.5. This principle states that memory references tend to cluster. Over a long period of time, the clusters in use change, but over a short period of time, the processor is primarily working with fixed clusters of memory references.

The principle of locality appears to be a valid one. Consider the following line of reasoning:

1. Except for branch and call instructions, which constitute only a small fraction of all program instructions, program execution is sequential. Hence, in most cases, the next instruction to be fetched immediately follows the last instruction fetched.

2. It is rare to have a long uninterrupted sequence of procedure calls followed by the corresponding sequence of returns. Rather, a program remains confined to a rather narrow window of procedure-invocation depth. Thus, over a short period of time references to instructions tend to be localized to a few procedures.

3. Most iterative constructs consist of a relatively small number of instructions repeated many times. For the duration of the iteration, computation is therefore confined to a small contiguous portion of a program.

4. In many programs, much of the computation involves processing data structures, such as arrays or sequences of records. In many cases, successive references to these data structures will be to closely located data items.

This line of reasoning has been confirmed in many studies. With reference to point (1), a variety of studies have analyzed the behavior of high-level language programs. Table 1.3 includes key results, measuring the appearance of various statement types during execution, from the following studies. The earliest study of programming language behavior, performed by Knuth [KNUT71], examined a collection of FORTRAN programs used as student exercises. Tanenbaum [TANE78] published measurements collected from over 300 procedures used in operating system programs and written in a language that supports structured programming (SAL). Patterson and Sequin [PATT82] analyzed a set of measurements taken from compilers and programs for typesetting, computer-aided design (CAD), sorting, and file

Table 1.3   Relative Dynamic Frequency of High-Level Language Operations

Study Language Workload	[HUCK83] Pascal Scientific	[KNUT71] FORTRAN Student	[PATT82] Pascal System	C System	[TANE78] SAL System
Assign	74	67	45	38	42
Loop	4	3	5	3	4
Call	1	3	15	12	12
IF	20	11	29	43	36
GOTO	2	9	—	3	—
Other	—	7	6	1	6

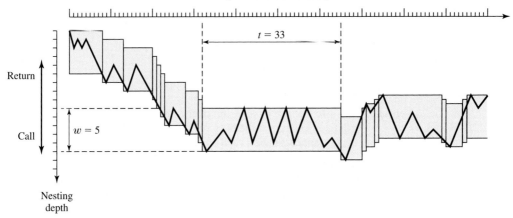

Figure 1.20   Example Call-Return Behavior of a Program

comparison. The programming languages C and Pascal were studied. Huck [HUCK83] ana-lyzed four programs intended to represent a mix of general-purpose scientific computing, including fast Fourier transform and the integration of systems of differential equations. There is good agreement in the results of this mixture of languages and applications that branching and call instructions represent only a fraction of statements executed during the lifetime of a program. Thus, these studies confirm assertion (1), from the preceding list.

With respect to assertion (2), studies reported in [PATT85] provide confirmation. This is illustrated in Figure 1.20, which shows call-return behavior. Each call is represented by the line moving down and to the right, and each return by the line moving up and to the right. In the figure, a *window* with depth equal to 5 is defined. Only a sequence of calls and returns with a net movement of 6 in either direction causes the window to move. As can be seen, the executing program can remain within a stationary window for long periods of time. A study by the same analysts of C and Pascal programs showed that a window of depth 8 would only need to shift on less than 1% of the calls or returns [TAMI83].

The principle of locality of reference continues to be validated in more recent studies. For example, Figure 1.21 illustrates the results of a study of Web page access patterns at a single site.

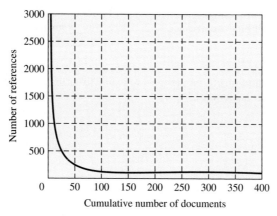

Figure 1.21   Locality of Reference for Web Pages
[BAEN97]

A distinction is made in the literature between spatial locality and temporal locality. **Spatial locality** refers to the tendency of execution to involve a number of memory locations that are clustered. This reflects the tendency of a processor to access instructions sequentially. Spatial location also reflects the tendency of a program to access data locations sequentially, such as when processing a table of data. **Temporal locality** refers to the tendency for a processor to access memory locations that have been used recently. For example, when an iteration loop is executed, the processor executes the same set of instructions repeatedly.

Traditionally, temporal locality is exploited by keeping recently used instruction and data values in cache memory and by exploiting a cache hierarchy. Spatial locality is generally exploited by using larger cache blocks and by incorporating prefetching mechanisms (fetching items whose use is expected) into the cache control logic. Recently, there has been considerable research on refining these techniques to achieve greater performance, but the basic strategies remain the same.

Operation of Two-Level Memory

The locality property can be exploited in the formation of a two-level memory. The upper-level memory (M1) is smaller, faster, and more expensive (per bit) than the lower-level memory (M2). M1 is used as a temporary store for part of the contents of the larger M2. When a memory reference is made, an attempt is made to access the item in M1. If this succeeds, then a quick access is made. If not, then a block of memory locations is copied from M2 to M1 and the access then takes place via M1. Because of locality, once a block is brought into M1, there should be a number of accesses to locations in that block, resulting in fast overall service.

To express the average time to access an item, we must consider not only the speeds of the two levels of memory but also the probability that a given reference can be found in M1. We have

$$T_s = H \times T_1 + (1 - H) \times (T_1 + T_2)$$
$$= T_1 + (1 - H) \times T_2 \tag{1.1}$$

where

T_s = average (system) access time
T_1 = access time of M1 (e.g., cache, disk cache)
T_2 = access time of M2 (e.g., main memory, disk)
H = hit ratio (fraction of time reference is found in M1)

Figure 1.15 shows average access time as a function of hit ratio. As can be seen, for a high percentage of hits, the average total access time is much closer to that of M1 than M2.

Performance

Let us look at some of the parameters relevant to an assessment of a two-level memory mechanism. First consider cost. We have

$$C_s = \frac{C_1 S_1 + C_2 S_2}{S_1 + S_2} \tag{1.2}$$

where

C_s = average cost per bit for the combined two-level memory
C_1 = average cost per bit of upper-level memory M1
C_2 = average cost per bit of lower-level memory M2
S_1 = size of M1
S_2 = size of M2

We would like $C_s \approx C_2$. Given that $C_1 \gg C_2$, this requires $S_1 \ll S_2$. Figure 1.22 shows the relationship.[7]

Next, consider access time. For a two-level memory to provide a significant performance improvement, we need to have T_s approximately equal to T_1 ($T_s \approx T_1$). Given that T_1 is much less than T_2 ($T_1 \ll T_2$), a hit ratio of close to 1 is needed.

So we would like M1 to be small to hold down cost, and large to improve the hit ratio and therefore the performance. Is there a size of M1 that satisfies both requirements to a reasonable extent? We can answer this question with a series of subquestions:

- What value of hit ratio is needed to satisfy the performance requirement?
- What size of M1 will assure the needed hit ratio?
- Does this size satisfy the cost requirement?

To get at this, consider the quantity T_1/T_s, which is referred to as the *access efficiency*. It is a measure of how close average access time (T_s) is to M1 access time (T_1). From Equation (1.1),

$$\frac{T_1}{T_s} = \frac{1}{1 + (1 - H)\dfrac{T_2}{T_1}} \tag{1.3}$$

In Figure 1.23, we plot T_1/T_s as a function of the hit ratio H, with the quantity T_2/T_1 as a parameter. A hit ratio in the range of 0.8 to 0.9 would seem to be needed to satisfy the performance requirement.

We can now phrase the question about relative memory size more exactly. Is a hit ratio of 0.8 or better reasonable for $S_1 \ll S_2$? This will depend on a number of factors, including the nature of the software being executed and the details of the design of the two-level memory. The main determinant is, of course, the degree of locality. Figure 1.24 suggests the effect of locality on the hit ratio. Clearly, if M1 is the same size as M2, then the hit ratio will be 1.0: All of the items in M2 are always stored also in M1. Now suppose that there is no locality; that is, references are completely random. In that case the hit ratio should be a strictly linear function of the relative memory size. For example, if M1 is half the size of M2, then at any time

---

[7]Note that both axes use a log scale. A basic review of log scales is in the math refresher document at the Computer Science Student Support Site at **WilliamStallings.com/StudentSupport.html**.

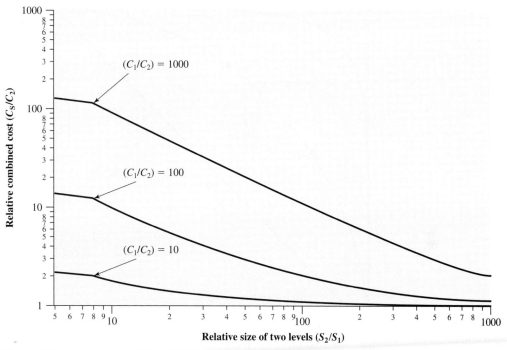

Figure 1.22   Relationship of Average Memory Cost to Relative Memory Size for a Two-Level Memory

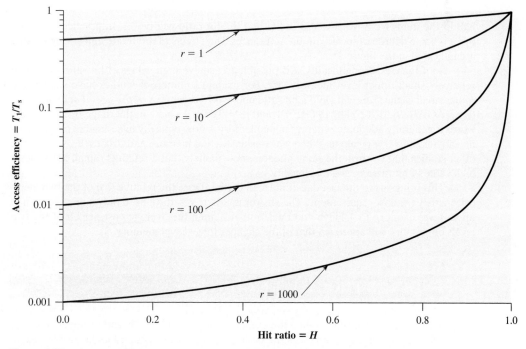

Figure 1.23   Access Efficiency as a Function of Hit Ratio ($r = T_2/T_1$)

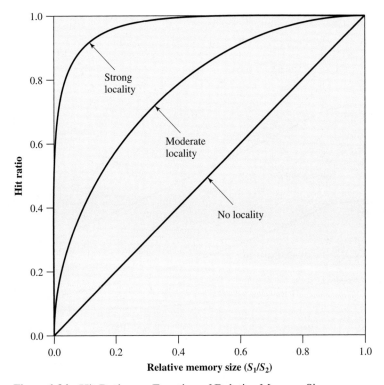

Figure 1.24   Hit Ratio as a Function of Relative Memory Size

half of the items from M2 are also in M1 and the hit ratio will be 0.5. In practice, however, there is some degree of locality in the references. The effects of moderate and strong locality are indicated in the figure.

So if there is strong locality, it is possible to achieve high values of hit ratio even with relatively small upper-level memory size. For example, numerous studies have shown that rather small cache sizes will yield a hit ratio above 0.75 *regardless of the size of main memory* (e.g., [AGAR89], [PRZY88], [STRE83], and [SMIT82]). A cache in the range of 1K to 128K words is generally adequate, whereas main memory is now typically in a range of hundreds of megabytes to over a gigabyte. When we consider virtual memory and disk cache, we will cite other studies that confirm the same phenomenon, namely that a relatively small M1 yields a high value of hit ratio because of locality.

This brings us to the last question listed earlier: Does the relative size of the two memories satisfy the cost requirement? The answer is clearly yes. If we need only a relatively small upper-level memory to achieve good performance, then the average cost per bit of the two levels of memory will approach that of the cheaper lower-level memory.

APPENDIX 1B PROCEDURE CONTROL

A common technique for controlling the execution of procedure calls and returns makes use of a stack. This appendix summarizes the basic properties of stacks and looks at their use in procedure control.

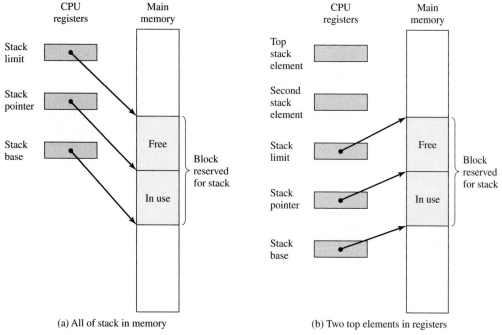

CPU registers | Main memory
Stack limit
Stack pointer
Stack base
Free
In use
Block reserved for stack

(a) All of stack in memory

CPU registers | Main memory
Top stack element
Second stack element
Stack limit
Stack pointer
Stack base
Free
In use
Block reserved for stack

(b) Two top elements in registers

Figure 1.25   Typical Stack Organization

Stack Implementation

A stack is an ordered set of elements, only one of which (the most recently added) can be accessed at a time. The point of access is called the *top* of the stack. The number of elements in the stack, or length of the stack, is variable. Items may only be added to or deleted from the top of the stack. For this reason, a stack is also known as a *pushdown list* or a *last-in-first-out (LIFO) list*.

The implementation of a stack requires that there be some set of locations used to store the stack elements. A typical approach is illustrated in Figure 1.25. A contiguous block of locations is reserved in main memory (or virtual memory) for the stack. Most of the time, the block is partially filled with stack elements and the remainder is available for stack growth. Three addresses are needed for proper operation, and these are often stored in processor registers:

- **Stack pointer:** Contains the address of the top of the stack. If an item is appended to (PUSH) or deleted from (POP) the stack, the pointer is decremented or incremented to contain the address of the new top of the stack.

- **Stack base:** Contains the address of the bottom location in the reserved block. This is the first location to be used when an item is added to an empty stack. If an attempt is made to POP an element when the stack is empty, an error is reported.

- **Stack limit:** Contains the address of the other end, or top, of the reserved block. If an attempt is made to PUSH an element when the stack is full, an error is reported.

Traditionally, and on most machines today, the base of the stack is at the high-address end of the reserved stack block, and the limit is at the low-address end. Thus, the stack grows from higher addresses to lower addresses.

Procedure Calls and Returns

A common technique for managing procedure calls and returns makes use of a stack. When the processor executes a call, it places (pushes) the return address on the stack. When it executes a return, it uses the address on top of the stack and removes (pops) that address from the stack. For the nested procedures of Figure 1.26, Figure 1.27 illustrates the use of a stack.

It is also often necessary to pass parameters with a procedure call. These could be passed in registers. Another possibility is to store the parameters in memory just after the Call instruction. In this case, the return must be to the location following the parameters. Both of these approaches have drawbacks. If registers are used, the called program and the calling program must be written to assure that the registers are used properly. The storing of parameters in memory makes it difficult to exchange a variable number of parameters.

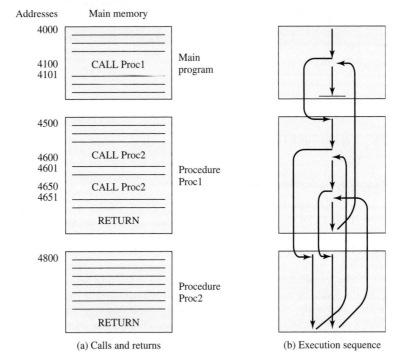

(a) Calls and returns   (b) Execution sequence

Figure 1.26   Nested Procedures

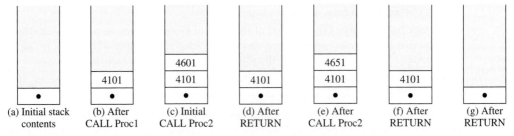

Figure 1.27   Use of Stack to Implement Nested Procedures of Figure 1.26

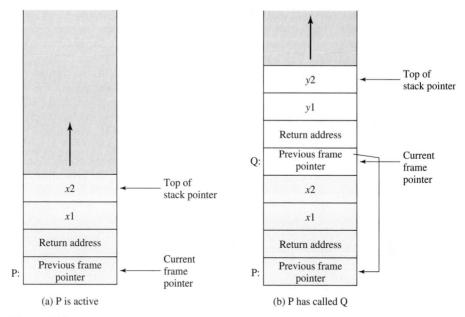

Figure 1.28   Stack Frame Growth Using Sample Procedures P and Q

A more flexible approach to parameter passing is the stack. When the processor executes a call, it not only stacks the return address, it stacks parameters to be passed to the called procedure. The called procedure can access the parameters from the stack. Upon return, return parameters can also be placed on the stack, *under* the return address. The entire set of parameters, including return address, that is stored for a procedure invocation is referred to as a **stack frame**.

An example is provided in Figure 1.28. The example refers to procedure P in which the local variables $x1$ and $x2$ are declared, and procedure Q, which can be called by P and in which the local variables $y1$ and $y2$ are declared. The first item stored in each stack frame is a pointer to the beginning of the previous frame. This is needed if the number or length of parameters to be stacked is variable. Next is stored the return point for the procedure that corresponds to this stack frame. Finally, space is allocated at the top of the stack frame for local variables. These local variables can be used for parameter passing. For example, suppose that when P calls Q, it passes one parameter value. This value could be stored in variable $y1$. Thus, in a high-level language, there would be an instruction in the P routine that looks like this:

$$CALL\ Q(y1)$$

When this call is executed, a new stack frame is created for Q (Figure 1.28b), which includes a pointer to the stack frame for P, the return address to P, and two local variables for Q, one of which is initialized to the passed parameter value from P. The other local variable, $y2$, is simply a local variable used by Q in its calculations. The need to include such local variables in the stack frame is discussed in the next subsection.

Reentrant Procedures

A useful concept, particularly in a system that supports multiple users at the same time, is that of the reentrant procedure. A reentrant procedure is one in which a single copy of the program code can be shared by multiple users during the same period of time. Reentrancy has two key aspects: The program code cannot modify itself and the local data for each user must be stored separately. A reentrant procedure can be interrupted and called by an interrupting program and still execute correctly upon return to the procedure. In a shared system, reentrancy allows more efficient use of main memory: One copy of the program code is kept in main memory, but more than one application can call the procedure.

Thus, a reentrant procedure must have a permanent part (the instructions that make up the procedure) and a temporary part (a pointer back to the calling program as well as memory for local variables used by the program). Each execution instance, called activation, of a procedure will execute the code in the permanent part but must have its own copy of local variables and parameters. The temporary part associated with a particular activation is referred to as an *activation record*.

The most convenient way to support reentrant procedures is by means of a stack. When a reentrant procedure is called, the activation record of the procedure can be stored on the stack. Thus, the activation record becomes part of the stack frame that is created on procedure call.

OPERATING SYSTEM OVERVIEW

We begin our study of operating systems with a brief history. This history is itself interesting and also serves the purpose of providing an overview of operating system principles. The first section examines the objectives and functions of operating systems. Then we look at how operating systems have evolved from primitive batch systems to sophisticated multitasking, multiuser systems. The remainder of the chapter looks at the history and general characteristics of the two operating systems that serve as examples throughout this book. All of the material in this chapter is covered in greater depth later in the book.

2.1 OPERATING SYSTEM OBJECTIVES AND FUNCTIONS

An operating system is a program that controls the execution of application programs and acts as an interface between applications and the computer hardware. It can be thought of as having three objectives:

- **Convenience:** An operating system makes a computer more convenient to use.
- **Efficiency:** An operating system allows the computer system resources to be used in an efficient manner.
- **Ability to evolve:** An operating system should be constructed in such a way as to permit the effective development, testing, and introduction of new system functions without interfering with service.

Let us examine these three aspects of an operating system in turn.

The Operating System as a User/Computer Interface

The hardware and software used in providing applications to a user can be viewed in a layered or hierarchical fashion, as depicted in Figure 2.1. The user of those applications, the end user, generally is not concerned with the details of computer hardware. Thus, the end user views a computer system in terms of a set of applications. An application can be expressed in a programming language and is developed by an application programmer. If one were to develop an application program as a set of machine instructions that is completely responsible for controlling the computer hardware, one would be faced with an overwhelmingly complex undertaking. To ease this chore, a set of system programs is provided. Some of these programs are referred to as utilities. These implement frequently used functions that assist in program creation, the management of files, and the control of I/O devices. A programmer will make use of these facilities in developing an application, and the application, while it is running, will invoke the utilities to perform certain functions. The most important system program is the operating system. The operating system masks the details of the hardware from the programmer and provides the programmer with a convenient interface for using the system. It acts as mediator, making it easier for the programmer and for application programs to access and use those facilities and services.

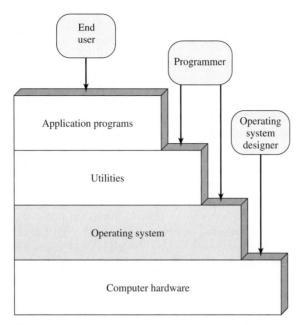

Figure 2.1 Layers and Views of a Computer System

Briefly, the operating system typically provides services in the following areas:

- **Program development:** The operating system provides a variety of facilities and services, such as editors and debuggers, to assist the programmer in creating programs. Typically, these services are in the form of utility programs that, while not strictly part of the core of the operating system, are supplied with the operating system and are referred to as application program development tools.

- **Program execution:** A number of steps need to be performed to execute a program. Instructions and data must be loaded into main memory, I/O devices and files must be initialized, and other resources must be prepared. The operating system handles these scheduling duties for the user.

- **Access to I/O devices:** Each I/O device requires its own peculiar set of instructions or control signals for operation. The operating system provides a uniform interface that hides these details so that programmers can access such devices using simple reads and writes.

- **Controlled access to files:** For file access, the operating system must reflect a detailed understanding of not only the nature of the I/O device (disk drive, tape drive) but also the structure of the data contained in the files on the storage medium. Further, in the case of a system with multiple users, the operating system may provide protection mechanisms to control access to the files.

- **System access:** For shared or public systems, the operating system controls access to the system as a whole and to specific system resources. The access function must provide protection of resources and data from unauthorized users and must resolve conflicts for resource contention.

- **Error detection and response:** A variety of errors can occur while a computer system is running. These include internal and external hardware errors, such as a memory error, or a device failure or malfunction; and various software errors, such as division by zero, attempt to access forbidden memory locations, and inability of the operating system to grant the request of an application. In each case, the operating system must provide a response that clears the error condition with the least impact on running applications. The response may range from ending the program that caused the error, to retrying the operation, to simply reporting the error to the application.

- **Accounting:** A good operating system will collect usage statistics for various resources and monitor performance parameters such as response time. On any system, this information is useful in anticipating the need for future enhancements and in tuning the system to improve performance. On a multiuser system, the information can be used for billing purposes.

The Operating System as Resource Manager

A computer is a set of resources for the movement, storage, and processing of data and for the control of these functions. The operating system is responsible for managing these resources.

Can we say that it is the operating system that controls the movement, storage, and processing of data? From one point of view, the answer is yes: By managing the computer's resources, the operating system is in control of the computer's basic functions. But this control is exercised in a curious way. Normally, we think of a control mechanism as something external to that which is controlled, or at least as something that is a distinct and separate part of that which is controlled. (For example, a residential heating system is controlled by a thermostat, which is separate from the heat-generation and heat-distribution apparatus.) This is not the case with the operating system, which as a control mechanism is unusual in two respects:

- The operating system functions in the same way as ordinary computer software; that is, it is a program or suite of programs executed by the processor.
- The operating system frequently relinquishes control and must depend on the processor to allow it to regain control.

The operating system is, in fact, a set of computer programs. Like other computer programs, it provides instructions for the processor. The key difference is in the intent of the program. The operating system directs the processor in the use of the other system resources and in the timing of its execution of other programs. But in order for the processor to do any of these things, it must cease executing the operating system program and execute other programs. Thus, the operating system relinquishes control for the processor to do some "useful" work and then resumes control long enough to prepare the processor to do the next piece of work. The mechanisms involved in all this should become clear as the chapter proceeds.

Figure 2.2 suggests the main resources that are managed by the operating system. A portion of the operating system is in main memory. This includes the **kernel**, or **nucleus**, which contains the most frequently used functions in the operating

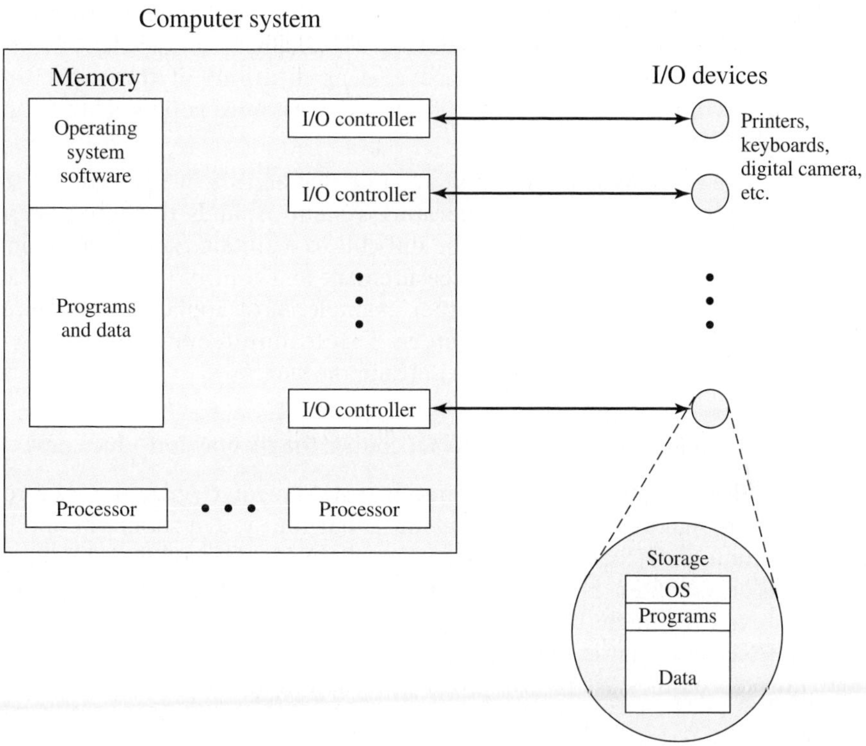

Computer system

Figure 2.2   The Operating System as Resource Manager

system and, at a given time, other portions of the operating system currently in use. The remainder of main memory contains user programs and data. The allocation of this resource (main memory) is controlled jointly by the operating system and memory management hardware in the processor, as we shall see. The operating system decides when an I/O device can be used by a program in execution and controls access to and use of files. The processor itself is a resource, and the operating system must determine how much processor time is to be devoted to the execution of a particular user program. In the case of a multiple-processor system, this decision must span all of the processors.

Ease of Evolution of an Operating System

A major operating system will evolve over time for a number of reasons:

- **Hardware upgrades plus new types of hardware:** For example, early versions of UNIX and the IBM OS/2 operating system did not employ a paging mechanism because they were run on machines without paging hardware.[1] More recent versions of these operating systems have been modified to exploit paging capabilities. Also, the use of graphics terminals

---

[1] Paging is introduced briefly later in this chapter and is discussed in detail in Chapter 7.

and page-mode terminals instead of line-at-a-time scroll mode terminals affects operating system design. For example, a graphics terminal typically allows the user to view several applications at the same time through "windows" on the screen. This requires more sophisticated support in the operating system.

- **New services:** In response to user demand or in response to the needs of system managers, the operating system expands to offer new services. For example, if it is found to be difficult to maintain good performance for users with existing tools, new measurement and control tools may be added to the operating system. As another example, most applications require the use of windows on the display screen. This feature requires major upgrades to the operating system if it does not support windows.

- **Fixes:** Any operating system has faults. These are discovered over the course of time and fixes are made. Of course, the fix may introduce new faults.

The need to change an operating system regularly places certain requirements on its design. An obvious statement is that the system should be modular in construction, with clearly defined interfaces between the modules, and that it should be well documented. For large programs, such as the typical contemporary operating system, what might be referred to as straightforward modularization is inadequate [DENN80a]. That is, much more must be done than simply partitioning a program into subroutines. We return to this topic later in this chapter.

2.2 THE EVOLUTION OF OPERATING SYSTEMS

In attempting to understand the key requirements for an operating system and the significance of the major features of a contemporary operating system, it is useful to consider how operating systems have evolved over the years.

Serial Processing

With the earliest computers, from the late 1940s to the mid-1950s, the programmer interacted directly with the computer hardware; there was no operating system. These machines were run from a console consisting of display lights, toggle switches, some form of input device, and a printer. Programs in machine code were loaded via the input device (e.g., a card reader). If an error halted the program, the error condition was indicated by the lights. The programmer could proceed to examine processor registers and main memory to determine the cause of the error. If the program proceeded to a normal completion, the output appeared on the printer.

These early systems presented two main problems:

- **Scheduling:** Most installations used a hardcopy sign-up sheet to reserve machine time. Typically, a user could sign up for a block of time in multiples of a half hour or so. A user might sign up for an hour and finish in 45 minutes; this would result in wasted computer processing time. On the other hand, the user might run into problems, not finish in the allotted time, and be forced to stop before resolving the problem.

- **Setup time:** A single program, called a **job**, could involve loading the compiler plus the high-level language program (source program) into memory, saving the compiled program (object program) and then loading and linking together the object program and common functions. Each of these steps could involve mounting or dismounting tapes or setting up card decks. If an error occurred, the hapless user typically had to go back to the beginning of the setup sequence. Thus, a considerable amount of time was spent just in setting up the program to run.

This mode of operation could be termed serial processing, reflecting the fact that users have access to the computer in series. Over time, various system software tools were developed to attempt to make serial processing more efficient. These include libraries of common functions, linkers, loaders, debuggers, and I/O driver routines that were available as common software for all users.

Simple Batch Systems

Early machines were very expensive, and therefore it was important to maximize machine utilization. The wasted time due to scheduling and setup time was unacceptable.

To improve utilization, the concept of a batch operating system was developed. It appears that the first batch operating system (and the first operating system of any kind) was developed in the mid-1950s by General Motors for use on an IBM 701 [WEIZ81]. The concept was subsequently refined and implemented on the IBM 704 by a number of IBM customers. By the early 1960s, a number of vendors had developed batch operating systems for their computer systems. IBSYS, the IBM operating system for the 7090/7094 computers, is particularly notable because of its widespread influence on other systems.

The central idea behind the simple batch processing scheme was the use of a piece of software known as the **monitor**. With this type of operating system, the user no longer has direct access to the machine. Instead, the user submits the job on cards or tape to a computer operator, who batches the jobs together sequentially and places the entire batch on an input device, for use by the monitor. Each program is constructed to branch back to the monitor when it completes processing, at which point the monitor automatically begins loading the next program.

To understand how this scheme works, let us look at it from two points of view: that of the monitor and that of the processor.

- **Monitor point of view:** The monitor controls the sequence of events. For this to be so, much of the monitor must always be in main memory and available for execution (Figure 2.3). That portion is referred to as the **resident monitor**. The rest of the monitor consists of utilities and common functions that are loaded as subroutines to the user program at the beginning of any job that requires them. The monitor reads in jobs one at a time from the input device (typically a card reader or magnetic tape drive). As it is read in, the current job is placed in the user program area, and control is passed to this job. When the job is completed, it returns control to the monitor, which immediately reads in the

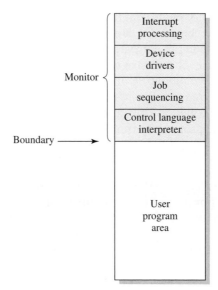

Figure 2.3   Memory Layout for a
Resident Monitor

next job. The results of each job are sent to an output device, such as a printer, for delivery to the user.

- **Processor point of view:** At a certain point, the processor is executing instructions from the portion of main memory containing the monitor. These instructions cause the next job to be read into another portion of main memory. Once a job has been read in, the processor will encounter a branch instruction in the monitor that instructs the processor to continue execution at the start of the user program. The processor will then execute the instructions in the user program until it encounters an ending or error condition. Either event causes the processor to fetch its next instruction from the monitor program. Thus the phrase "control is passed to a job" simply means that the processor is now fetching and executing instructions in a user program, and "control is returned to the monitor" means that the processor is now fetching and executing instructions from the monitor program.

The monitor performs a scheduling function: A batch of jobs is queued up, and jobs are executed as rapidly as possible, with no intervening idle time. The monitor improves job setup time as well. With each job, instructions are included in a primitive form of **job control language** (JCL). This is a special type of programming language used to provide instructions to the monitor. A simple example is that of a user submitting a program written in the programming language FORTRAN plus some data to be used by the program. All FORTRAN instructions and data are on a separate punched card or a separate record on tape. In addition to FORTRAN and data lines, the job includes job control instructions, which are denoted by the beginning '$'. The overall format of the job looks like this:

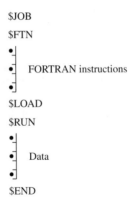

To execute this job, the monitor reads the $FTN line and loads the appropriate language compiler from its mass storage (usually tape). The compiler translates the user's program into object code, which is stored in memory or mass storage. If it is stored in memory, the operation is referred to as "compile, load, and go." If it is stored on tape, then the $LOAD instruction is required. This instruction is read by the monitor, which regains control after the compile operation. The monitor invokes the loader, which loads the object program into memory (in place of the compiler) and transfers control to it. In this manner, a large segment of main memory can be shared among different subsystems, although only one such subsystem could be executing at a time.

During the execution of the user program, any input instruction causes one line of data to be read. The input instruction in the user program causes an input routine that is part of the operating system to be invoked. The input routine checks to make sure that the program does not accidentally read in a JCL line. If this happens, an error occurs and control transfers to the monitor. At the completion of the user job, the monitor will scan the input lines until it encounters the next JCL instruction. Thus, the system is protected against a program with too many or too few data lines.

The monitor, or batch operating system, is simply a computer program. It relies on the ability of the processor to fetch instructions from various portions of main memory to alternately seize and relinquish control. Certain other hardware features are also desirable:

- **Memory protection:** While the user program is executing, it must not alter the memory area containing the monitor. If such an attempt is made, the processor hardware should detect an error and transfer control to the monitor. The monitor would then abort the job, print out an error message, and load in the next job.

- **Timer:** A timer is used to prevent a single job from monopolizing the system. The timer is set at the beginning of each job. If the timer expires, the user program is stopped, and control returns to the monitor.

- **Privileged instructions:** Certain machine-level instructions are designated privileged and can be executed only by the monitor. If the processor encounters such an instruction while executing a user program, an error occurs causing control to be transferred to the monitor. Among the privileged instructions are I/O instructions, so that the monitor retains control of all I/O devices. This prevents, for example, a user program from accidentally reading job control instructions from the next job. If a user program wishes to perform I/O, it must request that the monitor perform the operation for it.

- **Interrupts:** Early computer models did not have this capability. This feature gives the operating system more flexibility in relinquishing control to and regaining control from user programs.

Considerations of memory protection and privileged instructions lead to the concept of modes of operation. A user program executes in a **user mode**, in which certain areas of memory are protected from the user's use and in which certain instructions may not be executed. The monitor executes in a system mode, or what has come to be called **kernel mode**, in which privileged instructions may be executed and in which protected areas of memory may be accessed.

Of course, an operating system can be built without these features. But computer vendors quickly learned that the results were chaos, and so even relatively primitive batch operating systems were provided with these hardware features.

With a batch operating system, machine time alternates between execution of user programs and execution of the monitor. There have been two sacrifices: Some main memory is now given over to the monitor and some machine time is consumed by the monitor. Both of these are forms of overhead. Despite this overhead, the simple batch system improves utilization of the computer.

Multiprogrammed Batch Systems

Even with the automatic job sequencing provided by a simple batch operating system, the processor is often idle. The problem is that I/O devices are slow compared to the processor. Figure 2.4 details a representative calculation. The calculation concerns a program that processes a file of records and performs, on average, 100 machine instructions per record. In this example the computer spends over 96% of its time waiting for I/O devices to finish transferring data to and from the file. Figure 2.5a illustrates this situation, where we have a single program, referred to as uniprogramming. The processor spends a certain amount of time executing, until it reaches an I/O instruction. It must then wait until that I/O instruction concludes before proceeding.

This inefficiency is not necessary. We know that there must be enough memory to hold the operating system (resident monitor) and one user program. Suppose that there is room for the operating system and two user programs. When one job needs to wait for

Read one record from file	15 μs
Execute 100 instructions	1 μs
Write one record to file	15 μs
TOTAL	31 μs
Percent CPU utilization $= \frac{1}{31} = 0.032 = 3.2\%$	

Figure 2.4 System Utilization Example

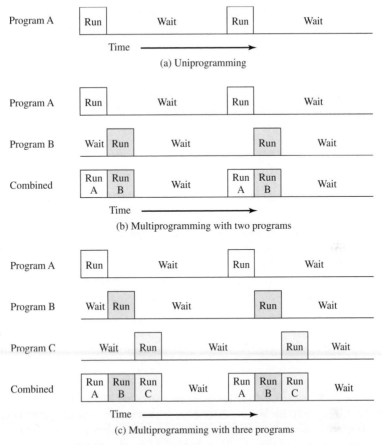

Figure 2.5   Multiprogramming Example

I/O, the processor can switch to the other job, which is likely not waiting for I/O (Figure 2.5b). Furthermore, we might expand memory to hold three, four, or more programs and switch among all of them (Figure 2.5c). The approach is known as **multiprogramming**, or **multitasking**. It is the central theme of modern operating systems.

   To illustrate the benefit of multiprogramming, we give a simple example. Consider a computer with 250 Mbytes of available memory (not used by the operating system), a disk, a terminal, and a printer. Three programs, JOB1, JOB2, and JOB3, are submitted for execution at the same time, with the attributes listed in Table 2.1. We assume minimal processor requirements for JOB2 and JOB3 and continuous disk and printer use by JOB3. For a simple batch environment, these jobs will be executed in sequence. Thus, JOB1 completes in 5 minutes. JOB2 must wait until the 5 minutes are over and then completes 15 minutes after that. JOB3 begins after 20 minutes and completes at 30 minutes from the time it was initially submitted. The average resource utilization, throughput, and response times are shown in the uniprogramming column of Table 2.2. Device-by-device utilization is illustrated in Figure 2.6a. It is evident that there is gross underutilization for all resources when averaged over the required 30-minute time period.

Table 2.1 Sample Program Execution Attributes

	JOB1	JOB2	JOB3
Type of job	Heavy compute	Heavy I/O	Heavy I/O
Duration	5 min	15 min	10 min
Memory required	50 M	100 M	75 M
Need disk?	No	No	Yes
Need terminal?	No	Yes	No
Need printer?	No	No	Yes

Table 2.2 Effects of Multiprogramming on Resource Utilization

	Uniprogramming	Multiprogramming
Processor use	20%	40%
Memory use	33%	67%
Disk use	33%	67%
Printer use	33%	67%
Elapsed time	30 min	15 min
Throughput	6 jobs/hr	12 jobs/hr
Mean response time	18 min	10 min

Now suppose that the jobs are run concurrently under a multiprogramming operating system. Because there is little resource contention between the jobs, all three can run in nearly minimum time while coexisting with the others in the computer (assuming that JOB2 and JOB3 are allotted enough processor time to keep their input and output operations active). JOB1 will still require 5 minutes to complete, but at the end of that time, JOB2 will be one-third finished and JOB3 half finished. All three jobs will have finished within 15 minutes. The improvement is evident when examining the multiprogramming column of Table 2.2, obtained from the histogram shown in Figure 2.6b.

As with a simple batch system, a multiprogramming batch system must rely on certain computer hardware features. The most notable additional feature that is useful for multiprogramming is the hardware that supports I/O interrupts and DMA (direct memory access). With interrupt-driven I/O or DMA, the processor can issue an I/O command for one job and proceed with the execution of another job while the I/O is carried out by the device controller. When the I/O operation is complete, the processor is interrupted and control is passed to an interrupt-handling program in the operating system. The operating system will then pass control to another job.

Multiprogramming operating systems are fairly sophisticated compared to single-program, or **uniprogramming**, systems. To have several jobs ready to run, they must be kept in main memory, requiring some form of **memory management**. In addition, if several jobs are ready to run, the processor must decide which one to run; this decision requires an algorithm for scheduling. These concepts are discussed later in this chapter.

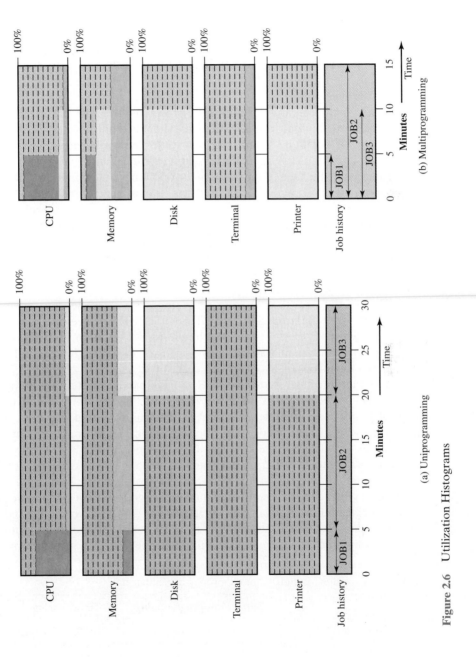

Figure 2.6 Utilization Histograms

Time-Sharing Systems

With the use of multiprogramming, batch processing can be quite efficient. However, for many jobs, it is desirable to provide a mode in which the user interacts directly with the computer. Indeed, for some jobs, such as transaction processing, an interactive mode is essential.

Today, the requirement for an interactive computing facility can be, and often is, met by the use of a dedicated personal computer or workstation. That option was not available in the 1960s, when most computers were big and costly. Instead, time sharing was developed.

Just as multiprogramming allows the processor to handle multiple batch jobs at a time, multiprogramming can also be used to handle multiple interactive jobs. In this latter case, the technique is referred to as **time sharing**, because processor time is shared among multiple users. In a time-sharing system, multiple users simultaneously access the system through terminals, with the operating system interleaving the execution of each user program in a short burst or quantum of computation. Thus, if there are n users actively requesting service at one time, each user will only see on the average $1/n$ of the effective computer capacity, not counting operating system overhead. However, given the relatively slow human reaction time, the response time on a properly designed system should be similar to that on a dedicated computer.

Both batch processing and time sharing use multiprogramming. The key differences are listed in Table 2.3.

One of the first time-sharing operating systems to be developed was the Compatible Time-Sharing System (CTSS) [CORB62], developed at MIT by a group known as Project MAC (Machine-Aided Cognition, or Multiple-Access Computers). The system was first developed for the IBM 709 in 1961 and later transferred to an IBM 7094.

Compared to later systems, CTSS is primitive. The system ran on a machine with 32,000 36-bit words of main memory, with the resident monitor consuming 5000 of that. When control was to be assigned to an interactive user, the user's program and data were loaded into the remaining 27,000 words of main memory. A program was always loaded to start at the location of the 5000th word; this simplified both the monitor and memory management. A system clock generated interrupts at a rate of approximately one every 0.2 seconds. At each clock interrupt, the operating system regained control and could assign the processor to another user. Thus, at regular time intervals, the current user would be preempted and another user loaded in. To preserve the old user program status for later resumption, the old user programs and data were written out to disk before the new user programs and

Table 2.3   Batch Multiprogramming versus Time Sharing

	Batch Multiprogramming	**Time Sharing**
Principal objective	Maximize processor use	Minimize response time
Source of directives to operating system	Job control language commands provided with the job	Commands entered at the terminal

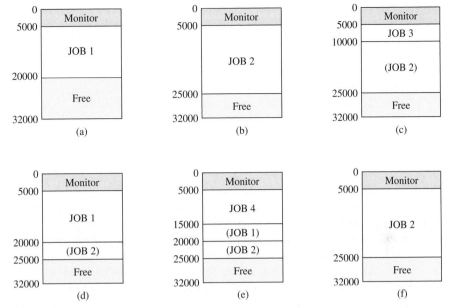

Figure 2.7   CTSS Operation

data were read in. Subsequently, the old user program code and data were restored in main memory when that program was next given a turn.

To minimize disk traffic, user memory was only written out when the incoming program would overwrite it. This principle is illustrated in Figure 2.7. Assume that there are four interactive users with the following memory requirements:

- JOB1: 15,000
- JOB2: 20,000
- JOB3: 5000
- JOB4: 10,000

Initially, the monitor loads in JOB1 and transfers control to it (a). Later, the monitor decides to transfer control to JOB2. Because JOB2 requires more memory than JOB1, JOB1 must be written out first, and then JOB2 can be loaded (b). Next, JOB3 is loaded in to be run. However, because JOB3 is smaller than JOB2, a portion of JOB2 can remain in memory, reducing disk write time (c). Later, the monitor decides to transfer control back to JOB1. An additional portion of JOB2 must be written out when JOB1 is loaded back into memory (d). When JOB4 is loaded, part of JOB1 and the portion of JOB2 remaining in memory are retained (e). At this point, if either JOB1 or JOB2 is activated, only a partial load will be required. In this example, it is JOB2 that runs next. This requires that JOB4 and the remaining resident portion of JOB1 be written out and that the missing portion of JOB2 be read in (f).

The CTSS approach is primitive compared to present-day time sharing, but it worked. It was extremely simple, which minimized the size of the monitor. Because a job was always loaded into the same locations in memory, there was no need for relocation techniques at load time (discussed subsequently). The technique of only writing out what was necessary minimized disk activity. Running on the 7094, CTSS supported a maximum of 32 users.

Time sharing and multiprogramming raise a host of new problems for the operating system. If multiple jobs are in memory, then they must be protected from interfering with each other by, for example, modifying each other's data. With multiple interactive users, the file system must be protected so that only authorized users have access to a particular file. The contention for resources, such as printers and mass storage devices, must be handled. These and other problems, with possible solutions, will be encountered throughout this text.

2.3   MAJOR ACHIEVEMENTS

Operating systems are among the most complex pieces of software ever developed. This reflects the challenge of trying to meet the difficult and in some cases competing objectives of convenience, efficiency, and ability to evolve. [DENN80a] proposes that there have been five major theoretical advances in the development of operating systems:

- Processes
- Memory management
- Information protection and security
- Scheduling and resource management
- System structure

Each advance is characterized by principles, or abstractions, developed to meet difficult practical problems. Taken together, these five areas span many of the key design and implementation issues of modern operating systems. The brief review of these five areas in this section serves as an overview of much of the rest of the text.

Processes

The concept of process is fundamental to the structure of operating systems. This term was first used by the designers of Multics in the 1960s [DALE68]. It is a somewhat more general term than job. Many definitions have been given for the term *process*, including

- A program in execution
- An instance of a program running on a computer
- The entity that can be assigned to and executed on a processor
- A unit of activity characterized by a single sequential thread of execution, a current state, and an associated set of system resources

This concept should become clearer as we proceed.

Three major lines of computer system development created problems in timing and synchronization that contributed to the development of the concept of the process: multiprogramming batch operation, time sharing, and real-time transaction systems. As we have seen, multiprogramming was designed to keep the processor and I/O devices, including storage devices, simultaneously busy to achieve maximum efficiency. The key mechanism is this: In response to signals indicating the completion of I/O transactions, the processor is switched among the various programs residing in main memory.

A second line of development was general-purpose time sharing. Here, the key design objective is to be responsive to the needs of the individual user and yet, for cost reasons, be able to support many users simultaneously. These goals are compatible because of the relatively slow reaction time of the user. For example, if a typical user needs an average of 2 seconds of processing time per minute, then close to 30 such users should be able to share the same system without noticeable interference. Of course, operating system overhead must be factored into such calculations.

Another important line of development has been real-time transaction processing systems. In this case, a number of users are entering queries or updates against a database. An example is an airline reservation system. The key difference between the transaction processing system and the time-sharing system is that the former is limited to one or a few applications, whereas users of a time-sharing system can engage in program development, job execution, and the use of various applications. In both cases, system response time is paramount.

The principal tool available to system programmers in developing the early multiprogramming and multiuser interactive systems was the interrupt. The activity of any job could be suspended by the occurrence of a defined event, such as an I/O completion. The processor would save some sort of context (e.g., program counter and other registers) and branch to an interrupt-handling routine, which would determine the nature of the interrupt, process the interrupt, and then resume user processing with the interrupted job or some other job.

The design of the system software to coordinate these various activities turned out to be remarkably difficult. With many jobs in progress at any one time, each of which involved numerous steps to be performed in sequence, it became impossible to analyze all of the possible combinations of sequences of events. In the absence of some systematic means of coordination and cooperation among activities, programmers resorted to ad hoc methods based on their understanding of the environment that the operating system had to control. These efforts were vulnerable to subtle programming errors whose effects could be observed only when certain relatively rare sequences of actions occurred. These errors were difficult to diagnose because they needed to be distinguished from application software errors and hardware errors. Even when the error was detected, it was difficult to determine the cause, because the precise conditions under which the errors appeared were very hard to reproduce. In general terms, there are four main causes of such errors [DENN80a]:

- **Improper synchronization:** It is often the case that a routine must be suspended awaiting an event elsewhere in the system. For example, a program that initiates an I/O read must wait until the data are available in a buffer before proceeding. In such cases, a signal from some other routine is required. Improper design of the signaling mechanism can result in signals being lost or duplicate signals being received.
- **Failed mutual exclusion:** It is often the case that more than one user or program will attempt to make use of a shared resource at the same time. For example, two users may attempt to edit the same file at the same time. If these accesses are not

controlled, an error can occur. There must be some sort of mutual exclusion mechanism that permits only one routine at a time to perform an update against the file. The implementation of such mutual exclusion is difficult to verify as being correct under all possible sequences of events.

- **Nondeterminate program operation:** The results of a particular program normally should depend only on the input to that program and not on the activities of other programs in a shared system. But when programs share memory, and their execution is interleaved by the processor, they may interfere with each other by overwriting common memory areas in unpredictable ways. Thus, the order in which various programs are scheduled may affect the outcome of any particular program.

- **Deadlocks:** It is possible for two or more programs to be hung up waiting for each other. For example, two programs may each require two I/O devices to perform some operation (e.g., disk to tape copy). One of the programs has seized control of one of the devices and the other program has control of the other device. Each is waiting for the other program to release the desired resource. Such a deadlock may depend on the chance timing of resource allocation and release.

What is needed to tackle these problems is a systematic way to monitor and control the various programs executing on the processor. The concept of the process provides the foundation. We can think of a process as consisting of three components:

- An executable program
- The associated data needed by the program (variables, work space, buffers, etc.)
- The execution context of the program

This last element is essential. The **execution context**, or **process state**, is the internal data by which the operating system is able to supervise and control the process. This internal information is separated from the process, because the operating system has information not permitted to the process. The context includes all of the information that the operating system needs to manage the process and that the processor needs to execute the process properly. The context includes the contents of the various processor registers, such as the program counter and data registers. It also includes information of use to the operating system, such as the priority of the process and whether the process is waiting for the completion of a particular I/O event.

Figure 2.8 indicates a way in which processes may be managed. Two processes, A and B, exist in portions of main memory. That is, a block of memory is allocated to each process that contains the program, data, and context information. Each process is recorded in a process list built and maintained by the operating system. The process list contains one entry for each process, which includes a pointer to the location of the block of memory that contains the process. The entry may also include part or all of the execution context of the process. The remainder of the execution context is stored elsewhere, perhaps with the process itself (as indicated in Figure 2.8) or frequently in a separate region of memory. The process index register contains the index into the process list of the process currently controlling the processor. The program counter points to the next instruction in that process to be executed. The base and limit registers define the region in memory occupied by the process:

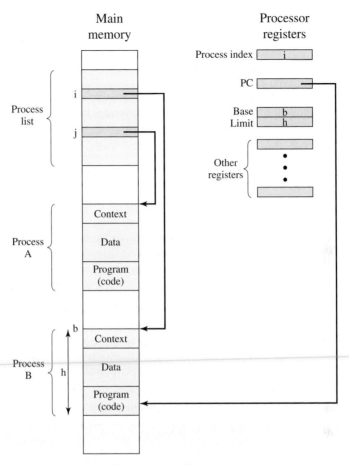

Figure 2.8   Typical Process Implementation

The base register is the starting address of the region of memory and the limit is the size of the region (in bytes or words). The program counter and all data references are interpreted relative to the base register and must not exceed the value in the limit register. This prevents interprocess interference.

In Figure 2.8, the process index register indicates that process B is executing. Process A was previously executing but has been temporarily interrupted. The contents of all the registers at the moment of A's interruption were recorded in its execution context. Later, the operating system can perform a process switch and resume execution of process A. The process switch consists of storing the context of B and restoring the context of A. When the program counter is loaded with a value pointing into A's program area, process A will automatically resume execution.

Thus, the process is realized as a data structure. A process can either be executing or awaiting execution. The entire **state** of the process at any instant is contained in its context. This structure allows the development of powerful techniques for ensuring coordination and cooperation among processes. New features can be designed and incorporated into the operating system (e.g., priority) by expanding the context to include any new information needed to support the feature. Throughout this book, we will see a number of examples where this process structure is employed to solve the problems raised by multiprogramming and resource sharing.

Memory Management

The needs of users can be met best by a computing environment that supports modular programming and the flexible use of data. System managers need efficient and orderly control of storage allocation. The operating system, to satisfy these requirements, has five principal storage management responsibilities:

- **Process isolation:** The operating system must prevent independent processes from interfering with each other's memory, both data and instructions.
- **Automatic allocation and management:** Programs should be dynamically allocated across the memory hierarchy as required. Allocation should be transparent to the programmer. Thus, the programmer is relieved of concerns relating to memory limitations, and the operating system can achieve efficiency by assigning memory to jobs only as needed.
- **Support of modular programming:** Programmers should be able to define program modules and to create, destroy, and alter the size of modules dynamically.
- **Protection and access control:** Sharing of memory, at any level of the memory hierarchy, creates the potential for one program to address the memory space of another. This is desirable when sharing is needed by particular applications. At other times, it threatens the integrity of programs and even of the operating system itself. The operating system must allow portions of memory to be accessible in various ways by various users.
- **Long-term storage:** Many application programs require means for storing information for extended periods of time, after the computer has been powered down.

Typically, operating systems meet these requirements with virtual memory and file system facilities. The file system implements a long-term store, with information stored in named objects, called files. The file is a convenient concept for the programmer and is a useful unit of access control and protection for the operating system.

Virtual memory is a facility that allows programs to address memory from a logical point of view, without regard to the amount of main memory physically available. Virtual memory was conceived to meet the requirement of having multiple user jobs reside in main memory concurrently, so that there would not be a hiatus between the execution of successive processes while one process was written out to secondary store and the successor process was read in. Because processes vary in size, if the processor switches among a number of processes it is difficult to pack them compactly into main memory. Paging systems were introduced, which allow processes to be comprised of a number of fixed-size blocks, called pages. A program references a word by means of a **virtual address** consisting of a page number and an offset within the page. Each page of a process may be located anywhere in main memory. The paging system provides for a dynamic mapping between the virtual address used in the program and a **real address**, or physical address, in main memory.

With dynamic mapping hardware available, the next logical step was to eliminate the requirement that all pages of a process reside in main memory simultaneously.

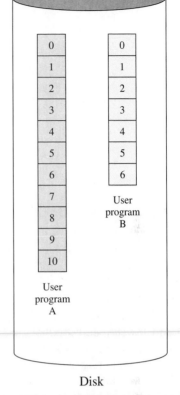

Main memory

Main memory consists of a number of fixed-length frames, each equal to the size of a page. For a program to execute, some or all of its pages must be in main memory.

Disk

Secondary memory (disk) can hold many fixed-length pages. A user program consists of some number of pages. Pages for all programs plus the operating system are on disk, as are files.

Figure 2.9   Virtual Memory Concepts

All the pages of a process are maintained on disk. When a process is executing, some of its pages are in main memory. If reference is made to a page that is not in main memory, the memory management hardware detects this and arranges for the missing page to be loaded. Such a scheme is referred to as virtual memory area and is depicted in Figure 2.9.

The processor hardware, together with the operating system, provides the user with a "virtual processor" that has access to a virtual memory. This store may be a linear address space or a collection of segments, which are variable-length blocks of contiguous addresses. In either case, programming language instructions can reference program and data locations in the virtual memory area. Process isolation can be achieved by giving each process a unique, nonoverlapping virtual memory. Memory sharing can be achieved by overlapping portions of two virtual memory spaces. Files are maintained in a long-term store. Files and portions of files may be copied into the virtual memory for manipulation by programs.

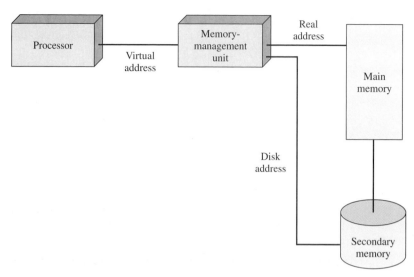

Figure 2.10 Virtual Memory Addressing

Figure 2.10 highlights the addressing concerns in a virtual memory scheme. Storage consists of directly addressable (by machine instructions) main memory and lower-speed auxiliary memory that is accessed indirectly by loading blocks into main memory. Address translation hardware (memory management unit) is interposed between the processor and memory. Programs reference locations using virtual addresses, which are mapped into real main memory addresses. If a reference is made to a virtual address not in real memory, then a portion of the contents of real memory is swapped out to auxiliary memory and the desired block of data is swapped in. During this activity, the process that generated the address reference must be suspended. The operating system designer needs to develop an address translation mechanism that generates little overhead and a storage allocation policy that minimizes the traffic between memory levels.

Information Protection and Security

The growth in the use of time-sharing systems and, more recently, computer networks has brought with it a growth in concern for the protection of information. The nature of the threat that concerns an organization will vary greatly depending on the circumstances. However, there are some general-purpose tools that can be built into computers and operating systems that support a variety of protection and security mechanisms. In general, we are concerned with the problem of controlling access to computer systems and the information stored in them.

Much of the work in security and protection as it relates to operating systems can be roughly grouped into four categories:

- **Availability:** Concerned with protecting the system against interruption.
- **Confidentiality:** Assures that users cannot read data for which access is unauthorized.

- **Data integrity:** Protection of data from unauthorized modification.
- **Authenticity:** Concerned with the proper verification of the identity of users and the validity of messages or data.

Scheduling and Resource Management

A key responsibility of the operating system is to manage the various resources available to it (main memory space, I/O devices, processors) and to schedule their use by the various active processes. Any resource allocation and scheduling policy must consider three factors:

- **Fairness:** Typically, we would like all processes that are competing for the use of a particular resource to be given approximately equal and fair access to that resource. This is especially so for jobs of the same class, that is, jobs of similar demands.
- **Differential responsiveness:** On the other hand, the operating system may need to discriminate among different classes of jobs with different service requirements. The operating system should attempt to make allocation and scheduling decisions to meet the total set of requirements. The operating system should also take these decisions dynamically. For example, if a process is waiting for the use of an I/O device, the operating system may wish to schedule that process for execution as soon as possible to free up the device for later demands from other processes.
- **Efficiency:** The operating system should attempt to maximize throughput, minimize response time, and, in the case of time sharing, accommodate as many users as possible. These criteria conflict; finding the right balance for a particular situation is an ongoing problem for operating system research.

Scheduling and resource management are essentially operations-research problems, and the mathematical results of that discipline can be applied. In addition, measurement of system activity is important to be able to monitor performance and make adjustments.

Figure 2.11 suggests the major elements of the operating system involved in the scheduling of processes and the allocation of resources in a multiprogramming environment. The operating system maintains a number of queues, each of which is simply a list of processes waiting for some resource. The short-term queue consists of processes that are in main memory (or at least an essential minimum portion of each is in main memory) and are ready to run as soon as the processor is made available. Any one of these processes could use the processor next. It is up to the short-term scheduler, or dispatcher, to pick one. A common strategy is to give each process in the queue some time in turn; this is referred to as a **round-robin** technique. In effect, the round-robin technique employs a circular queue. Another strategy is to assign priority levels to the various processes, with the scheduler selecting processes in priority order.

The long-term queue is a list of new jobs waiting to use the processor. The operating system adds jobs to the system by transferring a process from the long-term queue to the short-term queue. At that time, a portion of main memory must be allocated to the incoming process. Thus, the operating system must be sure that

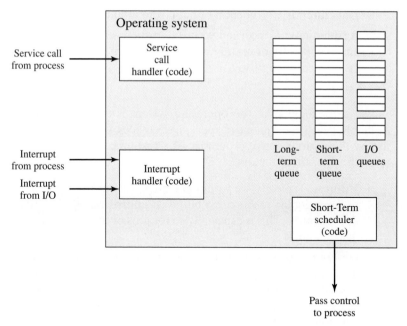

Figure 2.11 Key Elements of an Operating System for Multiprogramming

it does not overcommit memory or processing time by admitting too many processes to the system. There is an I/O queue for each I/O device. More than one process may request the use of the same I/O device. All processes waiting to use each device are lined up in that device's queue. Again, the operating system must determine which process to assign to an available I/O device.

The operating system receives control of the processor at the interrupt handler if an interrupt occurs. A process may specifically invoke some operating system service, such as an I/O device handler by means of a service call. In this case, a service call handler is the entry point into the operating system. In any case, once the interrupt or service call is handled, the short-term scheduler is invoked to pick a process for execution.

The foregoing is a functional description; details and modular design of this portion of the operating system will differ in various systems. Much of the research and development effort in operating systems has been directed at picking algorithms and data structures for this function that provide fairness, differential responsiveness, and efficiency.

System Structure

As more and more features have been added to operating systems, and as the underlying hardware has become more capable and versatile, the size and complexity of operating systems has grown. CTSS, put into operation at MIT in 1963, consisted of approximately 32,000 36-bit words of storage. OS/360, introduced a year later by IBM, had more than a million machine instructions. By 1975, the Multics system, developed by MIT and Bell Laboratories, had grown to more than 20 million instructions. It is true that more recently, some simpler operating systems have been introduced for smaller systems, but these have inevitably grown more complex as the underlying hardware and user requirements have grown. Thus, the UNIX of today is far more complex than the almost toy system put together by a few talented programmers in the early 1970s, and the simple MS-DOS has given way to the rich and complex power of OS/2 and Windows. For example, Windows NT 4.0 contains 16 million lines of code, and Windows 2000 has well over twice that number.

The size of a full-featured operating system, and the difficulty of the problem it addresses, has led to four unfortunate but all-too-common problems. First, operating systems are chronically late in being delivered. This goes for new operating systems and upgrades to older systems. Second, the systems have latent bugs that show up in the field and must be fixed and reworked. Third, performance is often not what was expected. Fourth, it has proved impossible to deploy a complex operating system that is not vulnerable to a variety of security attacks, including viruses, worms, and unauthorized access.

To manage the complexity of operating systems and to overcome these problems, there has been much focus over the years on the software structure of the operating system. Certain points seem obvious. The software must be modular. This will help organize the software development process and limit the effort of diagnosing and fixing errors. The modules must have well-defined interfaces to each other, and the interfaces must be as simple as possible. Again, this eases the programming burden. It also facilitates system evolution. With clean, minimal interfaces between modules, one module can be changed with minimal impact on other modules.

For large operating systems, which run from millions to tens of millions of lines of code, modular programming alone has not been found to be sufficient. Instead there has been increasing use of the concepts of hierarchical layers and information abstraction. The hierarchical structure of a modern operating system separates its functions according to their characteristic time scale and their level of abstraction. We can view the system as a series of levels. Each level performs a related subset of the functions required of the operating system. It relies on the next lower level to perform more primitive functions and to conceal the details of those functions. It provides services to the next higher layer. Ideally, the levels should be defined so that changes in one level do not require changes in other levels. Thus, we have decomposed one problem into a number of more manageable subproblems.

In general, lower layers deal with a far shorter time scale. Some parts of the operating system must interact directly with the computer hardware, where events can have a time scale as brief as a few billionths of a second. At the other end of the spectrum, parts of the operating system communicate with the user, who issues commands at a much more leisurely pace, perhaps one every few seconds. The use of a set of levels conforms nicely to this environment.

The way in which these principles are applied varies greatly among contemporary operating systems. However, it is useful at this point, for the purpose of gaining an overview of operating systems, to present a model of a hierarchical operating system. One proposed in [BROW84] and [DENN84] is useful, although it does not correspond to any particular operating system. The model is defined in Table 2.4 and consists of the following levels:

Table 2.4   Operating System Design Hierarchy

Level	Name	Objects	Example Operations
13	Shell	User programming environment	Statements in shell language
12	User processes	User processes	Quit, kill, suspend, resume
11	Directories	Directories	Create, destroy, attach, detach, search, list
10	Devices	External devices, such as printers, displays, and keyboards	Open, close, read, write
9	File system	Files	Create, destroy, open, close, read, write
8	Communications	Pipes	Create, destroy, open, close, read, write
7	Virtual memory	Segments, pages	Read, write, fetch
6	Local secondary store	Blocks of data, device channels	Read, write, allocate, free
5	Primitive processes	Primitive processes, semaphores, ready list	Suspend, resume, wait, signal
4	Interrupts	Interrupt-handling programs	Invoke, mask, unmask, retry
3	Procedures	Procedures, call stack, display	Mark stack, call, return
2	Instruction set	Evaluation stack, microprogram interpreter, scalar and array data	Load, store, add, subtract, branch
1	Electronic circuits	Registers, gates, buses, etc.	Clear, transfer, activate, complement

Grey shaded area represents hardware.

- **Level 1:** Consists of electronic circuits, where the objects that are dealt with are registers, memory cells, and logic gates. The operations defined on these objects are actions, such as clearing a register or reading a memory location.
- **Level 2:** The processor's instruction set. The operations at this level are those allowed in the machine language instruction set, such as add, subtract, load, and store.
- **Level 3:** Adds the concept of a procedure or subroutine, plus the call/return operations.
- **Level 4:** Introduces interrupts, which cause the processor to save the current context and invoke an interrupt-handling routine.

These first four levels are not part of the operating system but constitute the processor hardware. However, some elements of the operating system begin to appear at these levels, such as the interrupt-handling routines. It is at level 5 that we begin to reach the operating system proper and that the concepts associated with multiprogramming begin to appear.

- **Level 5:** The notion of a process as a program in execution is introduced at this level. The fundamental requirements on the operating system to support multiple processes include the ability to suspend and resume processes. This requires saving hardware registers so that execution can be switched from one process to another. In addition, if processes need to cooperate, then some method of synchronization is needed. One of the simplest techniques, and an important concept in operating system design, is the semaphore, a simple signaling technique that is explored in Chapter 5.
- **Level 6:** Deals with the secondary storage devices of the computer. At this level, the functions of positioning the read/write heads and the actual transfer of blocks of data occur. Level 6 relies on level 5 to schedule the operation and to notify the requesting process of completion of an operation. Higher levels are concerned with the address of the needed data on the disk and provide a request for the appropriate block to a device driver at level 5.
- **Level 7:** Creates a logical address space for processes. This level organizes the virtual address space into blocks that can be moved between main memory and secondary memory. Three schemes are in common use: those using fixed-size pages, those using variable-length segments, and those using both. When a needed block is not in main memory, logic at this level requests a transfer from level 6.

Up to this point, the operating system deals with the resources of a single processor. Beginning with level 8, the operating system deals with external objects such as peripheral devices and possibly networks and computers attached to the network. The objects at these upper levels are logical, named objects that can be shared among processes on the same computer or on multiple computers.

- **Level 8:** Deals with the communication of information and messages between processes. Whereas level 5 provided a primitive signal mechanism that allowed for the synchronization of processes, this level deals with a richer sharing of information. One of the most powerful tools for this purpose is the pipe, which is a logical channel for the flow of data between processes. A pipe is defined with its output from one process and its input into another process. It can also be used to link external devices or files to processes. The concept is discussed in Chapter 6.
- **Level 9:** Supports the long-term storage of named files. At this level, the data on secondary storage are viewed in terms of abstract, variable-length entities. This is in contrast to the hardware-oriented view of secondary storage in terms of tracks, sectors, and fixed-size blocks at level 6.
- **Level 10:** Provides access to external devices using standardized interfaces.
- **Level 11:** Is responsible for maintaining the association between the external and internal identifiers of the system's resources and objects. The external identifier is a name that can be employed by an application or user. The internal identifier is an address or other indicator that can be used by lower levels

of the operating system to locate and control an object. These associations are maintained in a directory. Entries include not only external/internal mapping, but also characteristics such as access rights.

- **Level 12:** Provides a full-featured facility for the support of processes. This goes far beyond what is provided at level 5. At level 5, only the processor register contents associated with a process are maintained, plus the logic for dispatching processes. At level 12, all of the information needed for the orderly management of processes is supported. This includes the virtual address space of the process, a list of objects and processes with which it may interact and the constraints of that interaction, parameters passed to the process upon creation, and any other characteristics of the process that might be used by the operating system to control the process.

- **Level 13:** Provides an interface to the operating system for the user. It is referred to as the **shell** because it separates the user from operating system details and presents the operating system simply as a collection of services. The shell accepts user commands or job control statements, interprets these, and creates and controls processes as needed. For example, the interface at this level could be implemented in a graphical manner, providing the user with commands through a list presented as a menu and displaying results using graphical output to a specific device such as a screen.

This hypothetical model of an operating system provides a useful descriptive structure and serves as an implementation guideline. The reader may refer back to this structure during the course of the book to observe the context of any particular design issue under discussion.

2.4   DEVELOPMENTS LEADING TO MODERN OPERATING SYSTEMS

Over the years, there has been a gradual evolution of operating system structure and capabilities. However, in recent years a number of new design elements have been introduced into both new operating systems and new releases of existing operating systems that create a major change in the nature of operating systems. These modern operating systems respond to new developments in hardware, new applications, and new security threats. Among the key hardware drivers are multiprocessor machines, greatly increased machine speed, high-speed network attachments, and increasing size and variety of memory storage devices. In the application arena, multimedia applications, Internet and Web access, and client/server computing have influenced operating system design. With respect to security, Internet access to computers has greatly increased the potential threat and increasingly sophisticated attacks, such as viruses, worms, and hacking techniques, have had a profound impact on operating system design.

The rate of change in the demands on operating systems requires not just modifications and enhancements to existing architectures but new ways of organizing the operating system. A wide range of different approaches and design elements has been tried in both experimental and commercial operating systems, but much of the work fits into the following categories:

- Microkernel architecture
- Multithreading
- Symmetric multiprocessing
- Distributed operating systems
- Object-oriented design

Most operating systems, until recently, featured a large **monolithic kernel**. Most of what is thought of as operating system functionality is provided in these large kernels, including scheduling, file system, networking, device drivers, memory management, and more. Typically, a monolithic kernel is implemented as a single process, with all elements sharing the same address space. A **microkernel architecture** assigns only a few essential functions to the kernel, including address spaces, interprocess communication (IPC), and basic scheduling. Other operating system services are provided by processes, sometimes called servers, that run in user mode and are treated like any other application by the microkernel. This approach decouples kernel and server development. Servers may be customized to specific application or environment requirements. The microkernel approach simplifies implementation, provides flexibility, and is well suited to a distributed environment. In essence, a microkernel interacts with local and remote server processes in the same way, facilitating construction of distributed systems.

Multithreading is a technique in which a process, executing an application, is divided into threads that can run concurrently. We can make the following distinction:

- **Thread:** A dispatchable unit of work. It includes a processor context (which includes the program counter and stack pointer) and its own data area for a stack (to enable subroutine branching). A thread executes sequentially and is interruptable so that the processor can turn to another thread.
- **Process:** A collection of one or more threads and associated system resources (such as memory containing both code and data, open files, and devices). This corresponds closely to the concept of a program in execution. By breaking a single application into multiple threads, the programmer has great control over the modularity of the application and the timing of application-related events.

Multithreading is useful for applications that perform a number of essentially independent tasks that do not need to be serialized. An example is a database server that listens for and processes numerous client requests. With multiple threads running within the same process, switching back and forth among threads involves less processor overhead than a major process switch between different processes. Threads are also useful for structuring processes that are part of the operating system kernel as described in subsequent chapters.

Until recently, virtually all single-user personal computers and workstations contained a single general-purpose microprocessor. As demands for performance increase and as the cost of microprocessors continues to drop, vendors have introduced computers with multiple microprocessors. To achieve greater efficiency and reliability, one technique is to employ **symmetric multiprocessing (SMP)**, a term that refers to a computer hardware architecture and also to the operating system behavior that exploits that architecture. A symmetric multiprocessor can be defined as a standalone computer system with the following characteristics:

1. There are multiple processors.
2. These processors share the same main memory and I/O facilities, interconnected by a communications bus or other internal connection scheme.
3. All processors can perform the same functions (hence the term *symmetric*).

The operating system of an SMP schedules processes or threads across all of the processors. SMP has a number of potential advantages over uniprocessor architecture, including the following:

- **Performance:** If the work to be done by a computer can be organized so that some portions of the work can be done in parallel, then a system with multiple processors will yield greater performance than one with a single processor of the same type. This is illustrated in Figure 2.12. With multiprogramming, only

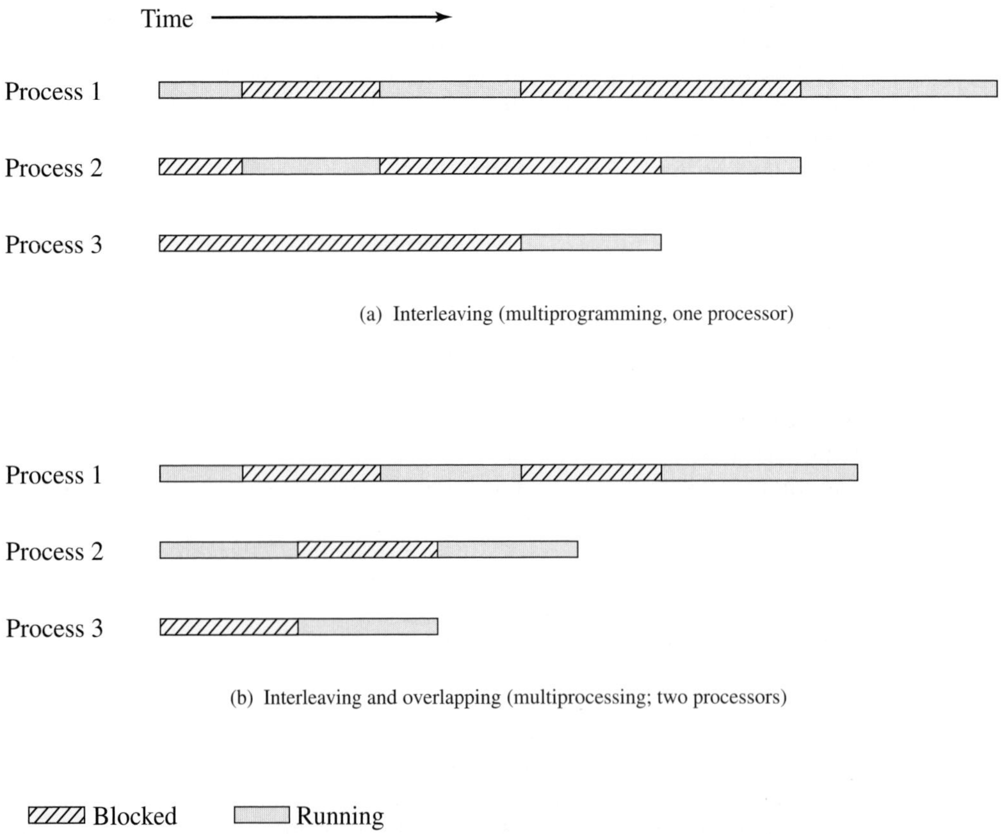

(a) Interleaving (multiprogramming, one processor)

(b) Interleaving and overlapping (multiprocessing; two processors)

▨ Blocked   ▭ Running

Figure 2.12   Multiprogramming and Multiprocessing

one process can execute at a time; meanwhile, all other processes are waiting for the processor. With multiprocessing, more than one process can be running simultaneously, each on a different processor.

- **Availability:** In a symmetric multiprocessor, because all processors can perform the same functions, the failure of a single processor does not halt the machine. Instead, the system can continue to function at reduced performance.

- **Incremental growth:** A user can enhance the performance of a system by adding an additional processor.

- **Scaling:** Vendors can offer a range of products with different price and performance characteristics based on the number of processors configured in the system.

It is important to note that these are potential, rather than guaranteed, benefits. The operating system must provide tools and functions to exploit the parallelism in an SMP system.

Multithreading and SMP are often discussed together, but the two are independent facilities. Even on a uniprocessor machine, multithreading is useful for structuring applications and kernel processes. An SMP machine is useful even for nonthreaded processes, because several processes can run in parallel. However, the two facilities complement each other and can be used effectively together.

An attractive feature of an SMP is that the existence of multiple processors is transparent to the user. The operating system takes care of scheduling of threads or processes on individual processors and of synchronization among processors. This book discusses the scheduling and synchronization mechanisms used to provide the single-system appearance to the user. A different problem is to provide the appearance of a single system for a cluster of separate computers—a multicomputer system. In this case, we are dealing with a collection of entities (computers), each with its own main memory, secondary memory, and other I/O modules. A **distributed operating system** provides the illusion of a single main memory space and a single secondary memory space, plus other unified access facilities, such as a distributed file system. Although clusters are becoming increasingly popular, and there are many cluster products on the market, the state of the art for distributed operating systems lags that of uniprocessor and SMP operating systems. We examine such systems in Part Six.

Another innovation in operating system design is the use of object-oriented technologies. **Object-oriented design** lends discipline to the process of adding modular extensions to a small kernel. At the operating system level, an object-based structure enables programmers to customize an operating system without disrupting system integrity. Object orientation also eases the development of distributed tools and full-blown distributed operating systems.

2.5 MICROSOFT WINDOWS OVERVIEW

In this section, we provide an overview of Microsoft Windows; we describe UNIX in the following section.

History

The story of Windows begins with a very different operating system, developed by Microsoft for the first IBM personal computer and referred to as MS-DOS or PC-DOS. The initial version, DOS 1.0, was released in August 1981. It consisted of 4000 lines of assembly language source code and ran in 8 Kbytes of memory using the Intel 8086 microprocessor.

When IBM developed a hard disk–based personal computer, the PC XT, Microsoft developed DOS 2.0, released in 1983. It contained support for the hard disk and provided for hierarchical directories. Heretofore, a disk could contain only one directory of files, supporting a maximum of 64 files. While this was adequate in the era of floppy disks, it was too limited for a hard disk, and the single-directory restriction was too clumsy. This new release allowed directories to contain subdirectories as well as files. The new release also contained a richer set of commands embedded in the operating system to provide functions that had to be performed by external programs provided as utilities with release 1. Among the capabilities added were several UNIX-like features, such as I/O redirection, which is the ability to change the input or output identity for a given application, and background printing. The memory-resident portion grew to 24 Kbytes.

When IBM announced the PC AT in 1984, Microsoft introduced DOS 3.0. The AT contained the Intel 80286 processor, which provided extended addressing and memory protection features. These were not used by DOS. To remain compatible with previous releases, the operating system simply used the 80286 as a "fast 8086." The operating system did provide support for new keyboard and hard disk peripherals. Even so, the memory requirement grew to 36 Kbytes. There were several notable upgrades to the 3.0 release. DOS 3.1, released in 1984, contained support for networking of PCs. The size of the resident portion did not change; this was achieved by increasing the amount of the operating system that could be swapped. DOS 3.3, released in 1987, provided support for the new line of IBM machines, the PS/2. Again, this release did not take advantage of the processor capabilities of the PS/2, provided by the 80286 and the 32-bit 80386 chips. The resident portion at this stage had grown to a minimum of 46 Kbytes, with more required if certain optional extensions were selected.

By this time, DOS was being used in an environment far beyond its capabilities. The introduction of the 80486 and then the Intel Pentium chip provided power and features that simply could not be exploited by the simple-minded DOS. Meanwhile, beginning in the early 1980s, Microsoft began development of a graphical user interface (GUI) that would be interposed between the user and DOS. Microsoft's intent was to compete with Macintosh, whose operating system was unsurpassed for ease of use. By 1990, Microsoft had a version of the GUI, known as Windows 3.0, which incorporated some of the user-friendly features of Macintosh. However, it was still hamstrung by the need to run on top of DOS.

After an abortive attempt by Microsoft to develop with IBM a next-generation operating system, which would exploit the power of the new microprocessors and which would incorporate the ease-of-use features of Windows, Microsoft struck out on its own and developed a new operating system from the ground up, Windows NT. Windows NT exploits the capabilities of contemporary microprocessors and provides multitasking in a single-user or multiple-user environment.

The first version of Windows NT (3.1) was released in 1993, with the same GUI as Windows 3.1, another Microsoft operating system (the follow-on to Windows 3.0). However, NT 3.1 was a new 32-bit operating system with the ability to support older DOS and Windows applications as well as provide OS/2 support.

After several versions of NT 3.x, Microsoft released NT 4.0. NT 4.0 has essentially the same internal architecture as 3.x. The most notable external change is that NT 4.0 provides the same user interface as Windows 95. The major architectural change is that several graphics components that ran in user mode as part of the Win32 subsystem in 3.x have been moved into the Windows NT Executive, which runs in kernel mode. The benefit of this change is to speed up the operation of these important functions. The potential drawback is that these graphics functions now have access to low-level system services, which could impact the reliability of the operating system.

In 2000, Microsoft introduced the next major upgrade, now called Windows 2000. Again, the underlying Executive and kernel architecture is fundamentally the same as in NT 4.0, but new features have been added. The emphasis in Windows 2000 is the addition of services and functions to support distributed processing. The central element of Windows 2000's new features is Active Directory, which is a distributed directory service able to map names of arbitrary objects to any kind of information about those objects.

One final general point to make about Windows 2000 is the distinction between Windows 2000 Server and Windows 2000 desktop. In essence, the kernel and executive architecture and services remain the same, but Server includes some services required to use as a network server.

In 2001, the latest desktop version of Windows was released, known as Windows XP. Both home PC and business workstation versions of XP are offered. Also in 2001, a 64-bit version of XP was introduced. In 2003, Microsoft introduced a new server version, known as Windows Server 2003; both 32-bit and 64 bit versions are available. The 64-bit versions of XP and Server 2003 are designed specifically for the 64-bit Intel Itanium hardware.

Single-User Multitasking

Windows (from Windows 2000 onward) is a significant example of what has become the new wave in microcomputer operating systems (other examples are OS/2 and MacOS). Windows was driven by a need to exploit the processing capabilities of today's 32-bit microprocessors, which rival mainframes and minicomputers of just a few years ago in speed, hardware sophistication, and memory capacity.

One of the most significant features of these new operating systems is that, although they are still intended for support of a single interactive user, they are multitasking operating systems. Two main developments have triggered the need for multitasking on personal computers, workstations, and servers. First, with the increased speed and memory capacity of microprocessors, together with the support for virtual memory, applications have become more complex and interrelated. For example, a user may wish to employ a word processor, a drawing program, and a spreadsheet application simultaneously to produce a document. Without multitasking, if a user wishes to create a drawing and paste it into a word processing document, the following steps are required:

1. Open the drawing program.
2. Create the drawing and save it in a file or on a temporary clipboard.
3. Close the drawing program.
4. Open the word processing program.
5. Insert the drawing in the correct location.

If any changes are desired, the user must close the word processing program, open the drawing program, edit the graphic image, save it, close the drawing program, open the word processing program, and insert the updated image. This becomes tedious very quickly. As the services and capabilities available to users become more powerful and varied, the single-task environment becomes more clumsy and user unfriendly. In a multitasking environment, the user opens each application as needed, and leaves it open. Information can be moved around among a number of applications easily. Each application has one or more open windows, and a graphical interface with a pointing device such as a mouse allows the user to navigate quickly in this environment.

A second motivation for multitasking is the growth of client/server computing. With client/server computing, a personal computer or workstation (client) and a host system (server) are used jointly to accomplish a particular application. The two are linked, and each is assigned that part of the job that suits its capabilities. Client/server can be achieved in a local area network of personal computers and servers or by means of a link between a user system and a large host such as a mainframe. An application may involve one or more personal computers and one or more server devices. To provide the required responsiveness, the operating system needs to support sophisticated real-time communication hardware and the associated communications protocols and data transfer architectures while at the same time supporting ongoing user interaction.

The foregoing remarks apply to the Professional version of Windows. The Server version is also multitasking but may support multiple users. It supports multiple local server connections as well as providing shared services used by multiple users on the network. As an Internet server, Windows may support thousands of simultaneous Web connections.

Architecture

Figure 2.13 illustrates the overall structure of Windows 2000; later releases of Windows have essentially the same structure at this level of detail. Its modular structure gives Windows considerable flexibility. It is designed to execute on a variety of hardware platforms and supports applications written for a variety of other operating systems. As of this writing, Windows is only implemented on the Intel Pentium/x86 and Itanium hardware platforms.

As with virtually all operating systems, Windows separates application-oriented software from operating system software. The latter, which includes the Executive, the kernel, device drivers, and the hardware abstraction layer, runs in kernel mode. Kernel

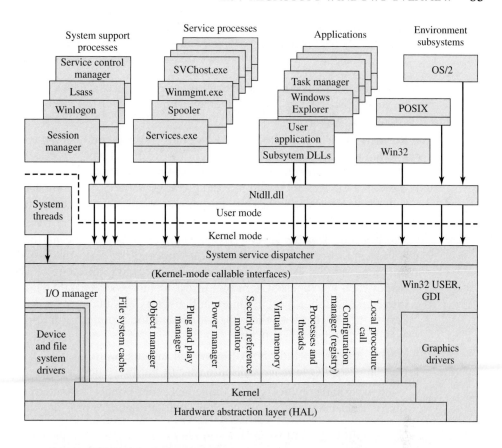

Lsass = local security authentication server   Colored area indicates Executive
POSIX = portable operating system interface
GDI = graphics device interface
DLL = dynamic link libraries

Figure 2.13   Windows 2000 Architecture [SOLO00]

mode software has access to system data and to the hardware. The remaining software, running in user mode, has limited access to system data.

Operating System Organization Windows does not have a pure microkernel architecture but what Microsoft refers to as a modified microkernel architecture. As with a pure microkernel architecture, Windows is highly modular. Each system function is managed by just one component of the operating system. The rest of the operating system and all applications access that function through the responsible component using a standard interface. Key system data can only be accessed through the appropriate function. In principle, any module can be removed, upgraded, or replaced without rewriting the entire system or its standard application program interface (APIs). However, unlike a pure microkernel system, Windows is configured so that many of the system functions outside the microkernel run in kernel mode. The reason is performance. The Windows developers found that using the pure microkernel approach, many non-microkernel functions required several process or thread switches, mode switches, and the use of extra memory buffers. The kernel-mode components of Windows are the following:

- **Executive:** Contains the base operating system services, such as memory management, process and thread management, security, I/O, and interprocess communication.

- **Kernel:** Consists of the most used and most fundamental components of the operating system. The kernel manages thread scheduling, process switching, exception and interrupt handling, and multiprocessor synchronization. Unlike the rest of the Executive and the user level, the kernel's own code does not run in threads. Hence, it is the only part of the operating system that is not preemptible or pageable.

- **Hardware abstraction layer (HAL):** Maps between generic hardware commands and responses and those unique to a specific platform. It isolates the operating system from platform-specific hardware differences. The HAL makes each machine's system bus, direct memory access (DMA) controller, interrupt controller, system timers, and memory module look the same to the kernel. It also delivers the support needed for symmetric multiprocessing (SMP), explained subsequently.

- **Device drivers:** Include both file system and hardware device drivers that translate user I/O function calls into specific hardware device I/O requests.

- **Windowing and graphics system:** Implements the graphical user interface (GUI) functions, such as dealing with windows, user interface controls, and drawing.

The Windows Executive includes modules for specific system functions and provides an API for user-mode software. Following is a brief description of each of the Executive modules:

- **I/O manager:** Provides a framework through which I/O devices are accessible to applications and is responsible for dispatching to the appropriate device drivers for further processing. The I/O manager implements all the Windows I/O APIs and enforces security and naming for devices and file systems (using the object manager). Windows I/O is discussed in Chapter 11.

- **Cache manager:** Improves the performance of file-based I/O by causing recently referenced disk data to reside in main memory for quick access, and by deferring disk writes by holding the updates in memory for a short time before sending them to the disk.

- **Object manager:** Creates, manages, and deletes Windows Executive objects and abstract data types that are used to represent resources such as processes, threads, and synchronization objects. It enforces uniform rules for retaining, naming, and setting the security of objects. The object manager also creates object handles, which consist of access control information and a pointer to the object. Windows objects are discussed later in this section.

- **Plug and play manager:** Determines which drivers are required to support a particular device and loads those drivers.

- **Power manager:** Coordinates power management among various devices and can be configured to reduce power consumption by putting the processor to sleep.

- **Security reference monitor:** Enforces access-validation and audit-generation rules. The Windows object-oriented model allows for a consistent and uniform view of security, right down to the fundamental entities that make up the Executive. Thus, Windows uses the same routines for access validation and for audit checks for all protected objects, including files, processes, address spaces, and I/O devices. Windows security is discussed in Chapter 15.

- **Virtual memory manager:** Maps virtual addresses in the process's address space to physical pages in the computer's memory. Windows virtual memory management is described in Chapter 8.

- **Process/thread manager:** Creates and deletes objects and tracks process and thread objects. Windows process and thread management are described in Chapter 4.

- **Configuration manager:** Responsible for implementing and managing the system registry, which is the repository for both systemwide and per-user settings of various parameters.

- **Local procedure call (LPC) facility:** Enforces a client/server relationship between applications and executive subsystems within a single system, in a manner similar to a remote procedure call (RPC) facility used for distributed processing.

User–Mode Processes Four basic types of user-mode processes are supported by Windows:

- **Special system support processes:** Include services not provided as part of the Windows operating system, such as the logon process and the session manager.

- **Service processes:** Other Windows services such as the event logger.

- **Environment subsystems:** Expose the native Windows services to user applications and thus provide an operating system environment or personality. The supported subsystems are Win32, Posix, and OS/2. Each environment subsystem includes dynamic link libraries (DLLs) that convert the user application calls to Windows calls.

- **User applications:** Can be one of five types: Win32, Posix, OS/2, Windows 3.1, or MS-DOS.

Windows is structured to support applications written for Windows 2000 and later releases, Windows 98, and several other operating systems. Windows provides this support using a single, compact Executive through protected environment subsystems. The protected subsystems are those parts of Windows that interact with the end user. Each subsystem is a separate process, and the Executive protects its address space from that of other subsystems and applications. A protected subsystem provides a graphical or command-line user interface that defines the look and feel of the operating system for a user. In addition, each protected subsystem provides the API for that particular operating environment.

This means that applications created for a particular operating environment may run unchanged on Windows, because the operating system interface that they see is the same as that for which they were written. So, for example, OS/2-based applications can run under the Windows operating system without modification. Furthermore, because the Windows system is itself designed to be platform independent, through the use of the hardware abstraction layer (HAL), it should be relatively easy to port both the protected subsystems and the applications they support from one hardware platform to another. In many cases, a recompile is all that should be required.

The most important subsystem is Win32. Win32 is the API implemented on both Windows 2000 and later releases and Windows 98. Some of the features of Win32 are not available in Windows 98, but those features implemented on Windows 98 are identical with those of Windows 2000 and later releases.

Client/Server Model

The Executive, the protected subsystems, and the applications are structured using the client/server computing model, which is a common model for distributed computing and which is discussed in Part Six. This same architecture can be adopted for use internal to a single system, as is the case with Windows.

Each environment subsystem and executive service subsystem is implemented as one or more processes. Each process waits for a request from a client for one of its services (for example, memory services, process creation services, or processor scheduling services). A client, which can be an application program or another operating system module, requests a service by sending a message. The message is routed through the Executive to the appropriate server. The server performs the requested operation and returns the results or status information by means of another message, which is routed through the Executive back to the client.

Advantages of a client/server architecture include the following:

- It simplifies the Executive. It is possible to construct a variety of APIs without any conflicts or duplications in the Executive. New APIs can be added easily.

- It improves reliability. Each executive services module runs on a separate process, with its own partition of memory, protected from other modules. Furthermore, the clients cannot directly access hardware or modify memory in which the Executive is stored. A single server can fail without crashing or corrupting the rest of the operating system.

- It provides a uniform means for applications to communicate with the Executive via LPCs without restricting flexibility. The message-passing process is hidden from the client applications by function stubs, which are nonexecutable placeholders kept in dynamic link libraries (DLLs). When an application makes an API call to an environment subsystem, the stub in the client application packages the parameters for the call and sends them as a message to a server subsystem that implements the call.

- It provides a suitable base for distributed computing. Typically, distributed computing makes use of a client/server model, with remote procedure calls implemented using distributed client and server modules and the exchange of messages between clients and servers. With Windows, a local server can pass a message on to a remote server for processing on behalf of local client applications. Clients need not know whether a request is serviced locally or remotely. Indeed, whether a request is serviced locally or remotely can change dynamically based on current load conditions and on dynamic configuration changes.

Threads and SMP

Two important characteristics of Windows are its support for threads and for symmetric multiprocessing (SMP), both of which were introduced in Section 2.4. [CUST93] lists the following features of Windows that support threads and SMP:

- Operating system routines can run on any available processor, and different routines can execute simultaneously on different processors.
- Windows supports the use of multiple threads of execution within a single process. Multiple threads within the same process may execute on different processors simultaneously.
- Server processes may use multiple threads to process requests from more than one client simultaneously.
- Windows provides mechanisms for sharing data and resources between processes and flexible interprocess communication capabilities.

Windows Objects

Windows draws heavily on the concepts of object-oriented design. This approach facilitates the sharing of resources and data among processes and the protection of resources from unauthorized access. Among the key object-oriented concepts used by Windows are the following:

- **Encapsulation:** An object consists of one or more items of data, called attributes, and one or more procedures that may be performed on those data, called services. The only way to access the data in an object is by invoking one of the object's services. Thus, the data in the object can easily be protected from unauthorized use and from incorrect use (e.g., trying to execute a nonexecutable piece of data).
- **Object class and instance:** An object class is a template that lists the attributes and services of an object and defines certain object characteristics. The operating system can create specific instances of an object class as needed. For example, there is a single process object class and one process object for every currently active process. This approach simplifies object creation and management.
- **Inheritance:** This is not supported at the user level but is supported to some extent within the Executive. For example, Directory objects are examples of container objects. One property of a container object is that the objects they contain can inherit properties from the container itself. As an example, suppose you have a directory in the file system that has its compressed flag set.

Then any files you might create within that directory container will also have their compressed flag set.

- **Polymorphism:** Internally, Windows uses a common set of API functions to manipulate objects of any type; this is a feature of polymorphism, as defined in Appendix B. However, Windows is not completely polymorphic because there are many APIs that are specific to specific object types.

The reader unfamiliar with object-oriented concepts should review Appendix B at the end of this book.

Not all entities in Windows are objects. Objects are used in cases where data are intended for user mode access or when data access is shared or restricted. Among the entities represented by objects are files, processes, threads, semaphores, timers, and windows. Windows creates and manages all types of objects in a uniform way, via the object manager. The object manager is responsible for creating and destroying objects on behalf of applications and for granting access to an object's services and data.

Each object within the Executive, sometimes referred to as a kernel object (to distinguish from user-level objects not of concern to the Executive), exists as a memory block allocated by the kernel and is accessible only by the kernel. Some elements of the data structure (e.g., object name, security parameters, usage count) are common to all object types, while other elements are specific to a particular object type (e.g., a thread object's priority). These kernel object data structures are accessible only by the kernel; it is impossible for an application to locate these data structures and read or write them directly. Instead, applications manipulate objects indirectly through the set of object manipulation functions supported by the Executive. When an object is created, the application that requested the creation receives back a handle for the object. In essence a handle is a pointer to the referenced object. This handle can then be used by any thread within the same process to invoke Win32 functions that work with objects.

Objects may have security information associated with them, in the form of a Security Descriptor (SD). This security information can be used to restrict access to the object. For example, a process may create a named semaphore object with the intent that only certain users should be able to open and use that semaphore. The SD for the semaphore object can list those users that are allowed (or denied) access to the semaphore object along with the sort of access permitted (read, write, change, etc.).

In Windows, objects may be either named or unnamed. When a process creates an unnamed object, the object manager returns a handle to that object, and the handle is the only way to refer to it. Named objects have a name that other processes can use to obtain a handle to the object. For example, if process A wishes to synchronize with process B, it could create a named event object and pass the name of the event to B. Process B could then open and use that event object. However, if A simply wished to use the event to synchronize two threads within itself, it would create an unnamed event object, because there is no need for other processes to be able to use that event.

As an example of the objects managed by Windows, we list the two categories of objects managed by the kernel;

- **Control objects:** Used to control the operation of the kernel in areas not affecting dispatching and synchronization. Table 2.5 lists the kernel control objects.

Table 2.5 Windows Microkernel Control Objects [MS96]

Asynchronous Procedure Call	Used to break into the execution of a specified thread and to cause a procedure to be called in a specified processor mode.
Interrupt	Used to connect an interrupt source to an interrupt service routine by means of an entry in an Interrupt Dispatch Table (IDT). Each processor has an IDT that is used to dispatch interrupts that occur on that processor.
Process	Represents the virtual address space and control information necessary for the execution of a set of thread objects. A process contains a pointer to an address map, a list of ready threads containing thread objects, a list of threads belonging to the process, the total accumulated time for all threads executing within the process, and a base priority.
Profile	Used to measure the distribution of run time within a block of code. Both user and system code can be profiled.

- **Dispatcher objects:** Control the dispatching and synchronization of system operations. These are described in Chapter 6.

Windows is not a full-blown object-oriented operating system. It is not implemented in an object-oriented language. Data structures that reside completely within one Executive component are not represented as objects. Nevertheless, Windows illustrates the power of object-oriented technology and represents the increasing trend toward the use of this technology in operating system design.

2.6 TRADITIONAL UNIX SYSTEMS

History

The history of UNIX is an oft-told tale and will not be repeated in great detail here. Instead, we provide a brief summary.

UNIX was initially developed at Bell Labs and became operational on a PDP-7 in 1970. Some of the people involved at Bell Labs had also participated in the time-sharing work being done at MIT's Project MAC. That project led to the development of first CTSS and then Multics. Although it is common to say that the original UNIX was a scaled-down version of Multics, the developers of UNIX actually claimed to be more influenced by CTSS [RITC78]. Nevertheless, UNIX incorporated many ideas from Multics.

Work on UNIX at Bell Labs, and later elsewhere, produced a series of versions of UNIX. The first notable milestone was porting the UNIX system from the PDP-7 to the PDP-11. This was the first hint that UNIX would be an operating system for all computers. The next important milestone was the rewriting of UNIX in the programming language C. This was an unheard-of strategy at the time. It was generally felt that something as complex as an operating system, which must deal with time-critical events, had to be written exclusively in assembly language. The C implementation demonstrated the advantages of using a high-level language for most if not all of the system code. Today, virtually all UNIX implementations are written in C.

These early versions of UNIX were popular within Bell Labs. In 1974, the UNIX system was described in a technical journal for the first time [RITC74]. This spurred great interest in the system. Licenses for UNIX were provided to commercial institutions as well as universities. The first widely available version outside Bell Labs was Version 6, in 1976. The follow-on Version 7, released in 1978, is the ancestor of most modern UNIX systems. The most important of the non-AT&T systems to be developed was done at the University of California at Berkeley, called UNIX BSD (Berkeley Software Distribution), running first on PDP and then VAX machines. AT&T continued to develop and refine the system. By 1982, Bell Labs had combined several AT&T variants of UNIX into a single system, marketed commercially as UNIX System III. A number of features was later added to the operating system to produce UNIX System V.

Description

Figure 2.14 provides a general description of the UNIX architecture. The underlying hardware is surrounded by the operating system software. The operating system is often called the system kernel, or simply the kernel, to emphasize its isolation from the user and applications. This portion of UNIX is what we will be concerned with in our use of UNIX as an example in this book. However, UNIX comes equipped with a number of user services and interfaces that are considered part of the system. These can be grouped into the shell, other interface software, and the components of the C compiler (compiler, assembler, loader). The layer outside of this consists of user applications and the user interface to the C compiler.

A closer look at the kernel is provided in Figure 2.15. User programs can invoke operating system services either directly or through library programs. The system call interface is the boundary with the user and allows higher-level software

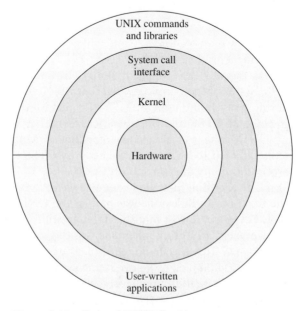

Figure 2.14   General UNIX Architecture

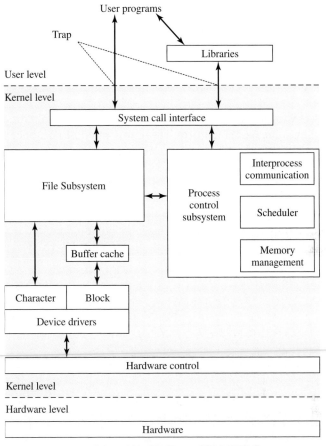

Figure 2.15 Traditional UNIX Kernel [BACH86]

to gain access to specific kernel functions. At the other end, the operating system contains primitive routines that interact directly with the hardware. Between these two interfaces, the system is divided into two main parts, one concerned with process control and the other concerned with file management and I/O. The process control subsystem is responsible for memory management, the scheduling and dispatching of processes, and the synchronization and interprocess communication of processes. The file system exchanges data between memory and external devices either as a stream of characters or in blocks. To achieve this, a variety of device drivers are used. For block-oriented transfers, a disk cache approach is used: A system buffer in main memory is interposed between the user address space and the external device.

The description in this subsection has dealt with what might be termed traditional UNIX systems; [VAHA96] uses this term to refer to System V Release 3 (SVR3), 4.3BSD, and earlier versions. The following general statements may be made about a traditional UNIX system. It is designed to run on a single processor and lacks the ability to protect its data structures from concurrent access by multiple processors. Its kernel is not very versatile, supporting a single type of file system, process scheduling policy, and executable file format. The traditional UNIX kernel is not designed to be extensible and has few facilities for code reuse. The result is that, as new features were added to the various UNIX versions, much new code had to be added, yielding a bloated and unmodular kernel.

2.7   MODERN UNIX SYSTEMS

As UNIX evolved, the number of different implementations proliferated, each providing some useful features. There was a need to produce a new implementation that unified many of the important innovations, added other modern operating system design features, and produced a more modular architecture. Typical of the modern UNIX kernel is the architecture depicted in Figure 2.16. There is a small core of facilities, written in a modular fashion, that provide functions and services needed by a number of operating system processes. Each of the outer circles represents functions and an interface that may be implemented in a variety of ways.

We now turn to some examples of modern UNIX systems.

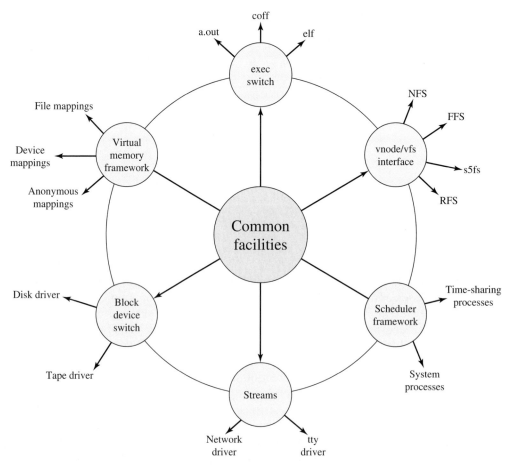

Figure 2.16   Modern UNIX Kernel [VAHA96]

System V Release 4 (SVR4)

SVR4, developed jointly by AT&T and Sun Microsystems, combines features from SVR3, 4.3BSD, Microsoft Xenix System V, and SunOS. It was almost a total rewrite of the System V kernel and produced a clean, if complex, implementation. New features in the release include real-time processing support, process scheduling classes, dynamically allocated data structures, virtual memory management, virtual file system, and a preemptive kernel.

SVR4 draws on the efforts of both commercial and academic designers and was developed to provide a uniform platform for commercial UNIX deployment. It has succeeded in this objective and is perhaps the most important UNIX variant. It incorporates most of the important features ever developed on any UNIX system and does so in an integrated, commercially viable fashion. SVR4 is running on machines ranging from 32-bit microprocessors up to supercomputers. Many of the UNIX examples in this book are from SVR4.

Solaris 9

Solaris is Sun's SVR4-based UNIX release, with the latest version being 9. Solaris provides all of the features of SVR4 plus a number of more advanced features, such as a fully preemptable, multithreaded kernel, full support for SMP, and an object-oriented interface to file systems. Solaris is the most widely used and most successful commercial UNIX implementation. For some operating system features, Solaris provides the UNIX examples in this book.

4.4BSD

The Berkeley Software Distribution (BSD) series of UNIX releases have played a key role in the development of operating system design theory. 4.xBSD is widely used in academic installations and has served as the basis of a number of commercial UNIX products. It is probably safe to say that BSD is responsible for much of the popularity of UNIX and that most enhancements to UNIX first appeared in BSD versions.

4.4BSD was the final version of BSD to be released by Berkeley, with the design and implementation organization subsequently dissolved. It is a major upgrade to 4.3BSD and includes a new virtual memory system, changes in the kernel structure, and a long list of other feature enhancements.

The latest version of the Macintosh operating system, Mac OS X, is based on 4.4BSD.

2.8 LINUX

History

Linux started out as a UNIX variant for the IBM PC (Intel 80386) architecture. Linus Torvalds, a Finnish student of computer science, wrote the initial version. Torvalds posted an early version of Linux on the Internet in 1991. Since then, a number of people, collaborating over the Internet, have contributed to the development of Linux, all under the control of Torvalds. Because Linux is free and the source code is available, it became an early alternative to other UNIX workstations, such as those offered by Sun Microsystems and IBM. Today, Linux is a full-featured UNIX system that runs on all of these platforms and more, including Intel Pentium and Itanium, and the Motorola/IBM PowerPC.

Key to the success of Linux has been the availability of free software packages under the auspices of the Free Software Foundation (FSF). FSF's goal is stable, platform-independent software that is free, high quality, and embraced by the user community. FSF's GNU project provides tools for software developers, and the GNU Public License (GPL) is the FSF seal of approval. Torvalds used GNU tools in developing his kernel, which he then released under the GPL. Thus, the Linux distributions that you see today are the product of FSF's GNU project, Torvald's individual effort, and many collaborators all over the world.

In addition to its use by many individual programmers, Linux has now made significant penetration into the corporate world. This is not only because of the free software, but also because of the quality of the Linux kernel. Many talented programmers have contributed to the current version, resulting in a technically impressive product. Moreover, Linux is highly modular and easily configured. This makes it easy to squeeze optimal performance from a variety of hardware platforms. Plus, with the source code available, vendors can tweak applications and utilities to meet specific requirements. Throughout this book, we will provide details of Linux kernel internals.

Modular Structure

Most UNIX kernels are monolithic. Recall from earlier in this chapter that a monolithic kernel is one that includes virtually all of the operating system functionality in one large block of code that runs as a single process with a single address space. All the functional components of the kernel have access to all of its internal data structures and routines. If changes are made to any portion of a typical monolithic operating system, all the modules and routines must be relinked and reinstalled and the system rebooted before the changes can take effect. As a result, any modification, such as adding a new device driver or file system function, is difficult. This problem is especially acute for Linux, for which development is global and done by a loosely associated group of independent programmers.

Although Linux does not use a microkernel approach, it achieves many of the potential advantages of this approach by means of its particular modular architecture. Linux is structured as a collection of modules, a number of which can be automatically loaded and unloaded on demand. These relatively independent blocks are referred to as **loadable modules** [GOYE99]. In essence, a module is an object file whose code can be linked to and unlinked from the kernel at runtime. Typically, a module implements some specific function, such as a filesystem, a device driver, or some other feature of the kernel's upper layer. A module does not execute as its own process or thread, although it can create kernel threads for various purposes as necessary. Rather, a module is executed in kernel mode on behalf of the current process.

Thus, although Linux may be considered monolithic, its modular structure overcomes some of the difficulties in developing and evolving the kernel.

The Linux loadable modules have two important characteristics:

- **Dynamic linking:** A kernel module can be loaded and linked into the kernel while the kernel is already in memory and executing. A module can also be unlinked and removed from memory at any time.
- **Stackable modules:** The modules are arranged in a hierarchy. Individual modules serve as libraries when they are referenced by client modules higher up in the hierarchy, and as clients when they reference modules further down.

Dynamic linking [FRAN97] facilitates configuration and saves kernel memory. In Linux, a user program or user can explicitly load and unload kernel modules using the insmod and rmmod commands. The kernel itself monitors the need for particular functions and can load and unload modules as needed. With stackable modules, dependencies between modules can be defined. This has two benefits:

1. Code common to a set of similar modules (e.g., drivers for similar hardware) can be moved into a single module, reducing replication.
2. The kernel can make sure that needed modules are present, refraining from unloading a module on which other running modules depend, and loading any additional required modules when a new module is loaded.

Figure 2.17 is an example that illustrates the structures used by Linux to manage modules. The figure shows the list of kernel modules after only two modules have been loaded: FAT and VFAT. Each module is defined by two tables, the module table and the symbol table. The module table includes the following elements:

- *next: Pointer to the following module. All modules are organized into a linked list. The list begins with a pseudomodule (not shown in Figure 2.17).
- *name: Pointer to module name.
- size: Module size in memory pages.
- usecount: Module usage counter. The counter is incremented when an operation involving the module's functions is started and decremented when the operation terminates.
- flags: Module flags.
- nsyms: Number of exported symbols.
- ndeps: Number of referenced modules
- *syms: Pointer to this module's symbol table.
- *deps: Pointer to list of modules the are referenced by this module.
- *refs: Pointer to list of modules that use this module.

The symbol table defines those symbols controlled by this module that are used elsewhere.

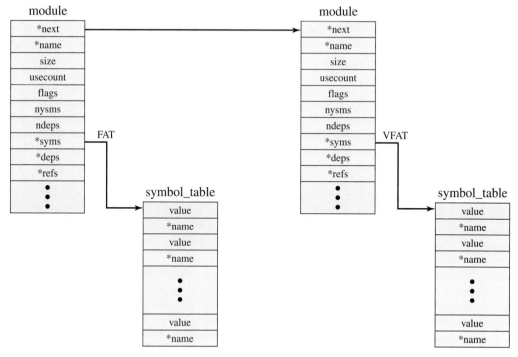

Figure 2.17   Example List of Linux Kernel Modules

Figure 2.17 shows that the VFAT module was loaded after the FAT module and that the VFAT module is dependent on the FAT module.

Kernel Components

Figure 2.18, taken from [MOSB02] shows the main components of the Linux kernel as implemented on an IA-64 architecture (e.g., Intel Itanium). The figure shows several processes running on top of the kernel. Each box indicates a separate process, while each squiggly line with an arrowhead represents a thread of execution.[2] The kernel itself consists of an interacting collection of components, with arrows indicating the main interactions. The underlying hardware is also depicted as a set of components with arrows indicating which kernel components use or control which hardware components. All of the kernel components, of course, execute on the CPU but, for simplicity, these relationships are not shown.

Briefly, the principal kernel components are the following:

- **Signals:** The kernel uses signals to call into a process. For example, signals are used to notify a process of certain faults, such as division by zero. Table 2.6 gives a few examples of signals.

---

[2]In Linux, there is no distinction between the concepts of processes and threads. However, multiple threads in Linux can be grouped together in such a way that, effectively, you can have a single process comprising multiple threads. These matters are discussed in Chapter 4.

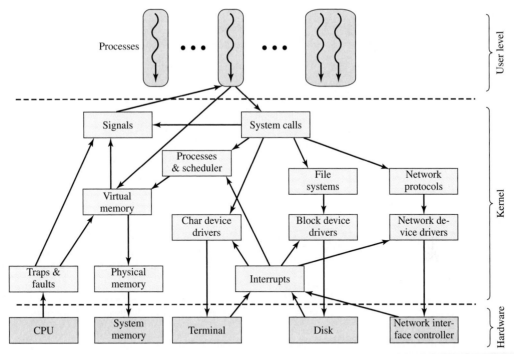

Figure 2.18 Linux Kernel Components

Table 2.6 Some Linux Signals

SIGHUP	Terminal hangup	SIGCONT	Continue
SIGQUIT	Keyboard quit	SIGTSTP	Keyboard stop
SIGTRAP	Trace trap	SIGTTOU	Terminal write
SIGBUS	Bus error	SIGXCPU	CPU limit exceeded
SIGKILL	Kill signal	SIGVTALRM	Virtual alarm clock
SIGSEGV	Segmentation violation	SIGWINCH	Window size unchanged
SIGPIPT	Broken pipe	SIGPWR	Power failure
SIGTERM	Termination	SIGRTMIN	First real-time signal
SIGCHLD	Child status unchanged	SIGRTMAX	Last real-time signal

- **System calls:** The system call is the means by which a process requests a specific kernel service. There are several hundred system calls, which can be roughly grouped into six categories: filesystem, process, scheduling, interprocess communication, socket (networking), and miscellaneous. Table 2.7 defines a few examples in each category.
- **Processes and scheduler:** Creates, manages, and schedules processes.
- **Virtual memory:** Allocates and manages virtual memory for processes.

Table 2.7 Some Linux System Calls

Filesystem related	
close	Close a file descriptor.
link	Make a new name for a file.
open	Open and possibly create a file or device.
read	Read from a file descriptor.
write	Read from a file descriptor
Process related	
execve	Execute program.
exit	Terminate the calling process.
getpid	Get process identification.
setuid	Set user identity of the current process.
prtrace	Provides a means by which a parent process my observe and control the execution of another process, and examine and change its core image and registers.
Scheduling related	
sched_getparam	Sets the scheduling parameters associated with the scheduling policy for the process identified by pid.
sched_get_priority_max	Returns the maximum priority value that can be used with the scheduling algorithm identified by policy.
sched_setscheduler	Sets both the scheduling policy (e.g., FIFO) and the associated parameters for the process pid.
sched_rr_get_interval	Writes into the timespec structure pointed to by the parameter tp the round robin time quantum for the process pid.
sched_yield	A process can relinquish the processor voluntarily without blocking via this system call. The process will then be moved to the end of the queue for its static priority and a new process gets to run.
Interprocess Communication (IPC) related	
msgrcv	A message buffer structure is allocated to receive a message. The system call then reads a message from the message queue specified by msqid into the newly created message buffer.
semctl	Performs the control operation specified by cmd on the semaphore set semid.
semop	Performs operations on selected members of the semaphore set semid.
shmat	Attaches the shared memory segment identified by shmid to the data segment of the calling process.
shmctl	Allows the user to receive information on a shared memory segment, set the owner, group, and permissions of a shared memory segment, or destroy a segment.

	Socket (networking) related
bind	Assigns the local IP address and port for a socket. Returns 0 for success and –1 for error.
connect	Establishes a connection between the given socket and the remote socket associated with sockaddr.
gethostname	Returns local host name.
send	Send the bytes contained in buffer pointed to by *msg over the given socket.
setsockopt	Sets the options on a socket
	Miscellaneous
create_module	Attempts to create a loadable module entry and reserve the kernel memory that will be needed to hold the module.
fsync	Copies all in-core parts of a file to disk, and waits until the device reports that all parts are on stable storage.
query_module	Requests information related to loadable modules from the kernel.
time	Returns the time in seconds since January 1, 1970.
vhangup	Simulates a hangup on the current terminal. This call arranges for other users to have a "clean" tty at login time.

- **File systems:** Provides a global, hierarchical namespace for files, directories, and other file related objects and provides file system functions.

- **Network protocols:** Supports the Sockets interface to users for the TCP/IP protocol suite.

- **Character device drivers:** Manages devices that require the kernel to send or receive data one byte at a time, such as terminals, modems, and printers.

- **Block device drivers:** Manages devices that read and write data in blocks, such as various forms of secondary memory (magnetic disks, CDROMs, etc.).

- **Network device drivers:** Manages network interface cards and communications ports that connect to network devices, such as bridges and routers.

- **Traps and faults:** Handles traps and faults generated by the CPU, such as a memory fault.

- **Physical memory:** Manages the pool of page frames in real memory and allocates pages for virtual memory.

- **Interrupts:** Handles interrupts from peripheral devices.

2.9 RECOMMENDED READING AND WEB SITES

As in the area of computer architecture, there are many books on operating systems. [SILB04], [NUTT04], and [TANE01] cover the basic principles using a number of important operating systems as case studies. [BRIN01] is an excellent collection of papers covering major advances in operating system design over the years.

An excellent treatment of UNIX internals, which provides a comparative analysis of a number of variants, is [VAHA96]. For UNIX SVR4, [GOOD94] provides a definitive treatment, with ample technical detail. For the academically popular Berkeley UNIX 4.4BSD, [MCKU96] is highly recommended. [MAUR01] provides a good treatment of Solaris internals. Two good treatments of Linux internals are [BOVE03] and [BAR00].

Although there are countless books on various versions of Windows, there is remarkably little material available on Windows internals. [SOLO00] provides an excellent treatment of Windows 2000 internals, and much of this material is valid for later versions. [BOSW03] provides some coverage in Windows 2003 internals.

BAR00   Bar, M. *Linux Internals*. New York, McGraw-Hill, 2000.

BOSW03   Boswell, W. *Inside Windows Server 2003*. Reading, MA: Addison-Wesley, 2003.

BOVE03   Bovet, D., and Cesati, M. *Understanding the Linux Kernel*. Sebastopol, CA: O'Reilly, 2003.

BRIN01   Brinch Hansen, P. *Classic Operating Systems: From Batch Processing to Distributed Systems*. New York: Springer-Verlag, 2001.

GOOD94   Goodheart, B., and Cox, J. *The Magic Garden Explained: The Internals of UNIX System V Release 4*. Englewood Cliffs, NJ: Prentice Hall, 1994.

MAUR01   Mauro, J., and McDougall, R. *Solaris Internals: Core Kernel Architecture*. Palo Alto, CA: Sun Microsystems Press, 2001.

MCKU96   McKusick, M.; Bostic, K.; Karels, M.; and Quartermain, J. *The Design and Implementation of the 4.4BSD UNIX Operating System*. Reading, MA: Addison-Wesley, 1996.

NUTT04   Nutt, G. *Operating System*. Reading, MA: Addison-Wesley, 2004.

SILB04   Silberschatz, A.; Galvin, P.; and Gagne, G. *Operating System Concepts with Java*. Reading, MA: Addison-Wesley, 2004.

SOLO00   Solomon, D. *Inside Microsoft Windows 2000*. Redmond, WA: Microsoft Press, 2000.

TANE01   Tanenbaum, A. *Modern Operating Systems*. Upper Saddle River, NJ: Prentice Hall, 2001.

VAHA96   Vahalia, U. *UNIX Internals: The New Frontiers*. Upper Saddle River, NJ: Prentice Hall, 1996.

Recommended Web Sites:

- **The Operating System Resource Center:** A useful collection of documents and papers on a wide range of operating system topics
- **Review of Operating Systems:** A comprehensive review of commercial, free, research and hobby operating systems
- **Operating System Technical Comparison:** Includes a substantial amount of information on a variety of operating systems
- **ACM Special Interest Group on Operating Systems:** Information on SIGOPS publications and conferences
- **IEEE Technical Committee on Operating Systems and Application Environments:** Includes an online newsletter and links to other sites
- **The comp.os.research FAQ:** Lengthy and worthwhile FAQ covering operating system design issues
- **UNIX Guru Universe:** Excellent source of UNIX information
- **Linux Documentation Project:** The name describes the site

2.10 KEY TERMS, REVIEW QUESTIONS, AND PROBLEMS

Key Terms

batch processing	multiprogrammed batch system	resident monitor
batch system	multiprogramming	round robin
execution context	multlitasking	scheduling
interrupt	multithreading	serial processing
job	nucleus	symmetric multiprocessing
job control language	operating system	task
kernel	physical address	thread
memory management	privileged instruction	time sharing
microkernel	process	time-sharing system
monitor	process state	uniprogramming
monolithic kernel	real address	virtual address

Review Questions

2.1   What are three objectives of an operating system design?

2.2   What is the kernel of an operating system?

2.3   What is multiprogramming?

2.4   What is a process?

2.5   How is the execution context of a process used by the operating system?

2.6   List and briefly explain five storage management responsibilities of a typical operating system.

2.7   Explain the distinction between a real address and a virtual address.

2.8   Describe the round-robin scheduling technique.

2.9   Explain the difference between a monolithic kernel and a microkernel.

2.10   What is multithreading?

Problems

2.1   Suppose that we have a multiprogrammed computer in which each job has identical characteristics. In one computation period, T, for a job, half the time is spent in I/O and the other half in processor activity. Each job runs for a total of N periods. Assume that a simple round-robin scheduling is used, and that I/O operations can overlap with processor operation. Define the following quantities:

- Turnaround time = actual time to complete a job.

- Throughput = average number of jobs completed per time period T.

- Processor utilization = percentage of time that the processor is active (not waiting).

Compute these quantities for one, two, and four simultaneous jobs, assuming that the period T is distributed in each of the following ways:
a.   I/O first half, processor second half
b.   I/O first and fourth quarters, processor second and third quarter

2.2   An I/O-bound program is one that, if run alone, would spend more time waiting for I/O than using the processor. A processor-bound program is the opposite. Suppose a short-term scheduling algorithm favors those programs that have used little processor time in the recent past. Explain why this algorithm favors I/O-bound programs and yet does not permanently deny processor time to processor-bound programs.

2.3   Contrast the scheduling policies you might use when trying to optimize a time-sharing system with those you would use to optimize a multiprogrammed batch system.

2.4   What is the purpose of system calls, and how do system calls relate to the operating system and to the concept of dual-mode (kernel mode and user mode) operation?

2.5   In IBM's mainframe operating system, OS/390, one of the major modules in the kernel is the System Resource Manager (SRM). This module is responsible for the allocation of resources among address spaces (processes). The SRM gives OS/390 a degree of sophistication unique among operating systems. No other mainframe operating system, and certainly no other type of operating system, can match the functions performed by SRM. The concept of resource includes processor, real memory, and I/O channels. SRM accumulates statistics pertaining to utilization of processor, channel, and various key data structures. Its purpose is to provide optimum performance based on performance monitoring and analysis. The installation sets forth various performance objectives, and these serve as guidance to the SRM, which dynamically modifies installation and job performance characteristics based on system utilization. In turn, the SRM provides reports that enable the trained operator to refine the configuration and parameter settings to improve user service.

This problem concerns one example of SRM activity. Real memory is divided into equal-sized blocks called frames, of which there may be many thousands. Each frame can hold a block of virtual memory referred to as a page. SRM receives control approximately 20 times per second and inspects each and every page frame. If the page has not been referenced or changed, a counter is incremented by 1. Over time, SRM averages these numbers to determine the average number of seconds that a page frame in the system goes untouched. What might be the purpose of this and what action might SRM take?

PART TWO

Processes

The fundamental task of any modern operating system is process management. The operating system must allocate resources to processes, enable processes to share and exchange information, protect the resources of each process from other processes, and enable synchronization among processes. To meet these requirements, the operating system must maintain a data structure for each process that describes the state and resource ownership of that process and that enables the operating system to exert process control.

On a multiprogramming uniprocessor, the execution of multiple processes can be interleaved in time. On a multiprocessor, not only may process execution be interleaved, but also multiple processes can execute simultaneously. Both interleaved and simultaneous execution are types of concurrency and lead to a host of difficult problems, both for the application programmer and the operating system.

In many contemporary operating systems, the difficulties of process management are compounded by the introduction of the concept of thread. In a multithreaded system, the process retains the attributes of resource ownership, while the attribute of multiple, concurrent execution streams is a property of threads running within a process.

ROAD MAP FOR PART TWO

Chapter 3 Process Description and Control

The focus of a traditional operating system is the management of processes. Each process is, at any time, in one of a number of execution states, including Ready, Running, and Blocked. The operating system keeps track of these execution states and manages the movement of processes among the states. For this purpose the operating system maintains rather elaborate data structures describing each process. The operating system must perform the scheduling function and provide facilities for process sharing and synchronization. Chapter 3 looks at the data structures and techniques used in a typical operating system for process management.

Chapter 4 Threads, SMP, and Microkernels

Chapter 4 covers three areas that characterize many contemporary operating systems and that represent advances over traditional operating system design. In many operating systems, the traditional concept of process has been split into two parts: one dealing with resource ownership (process) and one dealing with the stream of instruction execution (thread). A single process may contain multiple threads. A multithreaded organization has advantages both in the structuring of applications and in performance. Chapter 4 also examines the symmetric multiprocessor (SMP), which is a computer system with multiple processors, each of which is able to execute all application and system code. SMP organization enhances performance and reliability. SMP is often used in conjunction with multithreading but can have powerful performance benefits even without multithreading. Finally, Chapter-4 examines the microkernel, which is a style of operating system design that minimizes the amount of system code that runs in kernel mode. The advantages of this approach are analyzed.

Chapter 5 Concurrency: Mutual Exclusion and Synchronization

The two central themes of modern operating systems are multiprogramming and distributed processing. Fundamental to both these themes, and fundamental to the technology of operating system design, is concurrency. Chapter 5 looks at two aspects of concurrency control: mutual exclusion and synchronization. Mutual exclusion refers to the ability of multiple processes (or threads) to share code, resources, or data in such a way that only one process has access to the shared object at a time. Related to mutual exclusion is synchronization: the ability of multiple processes to coordinate their activities by the exchange of information. Chapter 5 provides a broad treatment of issues related to concurrency, beginning with a discussion of the design issues involved. The chapter provides a discussion of hardware support for concurrency and then looks at the most important mechanisms to support concurrency: semaphores, monitors, and message passing.

Chapter 6 Concurrency: Deadlock and Starvation

Chapter 6 looks at two additional aspects of concurrency control. *Deadlock* refers to a situation in which a set of two or more processes are waiting for other members of the set to complete an operation in order to proceed, but none of the members is able to proceed. Deadlock is a difficult phenomenon to anticipate, and there are no easy general solutions to this problem. Chapter 6 looks at the three major approaches to dealing with deadlock: prevention, avoidance, and detection. *Starvation* refers to a situation in which a process is ready to execute but is continuously denied access to a processor in deference to other processes. In large part, starvation is dealt with as a scheduling issue and is therefore treated in Part Four. Although Chapter 6 focuses on deadlock, starvation is addressed in the context that solutions to deadlock need to avoid the problem of starvation.

CHAPTER 3

PROCESS DESCRIPTION AND CONTROL

The design of an operating system must reflect certain general requirements. All multiprogramming operating systems, from single-user systems such as Windows 98 to mainframe systems such as IBM z/OS, which can support thousands of users, are built around the concept of the process. Most requirements that the operating system must meet can be expressed with reference to processes:

- The operating system must interleave the execution of multiple processes, to maximize processor utilization while providing reasonable response time.

- The operating system must allocate resources to processes in conformance with a specific policy (e.g., certain functions or applications are of higher priority) while at the same time avoiding deadlock.[1]

- The operating system may be required to support interprocess communication and user creation of processes, both of which may aid in the structuring of applications.

We begin our detailed study of operating systems with an examination of the way in which they represent and control processes. After an introduction to the concept of a process, the chapter discusses process states, which characterize the behavior of processes. Then we look at the data structures that the operating system uses to manage processes. These include data structures to represent the state of each process and data structures that record other characteristics of processes that the operating system needs to achieve its objectives. Next, we look at the ways in which the operating system uses these data structures to control process execution. Finally, we discuss process management in UNIX SVR4. Chapter 4 provides more modern examples of process management, namely Solaris, Windows, and Linux.

Note: In this chapter, reference is occasionally made to virtual memory. Much of the time, we can ignore this concept in dealing with processes, but at certain points in the discussion, virtual memory considerations are pertinent. Virtual memory is not discussed in detail until Chapter 8; a brief overview is provided in Chapter 2.

3.1 WHAT IS A PROCESS?

Background

Before defining the term *process*, it is useful to summarize some of the concepts introduced in Chapters 1 and 2:

1. A computer platform consists of a collection of hardware resources, such as the processor, main memory, I/O modules, timers, disk drives, and so on.

2. Computer applications are developed to perform some task. Typically, they accept input from the outside world, perform some processing, and generate output.

---

[1]Deadlock will be examined in Chapter 6. As a simple example, deadlock occurs if two processes need the same two resources to continue and each has ownership of one. Unless some action is taken, each process will wait indefinitely for the missing resource.

3. It is inefficient for applications to be written directly for a given hardware platform. The principal reasons for this are as follows:

   (a) Numerous applications can be developed for the same platform. Thus, it makes sense to develop common routines for accessing the computer's resources.

   (b) The processor itself provides only limited support for multiprogramming. Software is needed to manage the sharing of the processor and other resources by multiple applications at the same time.

   (c) When multiple applications are active at the same time, it is necessary to protect the data, I/O use, and other resource use of each application from the others.

4. The operating system was developed to provide a convenient feature rich, secure, and consistent interface for applications to use. The operating system is a layer of software between the applications and the computer hardware (Figure 2.1) that supports applications and utilities.

5. We can think of the operating system as providing a uniform, abstract representation of resources that can be requested and accessed by applications. Resources include main memory, network interfaces, file systems, and so on. Once the operating system has created these resource abstractions for applications to use, it must also manage their use. For example, an operating system may permit resource sharing and resource protection.

Now that we have the concepts of applications, system software, and resources, we are in a position to discuss how the operating system can, in an orderly fashion, manage the execution of applications so that

- Resources are made available to multiple applications.
- The physical processor is switched among multiple applications so all will appear to be progressing.
- The processor and I/O devices can be used efficiently.

The approach taken by all modern operating systems is to rely on a model in which the execution of an application corresponds to the existence of one or more processes.

Processes and Process Control Blocks

Recall from Chapter 2 that we suggested several definitions of the term *process*, including

- A program in execution
- An instance of a program running on a computer
- The entity that can be assigned to and executed on a processor
- A unit of activity characterized by the execution of a sequence of instructions, a current state, and an associated set of system resources

We can also think of a process as an entity that consists of a number of elements. Two essential elements of a process are **program code** (which may be shared with other processes that are executing the same program) and a **set of data** associated with that code. Let us suppose that the processor begins to execute this program code, and we refer to this executing entity as a process. At any given point in time, *while the program is executing*, this process can be uniquely characterized by a number of elements, including the following:

- **Identifier:** A unique identifier associated with this process, to distinguish it from all other processes.
- **State:** If the process is currently executing, it is in the running state.
- **Priority:** Priority level relative to other processes.
- **Program counter:** The address of the next instruction in the program to be executed.
- **Memory pointers:** Includes pointers to the program code and data associated with this process, plus any memory blocks shared with other processes.
- **Context data:** These are data that are present in registers in the processor while the process is executing.
- **I/O status information:** Includes outstanding I/O requests, I/O devices (e.g., tape drives) assigned to this process, a list of files in use by the process, and so on.
- **Accounting information:** May include the amount of processor time and clock time used, time limits, account numbers, and so on.

The information in the preceding list is stored in a data structure, typically called a **process control block** (Figure 3.1), that is created and managed by the operating system. The significant point about the process control block is that it contains sufficient information so that it is possible to interrupt a running process and later

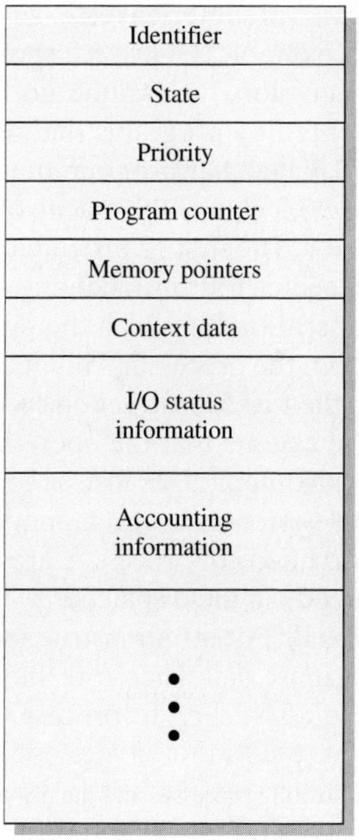

Identifier
State
Priority
Program counter
Memory pointers
Context data
I/O status information
Accounting information
⋮

Figure 3.1 Simplified Process Control Block

resume execution as if the interruption had not occurred. The process control block is the key tool that enables the operating system to support multiple processes and to provide for multiprocessing. When a process is interrupted, the current values of the program counter and the processor registers (context data) are saved in the appropriate fields of the corresponding process control block, and the state of the process is changed to some other value, such as *blocked* or *ready* (described subsequently). The operating system is now free to put some other process in the running state. The program counter and context data for this process are loaded into the processor registers and this process now begins to execute.

Thus, we can say that a process consists of program code and associated data plus a process control block. For a single-processor computer, at any given time, at most one process is executing and that process is in the *running* state.

3.2 PROCESS STATES

As just discussed, for a program to be executed, a process, or task, is created for that program. From the processor's point of view, it executes instructions from its repertoire in some sequence dictated by the changing values in the program counter register. Over time, the program counter may refer to code in different programs that are part of different processes. From the point of view of an individual program, its execution involves a sequence of instructions within that program.

We can characterize the behavior of an individual process by listing the sequence of instructions that execute for that process. Such a listing is referred to as a **trace** of the process. We can characterize the behavior of the processor by showing how the traces of the various processes are interleaved.

Let us consider a very simple example. Figure 3.2 shows a memory layout of three processes. To simplify the discussion, we assume no use of virtual memory; thus all three processes are represented by programs that are fully loaded in main memory. In addition, there is a small **dispatcher** program that switches the processor from one process to another. Figure 3.3 shows the traces of each of the processes during the early part of their execution. The first 12 instructions executed in processes A and C are shown. Process B executes four instructions, and we assume that the fourth instruction invokes an I/O operation for which the process must wait.

Now let us view these traces from the processor's point of view. Figure 3.4 shows the interleaved traces resulting from the first 52 instruction cycles (for convenience, the instruction cycles are numbered). We assume that the operating system only allows a process to continue execution for a maximum of six instruction cycles, after which it is interrupted; this prevents any single process from monopolizing processor time. As Figure 3.4 shows, the first six instructions of process A are executed, followed by a time-out and the execution of some code in the dispatcher, which executes six instructions before turning control to process B.[2] After four instructions are executed, process B requests an I/O action for which it must wait. Therefore, the processor stops executing process B and moves on, via the dispatcher, to process C. After a time-out, the

---

[2]The small numbers of instructions executed for the processes and the dispatcher are unrealistically low; they are used in this simplified example to clarify the discussion.

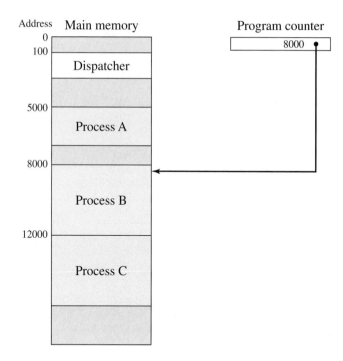

Figure 3.2 Snapshot of Example Execution (Figure 3.4) at Instruction Cycle 13

5000	8000	12000
5001	8001	12001
5002	8002	12002
5003	8003	12003
5004		12004
5005		12005
5006		12006
5007		12007
5008		12008
5009		12009
5010		12010
5011		12011
(a) Trace of Process A	**(b) Trace of Process B**	**(c) Trace of Process C**

5000 = Starting address of program of Process A
8000 = Starting address of program of Process B
12000 = Starting address of program of Process C

Figure 3.3 Traces of Processes of Figure 3.2

processor moves back to process A. When this process times out, process B is still waiting for the I/O operation to complete, so the dispatcher moves on to process C again.

A Two-State Process Model

The operating system's principal responsibility is controlling the execution of processes; this includes determining the interleaving pattern for execution and allocating

1	5000	27	12004
2	5001	28	12005
3	5002		————————Timeout
4	5003	29	100
5	5004	30	101
6	5005	31	102
————————Timeout		32	103
7	100	33	104
8	101	34	105
9	102	35	5006
10	103	36	5007
11	104	37	5008
12	105	38	5009
13	8000	39	5010
14	8001	40	5011
15	8002		————————Timeout
16	8003	41	100
————————I/O request		42	101
17	100	43	102
18	101	44	103
19	102	45	104
20	103	46	105
21	104	47	12006
22	105	48	12007
23	12000	49	12008
24	12001	50	12009
25	12002	51	12010
26	12003	52	12011
			————————Timeout

100 = Starting address of dispatcher program
Shaded areas indicate execution of dispatcher process;
first and third columns count instruction cycles;
second and fourth columns show address of instruction being executed.

Figure 3.4   Combined Trace of Processes of Figure 3.2

resources to processes. The first step in designing an operating system to control processes is to describe the behavior that we would like the processes to exhibit.

We can construct the simplest possible model by observing that, at any time, a process is either being executed by a processor or not. In this model, a process may be in one of two states: Running or Not Running, as shown in Figure 3.5a. When the operating system creates a new process, it creates a process control block for the process and enters that process into the system in the Not Running state. The process exists, is known to the operating system, and is waiting for an opportunity to execute. From time to time, the currently running process will be interrupted and the dispatcher portion of the operating system will select some other process to run. The former process moves from the Running state to the Not Running state, and one of the other processes moves to the Running state.

From this simple model, we can already begin to appreciate some of the design elements of the operating system. Each process must be represented in some way so that the operating system can keep track of it. That is, there must be some information relating to each process, including current state and location in memory; this is the process control block. Processes that are not running must be kept in some sort of

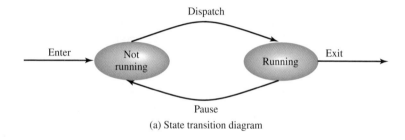

(a) State transition diagram

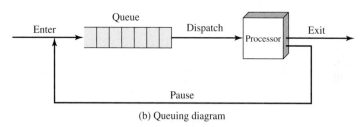

(b) Queuing diagram

Figure 3.5   Two-State Process Model

queue, waiting their turn to execute. Figure 3.5b suggests a structure. There is a single queue in which each entry is a pointer to the process control block of a particular process. Alternatively, the queue may consist of a linked list of data blocks, in which each block represents one process; we will explore this latter implementation subsequently.

We can describe the behavior of the dispatcher in terms of this queuing diagram. A process that is interrupted is transferred to the queue of waiting processes. Alternatively, if the process has completed or aborted, it is discarded (exits the system). In either case, the dispatcher then selects a process from the queue to execute.

The Creation and Termination of Processes

Before attempting to refine our simple two-state model, it will be useful to discuss the creation and termination of processes; ultimately, and regardless of the model of process behavior that is used, the life of a process is bounded by its creation and termination.

Process Creation   When a new process is to be added to those currently being managed, the operating system builds the data structures that are used to manage the process (as described in Section 3.3) and allocates address space in main memory to the process. These actions constitute the creation of a new process.

Four common events lead to the creation of a process, as indicated in Table 3.1. In a batch environment, a process is created in response to the submission of a job. In an interactive environment, a process is created when a new user attempts to log on. In both cases, the operating system is responsible for the creation of the new process. An operating system may also create a process on behalf of an application. For example, if a user requests that a file be printed, the operating system can create a process that will manage the printing. The requesting process can thus proceed independently of the time required to complete the printing task.

Table 3.1 Reasons for Process Creation

New batch job	The operating system is provided with a batch job control stream, usually on tape or disk. When the operating system is prepared to take on new work, it will read the next sequence of job control commands.
Interactive logon	A user at a terminal logs on to the system.
Created by OS to provide a service	The operating system can create a process to perform a function on behalf of a user program, without the user having to wait (e.g., a process to control printing).
Spawned by existing process	For purposes of modularity or to exploit parallelism, a user program can dictate the creation of a number of processes.

Traditionally, the operating system created all processes in a way that was transparent to the user or application program, and this is still commonly found with many contemporary operating systems. However, it can be useful to allow one process to cause the creation of another. For example, an application process may generate another process to receive data that the application is generating and to organize those data into a form suitable for later analysis. The new process runs in parallel to the original process and is activated from time to time when new data are available. This arrangement can be very useful in structuring the application. As another example, a server process (e.g., print server, file server) may generate a new process for each request that it handles. When the operating system creates a process at the explicit request of another process, the action is referred to as **process spawning**.

When one process spawns another, the former is referred to as the **parent process**, and the spawned process is referred to as the **child process**. Typically, the "related" processes need to communicate and cooperate with each other. Achieving this cooperation is a difficult task for the programmer; this topic is discussed in Chapter 5.

Process Termination Table 3.2 summarizes typical reasons for process termination. Any computer system must provide a means for a process to indicate its completion. A batch job should include a Halt instruction or an explicit operating system service call for termination. In the former case, the Halt instruction will generate an interrupt to alert the operating system that a process has completed. For an interactive application, the action of the user will indicate when the process is completed. For example, in a time-sharing system, the process for a particular user is to be terminated when the user logs off or turns off his or her terminal. On a personal computer or workstation, a user may quit an application (e.g., word processing or spreadsheet). All of these actions ultimately result in a service request to the operating system to terminate the requesting process.

Additionally, a number of error and fault conditions can lead to the termination of a process. Table 3.2 lists some of the more commonly recognized conditions.[3]

---

[3]A forgiving operating system might, in some cases, allow the user to recover from a fault without terminating the process. For example, if a user requests access to a file and that access is denied, the operating system might simply inform the user that access is denied and allow the process to proceed.

Table 3.2   Reasons for Process Termination

Normal completion	The process executes an OS service call to indicate that it has completed running.
Time limit exceeded	The process has run longer than the specified total time limit. There are a number of possibilities for the type of time that is measured. These include total elapsed time ("wall clock time"), amount of time spent executing, and, in the case of an interactive process, the amount of time since the user last provided any input.
Memory unavailable	The process requires more memory than the system can provide.
Bounds violation	The process tries to access a memory location that it is not allowed to access.
Protection error	The process attempts to use a resource such as a file that it is not allowed to use, or it tries to use it in an improper fashion, such as writing to a read-only file.
Arithmetic error	The process tries a prohibited computation, such as division by zero, or tries to store numbers larger than the hardware can accommodate.
Time overrun	The process has waited longer than a specified maximum for a certain event to occur.
I/O failure	An error occurs during input or output, such as inability to find a file, failure to read or write after a specified maximum number of tries (when, for example, a defective area is encountered on a tape), or invalid operation (such as reading from the line printer).
Invalid instruction	The process attempts to execute a nonexistent instruction (often a result of branching into a data area and attempting to execute the data).
Privileged instruction	The process attempts to use an instruction reserved for the operating system.
Data misuse	A piece of data is of the wrong type or is not initialized.
Operator or OS intervention	For some reason, the operator or the operating system has terminated the process (for example, if a deadlock exists).
Parent termination	When a parent terminates, the operating system may automatically terminate all of the offspring of that parent.
Parent request	A parent process typically has the authority to terminate any of its offspring.

Finally, in some operating systems, a process may be terminated by the process that created it or when the parent process is itself terminated.

A Five-State Model

If all processes were always ready to execute, then the queuing discipline suggested by Figure 3.5b would be effective. The queue is a first-in-first-out list and the processor operates in **round-robin** fashion on the available processes (each process in the queue is given a certain amount of time, in turn, to execute and then returned to the queue, unless blocked). However, even with the simple example that we have described, this implementation is inadequate: Some processes in the Not Running state are ready to execute, while others are blocked, waiting for an I/O operation to complete. Thus, using a single queue, the dispatcher could not just select the process

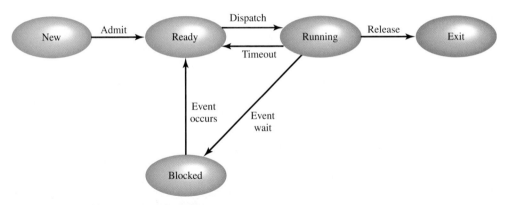

Figure 3.6 Five-State Process Model

at the oldest end of the queue. Rather, the dispatcher would have to scan the list looking for the process that is not blocked and that has been in the queue the longest.

A more natural way to handle this situation is to split the Not Running state into two states: Ready and Blocked. This is shown in Figure 3.6. For good measure, we have added two additional states that will prove useful. The five states in this new diagram are as follows:

- **Running:** The process that is currently being executed. For this chapter, we will assume a computer with a single processor, so at most one process at a time can be in this state.
- **Ready:** A process that is prepared to execute when given the opportunity.
- **Blocked:** A process that cannot execute until some event occurs, such as the completion of an I/O operation.
- **New:** A process that has just been created but has not yet been admitted to the pool of executable processes by the operating system. Typically, a new process has not yet been loaded into main memory, although its process control block has been created.
- **Exit:** A process that has been released from the pool of executable processes by the operating system, either because it halted or because it aborted for some reason.

The New and Exit states are useful constructs for process management. The New state corresponds to a process that has just been defined. For example, if a new user attempts to log onto a time-sharing system or a new batch job is submitted for execution, the operating system can define a new process in two stages. First, the operating system performs the necessary housekeeping chores. An identifier is associated with the process. Any tables that will be needed to manage the process are allocated and built. At this point, the process is in the New state. This means that the operating system has performed the necessary actions to create the process but has not committed itself to the execution of the process. For example, the operating system may limit the number of processes that may be in the system for reasons of performance or main memory limitation. While a process is in the new state, information concerning the process that is needed by the operating system is maintained in control tables in main memory. However, the process itself is not in main memory. That is, the code of the program to be executed is not in main memory, and no space has been allocated for the data associated with that program. While the process is in the New state, the program remains in secondary storage, typically disk storage.[4]

Similarly, a process exits a system in two stages. First, a process is terminated when it reaches a natural completion point, when it aborts due to an unrecoverable error, or when another process with the appropriate authority causes the process to abort. Termination moves the process to the exit state. At this point, the process is no longer eligible for execution. The tables and other information associated with the job are temporarily preserved by the operating system, which provides time for auxiliary or support programs to extract any needed information. For example, an accounting program may need to record the processor time and other resources utilized by the process for billing purposes. A utility program may need to extract information about the history of the process for purposes related to performance or utilization analysis. Once these programs have extracted the needed information, the operating system no longer needs to maintain any data relating to the process and the process is deleted from the system.

Figure 3.6 indicates the types of events that lead to each state transition for a process; the possible transitions are as follows:

- **Null → New:** A new process is created to execute a program. This event occurs for any of the reasons listed in Table 3.1.

- **New → Ready:** The operating system will move a process from the New state to the Ready state when it is prepared to take on an additional process. Most systems set some limit based on the number of existing processes or the amount of virtual memory committed to existing processes. This limit assures that there are not so many active processes as to degrade performance.

- **Ready → Running:** When it is time to select a new process to run, the operating system chooses one of the processes in the Ready state. This is the job of the scheduler or dispatcher. Scheduling is explored in Part Four.

- **Running → Exit:** The currently running process is terminated by the operating system if the process indicates that it has completed or if it aborts. See Table 3.2.

- **Running → Ready:** The most common reason for this transition is that the running process has reached the maximum allowable time for uninterrupted execution; virtually all multiprogramming operating systems impose this type of time discipline. There are several other alternative causes for this transition, which are not implemented in all operating systems. Of particular importance is the case in which the operating system assigns different levels of priority to different processes. Suppose, for example, that process A is running at a given priority level, and process B, at a higher priority level, is blocked. If the operating system learns that the event upon which process B has been waiting has occurred,

---

[4]In the discussion in this paragraph, we ignore the concept of virtual memory. In systems that support virtual memory, when a process moves from New to Ready, its program code and data are loaded into virtual memory. Virtual memory was briefly discussed in Chapter 2 and is examined in detail in Chapter 8.

moving B to a ready state, then it can interrupt process A and dispatch process B. We say that the operating system has **preempted** process A.[5] Finally, a process may voluntarily release control of the processor. An example is a background process that performs some accounting or maintenance function periodically.

- **Running** → **Blocked:** A process is put in the Blocked state if it requests something for which it must wait. A request to the operating system is usually in the form of a system service call; that is, a call from the running program to a procedure that is part of the operating system code. For example, a process may request a service from the operating system that the operating system is not prepared to perform immediately. It can request a resource, such as a file or a shared section of virtual memory, that is not immediately available. Or the process may initiate an action, such as an I/O operation, that must be completed before the process can continue. When processes communicate with each other, a process may be blocked when it is waiting for another process to provide data or waiting for a message from another process.

- **Blocked** → **Ready:** A process in the Blocked state is moved to the Ready state when the event for which it has been waiting occurs.

- **Ready** → **Exit:** For clarity, this transition is not shown on the state diagram. In some systems, a parent may terminate a child process at any time. Also, if a parent terminates, all child processes associated with that parent may be terminated.

- **Blocked** → **Exit:** The comments under the preceding item apply.

Returning to our simple example, Figure 3.7 shows the transition of each process among the states. Figure 3.8a suggests the way in which a queuing discipline might be implemented with two queues: a Ready queue and a Blocked queue. As each process is admitted to the system, it is placed in the Ready queue. When it is time for the operating system to choose another process to run, it selects one from the Ready queue. In the absence of any priority scheme, this can be a simple first-in-first-out queue. When a running process is removed from execution, it is either terminated or placed in the Ready or Blocked queue, depending on the circumstances. Finally, when an event occurs, any process in the Blocked queue that has been waiting on that event only is moved to the Ready queue.

This latter arrangement means that, when an event occurs, the operating system must scan the entire blocked queue, searching for those processes waiting on that event. In a large operating system, there could be hundreds or even thousands of processes in that queue. Therefore, it would be more efficient to have a number of queues, one for each event. Then, when the event occurs, the entire list of processes in the appropriate queue can be moved to the Ready state (Figure 3.8b).

One final refinement: If the dispatching of processes is dictated by a priority scheme, then it would be convenient to have a number of Ready queues, one for each priority level. The operating system could then readily determine which is the highest-priority ready process that has been waiting the longest.

---

[5]In general, the term *preemption* is defined to be the reclaiming of a resource from a process before the process is finished using it. In this case, the resource is the processor itself. The process is executing and could continue to execute but is preempted so that another process can be executed.

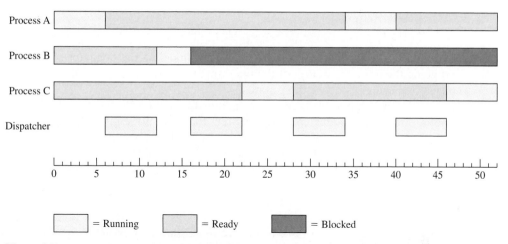

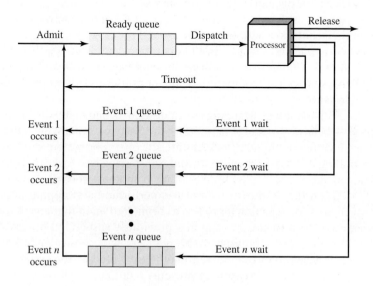

Figure 3.7 Process States for Trace of Figure 3.4

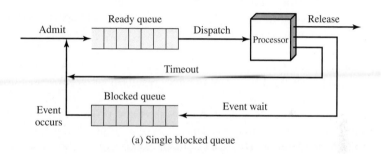

(a) Single blocked queue

(b) Multiple blocked queues

Figure 3.8 Queuing Model for Figure 3.6

Suspended Processes

The Need for Swapping   The three principal states just described (Ready, Running, Blocked) provide a systematic way of modeling the behavior of processes and guide the implementation of the operating system. Some operating systems are constructed using just these three states.

However, there is good justification for adding other states to the model. To see the benefit of these new states, consider a system that does not employ virtual memory. Each process to be executed must be loaded fully into main memory. Thus, in Figure 3.8b, all of the processes in all of the queues must be resident in main memory.

Recall that the reason for all of this elaborate machinery is that I/O activities are much slower than computation and therefore the processor in a uniprogramming system is idle most of the time. But the arrangement of Figure 3.8b does not entirely solve the problem. It is true that, in this case, memory holds multiple processes and that the processor can move to another process when one process is blocked. But the processor is so much faster than I/O that it will be common for all of the processes in memory to be waiting for I/O. Thus, even with multiprogramming, a processor could be idle most of the time.

What to do? Main memory could be expanded to accommodate more processes. But there are two flaws in this approach. First, there is a cost associated with main memory, that, though small on a per-byte basis, begins to add up as we get into the gigabytes of storage. Second, the appetite of programs for memory has grown as fast as the cost of memory has dropped. So larger memory results in larger processes, not more processes.

Another solution is swapping, which involves moving part or all of a process from main memory to disk. When none of the processes in main memory is in the Ready state, the operating system swaps one of the blocked processes out onto disk into a suspend queue. This is a queue of existing processes that have been temporarily kicked out of main memory, or suspended. The operating system then brings in another process from the suspend queue, or it honors a new-process request. Execution then continues with the newly arrived process.

Swapping, however, is an I/O operation, and therefore there is the potential for making the problem worse, not better. But because disk I/O is generally the fastest I/O on a system (e.g., compared to tape or printer I/O), swapping will usually enhance performance.

With the use of swapping as just described, one other state must be added to our process behavior model (Figure 3.9a): the Suspend state. When all of the processes in main memory are in the Blocked state, the operating system can suspend one process by putting it in the Suspend state and transferring it to disk. The space that is freed in main memory can then be used to bring in another process.

When the operating system has performed a swapping-out operation, it has two choices for selecting a process to bring into main memory: It can admit a newly created process or it can bring in a previously suspended process. It would appear that the preference should be to bring in a previously suspended process, to provide it with service rather than increasing the total load on the system.

But this line of reasoning presents a difficulty. All of the processes that have been suspended were in the Blocked state at the time of suspension. It clearly would not do any good to bring a blocked process back into main memory, because it is still

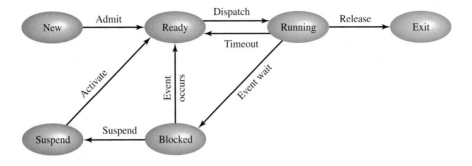

(a) With one Suspend state

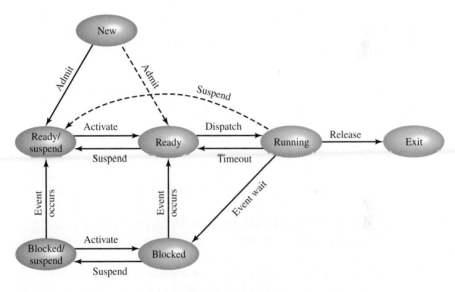

(b) With two Suspend states

Figure 3.9 Process State Transition Diagram with Suspend States

not ready for execution. Recognize, however, that each process in the Suspend state was originally blocked on a particular event. When that event occurs, the process is not blocked and is potentially available for execution.

Therefore, we need to rethink this aspect of the design. There are two independent concepts here: whether a process is waiting on an event (blocked or not) and whether a process has been swapped out of main memory (suspended or not). To accommodate this 2×2 combination, we need four states:

- **Ready:** The process is in main memory and available for execution.
- **Blocked:** The process is in main memory and awaiting an event.
- **Blocked/Suspend:** The process is in secondary memory and awaiting an event.
- **Ready/Suspend:** The process is in secondary memory but is available for execution as soon as it is loaded into main memory.

Before looking at a state transition diagram that encompasses the two new suspend states, one other point should be mentioned. The discussion so far has assumed that virtual memory is not in use and that a process is either all in main memory or all out of main memory. With a virtual memory scheme, it is possible to execute a process that is only partially in main memory. If reference is made to a process address that is not in main memory, then the appropriate portion of the process can be brought in. The use of virtual memory would appear to eliminate the need for explicit swapping, because any desired address in any desired process can be moved in or out of main memory by the memory management hardware of the processor. However, as we shall see in Chapter 8, the performance of a virtual memory system can collapse if there is a sufficiently large number of active processes, all of which are partially in main memory. Therefore, even in a virtual memory system, the operating system will need to swap out processes explicitly and completely from time to time in the interests of performance.

Let us look now, in Figure 3.9b, at the state transition model that we have developed. (The dashed lines in the figure indicate possible but not necessary transitions.) Important new transitions are the following:

- **Blocked → Blocked/Suspend:** If there are no ready processes, then at least one blocked process is swapped out to make room for another process that is not blocked. This transition can be made even if there are ready processes available, if the operating system determines that the currently running process or a ready process that it would like to dispatch requires more main memory to maintain adequate performance.

- **Blocked/Suspend → Ready/Suspend:** A process in the Blocked/Suspend state is moved to the Ready/Suspend state when the event for which it has been waiting occurs. Note that this requires that the state information concerning suspended processes must be accessible to the operating system.

- **Ready/Suspend → Ready:** When there are no ready processes in main memory, the operating system will need to bring one in to continue execution. In addition, it might be the case that a process in the Ready/Suspend state has higher priority than any of the processes in the Ready state. In that case, the operating system designer may dictate that it is more important to get at the higher-priority process than to minimize swapping.

- **Ready → Ready/Suspend:** Normally, the operating system would prefer to suspend a blocked process rather than a ready one, because the ready process can now be executed, whereas the blocked process is taking up main memory space and cannot be executed. However, it may be necessary to suspend a ready process if that is the only way to free up a sufficiently large block of main memory. Also, the operating system may choose to suspend a lower-priority ready process rather than a higher-priority blocked process if it believes that the blocked process will be ready soon.

Several other transitions that are worth considering are the following:

- **New → Ready/Suspend and New → Ready:** When a new process is created, it can either be added to the Ready queue or the Ready/Suspend queue. In either case, the operating system must create a process control block and allocate an address space to the process. It might be preferable for the operating system to perform these housekeeping duties at an early time, so that it can maintain a large pool of processes that are not blocked. With this strategy, there would often be insufficient room in main memory for a new process; hence the use of the (New → Ready/Suspend) transition. On the other hand, we could argue that a just-in-time philosophy of creating processes as late as possible reduces operating system overhead and allows that operating system to perform the process-creation duties at a time when the system is clogged with blocked processes anyway.

- **Blocked/Suspend → Blocked:** Inclusion of this transition may seem to be poor design. After all, if a process is not ready to execute and is not already in main memory, what is the point of bringing it in? But consider the following scenario: A process terminates, freeing up some main memory. There is a process in the Blocked/Suspend queue with a higher priority than any of the processes in the Ready/Suspend queue and the operating system has reason to believe that the blocking event for that process will occur soon. Under these circumstances, it would seem reasonable to bring a blocked process into main memory in preference to a ready process.

- **Running → Ready/Suspend:** Normally, a running process is moved to the Ready state when its time allocation expires. If, however, the operating system is preempting the process because a higher-priority process on the Blocked/Suspend queue has just become unblocked, the operating system could move the running process directly to the Ready/Suspend queue and free some main memory.

- **Any State → Exit:** Typically, a process terminates while it is running, either because it has completed or because of some fatal fault condition. However, in some operating systems, a process may be terminated by the process that created it or when the parent process is itself terminated. If this is allowed, then a process in any state can be moved to the Exit state.

Other Uses of Suspension So far, we have equated the concept of a suspended process with that of a process that is not in main memory. A process that is not in main memory is not immediately available for execution, whether or not it is awaiting an event.

We can generalize the concept of a suspended process. Let us define a suspended process as having the following characteristics:

1. The process is not immediately available for execution.
2. The process may or may not be waiting on an event. If it is, this blocked condition is independent of the suspend condition, and occurrence of the blocking event does not enable the process to be executed immediately.
3. The process was placed in a suspended state by an agent: either itself, a parent process, or the operating system, for the purpose of preventing its execution.
4. The process may not be removed from this state until the agent explicitly orders the removal.

Table 3.3 lists some reasons for the suspension of a process. One reason that we have discussed is to provide memory space either to bring in a Ready/Suspended process or to increase the memory allocated to other Ready processes. The

Table 3.3   Reasons for Process Suspension

Swapping	The operating system needs to release sufficient main memory to bring in a process that is ready to execute.
Other OS reason	The operating system may suspend a background or utility process or a process that is suspected of causing a problem.
Interactive user request	A user may wish to suspend execution of a program for purposes of debugging or in connection with the use of a resource.
Timing	A process may be executed periodically (e.g., an accounting or system monitoring process) and may be suspended while waiting for the next time interval.
Parent process request	A parent process may wish to suspend execution of a descendent to examine or modify the suspended process, or to coordinate the activity of various descendants.

operating system may have other motivations for suspending a process. For example, an auditing or tracing process may be employed to monitor activity on the system; the process may be used to record the level of utilization of various resources (processor, memory, channels) and the rate of progress of the user processes in the system. The operating system, under operator control, may turn this process on and off from time to time. If the operating system detects or suspects a problem, it may suspend a process. One example of this is deadlock, which is discussed in Chapter 6. As another example, a problem is detected on a communications line, and the operator has the operating system suspend the process that is using the line while some tests are run.

Another set of reasons concerns the actions of an interactive user. For example, if a user suspects a bug in the program, he or she may debug the program by suspending its execution, examining and modifying the program or data, and resuming execution. Or there may be a background process that is collecting trace or accounting statistics, which the user may wish to be able to turn on and off.

Timing considerations may also lead to a swapping decision. For example, if a process is to be activated periodically but is idle most of the time, then it should be swapped out between uses. A program that monitors utilization or user activity is an example.

Finally, a parent process may wish to suspend a descendent process. For example, process A may spawn process B to perform a file read. Subsequently, process B encounters an error in the file read procedure and reports this to process A. Process A suspends process B to investigate the cause.

In all of these cases, the activation of a suspended process is requested by the agent that initially requested the suspension.

3.3 PROCESS DESCRIPTION

The operating system controls events within the computer system. It schedules and dispatches processes for execution by the processor, allocates resources to processes, and responds to requests by user processes for basic services. Fundamentally, we can

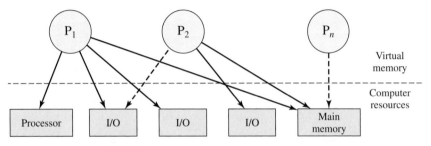

Figure 3.10   Processes and Resources (resource allocation at one snapshot in time)

think of the operating system as that entity that manages the use of system resources by processes.

This concept is illustrated in Figure 3.10. In a multiprogramming environment, there are a number of processes $(P_1, \ldots P_n)$ that have been created and exist in virtual memory. Each process, during the course of its execution, needs access to certain system resources, including the processor, I/O devices, and main memory. In the figure, process P_1 is running; at least part of the process is in main memory, and it has control of two I/O devices. Process P_2 is also in main memory but is blocked waiting for an I/O device allocated to P_1. Process P_n has been swapped out and is therefore suspended.

We explore the details of the management of these resources by the operating system on behalf of the processes in later chapters. Here we are concerned with a more fundamental question: What information does the operating system need to control processes and manage resources for them?

Operating System Control Structures

If the operating system is to manage processes and resources, it must have information about the current status of each process and resource. The universal approach to providing this information is straightforward: The operating system constructs and maintains tables of information about each entity that it is managing. A general idea of the scope of this effort is indicated in Figure 3.11, which shows four different types of tables maintained by the operating system: memory, I/O, file, and process. Although the details will differ from one operating system to another, fundamentally, all operating systems maintain information in these four categories.

Memory tables are used to keep track of both main (real) and secondary (virtual) memory. Some of main memory is reserved for use by the operating system; the remainder is available for use by processes. Processes are maintained on secondary memory using some sort of virtual memory or simple swapping mechanism. The memory tables must include the following information:

- The allocation of main memory to processes
- The allocation of secondary memory to processes
- Any protection attributes of blocks of main or virtual memory, such as which processes may access certain shared memory regions
- Any information needed to manage virtual memory

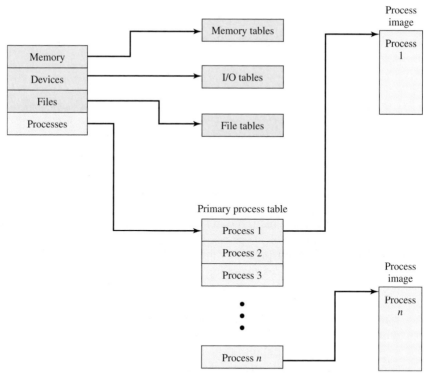

Figure 3.11 General Structure of Operating System Control Tables

We will look at the information structures for memory management in detail in Part Three.

I/O tables are used by the operating system to manage the I/O devices and channels of the computer system. At any given time, an I/O device may be available or assigned to a particular process. If an I/O operation is in progress, the operating system needs to know the status of the I/O operation and the location in main memory being used as the source or destination of the I/O transfer. I/O management is examined in Chapter 11.

The operating system may also maintain **file tables**. These tables provide information about the existence of files, their location on secondary memory, their current status, and other attributes. Much, if not all, of this information may be maintained and used by a file management system, in which case the operating system has little or no knowledge of files. In other operating systems, much of the detail of file management is managed by the operating system itself. This topic is explored in Chapter 12.

Finally, the operating system must maintain **process tables** to manage processes. The remainder of this section is devoted to an examination of the required process tables. Before proceeding to this discussion, two additional points should be made. First, although Figure 3.11 shows four distinct sets of tables, it should be clear that these tables must be linked or cross-referenced in some fashion. Memory, I/O, and files are managed on behalf of processes, so there must be some reference to these resources, directly or indirectly, in the process tables. The files referred to in the file tables are accessible via an I/O device and will, at some times, be in main or virtual memory. The tables themselves must be accessible by the operating system and therefore are subject to memory management.

Second, how does the operating system know to create the tables in the first place? Clearly, the operating system must have some knowledge of the basic environment, such as how much main memory exists, what are the I/O devices and what are their identifiers, and so on. This is an issue of configuration. That is, when the operating system is initialized, it must have access to some configuration data that define the basic environment, and these data must be created outside the operating system, with human assistance or by some autoconfiguration software.

Process Control Structures

Consider what the operating system must know if it is to manage and control a process. First, it must know where the process is located, and second, it must know the attributes of the process that are necessary for its management (e.g., process ID and process state).

Process Location Before we can deal with the questions of where a process is located or what its attributes are, we need to address an even more fundamental question: What is the physical manifestation of a process? At a minimum, a process must include a program or set of programs to be executed. Associated with these programs is a set of data locations for local and global variables and any defined constants. Thus, a process will consist of at least sufficient memory to hold the programs and data of that process. In addition, the execution of a program typically involves a stack (see Appendix 1B) that is used to keep track of procedure calls and parameter passing between procedures. Finally, each process has associated with it a number of attributes that are used by the operating system for process control. Typically, the collection of attributes is referred to as a **process control block**.[6] We can refer to this collection of program, data, stack, and attributes as the **process image** (Table 3.4).

The location of a process image will depend on the memory management scheme being used. In the simplest case, the process image is maintained as a contiguous, or continuous, block of memory. This block is maintained in secondary memory, usually disk. So that the operating system can manage the process, at least a small portion of its image must be maintained in main memory. To execute the process, the entire process image must be loaded into main memory or at least virtual memory. Thus, the operating system needs to know the location of each process on disk and, for each such process that is in main memory, the location of that process in main memory. We saw a slightly more complex variation on this scheme with the CTSS operating system, in Chapter 2. With CTSS, when a process is swapped out, part of the process image may remain in main memory. Thus, the operating system must keep track of which portions of the image of each process are still in main memory.

---

[6]Other commonly used names for this data structure are task control block, process descriptor, and task descriptor.

Table 3.4   Typical Elements of a Process Image

User Data

The modifiable part of the user space. May include program data, a user stack area, and programs that may be modified.

User Program

The program to be executed.

System Stack

Each process has one or more last-in-first-out (LIFO) system stacks associated with it. A stack is used to store parameters and calling addresses for procedure and system calls.

Process Control Block

Data needed by the operating system to control the process (see Table 3.5).

Modern operating systems presume paging hardware that allows noncontiguous physical memory to support partially resident processes. At any given time, a portion of a process image may be in main memory, with the remainder in secondary memory.[7] Therefore, process tables maintained by the operating system must show the location of each page of each process image.

Figure 3.11 depicts the structure of the location information in the following way. There is a primary process table with one entry for each process. Each entry contains, at least, a pointer to a process image. If the process image contains multiple blocks, this information is contained directly in the primary process table or is available by cross-reference to entries in memory tables. Of course, this depiction is generic; a particular operating system will have its own way of organizing the location information.

Process Attributes   A sophisticated multiprogramming system requires a great deal of information about each process. As was explained, this information can be considered to reside in a process control block. Different systems will organize this information in different ways, and several examples of this appear at the end of this chapter and the next. For now, let us simply explore the type of information that might be of use to an operating system without considering in any detail how that information is organized.

Table 3.5 lists the typical categories of information required by the operating system for each process. You may be somewhat surprised at the quantity of information required. As you gain a greater appreciation of the responsibilities of the operating system, this list should appear more reasonable.

We can group the process control block information into three general categories:

- Process identification
- Processor state information
- Process control information

---

[7]This brief discussion slides over some details. In particular, in a system that uses virtual memory, all of the process image for an active process is always in secondary memory. When a portion of the image is loaded into main memory, it is copied rather than moved. Thus, the secondary memory retains a copy of all segments and/or pages. However, if the main memory portion of the image is modified, the secondary copy will be out of date until the main memory portion is copied back onto disk.

Table 3.5 Typical Elements of a Process Control Block

Process Identification

Identifiers

Numeric identifiers that may be stored with the process control block include
- Identifier of this process
- Identifier of the process that created this process (parent process)
- User identifier

Processor State Information

User-Visible Registers

A user-visible register is one that may be referenced by means of the machine language that the processor executes while in user mode. Typically, there are from 8 to 32 of these registers, although some RISC implementations have over 100.

Control and Status Registers

These are a variety of processor registers that are employed to control the operation of the processor. These include
- *Program counter:* Contains the address of the next instruction to be fetched
- *Condition codes:* Result of the most recent arithmetic or logical operation (e.g., sign, zero, carry, equal, overflow)
- *Status information:* Includes interrupt enabled/disabled flags, execution mode

Stack Pointers

Each process has one or more last-in-first-out (LIFO) system stacks associated with it. A stack is used to store parameters and calling addresses for procedure and system calls. The stack pointer points to the top of the stack.

Process Control Information

Scheduling and State Information

This is information that is needed by the operating system to perform its scheduling function. Typical items of information:
- *Process state:* Defines the readiness of the process to be scheduled for execution (e.g., running, ready, waiting, halted).
- *Priority:* One or more fields may be used to describe the scheduling priority of the process. In some systems, several values are required (e.g., default, current, highest-allowable)
- *Scheduling-related information:* This will depend on the scheduling algorithm used. Examples are the amount of time that the process has been waiting and the amount of time that the process executed the last time it was running.
- *Event:* Identity of event the process is awaiting before it can be resumed.

Data Structuring

A process may be linked to other process in a queue, ring, or some other structure. For example, all processes in a waiting state for a particular priority level may be linked in a queue. A process may exhibit a parent-child (creator-created) relationship with another process. The process control block may contain pointers to other processes to support these structures.

Interprocess Communication

Various flags, signals, and messages may be associated with communication between two independent processes. Some or all of this information may be maintained in the process control block.

Process Privileges

Processes are granted privileges in terms of the memory that may be accessed and the types of instructions that may be executed. In addition, privileges may apply to the use of system utilities and services.

Memory Management

This section may include pointers to segment and/or page tables that describe the virtual memory assigned to this process.

Resource Ownership and Utilization

Resources controlled by the process may be indicated, such as opened files. A history of utilization of the processor or other resources may also be included; this information may be needed by the scheduler.

With respect to **process identification**, in virtually all operating systems, each process is assigned a unique numeric identifier, which may simply be an index into the primary process table (Figure 3.11); otherwise there must be a mapping that allows the operating system to locate the appropriate tables based on the process identifier. This identifier is useful in several ways. Many of the other tables controlled by the operating system may use process identifiers to cross-reference process tables. For example, the memory tables may be organized so as to provide a map of main memory with an indication of which process is assigned to each region. Similar references will appear in I/O and file tables. When processes communicate with one another, the process identifier informs the operating system of the destination of a particular communication. When processes are allowed to create other processes, identifiers indicate the parent and descendents of each process.

In addition to these process identifiers, a process may be assigned a user identifier that indicates the user responsible for the job.

Processor state information consists of the contents of processor registers. While a process is running, of course, the information is in the registers. When a process is interrupted, all of this register information must be saved so that it can be restored when the process resumes execution. The nature and number of registers involved depend on the design of the processor. Typically, the register set will include user-visible registers, control and status registers, and stack pointers. These are described in Chapter 1.

Of particular note, all processor designs include a register or set of registers, often known as the program status word (PSW), that contains status information. The PSW typically contain condition codes plus other status information. A good example of a processor status word is that on Pentium processors, referred to as the EFLAGS register (shown in Figure 3.12 and Table 3.6). This structure is used by any operating system (including UNIX and Windows) running on a Pentium processors.

The third major category of information in the process control block can be called, for want of a better name, **process control information**. This is the additional information needed by the operating system to control and coordinate the various

31							21		16	15										0
		I D	V I P	V I F	A C	V M	R F		N T	IO PL	O F	D F	I F	T F	S F	Z F		A F		P F		C F

ID	=	Identification flag
VIP	=	Virtual interrupt pending
VIF	=	Virtual interrupt flag
AC	=	Alignment check
VM	=	Virtual 8086 mode
RF	=	Resume flag
NT	=	Nested task flag
IOPL	=	I/O privilege level
OF	=	Overflow flag
DF	=	Direction flag
IF	=	Interrupt enable flag
TF	=	Trap flag
SF	=	Sign flag
ZF	=	Zero flag
AF	=	Auxiliary carry flag
PF	=	Parity flag
CF	=	Carry flag

Figure 3.12 Pentium II EFLAGS Register

Table 3.6 Pentium EFLAGS Register Bits

Control Bits

AC (Alignment check)
Set if a word or doubleword is addressed on a nonword or non-doubleword boundary.

ID (Identification flag)
If this bit can be set and cleared, this processor supports the CPUID instruction. This instruction provides information about the vendor, family, and model.

RF (Resume flag)
Allows the programmer to disable debug exceptions so that the instruction can be restarted after a debug exception without immediately causing another debug exception.

IOPL (I/O privilege level)
When set, causes the processor to generate an exception on all accesses to I/O devices during protected mode operation.

DF (Direction flag)
Determines whether string processing instructions increment or decrement the 16-bit half-registers SI and DI (for 16-bit operations) or the 32-bit registers ESI and EDI (for 32-bit operations).

IF (Interrupt enable flag)
When set, the processor will recognize external interrupts.

TF (Trap flag)
When set, causes an interrupt after the execution of each instruction. This is used for debugging.

Operating Mode Bits

NT (Nested task flag)
Indicates that the current task is nested within another task in protected mode operation.

VM (Virtual 8086 mode)
Allows the programmer to enable or disable virtual 8086 mode, which determines whether the processor runs as an 8086 machine.

VIP (Virtual interrupt pending)
Used in virtual 8086 mode to indicate that one or more interrupts are awaiting service.

VIF (Virtual interrupt flag)
Used in virtual 8086 mode instead of IF.

Condition Codes

AF (Auxiliary carry flag)
Represents carrying or borrowing between half-bytes of an 8-bit arithmetic or logic operation using the AL register.

CF (Carry flag)
Indicates carrying our or borrowing into the leftmost bit position following an arithmetic operation. Also modified by some of the shift and rotate operations.

OF (Overflow flag)
Indicates an arithmetic overflow after an addition or subtraction.

PF (Parity flag)
Parity of the result of an arithmetic or logic operation. 1 indicates even parity; 0 indicates odd parity.

SF (Sign flag)
Indicates the sign of the result of an arithmetic or logic operation.

ZF (Zero flag)
Indicates that the result of an arithmetic or logic operation is 0

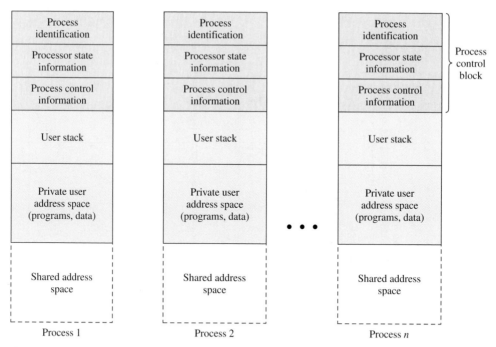

Figure 3.13   User Processes in Virtual Memory

active processes. The last part of Table 3.5 indicates the scope of this information. As we examine the details of operating system functionality in succeeding chapters, the need for the various items on this list should become clear.

Figure 3.13 suggests the structure of process images in virtual memory. Each process image consists of a process control block, a user stack, the private address space of the process, and any other address space that the process shares with other processes. In the figure, each process image appears as a contiguous range of addresses. In an actual implementation, this may not be the case; it will depend on the memory-management scheme and the way in which control structures are organized by the operating system.

As indicated in Table 3.5, the process control block may contain structuring information, including pointers that allow the linking of process control blocks. Thus, the queues that were described in the preceding section could be implemented as linked lists of process control blocks. For example, the queuing structure of Figure 3.8a could be implemented as suggested in Figure 3.14.

The Role of the Process Control Block   The process control block is the most important data structure in an operating system. Each process control block contains all of the information about a process that is needed by the operating system. The blocks are read and/or modified by virtually every module in the operating system, including those involved with scheduling, resource allocation, interrupt processing, and performance monitoring and analysis. One can say that the set of process control blocks defines the state of the operating system.

This brings up an important design issue. A number of routines within the operating system will need access to information in process control blocks. The provision of

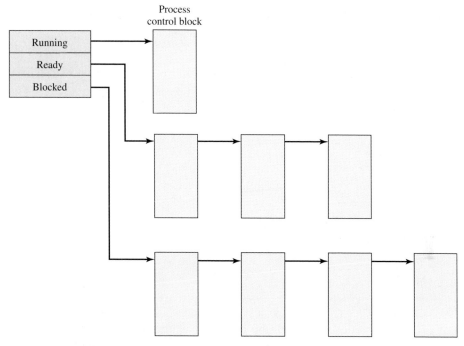

Figure 3.14 Process List Structures

direct access to these tables is not difficult. Each process is equipped with a unique ID, and this can be used as an index into a table of pointers to the process control blocks. The difficulty is not access but rather protection. Two problems present themselves:

- A bug in a single routine, such as an interrupt handler, could damage process control blocks, which could destroy the system's ability to manage the affected processes.
- A design change in the structure or semantics of the process control block could affect a number of modules in the operating system.

These problems can be addressed by requiring all routines in the operating system to go through a handler routine, the only job of which is to protect process control blocks, and which is the sole arbiter for reading and writing these blocks. The tradeoff in the use of such a routine involves performance issues and the degree to which the remainder of the system software can be trusted to be correct.

3.4 PROCESS CONTROL

Modes of Execution

Before continuing with our discussion of the way in which the operating system manages processes, we need to distinguish between the mode of processor execution normally associated with the operating system and that normally associated with user programs. Most processors support at least two modes of execution.

Table 3.7   Typical Functions of an Operating System Kernel

Process Management
• Process creation and termination
• Process scheduling and dispatching
• Process switching
• Process synchronization and support for interprocess communication
• Management of process control blocks
Memory Management
• Allocation of address space to processes
• Swapping
• Page and segment management
I/O Management
• Buffer management
• Allocation of I/O channels and devices to processes
Support Functions
• Interrupt handling
• Accounting
• Monitoring

Certain instructions can only be executed in the more-privileged mode. These would include reading or altering a control register, such as the program status word; primitive I/O instructions; and instructions that relate to memory management. In addition, certain regions of memory can only be accessed in the more-privileged mode.

The less-privileged mode is often referred to as the **user mode**, because user programs typically would execute in this mode. The more-privileged mode is referred to as the **system mode**, **control mode**, or **kernel mode**. This last term refers to the kernel of the operating system, which is that portion of the operating system that encompasses the important system functions. Table 3.7 lists the functions typically found in the kernel of an operating system.

The reason for using two modes should be clear. It is necessary to protect the operating system and key operating system tables, such as process control blocks, from interference by user programs. In the kernel mode, the software has complete control of the processor and all its instructions, registers, and memory. This level of control is not necessary and for safety is not desirable for user programs.

Two questions arise: How does the processor know in which mode it is to be executing and how is the mode changed? Regarding the first question, typically there is a bit in the program status word (PSW) that indicates the mode of execution. This bit is changed in response to certain events. Typically, when a user makes a call to an operating system service or when an interrupt triggers execution of an operating system route, the mode is set to the kernel mode and, upon return from the service to the user process, the mode is set to user mode. As an example, consider the Intel Itanium processor, which implements the 64-bit IA-64 architecture. The processor has a processor status register (psr) that includes a 2-bit cpl (current privilege level) field. Level 0 is the most privileged level, while level 3 is the least privileged level. Most operating systems, such as Linux, use level 0 for the kernel and one other level for user mode. When an interrupt occurs, the processor clears most of the bits in the psr, including the cpl field. This automatically sets the cpl to level 0. At the end of the interrupt-handling routine, the final instruction that is executed is irt (interrupt return). This instruction causes the processor to restore the psr of the interrupted program, which restores the privilege level of that program. A similar sequence occurs when an application places a system call. For the Itanium, an application places a system call by placing the system call identifier and the system call arguments in a predefined area and then executing a special instruction that has the effect of interrupting execution at the user level and transferring control to the kernel.

Process Creation

In Section 3.1, we discussed the events that lead to the creation of a new process. Having discussed the data structures associated with a process, we are now in a position to describe briefly the steps involved in actually creating the process.

Once the operating system decides, for whatever reason (Table 3.1), to create a new process, it can proceed as follows:

1. **Assign a unique process identifier to the new process.** At this time, a new entry is added to the primary process table, which contains one entry per process.

2. **Allocate space for the process.** This includes all elements of the process image. Thus, the operating system must know how much space is needed for the private user address space (programs and data) and the user stack. These values can be assigned by default based on the type of process, or they can be set based on user request at job creation time. If a process is spawned by another process, the parent process can pass the needed values to the operating system as part of the process-creation request. If any existing address space is to be shared by this new process, the appropriate linkages must be set up. Finally, space for a process control block must be allocated.

3. **Initialize the process control block.** The process identification portion contains the ID of this process plus other appropriate IDs, such as that of the parent process. The processor state information portion will typically be initialized with most entries zero, except for the program counter (set to the program entry point) and system stack pointers (set to define the process stack boundaries). The process control information portion is initialized based on standard default values plus attributes that have been requested for this process. For example, the process state would typically be initialized to Ready or Ready/Suspend. The priority may be set by default to the lowest priority unless an explicit request is made for a higher priority. Initially, the process may own no resources (I/O devices, files) unless there is an explicit request for these or unless they are inherited from the parent.

4. **Set the appropriate linkages.** For example, if the operating system maintains each scheduling queue as a linked list, then the new process must be put in the Ready or Ready/Suspend list.

5. **Create or expand other data structures.** For example, the operating system may maintain an accounting file on each process to be used subsequently for billing and/or performance assessment purposes.

Process Switching

On the face of it, the function of process switching would seem to be straightforward. At some time, a running process is interrupted and the operating system assigns another process to the Running state and turns control over to that process. However, several design issues are raised. First, what events trigger a process switch? Another issue is that we must recognize the distinction between mode switching and process switching. Finally, what must the operating system do to the various data structures under its control to achieve a process switch?

When to Switch Processes A process switch may occur any time that the operating system has gained control from the currently running process. Table 3.8 suggests the possible events that may give control to the operating system.

First, let us consider system interrupts. Actually, we can distinguish, as many systems do, two kinds of system interrupts, one of which is simply referred to as an interrupt, and the other as a trap. The former is due to some sort of event that is external to and independent of the currently running process, such as the completion of an I/O operation. The latter relates to an error or exception condition generated within the currently running process, such as an illegal file access attempt. With an ordinary **interrupt**, control is first transferred to an interrupt handler, which does some basic housekeeping and then branches to an operating system routine that is concerned with the particular type of interrupt that has occurred. Examples include the following:

- **Clock interrupt:** The operating system determines whether the currently running process has been executing for the maximum allowable unit of time, referred to as a **time slice**. That is, a time slice is the maximum amount of time that a process can execute before being interrupted. If so, this process must be switched to a Ready state and another process dispatched.

- **I/O interrupt:** The operating system determines what I/O action has occurred. If the I/O action constitutes an event for which one or more processes are waiting, then the operating system moves all of the corresponding blocked processes to the Ready state (and Blocked/Suspend processes to the Ready/Suspend state). The operating system must then decide whether to resume execution of the process currently in the Running state or to preempt that process for a higher-priority Ready process.

Table 3.8 Mechanisms for Interrupting the Execution of a Process

Mechanism	Cause	Use
Interrupt	External to the execution of the current instruction	Reaction to an asynchronous external event
Trap	Associated with the execution of the current instruction	Handling of an error or an exception condition
Supervisor call	Explicit request	Call to an operating system function

- **Memory fault:** The processor encounters a virtual memory address reference for a word that is not in main memory. The operating system must bring in the block (page or segment) of memory containing the reference from secondary memory to main memory. After the I/O request is issued to bring in the block of memory, the process with the memory fault is placed in a blocked state; the operating system then performs a process switch to resume execution of another process. After the desired block is brought into memory, that process is placed in the Ready state.

With a **trap**, the operating system determines if the error or exception condition is fatal. If so, then the currently running process is moved to the Exit state and a process switch occurs. If not, then the action of the operating system will depend on the nature of the error and the design of the operating system. It may attempt some recovery procedure or simply notify the user. It may do a process switch or resume the currently running process.

Finally, the operating system may be activated by a **supervisor call** from the program being executed. For example, a user process is running and an instruction is executed that requests an I/O operation, such as a file open. This call results in a transfer to a routine that is part of the operating system code. The use of a system call may place the user process in the Blocked state.

Mode Switching In Chapter 1, we discussed the inclusion of an interrupt stage as part of the instruction cycle. Recall that, in the interrupt stage, the processor checks to see if any interrupts are pending, indicated by the presence of an interrupt signal. If no interrupts are pending, the processor proceeds to the fetch stage and fetches the next instruction of the current program in the current process. If an interrupt is pending, the processor does the following:

1. It sets the program counter to the starting address of an interrupt handler program.

2. It switches from user mode to kernel mode so that the interrupt processing code may include privileged instructions.

The processor now proceeds to the fetch stage and fetches the first instruction of the interrupt handler program, which will service the interrupt. At this point, typically, the context of the process that has been interrupted is saved into that process control block of the interrupted program.

One question that may now occur to you is, What constitutes the context that is saved? The answer is that it must include any information that may be altered by the execution of the interrupt handler and that will be needed to resume the program that was interrupted. Thus, the portion of the process control block that was referred to as processor state information must be saved. This includes the program counter, other processor registers, and stack information.

Does anything else need to be done? That depends on what happens next. The interrupt handler is typically a short program that performs a few basic tasks related to an interrupt. For example, it resets the flag or indicator that signals the presence of an interrupt. It may send an acknowledgment to the entity that issued the interrupt, such as an I/O module. And it may do some basic housekeeping relating to the effects of the event that caused the interrupt. For example, if the interrupt relates to an I/O event, the interrupt handler will check for an error condition. If an error has occurred, the interrupt handler may send a signal to the process that originally requested the I/O operation. If the interrupt is by the clock, then the handler will hand control over to the dispatcher, which will want to pass control to another process because the time slice allotted to the currently running process has expired.

What about the other information in the process control block? If this interrupt is to be followed by a switch to another process, then some work will need to be done. However, in most operating systems, the occurrence of an interrupt does not necessarily mean a process switch. It is possible that, after the interrupt handler has executed, the currently running process will resume execution. In that case, all that is necessary is to save the processor state information when the interrupt occurs and restore that information when control is returned to the program that was running. Typically, the saving and restoring functions are performed in hardware.

Change of Process State   It is clear, then, that the mode switch is a concept distinct from that of the process switch.[8] A mode switch may occur without changing the state of the process that is currently in the Running state. In that case, the context saving and subsequent restoral involve little overhead. However, if the currently running process is to be moved to another state (Ready, Blocked, etc.), then the operating system must make substantial changes in its environment. The steps involved in a full process switch are as follows:

1. Save the context of the processor, including program counter and other registers.
2. Update the process control block of the process that is currently in the Running state. This includes changing the state of the process to one of the other states (Ready; Blocked; Ready/Suspend; or Exit). Other relevant fields must also be updated, including the reason for leaving the Running state and accounting information.
3. Move the process control block of this process to the appropriate queue (Ready; Blocked on Event i; Ready/Suspend).
4. Select another process for execution; this topic is explored in Part Four.
5. Update the process control block of the process selected. This includes changing the state of this process to Running.
6. Update memory-management data structures. This may be required, depending on how address translation is managed; this topic is explored in Part Three.
7. Restore the context of the processor to that which existed at the time the selected process was last switched out of the Running state, by loading in the previous values of the program counter and other registers.

---

[8]The term *context switch* is often found in OS literature and textbooks. Unfortunately, although most of the literature uses this term to mean what is here called a process switch, other sources use it to mean a mode switch or even a thread switch (defined in the next chapter). To avoid ambiguity, the term is not used in this book.

Thus, the process switch, which involves a state change, requires more effort than a mode switch.

Execution of the Operating System

In Chapter 2, we pointed out two intriguing facts about operating systems:

- The operating system functions in the same way as ordinary computer software in the sense that the operating system is a set of programs executed by the processor.
- The operating system frequently relinquishes control and depends on the processor to restore control to the operating system.

If the operating system is just a collection of programs and if it is executed by the processor just like any other program, is the operating system a process? If so, how is it controlled? These interesting questions have inspired a number of design approaches. Figure 3.15 illustrates a range of approaches that are found in various contemporary operating systems.

Nonprocess Kernel One traditional approach, which is common on many older operating systems, is to execute the kernel of the operating system outside of any process (Figure 3.15a). With this approach, when the currently running process is interrupted or issues a supervisor call, the mode context of this process is saved and control is passed to the kernel. The operating system has its own region of memory to use and its own system stack for controlling procedure calls and returns. The operating system can perform any desired functions and restore the context of the

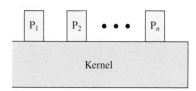

(a) Separate kernel

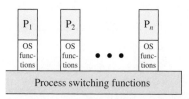

(b) OS functions execute within user processes

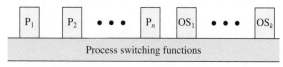

(c) OS functions execute as separate processes

Figure 3.15 Relationship between Operating System and User Processes

interrupted process, which causes execution to resume in the interrupted user process. Alternatively, the operating system can complete the function of saving the environment of the process and proceed to schedule and dispatch another process. Whether this happens depends on the reason for the interruption and the circumstances at the time.

In any case, the key point here is that the concept of process is considered to apply only to user programs. The operating system code is executed as a separate entity that operates in privileged mode.

Execution within User Processes An alternative that is common with operating systems on smaller machines (PCs, workstations) is to execute virtually all operating system software in the context of a user process. The view is that the operating system is primarily a collection of routines that the user calls to perform various functions, executed within the environment of the user's process. This is illustrated in Figure 3.15b. At any given point, the operating system is managing n process images. Each image includes not only the regions illustrated in Figure 3.13, but also program, data, and stack areas for kernel programs.

Figure 3.16 suggests a typical process image structure for this strategy. A separate kernel stack is used to manage calls/returns while the process is in kernel mode. Operating system code and data are in the shared address space and are shared by all user processes.

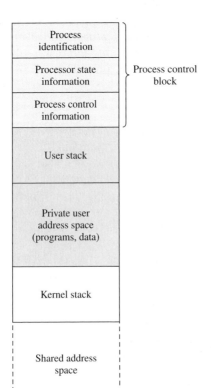

Figure 3.16   Process Image: Operating System Executes within User Space

When an interrupt, trap, or supervisor call occurs, the processor is placed in kernel mode and control is passed to the operating system. For this purpose, the mode context is saved and a mode switch takes place to an operating system routine. However, execution continues within the current user process. Thus, a process switch is not performed, just a mode switch within the same process.

If the operating system, upon completion of its work, determines that the current process should continue to run, then a mode switch resumes the interrupted program within the current process. This is one of the key advantages of this approach: A user program has been interrupted to employ some operating system routine, and then resumed, and all of this has occurred without incurring the penalty of two process switches. If, however, it is determined that a process switch is to occur rather than returning to the previously executing program, then control is passed to a process-switching routine. This routine may or may not execute in the current process, depending on system design. At some point, however, the current process has to be placed in a non-running state and another process designated as the running process. During this phase, it is logically most convenient to view execution as taking place outside of all processes.

In a way, this view of the operating system is remarkable. Simply put, at certain points in time, a process will save its state information, choose another process to run from among those that are ready, and relinquish control to that process. The reason this is not an arbitrary and indeed chaotic situation is that during the critical time, the code that is executed in the user process is shared operating system code and not user code. Because of the concept of user mode and kernel mode, the user cannot tamper with or interfere with the operating system routines, even though they are executing in the user's process environment. This further reminds us that there is a distinction between the concepts of process and program and that the relationship between the two is not one to one. Within a process, both a user program and operating system programs may execute, and the operating system programs that execute in the various user processes are identical.

Process–Based Operating System Another alternative, illustrated in Figure 3.15c, is to implement the operating system as a collection of system processes. As in the other options, the software that is part of the kernel executes in a kernel mode. In this case, however, major kernel functions are organized as separate processes. Again, there may be a small amount of process-switching code that is executed outside of any process.

This approach has several advantages. It imposes a program design discipline that encourages the use of a modular operating system with minimal, clean interfaces between the modules. In addition, some noncritical operating system functions are conveniently implemented as separate processes. For example, we mentioned earlier a monitor program that records the level of utilization of various resources (processor, memory, channels) and the rate of progress of the user processes in the system. Because this program does not provide a particular service to any active process, it can only be invoked by the operating system. As a process, the function can run at an assigned priority level and be interleaved with other processes under dispatcher control. Finally, implementing the operating system as a set of processes is useful in a multiprocessor or multicomputer environment, in which some of the operating system services can be shipped out to dedicated processors, improving performance.

3.5 UNIX SVR4 PROCESS MANAGEMENT

UNIX System V makes use of a simple but powerful process facility that is highly visible to the user. UNIX follows the model of Figure 3.15b, in which most of the operating system executes within the environment of a user process. Thus, two modes, user and kernel, are required. UNIX uses two categories of processes: system processes and user processes. System processes run in kernel mode and execute operating system code to perform administrative and housekeeping functions, such as allocation of memory and process swapping. User processes operate in user mode to execute user programs and utilities and in kernel mode to execute instructions that belong to the kernel. A user process enters kernel mode by issuing a system call, when an exception (fault) is generated, or when an interrupt occurs.

Process States

A total of nine process states are recognized by the UNIX operating system; these are listed in Table 3.9 and a state transition diagram is shown in Figure 3.17 (based on figure in [BACH86]). This figure is similar to Figure 3.9b, with the two UNIX sleeping states corresponding to the two blocked states. The differences can be summarized quickly:

- UNIX employs two Running states to indicate whether the process is executing in user mode or kernel mode.
- A distinction is made between the two states: (Ready to Run, in Memory) and (Preempted). These are essentially the same state, as indicated by the dotted line joining them. The distinction is made to emphasize the way in which the preempted state is entered. When a process is running in kernel mode (as a result of a supervisor call, clock interrupt, or I/O interrupt), there will come a time when the kernel has completed its work and is ready to return control to the user program. At this point, the kernel may decide to preempt the current process in favor of

Table 3.9   UNIX Process States

User Running	Executing in user mode.
Kernel Running	Executing in kernel mode.
Ready to Run, in Memory	Ready to run as soon as the kernel schedules it.
Asleep in Memory	Unable to execute until an event occurs; process is in main memory (a blocked state).
Ready to Run, Swapped	Process is ready to run, but the swapper must swap the process into main memory before the kernel can schedule it to execute.
Sleeping, Swapped	The process is awaiting an event and has been swapped to secondary storage (a blocked state).
Preempted	Process is returning from kernel to user mode, but the kernel preempts it and does a process switch to schedule another process.
Created	Process is newly created and not yet ready to run.
Zombie	Process no longer exists, but it leaves a record for its parent process to collect.

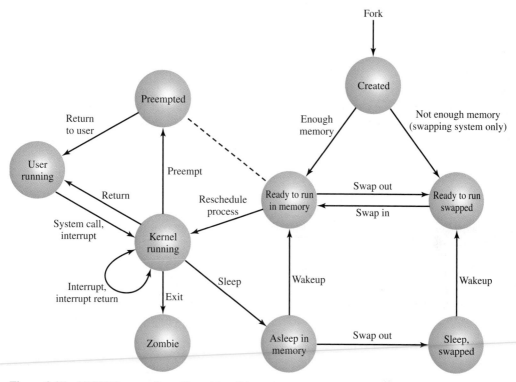

Figure 3.17   UNIX Process State Transition Diagram

one that is ready and of higher priority. In that case, the current process moves to the preempted state. However, for purposes of dispatching, those processes in the preempted state and those in the Ready to Run, in Memory state form one queue.

Preemption can only occur when a process is about to move from kernel mode to user mode. While a process is running in kernel mode, it may not be preempted. This makes UNIX unsuitable for real-time processing. A discussion of the requirements for real-time processing is provided in Chapter 10.

Two processes are unique in UNIX. Process 0 is a special process that is created when the system boots; in effect, it is predefined as a data structure loaded at boot time. It is the swapper process. In addition, process 0 spawns process 1, referred to as the init process; all other processes in the system have process 1 as an ancestor. When a new interactive user logs onto the system, it is process 1 that creates a user process for that user. Subsequently, the user process can create child processes in a branching tree, so that any particular application can consist of a number of related processes.

Process Description

A process in UNIX is a rather complex set of data structures that provide the operating system with all of the information necessary to manage and dispatch processes. Table 3.10 summarizes the elements of the process image, which are organized into three parts: user-level context, register context, and system-level context.

Table 3.10   UNIX Process Image

User-Level Context	
Process text	Executable machine instructions of the program
Process data	Data accessible by the program of this process
User stack	Contains the arguments, local variables, and pointers for functions executing in user mode
Shared memory	Memory shared with other processes, used for interprocess communication
Register Context	
Program counter	Address of next instruction to be executed; may be in kernel or user memory space of this process
Processor status register	Contains the hardware status at the time of preemption; contents and format are hardware dependent
Stack pointer	Points to the top of the kernel or user stack, depending on the mode of operation at the time or preemption
General-purpose registers	Hardware dependent
System-Level Context	
Process table entry	Defines state of a process; this information is always accessible to the operating system
U (user) area	Process control information that needs to be accessed only in the context of the process
Per process region table	Defines the mapping from virtual to physical addresses; also contains a permission field that indicates the type of access allowed the process: read-only, read-write, or read-execute
Kernel stack	Contains the stack frame of kernel procedures as the process executes in kernel mode

The **user-level context** contains the basic elements of a user's program and can be generated directly from a compiled object file. The user's program is separated into text and data areas; the text area is read-only and is intended to hold the program's instructions. While the process is executing, the processor uses the user stack area for procedure calls and returns and parameter passing. The shared memory area is a data area that is shared with other processes. There is only one physical copy of a shared memory area, but, by the use of virtual memory, it appears to each sharing process that the shared memory region is in its address space. When a process is not running, the processor status information is stored in the **register context** area.

The **system-level context** contains the remaining information that the operating system needs to manage the process. It consists of a static part, which is fixed in size and stays with a process throughout its lifetime, and a dynamic part, which varies in size through the life of the process. One element of the static part is the process table entry. This is actually part of the process table maintained by the operating system, with one entry per process. The process table entry contains process control information that is accessible to the kernel at all times; hence, in a virtual memory system, all process table entries are maintained in main memory. Table 3.11 lists the contents of a process table entry. The user area, or U area, contains additional process control information that is needed by the kernel when it is executing in the context of this process; it is also used when paging processes to and from memory. Table 3.12 shows the contents of this table.

Table 3.11   UNIX Process Table Entry

Process status	Current state of process.
Pointers	To U area and process memory area (text, data, stack).
Process size	Enables the operating system to know how much space to allocate the process.
User identifiers	The **real user ID** identifies the user who is responsible for the running process. The **effective user ID** may be used by a process to gain temporary privileges associated with a particular program; while that program is being executed as part of the process, the process operates with the effective user ID.
Process identifiers	ID of this process; ID of parent process. These are set up when the process enters the Created state during the fork system call.
Event descriptor	Valid when a process is in a sleeping state; when the event occurs, the process is transferred to a ready-to-run state.
Priority	Used for process scheduling.
Signal	Enumerates signals sent to a process but not yet handled.
Timers	Include process execution time, kernel resource utilization, and user-set timer used to send alarm signal to a process.
P_link	Pointer to the next link in the ready queue (valid if process is ready to execute).
Memory status	Indicates whether process image is in main memory or swapped out. If it is in memory, this field also indicates whether it may be swapped out or is temporarily locked into main memory.

The distinction between the process table entry and the U area reflects the fact that the UNIX kernel always executes in the context of some process. Much of the time, the kernel will be dealing with the concerns of that process. However, some of the time, such as when the kernel is performing a scheduling algorithm preparatory to dispatching another process, it will need access to information about other

Table 3.12   UNIX U Area

Process table pointer	Indicates entry that corresponds to the U area.
User identifiers	Real and effective user IDs. Used to determine user privileges.
Timers	Record time that the process (and its descendants) spent executing in user mode and in kernel mode.
Signal-handler array	For each type of signal defined in the system, indicates how the process will react to receipt of that signal (exit, ignore, execute specified user function).
Control terminal	Indicates login terminal for this process, if one exists.
Error field	Records errors encountered during a system call.
Return value	Contains the result of system calls.
I/O parameters	Describe the amount of data to transfer, the address of the source (or target) data array in user space, and file offsets for I/O.
File parameters	Current directory and current root describe the file system environment of the process.
User file descriptor table	Records the files the process has open.
Limit fields	Restrict the size of the process and the size of a file it can write.
Permission modes fields	Mask mode settings on files the process creates.

processes. The information in a process table can be accessed when the given process is not the current one.

The third static portion of the system-level context is the per process region table, which is used by the memory management system. Finally, the kernel stack is the dynamic portion of the system-level context. This stack is used when the process is executing in kernel mode and contains the information that must be saved and restored as procedure calls and interrupts occur.

Process Control

Process creation in UNIX is made by means of the kernel system call, fork( ). When a process issues a fork request, the operating system performs the following functions [BACH86]:

1. It allocates a slot in the process table for the new process.
2. It assigns a unique process ID to the child process.
3. It makes a copy of the process image of the parent, with the exception of any shared memory.
4. It increments counters for any files owned by the parent, to reflect that an additional process now also owns those files.
5. It assigns the child process to the Ready to Run state.
6. It returns the ID number of the child to the parent process, and a 0 value to the child process.

All of this work is accomplished in kernel mode in the parent process. When the kernel has completed these functions it can do one of the following, as part of the dispatcher routine:

1. Stay in the parent process. Control returns to user mode at the point of the fork call of the parent.
2. Transfer control to the child process. The child process begins executing at the same point in the code as the parent, namely at the return from the fork call.
3. Transfer control to another process. Both parent and child are left in the Ready to Run state.

It is perhaps difficult to visualize this method of process creation because both parent and child are executing the same passage of code. The difference is this: When the return from the fork occurs, the return parameter is tested. If the value is zero, then this is the child process, and a branch can be executed to the appropriate user program to continue execution. If the value is nonzero, then this is the parent process, and the main line of execution can continue.

3.6 SUMMARY

The most fundamental concept in a modern operating system is the process. The principal function of the operating system is to create, manage, and terminate processes. While processes are active, the operating system must see that each is allocated time for execution by the processor, coordinate their activities, manage conflicting demands, and allocate system resources to processes.

To perform its process management functions, the operating system maintains a description of each process, or process image, which includes the address space within which the process executes, and a process control block. The latter contains all of the information that is required by the operating system to manage the process, including its current state, resources allocated to it, priority, and other relevant data.

During its lifetime, a process moves among a number of states. The most important of these are Ready, Running, and Blocked. A ready process is one that is not currently executing but that is ready to be executed as soon as the operating system dispatches it. The running process is that process that is currently being executed by the processor. In a multiple-processor system, more than one process can be in this state. A blocked process is waiting for the completion of some event, such as an I/O operation.

A running process is interrupted either by an interrupt, which is an event that occurs outside the process and that is recognized by the processor, or by executing a supervisor call to the operating system. In either case, the processor performs a mode switch, transferring control to an operating system routine. The operating system, after it has completed necessary work, may resume the interrupted process or switch to some other process.

3.7   RECOMMENDED READINGS

All of the textbooks listed in Section 2.9 cover the material of this chapter. Good descriptions of UNIX process management are found in [GOOD94] and [GRAY97]. [NEHM75] is an interesting discussion of process states and the operating system primitives needed for process dispatching.

GOOD94   Goodheart, B., and Cox, J. *The Magic Garden Explained: The Internals of UNIX System V Release 4*. Englewood Cliffs, NJ: Prentice Hall, 1994.

GRAY97   Gray, J. *Interprocess Communications in Unix: The Nooks and Crannies*. Upper Saddle River, NJ: Prentice Hall, 1997.

NEHM75   Nehmer, J. "Dispatcher Primitives for the Construction of Operating System Kernels." *Acta Informatica*, vol 5, 1975.

3.8   KEY TERMS, REVIEW QUESTIONS, AND PROBLEMS

Key Terms

blocked state	privileged mode	suspend state
child process	process	swapping
exit state	process control block	system mode
interrupt	process image	task
kernel mode	process switch	trace
mode switch	program status word	trap
new state	ready state	user mode
parent process	round robin	
preempt	running state	

Review Questions

3.1 What is an instruction trace?

3.2 What common events lead to the creation of a process?

3.3 For the processing model of Figure 3.6, briefly define each state.

3.4 What does it mean to preempt a process?

3.5 What is swapping and what is its purpose?

3.6 Why does Figure 3.9b have two blocked states?

3.7 List four characteristics of a suspended process.

3.8 For what types of entities does the operating system maintain tables of information for management purposes?

3.9 List three general categories of information in a process control block.

3.10 Why are two modes (user and kernel) needed?

3.11 What are the steps performed by an operating system to create a new process?

3.12 What is the difference between an interrupt and a trap?

3.13 Give three examples of an interrupt.

3.14 What is the difference between a mode switch and a process switch?

Problems

3.1 Name five major activities of an operating system with respect to process management, and briefly describe why each is required.

3.2 In [PINK89], the following states are defined for processes: execute (running), active (ready), blocked, and suspend. A process is blocked if it is waiting for permission to use a resource, and it is suspended if it is waiting for an operation to be completed on a resource it has already acquired. In many operating systems, these two states are lumped together as the blocked state, and the suspended state has the definition we have used in this chapter. Compare the relative merits of the two sets of definitions.

3.3 For the seven-state process model of Figure 3.9b, draw a queuing diagram similar to that of Figure 3.8b.

3.4 Consider the state transition diagram of Figure 3.9b. Suppose that it is time for the operating system to dispatch a process and that there are processes in both the Ready state and the Ready/Suspend state, and that at least one process in the Ready/Suspend state has higher scheduling priority than any of the processes in the Ready state. Two extreme policies are (1) always dispatch from a process in the Ready state, to minimize swapping; and (2) always give preference to the highest-priority process, even though that may mean swapping when swapping is not necessary. Suggest an intermediate policy that tries to balance the concerns of priority and performance.

3.5 Table 3.13 shows the process states for the VAX/VMS operating system.
   a. Can you provide a justification for the existence of so many distinct wait states?
   b. Why do the following states not have resident and swapped-out versions: page fault wait, collided page wait, common event wait, free page wait, and resource wait?
   c. Draw the state transition diagram and indicate the action or occurrence that causes each transition.

3.6 The VAX/VMS operating system makes use of four processor access modes to facilitate the protection and sharing of system resources among processes. The access mode determines

   • **Instruction execution privileges:** What instructions the processor may execute
   • **Memory access privileges:** Which locations in virtual memory the current instruction may access

Table 3.13   VAX/VMS Process States

Process State	Process Condition
Currently Executing	Running process.
Computable (resident)	Ready and resident in main memory.
Computable (outswapped)	Ready, but swapped out of main memory.
Page Fault Wait	Process has referenced a page not in main memory and must wait for the page to be read in.
Collided Page Wait	Process has referenced a shared page that is the cause of an existing page fault wait in another process, or a private page that is in the process of being read in or written out.
Common Event Wait	Waiting for shared event flag (event flags are single-bit interprocess signaling mechanisms).
Free Page Wait	Waiting for a free page in main memory to be added to the collection of pages in main memory devoted to this process (the working set of the process).
Hibernate Wait (resident)	Process puts itself in a wait state.
Hibernate Wait (outswapped)	Hibernating process is swapped out of main memory.
Local Event Wait (resident)	Process in main memory and waiting for local event flag (usually I/O completion).
Local Event Wait (outswapped)	Process in local event wait is swapped out of main memory.
Suspended Wait (resident)	Process is put into a wait state by another process.
Suspended Wait (outswapped)	Suspended process is swapped out of main memory.
Resource Wait	Process waiting for miscellaneous system resource

The four modes are

- **Kernel:** Executes the kernel of the VMS operating system, which includes memory management, interrupt handling, and I/O operations
- **Executive:** Executes many of the operating system service calls, including file and record (disk and tape) management routines
- **Supervisor:** Executes other operating system services, such as responses to user commands
- **User:** Executes user programs, plus utilities such as compilers, editors, linkers, and debuggers

A process executing in a less-privileged mode often needs to call a procedure that executes in a more-privileged mode; for example, a user program requires an operating system service. This call is achieved by using a change-mode (CHM) instruction, which causes an interrupt that transfers control to a routine at the new access mode. A return is made by executing the REI (return from exception or interrupt) instruction.

   a. A number of operating systems have two modes, kernel and user. What are the advantages and disadvantages of providing four modes instead of two?
   b. Can you make a case for even more than four modes?

3.7   The VMS scheme discussed in the preceding problem is often referred to as a ring protection structure, as illustrated in Figure 3.18. Indeed, the simple kernel/user scheme, as described in Section 3.3, is a two-ring structure. [SILB04] points out a problem with this approach:

> The main disadvantage of the ring (hierarchical) structure is that it does not allow us to enforce the need-to-know principle. In particular, if an object must be accessible in domain D_j but not accessible in domain D_i, then we must have $j < i$. But this means that every segment accessible in D_i is also accessible in D_j.

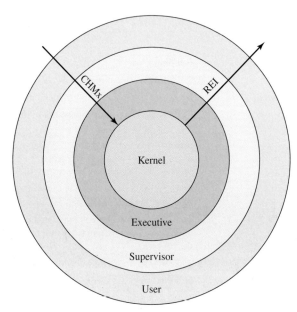

Figure 3.18 VAX/VMS Access Modes

    a. Explain clearly what the problem is that is referred to in the preceding quote.

    b. Suggest a way that a ring-structured operating system can deal with this problem.

3.8 Figure 3.7b suggests that a process can only be in one event queue at a time.

    a. Is it possible that you would want to allow a process to wait on more than one event at the same time? Provide an example.

    b. In that case, how would you modify the queuing structure of the figure to support this new feature?

3.9 In a number of early computers, an interrupt caused the register values to be stored in fixed locations associated with the given interrupt signal. Under what circumstances is this a practical technique? Explain why it is inconvenient in general.

3.10 In Section 3.4, it was stated that UNIX is unsuitable for real-time applications because a process executing in kernel mode may not be preempted. Elaborate.

Programming Project One: Developing a Shell

The Shell or Command Line Interpreter is the fundamental User interface to an Operating System. Your first project is to write a simple shell - **myshell** - that has the following properties:

1. The shell must support the following internal commands:

   i. cd <directory> - change the current default directory to **<directory>**. If the **<directory>** argument is not present, report the current directory. If the directory does not exist an appropriate error should be reported. This command should also change the PWD environment variable.

   ii. **clr** - clear the screen.

   iii. **dir <directory>** - list the contents of directory **<directory>**

   iv. **environ** - list all the environment strings

   v. **echo <comment>** - display **<comment>** on the display followed by a new line (multiple spaces/tabs may be reduced to a single space)

   vi. **help** - display the user manual using the **more** filter

   vii. **pause** - pause operation of the shell until **'Enter'** is pressed.

   viii. **quit** - quit the shell

   ix. The shell environment should contain **shell=<pathname>/ myshell** where **<pathname>/myshell** is the full path for the shell executable (not a hardwired path back to your directory, but the one from which it was executed)

2. All other command line input is interpreted as program invocation which should be done by the shell **forking** and **executing** the programs as its own child processes. The programs should be executed with an environment that contains the entry:

   parent=<pathname>/myshell where **<pathname>/myshell** is as described in 1.ix.above.

3. The shell must be able to take its command line input from a file. i.e. if the shell is invoked with a command line argument:

   programname arg1 arg2 < inputfile > outputfile

   then **batchfile** is assumed to contain a set of command lines for the shell to process. When the end-of-file is reached, the shell should exit. Obviously, if the shell is invoked without a command line argument it solicits input from the user via a prompt on the display.

4. The shell must support i/o-redirection on either or both *stdin* and/or *stdout*. i.e. the command line:

   stdout redirection should also be possible for the internal commands:
   dir, environ, echo, & help.

will execute the program **programname** with arguments **arg1** and **arg2**, the *stdin FILE stream* replaced by **inputfile** and the *stdout FILE stream* replaced by **outputfile**.

stdout redirection should also be possible for the internal commands: **dir, environ, echo, & help**.

With output redirection, if the redirection character is **>** then the **outputfile** is created if it does not exist and truncated if it does. If the redirection token is **>>** then **outputfile** is created if it does not exist and appended to if it does.

5. The shell must support background execution of programs. An ampersand (**&**) at the end of the command line indicates that the shell should return to the command line prompt immediately after launching that program.

6. The command line prompt must contain the pathname of the current directory.

Note: you can assume that all command line arguments (including the redirection symbols, **<, > & >>** and the background execution symbols, **&**) will be delimited from other command line arguments by white space - one or more spaces and/or tabs (see the command line in 4. above).

Project Requirements

1. Design a simple command line shell that satisfies the above criteria and implement it on the specified UNIX platform.

2. Write a simple manual describing how to use the shell. The manual should contain enough detail for a beginner to UNIX to use it. For example, you should explain the concepts of i/o redirection, the program environment, and background program execution. The manual MUST be named **readme** and must be a simple text document capable of being read by a standard Text Editor.
For an example of the sort of depth and type of description required, you should have a look at the on-line manuals for **csh** and **tcsh** (**man csh, man tcsh**). These shells obviously have much more functionality than yours and thus, your manuals don't have to be quite so large. You should NOT include building instructions, included file lists or source code - we can find that out from the other files you submit. This should be an Operator's manual not a Developer's manual.

3. The source code **MUST** be extensively commented and appropriately structured to allow your peers to understand and easily maintain the code. Properly commented and laid out code is much easier to interpret and it is in your interests to ensure that the person marking your project is able to understand your coding without having to perform mental gymnastics!

4. Details of submission procedures will be supplied well before the deadline.

5. The submission should contain only source code file(s), include file(s), a `makefile` (all lower case please), and the `readme file` (all lower case please). No executable program should be included. The marker will be automatically rebuilding your shell program from the source code provided. If the submitted code does not compile it can not be marked!

6. The `makefile` (all lower case please) **MUST** generate the binary file `myshell` (all lower case please). A sample `makefile` would be:

> \# Joe Citizen, s1234567 - Operating Systems Project 1
> \# CompLab1/01 tutor: Fred Bloggs
> myshell: myshell.c utility.c myshell.h
> gcc -Wall myshell.c utility.c -o myshell

The program `myshell` is then generated by just typing `make` at the command line prompt.

Note: the fourth line in the above `makefile` **MUST** begin with a tab

7. In the instance shown above, the files in the submitted directory would be:

> makefile
> myshell.c
> utility.c
> myshell.h
> readme

Submission

A `makefile` is required. All files in your submission will be copied to the same directory, therefore do not include any paths in your `makefile`. The `makefile` should include all dependencies that build your program. If a library is included, your `makefile` should also build the library.

To make this clear: *do not hand in any binary or object code files*. All that is required is your source code, a `makefile` and `readme` file. Test your project by copying the source code only into an empty directory and then compile it by entering the command `make`.

We shall be using a shell script that copies your files to a test directory, deletes any pre-existing `myshell`, `*.a`, and/or `*.o` files, performs a `make`, copies a set of test files to the test directory, and then exercises your shell with a standard set of test scripts through *stdin* and command line arguments. If this sequence fails due to wrong names, wrong case for names, wrong version of source code that fails to compile, non-existence of files etc then the marking sequence will also stop. In this instance, the only marks that can be awarded will be for the tests completed at that point and the source code and manual.

Required Documentation

Firstly, your source code will be assessed and marked as well as `readme` manual. Commenting is definitely required in your source code. The user manual can be presented in a format of your choice (within the limitations of being displayable by a simple Text Editor). Again, the manual should contain enough detail for a beginner to UNIX to use the shell. For example, you should explain the concepts of i/o redirection, the program environment and background execution. The manual **MUST** be named `readme` (all lower case please, **NO** `.txt` extension).

CHAPTER 4

THREADS, SMP, AND MICROKERNELS

This chapter examines some more advanced concepts related to process management, which are found in a number of contemporary operating systems. First, we show that the concept of process is more complex and subtle than presented so far and in fact embodies two separate and potentially independent concepts: one relating to resource ownership and one relating to execution. This distinction has led to the development, in many operating systems, of a construct known as the **thread**. After examining threads, we look at **symmetric multiprocessing** (SMP). With SMP, the operating system must be able simultaneously to schedule different processes on multiple processors. Finally, we introduce the concept of the **microkernel**, which is an effective means of structuring the operating system to support process management and its other tasks.

4.1 PROCESSES AND THREADS

The discussion so far has presented the concept of a process as embodying two characteristics:

- **Resource ownership:** A process includes a virtual address space to hold the process image; recall from Chapter 3 that the process image is the collection of program, data, stack, and attributes defined in the process control block. From time to time, a process may be allocated control or ownership of resources, such as main memory, I/O channels, I/O devices, and files. The operating system performs a protection function to prevent unwanted interference between processes with respect to resources.

- **Scheduling/execution:** The execution of a process follows an execution path (trace) through one or more programs. This execution may be interleaved with that of other processes. Thus, a process has an execution state (Running, Ready, etc.) and a dispatching priority and is the entity that is scheduled and dispatched by the operating system.

In most traditional operating systems, these two characteristics are indeed the essence of a process. However, some thought should convince the reader that these two characteristics are independent and could be treated independently by the operating system. This is done in a number of operating systems, particularly recently developed systems. To distinguish the two characteristics, the unit of dispatching is usually referred to as a **thread**, or **lightweight process**, while the unit of resource ownership is usually still referred to as a **process**, or **task**.[1]

Multithreading

Multithreading refers to the ability of an operating system to support multiple threads of execution within a single process. The traditional approach of a single

---

[1] Alas, even this degree of consistency cannot be maintained. In IBM's mainframe operating systems, the concepts of address space and task, respectively, correspond roughly to the concepts of process and thread that we describe in this section. Also, in the literature, the term *lightweight process* is used as either (1) equivalent to the term *thread*, (2) a particular type of thread known as a kernel-level thread, or (3) in the case of Solaris, an entity that maps user-level threads to kernel-level threads.

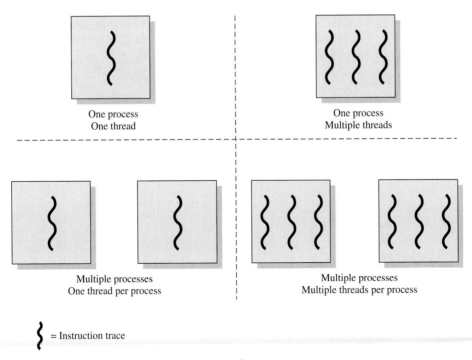

One process
One thread

One process
Multiple threads

Multiple processes
One thread per process

Multiple processes
Multiple threads per process

⟨ = Instruction trace

Figure 4.1   Threads and Processes [ANDE97]

thread of execution per process, in which the concept of a thread is not recognized, is referred to as a single-threaded approach. The two arrangements shown in the left half of Figure 4.1 are single-threaded approaches. MS-DOS is an example of an operating system that supports a single user process and a single thread. Other operating systems, such as many flavors of UNIX, support multiple user processes but only support one thread per process. The right half of Figure 4.1 depicts multithreaded approaches. A Java run-time environment is an example of a system of one process with multiple threads. Of interest in this section is the use of multiple processes, each of which support multiple threads. This approach is taken in Windows, Solaris, Mach, and OS/2, among others. In this section we give a general description of multithreading; the details of the Windows, Solaris, and Linux approaches are discussed later in this chapter.

In a multithreaded environment, a process is defined as the unit of resource allocation and a unit of protection. The following are associated with processes:

- A virtual address space that holds the process image
- Protected access to processors, other processes (for interprocess communication), files, and I/O resources (devices and channels)

Within a process, there may be one or more threads, each with the following:

- A thread execution state (Running, Ready, etc.).
- A saved thread context when not running; one way to view a thread is as an independent program counter operating within a process.

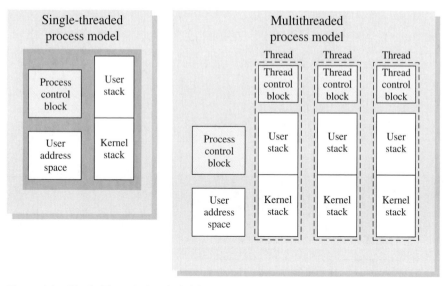

Figure 4.2   Single Threaded and Multithreaded Process Models

- An execution stack.
- Some per-thread static storage for local variables.
- Access to the memory and resources of its process, shared with all other threads in that process.

Figure 4.2 illustrates the distinction between threads and processes from the point of view of process management. In a single-threaded process model (i.e., there is no distinct concept of thread), the representation of a process includes its process control block and user address space, as well as user and kernel stacks to manage the call/return behavior of the execution of the process. While the process is running, processor registers are controlled by that process, and the contents of these registers are saved when the process is not running. In a multithreaded environment, there is still a single process control block and user address space associated with the process, but now there are separate stacks for each thread, as well as a separate control block for each thread containing register values, priority, and other thread-related state information.

Thus, all of the threads of a process share the state and resources of that process. They reside in the same address space and have access to the same data. When one thread alters an item of data in memory, other threads see the results if and when they access that item. If one thread opens a file with read privileges, other threads in the same process can also read from that file.

The key benefits of threads derive from the performance implications:

1. It takes far less time to create a new thread in an existing process than to create a brand-new process. Studies done by the Mach developers show that thread creation is ten times faster than process creation in UNIX [TEVA87].
2. It takes less time to terminate a thread than a process.
3. It takes less time to switch between two threads within the same process.

4. Threads enhance efficiency in communication between different executing programs. In most operating systems, communication between independent processes requires the intervention of the kernel to provide protection and the mechanisms needed for communication. However, because threads within the same process share memory and files, they can communicate with each other without invoking the kernel.

Thus, if there is an application or function that should be implemented as a set of related units of execution, it is far more efficient to do so as a collection of threads rather than a collection of separate processes.

An example of an application that could make use of threads is a file server. As each new file request comes in, a new thread can be spawned for the file management program. Because a server will handle many requests, many threads will be created and destroyed in a short period. If the server runs on a multiprocessor machine, then multiple threads within the same process can be executing simultaneously on different processors. Further, because processes or threads in a file server must share file data and therefore coordinate their actions, it is faster to use threads and shared memory than processes and message passing for this coordination.

The thread construct is also sometimes useful on a single processor to simplify the structure of a program that is logically doing several different functions.

[LETW88] gives four examples of the uses of threads in a single-user multiprocessing system:

- **Foreground and background work:** For example, in a spreadsheet program, one thread could display menus and read user input, while another thread executes user commands and updates the spreadsheet. This arrangement often increases the perceived speed of the application by allowing the program to prompt for the next command before the previous command is complete.

- **Asynchronous processing:** Asynchronous elements in the program can be implemented as threads. For example, as a protection against power failure, one can design a word processor to write its random access memory (RAM) buffer to disk once every minute. A thread can be created whose sole job is periodic backup and that schedules itself directly with the operating system; there is no need for fancy code in the main program to provide for time checks or to coordinate input and output.

- **Speed of execution:** A multithreaded process can compute one batch of data while reading the next batch from a device. On a multiprocessor system, multiple threads from the same process may be able to execute simultaneously. Thus, even though one thread may be blocked for an I/O operation to read in a batch of data, another thread may be executing.

- **Modular program structure:** Programs that involve a variety of activities or a variety of sources and destinations of input and output may be easier to design and implement using threads.

In an operating system that supports threads, scheduling and dispatching is done on a thread basis; hence most of the state information dealing with execution is maintained in thread-level data structures. There are, however, several actions that affect all of the threads in a process and that the operating system must manage at the process level. Suspension involves swapping the address space of one process out of main memory to make room for the address space of another process. Because all threads in a process share the same address space, all threads are suspended at the same time. Similarly, termination of a process terminates all threads within that process.

Thread Functionality

Like processes, threads have execution states and may synchronize with one another. We look at these two aspects of thread functionality in turn.

Thread States   As with processes, the key states for a thread are Running, Ready, and Blocked. Generally, it does not make sense to associate suspend states with threads because such states are process-level concepts. In particular, if a process is swapped out, all of its threads are necessarily swapped out because they all share the address space of the process.

There are four basic thread operations associated with a change in thread state [ANDE97]:

- **Spawn:** Typically, when a new process is spawned, a thread for that process is also spawned. Subsequently, a thread within a process may spawn another thread within the same process, providing an instruction pointer and arguments for the new thread. The new thread is provided with its own register context and stack space and placed on the ready queue.

- **Block:** When a thread needs to wait for an event, it will block (saving its user registers, program counter, and stack pointers). The processor may now turn to the execution of another ready thread in the same or a different process.

- **Unblock:** When the event for which a thread is blocked occurs, the thread is moved to the ready queue.

- **Finish:** When a thread completes, its register context and stacks are deallocated.

A significant issue is whether the blocking of a thread results in the blocking of the entire process. In other words, if one thread in a process is blocked, does this prevent the running of any other thread in the same process even if that other thread is in a ready state? Clearly, some of the flexibility and power of threads is lost if the one blocked thread blocks an entire process.

We return to this issue subsequently in our discussion of user-level versus kernel-level threads, but for now let us consider the performance benefits of threads that do not block an entire process. Figure 4.3 (based on one in [KLEI96]) shows a program that performs two remote procedure calls (RPCs)[2] to two different hosts to obtain a combined result. In a single-threaded program, the results are obtained in sequence, so that the program has to wait for a response from each server in turn. Rewriting the program to use a separate thread for each RPC results in a substantial

---

[2] An RPC is a technique by which two programs, which may execute on different machines, interact using procedure call/return syntax and semantics. Both the called and calling program behave as if the partner program were running on the same machine. RPCs are often used for client/server applications and are discussed in Chapter 13.

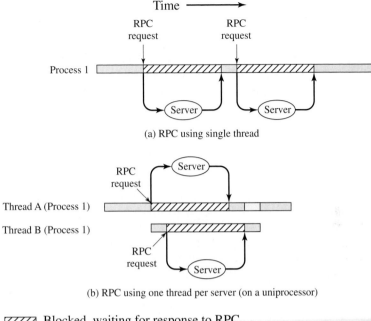

(a) RPC using single thread

(b) RPC using one thread per server (on a uniprocessor)

▨▨▨ Blocked, waiting for response to RPC

▭ Blocked, waiting for processor, which is in use by Thread B

▭ Running

Figure 4.3   Remote Procedure Call (RPC) Using Threads

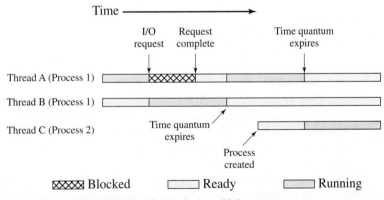

▨▨▨ Blocked   ▭ Ready   ▭ Running

Figure 4.4   Multithreading Example on a Uniprocessor

speedup. Note that if this program operates on a uniprocessor, the requests must be generated sequentially and the results processed in sequence; however, the program waits concurrently for the two replies.

On a uniprocessor, multiprogramming enables the interleaving of multiple threads within multiple processes. In the example of Figure 4.4, three threads in two processes are interleaved on the processor. Execution passes from one thread to another either when the currently running thread is blocked or its time slice is exhausted.[3]

Thread Synchronization All of the threads of a process share the same address space and other resources, such as open files. Any alteration of a resource by one thread affects the environment of the other threads in the same process. It is therefore necessary to synchronize the activities of the various threads so that they do not interfere with each other or corrupt data structures. For example, if two threads each try to add an element to a doubly linked list, one element may be lost or the list may end up malformed.

The issues raised and the techniques used in the synchronization of threads are, in general, the same as for the synchronization of processes. These issues and techniques are the subject of Chapters 5 and 6.

Example—Adobe PageMaker

An example of the use of threads is the Adobe PageMaker application running under a shared system. PageMaker is a writing, design, and production tool for desktop publishing. The thread structure for PageMaker used in OS/2, shown in Figure 4.5 [KRON90], was chosen to optimize the responsiveness of the application (similar thread structures would be found on other operating systems). Three threads are always active: an event-handling thread, a screen-redraw thread, and a service thread.

Generally, OS/2 is less responsive in managing windows if any input message requires too much processing. The OS/2 guidelines state that no message should require more than 0.1 s processing time. For example, calling a subroutine to print a page while processing a print command would prevent the system from dispatching any further message to any applications, slowing performance. To meet this criterion, time-consuming user operations in PageMaker—printing, importing data, and flowing text—are performed by a service thread. Program initialization is also largely performed by the service thread, which absorbs the idle time while the user invokes the dialogue to create a new document or open an existing document. A separate thread waits on new event messages.

Synchronizing the service thread and event-handling thread is complicated because a user may continue to type or move the mouse, which activates the event-handling thread, while the service thread is still busy. If this conflict occurs, PageMaker filters these messages and accepts only certain basic ones, such as window resize.

The service thread sends a message to the event-handling thread to indicate completion of its task. Until this occurs, user activity in PageMaker is restricted. The program indicates this by disabling menu items and displaying a "busy" cursor. The user is free to switch to other applications, and when the busy cursor is moved to another window, it will change to the appropriate cursor for that application.

The screen redraw function is handled by a separate thread. This is done for two reasons:

---

[3]In this example, thread C begins running after thread A exhausts its time quantum, even though thread B is also ready to run. The choice between B and C is a scheduling decision, a topic covered in Part Four.

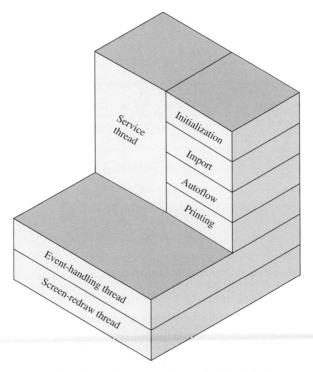

Figure 4.5   Thread Structure for Adobe PageMaker

1. PageMaker does not limit the number of objects appearing on a page; thus, processing a redraw request can easily exceed the guideline of 0.1 s.

2. Using a separate thread allows the user to abort drawing. In this case, when the user rescales a page, the redraw can proceed immediately. The program is less responsive if it completes an outdated display before commencing with a display at the new scale.

Dynamic scrolling—redrawing the screen as the user drags the scroll indicator—is also possible. The event-handling thread monitors the scroll bar and redraws the margin rulers (which redraw quickly and give immediate positional feedback to the user). Meanwhile, the screen-redraw thread constantly tries to redraw the page and catch up.

Implementing dynamic redraw without the use of multiple threads places a greater burden on the application to poll for messages at various points. Multithreading allows concurrent activities to be separated more naturally in the code.

User-Level and Kernel-Level Threads

There are two broad categories of thread implementation: user-level threads (ULTs) and kernel-level threads (KLTs).[4] The latter are also referred to in the literature as *kernel-supported threads* or *lightweight processes*.

---

[4]The acronyms ULT and KLT are unique to this book and introduced for conciseness.

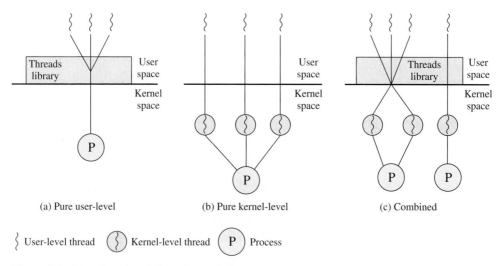

(a) Pure user-level   (b) Pure kernel-level   (c) Combined

} User-level thread   Kernel-level thread   P Process

Figure 4.6   User-Level and Kernel-Level Threads

User-Level Threads In a pure ULT facility, all of the work of thread management is done by the application and the kernel is not aware of the existence of threads. Figure 4.6a illustrates the pure ULT approach. Any application can be programmed to be multithreaded by using a threads library, which is a package of routines for ULT management. The threads library contains code for creating and destroying threads, for passing messages and data between threads, for scheduling thread execution, and for saving and restoring thread contexts.

By default, an application begins with a single thread and begins running in that thread. This application and its thread are allocated to a single process managed by the kernel. At any time that the application is running (the process is in the Running state), the application may spawn a new thread to run within the same process. Spawning is done by invoking the spawn utility in the threads library. Control is passed to that utility by a procedure call. The threads library creates a data structure for the new thread and then passes control to one of the threads within this process that is in the Ready state, using some scheduling algorithm. When control is passed to the library, the context of the current thread is saved, and when control is passed from the library to a thread, the context of that thread is restored. The context essentially consists of the contents of user registers, the program counter, and stack pointers.

All of the activity described in the preceding paragraph takes place in user space and within a single process. The kernel is unaware of this activity. The kernel continues to schedule the process as a unit and assigns a single execution state (Ready, Running, Blocked, etc.) to that process. The following examples should clarify the relationship between thread scheduling and process scheduling. Suppose that process B is executing in its thread 2; the states of the process and two ULTs that are part of the process are shown in Figure 4.7a. Each of the following is a possible occurrence:

1. The application executing in thread 2 makes a system call that blocks B. For example, an I/O call is made. This causes control to transfer to the kernel. The kernel invokes the I/O action, places process B in the Blocked state, and switches

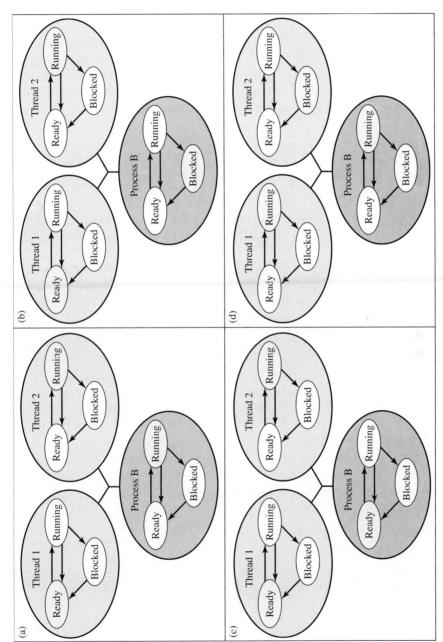

Figure 4.7 Examples of the Relationships between User-Level Thread States and Process States

to another process. Meanwhile, according to the data structure maintained by the threads library, thread 2 of process B is still in the Running state. It is important to note that thread 2 is not actually running in the sense of being executed on a processor; but it is perceived as being in the Running state by the threads library. The corresponding state diagrams are shown in Figure 4.7b.

2. A clock interrupt passes control to the kernel and the kernel determines that the currently running process (B) has exhausted its time slice. The kernel places process B in the Ready state and switches to another process. Meanwhile, according to the data structure maintained by the threads library, thread 2 of process B is still in the Running state. The corresponding state diagrams are shown in Figure 4.7c.

3. Thread 2 has reached a point where it needs some action performed by thread 1 of process B. Thread 2 enters a Blocked state and thread 1 transitions from Ready to Running. The process itself remains in the Running state. The corresponding state diagrams are shown in Figure 4.7d.

In cases 1 and 2 (Figures 4.7b and 4.7c), when the kernel switches control back to process B, execution resumes in thread 2. Also note that a process can be interrupted, either by exhausting its time slice or by being preempted by a higher-priority process, while it is executing code in the threads library. Thus, a process may be in the midst of a thread switch from one thread to another when interrupted. When that process is resumed, execution continues within the threads library, which completes the thread switch and transfers control to a new thread within that process.

There are a number of advantages to the use of ULTs instead of KLTs, including the following:

1. Thread switching does not require kernel mode privileges because all of the thread management data structures are within the user address space of a single process. Therefore, the process does not switch to the kernel mode to do thread management. This saves the overhead of two mode switches (user to kernel; kernel back to user).

2. Scheduling can be application specific. One application may benefit most from a simple round-robin scheduling algorithm, while another might benefit from a priority-based scheduling algorithm. The scheduling algorithm can be tailored to the application without disturbing the underlying OS scheduler.

3. ULTs can run on any operating system. No changes are required to the underlying kernel to support ULTs. The threads library is a set of application-level utilities shared by all applications.

There are two distinct disadvantages of ULTs compared to KLTs:

1. In a typical operating system, many system calls are blocking. As a result, when a ULT executes a system call, not only is that thread blocked, but also all of the threads within the process are blocked.

2. In a pure ULT strategy, a multithreaded application cannot take advantage of multiprocessing. A kernel assigns one process to only one processor at a time. Therefore, only a single thread within a process can execute at a time. In effect,

we have application-level multiprogramming within a single process. While this multiprogramming can result in a significant speedup of the application, there are applications that would benefit from the ability to execute portions of code concurrently.

There are ways to work around these two problems. For example, both problems can be overcome by writing an application as multiple processes rather than multiple threads. But this approach eliminates the main advantage of threads: Each switch becomes a process switch rather than a thread switch, resulting in much greater overhead.

Another way to overcome the problem of blocking threads is to use a technique referred to as jacketing. The purpose of jacketing is to convert a blocking system call into a nonblocking system call. For example, instead of directly calling a system I/O routine, a thread calls an application-level I/O jacket routine. Within this jacket routine is code that checks to determine if the I/O device is busy. If it is, the thread enters the Blocked state and passes control (through the threads library) to another thread. When this thread later is given control again, it checks the I/O device again.

Kernel-Level Threads   In a pure KLT facility, all of the work of thread management is done by the kernel. There is no thread management code in the application area, simply an application programming interface (API) to the kernel thread facility. Windows is an example of this approach.

Figure 4.6b depicts the pure KLT approach. Any application can be programmed to be multithreaded. All of the threads within an application are supported within a single process. The kernel maintains context information for the process as a whole and for individual threads within the process. Scheduling by the kernel is done on a thread basis. This approach overcomes the two principal drawbacks of the ULT approach. First, the kernel can simultaneously schedule multiple threads from the same process on multiple processors. Second, if one thread in a process is blocked, the kernel can schedule another thread of the same process. Another advantage of the KLT approach is that kernel routines themselves can be multithreaded.

The principal disadvantage of the KLT approach compared to the ULT approach is that the transfer of control from one thread to another within the same process requires a mode switch to the kernel. To illustrate the differences, Table 4.1 shows the results of measurements taken on a uniprocessor VAX machine running a UNIX-like operating system. The two benchmarks are as follows: Null Fork, the time to create, schedule, execute, and complete a process/thread that invokes the null procedure (i.e., the overhead of forking a process/thread); and Signal-Wait, the time for a process/thread to signal a waiting process/thread and then wait on a condition (i.e., the overhead of synchronizing two processes/threads together).

Table 4.1   Thread and Process Operation Latencies (μs) [ANDE92]

Operation	User-Level Threads	Kernel-Level Threads	Processes
Null Fork	34	948	11,300
Signal Wait	37	441	1,840

We see that there is an order of magnitude or more of difference between ULTs and KLTs and similarly between KLTs and processes.

Thus, on the face of it, while there is a significant speedup by using KLT multi-threading compared to single-threaded processes, there is an additional significant speedup by using ULTs. However, whether or not the additional speedup is realized depends on the nature of the applications involved. If most of the thread switches in an application require kernel mode access, then a ULT-based scheme may not perform much better than a KLT-based scheme.

Combined Approaches   Some operating systems provide a combined ULT/KLT facility (Figure 4.6c). Solaris is the principal example of this. In a combined system, thread creation is done completely in user space, as is the bulk of the scheduling and synchronization of threads within an application. The multiple ULTs from a single application are mapped onto some (smaller or equal) number of KLTs. The programmer may adjust the number of KLTs for a particular application and machine to achieve the best overall results.

In a combined approach, multiple threads within the same application can run in parallel on multiple processors, and a blocking system call need not block the entire process. If properly designed, this approach should combine the advantages of the pure ULT and KLT approaches while minimizing the disadvantages.

Other Arrangements

As we have said, the concepts of resource allocation and dispatching unit have traditionally been embodied in the single concept of the process; that is, as a 1 : 1 relationship between threads and processes. Recently, there has been much interest in providing for multiple threads within a single process, which is a many-to-one relationship. However, as Table 4.2 shows, the other two combinations have also been investigated, namely, a many-to-many relationship and a one-to-many relationship.

Table 4.2   Relationship Between Threads and Processes

Threads:Processes	Description	Example Systems
1:1	Each thread of execution is a unique process with its own address space and resources.	Traditional UNIX implementations
M:1	A process defines an address space and dynamic resource ownership. Multiple threads may be created and executed within that process.	Windows NT, Solaris, Linux OS/2, OS/390, MACH
1:M	A thread may migrate from one process environment to another. This allows a thread to be easily moved among distinct systems.	Ra (Clouds), Emerald
M:N	Combines attributes of M:1 and 1:M cases.	TRIX

Many-to-Many Relationship The idea of having a many-to-many relationship between threads and processes has been explored in the experimental operating system TRIX [SIEB83, WARD80]. In TRIX, there are the concepts of domain and thread. A domain is a static entity, consisting of an address space and "ports" through which messages may be sent and received. A thread is a single execution path, with an execution stack, processor state, and scheduling information.

As with the multithreading approaches discussed so far, multiple threads may execute in a single domain, providing the efficiency gains discussed earlier. However, it is also possible for a single user activity, or application, to be performed in multiple domains. In this case, a thread exists that can move from one domain to another.

The use of a single thread in multiple domains seems primarily motivated by a desire to provide structuring tools for the programmer. For example, consider a program that makes use of an I/O subprogram. In a multiprogramming environment that allows user-spawned processes, the main program could generate a new process to handle I/O and then continue to execute. However, if the future progress of the main program depends on the outcome of the I/O operation, then the main program will have to wait for the other I/O program to finish. There are several ways to implement this application:

1. The entire program can be implemented as a single process. This is a reasonable and straightforward solution. There are drawbacks related to memory management. The process as a whole may require considerable main memory to execute efficiently, whereas the I/O subprogram requires a relatively small address space to buffer I/O and to handle the relatively small amount of program code. Because the I/O program executes in the address space of the larger program, either the entire process must remain in main memory during the I/O operation or the I/O operation is subject to swapping. This memory-management effect would also exist if the main program and the I/O subprogram were implemented as two threads in the same address space.

2. The main program and I/O subprogram can be implemented as two separate processes. This incurs the overhead of creating the subordinate process. If the I/O activity is frequent, one must either leave the subordinate process alive, which consumes management resources, or frequently create and destroy the subprogram, which is inefficient.

3. Treat the main program and the I/O subprogram as a single activity that is to be implemented as a single thread. However, one address space (domain) could be created for the main program and one for the I/O subprogram. Thus, the thread can be moved between the two address spaces as execution proceeds. The operating system can manage the two address spaces independently, and no process creation overhead is incurred. Furthermore, the address space used by the I/O subprogram could also be shared by other simple I/O programs.

The experiences of the TRIX developers indicate that the third option has merit and may be the most effective solution for some applications.

One-to-Many Relationship In the field of distributed operating systems (designed to control distributed computer systems), there has been interest in the concept of a thread as primarily an entity that can move among address spaces.[5] A notable example of this research is the Clouds operating system, and especially its kernel, known as Ra [DASG92]. Another example is the Emerald system [STEE95].

A thread in Clouds is a unit of activity from the user's perspective. A process is a virtual address space with an associated process control block. Upon creation, a thread starts executing in a process by invoking an entry point to a program in that process. Threads may move from one address space to another and actually span machine boundaries (i.e., move from one computer to another). As a thread moves, it must carry with it certain information, such as the controlling terminal, global parameters, and scheduling guidance (e.g., priority).

The Clouds approach provides an effective way of insulating a user and programmer from the details of the distributed environment. A user's activity may be represented as a single thread, and the movement of that thread among machines may be dictated by the operating system for a variety of system-related reasons, such as the need to access a remote resource, and load balancing.

4.2 SYMMETRIC MULTIPROCESSING

Traditionally, the computer has been viewed as a sequential machine. Most computer programming languages require the programmer to specify algorithms as sequences of instructions. A processor executes programs by executing machine instructions in a sequence and one at a time. Each instruction is executed in a sequence of operations (fetch instruction, fetch operands, perform operation, store results).

This view of the computer has never been entirely true. At the micro-operation level, multiple control signals are generated at the same time. Instruction pipelining, at least to the extent of overlapping fetch and execute operations, has been around for a long time. Both of these are examples of performing functions in parallel.

As computer technology has evolved and as the cost of computer hardware has dropped, computer designers have sought more and more opportunities for parallelism, usually to improve performance and, in some cases, to improve reliability. In this book, we examine the two most popular approaches to providing parallelism by replicating processors: symmetric multiprocessors (SMPs) and clusters. SMPs are discussed in this section; clusters are examined in Part Six.

SMP Architecture

It is useful to see where SMP architectures fit into the overall category of parallel processors. A taxonomy that highlights parallel processor systems first introduced by Flynn [FLYN72] is still the most common way of categorizing such systems. Flynn proposed the following categories of computer systems:

- **Single instruction single data (SISD) stream:** A single processor executes a single instruction stream to operate on data stored in a single memory.

---

[5]The movement of processes or threads among address spaces, or thread migration, on different machines has become a hot topic in recent years. We explore this topic in Chapter 14.

- **Single instruction multiple data (SIMD) stream:** A single machine instruction controls the simultaneous execution of a number of processing elements on a lockstep basis. Each processing element has an associated data memory, so that each instruction is executed on a different set of data by the different processors. Vector and array processors fall into this category.
- **Multiple instruction single data (MISD) stream:** A sequence of data is transmitted to a set of processors, each of which executes a different instruction sequence. This structure has never been implemented.
- **Multiple instruction multiple data (MIMD) stream:** A set of processors simultaneously execute different instruction sequences on different data sets.

With the MIMD organization, the processors are general purpose, because they must be able to process all of the instructions necessary to perform the appropriate data transformation. MIMDs can be further subdivided by the means in which the processors communicate (Figure 4.8). If the processors each have a dedicated memory, then each processing element is a self-contained computer. Communication among the computers is either via fixed paths or via some network facility. Such a system is known as a **cluster**, or multicomputer. If the processors share a common memory, then each processor accesses programs and data stored in the shared memory, and processors communicate with each other via that memory; such a system is known as a **shared-memory multiprocessor**.

One general classification of shared-memory multiprocessors is based on how processes are assigned to processors. The two fundamental approaches are master/slave and symmetric. With a **master/slave** architecture, the operating system kernel always runs on a particular processor. The other processors may only execute user programs and perhaps operating system utilities. The master is responsible for scheduling processes or threads. Once a process/thread is active, if the slave needs service (e.g., an I/O call), it must send a request to the master and wait for the service to be performed. This approach is quite simple and requires little enhancement

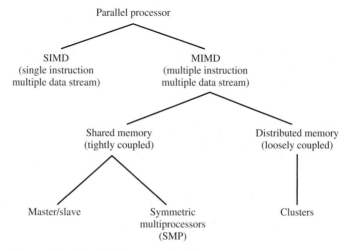

Figure 4.8 Parallel Processor Architectures

to a uniprocessor multiprogramming operating system. Conflict resolution is simplified because one processor has control of all memory and I/O resources. The disadvantages of this approach are as follows:

- A failure of the master brings down the whole system.
- The master can become a performance bottleneck, because it alone must do all scheduling and process management.

In a **symmetric multiprocessor (SMP)**, the kernel can execute on any processor, and typically each processor does self-scheduling from the pool of available processes or threads. The kernel can be constructed as multiple processes or multiple threads, allowing portions of the kernel to execute in parallel. The SMP approach complicates the operating system. It must ensure that two processors do not choose the same process and that processes are not somehow lost from the queue. Techniques must be employed to resolve and synchronize claims to resources.

The design of both SMPs and clusters is complex, involving issues relating to physical organization, interconnection structures, interprocessor communication, operating system design, and application software techniques. Our concern here, and later in our discussion of clusters (Chapter 13), is primarily with operating system design issues, although in both cases we touch briefly on organization.

SMP Organization

Figure 4.9 illustrates the general organization of an SMP. There are multiple processors, each of which contains its own control unit, arithmetic-logic unit, and registers. Each processor has access to a shared main memory and the I/O devices through some form of interconnection mechanism; a shared bus is a common facility. The processors can communicate with each other through memory (messages and status information left in shared address spaces). It may also be possible for processors to exchange signals directly. The memory is often organized so that multiple simultaneous accesses to separate blocks of memory are possible.

In modern machines, processors generally have at least one level of cache memory that is private to the processor. This use of cache introduces some new design considerations. Because each local cache contains an image of a portion of main memory, if a word is altered in one cache, it could conceivably invalidate a word in another cache. To prevent this, the other processors must be alerted that an update has taken place. This problem is known as the cache coherence problem and is typically addressed in hardware rather than by the operating system.[6]

Multiprocessor Operating System Design Considerations

An SMP operating system manages processor and other computer resources so that the user may view the system in the same fashion as a multiprogramming uniprocessor system. A user may construct applications that use multiple processes or multiple threads within processes without regard to whether a single processor or multiple processors will be available. Thus a multiprocessor operating system must

---

[6]A description of hardware-based cache coherency schemes is provided in [STAL03].

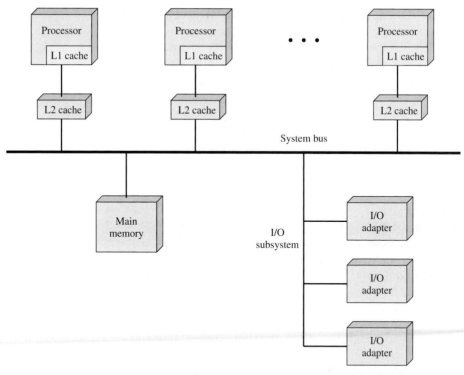

Figure 4.9   Symmetric Multiprocessor Organization

provide all the functionality of a multiprogramming system plus additional features to accommodate multiple processors. The key design issues include the following:

- **Simultaneous concurrent processes or threads:** Kernel routines need to be reentrant to allow several processors to execute the same kernel code simultaneously. With multiple processors executing the same or different parts of the kernel, kernel tables and management structures must be managed properly to avoid deadlock or invalid operations.

- **Scheduling:** Scheduling may be performed by any processor, so conflicts must be avoided. If kernel-level multithreading is used, then the opportunity exists to schedule multiple threads from the same process simultaneously on multiple processors. Multiprocessor scheduling is examined in Chapter 10.

- **Synchronization:** With multiple active processes having potential access to shared address spaces or shared I/O resources, care must be taken to provide effective synchronization. Synchronization is a facility that enforces mutual exclusion and event ordering. A common synchronization mechanism used in multiprocessor operating systems is locks, described in Chapter 5.

- **Memory management:** Memory management on a multiprocessor must deal with all of the issues found on uniprocessor machines and is discussed in Part Three. In addition, the operating system needs to exploit the available hardware parallelism, such as multiported memories, to achieve the best performance. The paging mechanisms on different processors must be coordinated to enforce consistency when several processors share a page or segment and to decide on page replacement.

- **Reliability and fault tolerance:** The operating system should provide graceful degradation in the face of processor failure. The scheduler and other portions of the operating system must recognize the loss of a processor and restructure management tables accordingly.

Because multiprocessor operating system design issues generally involve extensions to solutions to multiprogramming uniprocessor design problems, we do not treat multiprocessor operating systems separately. Rather, specific multiprocessor issues are addressed in the proper context throughout this book.

4.3 MICROKERNELS

A concept that has received much attention recently is the microkernel. A microkernel is a small operating system core that provides the foundation for modular extensions. The term is somewhat fuzzy, however, and there are a number of questions about microkernels that are answered differently by different operating system design teams. These questions include how small a kernel must be to qualify as a microkernel, how to design device drivers to get the best performance while abstracting their functions from the hardware, whether to run nonkernel operations in kernel or user space, and whether to keep existing subsystem code (e.g., a version of UNIX) or start from scratch.

The microkernel approach was popularized by its use in the Mach operating system. In theory, this approach provides a high degree of flexibility and modularity. A number of products now boast microkernel implementations, and this general design approach is likely to be seen in most of the personal computer, workstation, and server operating systems developed in the near future.

Microkernel Architecture

The early operating systems developed in the mid to late 1950s were designed with little concern about structure. No one had experience in building truly large software systems, and the problems caused by mutual dependence and interaction were grossly underestimated. In these **monolithic operating systems**, virtually any procedure can call any other procedure. Such lack of structure was unsustainable as operating systems grew to massive proportions. For example, the first version of OS/360 contained over a million lines of code; Multics, developed later, grew to 20 million lines of code [DENN84]. As we discussed in Section 2.3, modular programming techniques were needed to handle this scale of software development. Specifically, **layered operating systems**[7] (Figure 4.10a) were developed in which functions are

---

[7]As usual, the terminology in this area is not consistently applied in the literature. The term *monolithic operating system* is often used to refer to both of the two types of operating systems that I have referred to as *monolithic* and *layered*.

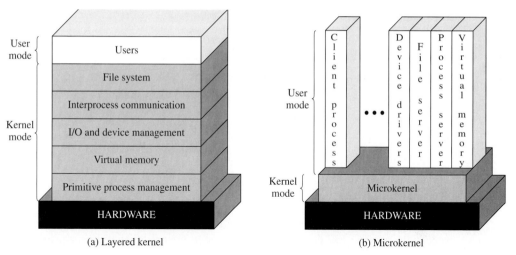

Figure 4.10   Kernel Architecture

organized hierarchically and interaction only takes place between adjacent layers. With the layered approach, most or all of the layers execute in kernel mode.

Problems remain even with the layered approach. Each layer possesses considerable functionality. Major changes in one layer can have numerous effects, many difficult to trace, on code in adjacent layers (above and below). As a result, it is difficult to implement tailored versions of a base operating system with a few functions added or subtracted. And security is difficult to build in because of the many interactions between adjacent layers.

The philosophy underlying the **microkernel** is that only absolutely essential core operating system functions should be in the kernel. Less essential services and applications are built on the microkernel and execute in user mode. Although the dividing line between what is in and what is outside the microkernel varies from one design to the next, the common characteristic is that many services that traditionally have been part of the operating system are now external subsystems that interact with the kernel and with each other; these include device drivers, file systems, virtual memory manager, windowing system, and security services.

A microkernel architecture replaces the traditional vertical, layered stratification of an operating system with a horizontal one (Figure 4.10b). Operating system components external to the microkernel are implemented as server processes; these interact with each other on a peer basis, typically by means of messages passed through the microkernel. Thus, the microkernel functions as a message exchange: It validates messages, passes them between components, and grants access to hardware. The microkernel also performs a protection function; it prevents message passing unless exchange is allowed.

For example, if an application wishes to open a file, it sends a message to the file system server. If it wishes to create a process or thread, it sends a message to the process server. Each of the servers can send messages to other servers and can invoke the primitive functions in the microkernel. This is a client/server architecture within a single computer.

Benefits of a Microkernel Organization

A number of advantages for the use of microkernels have been reported in the literature (e.g., [FINK97], [LIED96a], [WAYN94a]). These include

- Uniform interfaces
- Extensibility
- Flexibility
- Portability
- Reliability
- Distributed system support
- Support for object-oriented operating systems (OOOS)

Microkernel design imposes a **uniform interface** on requests made by a process. Processes need not distinguish between kernel-level and user-level services because all such services are provided by means of message passing.

Any operating system will inevitably need to acquire features not in its current design, as new hardware devices and new software techniques are developed. The microkernel architecture facilitates **extensibility**, allowing the addition of new services as well as the provision of multiple services in the same functional area. For example, there may be multiple file organizations for diskettes; each organization can be implemented as a user-level process rather than having multiple file services available in the kernel. Thus, users can choose from a variety of services the one that provides the best fit to the user's needs. With the microkernel architecture, when a new feature is added only selected servers need to be modified or added. The impact of new or modified servers is restricted to a subset of the system. Further, modifications do not require building a new kernel.

Related to the extensibility of the microkernel architecture is its **flexibility**. Not only can new features be added to the operating system, but existing features can be subtracted to produce a smaller, more efficient implementation. A microkernel-based operating system is not necessarily a small system. Indeed, the structure lends itself to adding a wide range of features. But not everyone needs, for example, a high level of security or the ability to do distributed computing. If substantial (in terms of memory requirements) features are made optional, the base product will appeal to a wider variety of users.

Intel's near monopoly of many segments of the computer platform market is unlikely to be sustained indefinitely. Thus, **portability** becomes an attractive feature of an operating system. In the microkernel architecture, all or at least much of the processor-specific code is in the microkernel. Thus, changes needed to port the system to a new processor are fewer and tend to be arranged in logical groupings.

The larger the size of a software product, the more difficult it is to ensure its reliability. Although modular design helps to enhance **reliability**, even greater gains can be achieved with a microkernel architecture. A small microkernel can be rigorously tested. Its use of a small number of application programming interfaces (APIs) improves the chance of producing quality code for the operating system services outside the kernel. The system programmer has a limited number of APIs to master and limited means of interacting with and therefore adversely affecting other system components.

The microkernel lends itself to **distributed system support**, including clusters controlled by a distributed operating system. When a message is sent from a client to a server process, the message must include an identifier of the requested service. If a distributed system (e.g., a cluster) is configured so that all processes and services have unique identifiers, then in effect there is a single system image at the microkernel level. A process can send a message without knowing on which machine the target service resides. We return to this point in our discussion of distributed systems in Part Six.

A microkernel architecture works well in the context of an **object-oriented operating system**. An object-oriented approach can lend discipline to the design of the microkernel and to the development of modular extensions to the operating system. As a result, a number of microkernel design efforts are moving in the direction of object orientation [WAYN94b]. One promising approach to marrying the microkernel architecture with OOOS principles is the use of components [MESS96]. Components are objects with clearly defined interfaces that can be interconnected to form software in a building block fashion. All interaction between components uses the component interface. Other systems, such as Windows, do not rely exclusively or fully on object-oriented methods but have incorporated object-oriented principles into the microkernel design.

Microkernel Performance

One potential disadvantage of microkernels that is often cited is that of performance. It takes longer to build and send a message via the microkernel, and accept and decode the reply, than to make a single service call. However, other factors come into play so that it is difficult to generalize about the performance penalty, if any.

Much depends on the size and functionality of the microkernel. [LIED96a] summarizes a number of studies that reveal a substantial performance penalty for what might be called first-generation microkernels. These penalties persisted despite efforts to optimize the microkernel code. One response to this problem was to enlarge the microkernel by reintegrating critical servers and drivers back into the operating system. Prime examples of this approach are Mach and Chorus. Selectively increasing the functionality of the microkernel reduces the number of user-kernel mode switches and the number of address-space process switches. However, this workaround reduces the performance penalty at the expense of the strengths of microkernel design: minimal interfaces, flexibility, and so on.

Another approach is to make the microkernel not larger but smaller. [LIED96b] argues that, properly designed, a very small microkernel eliminates the performance penalty and improves flexibility and reliability. To give an idea of the sizes involved, a typical first-generation microkernel consists of 300 Kbytes of code and 140 system call interfaces. An example of a small second generation microkernels is L4 [HART97, LIED95], which consists of 12 Kbytes of code and 7 system calls. Experience with these systems indicates that they can perform as well or better than a layered operating system such as UNIX.

Microkernel Design

Because different microkernels exhibit a range of functionality and size, no hard-and-fast rules can be stated concerning what functions are provided by the microkernel and what structure is implemented. In this section, we present a minimal set of microkernel functions and services, to give a feel for microkernel design.

The microkernel must include those functions that depend directly on the hardware and those functions needed to support the servers and applications operating in user mode. These functions fall into the general categories of low-level memory management, interprocess communication (IPC), and I/O and interrupt management.

Low–Level Memory Management The microkernel has to control the hardware concept of address space to make it possible to implement protection at the process level. As long as the microkernel is responsible for mapping each virtual page to a physical frame, the bulk of memory management, including the protection of the address space of one process from another and the page replacement algorithm and other paging logic, can be implemented outside the kernel. For example, a virtual memory module outside the microkernel decides when to bring a page into memory and which page already in memory is to be replaced; the microkernel maps these page references into a physical address in main memory.

The concept that paging and virtual memory management can be performed external to the kernel was introduced with Mach's external pager [YOUN87]. Figure 4.11 illustrates the operation of an external pager. When a thread in the application references a page not in main memory, a page fault occurs and execution traps to the kernel. The kernel then sends a message to the pager process indicating which page has been referenced. The pager can decide to load that page and allocate a page frame for that purpose. The pager and the kernel must interact to map the pager's logical operations onto physical memory. Once the page is available, the pager sends a resume message to the application.

This technique enables a nonkernel process to map files and databases into user address spaces without invoking the kernel. Application-specific memory sharing policies can be implemented outside the kernel.

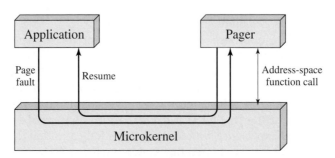

Figure 4.11 Page Fault Processing

[LIED95] suggests a set of just three microkernel operations that can support external paging and virtual memory management:

- **Grant:** The owner of an address space (a process) can grant a number of its pages to another process. The kernel removes these pages from the grantor's address space and assigns them to the designated process.

- **Map:** A process can map any of its pages into the address space of another process, so that both processes have access to the pages. This creates shared memory between the two processes. The kernel maintains the assignment of these pages to the original owner but provides a mapping to permit access by other processes.

- **Flush:** A process can reclaim any pages that were granted or mapped to other processes.

To begin, the kernel allocates all available physical memory as resources to a base system process. As new processes are created, pages from the original total address space can be granted or mapped to the new process. Such a scheme could support multiple virtual memory schemes simultaneously.

Interprocess Communication The basic form of communication between processes or threads in a microkernel operating system is messages. A **message** includes a header that identifies the sending and receiving process and a body that contains direct data, a pointer to a block of data, or some control information about the process. Typically, we can think of IPC as being based on ports associated with processes. A **port** is, in essence, a queue of messages destined for a particular process; a process may have multiple ports. Associated with the port is a list of capabilities indicating what processes may communicate with this process. Port identities and capabilities are maintained by the kernel. A process can grant new access to itself by sending a message to the kernel indicating the new port capability.

A note about message passing is appropriate here. Message passing between separate processes with nonoverlapping address spaces involves memory-to-memory copying and thus is bounded by memory speeds and does not scale with processor speeds. Thus, current OS research reflects an interest in thread-based IPC and memory-sharing schemes such as page remapping (a single page shared by multiple processes).

I/O and Interrupt Management With a microkernel architecture, it is possible to handle hardware interrupts as messages and to include I/O ports in address spaces. The microkernel can recognize interrupts but does not handle them. Rather, it generates a message for the user-level process currently associated with that interrupt. Thus, when an interrupt is enabled, a particular user-level process is assigned to the interrupt and the kernel maintains the mapping. Transforming interrupts into messages must be done by the microkernel, but the microkernel is not involved in device-specific interrupt handling.

[LIED96a] suggests viewing hardware as a set of threads that have unique thread identifiers and send messages (consisting simply of the thread ID) to associated software threads in user space. A receiving thread determines whether the message comes from an interrupt and determines the specific interrupt. The general structure of such user-level code is the following:

```
driver thread:
        do
                waitFor (msg, sender) ;
                if (sender == my_hardware_interrupt)
                {
                        read/write I/O ports;
                        reset hardware interrupt
                }
                else • • •
        while (true);
```

4.4 WINDOWS THREAD AND SMP MANAGEMENT

Windows process design is driven by the need to provide support for a variety of operating system environments. Processes supported by different operating system environments differ in a number of ways, including the following:

- How processes are named
- Whether threads are provided within processes
- How processes are represented
- How process resources are protected
- What mechanisms are used for interprocess communication and synchronization
- How processes are related to each other

Accordingly, the native process structures and services provided by the Windows kernel are relatively simple and general purpose, allowing each operating system subsystem to emulate a particular process structure and functionality. Important characteristics of Windows processes are the following:

- Windows processes are implemented as objects.
- An executable process may contain one or more threads.
- Both process and thread objects have built-in synchronization capabilities.

Figure 4.12, based on one in [SOLO00], illustrates the way in which a process relates to the resources it controls or uses. Each process is assigned a security access token, called the primary token of the process. When a user first logs on, Windows creates an access token that includes a security ID for the user. Every process that is created by or runs on behalf of this user has a copy of this access token. Windows uses the token to validate the user's ability to access secured objects or to perform restricted functions on the system and on secured objects. The access token controls whether the process can change its own attributes. In this

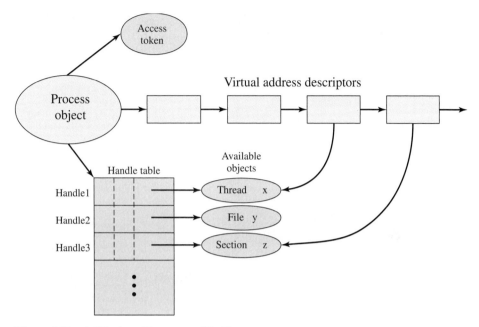

Figure 4.12   A Windows Process and Its Resources

case, the process does not have a handle opened to its access token. If the process attempts to open such a handle, the security system determines whether this is permitted and therefore whether the process may change its own attributes.

Also related to the process is a series of blocks that define the virtual address space currently assigned to this process. The process cannot directly modify these structures but must rely on the virtual memory manager, which provides a memory-allocation service for the process.

Finally, the process includes an object table, with handles to other objects known to this process. One handle exists for each thread contained in this object. Figure 4.12 shows a single thread. In addition, the process has access to a file object and to a section object that defines a section of shared memory.

Process and Thread Objects

The object-oriented structure of Windows facilitates the development of a general-purpose process facility. Windows makes use of two types of process-related objects: processes and threads. A process is an entity corresponding to a user job or application that owns resources, such as memory, and opens files. A thread is a dispatchable unit of work that executes sequentially and is interruptible, so that the processor can turn to another thread.

Each Windows process is represented by an object whose general structure is shown in Figure 4.13a. Each process is defined by a number of attributes and encapsulates a number of actions, or services, that it may perform. A process will perform a service upon receipt of the appropriate message; the only way to invoke such a service is by means of messages to a process object that provides that service. When Windows creates a new process, it uses the object class, or type, defined for the Windows process

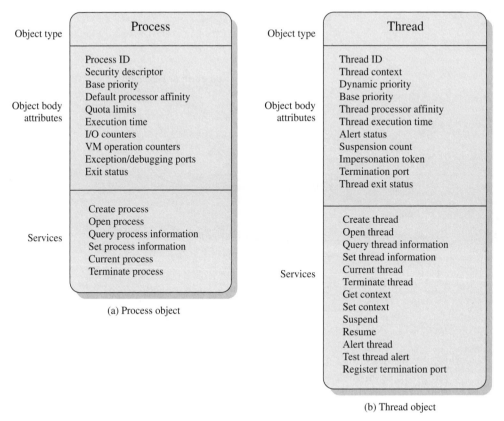

Figure 4.13   Windows Process and Thread Objects

as a template to generate a new object instance. At the time of creation, attribute values are assigned. Table 4.3 gives a brief definition of each of the object attributes for a process object.

A Windows process must contain at least one thread to execute. That thread may then create other threads. In a multiprocessor system, multiple threads from the same process may execute in parallel. Figure 4.13b depicts the object structure for a thread object, and Table 4.4 defines the thread object attributes. Note that some of the attributes of a thread resemble those of a process. In those cases, the thread attribute value is derived from the process attribute value. For example, the *thread processor affinity* is the set of processors in a multiprocessor system that may execute this thread; this set is equal to or a subset of the *process processor affinity*.

Note that one of the attributes of a thread object is context. This information enables threads to be suspended and resumed. Furthermore, it is possible to alter the behavior of a thread by altering its context when it is suspended.

Multithreading

Windows supports concurrency among processes because threads in different processes may execute concurrently. Moreover, multiple threads within the same

Table 4.3   Windows Process Object Attributes

Process ID	A unique value that identifies the process to the operating system.
Security Descriptor	Describes who created an object, who can gain access to or use the object, and who is denied access to the object.
Base priority	A baseline execution priority for the process's threads.
Default processor affinity	The default set of processors on which the process's threads can run.
Quota limits	The maximum amount of paged and nonpaged system memory, paging file space, and processor time a user's processes can use.
Execution time	The total amount of time all threads in the process have executed.
I/O counters	Variables that record the number and type of I/O operations that the process's threads have performed.
VM operation counters	Variables that record the number and types of virtual memory operations that the process's threads have performed.
Exception/debugging ports	Interprocess communication channels to which the process manager sends a message when one of the process's threads causes an exception.
Exit status	The reason for a process's termination.

Table 4.4   Windows Thread Object Attributes

Thread ID	A unique value that identifies a thread when it calls a server.
Thread context	The set of register values and other volatile data that defines the execution state of a thread.
Dynamic priority	The thread's execution priority at any given moment.
Base priority	The lower limit of the thread's dynamic priority.
Thread processor affinity	The set of processors on which the thread can run, which is a subset or all of the processor affinity of the thread's process.
Thread execution time	The cumulative amount of time a thread has executed in user mode and in kernel mode.
Alert status	A flag that indicates whether the thread should execute an asynchronous procedure call.
Suspension count	The number of times the thread's execution has been suspended without being resumed.
Impersonation token	A temporary access token allowing a thread to perform operations on behalf of another process (used by subsystems).
Termination port	An interprocess communication channel to which the process manager sends a message when the thread terminates (used by subsystems).
Thread exit status	The reason for a thread's termination.

process may be allocated to separate processors and execute concurrently. A multithreaded process achieves concurrency without the overhead of using multiple processes. Threads within the same process can exchange information through their common address space and have access to the shared resources of the process. Threads in different processes can exchange information through shared memory that has been set up between the two processes.

An object-oriented multithreaded process is an efficient means of implementing a server application. For example, one server process can service a number of clients. Each client request triggers the creation of a new thread within the server.

Thread States

An existing Windows thread is in one of six states (Figure 4.14):

- **Ready:** May be scheduled for execution. The microkernel dispatcher keeps track of all ready threads and schedules in priority order.

- **Standby:** A standby thread has been selected to run next on a particular processor. The thread waits in this state until that processor is made available. If the standby thread's priority is high enough, the running thread on that processor may be preempted in favor of the standby thread. Otherwise, the standby thread waits until the running thread blocks or finishes its time slice.

- **Running:** Once the microkernel performs a thread or process switch, the standby thread enters the running state and begins execution and continues execution until it is preempted, exhausts its time slice, blocks, or terminates. In the first two cases, it goes back to the ready state.

- **Waiting:** A thread enters the waiting state when (1) it is blocked on an event (e.g., I/O), (2) it voluntarily waits for synchronization purposes, or (3) an environment subsystem directs the thread to suspend itself. When the waiting condition is satisfied, the thread moves to the Ready state if all of its resources are available.

- **Transition:** A thread enters this state after waiting if it is ready to run but the resources are not available. For example, the thread's stack may be paged out of memory. When the resources are available, the thread goes to the Ready state.

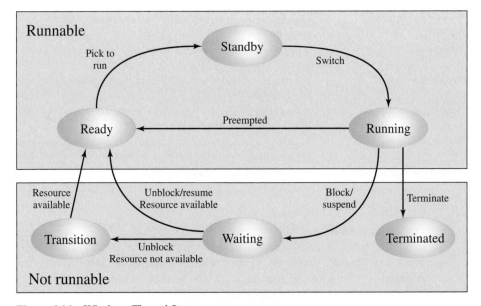

Figure 4.14   Windows Thread States

- **Terminated:** A thread can be terminated by itself, by another thread, or when its parent process terminates. Once housekeeping chores are completed, the thread is removed from the system, or it may be retained by the executive[8] for future reinitialization.

Support for OS Subsystems

The general-purpose process and thread facility must support the particular process and thread structures of the various OS clients. It is the responsibility of each OS subsystem to exploit the Windows process and thread features to emulate the process and thread facilities of its corresponding operating system. This area of process/thread management is complicated, and we give only a brief overview here.

Process creation begins with a request for a new process from an application. The application issues a create-process request to the corresponding protected subsystem, which passes the request to the Windows executive. The executive creates a process object and returns a handle to that object to the subsystem. When Windows creates a process, it does not automatically create a thread. In the case of Win32 and OS/2, a new process is always created with a thread. Therefore, for these operating systems, the subsystem calls the Windows process manager again to create a thread for the new process, receiving a thread handle back from Windows. The appropriate thread and process information are then returned to the application. In the case of 16-bit Windows and POSIX, threads are not supported. Therefore, for these operating systems, the subsystem obtains a thread for the new process from Windows so that the process may be activated but returns only process information to the application. The fact that the application process is implemented using a thread is not visible to the application.

When a new process is created in Win32 or OS/2, the new process inherits many of its attributes from the creating process. However, in the Windows environment, this process creation is done indirectly. An application client process issues its process creation request to the OS subsystem; then a process in the subsystem in turn issues a process request to the Windows executive. Because the desired effect is that the new process inherits characteristics of the client process and not of the server process, Windows enables the subsystem to specify the parent of the new process. The new process then inherits the parent's access token, quota limits, base priority, and default processor affinity.

Symmetric Multiprocessing Support

Windows supports an SMP hardware configuration. The threads of any process, including those of the executive, can run on any processor. In the absence of affinity restrictions, explained in the next paragraph, the microkernel assigns a ready thread to the next available processor. This assures that no processor is idle or is executing a lower-priority thread when a higher-priority thread is ready. Multiple threads from the same process can be executing simultaneously on multiple processors.

---

[8]The Windows executive is described in Chapter 2. It contains the base operating system services, such as memory management, process and thread management, security, I/O, and interprocess communication.

As a default, the microkernel uses the policy of **soft affinity** in assigning threads to processors: The dispatcher tries to assign a ready thread to the same processor it last ran on. This helps reuse data still in that processor's memory caches from the previous execution of the thread. It is possible for an application to restrict its thread execution to certain processors (**hard affinity**).

4.5 SOLARIS THREAD AND SMP MANAGEMENT

Solaris implements an unusual multilevel thread support designed to provide considerable flexibility in exploiting processor resources.

Multithreaded Architecture

Solaris makes use of four separate thread-related concepts:

- **Process:** This is the normal UNIX process and includes the user's address space, stack, and process control block.
- **User-level threads:** Implemented through a threads library in the address space of a process, these are invisible to the operating system. User-level threads (ULTs)[9] are the interface for application parallelism.
- **Lightweight processes:** A lightweight process (LWP) can be viewed as a mapping between ULTs and kernel threads. Each LWP supports one or more ULTs and maps to one kernel thread. LWPs are scheduled by the kernel independently and may execute in parallel on multiprocessors.
- **Kernel threads:** These are the fundamental entities that can be scheduled and dispatched to run on one of the system processors.

Figure 4.15 illustrates the relationship among these four entities. Note that there is always exactly one kernel thread for each LWP. An LWP is visible within a process to the application. Thus, LWP data structures exist within their respective process address space. At the same time, each LWP is bound to a single dispatchable kernel thread, and the data structure for that kernel thread is maintained within the kernel's address space.

In our example, process 1 consists of a single ULT bound to a single LWP. Thus, there is a single thread of execution, corresponding to a traditional UNIX process. When concurrency is not required within a single process, an application uses this process structure. Process 2 corresponds to a pure ULT strategy. All of the ULTs are supported by a single kernel thread, and therefore only one ULT can execute at a time. This structure is useful for an application that can best be programmed in a way that expresses concurrency but for which it is not necessary to have parallel execution of multiple threads. Process 3 shows multiple threads multiplexed on a lesser number of LWPs. In general, Solaris allows applications to

---

[9]Again, the acronym ULT is unique to this book and is not found in the Solaris literature.

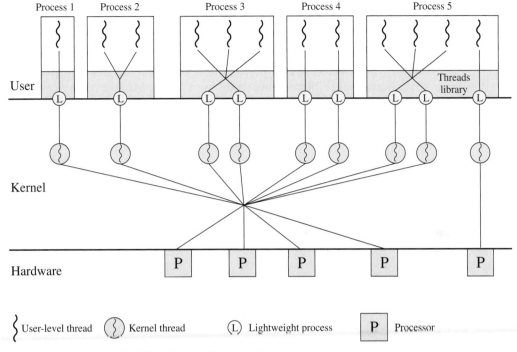

Figure 4.15 Solaris Multithreaded Architecture Example

multiplex ULTs on a lesser or equal number of LWPs. This enables the application to specify the degree of parallelism at the kernel level that will support this process. Process 4 has its threads permanently bound to LWPs in a one-to-one mapping. This structure makes the kernel-level parallelism fully visible to the application. It is useful if threads will typically or frequently be suspended in a blocking fashion. Process 5 shows both a mapping of multiple ULTs onto multiple LWPs and the binding of a ULT to a LWP. In addition, one LWP is bound to a particular processor.

Not shown in the figure is the presence of kernel threads that are not associated with LWPs. The kernel creates, runs, and destroys these kernel threads to execute specific system functions. The use of kernel threads rather than kernel processes to implement system functions reduces the overhead of switching within the kernel (from a process switch to a thread switch).

Motivation

The combination of user-level and kernel-level threads gives the application programmer the opportunity to exploit concurrency in a way that is most efficient and most appropriate to a given application.

Some programs have logical parallelism that can be exploited to simplify and structure the code but do not need hardware parallelism. For example, an application that employs multiple windows, only one of which is active at a time, could with advantage be implemented as a set of ULTs on a single LWP. The advantage of restricting such applications to ULTs is efficiency. ULTs may be created, destroyed, blocked, activated, and so on without involving the kernel. If each ULT were known to the kernel, the kernel would have to allocate kernel data structures for each one and perform thread switching. As we have seen (Table 4.1), kernel-level thread switching is more expensive than user-level thread switching.

If an application involves threads that may block, such as when performing I/O, then having multiple LWPs to support an equal or greater number of ULTs is attractive. Neither the application nor the threads library need perform contortions to allow other threads within the same process to execute. Instead, if one thread in a process blocks, other threads within the process may run on the remaining LWPs.

Mapping ULTs one-to-one to LWPs is effective for some applications. For example, a parallel array computation could divide the rows of its arrays among different threads. If there is exactly one ULT per LWP, then no thread switching is required for the computation to proceed.

A mixture of threads that are permanently bound to LWPs and unbound threads (multiple threads sharing multiple LWPs) is appropriate for some applications. For example, a real-time application may want some threads to have system wide priority and real-time scheduling, while other threads perform background functions and can share one or a small pool of LWPs.

Process Structure

Figure 4.16 compares, in general terms, the process structure of a traditional UNIX system with that of Solaris. On a typical UNIX implementation, the process structure includes the process ID; the user IDs; a signal dispatch table, which the kernel uses to decide what to do when sending a signal to a process; file descriptors, which describe the state of files in use by this process; a memory map, which defines the address space for this process; and a processor state structure, which includes the kernel stack for this process. Solaris retains this basic structure but replaces the processor state block with a list of structures containing one data block for each LWP.

The LWP data structure includes the following elements:

- An LWP identifier
- The priority of this LWP and hence the kernel thread that supports it
- A signal mask that tells the kernel which signals will be accepted
- Saved values of user-level registers (when the LWP is not running)
- The kernel stack for this LWP, which includes system call arguments, results, and error codes for each call level
- Resource usage and profiling data
- Pointer to the corresponding kernel thread
- Pointer to the process structure

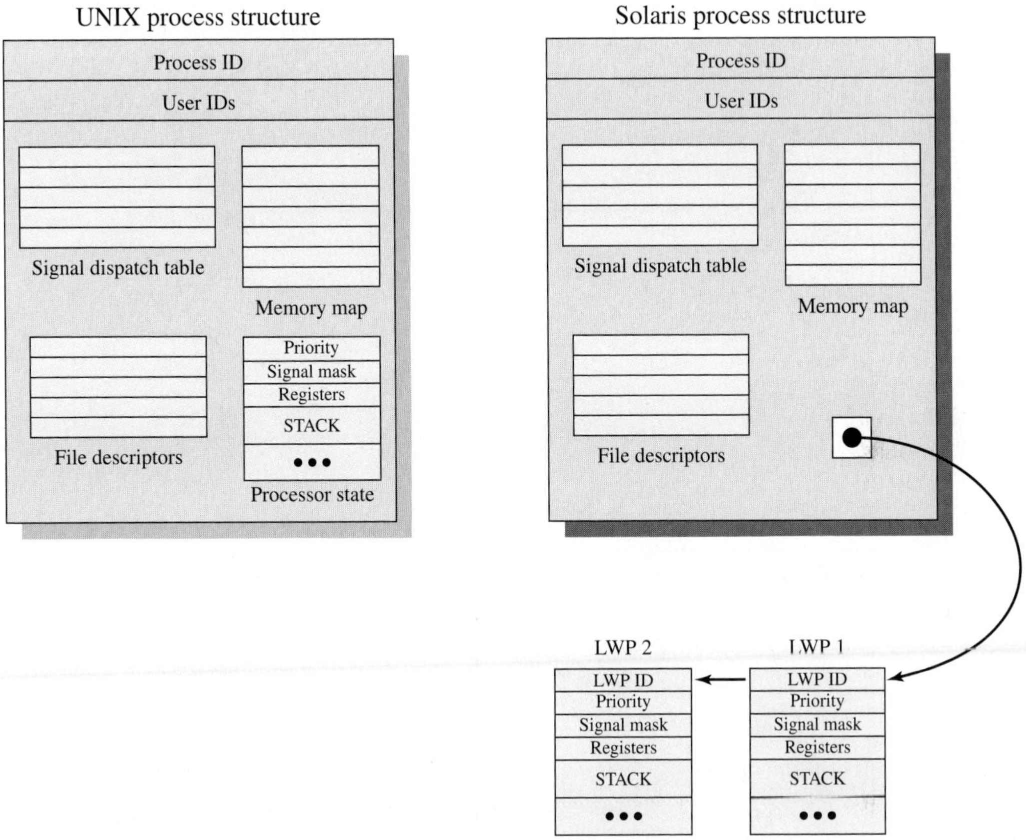

UNIX process structure

Solaris process structure

Process ID

User IDs

Signal dispatch table

Memory map

Priority
Signal mask
Registers

STACK

File descriptors

• • •

Processor state

Process ID

User IDs

Signal dispatch table

Memory map

File descriptors

LWP 2

LWP ID
Priority
Signal mask
Registers

STACK

• • •

LWP 1

LWP ID
Priority
Signal mask
Registers

STACK

• • •

Figure 4.16 Process Structure in Traditional UNIX and Solaris [LEWI96]

Thread Execution

Figure 4.17 shows a simplified view of both ULT and LWP execution states. The execution of user-level threads is managed by the threads library. Let us first consider unbound threads, that is, threads that share a number of LWPs. An unbound thread can be in one of four states: runnable, active, sleeping, or stopped. A ULT in the active state is currently assigned to a LWP and executes while the underlying kernel thread executes. A number of events may cause the ULT to leave the active state. Let us consider an active ULT called T1. The following events may occur:

- **Synchronization:** T1 invokes one of the concurrency primitives discussed in Chapter 5 to coordinate its activity with other threads and to enforce mutual exclusion. T1 is placed in the sleeping state. When the synchronization condition is met, T1 is moved to the runnable state.

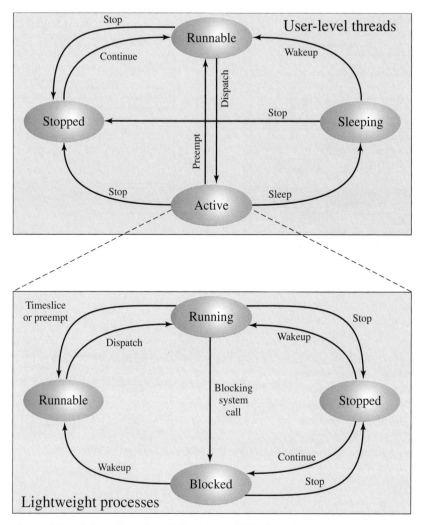

Figure 4.17 Solaris User-Level Thread and LWP States

- **Suspension:** Any thread (including T1) may cause T1 to be suspended and placed in the stopped state. T1 remains in that state until another thread issues a continue request, which moves it to the runnable state.

- **Preemption:** An active thread (T1 or some other thread) does something that causes another thread (T2) of higher priority to become runnable. If T1 is the lowest-priority active thread, it is preempted and moved to the runnable state, and T2 is assigned to the LWP made available.

- **Yielding:** If T1 executes the `thr_yield()` library command, the threads scheduler in the library will look to see if there is another runnable thread (T2) of the same priority. If so, T1 is placed in the runnable state and T2 is assigned to the LWP that is freed. If not, T1 continues to run.

In all of the preceding cases, when T1 is moved out of the active state, the threads library selects another unbound thread in the runnable state and runs it on the newly available LWP.

Figure 4.17 also shows the state diagram for an LWP. We can view this state diagram as a detailed description of the ULT active state, because an unbound thread only has an LWP assigned to it when it is in the Active state. The LWP state diagram is reasonably self-explanatory. An active thread is only executing when its LWP is in the Running state. When an active thread executes a blocking system call, the LWP enters the Blocked state. However, the ULT remains bound to that LWP and, as far as the threads library is concerned, that ULT remains active.

With bound threads, the relationship between ULT and LWP is slightly different. For example, if a bound ULT moves to the Sleeping state awaiting a synchronization event, its LWP must also stop running. This is accomplished by having the LWP block on a kernel-level synchronization variable.

Interrupts as Threads

Most operating systems contain two fundamental forms of concurrent activity: processes and interrupts. Processes (or threads) cooperate with each other and manage the use of shared data structures by means of a variety of primitives that enforce mutual exclusion (only one process at a time can execute certain code or access certain data) and that synchronize their execution. Interrupts are synchronized by preventing their handling for a period of time. Solaris unifies these two concepts into a single model, namely kernel threads and the mechanisms for scheduling and executing kernel threads. To do this, interrupts are converted to kernel threads.

The motivation for converting interrupts to threads is to reduce overhead. Interrupt handlers often manipulate data shared by the rest of the kernel. Therefore, while a kernel routine that accesses such data is executing, interrupts must be blocked, even though most interrupts will not affect that data. Typically, the way this is done is for the routine to set the interrupt priority level higher to block interrupts and then lower the priority level after access is completed. These operations take time. The problem is magnified on a multiprocessor system. The kernel must protect more objects and may need to block interrupts on all processors.

The solution in Solaris can be summarized as follows:

1. Solaris employs a set of kernel threads to handle interrupts. As with any kernel thread, an interrupt thread has its own identifier, priority, context, and stack.

2. The kernel controls access to data structures and synchronizes among interrupt threads using mutual exclusion primitives, of the type discussed in Chapter 5. That is, the normal synchronization techniques for threads are used in handling interrupts.

3. Interrupt threads are assigned higher priorities than all other types of kernel threads.

When an interrupt occurs, it is delivered to a particular processor and the thread that was executing on that processor is pinned. A pinned thread cannot move to another processor and its context is preserved; it is simply suspended until the interrupt is processed. The processor then begins executing an interrupt thread. There is a pool of deactivated interrupt threads available, so that a new thread creation is not required. The interrupt thread then executes to handle the interrupt. If the handler routine needs access to a data structure that is currently locked in some fashion for use by another executing thread, the interrupt thread must wait for access to that data structure. An interrupt thread can only be preempted by another interrupt thread of higher priority.

Experience with Solaris interrupt threads indicates that this approach provides superior performance to the traditional interrupt-handling strategy [KLEI95].

4.6 LINUX PROCESS AND THREAD MANAGEMENT

Linux Tasks

A process, or task, in Linux is represented by a `task_struct` data structure. The `task_struct` data structure contains information in a number of categories:

- **State:** The execution state of the process (executing, ready, suspended, stopped, zombie). This is described subsequently.
- **Scheduling information:** Information needed by Linux to schedule processes. A process can be normal or real time and has a priority. Real-time processes are scheduled before normal processes, and within each category, relative priorities can be used. A counter keeps track of the amount of time a process is allowed to execute.
- **Identifiers:** Each process has a unique process identifier and also has user and group identifiers. A group identifier is used to assign resource access privileges to a group of processes.
- **Interprocess communication:** Linux supports the IPC mechanisms found in UNIX SVR4, described in Chapter 6.
- **Links:** Each process includes a link to its parent process, links to its siblings (processes with the same parent), and links to all of its children.
- **Times and timers:** Includes process creation time and the amount of processor time so far consumed by the process. A process may also have associated one or more interval timers. A process defines an interval timer by means of a system call; as a result a signal is sent to the process when the timer expires. A timer may be single use or periodic.
- **File system:** Includes pointers to any files opened by this process, as well as pointers to the current and the root directories for this process.
- **Address space:** Defines the virtual address space assigned to this process.
- **Processor-specific context:** The registers and stack information that constitute the context of this process.

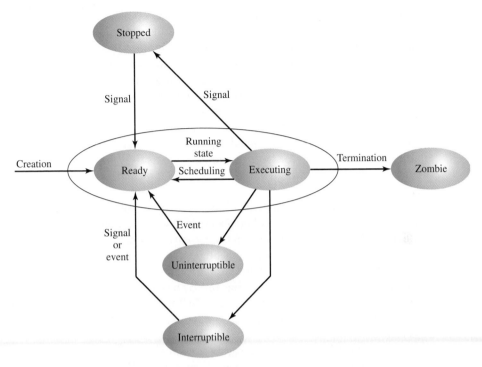

Figure 4.18   Linux Process/Thread Model

Figure 4.18 shows the execution states of a process. These are as follows:

- **Running:** This state value corresponds to two states. A Running process is either executing or it is ready to execute.
- **Interruptible:** This is a blocked state, in which the process is waiting for an event, such as the end of an I/O operation, the availability of a resource, or a signal from another process.
- **Uninterruptible:** This is another blocked state. The difference between this and the Interruptible state is that in an uninterruptible state, a process is waiting directly on hardware conditions and therefore will not handle any signals.
- **Stopped:** The process has been halted and can only resume by positive action from another process. For example, a process that is being debugged can be put into the Stopped state.
- **Zombie:** The process has been terminated but, for some reason, still must have its task structure in the process table.

Linux Threads

Traditional UNIX systems support a single thread of execution per process, while modern UNIX systems typically provide support for multiple kernel-level threads per process. As with traditional UNIX systems, older versions of the Linux kernel offered no support for multithreading. Instead, applications would need to be written with a set of user-level library functions, the most popular of which is known as *pthread (POSIX thread) libraries*, with all of the threads mapping into a single kernel-level process. We have seen that modern versions of UNIX offer kernel-level threads. Linux provides a unique solution in that it does not recognize a distinction between threads and processes. Using a mechanism similar to the lightweight processes of Solaris, user-level threads are mapped into kernel-level processes. Multiple user-level threads that constitute a single user-level process are mapped into Linux kernel-level processes that share the same group ID. This enables these processes to share resources such as files and memory and to avoid the need for a context switch when the scheduler switches among processes in the same group.

A new process is created in Linux by copying the attributes of the current process. A new process can be *cloned* so that it shares resources, such as files, signal handlers, and virtual memory. When the two processes share the same virtual memory, they function as threads within a single process. However, no separate type of data structure is defined for a thread. In place of the usual **fork()** command, processes are created in Linux using the **clone()** command. This command includes a set of flags as arguments, defined in Table 4.5. The traditional **fork()** system call is implemented by Linux as a **clone()** system call with all of the clone flags cleared.

When the Linux kernel performs a switch from one process to another, it checks whether the address of the page directory of the current process is the same as that of the to-be-scheduled process. If they are, then they are sharing the same address space, so that a context switch is basically just a jump from one location of code to another location of code.

Although cloned processes that are part of the same process group can share the same memory space, they cannot share the same user stacks. Thus the **clone()** call creates separate stack spaces for each process.

4.7 SUMMARY

Some operating systems distinguish the concepts of process and thread, the former related to resource ownership and the latter related to program execution. This approach may lead to improved efficiency and coding convenience. In a multithreaded system, multiple concurrent threads may be defined within a single process. This may be done using either user-level threads or kernel-level threads. User-level threads are unknown to the operating system and are created and managed by a threads library that runs in the user space of a process. User-level threads are very efficient because a mode switch is not required to switch from one thread to another. However, only a single user-level thread within a process can execute at a time, and if one thread blocks, the entire process is blocked. Kernel-level threads are threads within a process that are maintained by the kernel. Because they are recognized by the kernel, multiple threads within the same process can execute in parallel on a multiprocessor and the blocking of a thread does not block the entire process. However, a mode switch is required to switch from one thread to another.

Table 4.5   Linux clone () flags

CLONE_CLEARID	Clear the task ID.
CLONE_DETACHED	The parent does not want a SIGCHLD signal sent on exit.
CLONE_FILES	Shares the table that identifies the open files.
CLONE_FS	Shares the table that identifies the root directory and the current working directory, as well as the value of the bit mask used to mask the initial file permissions of a new file.
CLONE_IDLETASK	Set PID to zero, which refers to an idle task. The idle task is employed when all available tasks are blocked waiting for resources.
CLONE_NEWNS	Create a new namespace for the child.
CLONE_PARENT	Caller and new task share the same parent process.
CLONE_PTRACE	If the parent process is being traced, the child process will also be traced.
CLONE_SETTID	Write the TID back to user space.
CLONE_SETTLS	Create a new TLS for the child.
CLONE_SIGHAND	Shares the table that identifies the signal handlers.
CLONE_SYSVSEM	Shares System V SEM_UNDO semantics.
CLONE_THREAD	Inserts this process into the same thread group of the parent. If this flag is true, it implicitly enforces CLONE_PARENT.
CLONE_VFORK	If set, the parent does not get scheduled for execution until the child invokes the *execve()* system call.
CLONE_VM	Shares the address space (memory descriptor and all page tables).

Symmetric multiprocessing is a method of organizing a multiprocessor system such that any process (or thread) can run on any processor; this includes kernel code and processes. An SMP architecture raises new operating system design issues and provides greater performance than a uniprocessor system under similar conditions.

In recent years, there has been much interest in the microkernel approach to operating system design. In its pure form, a microkernel operating system consists of a very small microkernel that runs in kernel mode and that contains only the most essential and critical operating system functions. Other operating system functions are implemented to execute in user mode and to use the microkernel for critical services. The microkernel design leads to a flexible and highly modular implementation. However, questions remain about the performance of such an architecture.

4.8 RECOMMENDED READINGS

[LEWI96] and [KLEI96] provide good overviews of thread concepts and a discussion of programming strategies; the former focuses more on concepts and the latter more on programming, but both provide useful coverage of both topics. [PHAM96] discusses the Windows NT thread facility in depth. Good coverage of UNIX threads concepts is found in [ROBB04].

[MUKH96] provides a good discussion of operating system design issues for SMPs. [CHAP97] contains five articles on recent design directions for multiprocessor operating systems. Worthwhile discussions of the principles of microkernel design are contained in [LIED95] and [LIED96]; the latter focuses on performance issues.

CHAP97 Chapin, S., and Maccabe, A., eds. "Multiprocessor Operating Systems: Harnessing the Power." Special issue of *IEEE Concurrency*, April–June 1997.

KLEI96 Kleiman, S.; Shah, D.; and Smallders, B. *Programming with Threads.* Upper Saddle River, NJ: Prentice Hall, 1996.

LEWI96 Lewis, B., and Berg, D. *Threads Primer.* Upper Saddle River, NJ: Prentice Hall, 1996.

LIED95 Liedtke, J. "On μ-Kernel Construction." *Proceedings of the Fifteenth ACM Symposium on Operating Systems Principles*, December 1995.

LIED96 Liedtke, J. "Toward Real Microkernels." *Communications of the ACM*, September 1996.

MUKH96 Mukherjee, B., and Karsten, S. "Operating Systems for Parallel Machines." in *Parallel Computers: Theory and Practice.* Edited by T. Casavant, P. Tvrkik, and F. Plasil. Los Alamitos, CA: IEEE Computer Society Press, 1996.

PHAM96 Pham, T., and Garg, P. *Multithreaded Programming with Windows NT.* Upper Saddle River, NJ: Prentice Hall, 1996.

ROBB04 Robbins, K., and Robbins, S. *UNIX Systems Programming: Communication, Concurrency, and Threads.* Upper Saddle River, NJ: Prentice Hall, 2004.

4.9 KEY TERMS, REVIEW QUESTIONS, AND PROBLEMS

Key Terms

kernel-level thread (KLT)	multithreading	task
lightweight process	port	thread
message	process	user-level thread (ULT)
microkernel	symmetric multiprocessor	
monolithic operating system	(SMP)	

Review Questions

4.1 Table 3.5 lists typical elements found in a process control block for an unthreaded operating system. Of these, which should belong to a thread control block and which should belong to a process control block for a multithreaded system?

4.2 List reasons why a mode switch between threads may be cheaper than a mode switch between processes.

4.3 What are the two separate and potentially independent characteristics embodied in the concept of process?

4.4 Give four general examples of the use of threads in a single-user multiprocessing system.

4.5 What resources are typically shared by all of the threads of a process?

4.6 List three advantages of ULTs over KLTs.

4.7 List two disadvantages of ULTs compared to KLTs.

4.8 Define jacketing.

4.9 Briefly define the various architectures named in Figure 4.8.

4.10 List the key design issues for an SMP operating system.

4.11 Give examples of services and functions found in a typical monolithic operating system that may be external subsystems to a microkernel operating system.

4.12 List and briefly explain seven potential advantages of a microkernel design compared to a monolithic design.

4.13 Explain the potential performance disadvantage of a microkernel operating system.

4.14 List three functions you would expect to find even in a minimal microkernel operating system.

4.15 What is the basic form of communications between processes or threads in a microkernel operating system?

Problems

4.1 It was pointed out that two advantages of using multiple threads within a process are that (1) less work is involved in creating a new thread within an existing process than in creating a new process, and (2) communication among threads within the same process is simplified. Is it also the case that a mode switch between two threads within the same process involves less work than a mode switch between two threads in different processes?

4.2 In the discussion of ULTs versus KLTs, it was pointed out that a disadvantage of ULTs is that when a ULT executes a system call, not only is that thread blocked, but also all of the threads within the process are blocked. Why is that so?

4.3 In OS/2, what is commonly embodied in the concept of process in other operating systems is split into three separate types of entities: session, processes, and threads. A session is a collection of one or more processes associated with a user interface (keyboard, display, mouse). The session represents an interactive user application, such as a word processing program or a spreadsheet. This concept allows the personal-computer user to open more than one application, giving each one or more windows on the screen. The operating system must keep track of which window, and therefore which session, is active, so that keyboard and mouse input are routed to the appropriate session. At any time, one session is in foreground mode, with other sessions in background mode. All keyboard and mouse input is directed to one of the processes of the foreground session, as dictated by the applications. When a session is in foreground mode, a process performing video output sends it directly to the hardware video buffer and thence to the user's screen. When the session is moved to the background, the hardware video buffer is saved to a logical video buffer for that session. While a session is in background, if any of the threads of any of the processes of that session executes and produces screen output, that output is directed to the logical video buffer. When the session returns to foreground, the screen is updated to reflect the current contents of the logical video buffer for the new foreground session.

There is a way to reduce the number of process-related concepts in OS/2 from three to two. Eliminate sessions, and associate the user interface (keyboard, mouse, screen) with processes. Thus one process at a time is in foreground mode. For further structuring, processes can be broken up into threads.

a. What benefits are lost with this approach?

b. If you go ahead with this modification, where do you assign resources (memory, files, etc.): at the process or thread level?

4.4 Consider an environment in which there is a one-to-one mapping between user-level threads and kernel-level threads that allows one or more threads within a process to issue blocking system calls while other threads continue to run. Explain why this model can make multithreaded programs run faster than their single-threaded counterparts on a uniprocessor machine.

4.5   If a process exits and there are still threads of that process running, will they continue to run?

4.6   The OS/390 mainframe operating system is structured around the concepts of address space and task. Roughly speaking, a single address space corresponds to a single application and corresponds more or less to a process in other operating systems. Within an address space, a number of tasks may be generated and execute concurrently; this corresponds roughly to the concept of multithreading. Two data structures are key to managing this task structure. An address space control block (ASCB) contains information about an address space needed by OS/390 whether or not that address space is executing. Information in the ASCB includes dispatching priority, real and virtual memory allocated to this address space, the number of ready tasks in this address space, and whether each is swapped out. A task control block (TCB) represents a user program in execution. It contains information needed for managing a task within an address space, including processor status information, pointers to programs that are part of this task, and task execution state. ASCBs are global structures maintained in system memory, while TCBs are local structures maintained within their address space. What is the advantage of splitting the control information into global and local portions?

4.7   A multiprocessor with eight processors has 20 attached tape drives. There is a large number of jobs submitted to the system that each require a maximum of four tape drives to complete execution. Assume that each job starts running with only three tape drives for a long period before requiring the fourth tape drive for a short period toward the end of its operation. Also assume an endless supply of such jobs.

    a.   Assume the scheduler in the OS will not start a job unless there are four tape drives available. When a job is started, four drives are assigned immediately and are not released until the job finishes. What is the maximum number of jobs that can be in progress at once? What is the maximum and minimum number of tape drives that may be left idle as a result of this policy?

    b.   Suggest an alternative policy to improve tape drive utilization and at the same time avoid system deadlock. What is the maximum number of jobs that can be in progress at once? What are the bounds on the number of idling tape drives?

4.8   In the description of Solaris ULT states, it was stated that a ULT may yield to another thread of the same priority. Isn't it possible that there will be a runnable thread of higher priority and that therefore the yield function should result in yielding to a thread of the same or higher priority?

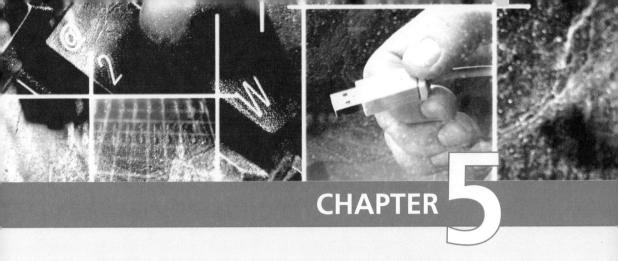

CHAPTER 5

CONCURRENCY: MUTUAL EXCLUSION AND SYNCHRONIZATION

The central themes of operating system design are all concerned with the management of processes and threads:

- **Multiprogramming:** The management of multiple processes within a uniprocessor system.
- **Multiprocessing:** The management of multiple processes within a multiprocessor.
- **Distributed processing:** The management of multiple processes executing on multiple, distributed computer systems. The recent proliferation of clusters is a prime example of this type of system.

Fundamental to all of these areas, and fundamental to operating system design, is concurrency. Concurrency encompasses a host of design issues, including communication among processes, sharing of and competing for resources, synchronization of the activities of multiple processes, and allocation of processor time to processes. We shall see that these issues arise not just in multiprocessing and distributed processing environments but even in single-processor multiprogramming systems.

Concurrency arises in three different contexts:

- **Multiple applications:** Multiprogramming was invented to allow processing time to be dynamically shared among a number of active applications.
- **Structured applications:** As an extension of the principles of modular design and structured programming, some applications can be effectively programmed as a set of concurrent processes.
- **Operating system structure:** The same structuring advantages apply to the systems programmer, and we have seen that operating systems are themselves often implemented as a set of processes or threads.

Because of the importance of this topic, four chapters of this book focus on concurrency-related issues. This chapter and the next deal with concurrency in multiprogramming and multiprocessing systems. Chapters 13 and 14 examine concurrency issues related to distributed processing. Although the remainder of this book covers a number of other important topics in operating system design, concurrency will play a major role in our consideration of all of these other topics.

This chapter begins with an introduction to the concept of concurrency and the implications of the execution of multiple concurrent processes.[1] We find that the basic requirement for support of concurrent processes is the ability to enforce mutual exclusion; that is, the ability to exclude all other processes from a course of action while one process is granted that ability. Next, we examine some hardware mechanisms that can support mutual exclusion. Then we look at solutions that do not involve busy waiting and that can be supported either by the operating system or enforced by language compilers. We examine three approaches: semaphores, monitors, and message passing.

Two classic problems in concurrency are used to illustrate the concepts and compare the approaches presented in this chapter. The producer/consumer problem is introduced early on and is used as a running example. The chapter closes with the readers/writers problem.

---

[1]For simplicity, we generally refer to the concurrent execution of *processes*. In fact, as we have seen in the preceding chapter, in some systems the fundamental unit of concurrency is a thread rather than a process.

Table 5.1   Some Key Terms Related to Concurrency

critical section	A section of code within a process that requires access to shared resources and that may not be executed while another process is in a corresponding section of code.
deadlock	A situation in which two or more processes are unable to proceed because each is waiting for one of the others to do something.
livelock	A situation in which two or more processes continuously change their state in response to changes in the other process(es) without doing any useful work.
mutual exclusion	The requirement that when one process is in a critical section that accesses shared resources, no other process may be in a critical section that accesses any of those shared resources.
race condition	A situation in which multiple threads or processes read and write a shared data item and the final result depends on the relative timing of their execution.
starvation	A situation in which a runnable process is overlooked indefinitely by the scheduler; although it is able to proceed, it is never chosen.

Our discussion of concurrency continues in Chapter 6, and we defer a discussion of the concurrency mechanisms of our example systems until the end of that chapter. Table 5.1 lists some key terms related to concurrency.

5.1 PRINCIPLES OF CONCURRENCY

In a single-processor multiprogramming system, processes are interleaved in time to yield the appearance of simultaneous execution (Figure 2.12a). Even though actual parallel processing is not achieved, and even though there is a certain amount of overhead involved in switching back and forth between processes, interleaved execution provides major benefits in processing efficiency and in program structuring. In a multiple-processor system, it is possible not only to interleave the execution of multiple processes but also to overlap them (Figure 2.12b).

At first glance, it may seem that interleaving and overlapping represent fundamentally different modes of execution and present different problems. In fact, both techniques can be viewed as examples of concurrent processing, and both present the same problems. In the case of a uniprocessor, the problems stem from a basic characteristic of multiprogramming systems: The relative speed of execution of processes cannot be predicted. It depends on the activities of other processes, the way in which the operating system handles interrupts, and the scheduling policies of the operating system. The following difficulties arise:

1. The sharing of global resources is fraught with peril. For example, if two processes both make use of the same global variable and both perform reads and writes on that variable, then the order in which the various reads and writes are executed is critical. An example of this problem is shown in the following subsection.

2. It is difficult for the operating system to manage the allocation of resources optimally. For example, process A may request use of, and be granted control of, a particular I/O channel and then be suspended before using that channel. It may be undesirable for the operating system simply to lock the channel and prevent

its use by other processes; indeed this may lead to a deadlock condition, as described in Chapter 6.

3. It becomes very difficult to locate a programming error because results are typically not deterministic and reproducible (e.g., see [LEBL87, CARR89, SHEN02] for a discussion of this point).

All of the foregoing difficulties present themselves in a multiprocessor system as well, because here too the relative speed of execution of processes is unpredictable. A multiprocessor system must also deal with problems arising from the simultaneous execution of multiple processes. Fundamentally, however, the problems are the same as those for uniprocessor systems. This should become clear as the discussion proceeds.

A Simple Example

Consider the following procedure:

```
void echo()
{
        chin = getchar();
        chout = chin;
        putchar(chout);
}
```

This procedure shows the essential elements of a program that will provide a character echo procedure; input is obtained from a keyboard one keystroke at a time. Each input character is stored in variable **chin**. It is then transferred to variable **chout** and sent to the display. Any program can call this procedure repeatedly to accept user input and display it on the user's screen.

Now consider that we have a single-processor multiprogramming system supporting a single user. The user can jump from one application to another, and each application uses the same keyboard for input and the same screen for output. Because each application needs to use the procedure **echo**, it makes sense for it to be a shared procedure that is loaded into a portion of memory global to all applications. Thus, only a single copy of the **echo** procedure is used, saving space.

The sharing of main memory among processes is useful to permit efficient and close interaction among processes. However, such sharing can lead to problems. Consider the following sequence:

1. Process P1 invokes the **echo** procedure and is interrupted immediately after **getchar** returns its value and stores it in **chin**. At this point, the most recently entered character, x, is stored in variable **chin**.

2. Process P2 is activated and invokes the **echo** procedure, which runs to conclusion, inputting and then displaying a single character, y, on the screen.

3. Process P1 is resumed. By this time, the value x has been overwritten in **chin** and therefore lost. Instead, **chin** contains y, which is transferred to **chout** and displayed.

Thus, the first character is lost and the second character is displayed twice. The essence of this problem is the shared global variable, `chin`. Multiple processes have access to this variable. If one process updates the global variable and then is interrupted, another process may alter the variable before the first process can use its value. Suppose, however, that we say that only one process at a time may be in that procedure. Then the foregoing sequence would result in the following:

1. Process P1 invokes the `echo` procedure and is interrupted immediately after the conclusion of the input function. At this point, the most recently entered character, x, is stored in variable `chin`.

2. Process P2 is activated and invokes the `echo` procedure. However, because P1 is still inside the `echo` procedure, although currently suspended, P2 is blocked from entering the procedure. Therefore, P2 is suspended awaiting the availability of the `echo` procedure.

3. At some later time, process P1 is resumed and completes execution of `echo`. The proper character, x, is displayed.

4. When P1 exits `echo`, this removes the block on P2. When P2 is later resumed, the `echo` procedure is successfully invoked.

The lesson to be learned from this example is that it is necessary to protect shared global variables (and other shared global resources) and that the only way to do that is to control the code that accesses the variable. If we impose the discipline that only one process at a time may enter `echo` and that once in `echo` the procedure must run to completion before it is available for another process, then the type of error just discussed will not occur. How that discipline may be imposed is a major topic of this chapter.

This problem was stated with the assumption that there was a single-processor, multiprogramming operating system. The example demonstrates that the problems of concurrency occur even when there is a single processor. In a multiprocessor system, the same problems of protected shared resources arise, and the same solutions work. First, suppose that there is no mechanism for controlling access to the shared global variable:

1. Processes P1 and P2 are both executing, each on a separate processor. Both processes invoke the `echo` procedure.

2. The following events occur; events on the same line take place in parallel:

Process P1	**Process P2**
•	•
chin = getchar();	•
•	chin = getchar();
chout = chin;	chout = chin;
putchar(chout);	•
•	putchar(chout);
•	•

The result is that the character input to P1 is lost before being displayed, and the character input to P2 is displayed by both P1 and P2. Again, let us add the capability of enforcing the discipline that only one process at a time may be in echo. Then the following sequence occurs:

1. Processes P1 and P2 are both executing, each on a separate processor. P1 invokes the **echo** procedure.

2. While P1 is inside the **echo** procedure, P2 invokes **echo**. Because P1 is still inside the **echo** procedure (whether P1 is suspended or executing), P2 is blocked from entering the procedure. Therefore, P2 is suspended awaiting the availability of the **echo** procedure.

3. At a later time, process P1 completes execution of **echo**, exits that procedure, and continues executing. Immediately upon the exit of P1 from **echo**, P2 is resumed and begins executing **echo**.

In the case of a uniprocessor system, the reason we have a problem is that an interrupt can stop instruction execution anywhere in a process. In the case of a multiprocessor system, we have that same condition and, in addition, a problem can be caused because two processes may be executing simultaneously and both trying to access the same global variable. However, the solution to both types of problem is the same: control access to the shared resource.

Race Condition

A race condition occurs when multiple processes or threads read and write data items so that the final result depends on the order of execution of instructions in the multiple processes. Let us consider two simple examples.

As a first example, suppose that two processes, P1 and P2, share the global variable **a**. At some point in its execution, P1 updates **a** to the value 1, and at some point in its execution, P2 updates **a** to the value 2. Thus, the two tasks are in a race to write variable **a**. In this example the "loser" of the race (the process that updates last) determines the final value of **a**.

For our second example, consider two process, P3 and P4, that share global variables **b** and **c**, with initial values **b** = 1 and **c** = 2. At some point in its execution, P3 executes the assignment **b** = **b** + **c**, and at some point in its execution, P4 executes the assignment **c** = **b** + **c**. Note that the two processes update different variables. However, the final values of the two variables depend on the order in which the two processes execute these two assignments. If P3 executes its assignment statement first, then the final values are **b** = 3 and **c** = 5. If P4 executes its assignment statement first, then the final values are **b** = 4 and **c** = 3.

Appendix A includes a discussion of race conditions using semaphores as an example.

Operating System Concerns

What design and management issues are raised by the existence of concurrency? We can list the following concerns:

1. The operating system must be able to keep track of the various processes. This is done with the use of process control blocks and was described in Chapter 4.

2. The operating system must allocate and deallocate various resources for each active process. These resources include

   - **Processor time:** This is the scheduling function, discussed in Part Four.
   - **Memory:** Most operating systems use a virtual memory scheme. The topic is addressed in Part Three.
   - **Files:** Discussed in Chapter 12.
   - **I/O devices:** Discussed in Chapter 11.

3. The operating system must protect the data and physical resources of each process against unintended interference by other processes. This involves techniques that relate to memory, files, and I/O devices. A general treatment of protection is found in Chapter 15.

4. The functioning of a process, and the output it produces, must be independent of the speed at which its execution is carried out relative to the speed of other concurrent processes. This is the subject of this chapter.

To understand how the issue of speed independence can be addressed, we need to look at the ways in which processes can interact.

Process Interaction

We can classify the ways in which processes interact on the basis of the degree to which they are aware of each other's existence. Table 5.2 lists three possible degrees of awareness plus the consequences of each:

- **Processes unaware of each other:** These are independent processes that are not intended to work together. The best example of this situation is the multiprogramming of multiple independent processes. These can either be batch jobs or interactive sessions or a mixture. Although the processes are not working together, the operating system needs to be concerned about **competition** for resources. For example, two independent applications may both want to access the same disk or file or printer. The operating system must regulate these accesses.

- **Processes indirectly aware of each other:** These are processes that are not necessarily aware of each other by their respective process IDs but that share access to some object, such as an I/O buffer. Such processes exhibit **cooperation** in sharing the common object.

- **Processes directly aware of each other:** These are processes that are able to communicate with each other by process ID and that are designed to work jointly on some activity. Again, such processes exhibit **cooperation**.

Conditions will not always be as clear-cut as suggested in Table 5.2. Rather, several processes may exhibit aspects of both competition and cooperation. Nevertheless, it is productive to examine each of the three items in the preceding list separately and determine their implications for the operating system.

Competition among Processes for Resources Concurrent processes come into conflict with each other when they are competing for the use of the same resource. In its pure form, we can describe the situation as follows. Two or more

Table 5.2 Process Interaction

Degree of Awareness	Relationship	Influence that one Process Has on the Other	Potential Control Problems
Processes unaware of each other	Competition	• Results of one process independent of the action of others • Timing of process may be affected	• Mutual exclusion • Deadlock (renewable resource) • Starvation
Processes indirectly aware of each other (e.g., shared object)	Cooperation by sharing	• Results of one process may depend on information obtained from others • Timing of process may be affected	• Mutual exclusion • Deadlock (renewable resource) • Starvation • Data coherence
Processes directly aware of each other (have communication primitives available to them)	Cooperation by communication	• Results of one process may depend on information obtained from others • Timing of process may be affected	• Deadlock (consumable resource) • Starvation

processes need to access a resource during the course of their execution. Each process is unaware of the existence of the other processes, and each is to be unaffected by the execution of the other processes. It follows from this that each process should leave the state of any resource that it uses unaffected. Examples of resources include I/O devices, memory, processor time, and the clock.

There is no exchange of information between the competing processes. However, the execution of one process may affect the behavior of competing processes. In particular, if two processes both wish access to a single resource, then one process will be allocated that resource by the operating system, and the other will have to wait. Therefore, the process that is denied access will be slowed down. In an extreme case, the blocked process may never get access to the resource and hence will never terminate successfully.

In the case of competing processes three control problems must be faced. First is the need for **mutual exclusion**. Suppose two or more processes require access to a single nonsharable resource, such as a printer. During the course of execution, each process will be sending commands to the I/O device, receiving status information, sending data, and/or receiving data. We will refer to such a resource as a **critical resource**, and the portion of the program that uses it a **critical section** of the program. It is important that only one program at a time be allowed in its critical section. We cannot simply rely on the operating system to understand and enforce this restriction because the detailed requirements may not be obvious. In the case of the printer, for example, we want any individual process to have control of the printer while it prints an entire file. Otherwise, lines from competing processes will be interleaved.

The enforcement of mutual exclusion creates two additional control problems. One is that of **deadlock**. For example, consider two processes, P1 and P2, and two resources, R1 and R2. Suppose that each process needs access to both resources to perform part of its function. Then it is possible to have the following situation: the operating system assigns R1 to P2, and R2 to P1. Each process is waiting for one of the two resources. Neither will release the resource that it already owns until it has acquired the other resource and performed the function requiring both resources. The two processes are deadlocked.

A final control problem is **starvation**. Suppose that three processes (P1, P2, P3) each require periodic access to resource R. Consider the situation in which P1 is in possession of the resource, and both P2 and P3 are delayed, waiting for that resource. When P1 exits its critical section, either P2 or P3 should be allowed access to R. Assume that the operating system grants access to P3 and that P1 again requires access before completing its critical section. If the operating system grants access to P1 after P3 has finished, and subsequently alternately grants access to P1 and P3, then P2 may indefinitely be denied access to the resource, even though there is no deadlock situation.

Control of competition inevitably involves the operating system because it is the operating system that allocates resources. In addition, the processes themselves will need to be able to express the requirement for mutual exclusion in some fashion, such as locking a resource prior to its use. Any solution will involve some support from the operating system, such as the provision of the locking facility. Figure 5.1 illustrates the mutual exclusion mechanism in abstract terms. There are n processes to be executed concurrently. Each process includes (1) a critical section that operates on some resource Ra, and (2) additional code preceding and following the critical section that does not involve access to Ra. Because all processes access the same resource Ra, it is desired that only one process at a time be in its critical section. To enforce mutual exclusion, two functions are provided: **entercritical** and **exitcritical**. Each function takes as an argument the name of the resource that is the subject of

/* PROCESS 1 */	/* PROCESS 2 */	/* PROCESS n */
void P1	**void** P2	**void** Pn
{	{	{
while (true)	**while** (true)	**while** (true)
{	{	{
/* preceding code */;	/* preceding code */;	/* preceding code */;
entercritical (Ra);	entercritical (Ra);	entercritical (Ra);
/* critical section */;	/* critical section */;	/* critical section */;
exitcritical (Ra);	exitcritical (Ra);	exitcritical (Ra);
/* following code */;	/* following code */;	/* following code */;
}	}	}
}	}	}

Figure 5.1 Illustration of Mutual Exclusion

competition. Any process that attempts to enter its critical section while another process is in its critical section, for the same resource, is made to wait.

It remains to examine specific mechanisms for providing the functions `entercritical` and `exitcritical`. For the moment, we defer this issue while we consider the other cases of process interaction.

Cooperation among Processes by Sharing The case of cooperation by sharing covers processes that interact with other processes without being explicitly aware of them. For example, multiple processes may have access to shared variables or to shared files or databases. Processes may use and update the shared data without reference to other processes but know that other processes may have access to the same data. Thus the processes must cooperate to ensure that the data they share are properly managed. The control mechanisms must ensure the integrity of the shared data.

Because data are held on resources (devices, memory), the control problems of mutual exclusion, deadlock, and starvation are again present. The only difference is that data items may be accessed in two different modes, reading and writing, and only writing operations must be mutually exclusive.

However, over and above these problems, a new requirement is introduced: that of data coherence. As a simple example, consider a bookkeeping application in which various data items may be updated. Suppose two items of data a and b are to be maintained in the relationship $a = b$. That is, any program that updates one value must also update the other to maintain the relationship. Now consider the following two processes:

P1:
$$a = a + 1;$$
$$b = b + 1;$$

P2:
$$b = 2 * b;$$
$$a = 2 * a;$$

If the state is initially consistent, each process taken separately will leave the shared data in a consistent state. Now consider the following concurrent execution, in which the two processes respect mutual exclusion on each individual data item (a and b):

$$a = a + 1;$$
$$b = 2 * b;$$
$$b = b + 1;$$
$$a = 2 * a;$$

At the end of this execution sequence, the condition $a = b$ no longer holds. For example, if we start with $a = b = 1$, at the end of this execution sequence we have $a = 4$ and $b = 3$. The problem can be avoided by declaring the entire sequence in each process to be a critical section.

Thus we see that the concept of critical section is important in the case of cooperation by sharing. The same abstract functions of **entercritical** and **exitcritical** discussed earlier (Figure 5.1) can be used here. In this case, the argument for the functions could be a variable, a file, or any other shared object. Furthermore, if critical sections are used to provide data integrity, then there may be no specific resource or variable that can be identified as an argument. In that case, we can think of the argument as being an identifier that is shared among concurrent processes to identify critical sections that must be mutually exclusive.

Cooperation among Processes by Communication In the first two cases that we have discussed, each process has its own isolated environment that does not include the other processes. The interactions among processes are indirect. In both cases, there is a sharing. In the case of competition, they are sharing resources without being aware of the other processes. In the second case, they are sharing values, and although each process is not explicitly aware of the other processes, it is aware of the need to maintain data integrity. When processes cooperate by communication, however, the various processes participate in a common effort that links all of the processes. The communication provides a way to synchronize, or coordinate, the various activities.

Typically, communication can be characterized as consisting of messages of some sort. Primitives for sending and receiving messages may be provided as part of the programming language or provided by the system kernel of the operating system.

Because nothing is shared between processes in the act of passing messages, mutual exclusion is not a control requirement for this sort of cooperation. However, the problems of deadlock and starvation are present. As an example of deadlock, two processes may be blocked, each waiting for a communication from the other. As an example of starvation, consider three processes, P1, P2, and P3, that exhibit the following behavior. P1 is repeatedly attempting to communicate with either P2 or P3, and P2 and P3 are both attempting to communicate with P1. A sequence could arise in which P1 and P2 exchange information repeatedly, while P3 is blocked waiting for a communication from P1. There is no deadlock, because P1 remains active, but P3 is starved.

Requirements for Mutual Exclusion

Any facility or capability that is to provide support for mutual exclusion should meet the following requirements:

1. Mutual exclusion must be enforced: Only one process at a time is allowed into its critical section, among all processes that have critical sections for the same resource or shared object.

2. A process that halts in its noncritical section must do so without interfering with other processes.

3. It must not be possible for a process requiring access to a critical section to be delayed indefinitely: no deadlock or starvation.

4. When no process is in a critical section, any process that requests entry to its critical section must be permitted to enter without delay.

5. No assumptions are made about relative process speeds or number of processors.

6. A process remains inside its critical section for a finite time only.

There are a number of ways in which the requirements for mutual exclusion can be satisfied. One way is to leave the responsibility with the processes that wish to execute concurrently. Thus processes, whether they are system programs or application programs, would be required to coordinate with one another to enforce mutual exclusion, with no support from the programming language or the operating system. We can refer to these as software approaches. Although this approach is prone to high processing overhead and bugs, it is nevertheless useful to examine such approaches to gain a better understanding of the complexity of concurrent processing. This topic is covered in Appendix A. A second approach involves the use of special-purpose machine instructions. These have the advantage of reducing overhead but nevertheless will be shown to be unattractive as a general-purpose solution; they are covered in Section 5.2. A third approach is to provide some level of support within the operating system or a programming language. Three of the most important such approaches are examined in Sections 5.3 through 5.5.

5.2 MUTUAL EXCLUSION: HARDWARE SUPPORT

A number of software algorithms for enforcing mutual exclusion have been developed, of which the best known is Dekker's algorithm. The software approach is likely to have high processing overhead and the risk of logical errors is significant. However, a study of these algorithms illustrates many of the basic concepts and potential problems in developing concurrent programs. For the interested reader, Appendix A includes a discussion of software approaches. In this section, we look at several interesting hardware approaches to mutual exclusion.

Interrupt Disabling

In a uniprocessor machine, concurrent processes cannot be overlapped; they can only be interleaved. Furthermore, a process will continue to run until it invokes an operating system service or until it is interrupted. Therefore, to guarantee mutual exclusion, it is sufficient to prevent a process from being interrupted. This capability can be provided in the form of primitives defined by the system kernel for disabling and enabling interrupts. A process can then enforce mutual exclusion in the following way (compare Figure 5.1):

```
while (true)
{
        /* disable interrupts */;
        /* critical section */;
        /* enable interrupts */;
        /* remainder */;
}
```

Because the critical section cannot be interrupted, mutual exclusion is guaranteed. The price of this approach, however, is high. The efficiency of execution could be noticeably degraded because the processor is limited in its ability to interleave programs. A second problem is that this approach will not work in a multiprocessor architecture. When the computer system includes more than one processor, it is possible (and typical) for more than one process to be executing at a time. In this case, disabled interrupts do not guarantee mutual exclusion.

Special Machine Instructions

In a multiprocessor configuration, several processors share access to a common main memory. In this case, there is not a master/slave relationship; rather the processors behave independently in a peer relationship. There is no interrupt mechanism between processors on which mutual exclusion can be based.

At a hardware level, as was mentioned, access to a memory location excludes any other access to that same location. With this as a foundation, processor designers have proposed several machine instructions that carry out two actions atomically,[2] such as reading and writing or reading and testing, of a single memory location with one instruction fetch cycle. During execution of the instruction, access to the memory location is blocked for any other instruction referencing that location. Typically, these actions are performed in a single instruction cycle.

In this section, we look at two of the most commonly implemented instructions. Others are described in [RAYN86] and [STON93].

Test and Set Instruction The test and set instruction can be defined as follows:

```
boolean testset (int i)
{
    if (i == 0)
    {
        i = 1;
        return true;
    }
    else
    {
        return false;
    }
}
```

The instruction tests the value of its argument *i*. If the value is 0, then the instruction replaces the value by 1 and returns true. Otherwise, the value is not changed and false is returned. The entire `testset` function is carried out atomically; that is, it is not subject to interruption.

Figure 5.2a shows a mutual exclusion protocol based on the use of this instruction. The construct `parbegin` (P1, P2, . . . , P*n*) means the following: suspend the execution of the main program; initiate concurrent execution of procedures P1, P2, . . . , P*n*; when all of P1, P2, . . . , P*n* have terminated, resume the main program. A shared variable `bolt` is initialized to 0. The only process that may enter its critical section is one

---

[2]The term *atomic* means the instruction is treated as a single step that cannot be interrupted.

```
/* program mutualexclusion */                /* program mutualexclusion */
const int n = /* number of processes */;     int const n = /* number of processes**/;
int bolt;                                     int bolt;
void P(int i)                                 void P(int i)
{                                             {
    while (true)                                  int keyi = 1;
    {                                             while (true)
        while (!testset (bolt))                   {
            /* do nothing */;                         do exchange (keyi, bolt)
        /* critical section */;                       while (keyi != 0)
        bolt = 0;                                     /* critical section */;
        /* remainder */                               exchange (keyi, bolt);
    }                                                 /* remainder */
}                                                 }
void main()                                   }
{                                             void main()
    bolt = 0;                                 {
    parbegin (P(1), P(2), . . . ,P(n));           bolt = 0;
}                                                 parbegin (P(1), P(2), . . ., P(n));
                                              }
```

(a) Test and set instruction	**(b) Exchange instruction**

Figure 5.2 Hardware Support for Mutual Exclusion

that finds `bolt` equal to 0. All other processes attempting to enter their critical section go into a busy waiting mode. The term **busy waiting**, or **spin waiting**, refers to a technique in which a process can do nothing until it gets permission to enter its critical section but continues to execute an instruction or set of instructions that tests the appropriate variable to gain entrance. When a process leaves its critical section, it resets `bolt` to 0; at this point one and only one of the waiting processes is granted access to its critical section. The choice of process depends on which process happens to execute the `testset` instruction next.

Exchange Instruction The exchange instruction can be defined as follows:

```
void exchange (int register, int memory)
{
        int     temp;
        temp = memory;
        memory = register;
        register = temp;
}
```

The instruction exchanges the contents of a register with that of a memory location. Both the Intel IA-32 architecture (Pentium) and the IA-64 architecture (Itanium) contain an XCHG instruction.

Figure 5.2b shows a mutual exclusion protocol based on the use of an exchange instruction. A shared variable *bolt* is initialized to 0. Each process uses a local variable *key* that is initialized to 1. The only process that may enter its critical section is one that finds *bolt* equal to 0. It excludes all other processes from the critical section by setting *bolt* to 1. When a process leaves its critical section, it resets *bolt* to 0, allowing another process to gain access to its critical section.

Note that the following expression always holds because of the way in which the variables are initialized and because of the nature of the **exchange** algorithm:

$$bolt + \sum_i key_i = n$$

If *bolt* = 0, then no process is in its critical section. If *bolt* = 1, then exactly one process is in its critical section, namely the process whose *key* value equals 0.

Properties of the Machine-Instruction Approach The use of a special machine instruction to enforce mutual exclusion has a number of advantages:

- It is applicable to any number of processes on either a single processor or multiple processors sharing main memory.
- It is simple and therefore easy to verify.
- It can be used to support multiple critical sections; each critical section can be defined by its own variable.

There are some serious disadvantages:

- **Busy waiting is employed.** Thus, while a process is waiting for access to a critical section, it continues to consume processor time.
- **Starvation is possible.** When a process leaves a critical section and more than one process is waiting, the selection of a waiting process is arbitrary. Thus, some process could indefinitely be denied access.
- **Deadlock is possible.** Consider the following scenario on a single-processor system. Process P1 executes the special instruction (e.g., testset, exchange) and enters its critical section. P1 is then interrupted to give the processor to P2, which has higher priority. If P2 now attempts to use the same resource as P1, it will be denied access because of the mutual exclusion mechanism. Thus it will go into a busy waiting loop. However, P1 will never be dispatched because it is of lower priority than another ready process, P2.

Because of the drawbacks of both the software and hardware solutions just outlined, we need to look for other mechanisms.

5.3 SEMAPHORES

We now turn to operating system and programming language mechanisms that are used to provide concurrency. We begin, in this section, with semaphores. The next two sections discuss monitors and message passing.

The first major advance in dealing with the problems of concurrent processes came in 1965 with Dijkstra's treatise [DIJK65]. Dijkstra was concerned with the design of an operating system as a collection of cooperating sequential processes and with the development of efficient and reliable mechanisms for supporting cooperation. These mechanisms can just as readily be used by user processes if the processor and operating system make the mechanisms available.

The fundamental principle is this: Two or more processes can cooperate by means of simple signals, such that a process can be forced to stop at a specified place until it has received a specific signal. Any complex coordination requirement can be satisfied by the appropriate structure of signals. For signaling, special variables called semaphores are used. To transmit a signal via semaphore **s**, a process executes the primitive **semSignal(s)**. To receive a signal via semaphore **s**, a process executes the primitive **semWait(s)**; if the corresponding signal has not yet been transmitted, the process is suspended until the transmission takes place.[3]

To achieve the desired effect, we can view the semaphore as a variable that has an integer value upon which only three operations are defined:

1. A semaphore may be initialized to a nonnegative value.
2. The **semWait** operation decrements the semaphore value. If the value becomes negative, then the process executing the **semWait** is blocked. Otherwise, the process continues execution.
3. The **semSignal** operation increments the semaphore value. If the value is less than or equal to zero, then a process blocked by a **semWait** operation is unblocked.

Other than these three operations, there is no way to inspect or manipulate semaphores. Figure 5.3 suggests a more formal definition of the primitives for semaphores. The **semWait** and **semSignal** primitives are assumed to be atomic. A more restricted version, known as the **binary semaphore** or **mutex**, is defined in Figure 5.4. A binary semaphore may only take on the values 0 and 1 and can be defined by the following three operations:

1. A binary semaphore may be initialized to 0 or 1.
2. The **semWaitB** operation checks the semaphore value. If the value is zero, then the process executing the **semWaitB** is blocked. If the value is one, then the value is changed to zero and the process continues execution.
3. The **semSignalB** operation checks to see if any processes are blocked on this semaphore. If so, then a process blocked by a **semWaitB** operation is unblocked. If no processes are blocked, then the value of the semaphore is set to one.

In principle, it should be easier to implement the binary semaphore, and it can be shown that it has the same expressive power as the general semaphore (see Problem 5.9). To contrast the two types of semaphores, the non-binary semaphore is often referred to as either a **counting semaphore** or a **general semaphore**.

For both counting semaphores and binary semaphores, a queue is used to hold processes waiting on the semaphore. The question arises of the order in which

---

[3]In Dijkstra's original paper and in much of the literature, the letter **P** is used for **semWait** and the letter **V** for **semSignal**; these are the initials of the Dutch words for test (*proberen*) and increment (*verhogen*). In some of the literature, the terms **wait** and **signal** are used. This book uses **semWait** and **semSignal** for clarity, and to avoid confusion with similar wait and signal operations in monitors, discussed subsequently.

```
struct semaphore {
    int count;
    queueType queue;
}
void semWait(semaphore s)
{
    s.count−−;
    if (s.count < 0)
    {
        place this process in s.queue;
        block this process
    }
}
void semSignal(semaphore s)
{
    s.count++;
    if (s.count <= 0)
    {
        remove a process P from s.queue;
        place process P on ready list;
    }
}
```

Figure 5.3   A Definition of Semaphore Primitives

```
struct binary_semaphore {
    enum {zero, one} value;
    queueType queue;
};
void semWaitB(binary_semaphore s)
{
    if (s.value ==  1)
        s.value = 0;
    else
        {
            place this process in s.queue;
            block this process;
        }
}
void semSignalB(semaphore s)
{
    if (s.queue is empty())
        s.value = 1;
    else
    {
        remove a process P from s.queue;
        place process P on ready list;
    }
}
```

Figure 5.4   A Definition of Binary Semaphore Primitives

processes are removed from such a queue. The fairest policy is first-in-first-out (FIFO): The process that has been blocked the longest is released from the queue first; a semaphore whose definition includes this policy is called a **strong semaphore**. A semaphore that does not specify the order in which processes are removed from the queue is a **weak semaphore**. Figure 5.5, based on one in [DENN84], is an example of the operation of a strong semaphore. Here processes A, B, and C depend on a result from process D. Initially (1), A is running; B, C, and D are ready; and the semaphore count is 1, indicating that one of D's results is available. When A issues a `semWait` instruction on semaphore s, the semaphore decrements to 0, and A and can continue to execute; subsequently it rejoins the ready queue. Then B runs (2), eventually issues a `semWait` instruction, and is blocked, allowing D to run (3). When D completes a new result, it issues a `semSignal` instruction, which allows B to move to the ready queue (4). D rejoins the ready queue and C begins to run (5) but is blocked when it issues a `semWait` instruction. Similarly, A and B run and are blocked on the semaphore, allowing D to resume execution (6). When D has a result, it issues a `semSignal`, which transfers C to the ready queue. Later cycles of D will release A and B from the Blocked state.

For the mutual exclusion algorithm discussed in the next subsection and illustrated in Figure 5.6, strong semaphores guarantee freedom from starvation, while weak semaphores do not. We will assume strong semaphores because they are more convenient and because this is the form of semaphore typically provided by operating systems.

Mutual Exclusion

Figure 5.6 shows a straightforward solution to the mutual exclusion problem using a semaphore s (compare Figure 5.1). Consider n processes, identified in the array $P(i)$, all of which need access to the same resource. Each process has a critical section used to access the resource. In each process, a semWait(s) is executed just before entering its critical section. If the value of s becomes negative, the process is blocked. If the value is 1, then it is decremented to 0 and the process immediately enters its critical section; because s is no longer positive, no other process will be able to enter its critical section.

The semaphore is initialized to 1. Thus, the first process that executes a `semWait` will be able to enter the critical section immediately, setting the value of s to 0. Any other process attempting to enter the critical section will find it busy and will be blocked, setting the value of s to -1. Any number of processes may attempt entry; each such unsuccessful attempt results in a further decrement of the value of s. When the process that initially entered its critical section departs, s is incremented and one of the blocked processes (if any) is removed from the queue of blocked processes associated with the semaphore and put in the Ready state. When it is next scheduled by the operating system, it may enter the critical section.

Figure 5.7, based on one in [BACO03], shows a possible sequence for three processes using the mutual exclusion discipline of Figure 5.6. In this example three processes (A, B, C) access a shared resource protected by the semaphore *lock*. Process A executes `semWait(lock)`; because the semaphore has a value of 1 at the time of the `semWait` operation, A can immediately enter its critical section and the semaphore takes on the value 0. While A is in its critical section, both B and C perform a `semWait` operation and are blocked pending the availability of the semaphore. When

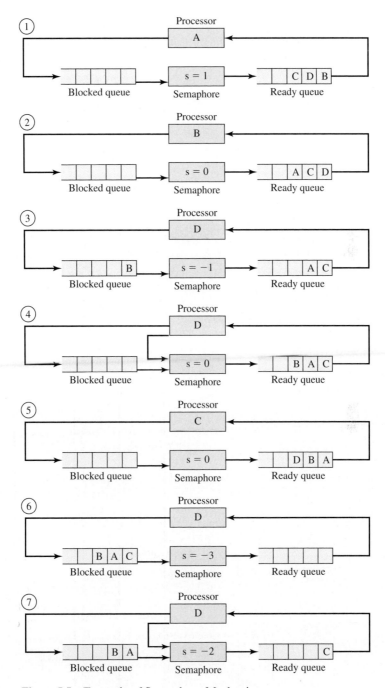

Figure 5.5   Example of Semaphore Mechanism

```
/* program mutualexclusion */
const int n = /* number of processes  */;
semaphore s = 1;
void P(int i)
{
    while (true)
    {
        semWait(s);
        /* critical section  */;
        semSignal(s);
        /* remainder  */;
    }
}
void main()
{
    parbegin (P(1), P(2), ..., P(n));
}
```

Figure 5.6   Mutual Exclusion Using Semaphores

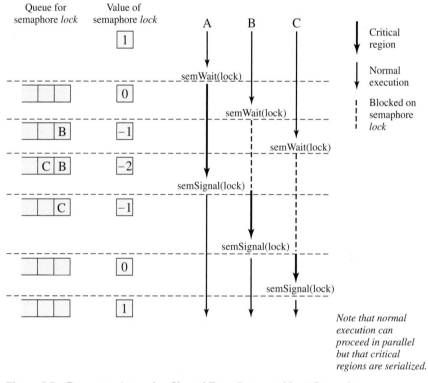

Figure 5.7   Processes Accessing Shared Data Protected by a Semaphore

A exits its critical section and performs **semSignal(lock)**, B, which was the first process in the queue, can now enter its critical section.

The program of Figure 5.6 can equally well handle a requirement that more than one process be allowed in its critical section at a time. This requirement is met simply by initializing the semaphore to the specified value. Thus, at any time, the value of *s.count* can be interpreted as follows:

- *s.count* ≥ 0: *s.count* is the number of processes that can execute **semWait(s)** without suspension (if no **semSignal(s)** is executed in the meantime). Such situations will allow semaphores to support synchronization as well as mutual exclusion.

- *s.count* < 0: the magnitude of *s.count* is the number of processes suspended in *s.queue*.

The Producer/Consumer Problem

We now examine one of the most common problems faced in concurrent processing: the producer/consumer problem. The general statement is this: There are one or more producers generating some type of data (records, characters) and placing these in a buffer. There is a single consumer that is taking items out of the buffer one at a time. The system is to be constrained to prevent the overlap of buffer operations. That is, only one agent (producer or consumer) may access the buffer at any one time. We will look at a number of solutions to this problem to illustrate both the power and the pitfalls of semaphores.

To begin, let us assume that the buffer is infinite and consists of a linear array of elements. In abstract terms, we can define the producer and consumer functions as follows:

```
producer:                      consumer:
while (true)                   while (true)
{                              {
    /* produce item v */;          while (in <= out)
    b[in] = v;                         /* do nothing */;
    in++;                          w = b[out];
}                                  out++;
                                   /* consume item w */

                               }
```

Figure 5.8 illustrates the structure of buffer **b**. The producer can generate items and store them in the buffer at its own pace. Each time, an index (*in*) into the buffer is incremented. The consumer proceeds in a similar fashion but must make sure that it does not attempt to read from an empty buffer. Hence, the consumer makes sure that the producer has advanced beyond it (*in* > *out*) before proceeding.

Let us try to implement this system using binary semaphores. Figure 5.9 is a first attempt. Rather than deal with the indices *in* and *out*, we can simply keep track of the number of items in the buffer, using the integer variable *n*(=*in* − *out*). The semaphore *s* is used to enforce mutual exclusion; the semaphore *delay* is used to force the consumer to **semWait** if the buffer is empty.

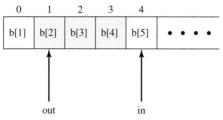

Figure 5.8   Infinite Buffer for the Producer/Consumer Problem

Note: Shaded area indicates portion of buffer that is occupied

```
/* program producerconsumer */
int n;
binary_semaphore s = 1;
binary_semaphore delay = 0;
void producer()
{
    while (true)
    {
        produce();
        semWaitB(s);
        append();
        n++;
        if (n==1)
            semSignalB(delay);
        semSignalB(s);
    }
}
void consumer()
{
    semWaitB(delay);
    while (true)
    {
        semWaitB(s);
        take();
        n--;
        semSignalB(s);
        consume();
        if (n==0)
            semWaitB(delay);
    }
}
void main()
{
    n = 0;
    parbegin (producer, consumer);
}
```

Figure 5.9   An Incorrect Solution to the Infinite-Buffer Producer/Consumer Problem Using Binary Semaphores

This solution seems rather straightforward. The producer is free to add to the buffer at any time. It performs **semWaitB(s)** before appending and **semSignalB(s)** afterward to prevent the consumer or any other producer from accessing the buffer during the append operation. Also, while in the critical section, the producer increments the value of n. If $n = 1$, then the buffer was empty just prior to this append, so the producer performs **semSignalB(*delay*)** to alert the consumer of this fact. The consumer begins by waiting for the first item to be produced, using **semWaitB(*delay*)**. It then takes an item and decrements n in its critical section. If the producer is able to stay ahead of the consumer (a common situation), then the consumer will rarely block on the semaphore *delay* because n will usually be positive. Hence both producer and consumer run smoothly.

There is, however, a flaw in this program. When the consumer has exhausted the buffer, it needs to reset the *delay* semaphore so that it will be forced to wait until the producer has placed more items in the buffer. This is the purpose of the statement: **if** n **== 0 semWaitB(*delay*)**. Consider the scenario outlined in Table 5.3. In line 14, the consumer fails to execute the **semWaitB** operation. The consumer did indeed exhaust the buffer and set n to 0 (line 8), but the producer has incremented n before the consumer can test it in line 14. The result is a **semSignalB** not matched by a prior **semWaitB**. The value of -1 for n in line 20 means that the consumer has consumed an item from the buffer that does not exist. It would not do simply to move the conditional statement inside the critical section of the consumer because this could lead to deadlock (e.g., after line 8 of the table).

A fix for the problem is to introduce an auxiliary variable that can be set in the consumer's critical section for use later on. This is shown in Figure 5.10. A careful trace of the logic should convince you that deadlock can no longer occur.

A somewhat cleaner solution can be obtained if general semaphores (also called counting semaphores) are used, as shown in Figure 5.11. The variable n is now a semaphore. Its value still is equal to the number of items in the buffer. Suppose now that in transcribing this program, a mistake is made and the operations **semSignal(s)** and **semSignal(n)** are interchanged. This would require that the **semSignal(n)** operation be performed in the producer's critical section without interruption by the consumer or another producer. Would this affect the program? No, because the consumer must wait on both semaphores before proceeding in any case.

Now suppose that the **semWait(n)** and **semWait(s)** operations are accidentally reversed. This produces a serious, indeed a fatal, flaw. If the consumer ever enters its critical section when the buffer is empty ($n.count = 0$), then no producer can ever append to the buffer and the system is deadlocked. This is a good example of the subtlety of semaphores and the difficulty of producing correct designs.

Finally, let us add a new and realistic restriction to the producer/consumer problem: namely, that the buffer is finite. The buffer is treated as a circular storage (Figure 5.12), and pointer values must be expressed modulo the size of the buffer. The following relationships hold:

Block on:	Unblock on:
Producer: insert in full buffer	Consumer: item inserted
Consumer: remove from empty buffer	Producer: item removed

Table 5.3   Possible Scenario for the Program of Figure 5.9

	Producer	Consumer	s	n	Delay
1			1	0	0
2	semWaitB(s)		0	0	0
3	n++		0	1	0
4	**if** (n==1) (semSignalB(delay))		0	1	1
5	semSignalB(s)		1	1	1
6		semWaitB(delay)	1	1	0
7		semWaitB(s)	0	1	0
8		n−−	0	0	0
9		semSignalB(s)	1	0	0
10	semWaitB(s)		0	0	0
11	n++		0	1	0
12	**if** (n==1) (semSignalB(delay))		0	1	1
13	semSignalB(s)		1	1	1
14		**if** (n==1) (semWaitB(delay))	1	1	1
15		semWaitB(s)	0	1	1
16		n−−	0	0	1
17		semSignalB(s)	1	0	1
18		**if** (n==1) (semWaitB(delay))	1	0	0
19		semWaitB(s)	0	0	0
20		n−−	0	−1	0
21		semSignalB(s)	1	−1	0

White areas represent the critical section controlled by semaphores.

The producer and consumer functions can be expressed as follows (variable *in* and *out* are initialized to 0):

```
producer:                      consumer:
while (true)                   while (true)
{                              {
    /* produce item v */           while (in == out)
    while ((in + 1) % n == out)    /* do nothing */;
        /* do nothing */;          w = b[out];
    b[in] = v;                     out = (out + 1) % n;
    in = (in + 1) % n;             /* consume item w */;
}                              }
```

Figure 5.13 shows a solution using general semaphores. The semaphore *e* has been added to keep track of the number of empty spaces.

```
/* program producerconsumer */
int n;
binary_semaphore s = 1;
binary_semaphore delay = 0;
void producer()
{
    while (true)
    {
        produce();
        semWaitB(s);
        append();
        n++;
        if (n==1) semSignalB(delay);
        semSignalB(s);
    }
}
void consumer()
{
    int m; /* a local variable */
    semWaitB(delay);
    while (true)
    {
        semWaitB(s);
        take();
        n    ;
        m = n;
        semSignalB(s);
        consume();
        if (m==0) semWaitB(delay);
    }
}
void main()
{
    n = 0;
    parbegin (producer, consumer);
}
```

Figure 5.10   A Correct Solution to the Infinite-Buffer Producer/
Consumer Problem Using Binary Semaphores

Another instructive example in the use of semaphores is the barbershop problem, described in Appendix A. Appendix A also includes additional examples of the problem of race conditions when using semaphores.

Implementation of Semaphores

As was mentioned earlier, it is imperative that the **semWait** and **semSignal** operations be implemented as atomic primitives. One obvious way is to implement them in hardware or firmware. Failing this, a variety of schemes have been suggested. The essence of the problem is one of mutual exclusion: Only one process at a time may manipulate a semaphore with either a **semWait** or **semSignal** operation. Thus, any of the software schemes, such as Dekker's algorithm or Peterson's

```
/* program  producerconsumer */
semaphore n = 0;
semaphore s = 1;
void producer()
{
    while (true)
    {
        produce();
        semWait(s);
        append();
        semSignal(s);
        semSignal(n);
    }
}
void consumer()
{
    while (true)
    {
        semWait(n);
        semWait(s);
        take();
        semSignal(s);
        consume();
    }
}
void main()
{
    parbegin (producer, consumer);
}
```

Figure 5.11 A Solution to the Infinite-Buffer Producer/Consumer Problem Using Semaphores

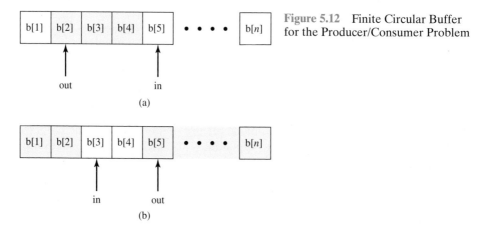

Figure 5.12 Finite Circular Buffer for the Producer/Consumer Problem

algorithm (Appendix A), could be used; this would entail a substantial processing overhead. Another alternative is to use one of the hardware-supported schemes for mutual exclusion. For example, Figure 5.14a shows the use of a test and set instruction. In this implementation, the semaphore is again a structure, as in Figure 5.3,

```
/* program boundedbuffer */
const int sizeofbuffer = /* buffer size */;
semaphore s = 1;
semaphore n= 0;
semaphore        e= sizeofbuffer;
void producer()
{
    while (true)
    {
        produce();
        semWait(e);
        semWait(s);
        append();
        semSignal(s);
        semSignal(n)
    }
}
void consumer()
{
    while (true)
    {
        semWait(n);
        semWait(s);
        take();
        semSignal(s);
        semSignal(e);
        consume();
    }
}
void main()
{
    parbegin (producer, consumer);
}
```

Figure 5.13   A Solution to the Bounded-Buffer Producer/Consumer Problem Using Semaphores

but now includes a new integer component, *s.flag*. Admittedly, this involves a form of busy waiting. However, the `semWait` and `semSignal` operations are relatively short, so the amount of busy waiting involved should be minor.

For a single-processor system, it is possible to inhibit interrupts for the duration of a `semWait` or `semSignal` operation, as suggested in Figure 5.14b. Once again, the relatively short duration of these operations means that this approach is reasonable.

5.4 MONITORS

Semaphores provide a primitive yet powerful and flexible tool for enforcing mutual exclusion and for coordinating processes. However, as Figure 5.9 suggests, it may be difficult to produce a correct program using semaphores. The difficulty is

```
semWait(s)
{
    while (!testset(s.flag))
        /* do nothing */;
    s.count--;
    if (s.count < 0)
    {
        place this process in s.queue;
        block this process (must also set s.flag to 0)
    }
    else
        s.flag = 0;
}
semSignal(s)
{
    while (!testset(s.flag))
        /* do nothing */;
    s.count++;
    if (s.count <= 0)
    {
        remove a process P from s.queue;
        place process P on ready list
    }
    s.flag = 0;
}
```

```
semWait(s)
{
    inhibit interrupts;
    s.count--;
    if (s.count < 0)
    {
        place this process in s.queue;
        block this process and allow interrupts
    }
    else
        allow interrupts;
}
semSignal(s)
{
    inhibit interrupts;
    s.count++;
    if (s.count <= 0)
    {
        remove a process P from s.queue;
        place process P on ready list
    }
    allow interrupts;
}
```

(a) Testset Instruction   **(b) Interrupts**

Figure 5.14   Two Possible Implementations of Semaphores

that **semWait** and **semSignal** operations may be scattered throughout a program and it is not easy to see the overall effect of these operations on the semaphores they affect.

The monitor is a programming-language construct that provides equivalent functionality to that of semaphores and that is easier to control. The concept was first formally defined in [HOAR74]. The monitor construct has been implemented in a number of programming languages, including Concurrent Pascal, Pascal-Plus, Modula-2, Modula-3, and Java. It has also been implemented as a program library. This allows programmers to put monitor locks on any object. In particular, for something like a linked list, you may want to lock all linked lists with one lock, or have one lock for each list, or have one lock for each element of each list.

We begin with a look at Hoare's version and then examine a refinement.

Monitor with Signal

A monitor is a software module consisting of one or more procedures, an initialization sequence, and local data. The chief characteristics of a monitor are the following:

1. The local data variables are accessible only by the monitor's procedures and not by any external procedure.

2. A process enters the monitor by invoking one of its procedures.

3. Only one process may be executing in the monitor at a time; any other process that has invoked the monitor is blocked, waiting for the monitor to become available.

The first two characteristics are reminiscent of those for objects in object-oriented software. Indeed, an object-oriented operating system or programming language can readily implement a monitor as an object with special characteristics.

By enforcing the discipline of one process at a time, the monitor is able to provide a mutual exclusion facility. The data variables in the monitor can be accessed by only one process at a time. Thus, a shared data structure can be protected by placing it in a monitor. If the data in a monitor represent some resource, then the monitor provides a mutual exclusion facility for accessing the resource.

To be useful for concurrent processing, the monitor must include synchronization tools. For example, suppose a process invokes the monitor and, while in the monitor, must be blocked until some condition is satisfied. A facility is needed by which the process is not only blocked but releases the monitor so that some other process may enter it. Later, when the condition is satisfied and the monitor is again available, the process needs to be resumed and allowed to reenter the monitor at the point of its suspension.

A monitor supports synchronization by the use of **condition variables** that are contained within the monitor and accessible only within the monitor. Condition variables are a special data type in monitors, which are operated on by two functions:

- **cwait(c)**: Suspend execution of the calling process on condition *c*. The monitor is now available for use by another process.
- **csignal(c)**: Resume execution of some process blocked after a **cwait** on the same condition. If there are several such processes, choose one of them; if there is no such process, do nothing.

Note that monitor *wait* and *signal* operations are different from those for the semaphore. If a process in a monitor signals and no task is waiting on the condition variable, the signal is lost.

Figure 5.15 illustrates the structure of a monitor. Although a process can enter the monitor by invoking any of its procedures, we can think of the monitor as having a single entry point that is guarded so that only one process may be in the monitor at a time. Other processes that attempt to enter the monitor join a queue of processes blocked waiting for monitor availability. Once a process is in the monitor, it may temporarily block itself on condition *x* by issuing **cwait(x)**; it is then placed in a queue of processes waiting to reenter the monitor when the condition changes, and resume execution at the point in its program following the **cwait(x)** call.

If a process that is executing in the monitor detects a change in condition variable **x**, it issues **csignal(x)**, which alerts the corresponding condition queue that the condition has changed.

As an example of the use of a monitor, let us return to the bounded-buffer producer/consumer problem. Figure 5.16 shows a solution using a monitor. The monitor module, **boundedbuffer**, controls the buffer used to store and retrieve characters. The monitor includes two condition variables (declared with the

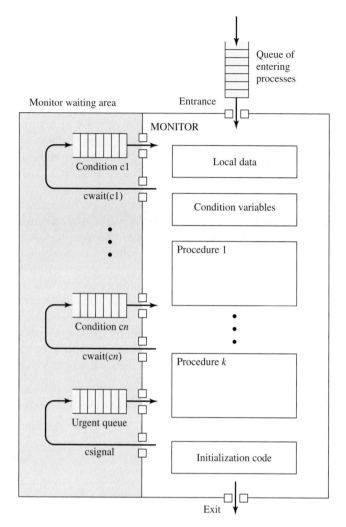

Figure 5.15 Structure of a Monitor

construct **cond**) : *notfull* is true when there is room to add at least one character to the buffer, and *notempty* is true when there is at least one character in the buffer.

A producer can add characters to the buffer only by means of the procedure **append** inside the monitor; the producer does not have direct access to *buffer*. The procedure first checks the condition *notfull* to determine if there is space available in the buffer. If not, the process executing the monitor is blocked on that condition. Some other process (producer or consumer) may now enter the monitor. Later, when the buffer is no longer full, the blocked process may be removed from the queue, reactivated, and resume processing. After placing a character in the buffer, the process signals the *notempty* condition. A similar description can be made of the consumer function.

This example points out the division of responsibility with monitors compared to semaphores. In the case of monitors, the monitor construct itself enforces mutual

```
/* program producerconsumer */
monitor boundedbuffer;
char buffer [N];                                                  /* space for N items */
int nextin, nextout;                                             /* buffer pointers */
int count;                                               /* number of items in buffer */
cond notfull, notempty;               /* condition variables for synchronization */

void append (char x)
{
    if (count == N)
        cwait(notfull);                          /* buffer is full; avoid overflow */
    buffer[nextin] = x;
    nextin = (nextin + 1) % N;
    count++;
    /* one more item in buffer */
    csignal(notempty);                         /* resume any waiting consumer */
}
void take (char x)
{
    if (count == 0)
        cwait(notempty);                       /* buffer is empty; avoid underflow */
    x = buffer[nextout];
    nextout = (nextout + 1) % N;
    count--;                                     /* one fewer item in buffer */
    csignal(notfull);                          /* resume any waiting producer */
}
{                                                          /* monitor body */
    nextin = 0; nextout = 0; count = 0;                 /* buffer initially empty */
}
```

```
void producer()
char x;
{
    while (true)
    {
    produce(x);
    append(x);
    }
}
void consumer()
{
    char x;
    while (true)
    {
        take(x);
        consume(x);
    }
}
void main()
{
    parbegin (producer, consumer);
}
```

Figure 5.16   A Solution to the Bounded-Buffer Producer/Consumer Problem Using a Monitor

exclusion: It is not possible for both a producer and a consumer simultaneously to access the buffer. However, the programmer must place the appropriate **cwait** and **csignal** primitives inside the monitor to prevent processes from depositing items in a full buffer or removing them from an empty one. In the case of semaphores, both mutual exclusion and synchronization are the responsibility of the programmer.

Note that in Figure 5.16, a process exits the monitor immediately after executing the **csignal** function. If the **csignal** does not occur at the end of the procedure, then, in Hoare's proposal, the process issuing the signal is blocked to make the monitor available and placed in a queue until the monitor is free. One possibility at this point would be to place the blocked process in the entrance queue, so that it would have to compete for access with other processes that had not yet entered the monitor. However, because a process blocked on a **csignal** function has already partially performed its task in the monitor, it makes sense to give this process precedence over newly entering processes by setting up a separate urgent queue (Figure 5.15). One language that uses monitors, Concurrent Pascal, requires that **csignal** only appear as the last operation executed by a monitor procedure.

If there are no processes waiting on condition x, then the execution of **csignal(x)** has no effect.

As with semaphores, it is possible to make mistakes in the synchronization function of monitors. For example, if either of the **csignal** functions in the **boundedbuffer** monitor are omitted, then processes entering the corresponding condition queue are permanently hung up. The advantage that monitors have over semaphores is that all of the synchronization functions are confined to the monitor. Therefore, it is easier to verify that the synchronization has been done correctly and to detect bugs. Furthermore, once a monitor is correctly programmed, access to the protected resource is correct for access from all processes. In contrast, with semaphores, resource access is correct only if all of the processes that access the resource are programmed correctly.

Alternate Model of Monitors with Notify and Broadcast

Hoare's definition of monitors [HOAR74] requires that if there is at least one process in a condition queue, a process from that queue runs immediately when another process issues a **csignal** for that condition. Thus, the process issuing the **csignal** must either immediately exit the monitor or be blocked on the monitor.

There are two drawbacks to this approach:

1. If the process issuing the **csignal** has not finished with the monitor, then two additional process switches are required: one to block this process and another to resume it when the monitor becomes available.

2. Process scheduling associated with a signal must be perfectly reliable. When a **csignal** is issued, a process from the corresponding condition queue must be activated immediately and the scheduler must ensure that no other process enters the monitor before activation. Otherwise, the condition under which the process was activated could change. For example, in Figure 5.16, when a **csignal(*notempty*)** is issued, a process from the *notempty* queue must be activated before a new consumer enters the monitor. Another example: a

producer process may append a character to an empty buffer and then fail before signaling; any processes in the *notempty* queue would be permanently hung up.

Lampson and Redell developed a different definition of monitors for the language Mesa [LAMP80]. Their approach overcomes the problems just listed and supports several useful extensions. The Mesa monitor structure is also used in the Modula-3 systems programming language [NELS91]. In Mesa, the `csignal` primitive is replaced by `cnotify`, with the following interpretation: When a process executing in a monitor executes `cnotify(x)`, it causes the *x* condition queue to be notified, but the signaling process continues to execute. The result of the notification is that the process at the head of the condition queue will be resumed at some convenient future time when the monitor is available. However, because there is no guarantee that some other process will not enter the monitor before the waiting process, the waiting process must recheck the condition. For example, the procedures in the `boundedbuffer` monitor would now have the code of Figure 5.17.

The **if** statements are replaced by **while** loops. Thus, this arrangement results in at least one extra evaluation of the condition variable. In return, however, there are no extra process switches, and no constraints on when the waiting process must run after a `cnotify`.

One useful refinement that can be associated with the `cnotify` primitive is a watchdog timer associated with each condition primitive. A process that has been waiting for the maximum time-out interval will be placed in a Ready state regardless of whether the condition has been notified. When activated, the process checks the condition and continues if the condition is satisfied. The time-out prevents the indefinite starvation of a process in the event that some other process fails before signaling a condition.

With the rule that a process is notified rather than forcibly reactivated, it is possible to add a `cbroadcast` primitive to the repertoire. The broadcast causes all

```
void append (char x)
{
    while(count == N)
        cwait(notfull);            /* buffer is full; avoid overflow */
    buffer[nextin] = x;
    nextin = (nextin + 1) % N;
    count++;                       /* one more item in buffer */
    cnotify(notempty);             /* notify any waiting consumer */
}
void take (char x)
{
    while(count == 0)
        cwait(notempty);           /* buffer is empty; avoid underflow */
    x = buffer[nextout];
    nextout = (nextout + 1) % N;
    count--;                       /* one fewer item in buffer */
    cnotify(notfull);              /* notify any waiting producer */
}
```

Figure 5.17   Bounded Buffer Monitor Code for Mesa Monitor

processes waiting on a condition to be placed in a Ready state. This is convenient in situations where a process does not know how many other processes should be reactivated. For example, in the producer/consumer program, suppose that both the **append** and the **take** functions can apply to variable length blocks of characters. In that case, if a producer adds a block of characters to the buffer, it need not know how many characters each waiting consumer is prepared to consume. It simply issues a **cbroadcast** and all waiting processes are alerted to try again.

In addition, a broadcast can be used when a process would have difficulty figuring out precisely which other process to reactivate. A good example is a memory manager. The manager has j bytes free; a process frees up an additional k bytes, but it does not know which waiting process can proceed with a total of $k + j$ bytes. Hence it uses broadcast, and all processes check for themselves if there is enough memory free.

An advantage of Lampson/Redell monitors over Hoare monitors is that the Lampson/Redell approach is less prone to error. In the Lampson/Redell approach, because each procedure checks the monitor variable after being signaled, with the use of the **while** construct, a process can signal or broadcast incorrectly without causing an error in the signaled program. The signaled program will check the relevant variable and, if the desired condition is not met, continue to wait.

Another advantage of the Lampson/Redell monitor is that it lends itself to a more modular approach to program construction. For example, consider the implementation of a buffer allocator. There are two levels of conditions to be satisfied for cooperating sequential processes:

1. Consistent data structures. Thus, the monitor enforces mutual exclusion and completes an input or output operation before allowing another operation on the buffer.

2. Level 1, plus enough memory for this process to complete its allocation request.

In the Hoare monitor, each signal conveys the level 1 condition but also carries the implicit message, "I have freed enough bytes for your particular allocate call to work now." Thus, the signal implicitly carries the level 2 condition. If the programmer later changes the definition of the level 2 condition, it will be necessary to reprogram all signaling processes. If the programmer changes the assumptions made by any particular waiting process (i.e., waiting for a slightly different level 2 invariant), it may be necessary to reprogram all signaling processes. This is unmodular and likely to cause synchronization errors (e.g., wake up by mistake) when the code is modified. The programmer has to remember to modify all procedures in the monitor every time a small change is made to the level 2 condition. With a Lampson/Redell monitor, a broadcast ensures the level 1 condition and carries a hint that level 2 might hold; each process should check the level 2 condition itself. If a change is made in the level 2 condition in either a waiter or a signaler, there is no possibility of erroneous wakeup because each procedure checks its own level 2 condition. Therefore, the level 2 condition can be hidden within each procedure. With the Hoare monitor, the level 2 condition must be carried from the waiter into the code of every signaling process, which violates data abstraction and interprocedural modularity principles.

5.5   MESSAGE PASSING

When processes interact with one another, two fundamental requirements must be satisfied: synchronization and communication. Processes need to be synchronized to enforce mutual exclusion; cooperating processes may need to exchange information. One approach to providing both of these functions is message passing. Message passing has the further advantage that it lends itself to implementation in distributed systems as well as in shared-memory multiprocessor and uniprocessor systems.

Message-passing systems come in many forms. In this section, we provide a general introduction that discusses features typically found in such systems. The actual function of message passing is normally provided in the form of a pair of primitives:

> send (destination, message)
> receive (source, message)

This is the minimum set of operations needed for processes to engage in message passing. A process sends information in the form of a *message* to another process designated by a *destination*. A process receives information by executing the **receive** primitive, indicating the *source* and the *message*.

A number of design issues relating to message-passing systems are listed in Table 5.4, and examined in the remainder of this section.

Table 5.4   Design Characteristics of Message Systems for Interprocessor Communication and Synchronization

Synchronization	Format
Send	Content
blocking	Length
nonblocking	fixed
Receive	variable
blocking	
nonblocking	
test for arrival	
Addressing	**Queuing Discipline**
Direct	FIFO
send	Priority
receive	
explicit	
implicit	
Indirect	
static	
dynamic	
ownership	

Synchronization

The communication of a message between two processes implies some level of synchronization between the two: the receiver cannot receive a message until it has been sent by another process. In addition, we need to specify what happens to a process after it issues a **send** or **receive** primitive.

Consider the **send** primitive first. When a **send** primitive is executed in a process, there are two possibilities: Either the sending process is blocked until the message is received, or it is not. Similarly, when a process issues a **receive** primitive, there are two possibilities:

1. If a message has previously been sent, the message is received and execution continues.

2. If there is no waiting message, then either (a) the process is blocked until a message arrives, or (b) the process continues to execute, abandoning the attempt to receive.

Thus, both the sender and receiver can be blocking or nonblocking. Three combinations are common, although any particular system will usually have only one or two combinations implemented:

- **Blocking send, blocking receive:** Both the sender and receiver are blocked until the message is delivered; this is sometimes referred to as a *rendezvous*. This combination allows for tight synchronization between processes.

- **Nonblocking send, blocking receive:** Although the sender may continue on, the receiver is blocked until the requested message arrives. This is probably the most useful combination. It allows a process to send one or more messages to a variety of destinations as quickly as possible. A process that must receive a message before it can do useful work needs to be blocked until such a message arrives. An example is a server process that exists to provide a service or resource to other processes.

- **Nonblocking send, nonblocking receive:** Neither party is required to wait.

The nonblocking **send** is more natural for many concurrent programming tasks. For example, if it is used to request an output operation, such as printing, it allows the requesting process to issue the request in the form of a message and then carry on. One potential danger of the nonblocking **send** is that an error could lead to a situation in which a process repeatedly generates messages. Because there is no blocking to discipline the process, these messages could consume system resources, including processor time and buffer space, to the detriment of other processes and the operating system. Also, the nonblocking **send** places the burden on the programmer to determine that a message has been received: Processes must employ reply messages to acknowledge receipt of a message.

For the **receive** primitive, the blocking version appears to be more natural for many concurrent programming tasks. Generally, a process that requests a message will need the expected information before proceeding. However, if a message is lost, which can happen in a distributed system, or if a process fails before it sends an anticipated message, a receiving process could be blocked indefinitely. This problem can be solved by the use of the nonblocking `receive`. However, the danger of this approach is that if a message is sent after a process has already executed a matching `receive`, the message will be lost. Other possible approaches are to allow a process to test whether a message is waiting before issuing a `receive` and allow a process to specify more than one source in a receive primitive. The latter approach is useful if a process is waiting for messages from more than one source and can proceed if any of these messages arrive.

Addressing

Clearly, it is necessary to have a way of specifying in the send primitive which process is to receive the message. Similarly, most implementations allow a receiving process to indicate the source of a message to be received.

The various schemes for specifying processes in `send` and `receive` primitives fall into two categories: direct addressing and indirect addressing. With **direct addressing**, the `send` primitive includes a specific identifier of the destination process. The `receive` primitive can be handled in one of two ways. One possibility is to require that the process explicitly designate a sending process. Thus, the process must know ahead of time from which process a message is expected. This will often be effective for cooperating concurrent processes. In other cases, however, it is impossible to specify the anticipated source process. An example is a printer-server process, which will accept a print request message from any other process. For such applications, a more effective approach is the use of implicit addressing. In this case, the *source* parameter of the `receive` primitive possesses a value returned when the receive operation has been performed.

The other general approach is **indirect addressing**. In this case, messages are not sent directly from sender to receiver but rather are sent to a shared data structure consisting of queues that can temporarily hold messages. Such queues are generally referred to as *mailboxes*. Thus, for two processes to communicate, one process sends a message to the appropriate mailbox and the other process picks up the message from the mailbox.

A strength of the use of indirect addressing is that, by decoupling the sender and receiver, it allows for greater flexibility in the use of messages. The relationship between senders and receivers can be one-to-one, many-to-one, one-to-many, or many-to-many (Figure 5.18). A **one-to-one** relationship allows a private communications link to be set up between two processes. This insulates their interaction from erroneous interference from other processes. A **many-to-one** relationship is useful for client/server interaction; one process provides service to a number of other processes. In this case, the mailbox is often referred to as a *port*. A **one-to-many** relationship allows for one sender and multiple receivers; it is useful for applications where a message or some information is to be broadcast to a set of processes. A **many-to-many** relationship allows multiple server processes to provide concurrent service to multiple clients.

The association of processes to mailboxes can be either static or dynamic. Ports are often statically associated with a particular process; that is, the port is created and assigned to the process permanently. Similarly, a one-to-one relationship is typically defined statically and permanently. When there are many senders, the association of a sender to a mailbox may occur dynamically. Primitives such as `connect` and `disconnect` may be used for this purpose.

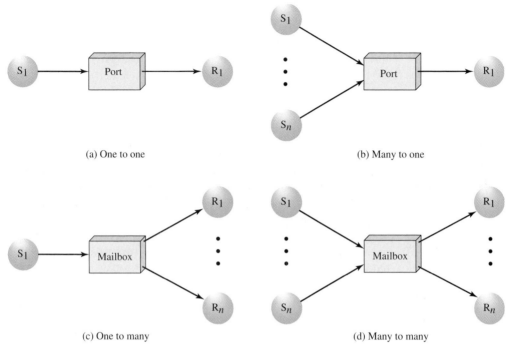

Figure 5.18 Indirect Process Communication

A related issue has to do with the ownership of a mailbox. In the case of a port, it is typically owned by and created by the receiving process. Thus, when the process is destroyed, the port is also destroyed. For the general mailbox case, the operating system may offer a create-mailbox service. Such mailboxes can be viewed either as being owned by the creating process, in which case they terminate with the process, or else as being owned by the operating system, in which case an explicit command will be required to destroy the mailbox.

Message Format

The format of the message depends on the objectives of the messaging facility and whether the facility runs on a single computer or on a distributed system. For some operating systems, designers have preferred short, fixed-length messages to minimize processing and storage overhead. If a large amount of data is to be passed, the data can be placed in a file and the message then simply references that file. A more flexible approach is to allow variable-length messages.

Figure 5.19 shows a typical message format for operating systems that support variable-length messages. The message is divided into two parts: a header, which contains information about the message, and a body, which contains the actual contents of the message. The header may contain an identification of the source and intended destination of the message, a length field, and a type field to discriminate among various types of messages. There may also be additional control information, such as a pointer field so that a linked list of messages can be created; a sequence

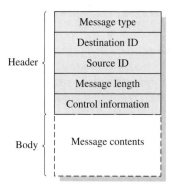

Figure 5.19   General Message Format

```
/* program mutualexclusion */
const int n = /* number of processes */;
void P(int i)
{
    message msg;
    while (true)
    {
        receive (box, msg);
        /* critical section */;
        send (box, msg);
        /* remainder */;
    }
}
void main()
{
    create_mailbox (box);
    send (box, null);
    parbegin (P(1), P(2), ..., P(n));
}
```

Figure 5.20   Mutual Exclusion Using Messages

number, to keep track of the number and order of messages passed between source and destination; and a priority field.

Queuing Discipline

The simplest queuing discipline is first-in-first-out, but this may not be sufficient if some messages are more urgent than others. An alternative is to allow the specifying of message priority, on the basis of message type or by designation by the sender. Another alternative is to allow the receiver to inspect the message queue and select which message to receive next.

Mutual Exclusion

Figure 5.20 shows one way in which message passing can be used to enforce mutual exclusion (compare Figures 5.1, 5.2, and 5.6). We assume the use of the blocking **receive** primitive and the nonblocking **send** primitive. A set of concurrent processes share a mailbox, box, which can be used by all processes to send and receive. The mailbox is initialized to contain a single message with null content. A process wishing to enter its critical section first attempts to receive a message. If the mailbox is empty, then the process is blocked. Once a process has acquired the message, it performs its critical section and then places the message back into the mailbox. Thus, the message functions as a token that is passed from process to process.

The preceding solution assumes that if more than one process performs the receive operation concurrently, then

- If there is a message, it is delivered to only one process and the others are blocked, or

- If the message queue is empty, all processes are blocked; when a message is available, only one blocked process is activated and given the message.

These assumptions are true of virtually all message-passing facilities.

As an example of the use of message passing, Figure 5.21 is a solution to the bounded-buffer producer/consumer problem. Using the basic mutual-exclusion power of message passing, the problem could have been solved with an algorithmic

```
const int
    capacity = /* buffering capacity */ ;
    null = /* empty message */ ;
int i;
void producer()
{   message pmsg;
    while (true)
    {
        receive (mayproduce, pmsg);
        pmsg = produce();
        send (mayconsume, pmsg);
    }
}
void consumer()
{   message cmsg;
    while (true)
    {
        receive (mayconsume, cmsg);
        consume (cmsg);
        send (mayproduce, null);
    }
}
void main()
{
    create_mailbox (mayproduce);
    create_mailbox (mayconsume);
    for (int i = 1; i <= capacity; i++)
        send (mayproduce, null);
    parbegin (producer, consumer);
}
```

Figure 5.21   A Solution to the Bounded-Buffer Producer/Consumer Problem Using Messages

structure similar to that of Figure 5.13. Instead, the program of Figure 5.21 takes advantage of the ability of message passing to be used to pass data in addition to signals. Two mailboxes are used. As the producer generates data, it is sent as messages to the mailbox *mayconsume*. As long as there is at least one message in that mailbox, the consumer can consume. Hence *mayconsume* serves as the buffer; the data in the buffer are organized as a queue of messages. The "size" of the buffer is determined by the global variable *capacity*. Initially, the mailbox *mayproduce* is filled with a number of null messages equal to the capacity of the buffer. The number of messages in *mayproduce* shrinks with each production and grows with each consumption.

This approach is quite flexible. There may be multiple producers and consumers, as long as all have access to both mailboxes. The system may even be distributed, with all producer processes and the *mayproduce* mailbox at one site and all the consumer processes and the *mayconsume* mailbox at another.

5.6 READERS/WRITERS PROBLEM

In dealing with the design of synchronization and concurrency mechanisms, it is useful to be able to relate the problem at hand to known problems and to be able to test any solution in terms of its ability to solve these known problems. In the literature, several problems have assumed importance and appear frequently, both because they are examples of common design problems and because of their educational value. One such problem is the producer/consumer problem, which has already been explored. In this section, we look at another classic problem: the readers/writers problem.

The readers/writers problem is defined as follows: There is a data area shared among a number of processes. The data area could be a file, a block of main memory, or even a bank of processor registers. There are a number of processes that only read the data area (readers) and a number that only write to the data area (writers). The following conditions must be satisfied:

1. Any number of readers may simultaneously read the file.
2. Only one writer at a time may write to the file.
3. If a writer is writing to the file, no reader may read it.

Before proceeding, let us distinguish this problem from two others: the general mutual exclusion problem and the producer/consumer problem. In the readers/writers problem readers do not also write to the data area, nor do writers read the data area. A more general case, which includes this case, is to allow any of the processes to read or write the data area. In that case, we can declare any portion of a process that accesses the data area to be a critical section and impose the general mutual exclusion solution. The reason for being concerned with the more restricted case is that more efficient solutions are possible for this case and that the less efficient solutions to the general problem are unacceptably slow. For example, suppose that the shared area is a library catalog. Ordinary users of the library read the catalog to locate a book. One or more librarians are able to update the catalog. In the general solution, every access to the catalog would be treated as a critical section, and users would be forced to read the catalog one at a time. This would clearly impose intolerable delays. At the same time, it is important to prevent writers from interfering with each other and it is also required to prevent reading while writing is in progress to prevent the access of inconsistent information.

Can the producer/consumer problem be considered simply a special case of the readers/writers problem with a single writer (the producer) and a single reader (the consumer)? The answer is no. The producer is not just a writer. It must read queue pointers to determine where to write the next item, and it must determine if the buffer is full. Similarly, the consumer is not just a reader, because it must adjust the queue pointers to show that it has removed a unit from the buffer.

We now examine two solutions to the problem.

Readers Have Priority

Figure 5.22 is a solution using semaphores, showing one instance each of a reader and a writer; the solution does not change for multiple readers and writers. The writer process is simple. The semaphore **wsem** is used to enforce mutual exclusion. As long as one writer is accessing the shared data area, no other writers and no readers may access it. The reader process also makes use of **wsem** to enforce mutual exclusion. However, to allow multiple readers, we require that, when there are no readers reading, the first reader that attempts to read should wait on **wsem**. When there is already at least one reader reading, subsequent readers need not wait before entering. The global variable **readcount** is used to keep track of the number of readers, and the semaphore **x** is used to assure that **readcount** is updated properly.

Writers Have Priority

In the previous solution, readers have priority. Once a single reader has begun to access the data area, it is possible for readers to retain control of the data area as long as there is at least one reader in the act of reading. Therefore, writers are subject to starvation.

Figure 5.23 shows a solution that guarantees that no new readers are allowed access to the data area once at least one writer has declared a desire to write. For writers, the following semaphores and variables are added to the ones already defined:

- A semaphore **rsem** that inhibits all readers while there is at least one writer desiring access to the data area
- A variable **writecount** that controls the setting of **rsem**
- A semaphore **y** that controls the updating of **writecount**

For readers, one additional semaphore is needed. A long queue must not be allowed to build up on **rsem**; otherwise writers will not be able to jump the queue. Therefore, only one reader is allowed to queue on **rsem,** with any additional readers queuing on semaphore **z**, immediately before waiting on **rsem**. Table 5.5 summarizes the possibilities.

An alternative solution, which gives writers priority and which is implemented using message passing, is shown in Figure 5.24. In this case, there is a controller process that has access to the shared data area. Other processes wishing to access the data area send a request message to the controller, are granted access with an "OK" reply message, and indicate completion of access with a "finished" message.

```
/* program readersandwriters */
int readcount;
semaphore x = 1, wsem = 1;
void reader()
{
    while (true)
    {
        semWait (x);
        readcount++;
        if (readcount == 1)
            semWait (wsem);
        semSignal (x);
        READUNIT();
        semWait (x);
        readcount--;
        if (readcount == 0)
            semSignal (wsem);
        semSignal (x);
    }
}
void writer()
{
    while (true)
    {
        semWait (wsem);
        WRITEUNIT();
        semSignal (wsem);
    }
}
void main()
{
    readcount = 0;
    parbegin (reader, writer);
}
```

Figure 5.22   A Solution to the Readers/Writers Problem
Using Semaphores: Readers Have Priority

The controller is equipped with three mailboxes, one for each type of message that it may receive.

The controller process services write request messages before read request messages to give writers priority. In addition, mutual exclusion must be enforced. To do this the variable *count* is used, which is initialized to some number greater than the maximum possible number of readers. In this example, we use a value of 100. The action of the controller can be summarized as follows:

- If *count* > 0, then no writer is waiting and there may or may not be readers active. Service all "finished" messages first to clear active readers. Then service write requests and then read requests.

- If *count* = 0, then the only request outstanding is a write request. Allow the writer to proceed and wait for a "finished" message.

```
/* program readersandwriters */
int    readcount, writecount;
semaphore x = 1, y = 1, z = 1, wsem = 1, rsem = 1;
void reader()
{
    while (true)
    {
      semWait (z);
        semWait (rsem);
          semWait (x);
              readcount++;
            if (readcount == 1)
                semWait (wsem);
          semSignal (x);
        semSignal (rsem);
      semSignal (z);
      READUNIT();
      semWait (x);
        readcount−−;
        if (readcount == 0)
          semSignal (wsem);
      semSignal (x);
    }
}
void writer ()
{
    while (true)
    {
      semWait (y);
        writecount++;
        if (writecount == 1)
            semWait (rsem);
      semSignal (y);
      semWait (wsem);
      WRITEUNIT();
      semSignal (wsem);
      semWait (y);
        writecount−−;
        if (writecount == 0)
            semSignal (rsem);
      semSignal (y);
    }
}
void main()
{
    readcount = writecount = 0;
    parbegin (reader, writer);
}
```

Figure 5.23   A Solution to the Readers/Writers Problem Using Semaphores: Writers Have Priority

Table 5.5   State of the Process Queues for Program of Figure 5.23

Readers only in the system	• *wsem* set • no queues
Writers only in the system	• *wsem* and *rsem* set • writers queue on wsem
Both readers and writers with read first	• *wsem* set by reader • *rsem* set by writer • all writers queue on *wsem* • one reader queues on *rsem* • other readers queue on *z*
Both readers and writers with write first	• *wsem* set by writer • *rsem* set by writer • writers queue on *wsem* • one reader queues on *rsem* • other readers queue on *z*

- If *count* < 0, then a writer has made a request and is being made to wait to clear all active readers. Therefore, only "finished" messages should be serviced.

5.7   SUMMARY

The central themes of modern operating systems are multiprogramming, multiprocessing, and distributed processing. Fundamental to these themes, and fundamental to the technology of operating system design, is concurrency. When multiple processes are executing concurrently, either actually in the case of a multiprocessor system or virtually in the case of a single-processor multiprogramming system, issues of conflict resolution and cooperation arise.

Concurrent processes may interact in a number of ways. Processes that are unaware of each other may nevertheless compete for resources, such as processor time or access to I/O devices. Processes may be indirectly aware of one another because they share access to a common object, such as a block of main memory or a file. Finally, processes may be directly aware of each other and cooperate by the exchange of information. The key issues that arise in these interactions are mutual exclusion and deadlock.

Mutual exclusion is a condition in which there is a set of concurrent processes, only one of which is able to access a given resource or perform a given function at any time. Mutual exclusion techniques can be used to resolve conflicts, such as competition for resources, and to synchronize processes so that they can cooperate. An example of the latter is the producer/consumer model, in which one process is putting data into a buffer and one or more processes are extracting data from that buffer.

One approach to supporting mutual exclusion involves the use of special-purpose machine instructions. This approach reduces overhead but is still inefficient because it uses busy waiting.

Another approach to supporting mutual exclusion is to provide features within the operating system. Two of the most common techniques are semaphores and message

```
void reader(int i)                          void  controller()
{                                           {
    message rmsg;                               while (true)
        while (true)                            {
        {                                           if (count > 0)
            rmsg = i;                               {
            send (readrequest, rmsg);                   if (!empty (finished))
            receive (mbox[i], rmsg);                    {
            READUNIT ();                                    receive (finished, msg);
            rmsg = i;                                       count++;
            send (finished, rmsg);                      }
        }                                               else if (!empty (writerequest))
}                                                       {
void writer(int j)                                          receive (writerequest, msg);
{                                                           writer_id = msg.id;
    message rmsg;                                            count = count – 100;
    while(true)                                          }
    {                                                   else if (!empty (readrequest))
        rmsg = j;                                       {
        send (writerequest, rmsg);                          receive (readrequest, msg);
        receive (mbox[j], rmsg);                            count – –;
        WRITEUNIT ();                                       send (msg.id, "OK");
        rmsg = j;                                       }
        send (finished, rmsg);                      }
    }                                               if (count == 0)
}                                                   {
                                                        send (writer_id, "OK");
                                                        receive (finished, msg);
                                                        count = 100;
                                                    }
                                                    while (count < 0)
                                                    {
                                                        receive (finished, msg);
                                                        count++;
                                                    }
                                                }
                                            }
```

Figure 5.24   A Solution to the Readers/Writers Problem Using Message Passing

facilities. Semaphores are used for signaling among processes and can be readily used to enforce a mutual-exclusion discipline. Messages are useful for the enforcement of mutual exclusion and also provide an effective means of interprocess communication.

5.8 RECOMMENDED READINGS

[BEN82] provides a very clear and even entertaining discussion of concurrency, mutual exclusion, semaphores, and other related topics. A more formal treatment, expanded to include distributed systems, is contained in [BEN90]. [AXFO88] is another readable and useful treatment; it also contains a number of problems with worked-out solutions. [RAYN86] is a comprehensive and lucid collection of algorithms for mutual exclusion, covering software (e.g., Dekker) and hardware approaches, as well as semaphores and messages. [HOAR85] is a very readable classic that presents a formal approach to defining sequential processes and concurrency. [LAMP86] is a lengthy formal treatment of mutual exclusion. [RUDO90] is a useful aid in understanding concurrency. [BACO03] is a well-organized treatment of concurrency. [BIRR89] provides a good practical introduction to programming using concurrency. [BUHR95] is an exhaustive survey of monitors. [KANG98] is an instructive analysis of 12 different scheduling policies for the readers/writers problem.

AXFO88   Axford, T. *Concurrent Programming: Fundamental Techniques for Real-Time and Parallel Software Design.* New York: Wiley, 1988.

BACO03   Bacon, J., and Harris, T. *Operating Systems: Concurrent and Distributed Software Design.* Reading, MA: Addison-Wesley, 1998.

BEN82   Ben-Ari, M. *Principles of Concurrent Programming.* Englewood Cliffs, NJ: Prentice Hall, 1982.

BEN90   Ben-Ari, M. *Principles of Concurrent and Distributed Programming.* Englewood Cliffs, NJ: Prentice Hall, 1990.

BIRR89   Birrell, A. *An Introduction to Programming with Threads.* SRC Research Report 35, Compaq Systems Research Center, Palo Alto, CA, January 1989. Available at **http://www.research.compaq.com/SRC**.

BUHR95   Buhr, P., and Fortier, M. "Monitor Classification." *ACM Computing Surveys*, March 1995.

HOAR85   Hoare, C. *Communicating Sequential Processes.* Englewood Cliffs, NJ: Prentice Hall, 1985.

KANG98   Kang, S., and Lee, J. "Analysis and Solution of Non-Preemptive Policies for Scheduling Readers and Writers." *Operating Systems Review*, July 1998.

LAMP86   Lamport, L. "The Mutual Exclusion Problem." *Journal of the ACM*, April 1986.

RAYN86   Raynal, M. *Algorithms for Mutual Exclusion.* Cambridge, MA: MIT Press, 1986.

RUDO90   Rudolph, B. "Self-Assessment Procedure XXI: Concurrency." *Communications of the ACM*, May 1990.

5.9   KEY TERMS, REVIEW QUESTIONS, AND PROBLEMS

Key Terms

binary semaphore	critical resource	mutex
blocking	critical section	nonblocking
busy waiting	deadlock	race condition
concurrent processes	general semaphore	semaphore
concurrency	message passing	starvation
coroutine	monitor	strong semaphore
counting semaphore	mutual exclusion	weak semaphore

Review Questions

5.1   List four design issues for which the concept of concurrency is relevant.

5.2   What are three contexts in which concurrency arises?

5.3   What is the basic requirement for the execution of concurrent processes?

5.4   List three degrees of awareness between processes and briefly define each.

5.5   What is the distinction between competing processes and cooperating processes?

5.6   List the three control problems associated with competing processes and briefly define each.

5.7   List the requirements for mutual exclusion.

5.8   What operations can be performed on a semaphore?

5.9   What is the difference between binary and general semaphores?

5.10   What is the difference between strong and weak semaphores?

5.11   What is a monitor?

5.12   What is the distinction between *blocking* and *nonblocking* with respect to messages?

5.13   What conditions are generally associated with the readers/writers problem?

Problems

5.1   Processes and threads provide a powerful structuring tool for implementing programs that would be much more complex as simple sequential programs. An earlier construct that is instructive to examine is the coroutine. The purpose of this problem is to introduce coroutines and compare them to processes. Consider this simple problem from [CONW63]:

> Read 80-column cards and print them on 125-character lines, with the following changes. After every card image an extra blank is inserted, and every adjacent pair of asterisks (**) on a card is replaced by the character ↑.

a.   Develop a solution to this problem as an ordinary sequential program. You will find that the program is tricky to write. The interactions among the various elements of the program are uneven because of the conversion from a length of 80 to 125; furthermore, the length of the card image, after conversion, will vary depending on the number of double asterisk occurrences. One way to improve clarity, and to minimize the potential for bugs, is to write the application as three separate procedures. The first procedure reads in card images, pads each image with a blank, and writes a stream of characters to a temporary file. After all of the cards have been read, the second procedure reads the temporary file, does the character substitution, and writes out a second temporary file. The third procedure reads the stream of characters from the second temporary file and prints lines of 125 characters each.

b.   The sequential solution is unattractive because of the overhead of I/O and temporary files. Conway proposed a new form of program structure, the coroutine, that allows the application to be written as three programs connected by one-character buffers (Figure 5.25). In a traditional **procedure**, there is a master/slave relationship between the called and calling procedure. The calling procedure may execute a call from any point in the procedure; the called procedure is begun at its entry point and returns to the calling procedure at the point of call. The **coroutine** exhibits a more symmetric relationship. As each call is made, execution takes up from the last active point in the called procedure. Because there is no sense in which a calling procedure is "higher" than the called, there is no return. Rather, any coroutine can pass control to any other coroutine with a resume command. The first time a coroutine is invoked, it is "resumed" at

```
char rs, sp;                          }void squash()
char inbuf[80];                       {
char outbuf[125];                         while (true)
void read()                               {
{                                             if (rs != "*")
    while (true)                              {
    {                                             sp = rs;
        READCARD (inbuf);                         RESUME print;
        for (int i=0; i < 80; i++)            }
        {                                     else
            rs = inbuf [i];                   {
            RESUME squash                         RESUME read;
        }                                         if (rs == "*")
        rs = " ";                                 {
        RESUME squash;                                sp = "↑";
    }                                                 RESUME print;
}                                                 }
void print()                                      else
{                                                 {
    while (true)                                      sp = "*";
    {                                                 RESUME print;
        for (int j = 0; j < 125; j++)                 sp = rs;
        {                                             RESUME print;
            outbuf [j] = sp;                      }
            RESUME squash                     }
        }                                     RESUME read;
        OUTPUT (outbuf);                  }
    }                                 }
}
```

Figure 5.25   An Application of Coroutines

its entry point. Subsequently, the coroutine is reactivated at the point of its own last resume command. Note that only one coroutine in a program can be in execution at one time and that the transition points are explicitly defined in the code, so this is not an example of concurrent processing. Explain the operation of the program in Figure 5.25.

c. The program does not address the termination condition. Assume that the I/O routine READCARD returns the value true if it has placed an 80-character image in *inbuf*; otherwise it returns false. Modify the program to include this contingency. Note that the last printed line may therefore contain less than 125 characters.

d. Rewrite the solution as a set of three processes using semaphores.

5.2 Consider a concurrent program with two processes, p and q, defined as follows. A, B, C, D, and E are arbitrary atomic (indivisible) statements. Assume that the main program (not shown) does a **parbegin** of the two processes.

```
void p()                    void q()
{                           {
    A;                          D;
    B;                          E;
    C;                      }
}
```

Show all the possible interleavings of the execution of the preceding two processes (show this by giving execution "traces" in terms of the atomic statements).

5.3   Consider the following program:

```
const int n = 50;
int tally;
void total()
{
    int count;
    for (count = 1; count <= n; count++)
    {
        tally++;
    }
}
void main()
{
    tally = 0;
    parbegin (total (), total ());
    write (tally);
}
```

a. Determine the proper lower bound and upper bound on the final value of the shared variable *tally* output by this concurrent program. Assume processes can execute at any relative speed and that a value can only be incremented after it has been loaded into a register by a separate machine instruction.

b. Suppose that an arbitrary number of these processes are permitted to execute in parallel under the assumptions of part (a). What effect will this modification have on the range of final values of *tally*?

5.4   Is busy waiting always less efficient (in terms of using processor time) than a blocking wait? Explain.

5.5   Consider the following program:

```
boolean blocked [2];
int turn;
void P (int id)
{
    while (true)
    {
        blocked[id] = true;
        while (turn != id)
        {
            while (blocked[1-id])
                /* do nothing */;
            turn = id;
        }
        /* critical section */
        blocked[id] = false;
        /* remainder */
    }
}
void main()
{
    blocked[0] = false;
    blocked[1] = false;
    turn = 0;
    parbegin (P(0), P(1));
}
```

This software solution to the mutual exclusion problem for two processes is proposed in [HYMA66]. Find a counterexample that demonstrates that this solution is incorrect. It is interesting to note that even the *Communications of the ACM* was fooled on this one.

5.6   Another software approach to mutual exclusion is Lamport's **bakery algorithm** [LAMP74], so called because it is based on the practice in bakeries and other shops in which every customer receives a numbered ticket on arrival, allowing each to be served in turn. The algorithm is as follows:

```
boolean choosing[n];
int number[n];
while (true)
{
    choosing[i] = true;
    number[i] = 1 + getmax(number[], n);
    choosing[i] = false;
    for (int j = 0; j < n; j++)
    {
        while (choosing[j])
        {};
        while ((number[j] != 0) && (number[j],j) < (number[i],i))
        {};
    }
        /* critical section */;
        number [i] = 0;
        /* remainder */;
}
```

The arrays *choosing* and *number* are initialized to false and 0 respectively. The *i*th element of each array may be read and written by process *i* but only read by other processes. The notation $(a, b) < (c, d)$ is defined as

$$(a < c) \text{ or } (a = c \text{ and } b < d)$$

a.   Describe the algorithm in words.
b.   Show that this algorithm avoids deadlock.
c.   Show that it enforces mutual exclusion.

5.7   When a special machine instruction is used to provide mutual exclusion in the fashion of Figure 5.2, there is no control over how long a process must wait before being granted access to its critical section. Devise an algorithm that uses the testset instruction but that guarantees that any process waiting to enter its critical section will do so within $n - 1$ turns, where n is the number of processes that may require access to the critical section and a "turn" is an event consisting of one process leaving the critical section and another process being granted access.

5.8   Consider the following definition of semaphores:

```
void semWait(s)
{
    if (s.count > 0)
    {
        s.count--;
    }
    else
    {
        place this process in s.queue;
        block;
    }
}
```

```
void semSignal (s)
{
    if (there is at least one process blocked on semaphore s)
    {
        remove a process P from s.queue;
        place process P on ready list;
    }
    else
        s.count++;
}
```

Compare this set of definitions with that of Figure 5.3. Note one difference: With the preceding definition, a semaphore can never take on a negative value. Is there any difference in the effect of the two sets of definitions when used in programs? That is, could you substitute one set for the other without altering the meaning of the program?

5.9   It should be possible to implement general semaphores using binary semaphores. We can use the operations **semWaitB** and **semSignalB** and two binary semaphores, **delay** and **mutex**. Consider the following:

```
void semWait(semaphore s)
{
    semWaitB(mutex);
    s−−;
    if (s < 0)
    {
        semSignalB(mutex);
        semWaitB(delay);
    }
    else
        SemsignalB(mutex);
}
void semSignal(semaphore s);
{
    semWaitB(mutex);
    s++;
    if (s <= 0)
        semSignalB(delay);
    semSignalB(mutex);
}
```

Initially, *s* is set to the desired semaphore value. Each **semWait** operation decrements *s*, and each **semSignal** operation increments *s*. The binary semaphore mutex, which is initialized to 1, assures that there is mutual exclusion for the updating of *s*. The binary semaphore delay, which is initialized to 0, is used to block processes.

There is a flaw in the preceding program. Demonstrate the flaw and propose a change that will fix it. *Hint:* Suppose two processes each call **semWait(s)** when s is initially 0, and after the first has just performed **semSignalB(mutex)** but not performed **semWaitB(delay)**, the second call to **semWait(s)** proceeds to the same point. All that you need to do is move a single line of the program.

5.10   In 1978, Dijkstra put forward the conjecture that there was no solution to the mutual exclusion problem avoiding starvation, applicable to an unknown but finite number of processes, using a finite number of weak semaphores. In 1979, J. M. Morris refuted this conjecture by publishing an algorithm using three weak semaphores. The behavior of the algorithm can be described as follows: If one or several process are waiting in a **semWait(S)** operation and another process is executing **semSignal(S)**, the value of the semaphore S is not modified and one of the waiting processes is unblocked independently of **semWait(S)**. Apart from the three semaphores, the algorithm uses two nonnegative integer variables as counters of the number of processes in certain sections of the algorithm. Thus, semaphores A and B are initialized to 1, while semaphore M and counters NA and NM are initialized to 0. The mutual exclusion semaphore B protects access to the shared variable NA. A process attempting to enter its critical section must cross two barriers represented by semaphores A and M. Counters NA and NM, respectively, contain the number of processes ready to cross barrier A and those having already crossed barrier A but not yet barrier M. In the second part of the protocol, the NM processes blocked at M will enter their critical sections one by one, using a cascade technique similar to that used in the first part. Define an algorithm that conforms to this description.

5.11 The following problem was once used on an exam:

Jurassic Park consists of a dinosaur museum and a park for safari riding. There are *m* passengers and *n* single-passenger cars. Passengers wander around the museum for a while, then line up to take a ride in a safari car. When a car is available, it loads the one passenger it can hold and rides around the park for a random amount of time. If the *n* cars are all out riding passengers around, then a passenger who wants to ride waits; if a car is ready to load but there are no waiting passengers, then the car waits. Use semaphores to synchronize the *m* passenger processes and the *n* car processes.

The following skeleton code was found on a scrap of paper on the floor of the exam room. Grade it for correctness. Ignore syntax and missing variable declarations. Remember that P and V correspond to **semWait** and **semSignal**.

```
resource Jurassic_Park()
    sem car_avail := 0, car_taken := 0, car_filled := 0, passenger_released := 0
    process passenger(i := 1 to num_passengers)
        do true -> nap(int(random(1000*wander_time)))
            P(car_avail); V(car_taken); P(car_filled)
            P(passenger_released)
        od
    end passenger
    process car(j := 1 to num_cars)
        do true -> V(car_avail); P(car_taken); V(car_filled)
            nap(int(random(1000*ride_time)))
            V(passenger_released)
        od
    end car
end Jurassic_Park
```

5.12 In the commentary on Figure 5.9 and Table 5.3, it was stated that "it would not do simply to move the conditional statement inside the critical section (controlled by s) of the consumer because this could lead to deadlock." Demonstrate this with a table similar to Table 5.3.

5.13 Consider the solution to the infinite-buffer producer/consumer problem defined in Figure 5.10. Suppose we have the (common) case in which the producer and consumer are running at roughly the same speed. The scenario could be
Producer: append; **semSignal**; produce; ...; append; **semSignal**; produce; ...
Consumer: consume; ...; take; **semWait**; consume; ...; take; semWait; ...

The producer always manages to append a new element to the buffer and signal during the consumption of the previous element by the consumer. The producer is always appending to an empty buffer and the consumer is always taking the sole item in the buffer. Although the consumer never blocks on the semaphore, a large number of calls to the semaphore mechanism is made, creating considerable overhead.

Construct a new program that will be more efficient under these circumstances. *Hints:* Allow *n* to have the value −1, which is to mean that not only is the buffer empty but that the consumer has detected this fact and is going to block until the producer supplies fresh data. The solution does not require the use of the local variable m found in Figure 5.10.

5.14 Consider Figure 5.13. Would the meaning of the program change if the following were interchanged?
   a. `semWait(e); semWait(s)`
   b. `semSignal(s); semSignal(n)`
   c. `semWait(n); semWait(s)`
   d. `semSignal(s); semSignal(e)`

5.15 In the discussion of the producer/consumer problem with finite buffer (Figure 5.12), note that our definition allows at most $n - 1$ entries in the buffer.
   a. Why is this?
   b. Modify the algorithm to remedy this deficiency.

5.16 This problem demonstrates the use of semaphores to coordinate three types of processes.[4] Santa Claus sleeps in his shop at the North Pole and can only be wakened by either (1) all nine reindeer being back from their vacation in the South Pacific, or (2) some of the elves having difficulties making toys; to allow Santa to get some sleep, the elves can only wake him when three of them have problems. When three elves are having their problems solved, any other elves wishing to visit Santa must wait for those elves to return. If Santa wakes up to find three elves waiting at his shop's door, along with the last reindeer having come back from the tropics, Santa has decided that the elves can wait until after Christmas, because it is more important to get his sleigh ready. (It is assumed that the reindeer do not want to leave the tropics, and therefore they stay there until the last possible moment.) The last reindeer to arrive must get Santa while the others wait in a warming hut before being harnessed to the sleigh. Solve this problem using semaphores.

5.17 Show that message passing and semaphores have equivalent functionality by
   a. Implementing message-passing using semaphores. *Hint:* Make use of a shared buffer area to hold mailboxes, each one consisting of an array of message slots.
   b. Implementing a semaphore using message passing. *Hint:* Introduce a separate synchronization process.

---

[4]I am grateful to John Trono of St. Michael's College in Vermont for supplying this problem.

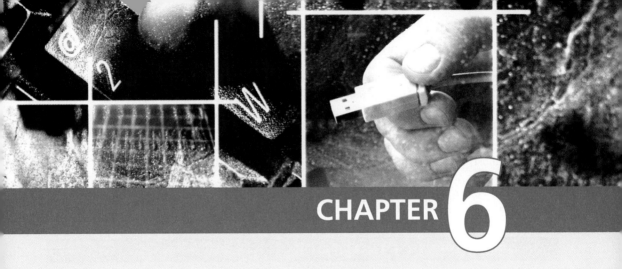

CHAPTER 6

CONCURRENCY: DEADLOCK AND STARVATION

This chapter continues our survey of concurrency by looking at two problems that plague all efforts to support concurrent processing: deadlock and starvation. We begin with a discussion of the underlying principles of deadlock and the related problem of starvation. Then we examine the three common approaches to dealing with deadlock: prevention, detection, and avoidance. We then look at one of the classic problems used to illustrate both synchronization and deadlock issues: the dining philosophers problem.

As with Chapter 5, the discussion in this chapter is limited to a consideration of concurrency and deadlock on a single system. Measures to deal with distributed deadlock problems are assessed in Chapter 14.

6.1 PRINCIPLES OF DEADLOCK

Deadlock can be defined as the *permanent* blocking of a set of processes that either compete for system resources or communicate with each other. A set of processes is deadlocked when each process in the set is blocked awaiting an event (typically the freeing up of some requested resource) that can only be triggered by another blocked process in the set. Deadlock is permanent because none of the events is ever triggered. Unlike other problems in concurrent process management, there is no efficient solution in the general case.

All deadlocks involve conflicting needs for resources by two or more processes. A common example is the traffic deadlock. Figure 6.1a shows a situation in which four cars have arrived at a four-way stop intersection at approximately the same time. The four quadrants of the intersection are the resources over which control is needed. In particular, if all four cars wish to go straight through the intersection, the resource requirements are as follows:

- Car 1, traveling north, needs quadrants a and b.
- Car 2 needs quadrants b and c.

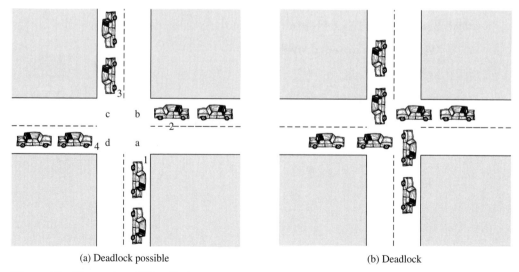

(a) Deadlock possible   (b) Deadlock

Figure 6.1 Illustration of Deadlock

- Car 3 needs quadrants c and d.
- Car 4 needs quadrants d and a.

The typical rule of the road is that a car at a four-way stop should defer to a car immediately to its right. This rule works if there are only two or three cars at the intersection. For example, if only the northbound and westbound cars arrive at the intersection, the northbound car will wait and the westbound car proceeds. However, if all four cars arrive at about the same time, each will refrain from entering the intersection, causing a deadlock. If all four cars ignore the rules and proceed (cautiously) into the intersection, then each car seizes one resource (one quadrant) but cannot proceed because the required second resource has already been seized by another car. Again, we have deadlock. Note also that because each car is closely followed by another car, reversing to eliminate the deadlock is not possible.

Let us now look at a depiction of deadlock involving processes and computer resources. Figure 6.2 (based on one in [BACO03]), which we refer to as a **joint progress diagram**, illustrates the progress of two processes competing for two resources. Each process needs exclusive use of both resources for a certain period of time. Two processes, P and Q, have the following general form:

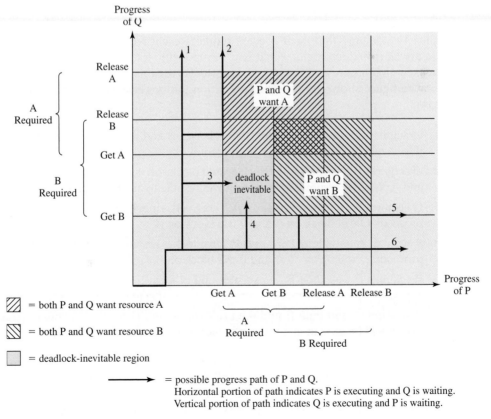

= both P and Q want resource A

= both P and Q want resource B

= deadlock-inevitable region

⟶ = possible progress path of P and Q.
Horizontal portion of path indicates P is executing and Q is waiting.
Vertical portion of path indicates Q is executing and P is waiting.

Figure 6.2 Example of Deadlock

Process P	**Process Q**
...	...
Get A	Get B
...	...
Get B	Get A
...	...
Release A	Release B
...	...
Release B	Release A
...	...

In Figure 6.2, the x-axis represents progress in the execution of P and the y-axis represents progress in the execution of Q. The joint progress of the two processes is therefore represented by a path that progresses from the origin in a northeasterly direction. For a uniprocessor system, only one process at a time may execute, and the path consists of alternating horizontal and vertical segments, with a horizontal segment representing a period when P executes and Q waits and a vertical segment representing a period when Q executes and P waits. The figure indicates areas in which both P and Q require resource A (upward slanted lines); both P and Q require resource B (downward slanted lines); and both P and Q require both resources. Because we assume that each process requires exclusive control of any resource, these are all forbidden regions; that is, it is impossible for any path representing the joint execution progress of P and Q to enter these regions.

The figure shows six different execution paths. These can be summarized as follows:

1. Q acquires B and then A and then releases B and A. When P resumes execution, it will be able to acquire both resources.
2. Q acquires B and then A. P executes and blocks on a request for A. Q releases B and A. When P resumes execution, it will be able to acquire both resources.
3. Q acquires B and then P acquires A. Deadlock is inevitable, because as execution proceeds, Q will block on A and P will block on B.
4. P acquires A and then Q acquires B. Deadlock is inevitable, because as execution proceeds, Q will block on A and P will block on B.
5. P acquires A and then B. Q executes and blocks on a request for B. P releases A and B. When Q resumes execution, it will be able to acquire both resources.
6. P acquires A and then B and then releases A and B. When Q resumes execution, it will be able to acquire both resources.

The gray-shaded area of Figure 6.2, which can be referred to as a **fatal region**, applies to the commentary on paths 3 and 4. If an execution path enters this fatal region, then deadlock is inevitable. Note that the existence of a fatal region depends on the logic of the two processes. However, deadlock is only inevitable if the joint progress of the two processes creates a path that enters the fatal region.

Whether or not deadlock occurs depends on both the dynamics of the execution and on the details of the application. For example, suppose that P does not need both resources at the same time so that the two processes have the following form:

Process P	**Process Q**
. . .	. . .
Get A	Get B
. . .	. . .
Release A	Get A
. . .	. . .
Get B	Release B
. . .	. . .
Release B	Release A
. . .	. . .

This situation is reflected in Figure 6.3. Some thought should convince you that regardless of the relative timing of the two processes, deadlock cannot occur.

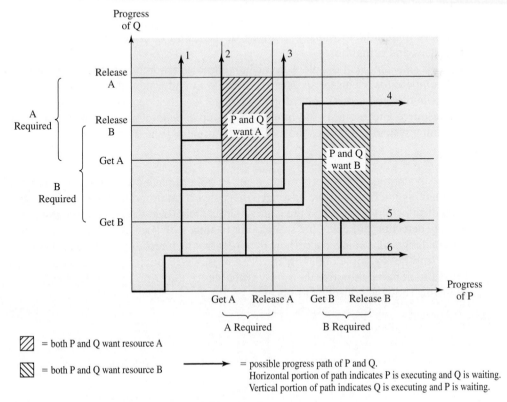

Figure 6.3   Example of No Deadlock [BACO03]

Process P		Process Q	
Step	**Action**	**Step**	**Action**
p_0	Request (D)	q_0	Request (T)
p_1	Lock (D)	q_1	Lock (T)
p_2	Request (T)	q_2	Request (D)
p_3	Lock (T)	q_3	Lock (D)
p_4	Perform function	q_4	Perform function
p_5	Unlock (D)	q_5	Unlock (T)
p_6	Unlock (T)	q_6	Unlock (D)

Figure 6.4   Example of Two Processes Competing for Reusable Resources

As shown, the joint progress diagram can be used to record the execution history of two processes that share resources. In cases where more than two processes may compete for the same resource, a higher-dimensional diagram would be required. The principles concerning fatal regions and deadlock would remain the same.

Reusable Resources

Two general categories of resources can be distinguished: reusable and consumable. A reusable resource is one that can be safely used by only one process at a time and is not depleted by that use. Processes obtain resource units that they later release for reuse by other processes. Examples of reusable resources include processors, I/O channels, main and secondary memory, devices, and data structures such as files, databases, and semaphores.

As an example of deadlock involving reusable resources, consider two processes that compete for exclusive access to a disk file D and a tape drive T. The programs engage in the operations depicted in Figure 6.4. Deadlock occurs if each process holds one resource and requests the other. For example, deadlock occurs if the multiprogramming system interleaves the execution of the two processes as follows:

$$p_0 \; p_1 \; q_0 \; q_1 \; p_2 \; q_2$$

It may appear that this is a programming error rather than a problem for the operating system designer. However, we have seen that concurrent program design is challenging. Such deadlocks do occur, and the cause is often embedded in complex program logic, making detection difficult. One strategy for dealing with such a deadlock is to impose system design constraints concerning the order in which resources can be requested.

Another example of deadlock with a reusable resource has to do with requests for main memory. Suppose the space available for allocation is 200 Kbytes, and the following sequence of requests occurs:

P1	**P2**
...	...
Request 80 Kbytes;	Request 70 Kbytes;
...	...
Request 60 Kbytes;	Request 80 Kbytes;

Deadlock occurs if both processes progress to their second request. If the amount of memory to be requested is not known ahead of time, it is difficult to deal with this type of deadlock by means of system design constraints. The best way to deal with this particular problem is, in effect, to eliminate the possibility by using virtual memory, which is discussed in Chapter 8.

Consumable Resources

A consumable resource is one that can be created (produced) and destroyed (consumed). Typically, there is no limit on the number of consumable resources of a particular type. An unblocked producing process may create any number of such resources. When a resource is acquired by a consuming process, the resource ceases to exist. Examples of consumable resources are interrupts, signals, messages, and information in I/O buffers.

As an example of deadlock involving consumable resources, consider the following pair of processes, in which each process attempts to receive a message from the other process and then send a message to the other process:

P1	**P2**
. . .	. . .
Receive (P2);	Receive (P1);
. . .	. . .
Send (P2, M1);	Send (P1, M2);

Deadlock occurs if the Receive is blocking (i.e., the receiving process is blocked until the message is received). Once again, a design error is the cause of the deadlock. Such errors may be quite subtle and difficult to detect. Furthermore, it may take a rare combination of events to cause the deadlock; thus a program could be in use for a considerable period of time, even years, before the deadlock actually occurs.

There is no single effective strategy that can deal with all types of deadlock. Table 6.1 summarizes the key elements of the most important approaches that have been developed: prevention, avoidance, and detection. We examine each of these in turn, after first introducing resource allocation graphs and then discussing the conditions for deadlock.

Resource Allocation Graphs

A useful tool in characterizing the allocation of resources to processes is the **resource allocation graph**, introduced by Holt [HOLT72]. The resource allocation graph is a directed graph that depicts a state of the system of resources and processes, with each process and each resource represented by a node. A graph edge directed from a process to a resource indicates a resource that has been requested by the process but not yet granted (Figure 6.5a). Within a resource node, a dot is shown for each instance of that resource. Examples of resource types that may have multiple instances are I/O devices that are allocated by a resource management module in the operating system. A graph edge directed from a reusable

Table 6.1 Summary of Deadlock Detection, Prevention, and Avoidance Approaches for Operating Systems [ISLO80]

Approach	Resource Allocation Policy	Different Schemes	Major Advantages	Major Disadvantages
Prevention	Conservative; undercommit resources	Requesting all resources at once	• Works well for processes that perform a single burst of activity • No preemption necessary	• Inefficient • Delays process initiation • Future resource requirements must be known by processes
		Preemption	• Convenient when applied to resources whose state can be saved and restored easily	• Preempts more often than necessary
		Resource ordering	• Feasible to enforce via compile-time checks • Needs no run-time computation since problem is solved in system design	• Disallows incremental resource requests
Avoidance	Midway between that of detection and prevention	Manipulate to find at least one safe path	• No preemption necessary	• Future resource requirements must be known by OS • Processes can be blocked for long periods
Detection	Very liberal; requested resources are granted where possible	Invoke periodically to test for deadlock	• Never delays process initiation • Facilitates online handling	• Inherent preemption losses

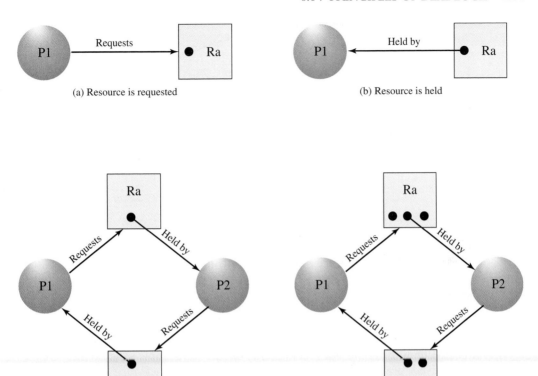

Figure 6.5   Examples of Resource Allocation Graphs

resource node dot to a process indicates a request that has been granted (Figure 6.5b); that is, the process has been assigned one unit of that resource. A graph edge directed from a consumable resource node dot to a process indicates that the process is the producer of that resource.

Figure 6.5c shows an example deadlock. There is only one unit each of resources Ra and Rb. Process P1 holds Rb and requests Ra, while P2 holds Ra but requests Rb. Figure 6.5d has the same topology as Figure 6.5c, but there is no deadlock because multiple units of each resource are available.

The resource allocation graph of Figure 6.6 corresponds to the deadlock situation in Figure 6.1b. Note that in this case, we do not have a simple situation in which two processes each have one resource the other needs. Rather, in this case, there is a circular chain of processes and resources that results in deadlock.

The Conditions for Deadlock

Three conditions of policy must be present for a deadlock to be possible:

1. **Mutual exclusion.** Only one process may use a resource at a time. No process may access a resource unit that has been allocated to another process.

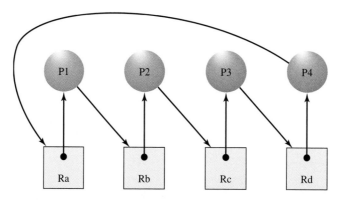

Figure 6.6   Resource Allocation Graph for Figure 6.1b

2. **Hold and wait.** A process may hold allocated resources while awaiting assignment of other resources.

3. **No preemption.** No resource can be forcibly removed from a process holding it.

In many ways these conditions are quite desirable. For example, mutual exclusion is needed to ensure consistency of results and the integrity of a database. Similarly, preemption should not be done arbitrarily. For example, when data resources are involved, preemption must be supported by a rollback recovery mechanism, which restores a process and its resources to a suitable previous state from which the process can eventually repeat its actions.

Deadlock can occur with these three conditions but might not exist with just these three conditions. For deadlock to actually take place, a fourth condition is required:

4. **Circular wait.** A closed chain of processes exists, such that each process holds at least one resource needed by the next process in the chain (e.g., Figure 6.5c and Figure 6.6).

The first three conditions are necessary but not sufficient for a deadlock to exist. The fourth condition is, actually, a potential consequence of the first three. That is, given that the first three conditions exist, a sequence of events may occur that lead to an unresolvable circular wait. The unresolvable circular wait is in fact the definition of deadlock. The circular wait listed as condition 4 is unresolvable because the first three conditions hold. Thus, the four conditions, taken together, constitute necessary and sufficient conditions for deadlock.[1]

To clarify this discussion, it is useful to return to the concept of the joint progress diagram, such as the one shown in Figure 6.2. Recall that we defined a fatal

---

[1]Virtually all textbooks simply list these four conditions as the conditions needed for deadlock, but such a presentation obscures some of the subtler issues. Item 4, the circular wait condition, is fundamentally different from the other three conditions. Items 1 through 3 are policy decisions, while item 4 is a circumstance that might occur depending on the sequencing of requests and releases by the involved processes. Linking circular wait with the three necessary conditions leads to inadequate distinction between prevention and avoidance. See [SHUB90] and [SHUB03] for a discussion.

region as one such that once the processes have progressed into that region, those processes will deadlock. A fatal region exists only if all of the first three conditions listed above are met. If one or more of these conditions are not met, there is no fatal region and deadlock cannot occur. Thus, these are necessary conditions for deadlock. For deadlock to occur, there must not only be a fatal region, but also a sequence of resource requests that has led into the fatal region. If a circular wait condition occurs, then in fact the fatal region has been entered. Thus, all four conditions listed above are sufficient for deadlock. To summarize,

Possibility of Deadlock	Existence of Deadlock
1. Mutual exclusion	**1.** Mutual exclusion
2. No preemption	**2.** No preemption
3. Hold and wait	**3.** Hold and wait
	4. Circular wait

Three general approaches exist for dealing with deadlock. First, one can **prevent** deadlock by adopting a policy that eliminates one of the conditions (conditions 1 through 4). Second, one can **avoid** deadlock by making the appropriate dynamic choices based on the current state of resource allocation. Third, one can attempt to **detect** the presence of deadlock (conditions 1 through 4 hold) and take action to recover. We discuss each of these approaches in turn.

6.2 DEADLOCK PREVENTION

The strategy of deadlock prevention is, simply put, to design a system in such a way that the possibility of deadlock is excluded. We can view deadlock prevention methods as falling into two classes. An indirect method of deadlock prevention is to prevent the occurrence of one of the three necessary conditions listed previously (items 1 through 3). A direct method of deadlock prevention is to prevent the occurrence of a circular wait (item 4). We now examine techniques related to each of the four conditions.

Mutual Exclusion

In general, the first of the four listed conditions cannot be disallowed. If access to a resource requires mutual exclusion, then mutual exclusion must be supported by the operating system. Some resources, such as files, may allow multiple accesses for reads but only exclusive access for writes. Even in this case, deadlock can occur if more than one process requires write permission.

Hold and Wait

The hold-and-wait condition can be prevented by requiring that a process request all of its required resources at one time and blocking the process until all requests can be granted simultaneously. This approach is inefficient in two ways. First, a process may be held up for a long time waiting for all of its resource requests to be filled, when in fact it could have proceeded with only some of the resources. Second, resources allocated to a process may remain unused for a considerable period, during which time they are denied to other processes. Another problem is that a process may not know in advance all of the resources that it will require.

There is also the practical problem created by the use of modular programming or a multithreaded structure for an application. An application would need to be aware of all resources that will be requested at all levels or in all modules to make the simultaneous request.

No Preemption

This condition can be prevented in several ways. First, if a process holding certain resources is denied a further request, that process must release its original resources and, if necessary, request them again together with the additional resource. Alternatively, if a process requests a resource that is currently held by another process, the operating system may preempt the second process and require it to release its resources. This latter scheme would prevent deadlock only if no two processes possessed the same priority.

This approach is practical only when applied to resources whose state can be easily saved and restored later, as is the case with a processor.

Circular Wait

The circular-wait condition can be prevented by defining a linear ordering of resource types. If a process has been allocated resources of type R, then it may subsequently request only those resources of types following R in the ordering.

To see that this strategy works, let us associate an index with each resource type. Then resource R_i precedes R_j in the ordering if $i < j$. Now suppose that two processes, A and B, are deadlocked because A has acquired R_i and requested R_j, and B has acquired R_j and requested R_i. This condition is impossible because it implies $i < j$ and $j < i$.

As with hold-and-wait prevention, circular-wait prevention may be inefficient, slowing down processes and denying resource access unnecessarily.

6.3 DEADLOCK AVOIDANCE

An approach to solving the deadlock problem that differs subtly from deadlock prevention is deadlock avoidance.[2] In **deadlock prevention**, we constrain resource requests to prevent at least one of the four conditions of deadlock. This is either done indirectly, by preventing one of the three necessary policy conditions (mutual exclusion, hold and wait, no preemption), or directly, by preventing circular wait. This leads to inefficient use of resources and inefficient execution of processes. **Deadlock avoidance**, on the other hand, allows the three necessary conditions but makes judicious choices to assure that the deadlock point is never reached. As such,

---

[2]The term *avoidance* is a bit confusing. In fact, one could consider the strategies discussed in this section to be examples of deadlock prevention because they indeed prevent the occurrence of a deadlock.

avoidance allows more concurrency than prevention. With deadlock avoidance, a decision is made dynamically whether the current resource allocation request will, if granted, potentially lead to a deadlock. Deadlock avoidance thus requires knowledge of future process resource requests.

In this section, we describe two approaches to deadlock avoidance:

- Do not start a process if its demands might lead to deadlock.
- Do not grant an incremental resource request to a process if this allocation might lead to deadlock.

Process Initiation Denial

Consider a system of n processes and m different types of resources. Let us define the following vectors and matrices:

Resource = $\mathbf{R} = (R_1, R_2, \cdots, R_m)$	total amount of each resource in the system
Available = $\mathbf{V} = (V_1, V_2, \cdots, V_m)$	total amount of each resource not allocated to any process
Claim = $\mathbf{C} = \begin{vmatrix} C_{11} & C_{12} & \cdots & C_{1m} \\ C_{21} & C_{22} & \cdots & C_{2m} \\ \vdots & \vdots & \vdots & \vdots \\ C_{n1} & C_{n2} & \cdots & C_{nm} \end{vmatrix}$	C_{ij} = requirement of process i for resource j
Allocation = $\mathbf{A} = \begin{vmatrix} A_{11} & A_{12} & \cdots & A_{1m} \\ A_{21} & A_{22} & \cdots & A_{2m} \\ \vdots & \vdots & \vdots & \vdots \\ A_{n1} & A_{n2} & \cdots & A_{nm} \end{vmatrix}$	A_{ij} = current allocation to process i of resource j

The matrix Claim gives the maximum requirement of each process for each resource, with one row dedicated to each process. This information must be declared in advance by a process for deadlock avoidance to work. Similarly, the matrix Allocation gives the current allocation to each process. The following relationships hold:

1. $R_j = V_j + \sum_{i=1}^{n} A_{ij}$, for all j All resources are either available or allocated.

2. $C_{ij} \leq R_j$, for all i, j No process can claim more than the total amount of resources in the system.

3. $A_{ij} \leq C_{ij}$, for all i, j No process is allocated more resources of any type than the process originally claimed to need.

With these quantities defined, we can define a deadlock avoidance policy that refuses to start a new process if its resource requirements might lead to deadlock. Start a new process P_{n+1} only if

$$R_j \geq C_{(n+1)j} + \sum_{i=1}^{n} C_{ij} \quad \text{for all } j$$

That is, a process is only started if the maximum claim of all current processes plus those of the new process can be met. This strategy is hardly optimal, because it assumes the worst: that all processes will make their maximum claims together.

Resource Allocation Denial

The strategy of resource allocation denial, referred to as the **banker's algorithm**,[3] was first proposed in [DIJK65]. Let us begin by defining the concepts of state and safe state. Consider a system with a fixed number of processes and a fixed number of resources. At any time a process may have zero or more resources allocated to it. The **state** of the system reflects the current allocation of resources to processes. Thus, the state consists of the two vectors, Resource and Available, and the two matrices, Claim and Allocation, defined earlier. A **safe state** is one in which there is at least one sequence of resource allocations to processes that does not result in a deadlock (i.e., all of the processes can be run to completion). An **unsafe state** is, of course, a state that is not safe.

The following example illustrates these concepts. Figure 6.7a shows the state of a system consisting of four processes and three resources. The total amount of resources R1, R2, and R3 are 9, 3, and 6 units, respectively. In the current state allocations have been made to the four processes, leaving 1 unit of R2 and 1 unit of R3 available. The question is, Is this a safe state? To answer this question, we ask an intermediate question: can any of the four processes be run to completion with the resources available? That is, can the difference between the maximum requirement and current allocation for any process be met with the available resources? In terms of the matrices and vectors introduced earlier, the condition to be met for process i is

$$C_{ij} - A_{ij} \leq V_j, \text{ for all } j$$

Clearly, this is not possible for P1, which has only 1 unit of R1 and requires 2 more units of R1, 2 units of R2, and 2 units of R3. However, by assigning one unit of R3 to process P2, P2 has its maximum required resources allocated and can run to completion. Let us assume that this is accomplished. When P2 completes, its resources can be returned to the pool of available resources. The resulting state is shown in Figure 6.7b. Now we can ask again if any of the remaining processes can be completed. In this case, each of the remaining processes could be completed. Suppose we

---

[3]Dijkstra used this name because of the analogy of this problem to one in banking, with customers who wish to borrow money corresponding to processes and the money to be borrowed corresponding to resources. Stated as a banking problem, the bank has a limited reserve of money to lend and a list of customers, each with a line of credit. A customer may choose to borrow against the line of credit a portion at a time, and there is no guarantee that the customer will make any repayment until after having taken out the maximum amount of loan. The banker can refuse a loan to a customer if there is a risk that the bank will have insufficient funds to make further loans that will permit the customers to repay eventually.

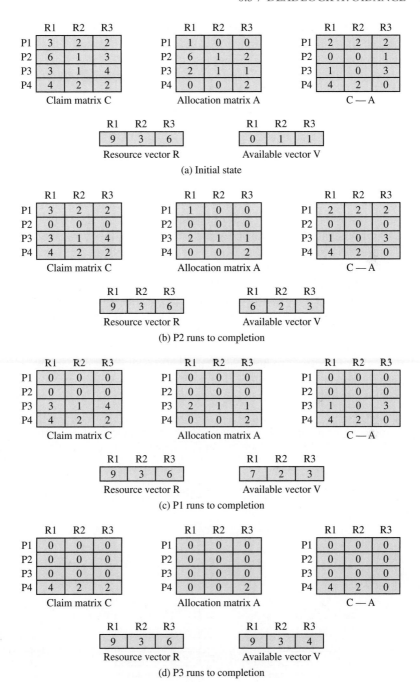

Figure 6.7   Determination of a Safe State

choose P1, allocate the required resources, complete P1, and return all of P1's resources to the available pool. We are left in the state shown in Figure 6.7c. Next, we can complete P3, resulting in the state of Figure 6.7d. Finally, we can complete P4. At this point, all of the processes have been run to completion. Thus, the state defined by Figure 6.7a is a safe state.

These concepts suggest the following deadlock avoidance strategy, which ensures that the system of processes and resources is always in a safe state. When a process makes a request for a set of resources, assume that the request is granted, update the system state accordingly, and then determine if the result is a safe state. If so, grant the request and, if not, block the process until it is safe to grant the request.

Consider the state defined in Figure 6.8a. Suppose P2 makes a request for one additional unit of R1 and one additional unit of R3. If we assume the request is granted, then the resulting state is that of Figure 6.7a. We have already seen that this is a safe state; therefore, it is safe to grant the request. Now let us return to the state of Figure 6.8a and suppose that P1 makes the request for one additional unit each of R1 and R3; if we assume that the request is granted, we are left in the state of Figure 6.8b. Is this a safe state? The answer is no, because each process will need at least one additional unit of R1, and there are none available. Thus, on the basis of deadlock avoidance, the request by P1 should be denied and P1 should be blocked.

It is important to point out that Figure 6.8b is not a deadlocked state. It merely has the potential for deadlock. It is possible, for example, that if P1 were run from this state that it would subsequently release one unit of R1 and one unit of R3 prior to

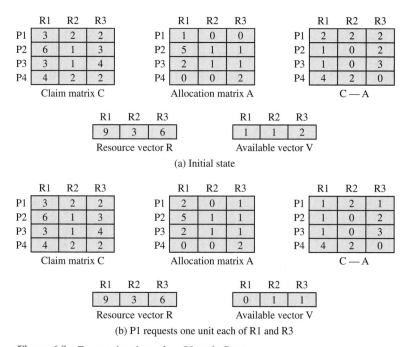

(a) Initial state

(b) P1 requests one unit each of R1 and R3

Figure 6.8   Determination of an Unsafe State

needing these resources again. If that happened, the system would return to a safe state. Thus, the deadlock avoidance strategy does not predict deadlock with certainty; it merely anticipates the possibility of deadlock and assures that there is never such a possibility.

Figure 6.9 gives an abstract version of the deadlock avoidance logic. The main algorithm is shown in part (b). With the state of the system defined by the data structure **state**, **request[*]** is a vector defining the resources requested by process *i*. First, a check is made to assure that the request does not exceed the original claim of the process. If the request is valid, the next step is to determine if it is possible to fulfill the request (i.e., there are sufficient resources available). If it is not possible, then the process is suspended. If it is possible, the final step is to determine if it is safe to fulfill the request. To do this, the resources are tentatively assigned to process *i* to form **newstate**. Then a test for safety is made using the algorithm in Figure 6.9c.

Deadlock avoidance has the advantage that it is not necessary to preempt and rollback processes, as in deadlock detection, and is less restrictive than deadlock prevention. However, it does have a number of restrictions on its use:

- The maximum resource requirement for each process must be stated in advance.
- The processes under consideration must be independent; that is, the order in which they execute must be unconstrained by any synchronization requirements.
- There must be a fixed number of resources to allocate.
- No process may exit while holding resources.

6.4 DEADLOCK DETECTION

Deadlock prevention strategies are very conservative; they solve the problem of deadlock by limiting access to resources and by imposing restrictions on processes. At the opposite extreme, deadlock detection strategies do not limit resource access or restrict process actions. With deadlock detection, requested resources are granted to processes whenever possible. Periodically, the operating system performs an algorithm that allows it to detect the circular wait condition described earlier in condition (4) and illustrated in Figure 6.6.

Deadlock Detection Algorithm

A check for deadlock can be made as frequently as each resource request or, less frequently, depending on how likely it is for a deadlock to occur. Checking at each resource request has two advantages: It leads to early detection, and the algorithm is relatively simple because it is based on incremental changes to the state of the system. On the other hand, such frequent checks consume considerable processor time.

A common algorithm for deadlock detection is one described in [COFF71]. The Allocation matrix and Available vector described in the previous section are used. In addition, a request matrix $\mathbf{Q}$ is defined such that Q_{ij} represents the amount of resources of type *j* requested by process *i*. The algorithm proceeds by marking

```
struct state
{
    int resource[m];
    int available[m];
    int claim[n][m];
    int alloc[n][m];
}
```

(a) global data structures

```
if (alloc [i,*] + request [*] > claim [i,*])
    < error >;                                        /* total request > claim*/
else if (request [*] > available [*])
    < suspend process >;
else                                                  /* simulate alloc */
{
    < define newstate by:
    alloc [i,*] = alloc [i,*] + request [*];
    available [*] = available [*] - request [*] >;
}
if (safe (newstate))
    < carry out allocation >;
else
{
    < restore original state >;
    < suspend process >;
}
```

(b) resource alloc algorithm

```
boolean safe (state S)
{
    int currentavail[m];
    process rest[<number of processes>];
    currentavail = available;
    rest = {all processes};
    possible = true;
    while (possible)
    {
        <find a process Pk in rest such that
            claim [k,*] – alloc [k,*] <= currentavail;>
        if (found)                                    /* simulate execution of Pk */
        {
            currentavail = currentavail + alloc [k,*];
            rest = rest - {Pk};
        }
        else
            possible = false;
    }
    return (rest == null);
}
```

(c) test for safety algorithm (banker's algorithm)

Figure 6.9   Deadlock Avoidance Logic

processes that are not deadlocked. Initially, all processes are unmarked. Then the following steps are performed:

1. Mark each process that has a row in the Allocation matrix of all zeros.
2. Initialize a temporary vector **W** to equal the Available vector.
3. Find an index i such that process i is currently unmarked and the ith row of **Q** is less than or equal to **W**. That is, $Q_{ik} \leq W_k$, for $1 \leq k \leq m$. If no such row is found, terminate the algorithm.
4. If such a row is found, mark process i and add the corresponding row of the allocation matrix to **W**. That is, set $W_k = W_k + A_{ik}$, for $1 \leq k \leq m$. Return to step 3.

A deadlock exists if and only if there are unmarked processes at the end of the algorithm. Each unmarked process is deadlocked. The strategy in this algorithm is to find a process whose resource requests can be satisfied with the available resources, and then assume that those resources are granted and that the process runs to completion and releases all of its resources. The algorithm then looks for another process to satisfy. Note that this algorithm does not guarantee to prevent deadlock; that will depend on the order in which future requests are granted. All that it does is determine if deadlock currently exists.

We can use Figure 6.10 to illustrate the deadlock detection algorithm. The algorithm proceeds as follows:

1. Mark P4, because P4 has no allocated resources.
2. Set **W** $= (0\,0\,0\,0\,1)$.
3. The request of process P3 is less than or equal to **W**, so mark P3 and set **W** $=$ **W** $+ (0\,0\,0\,1\,0) = (0\,0\,0\,1\,1)$.
4. No other unmarked process has a row in **Q** that is less than or equal to **W**. Therefore, terminate the algorithm.

The algorithm concludes with P1 and P2 unmarked, indicating that these processes are deadlocked.

Recovery

Once deadlock has been detected, some strategy is needed for recovery. The following are possible approaches, listed in order of increasing sophistication:

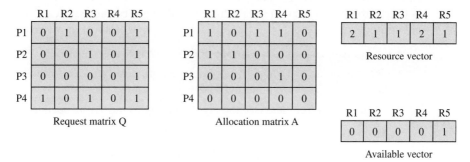

Figure 6.10   Example for Deadlock Detection

1. Abort all deadlocked processes. This is, believe it or not, one of the most common, if not the most common, solution adopted in operating systems.

2. Back up each deadlocked process to some previously defined checkpoint, and restart all processes. This requires that rollback and restart mechanisms be built in to the system. The risk in this approach is that the original deadlock may recur. However, the nondeterminancy of concurrent processing may ensure that this does not happen.

3. Successively abort deadlocked processes until deadlock no longer exists. The order in which processes are selected for abortion should be on the basis of some criterion of minimum cost. After each abortion, the detection algorithm must be reinvoked to see whether deadlock still exists.

4. Successively preempt resources until deadlock no longer exists. As in (3), a cost-based selection should be used, and reinvocation of the detection algorithm is required after each preemption. A process that has a resource preempted from it must be rolled back to a point prior to its acquisition of that resource.

For (3) and (4), the selection criteria could be one of the following. Choose the process with the

- least amount of processor time consumed so far
- least amount of output produced so far
- most estimated time remaining
- least total resources allocated so far
- lowest priority

Some of these quantities are easier to measure than others. Estimated time remaining is particularly suspect. Also, other than by means of the priority measure, there is no indication of the "cost" to the user, as opposed to the cost to the system as a whole.

6.5 AN INTEGRATED DEADLOCK STRATEGY

As Table 6.1 suggests, there are strengths and weaknesses to all of the strategies for dealing with deadlock. Rather than attempting to design an operating system facility that employs only one of these strategies, it might be more efficient to use different strategies in different situations. [HOWA73] suggests one approach:

- Group resources into a number of different resource classes.
- Use the linear ordering strategy defined previously for the prevention of circular wait to prevent deadlocks between resource classes.
- Within a resource class, use the algorithm that is most appropriate for that class.

As an example of this technique, consider the following classes of resources:

- **Swappable space:** Blocks of memory on secondary storage for use in swapping processes

- **Process resources:** Assignable devices, such as tape drives, and files
- **Main memory:** Assignable to processes in pages or segments
- **Internal resources:** Such as I/O channels

The order of the preceding list represents the order in which resources are assigned. The order is a reasonable one, considering the sequence of steps that a process may follow during its lifetime. Within each class, the following strategies could be used:

- **Swappable space:** Prevention of deadlocks by requiring that all of the required resources that may be used be allocated at one time, as in the hold-and-wait prevention strategy. This strategy is reasonable if the maximum storage requirements are known, which is often the case. Deadlock avoidance is also a possibility.

- **Process resources:** Avoidance will often be effective in this category, because it is reasonable to expect processes to declare ahead of time the resources that they will require in this class. Prevention by means of resource ordering within this class is also possible.

- **Main memory:** Prevention by preemption appears to be the most appropriate strategy for main memory. When a process is preempted, it is simply swapped to secondary memory, freeing space to resolve the deadlock.

- **Internal resources:** Prevention by means of resource ordering can be used.

6.6 DINING PHILOSOPHERS PROBLEM

We now turn to the dining philosophers problem, introduced by Dijkstra [DIJK71]. Five philosophers live in a house, where a table is laid for them. The life of each philosopher consists principally of thinking and eating, and through years of thought, all of the philosophers had agreed that the only food that contributed to their thinking efforts was spaghetti. Due to a lack of manual skill, each philosopher requires two forks to eat spaghetti.

The eating arrangements are simple (Figure 6.11): a round table on which is set a large serving bowl of spaghetti, five plates, one for each philosopher, and five forks. A philosopher wishing to eat goes to his or her assigned place at the table and, using the two forks on either side of the plate, takes and eats some spaghetti. The problem: Devise a ritual (algorithm) that will allow the philosophers to eat. The algorithm must satisfy mutual exclusion (no two philosophers can use the same fork at the same time) while avoiding deadlock and starvation (in this case, the term has literal as well as algorithmic meaning!).

This problem may not seem important or relevant in itself. However, it does illustrate basic problems in deadlock and starvation. Furthermore, attempts to develop solutions reveal many of the difficulties in concurrent programming (e.g., see [GING90]). In addition, the dining philosophers problem can be seen as representative of problems dealing with the coordination of shared resources, which may occur when an application includes concurrent threads of execution. Accordingly, this problem is a standard test case for evaluating approaches to synchronization.

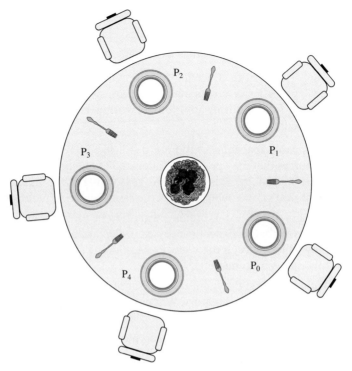

Figure 6.11 Dining Arrangement for Philosophers

Solution Using Semaphores

Figure 6.12 suggests a solution using semaphores. Each philosopher picks up first the fork on the left and then the fork on the right. After the philosopher is finished eating, the two forks are replaced on the table. This solution, alas, leads to deadlock: If all of the philosophers are hungry at the same time, they all sit down, they all pick up the fork on their left, and they all reach out for the other fork, which is not there. In this undignified position, all philosophers starve.

To overcome the risk of deadlock, we could buy five additional forks (a more sanitary solution!) or teach the philosophers to eat spaghetti with just one fork. As another approach, we could consider adding an attendant who only allows four philosophers at a time into the dining room. With at most four seated philosophers, at least one philosopher will have access to two forks. Figure 6.13 shows such a solution, again using semaphores. This solution is free of deadlock and starvation.

Solution Using a Monitor

Figure 6.14 shows a solution to the dining philosophers problem using a monitor. A vector of five condition variables is defined, one condition variable per fork. These condition variables are used to enable a philosopher to wait for the availability of a fork. In addition, there is a Boolean vector that records the availability status of each fork (**true** means the fork is available). The monitor consists of two procedures. The

```
/* program diningphilosophers */
semaphore fork [5] = {1};
int i;
void philosopher (int i)
{
    while (true)
    {
        think();
        wait (fork[i]);
        wait (fork [(i+1) mod 5]);
        eat();
        signal(fork [(i+1) mod 5]);
        signal(fork[i]);
    }
}
void main()
{
    parbegin (philosopher (0), philosopher (1), philosopher (2),
        philosopher (3), philosopher (4));
}
```

Figure 6.12 A First Solution to the Dining Philosophers Problem

```
/* program diningphilosophers */
semaphore fork[5] = {1};
semaphore room = {4};
int i;
void philosopher (int I)
{
    while (true)
    {
        think();
        wait (room);
        wait (fork[i]);
        wait (fork [(i+1) mod 5]);
        eat();
        signal (fork [(i+1) mod 5]);
        signal (fork[i]);
        signal (room);
    }
}
void main()
{
    parbegin (philosopher (0), philosopher (1), philosopher (2),
        philosopher (3), philosopher (4));
}
```

Figure 6.13 A Second Solution to the Dining Philosophers Problem

```
monitor dining_controller;
cond ForkReady[5];                              /* condition variable for synchronization */
boolean fork[5] = {true};                        /* availability status of each fork */
void get_forks(int pid)                          /* pid is the philosopher id number */
{
    int left = pid;
    int right = (pid++) % 5;
    /*grant the left fork*/
    if (!fork(left)
        cwait(ForkReady[left]);                  /* queue on condition variable */
    fork(left) = false;
    /*grant the right fork*/
    if (!fork(right)
        cwait(ForkReady[right]);                 /* queue on condition variable */
    fork(right) = false:
}
void release_forks(int pid)
{
    int left = pid;
    int right = (pid++) % 5;
    /*release the left fork*/
    if (empty(ForkReady[left])                   /*no one is waiting for this fork */
        fork(left) = true;
    else   /* awaken a process waiting on this fork */
        csignal(ForkReady[left]);
    /*release the right fork*/
    if (empty(ForkReady[right])                  /*no one is waiting for this fork */
        fork(right) = true;
    else                                         /* awaken a process waiting on this fork */
        csignal(ForkReady[right]);
}
```

```
void philosopher[k=0 to 4]                       /* the five philosopher clients */
{
    while (true)
    {
        <think>;
        get_forks(k);                            /* client requests two forks via monitor */
        <eat spaghetti>;
        release_forks(k);                        /* client releases forks via the monitor */
    }
}
```

Figure 6.14   A Solution to the Dining Philosophers Problem Using a Monitor

get_forks procedure is used by a philosopher to seize his or her left and right forks. If either fork is unavailable, the philosopher process is queued on the appropriate condition variable. This enables another philosopher process to enter the monitor. The **release-forks** procedure is used to make two forks available. Note that the structure of this solution is similar to that of the semaphore solution proposed in Figure 6.12. In both cases, a philosopher seizes first the left fork and then the right fork. Unlike the semaphore solution, this monitor solution does not suffer from deadlock, because only one process at a time may be in the monitor. For example, the first philosopher process to enter the monitor is guaranteed that it can pick up the right fork after it picks up the left fork before the next philosopher to the right has a chance to seize its left fork, which is this philosopher's right fork.

6.7 UNIX CONCURRENCY MECHANISMS

UNIX provides a variety of mechanisms for interprocessor communication and synchronization. Here, we look at the most important of these:

- Pipes
- Messages
- Shared memory
- Semaphores
- Signals

Pipes, messages, and shared memory can be used to communicate data between processes, whereas semaphores and signals are used to trigger actions by other processes.

Pipes

One of the most significant contributions of UNIX to the development of operating systems is the pipe. Inspired by the concept of coroutines [RITC84], a pipe is a circular buffer allowing two processes to communicate on the producer-consumer model. Thus, it is a first-in-first-out queue, written by one process and read by another.

When a pipe is created, it is given a fixed size in bytes. When a process attempts to write into the pipe, the write request is immediately executed if there is sufficient room; otherwise the process is blocked. Similarly, a reading process is blocked if it attempts to read more bytes than are currently in the pipe; otherwise the read request is immediately executed. The operating system enforces mutual exclusion: that is, only one process can access a pipe at a time.

There are two types of pipes: named and unnamed. Only related processes can share unnamed pipes, while either related or unrelated processes can share named pipes.

Messages

A message is a block of bytes with an accompanying type. UNIX provides **msgsnd** and **msgrcv** system calls for processes to engage in message passing. Associated with each process is a message queue, which functions like a mailbox.

The message sender specifies the type of message with each message sent, and this can be used as a selection criterion by the receiver. The receiver can either retrieve messages in first-in-first-out order or by type. A process will block when trying to send a message to a full queue. A process will also block when trying to read from an empty queue. If a process attempts to read a message of a certain type and fails because no message of that type is present, the process is not blocked.

Shared Memory

The fastest form of interprocess communication provided in UNIX is shared memory. This is a common block of virtual memory shared by multiple processes. Processes read and write shared memory using the same machine instructions they use to read and write other portions of their virtual memory space. Permission is read-only or read-write for a process, determined on a per-process basis. Mutual exclusion constraints are not part of the shared-memory facility but must be provided by the processes using the shared memory.

Semaphores

The semaphore system calls in UNIX System V are a generalization of the **semWait** and **semSignal** primitives defined in Chapter 5; several operations can be performed simultaneously and the increment and decrement operations can be values greater than 1. The kernel does all of the requested operations atomically; no other process may access the semaphore until all operations have completed.

A semaphore consists of the following elements:

- Current value of the semaphore
- Process ID of the last process to operate on the semaphore
- Number of processes waiting for the semaphore value to be greater than its current value
- Number of processes waiting for the semaphore value to be zero

Associated with the semaphore are queues of processes blocked on that semaphore.

Semaphores are actually created in sets, with a semaphore set consisting of one or more semaphores. There is a **semctl** system call that allows all of the semaphore values in the set to be set at the same time. In addition, there is a **sem_op** system call that takes as an argument a list of semaphore operations, each defined on one of the semaphores in a set. When this call is made, the kernel performs the indicated operations one at a time. For each operation, the actual function is specified by the value **sem_op**. The following are the possibilities:

- If **sem_op** is positive, the kernel increments the value of the semaphore and awakens all processes waiting for the value of the semaphore to increase.
- If **sem_op** is 0, the kernel checks the semaphore value. If the semaphore value equals 0, the kernel continues with the other operations on the list. Otherwise, the kernel increments the number of processes waiting for this semaphore to be 0 and suspends the process to wait for the event that the value of the semaphore equals 0.
- If **sem_op** is negative and its absolute value is less than or equal to the semaphore value, the kernel adds **sem_op** (a negative number) to the semaphore value. If the result is 0, the kernel awakens all processes waiting for the value of the semaphore to equal 0.

- If **sem_op** is negative and its absolute value is greater than the semaphore value, the kernel suspends the process on the event that the value of the semaphore increases.

This generalization of the semaphore provides considerable flexibility in performing process synchronization and coordination.

Signals

A signal is a software mechanism that informs a process of the occurrence of asynchronous events. A signal is similar to a hardware interrupt but does not employ priorities. That is, all signals are treated equally; signals that occur at the same time are presented to a process one at a time, with no particular ordering.

Processes may send each other signals, or the kernel may send signals internally. A signal is delivered by updating a field in the process table for the process to which the signal is being sent. Because each signal is maintained as a single bit, signals of a given type cannot be queued. A signal is processed just after a process wakes up to run or whenever the process is preparing to return from a system call. A process may respond to a signal by performing some default action (e.g., termination), executing a signal handler function, or ignoring the signal.

Table 6.2 lists signals defined for UNIX SVR4.

6.8 LINUX KERNEL CONCURRENCY MECHANISMS

Linux includes all of the concurrency mechanisms found in other UNIX systems, such as SVR4, including pipes, messages, shared memory, and signals. In addition, Linux 2.6 includes a rich set of concurrency mechanisms specifically intended for use when a thread is executing in kernel mode. That is, these are mechanisms used within the kernel to provide concurrency in the execution of kernel code. This section examines the Linux kernel concurrency mechanisms.

Atomic Operations

Linux provides a set of operations that guarantee atomic operations on a variable. These operations can be used to avoid simple race conditions. An atomic operation executes without interruption and without interference. On a uniprocessor system, a thread performing an atomic operation cannot be interrupted once the operation has started until the operation is finished. In addition, on a multiprocessor system, the variable being operated on is locked from access by other threads until this operation is completed.

Two types of atomic operations are defined in Linux: integer operations, which operate on an integer variable, and bitmap operations, which operate on one bit in a bitmap (Table 6.3). These operations must be implemented on any architecture that implements Linux. For some architectures, there are corresponding assembly language instructions for the atomic operations. On other architectures, an operation that locks the memory bus is used to guarantee that the operation is atomic.

Table 6.2   UNIX Signals

Value	Name	Description
01	SIGHUP	Hang up; sent to process when kernel assumes that the user of that process is doing no useful work
02	SIGINT	Interrupt
03	SIGQUIT	Quit; sent by user to induce halting of process and production of core dump
04	SIGILL	Illegal instruction
05	SIGTRAP	Trace trap; triggers the executioon of code for process tracing
06	SIGIOT	IOT instruction
07	SIGEMT	EMT instruction
08	SIGFPE	Floating-point exception
09	SIGKILL	Kill; terminate process
10	SIGBUS	Bus error
11	SIGSEGV	Segmentation violation; process attempts to access location outside its virtual address space
12	SIGSYS	Bad arument to system call
13	SIGPIPE	Write on a pipe that has no readers attached to it
14	SIGALRM	Alarm clock; issued when a process wishes to receive a signal after a period of time
15	SIGTERM	Software termination
16	SIGUSRI	User-defined signal 1
17	SIGUSR2	User-defined signal 2
18	SIGCHLD	Death of a child
19	SIGPWR	Power failure

For **atomic integer operations**, a special data type is used, `atomic_t`. The atomic integer operations can be used only on this data type, and no other operations are allowed on this data type. [LOVE04] lists the following advantages for these restrictions:

1. The atomic operations are never used on variables that might in some circumstances be unprotected from race conditions.

2. Variables of this data type are protected from improper use by nonatomic operations.

3. The compiler cannot erroneously optimize access to the value (e.g., by using an alias rather than the correct memory address).

4. This data type serves to hide architecture-specific differences in its implementation.

A typical use of the atomic integer data type is to implement counters.

Table 6.3   Linux Atomic Operations

Atomic Integer Operations	
ATOMIC_INT (int i)	At declaration: initialize an atomic_t to i
int atomic_read(atomic_t *v)	Read integer value of v
void atomic_set(atomic_t *v, int i)	Set the value of v to integer i
void atomic_add(int i, atomic_t *v)	Add i to v
void atomic_sub(int i, atomic_t *v)	Subtract i from v
void atomic_inc(atomic_t *v)	Add 1 to v
void atomic_dec(atomic_t *v)	Substract 1 from v
int atomic_sub_and_test(int i, atomic_t *v)	Substract i from v; return 1 if the result is zero; return 0 otherwise
int atomic_dec_and_test(atomic_t *v)	Add 1 to v; return 1 if the result is zero; return 0 otherwise
Atomic Bitmap Operations	
void set_bit(int nr, void* addr)	Set bit nr in the bitmap pointed to by addr
void clear_bit(int nr, void *addr)	Clear bit nr in the bitmap pointed to by addr
void change_bit(int nr, void *addr)	Invert bit nr in the bitmap pointed to by addr
int test_and_set_bit(int nr, void *addr)	Set bit nr in the bitmap pointed to by addr; return the old bit value
int test_and_clear_bit(int nr, void *addr)	Clear bit nr in the bitmap pointed to by addr; return the old bit value
int test_and_change_bit(int nr, void *addr)	Invert bit nr in the bitmap pointed to by addr; return the old bit value
int test_bit(int nr, void *addr)	Return the value of bit nr in the bitmap pointed to by addr

The **atomic bitmap operations** operate on one of a sequence of bits at an arbitrary memory location indicated by a pointer variable. Thus, there is no equivalent to the `atomic_t` data type needed for atomic integer operations.

Atomic operations are the simplest of the approaches to kernel synchronization. More complex locking mechanisms can be built on top of them.

Spinlocks

The most common technique used for protecting a critical section in Linux is the spinlock. Only one thread at a time can acquire a spinlock. Any other thread attempting to acquire the same lock will keep trying (spinning) until it can acquire the lock. In essence, a spinlock is built on an integer location in memory that is checked by each thread before it enters its critical section. If the value is 0, the thread sets the value to 1 and enters its critical section. If the value is nonzero, the thread continually checks the value until it is zero. The spinlock is easy to implement but has the disadvantage that locked-out threads continue to execute in a busy-waiting mode. Thus spinlocks are most effective in situations where the wait

Table 6.4   Linux Spinlocks

void spin_lock(spinlock_t *lock)	Acquires the specified lock, spinning if needed until it is available
void spin_lock_irq(spinlock_t *lock)	Like spin_lock, but also disables interrupts on the local processor
void spin_lock_irqsave(spinlock_t *lock, unsigned long flags)	Like spin_lock_irq, but also saves the current interrupt state in flags
void spin_lock_bh(spinlock_t *lock)	Like spin_lock, but also disables the execution of all bottom halves
void spin_unlock(spinlock_t *lock)	Releases given lock
void spin_unlock_irq(spinlock_t *lock)	Releases given lock and enables local interrupts
void spin_unlock_irqrestore(spinlock_t *lock, unsigned long flags)	Releases given lock and restores local interrupts to given previous state
void spin_unlock_bh(spinlock_t *lock)	Releases given lock and enables bottom halves
void spin_lock_init(spinlock_t *lock)	Initializes given spinlock
int spin_trylock(spinlock_t *lock)	Tries to acquire specified lock; returns nonzero if lock is currently held and zero otherwise
int spin_is_locked(spinlock_t *lock)	Returns nonzero if lock is currently held and zero otherwise

time for acquiring a lock is expected to be very short, say on the order of less than two context changes.

The basic form of use of a spinlock is the following:

```
spin_lock(&lock)
/* critical section */
spin_unlock(&lock)
```

Basic Spinlocks   The basic spinlock (as opposed to the reader-writer spinlock explained subsequently) comes in four flavors (Table 6.4):

- **Plain:** If the critical section of code is not executed by interrupt handlers or if the interrupts are disabled during the execution of the critical section, then the plain spinlock can be used. It does not affect the interrupt state on the processor on which it is run.
- **_irq:** If interrupts are always enabled, then this spinlock should be used.
- **_irqsave:** If it is not known if interrupts will be enabled or disabled at the time of execution, then this version should be used. When a lock is acquired, the current state of interrupts on the local processor is saved, to be restored when the lock is released.
- **_bh:** When an interrupt occurs, the minimum amount of work necessary is performed by the corresponding interrupt handler. A piece of code, called the *bottom half*, performs the remainder of the interrupt-related work, allowing the current interrupt to be enabled as soon as possible. The _bh spinlock is

used to disable and then enable bottom halves to avoid conflict with the protected critical section.

The plain spinlock is used if the programmer knows that the protected data is not accessed by an interrupt handler or bottom half. Otherwise, the appropriate nonplain spinlock is used.

Spinlocks are implemented differently on a uniprocessor machine versus a multiprocessor machine. For a uniprocessor system, the following considerations apply. If kernel preemption is turned off, so that a thread executing in kernel mode cannot be interrupted, then the locks are deleted at compile time; they are not needed. If kernel preemption is enabled, which does permit interrupts, then the spinlocks again compile away (that is, no test of a spinlock memory location occurs) but are simply implemented as code that enables/disables interrupts. On a multiple-processor machine, the spinlock is compiled into code that does in fact test the spinlock location. The use of the spinlock mechanism in the program allows it to be independent of whether it is executed on a uniprocessor or multiprocessor machine.

Reader-Writer Spinlock The reader-writer spinlock is a mechanism that allows a greater degree of concurrency within the kernel than the basic spinlock. The reader-writer spinlock allows multiple threads to have simultaneous access to the same data structure for reading only but gives exclusive access to the spinlock for a thread that intends to update the data structure. Each reader-writer spinlock consists of a 24-bit reader counter and an unlock flag, with the following interpretation:

Counter	Flag	Interpretation
0	1	The spinlock is released and available for use
0	0	Spinlock has been acquired for writing by one thread
$n(n > 0)$	0	Spinlock has been acquired for reading by n threads
$n(n > 0)$	1	Not valid

As with the basic spinlock, there are plain, _irq, and _irqsave versions of the reader-writer spinlock.

Note that the reader-writer spinlock favors readers over writers. If the spinlock is held for readers, then so long as there is at least one reader, the spinlock cannot be preempted by a writer. Furthermore, new readers may be added to the spinlock even while a writer is waiting.

Semaphores

At the user level, Linux provides a semaphore interface corresponding to that in UNIX SVR4. Internally, Linux provides an implementation of semaphores for its own use. That is, code that is part of the kernel can invoke kernel semaphores. These kernel semaphores cannot be accessed directly by the user program via system calls.

Table 6.5 Linux Semaphores

Traditional Semaphores	
void sema_init(struct semaphore *sem, int count)	Initializes the dynamically created semaphore to the given count
void init_MUTEX(struct semaphore *sem)	Initializes the dynamically created semaphore with a count of 1 (initially unlocked)
void init_MUTEX_LOCKED(struct semaphore *sem)	Initializes the dynamically created semaphore with a count of 0 (initially locked)
void down(struct semaphore *sem)	Attempts to acquire the given semaphore, entering uninterruptible sleep if semaphore is unavailable
int down_interruptible(struct semaphore *sem)	Attempts to acquire the given semaphore, entering interruptible sleep if semaphore is unavailable; returns -EINTR value if a signal other than the result of an up operation is received.
int down_trylock(struct semaphore *sem)	Attempts to acquire the given semaphore, and returns a nonzero value if semaphore is unavailable
void up(struct semaphore *sem)	Releases the given semaphore
Reader-Writer Semaphores	
void init_rwsem(struct rw_semaphore, *rwsem)	Initalizes the dynamically created semaphore with a count of 1
void down_read(struct rw_semaphore, *rwsem)	Down operation for readers
void up_read(struct rw_semaphore, *rwsem)	Up operation for readers
void down_write(struct rw_semaphore, *rwsem)	Down operation for writers
void up_write(struct rw_semaphore, *rwsem)	Up operation for writers

They are implemented as functions within the kernel and are thus more efficient than user-visible semaphores.

Linux provides three types of semaphore facilities in the kernel: binary semaphores, counting semaphores, and reader-writer semaphores.

Binary and Counting Semaphores The binary and counting semaphores defined in Linux 2.6 (Table 6.5) have the same functionality as described for such semaphores in Chapter 5. The function names **down** and **up** are used for the functions referred to in Chapter 5 as **semWait** and **semSignal**, respectively.

A counting semaphore is initialized using the **sema_init** function, which gives the semaphore a name and assigns an initial value to the semaphore. Binary semaphores, called MUTEXes in Linux, are initialized using the **init_MUTEX** and **init_MUTEX_LOCKED** functions, which initialize the semaphore to 1 or 0, respectively.

Linux provides three versions of the **down (semWait)** operation.

1. The **down** function corresponds to the traditional **semWait** operation. That is, the thread tests the semaphore and blocks if the semaphore is not available. The thread will awaken when a corresponding **up** operation on this semaphore

occurs. Note that this function name is used for an operation on either a counting semaphore or a binary semaphore.

2. The **down_interruptible** function allows the thread to receive and respond to a kernel signal while being blocked on the down operation. If the thread is woken up by a signal, the **down_interruptible** function increments the count value of the semaphore and returns an error code known in Linux as **-EINTR**. This alerts the thread that the invoked semaphore function has aborted. In effect, the thread has been forced to "give up" the semaphore. This feature is useful for device drivers and other services in which it is convenient to override a semaphore operation.

3. The **down_trylock** function makes it possible to try to acquire a semaphore without being blocked. If the semaphore is available, it is acquired. Otherwise, this function returns a nonzero value without blocking the thread.

Reader–Writer Semaphores The reader-writer semaphore divides users into readers and writers; it allows multiple concurrent readers (with no writers) but only a single writer (with no concurrent readers). In effect, the semaphore functions as a counting semaphore for readers but a binary semaphore (MUTEX) for writers. Table 6.5 shows the basic reader-writer semaphore operations. The reader-writer semaphore uses uninterruptible sleep, so there is only one version of each of the down operations.

Barriers

In some architectures, compilers and/or the processor hardware may reorder memory accesses in source code to optimize performance. These reorderings are done to optimize the use of the instruction pipeline in the processor. The reordering algorithms contain checks to ensure that data dependencies are not violated. For example, the code

```
a = 1;
b = 1;
```

may be reordered so that memory location **b** is updated before memory location **a** is updated. However, the code

```
a = 1;
b = a;
```

will not be reordered. Even so, there are occasions when it is important that reads or writes are executed in the order specified because of use of the information that is made by another thread or a hardware device.

To enforce the order in which instructions are executed, Linux provides the memory barrier facility. Table 6.6 lists the most important functions that are defined for this facility. The **rmb()** operation insures that no reads occur across the barrier defined by the place of the **rmb()** in the code. Similarly, the **wmb()** operation insures that no writes occur across the barrier defined by the place of the **wmb()** in the code. The **mb()** operation provides both a load and store barrier.

Table 6.6 Linux Memory Barrier Operations

rmb()	Prevents loads from being reordered across the barrier
wmb()	Prevents stores from being reordered across the barrier
mb()	Prevents loads and stores from being reordered across the barrier
barrier()	Prevents the compiler from reordering loads or stores across the barrier
smp_rmb()	On SMP, provides a **rmb**() and on UP provides a barrier()
smp_wmb()	On SMP, provides a **wmb**() and on UP provides a barrier()
smp_mb()	On SMP, provides a **mb**() and on UP provides a barrier()

SMP = symmetric multiprocessor
UP = uniprocessor

Two important points to note about the barrier operations:

1. The barriers relate to machine instructions, namely loads and stores. Thus the higher-level language instruction **a = b** involves both a load (read) from location **b** and a store (write) to location **a**.

2. The **rmb**, **wmb**, and **mb** operations dictate the behavior of both the compiler and the processor. In the case of the compiler, the barrier operation dictates that the compiler not reorder instructions during the compile process. In the case of the processor, the barrier operation dictates that any instructions pending in the pipeline before the barrier must be committed for execution before any instructions encountered after the barrier.

The **barrier()** operation is a lighter-weight version of the **mb()** operation, in that it only controls the compiler's behavior. This would be useful if it is known that the processor will not perform undesirable reorderings. For example, the Intel x86 processors do not reorder writes.

The **smp_rmb**, **smp_wmb**, and **smp_mb** operations provide an optimization for code that may be compiled on either a uniprocessor (UP) or a symmetric multiprocessor (SMP). These instructions are defined as the usual memory barriers for an SMP, but for a UP, they are all treated only as compiler barriers. The **smp_** operations are useful in situations in which the data dependencies of concern will only arise in an SMP context.

6.9 SOLARIS THREAD SYNCHRONIZATION PRIMITIVES

In addition to the concurrency mechanisms of UNIX SVR4, Solaris supports four thread synchronization primitives:

- Mutual exclusion (mutex) locks
- Semaphores
- Multiple readers, single writer (readers/writer) locks
- Condition variables

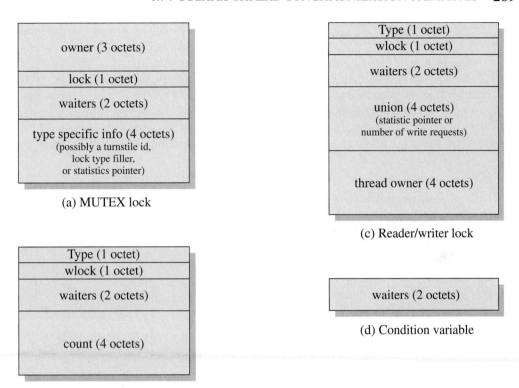

Figure 6.15 Solaris Synchronization Data Structures

Solaris implements these primitives within the kernel for kernel threads; they are also provided in the threads library for user-level threads. Figure 6.15 shows the data structures for these primitives. The initialization functions for the primitives fill in some of the data members. Once a synchronization object is created, there are essentially only two operations that can be performed: enter (acquire lock) and release (unlock). There are no mechanisms in the kernel or the threads library to enforce mutual exclusion or to prevent deadlock. If a thread attempts to access a piece of data or code that is supposed to be protected but does not use the appropriate synchronization primitive, then such access occurs. If a thread locks an object and then fails to unlock it, no kernel action is taken.

All of the synchronization primitives require the existence of a hardware instruction that allows an object to be tested and set in one atomic operation, as discussed in Section 5.3.

Mutual Exclusion Lock

A mutex is used to ensure only one thread at a time can access the resource protected by the mutex. The thread that locks the mutex must be the one that unlocks it. A thread attempts to acquire a mutex lock by executing the **mutex_enter** primitive. If **mutex_enter** cannot set the lock (because it is already set by another thread), the blocking action depends on type-specific information stored in the mutex object. The default blocking policy is a spin lock: A blocked thread polls the status of the lock while executing in a busy waiting loop. An interrupt-based blocking mechanism is optional. In this latter case, the mutex includes a `turnstile id` that identifies a queue of threads sleeping on this lock.

The operations on a mutex lock are as follows:

`mutex_enter()`	Acquires the lock, potentially blocking if it is already held
`mutex_exit()`	Releases the lock, potentially unblocking a waiter
`mutex_tryenter()`	Acquires the lock if it is not already held

The `mutex_tryenter()` primitive provides a nonblocking way of performing the mutual exclusion function. This enables the programmer to use a busy-wait approach for user-level threads, which avoids blocking the entire process because one thread is blocked.

Semaphores

Solaris provides classic counting semaphores, with the following primitives:

`sema_p()`	Decrements the semaphore, potentially blocking the thread
`sema_v()`	Increments the semaphore, potentially unblocking a waiting thread
`sema_tryp()`	Decrements the semaphore if blocking is not required

Again, the `sema_tryp()` primitive permits busy waiting.

Readers/Writer Lock

The readers/writer lock allows multiple threads to have simultaneous read-only access to an object protected by the lock. It also allows a single thread to access the object for writing at one time while excluding all readers. When the lock is acquired for writing it takes on the status of `write lock`: All threads attempting access for reading or writing must wait. If one or more readers have acquired the lock, its status is `read lock`. The primitives are as follows:

`rw_enter()`	Attempts to acquire a lock as reader or writer.
`rw_exit()`	Releases a lock as reader or writer.
`rw_tryenter()`	Acquires the lock if blocking is not required.
`rw_downgrade()`	A thread that has acquired a write lock converts it to a read lock. Any waiting writer remains waiting until this thread releases the lock. If there are no waiting writers, the primitive wakes up any pending readers.
`rw_tryupgrade()`	Attempts to convert a reader lock into a writer lock.

Condition Variables

A condition variable is used to wait until a particular condition is true. Condition variables must be used in conjunction with a mutex lock. This implements a monitor of the type illustrated in Figure 6.14. The primitives are as follows:

`cv_wait()`	Blocks until the condition is signaled
`cv_signal()`	Wakes up one of the threads blocked in `cv_wait()`
`cv_broadcast()`	Wakes up all of the threads blocked in `cv_wait()`

`cv_wait()` releases the associated mutex before blocking and reacquires it before returning. Because reacquisition of the mutex may be blocked by other threads waiting for the mutex, the condition that caused the wait must be retested. Thus, typical usage is as follows:

```
mutex_enter(&m)
• •
while (some_condition) {
   cv_wait(&cv, &m);
}
• •
mutex_exit(&m);
```

This allows the condition to be a complex expression, because it is protected by the mutex.

6.10 WINDOWS CONCURRENCY MECHANISMS

Windows XP and 2003 provide synchronization among threads as part of the object architecture. The two most important methods of synchronization are synchronization objects and critical section objects. Synchronization objects make use of wait functions. We first describe wait functions and then look at the two object types.

Wait Functions

The wait functions allow a thread to block its own execution. The wait functions do not return until the specified criteria have been met. The type of wait function determines the set of criteria used. When a wait function is called, it checks whether the wait criteria have been met. If the criteria have not been met, the calling thread enters the wait state. It uses no processor time while waiting for the criteria to be met.

The most straightforward type of wait function is one that waits on a single object. The `WaitForSingleObject` function requires a handle to one synchronization object. The function returns when one of the following occurs:

- The specified object is in the signaled state.
- The time-out interval elapses. The time-out interval can be set to `INFINITE` to specify that the wait will not time out.

Synchronization Objects

The mechanism used by the Windows executive to implement synchronization facilities is the family of synchronization objects, which are listed with brief descriptions in Table 6.7.

The first four object types in the table are specifically designed to support synchronization. The remaining object types have other uses but also may be used for synchronization.

Each synchronization object instance can be in either a signaled or unsignaled state. A thread can be blocked on an object in an unsignaled state; the thread is released when the object enters the signaled state. The mechanism is straightforward: A thread issues a wait request to the Windows executive, using the handle of the synchronization object. When an object enters the signaled state, the Windows executive releases all thread objects that are waiting on that synchronization object.

Table 6.7   Windows Synchronization Objects

Object Type	Definition	Set to Signaled State When	Effect on Waiting Threads
Event	An announcement that a system event has occurred	Thread sets the event	All released
Mutex	A mechanism that provides mutual exclusion capabilities; equivalent to a binary semaphore	Owning thread or other thread releases the mutex	One thread released
Semaphore	A counter that regulates the number of threads that can use a resource	Semaphore count drops to zero	All released
Waitable timer	A counter that records the passage of time	Set time arrives or time interval expires	All released
File change notification	A notification of any file system changes.	Change occurs in file system that matches filter criteria of this object	One thread released
Console input	A text window screen buffer (e.g., used to handle screen I/O for an MS-DOS application)	Input is available for processing	One thread released
Job	An instance of an opened file or I/O device	I/O operation completes	All released
Memory resource notification	A notification of change to a memory resource	Specified type of change occurs within physical memory	All released
Process	A program invocation, including the address space and resources required to run the program	Last thread terminates	All released
Thread	An executable entity within a process	Thread terminates	All released

Note: Colored rows correspond to objects that exist for the sole purpose of synchronization.

The **event object** is useful in sending a signal to a thread indicating that a particular event has occurred. For example, in overlapped input and output, the system sets a specified event object to the signaled state when the overlapped operation has been completed. The **mutex object** is used to enforce mutually exclusive access to a resource, allowing only one thread object at a time to gain access. It therefore functions as a binary semaphore. When the mutex object enters the signaled state, only one of the threads waiting on the mutex is released. Mutexes can be used to synchronize threads running in different processes. Like mutexes, **semaphore objects** may be shared by threads in multiple processes. The Windows semaphore is a counting semaphore. In essence, the **waitable timer object** signals at a certain time and/or at regular intervals.

Critical Section Objects

Critical section objects provide a synchronization mechanism similar to that provided by mutex objects, except that critical section objects can be used only by the threads of a single process. Event, mutex, and semaphore objects can also be used in a single-process application, but critical section objects provide a slightly faster, more efficient mechanism for mutual-exclusion synchronization.

The process is responsible for allocating the memory used by a critical section. Typically, this is done by simply declaring a variable of type `CRITICAL_SECTION`. Before the threads of the process can use it, initialize the critical section by using the `InitializeCriticalSection` or `InitializeCriticalSectionAndSpinCount` function.

A thread uses the `EnterCriticalSection` or `TryEnterCriticalSection` function to request ownership of a critical section. It uses the `LeaveCriticalSection` function to release ownership of a critical section. If the critical section object is currently owned by another thread, `EnterCriticalSection` waits indefinitely for ownership. In contrast, when a mutex object is used for mutual exclusion, the wait functions accept a specified time-out interval. The `TryEnterCriticalSection` function attempts to enter a critical section without blocking the calling thread.

6.11 SUMMARY

Deadlock is the blocking of a set of processes that either compete for system resources or communicate with each other. The blockage is permanent unless the operating system takes some extraordinary action, such as killing one or more processes or forcing one or more processes to backtrack. Deadlock may involve reusable resources or consumable resources. A reusable resource is one that is not depleted or destroyed by use, such as an I/O channel or a region of memory. A consumable resource is one that is destroyed when it is acquired by a process; examples include messages and information in I/O buffers.

There are three general approaches to dealing with deadlock: prevention, detection, and avoidance. Deadlock prevention guarantees that deadlock will not occur, by assuring that one of the necessary conditions for deadlock is not met. Deadlock detection is needed if the operating system is always willing to grant resource requests; periodically, the operating system must check for deadlock and take action to break the deadlock. Deadlock avoidance involves the analysis of each new resource request to determine if it could lead to deadlock, and granting it only if deadlock is not possible.

6.12 RECOMMENDED READINGS

The classic paper on deadlocks, [HOLT72], is still well worth a read, as is [COFF71]. Another good survey is [ISLO80]. [CORB96] is a thorough treatment of deadlock detection. [DIMI98] is a nice overview of deadlocks. Two recent papers by Levine [LEVI03a, LEVI03b] clarify some of the concepts used in discussions of deadlock. [SHUB03] is a useful overview of deadlock.

The concurrency mechanisms in UNIX SVR4, Linux, and Solaris 2 are well covered in [GRAY97], [LOVE04], and [MAUR01], respectively.

COFF71 Coffman, E.; Elphick, M.; and Shoshani, A. "System Deadlocks." *Computing Surveys*, June 1971.

CORB96 Corbett, J. "Evaluating Deadlock Detection Methods for Concurrent Software." *IEEE Transactions on Software Engineering*, March 1996.

DIMI98 Dimitoglou, G. "Deadlocks and Methods for Their Detection, Prevention, "and Recovery in Modern Operating Systems." *Operating Systems Review*, July 1998.

GRAY97 Gray, J. *Interprocess Communications in UNIX: The Nooks and Crannies.* Upper Saddle River, NJ: Prentice Hall, 1997.

HOLT72 Holt, R. "Some Deadlock Properties of Computer Systems." *Computing Surveys*, September 1972.

ISLO80 Isloor, S., and Marsland, T. "The Deadlock Problem: An Overview." *Computer*, September 1980.

LEVI03a Levine, G. "Defining Deadlock." *Operating Systems Review*, January 2003.

LEVI03b Levine, G. "Defining Deadlock with Fungible Resources." *Operating Systems Review*, July 2003.

LOVE04 Love, R. *Linux Kernel Development.* Indianapolis, IN: Sams Publishing, 2004.

MAUR01 Mauro, J., McDougall, R. *Solaris Internals.* Upper Saddle River, NJ: Prentice Hall PTR, 2001.

SHUB03 Shub, C. "A Unified Treatment of Deadlock." *Journal of Computing in Small Colleges*, October 2003. Available through the ACM digital library.

6.13 KEY TERMS, REVIEW QUESTIONS, AND PROBLEMS

Key Terms

banker's algorithm	deadlock prevention	pipe
circular wait	hold and wait	preemption
consumable resource	joint progress diagram	resource allocation graph
deadlock	memory barrier	reusable resource
deadlock avoidance	message	spinlock
deadlock detection	mutual exclusion	starvation

Review Questions

6.1 Give examples of reusable and consumable resources.

6.2 What are the three conditions that must be present for deadlock to be possible?

6.3 What are the four conditions that create deadlock?

6.4 How can the hold-and-wait condition be prevented?

6.5 List two ways in which the no-preemption condition can be prevented.

6.6 How can the circular wait condition be prevented?

6.7 What is the difference among deadlock avoidance, detection, and prevention?

Problems

6.1 Show that the four conditions of deadlock apply to Figure 6.1a.

6.2 For Figure 6.3, provide a narrative description of each of the six depicted paths, similar to the description of the paths of Figure 6.2 provided in Section 6.1.

6.3 It was stated that deadlock cannot occur for the situation reflected in Figure 6.3. Justify that statement.

6.4 Consider the following snapshot of a system. There are no outstanding unsatisfied requests for resources.

available

r1	r2	r3	r4
2	1	0	0

process	current allocation				maximum demand				still needs			
	r1	r2	r3	r4	r1	r2	r3	r4	r1	r2	r3	r4
p1	0	0	1	2	0	0	1	2				
p2	2	0	0	0	2	7	5	0				
p3	0	0	3	4	6	6	5	6				
p4	2	3	5	4	4	3	5	6				
p5	0	3	3	2	0	6	5	2				

a. Compute what each process still might request and display in the columns labeled "still needs."

b. Is this system currently in a safe or unsafe state? Why?

c. Is this system currently deadlocked? Why or why not?

d. Which processes, if any, are or may become deadlocked?

e. If a request from p3 arrives for (0, 1, 0, 0), can that request be safely granted immediately? In what state (deadlocked, safe, unsafe) would immediately granting that whole request leave the system? Which processes, if any, are or may become deadlocked if this whole request is granted immediately?

6.5 Apply the deadlock detection algorithm of Section 6.4 to the following data and show the results.

$$\text{Available} = (2\ \ 1\ \ 0\ \ 0)$$

$$\text{Request} = \begin{vmatrix} 2 & 0 & 0 & 1 \\ 1 & 0 & 1 & 0 \\ 2 & 1 & 0 & 0 \end{vmatrix} \quad \text{Allocation} = \begin{vmatrix} 0 & 0 & 1 & 0 \\ 2 & 0 & 0 & 1 \\ 0 & 1 & 2 & 0 \end{vmatrix}$$

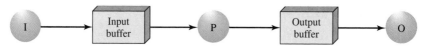

Figure 6.16 A Spooling System

6.6   A spooling system (Figure 6.16) consists of an input process I, user process P, and an output process O connected by two buffers. The processes exchange data in blocks of equal size. These blocks are buffered on a disk using a floating boundary between the input and the output buffers, depending on the speed of the processes. The communication primitives used ensure that the following resource constraint is satisfied:

$$i + o \leq max$$

where

$$max = \text{maximum number of block on disk}$$
$$i = \text{number of input blocks on disk}$$
$$o = \text{number of output blocks on disk}$$

The following is known about the processes:

1. As long as the environment supplies data, process I will eventually input it to the disk (provided disk space becomes available).
2. As long as input is available on the disk, process P will eventually consume it and output a finite amount of data on the disk for each block input (provided disk space becomes available).
3. As long as output is available on the disk, process O will eventually consume it. Show that this system can become deadlocked.

6.7   Suggest an additional resource constraint that will prevent the deadlock in Problem 6.6 but still permit the boundary between input and output buffers to vary in accordance with the present needs of the processes.

6.8   In THE multiprogramming system [DIJK68], a drum (precursor to the disk for secondary storage) is divided into input buffers, processing areas, and output buffers, with floating boundaries, depending on the speed of the processes involved. The current state of the drum can be characterized by the following parameters:

$$max = \text{maximum number of pages on drum}$$
$$i = \text{number of input pages on drum}$$
$$p = \text{number of processing pages on drum}$$
$$o = \text{number of output pages on drum}$$
$$reso = \text{minimum number of pages reserved for output}$$
$$resp = \text{minimum number of pages reserved for processing}$$

Formulate the necessary resource constraints that guarantee that the drum capacity is not exceeded and that a minimum number of pages is reserved permanently for output and processing.

6.9   In THE multiprogramming system, a page can make the following state transitions:
1. empty $\rightarrow$ input buffer   (input production)
2. input buffer $\rightarrow$ processing area   (input consumption)
3. processing area $\rightarrow$ output buffer   (output production)
4. output buffer $\rightarrow$ empty   (output consumption)
5. empty $\rightarrow$ processing area   (procedure call)
6. processing area $\rightarrow$ empty   (procedure return)
   a. Define the effect of these transitions in terms of the quantities i, o, and p.
   b. Can any of them lead to a deadlock if the assumptions made in Problem 6.6 about input processes, user processes, and output processes hold?

6.10   Consider a system with a total of 150 units of memory, allocated to three process-es as shown:

Process	Max	Hold
1	70	45
2	60	40
3	60	15

Apply the banker's algorithm to determine whether it would be safe to grant each of the following requests. If yes, indicate a sequence of terminations that could be guar-anteed possible. If no, show the reduction of the resulting allocation table.

  a.   A fourth process arrives, with a maximum memory need of 60 and an initial need of 25 units.
  b.   A fourth process arrives, with a maximum memory need of 60 and an initial need of 35 units.

6.11   Evaluate the banker's algorithm for its usefulness in an operating system.

6.12   A pipeline algorithm is implemented so that a stream of data elements of type **T** pro-duced by a process P_0 passes through a sequence of processes $P_1, P_2, \ldots, P_{n-1}$, which operates on the elements in that order.

  a.   Define a generalized message buffer that contains all the partially consumed data elements and write an algorithm for process P_i $(0 \le i \le n - 1)$, of the form

  repeat
     receive from predecessor;
     consume element;
     send to successor:
  forever

  Assume P_0 receives input elements sent by P_{n-1}. The algorithm should enable the processes to operate directly on messages stored in the buffer so that copying is unnecessary.

  b.   Show that the processes cannot be deadlocked with respect to the common buffer.

6.13 a.   Three processes share four resource units that can be reserved and released only one at a time. Each process needs a maximum of two units. Show that a deadlock cannot occur.

  b.   N processes share M resource units that can be reserved and released only one at a time. The maximum need of each process does not exceed M, and the sum of all maximum needs is less than $M + N$. Show that a deadlock cannot occur.

6.14   Consider a system consisting of four processes and a single resource. The current state of the claim and allocation matrices is

$$\mathbf{C} = \begin{vmatrix} 3 \\ 2 \\ 9 \\ 7 \end{vmatrix} \quad \mathbf{A} = \begin{vmatrix} 1 \\ 1 \\ 3 \\ 2 \end{vmatrix}$$

What is the minimum number of units of the resource needed to be available for this state to be safe?

6.15   Consider the following ways of handling deadlock: (1) banker's algorithm, (2) detect deadlock and kill thread, releasing all resources, (3) reserve all resources in advance, (4) restart thread and release all resources if thread needs to wait, (5) resource order-ing, and (6) detect deadlock and roll back thread's actions.

  a.   One criterion to use in evaluating different approaches to deadlock is which approach permits the greatest concurrency. In other words, which approach

```
monitor dining_controller;
enum states (thinking, hungry, eating} state[5];
cond needFork[5]                                        /* condition variable */
void get_forks(int pid)                                 /* pid is the philosopher id number */
{
    state[pid] = hungry;                                /* announce that I'm hungry */
    if (state[(pid+1) % 5] == eating
    || (state[(pid-1) % 5] == eating
    cwait(needFork[pid]);                               /* wait if either neighbor is eating */
    state[pid] = eating;                                /* proceed if neither neighbor is eating */
}
void release_forks(int pid)
{
    state[pid] = thinking;
    /* give right (higher) neighbor a chance to eat */
    if (state[(pid+1) % 5] == hungry)
    || (state[(pid+2) % 5]) != eating)
    csignal(needFork[pid+1]);
    /* give left (lower) neighbor a chance to eat */
    else if (state[(pid–1) % 5] == hungry)
    || (state[(pid–2) % 5]) != eating)
    csignal(needFork[pid–1]);
}
```

```
void philosopher[k=0 to 4]                              /* the five philosopher clients */
{
    while (true)
    {
        <think>;
        get_forks(k);                                   /* client requests two forks via monitor */
        <eat spaghetti>;
        release_forks(k);                               /* client releases forks via the monitor */
    }
}
```

Figure 6.17   Another Solution to the Dining Philosophers Problem Using a Monitor

allows the most threads to make progress without waiting when there is no dead-lock? Give a rank order from 1 to 6 for each of the ways of handling deadlock just listed, where 1 allows the greatest degree of concurrency. Comment on your ordering.

b.   Another criterion is efficiency; in other words, which requires the least processor overhead. Rank order the approaches from 1 to 6, with 1 being the most efficient, assuming that deadlock is a very rare event. Comment on your ordering. Does your ordering change if deadlocks occur frequently?

6.16   Comment on the following solution to the dining philosophers problem. A hungry philosopher first picks up his left fork; if his right fork is also available, he picks up his right fork and starts eating; otherwise he puts down his left fork again and repeats the cycle.

6.17   Suppose that there are two types of philosophers. One type always picks up his left fork first (a "lefty"), and the other type always picks up his right fork first (a "righty"). The behavior of a lefty is defined in Figure 6.12. The behavior of a righty is as follows:

begin
  repeat
        think;
        wait (fork[(i + 1) **mod** 5]);
        wait (fork[i]);
        eat;
        signal (fork[i]);
        signal (fork[(i + 1) **mod** 5]);
  forever
end;

Prove the following:
a. Any seating arrangement of lefties and righties with at least one of each avoids deadlock.
b. Any seating arrangement of lefties and righties with at least one of each prevents starvation.

6.18 Figure 6.17 shows another solution to the dining philosophers problem using monitors. Compare to Figure 6.14 and report your conclusions.

6.19 In Table 6.3, some of the Linux atomic operations do not involve two accesses to a variable, such as **atomic_read(atomic_t *v)**. A simple read operation is obviously atomic in any architecture. Therefore, why is this operation added to the repertoire of atomic operations?

6.20 Consider the following fragment of code on a Linux system.

        read_lock(&mr_rwlock);
        write_lock(&mr_rwlock);

Where **mr_rwlock** is a reader-writer lock. What is the effect of this code?

6.21 The two variables a and b have initial values of 1 and 2, respectively. The following code is for a Linux system:

Thread 1	Thread 2
a = 3;	—
mb();	—
b=4;	c = b;
—	rmb();
—	d = a;

What possible errors are avoided by the use of the memory barriers?

PART THREE

Memory

One of the most difficult aspects of operating system design is memory management. Although the cost of memory has dropped dramatically and, as a result, the size of main memory on modern machines has grown, reaching into the gigabyte range, there is never enough main memory to hold all of the programs and data structures needed by active processes and by the operating system. Accordingly, a central task of the operating system is to manage memory, which involves bringing in and swapping out blocks of data from secondary memory. However, memory I/O is a slow operation, and its speed relative to the processor's instruction cycle time lags further and further behind with each passing year. To keep the processor or processors busy and thus to maintain efficiency, the operating system must cleverly time the swapping in and swapping out to minimize the effect of memory I/O on performance.

Chapter 7 Memory Management

Chapter 7 provides an overview of the fundamental mechanisms used in memory management. First, the basic requirements of any memory management scheme are summarized. Then the use of memory partitioning is introduced. This technique is not much used except in special cases, such as kernel memory management. However, a review of memory partitioning illuminates many of the design issues involved in memory management. The remainder of the chapter deals with two techniques that form the basic building blocks of virtually all memory management systems: paging and segmentation.

Chapter 8 Virtual Memory

Virtual memory, based on the use of either paging or the combination of paging and segmentation, is the almost universal approach to memory management on contemporary machines. Virtual memory is a scheme that is transparent to the application processes and allows each process to behave as if it had unlimited memory at its disposal. To achieve this, the operating system creates for each process a virtual address space, or virtual memory, on disk. Part of the virtual memory is brought into real main memory as needed. In this way, many processes can share a relatively small amount of main memory. For virtual memory to work effectively, hardware mechanisms are needed to perform the basic paging and segmentation functions, such as address translation between virtual and real addresses. Chapter 8 begins with an overview of these hardware mechanisms. The remainder of the chapter is devoted to operating system design issues relating to virtual memory.

CHAPTER 7

MEMORY MANAGEMENT

In a uniprogramming system, main memory is divided into two parts: one part for the operating system (resident monitor, kernel) and one part for the program currently being executed. In a multiprogramming system, the "user" part of memory must be further subdivided to accommodate multiple processes. The task of subdivision is carried out dynamically by the operating system and is known as **memory management**.

Effective memory management is vital in a multiprogramming system. If only a few processes are in memory, then for much of the time all of the processes will be waiting for I/O and the processor will be idle. Thus memory needs to be allocated to ensure a reasonable supply of ready processes to consume available processor time.

We begin this chapter with a look at the requirements that memory management is intended to satisfy. Next, we approach the technology of memory management by looking at a variety of simple schemes that have been used. Our focus is the requirement that a program must be loaded into main memory to be executed. This discussion introduces some of the fundamental principles of memory management.

7.1 MEMORY MANAGEMENT REQUIREMENTS

While surveying the various mechanisms and policies associated with memory management, it is helpful to keep in mind the requirements that memory management is intended to satisfy. [LIST93] suggests five requirements:

- Relocation
- Protection
- Sharing
- Logical organization
- Physical organization

Relocation

In a multiprogramming system, the available main memory is generally shared among a number of processes. Typically, it is not possible for the programmer to know in advance which other programs will be resident in main memory at the time of execution of his or her program. In addition, we would like to be able to swap active processes in and out of main memory to maximize processor utilization by providing a large pool of ready processes to execute. Once a program has been swapped out to disk, it would be quite limiting to declare that when it is next swapped back in, it must be placed in the same main memory region as before. Instead, we may need to **relocate** the process to a different area of memory.

Thus, we cannot know ahead of time where a program will be placed, and we must allow that the program may be moved about in main memory due to swapping. These facts raise some technical concerns related to addressing, as illustrated in Figure 7.1. The figure depicts a process image. For simplicity, let us assume that the process image occupies a contiguous region of main memory. Clearly, the

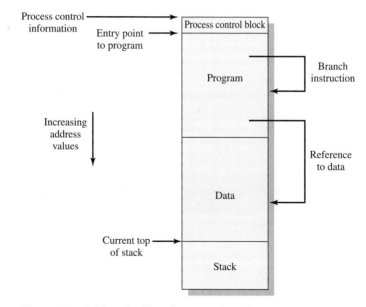

Figure 7.1 Addressing Requirements for a Process

operating system will need to know the location of process control information and of the execution stack, as well as the entry point to begin execution of the program for this process. Because the operating system is managing memory and is responsible for bringing this process into main memory, these addresses are easy to come by. In addition, however, the processor must deal with memory references within the program. Branch instructions contain an address to reference the instruction to be executed next. Data reference instructions contain the address of the byte or word of data referenced. Somehow, the processor hardware and operating system software must be able to translate the memory references found in the code of the program into actual physical memory addresses, reflecting the current location of the program in main memory.

Protection

Each process should be protected against unwanted interference by other processes, whether accidental or intentional. Thus, programs in other processes should not be able to reference memory locations in a process for reading or writing purposes without permission. In one sense, satisfaction of the relocation requirement increases the difficulty of satisfying the protection requirement. Because the location of a program in main memory is unpredictable, it is impossible to check absolute addresses at compile time to assure protection. Furthermore, most programming languages allow the dynamic calculation of addresses at run time (for example, by computing an array subscript or a pointer into a data structure). Hence all memory references generated by a process must be checked at run time to ensure that they refer only to the memory space allocated to that process. Fortunately, we shall see that mechanisms that support relocation also support the protection requirement.

Normally, a user process cannot access any portion of the operating system, neither program nor data. Again, usually a program in one process cannot branch to an instruction in another process. Without special arrangement, a program in one process cannot access the data area of another process. The processor must be able to abort such instructions at the point of execution.

Note that the memory protection requirement must be satisfied by the processor (hardware) rather than the operating system (software). This is because the operating system cannot anticipate all of the memory references that a program will make. Even if such anticipation were possible, it would be prohibitively time consuming to screen each program in advance for possible memory-reference violations. Thus, it is only possible to assess the permissibility of a memory reference (data access or branch) at the time of execution of the instruction making the reference. To accomplish this, the processor hardware must have that capability.

Sharing

Any protection mechanism must have the flexibility to allow several processes to access the same portion of main memory. For example, if a number of processes are executing the same program, it is advantageous to allow each process to access the same copy of the program rather than have its own separate copy. Processes that are cooperating on some task may need to share access to the same data structure. The memory-management system must therefore allow controlled access to shared areas of memory without compromising essential protection. Again, we will see that the mechanisms used to support relocation support sharing capabilities.

Logical Organization

Almost invariably, main memory in a computer system is organized as a linear, or one-dimensional, address space, consisting of a sequence of bytes or words. Secondary memory, at its physical level, is similarly organized. While this organization closely mirrors the actual machine hardware, it does not correspond to the way in which programs are typically constructed. Most programs are organized into modules, some of which are unmodifiable (read only, execute only) and some of which contain data that may be modified. If the operating system and computer hardware can effectively deal with user programs and data in the form of modules of some sort, then a number of advantages can be realized:

1. Modules can be written and compiled independently, with all references from one module to another resolved by the system at run time.

2. With modest additional overhead, different degrees of protection (read only, execute only) can be given to different modules.

3. It is possible to introduce mechanisms by which modules can be shared among processes. The advantage of providing sharing on a module level is that this corresponds to the user's way of viewing the problem, and hence it is easy for the user to specify the sharing that is desired.

The tool that most readily satisfies these requirements is segmentation, which is one of the memory-management techniques explored in this chapter.

Physical Organization

As we discussed in Section 1.5, computer memory is organized into at least two levels, referred to as main memory and secondary memory. Main memory provides fast access at relatively high cost. In addition, main memory is volatile; that is, it does not provide permanent storage. Secondary memory is slower and cheaper than main memory and is usually not volatile. Thus secondary memory of large capacity can be provided for long-term storage of programs and data, while a smaller main memory holds programs and data currently in use.

In this two-level scheme, the organization of the flow of information between main and secondary memory is a major system concern. The responsibility for this flow could be assigned to the individual programmer, but this is impractical and undesirable for two reasons:

1. The main memory available for a program plus its data may be insufficient. In that case, the programmer must engage in a practice known as **overlaying**, in which the program and data are organized in such a way that various modules can be assigned the same region of memory, with a main program responsible for switching the modules in and out as needed. Even with the aid of compiler tools, overlay programming wastes programmer time.

2. In a multiprogramming environment, the programmer does not know at the time of coding how much space will be available or where that space will be.

It is clear, then, that the task of moving information between the two levels of memory should be a system responsibility. This task is the essence of memory management.

7.2 MEMORY PARTITIONING

The principal operation of memory management is to bring processes into main memory for execution by the processor. In almost all modern multiprogramming systems, this involves a sophisticated scheme known as virtual memory. Virtual memory is, in turn, based on the use of one or both of two basic techniques: segmentation and paging. Before we can look at these virtual memory techniques, we must prepare the ground by looking at simpler techniques that do not involve virtual memory (Table 7.1). One of these techniques, partitioning, has been used in several variations in some now-obsolete operating systems. The other two techniques, simple paging and simple segmentation, are not used by themselves. However, it will clarify the discussion of virtual memory if we look first at these two techniques in the absence of virtual memory considerations.

Fixed Partitioning

In most schemes for memory management, we can assume that the operating system occupies some fixed portion of main memory and that the rest of main memory is available for use by multiple processes. The simplest scheme for managing this available memory is to partition it into regions with fixed boundaries.

Table 7.1   Memory Management Techniques

Technique	Description	Strengths	Weaknesses
Fixed Partitioning	Main memory is divided into a number of static partitions at system generation time. A process may be loaded into a partition of equal or greater size.	Simple to implement; little operating system overhead.	Inefficient use of memory due to internal fragmentation; maximum number of active processes is fixed.
Dynamic Partitioning	Partitions are created dynamically, so that each process is loaded into a partition of exactly the same size as that process.	No internal fragmentation; more efficient use of main memory.	Inefficient use of processor due to the need for compaction to counter external fragmentation.
Simple Paging	Main memory is divided into a number of equal-size frames. Each process is divided into a number of equal-size pages of the same length as frames. A process is loaded by loading all of its pages into available, not necessarily contiguous, frames.	No external fragmentation.	A small amount of internal fragmentation.
Simple Segmentation	Each process is divided into a number of segments. A process is loaded by loading all of its segments into dynamic partitions that need not be contiguous.	No internal fragmentation; improved memory utilization and reduced overhead compared to dynamic partitioning.	External fragmentation.
Virtual-Memory Paging	As with simple paging, except that it is not necessary to load all of the pages of a process. Nonresident pages that are needed are brought in later automatically.	No external fragmentation; higher degree of multiprogramming; large virtual address space.	Overhead of complex memory management.
Virtual-Memory Segmentation	As with simple segmentation, except that it is not necessary to load all of the segments of a process. Nonresident segments that are needed are brought in later automatically.	No internal fragmentation, higher degree of multiprogramming; large virtual address space; protection and sharing support.	Overhead of complex memory management.

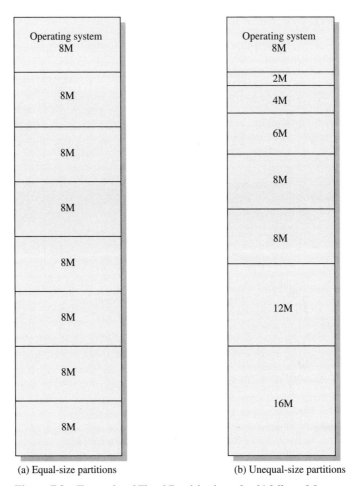

(a) Equal-size partitions   (b) Unequal-size partitions

Figure 7.2   Example of Fixed Partitioning of a 64-Mbyte Memory

Partition Sizes Figure 7.2 shows examples of two alternatives for fixed partitioning. One possibility is to make use of equal-size partitions. In this case, any process whose size is less than or equal to the partition size can be loaded into any available partition. If all partitions are full and no process is in the Ready or Running state, the operating system can swap a process out of any of the partitions and load in another process, so that there is some work for the processor.

There are two difficulties with the use of equal-size fixed partitions:

- A program may be too big to fit into a partition. In this case, the programmer must design the program with the use of overlays so that only a portion of the program need be in main memory at any one time. When a module is needed that is not present, the user's program must load that module into the program's partition, overlaying whatever programs or data are there.

- Main memory utilization is extremely inefficient. Any program, no matter how small, occupies an entire partition. In our example, there may be a program whose length is less than 2 Mbytes; yet it occupies an 8-Mbyte partition whenever it is swapped in. This phenomenon, in which there is wasted space internal to a partition due to the fact that the block of data loaded is smaller than the partition, is referred to as **internal fragmentation**.

Both of these problems can be lessened, though not solved, by using unequal-size partitions (Figure 7.2b). In this example, programs as large as 16 Mbytes can be accommodated without overlays. Partitions smaller than 8 Mbytes allow smaller programs to be accommodated with less internal fragmentation.

Placement Algorithm With equal-size partitions, the placement of processes in memory is trivial. As long as there is any available partition, a process can be loaded into that partition. Because all partitions are of equal size, it does not matter which partition is used. If all partitions are occupied with processes that are not ready to run, then one of these processes must be swapped out to make room for a new process. Which one to swap out is a scheduling decision; this topic is explored in Part Four.

With unequal-size partitions, there are two possible ways to assign processes to partitions. The simplest way is to assign each process to the smallest partition within which it will fit.[1] In this case, a scheduling queue is needed for each partition, to hold swapped-out processes destined for that partition (Figure 7.3a). The advantage of this approach is that processes are always assigned in such a way as to minimize wasted memory within a partition (internal fragmentation).

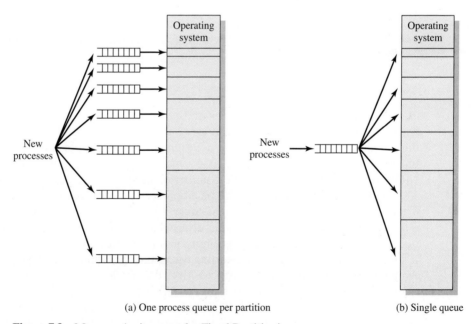

(a) One process queue per partition

(b) Single queue

Figure 7.3 Memory Assignment for Fixed Partitioning

---

[1]This assumes that one knows the maximum amount of memory that a process will require. This is not always the case. If it is not known how large a process may become, the only alternatives are an overlay scheme or the use of virtual memory.

Although this technique seems optimum from the point of view of an individual partition, it is not optimum from the point of view of the system as a whole. In Figure 7.2b, for example, consider a case in which there are no processes with a size between 12 and 16M at a certain point in time. In that case, the 16M partition will remain unused, even though some smaller process could have been assigned to it. Thus, a preferable approach would be to employ a single queue for all processes (Figure 7.3b). When it is time to load a process into main memory, the smallest available partition that will hold the process is selected. If all partitions are occupied, then a swapping decision must be made. Preference might be given to swapping out of the smallest partition that will hold the incoming process. It is also possible to consider other factors, such as priority, and a preference for swapping out blocked processes versus ready processes.

The use of unequal-size partitions provides a degree of flexibility to fixed partitioning. In addition, it can be said that fixed-partitioning schemes are relatively simple and require minimal operating system software and processing overhead. However, there are disadvantages:

- The number of partitions specified at system generation time limits the number of active (not suspended) processes in the system.
- Because partition sizes are preset at system generation time, small jobs will not utilize partition space efficiently. In an environment where the main storage requirement of all jobs is known beforehand, this may be reasonable, but in most cases, it is an inefficient technique.

The use of fixed partitioning is almost unknown today. One example of a successful operating system that did use this technique was an early IBM mainframe operating system, OS/MFT (Multiprogramming with a Fixed Number of Tasks).

Dynamic Partitioning

To overcome some of the difficulties with fixed partitioning, an approach known as dynamic partitioning was developed. Again, this approach has been supplanted by more sophisticated memory-management techniques. An important operating system that used this technique was IBM's mainframe operating system, OS/MVT (Multiprogramming with a Variable Number of Tasks).

With dynamic partitioning, the partitions are of variable length and number. When a process is brought into main memory, it is allocated exactly as much memory as it requires and no more. An example, using 64 Mbytes of main memory, is shown in Figure 7.4. Initially, main memory is empty, except for the operating system (a). The first three processes are loaded in, starting where the operating system ends and occupying just enough space for each process (b, c, d). This leaves a "hole" at the end of memory that is too small for a fourth process. At some point, none of the processes in memory is ready. The operating system swaps out process 2 (e), which leaves sufficient room to load a new process, process 4 (f). Because process 4 is smaller than process 2, another small hole is created. Later, a point is reached at which none of the processes in main memory is ready, but process 2, in the Ready-Suspend state, is available. Because there is insufficient room in memory for process 2, the operating system swaps process 1 out (g) and swaps process 2 back in (h).

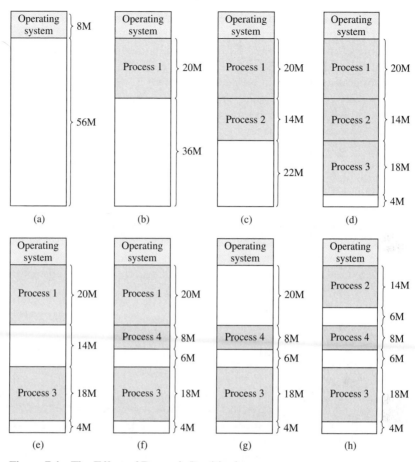

Figure 7.4 The Effect of Dynamic Partitioning

As this example shows, this method starts out well, but eventually it leads to a situation in which there are a lot of small holes in memory. As time goes on, memory becomes more and more fragmented, and memory utilization declines. This phenomenon is referred to as **external fragmentation**, indicating that the memory that is external to all partitions becomes increasingly fragmented. This is in contrast to internal fragmentation, referred to earlier.

One technique for overcoming external fragmentation is **compaction**: From time to time, the operating system shifts the processes so that they are contiguous and so that all of the free memory is together in one block. For example, in Figure 7.4h, compaction will result in a block of free memory of length 16M. This may well be sufficient to load in an additional process. The difficulty with compaction is that it is a time consuming procedure and wasteful of processor time. Note that compaction implies the need for a dynamic relocation capability. That is, it must be possible to move a program from one region to another in main memory without invalidating the memory references in the program (see Appendix 7A).

Placement Algorithm Because memory compaction is time consuming, the operating system designer must be clever in deciding how to assign processes to memory (how to plug the holes). When it is time to load or swap a process into main memory, and if there is more than one free block of memory of sufficient size, then the operating system must decide which free block to allocate.

Three placement algorithms that might be considered are best-fit, first-fit, and next-fit. All, of course, are limited to choosing among free blocks of main memory that are equal to or larger than the process to be brought in. **Best-fit** chooses the block that is closest in size to the request. **First-fit** begins to scan memory from the beginning and chooses the first available block that is large enough. **Next-fit** begins to scan memory from the location of the last placement, and chooses the next available block that is large enough.

Figure 7.5a shows an example memory configuration after a number of placement and swapping-out operations. The last block that was used was a 22-Mbyte block from which a 14-Mbyte partition was created. Figure 7.5b shows the difference between the best-, first-, and next-fit placement algorithms in satisfying a 16-Mbyte allocation request. Best-fit will search the entire list of available blocks

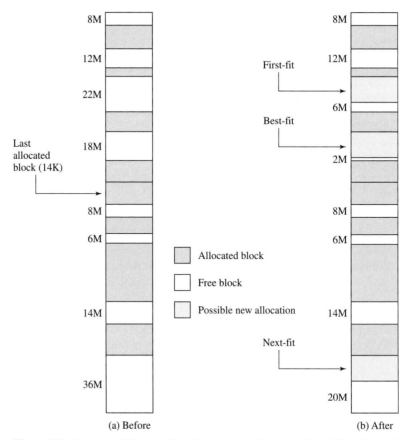

Figure 7.5 Example Memory Configuration before and after Allocation of 16-Mbyte Block

and make use of the 18-Mbyte block, leaving a 2-Mbyte fragment. First-fit results in a 6-Mbyte fragment, and next-fit results in a 20-Mbyte fragment.

Which of these approaches is best will depend on the exact sequence of process swappings that occurs and the size of those processes. However, some general comments can be made (see also [BREN89], [SHOR75], and [BAYS77]). The first-fit algorithm is not only the simplest but usually the best and fastest as well. The next-fit algorithm tends to produce slightly worse results than the first-fit. The next-fit algorithm will more frequently lead to an allocation from a free block at the end of memory. The result is that the largest block of free memory, which usually appears at the end of the memory space, is quickly broken up into small fragments. Thus, compaction may be required more frequently with next-fit. On the other hand, the first-fit algorithm may litter the front end with small free partitions that need to be searched over on each subsequent first-fit pass. The best-fit algorithm, despite its name, is usually the worst performer. Because this algorithm looks for the smallest block that will satisfy the requirement, it guarantees that the fragment left behind is as small as possible. Although each memory request always wastes the smallest amount of memory, the result is that main memory is quickly littered by blocks too small to satisfy memory allocation requests. Thus, memory compaction must be done more frequently than with the other algorithms.

Replacement Algorithm In a multiprogramming system using dynamic partitioning, there will come a time when all of the processes in main memory are in a blocked state and there is insufficient memory, even after compaction, for an additional process. To avoid wasting processor time waiting for an active process to become unblocked, the operating system will swap one of the processes out of main memory to make room for a new process or for a process in a Ready-Suspend state. Therefore, the operating system must choose which process to replace. Because the topic of replacement algorithms will be covered in some detail with respect to various virtual memory schemes, we defer a discussion of replacement algorithms until then.

Buddy System

Both fixed and dynamic partitioning schemes have drawbacks. A fixed partitioning scheme limits the number of active processes and may use space inefficiently if there is a poor match between available partition sizes and process sizes. A dynamic partitioning scheme is more complex to maintain and includes the overhead of compaction. An interesting compromise is the buddy system ([KNUT97], [PETE77]).

In a buddy system, memory blocks are available of size 2^K, $L \leq K \leq U$, where

2^L = smallest size block that is allocated

2^U = largest size block that is allocated; generally 2^U is the size of the entire memory available for allocation

To begin, the entire space available for allocation is treated as a single block of size 2^U. If a request of size s such that $2^{U-1} < s \leq 2^U$ is made, then the entire block is allocated. Otherwise, the block is split into two equal buddies of size 2^{U-1}. If $2^{U-2} < s \leq 2^{U-1}$, then the request is allocated to one of the two buddies. Otherwise, one of the buddies is split in half again. This process continues until the smallest block greater than or equal to s is generated and allocated to the request. At any time, the buddy system maintains a list of holes (unallocated blocks) of each size 2^i. A hole may be removed from the $(i + 1)$ list by splitting it in half to create two buddies of size 2^i in the i list. Whenever a pair of buddies on the i list both become unallocated, they are removed from that list and coalesced into a single block on the $(i + 1)$ list. Presented with a request for an allocation of size k such that $2^{i-1} < k \leq 2^i$, the following recursive algorithm (from [LIST93]) is used to find a hole of size 2^i:

```
void get_hole(int i)
{
    if (i == (U + 1))
        <failure>;
    if (<i_list empty>)
    {
        get_hole(i + 1);
        <split hole into buddies>;
        <put buddies on i_list>;
    }
    <take first hole on i_list>;
}
```

Figure 7.6 gives an example using a 1-Mbyte initial block. The first request, A, is for 100 Kbytes, for which a 128K block is needed. The initial block is divided into two 512K buddies. The first of these is divided into two 256K buddies, and the first of

1 Mbyte block	1M				
Request 100K	A = 128K	128K	256K	512K	
Request 240K	A = 128K	128K	B = 256K	512K	
Request 64K	A = 128K	C = 64K	64K	B = 256K	512K
Request 256K	A = 128K	C = 64K	64K	B = 256K	D = 256K	256K
Release B	A = 128K	C = 64K	64K	256K	D = 256K	256K
Release A	128K	C = 64K	64K	256K	D = 256K	256K
Request 75K	E = 128K	C = 64K	64K	256K	D = 256K	256K
Release C	E = 128K	128K	256K	D = 256K	256K
Release E	512K	D = 256K	256K
Release D	1M	

Figure 7.6   Example of Buddy System

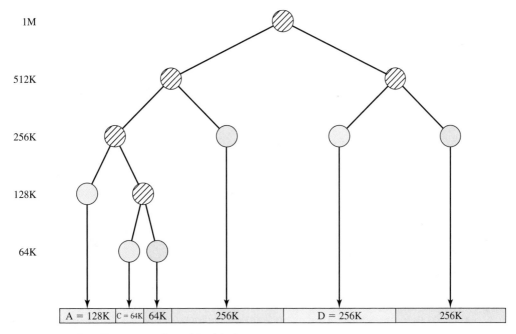

Figure 7.7   Tree Representation of Buddy System

these is divided into two 128K buddies, one of which is allocated to A. The next request, B, requires a 256K block. Such a block is already available and is allocated. The process continues with splitting and coalescing occurring as needed. Note that when E is released, two 128K buddies are coalesced into a 256K block, which is immediately coalesced with its buddy.

Figure 7.7 shows a binary tree representation of the buddy allocation immediately after the Release B request. The leaf nodes represent the current partitioning of the memory. If two buddies are leaf nodes, then at least one must be allocated; otherwise they would be coalesced into a larger block.

The buddy system is a reasonable compromise to overcome the disadvantages of both the fixed and variable partitioning schemes, but in contemporary operating systems, virtual memory based on paging and segmentation is superior. However, the buddy system has found application in parallel systems as an efficient means of allocation and release for parallel programs (e.g., see [JOHN92]). A modified form of the buddy system is used for UNIX kernel memory allocation (described in Chapter 8).

Relocation

Before we consider ways of dealing with the shortcomings of partitioning, we must clear up one loose end, which relates to the placement of processes in memory. When the fixed partition scheme of Figure 7.3a is used, we can expect that a process will always be assigned to the same partition. That is, whichever partition is selected when a new process is loaded will always be used to swap that process back into memory after it has been swapped out. In that case, a simple relocating loader, such as is described in Appendix 7A, can be used: When the process is first loaded, all relative memory references in the code are replaced by absolute main memory addresses, determined by the base address of the loaded process.

In the case of equal-size partitions (Figure 7.2), and in the case of a single process queue for unequal-size partitions (Figure 7.3b), a process may occupy different partitions during the course of its life. When a process image is first created, it is loaded into some partition in main memory. Later, the process may be swapped out; when it is subsequently swapped back in, it may be assigned to a different partition than the last time. The same is true for dynamic partitioning. Observe in Figures 7.4c and h that process 2 occupies two different regions of memory on the two occasions when it is brought in. Furthermore, when compaction is used, processes are shifted while they are in main memory. Thus, the locations (of instructions and data) referenced by a process are not fixed. They will change each time a process is swapped in or shifted. To solve this problem, a distinction is made among several types of addresses. A **logical address** is a reference to a memory location independent of the current assignment of data to memory; a translation must be made to a physical address before the memory access can be achieved. A **relative address** is a particular example of logical address, in which the address is expressed as a location relative to some known point, usually a value in a processor register. A **physical address**, or absolute address, is an actual location in main memory.

Programs that employ relative addresses in memory are loaded using dynamic run-time loading (see Appendix 7A for a discussion). Typically, all of the memory references in the loaded process are relative to the origin of the program. Thus a hardware mechanism is needed for translating relative addresses to physical main memory addresses at the time of execution of the instruction that contains the reference.

Figure 7.8 shows the way in which this address translation is typically accomplished. When a process is assigned to the Running state, a special processor register, sometimes called the base register, is loaded with the starting address in main memory of the program. There is also a "bounds" register that indicates the ending location of the program; these values must be set when the program is loaded into memory or when the process image is swapped in. During the course of execution of the process, relative addresses are encountered. These include the contents of the instruction register, instruction addresses that occur in branch and call instructions, and data addresses that occur in load and store instructions. Each such relative address goes through two steps of manipulation by the processor. First, the value in the base register is added to the relative address to produce an absolute address. Second, the resulting address is compared to the value in the bounds register. If the address is within bounds, then the instruction execution may proceed. Otherwise, an interrupt is generated to the operating system, which must respond to the error in some fashion.

The scheme of Figure 7.8 allows programs to be swapped in and out of memory during the course of execution. It also provides a measure of protection: Each process image is isolated by the contents of the base and bounds registers and safe from unwanted accesses by other processes.

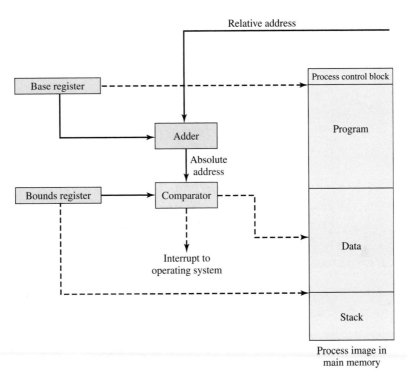

Figure 7.8 Hardware Support for Relocation

7.3 PAGING

Both unequal fixed-size and variable-size partitions are inefficient in the use of memory; the former results in internal fragmentation, the latter in external fragmentation. Suppose, however, that main memory is partitioned into equal fixed-size chunks that are relatively small, and that each process is also divided into small fixed-size chunks of the same size. Then the chunks of a process, known as **pages**, could be assigned to available chunks of memory, known as **frames**, or page frames. We show in this section that the wasted space in memory for each process is due to internal fragmentation consisting of only a fraction of the last page of a process. There is no external fragmentation.

Figure 7.9 illustrates the use of pages and frames. At a given point in time, some of the frames in memory are in use and some are free. A list of free frames is maintained by the operating system. Process A, stored on disk, consists of four pages. When it comes time to load this process, the operating system finds four free frames and loads the four pages of process A into the four frames (Figure 7.9b). Process B, consisting of three pages, and process C, consisting of four pages, are subsequently loaded. Then process B is suspended and is swapped out of main memory. Later, all of the processes in main memory are blocked, and the operating system needs to bring in a new process, process D, which consists of five pages.

Now suppose, as in this example, that there are not sufficient unused contiguous frames to hold the process. Does this prevent the operating system from loading D?

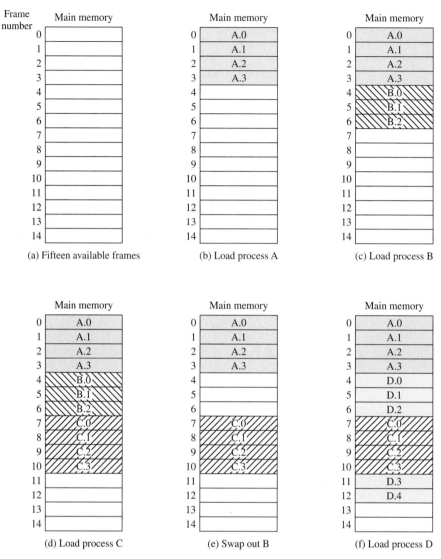

Figure 7.9   Assignment of Process Pages to Free Frames

The answer is no, because we can once again use the concept of logical address. A simple base address register will no longer suffice. Rather, the operating system maintains a **page table** for each process. The page table shows the frame location for each page of the process. Within the program, each logical address consists of a page number and an offset within the page. Recall that in the case of simple partition, a logical address is the location of a word relative to the beginning of the program; the processor translates that into a physical address. With paging, the logical-to-physical address translation is still done by processor hardware. Now the processor must know how to access the page table of the current process. Presented with a logical address (page number, offset), the processor uses the page table to produce a physical address (frame number, offset).

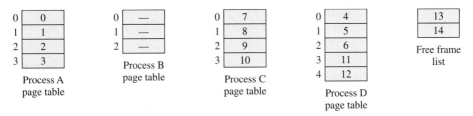

Figure 7.10 Data Structures for the Example of Figure 7.9 at Time Epoch (f)

Continuing our example, the five pages of process D are loaded into frames 4, 5, 6, 11, and 12. Figure 7.10 shows the various page tables at this time. A page table contains one entry for each page of the process, so that the table is easily indexed by the page number (starting at page 0). Each page table entry contains the number of the frame in main memory, if any, that holds the corresponding page. In addition, the operating system maintains a single free-frame list of all frames in main memory that are currently unoccupied and available for pages.

Thus we see that simple paging, as described here, is similar to fixed partitioning. The differences are that, with paging, the partitions are rather small; a program may occupy more than one partition; and these partitions need not be contiguous.

To make this paging scheme convenient, let us dictate that the page size, hence the frame size, must be a power of 2. With the use of a page size that is a power of 2, it is easy to demonstrate that the relative address, which is defined with reference to the origin of the program, and the logical address, expressed as a page number and offset, are the same. An example is shown in Figure 7.11. In this example, 16-bit addresses are used, and the page size is 1K = 1024 bytes. The relative address 1502, in binary form, is 0000010111011110. With a page size of 1K, an offset field of 10 bits is needed, leaving 6 bits for the page number. Thus a program can consist of a maximum of $2^6 = 64$ pages of 1K bytes each. As Figure 7.11b shows, relative address 1502 corresponds to an offset of 478 (0111011110) on page 1 (000001), which yields the same 16-bit number, 0000010111011110.

The consequences of using a page size that is a power of 2 are twofold. First, the logical addressing scheme is transparent to the programmer, the assembler, and the linker. Each logical address (page number, offset) of a program is identical to its relative address. Second, it is a relatively easy matter to implement a function in hardware to perform dynamic address translation at run time. Consider an address of $n + m$ bits, where the leftmost n bits are the page number and the rightmost m bits are the offset. In our example (Figure 7.11b), $n = 6$ and $m = 10$. The following steps are needed for address translation:

- Extract the page number as the leftmost n bits of the logical address.
- Use the page number as an index into the process page table to find the frame number, k.
- The starting physical address of the frame is $k \times 2^m$, and the physical address of the referenced byte is that number plus the offset. This physical address need not be calculated; it is easily constructed by appending the frame number to the offset.

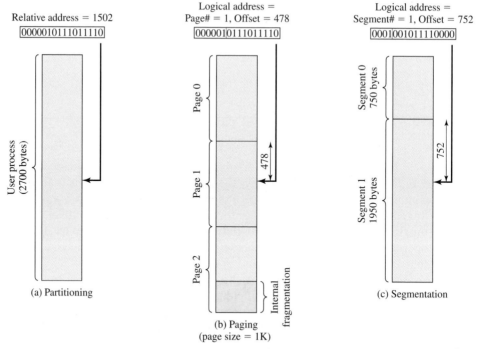

Figure 7.11 Logical Addresses

In our example, we have the logical address 0000010111011110, which is page number 1, offset 478. Suppose that this page is residing in main memory frame 6 = binary 000110. Then the physical address is frame number 6, offset 478 = 0001100111011110 (Figure 7.12a).

To summarize, with simple paging, main memory is divided into many small equal-size frames. Each process is divided into frame-size pages; smaller processes require fewer pages, larger processes require more. When a process is brought in, all of its pages are loaded into available frames, and a page table is set up. This approach solves many of the problems inherent in partitioning.

7.4 SEGMENTATION

A user program can be subdivided using segmentation, in which the program and its associated data are divided into a number of **segments**. It is not required that all segments of all programs be of the same length, although there is a maximum segment length. As with paging, a logical address using segmentation consists of two parts, in this case a segment number and an offset.

Because of the use of unequal-size segments, segmentation is similar to dynamic partitioning. In the absence of an overlay scheme or the use of virtual memory, it would be required that all of a program's segments be loaded into memory for execution. The difference, compared to dynamic partitioning, is that with segmentation a program may occupy more than one partition, and these partitions

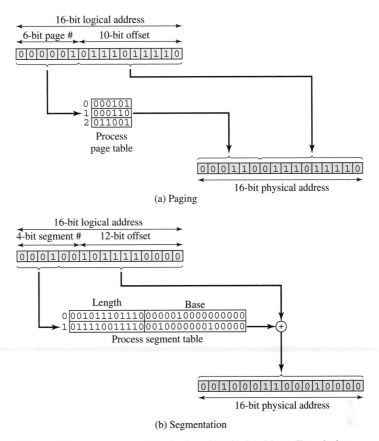

Figure 7.12   Examples of Logical-to-Physical Address Translation

need not be contiguous. Segmentation eliminates internal fragmentation but, like dynamic partitioning, it suffers from external fragmentation. However, because a process is broken up into a number of smaller pieces, the external fragmentation should be less.

Whereas paging is invisible to the programmer, segmentation is usually visible and is provided as a convenience for organizing programs and data. Typically, the programmer or compiler will assign programs and data to different segments. For purposes of modular programming, the program or data may be further broken down into multiple segments. The principal inconvenience of this service is that the programmer must be aware of the maximum segment size limitation.

Another consequence of unequal-size segments is that there is no simple relationship between logical addresses and physical addresses. Analogous to paging, a simple segmentation scheme would make use of a segment table for each process and a list of free blocks of main memory. Each segment table entry would have to give the starting address in main memory of the corresponding segment. The entry should also provide the length of the segment, to assure that invalid addresses are not used. When a process enters the Running state, the address of its segment table is loaded into a special register used by the memory-management hardware.

Consider an address of $n + m$ bits, where the leftmost n bits are the segment number and the rightmost m bits are the offset. In our example (Figure 7.11c), $n = 4$ and $m = 12$. Thus the maximum segment size is $2^{12} = 4096$. The following steps are needed for address translation:

- Extract the segment number as the leftmost n bits of the logical address.
- Use the segment number as an index into the process segment table to find the starting physical address of the segment.
- Compare the offset, expressed in the rightmost m bits, to the length of the segment. If the offset is greater than or equal to the length, the address is invalid.
- The desired physical address is the sum of the starting physical address of the segment plus the offset.

In our example, we have the logical address 0001001011110000, which is segment number 1, offset 752. Suppose that this segment is residing in main memory starting at physical address 0010000000100000. Then the physical address is 0010000000100000 + 001011110000 = 0010001100010000 (Figure 7.12b).

To summarize, with simple segmentation, a process is divided into a number of segments that need not be of equal size. When a process is brought in, all of its segments are loaded into available regions of memory, and a segment table is set up.

7.5 SUMMARY

One of the most important and complex tasks of an operating system is memory management. Memory management involves treating main memory as a resource to be allocated to and shared among a number of active processes. To use the processor and the I/O facilities efficiently, it is desirable to maintain as many processes in main memory as possible. In addition, it is desirable to free programmers from size restrictions in program development.

The basic tools of memory management are paging and segmentation. With paging, each process is divided into relatively small, fixed-size pages. Segmentation provides for the use of pieces of varying size. It is also possible to combine segmentation and paging in a single memory-management scheme.

7.6 RECOMMENDED READINGS

The operating system books recommended in Section 2.9 provide coverage of memory management.

Because partitioning has been supplanted by virtual memory techniques, most books offer only cursory coverage. One of the more complete and interesting treatments is in [MILE92]. A thorough discussion of partitioning strategies is found in [KNUT97].

The topics of linking and loading are covered in many books on program development, computer architecture, and operating systems. A particularly detailed treatment is [BECK90]. [CLAR98] also contains a good discussion. A thorough practical discussion of this topic, with numerous OS examples, is [LEVI99].

BECK90   Beck, L. *System Software*. Reading, MA: Addison-Wesley, 1990.

CLAR98   Clarke, D., and Merusi, D. *System Software Programming: The Way Things Work*. Upper Saddle River, NJ: Prentice Hall, 1998.

KNUT97   Knuth, D. *The Art of Computer Programming, Volume 1: Fundamental Algorithms*. Reading, MA: Addison-Wesley, 1997.

LEVI99   Levine, J. *Linkers and Loaders*. New York: Elsevier Science and Technology, 1999.

MILE92   Milenkovic, M. *Operating Systems: Concepts and Design*. New York: McGraw-Hill, 1992.

7.7 KEY TERMS, REVIEW QUESTIONS, AND PROBLEMS

Key Terms

absolute loading	linkage editor	physical address
buddy system	linking	physical organization
compaction	loading	protection
dynamic linking	logical address	relative address
dynamic partitioning	logical organization	relocatable loading
dynamic run-time loading	memory management	relocation
external fragmentation	page	segmentation
fixed partitioning	page table	sharing
frame	paging	
internal fragmentation	partitioning	

Review Questions

7.1 What requirements is memory management intended to satisfy?

7.2 Why is the capability to relocate processes desirable?

7.3 Why is it not possible to enforce memory protection at compile time?

7.4 What are some reasons to allow two or more processes to all have access to a particular region of memory?

7.5 In a fixed-partitioning scheme, what are the advantages of using unequal-size partitions?

7.6 What is the difference between internal and external fragmentation?

7.7 What are the distinctions among logical, relative, and physical addresses?

7.8 What is the difference between a page and a frame?

7.9 What is the difference between a page and a segment?

Problems

7.1 In Section 2.3, we listed five objectives of memory management, and in Section 7.1, we listed five requirements. Argue that each list encompasses all of the concerns addressed in the other.

7.2 Consider a fixed partitioning scheme with equal-size partitions of 2^{16} bytes and a total main memory size of 2^{24} bytes. A process table is maintained that includes a pointer to a partition for each resident process. How many bits are required for the pointer?

7.3 Consider a dynamic partitioning scheme. Show that, on average, the memory contains half as many holes as segments.

7.4 To implement the various placement algorithms discussed for dynamic partitioning (Section 7.2), a list of the free blocks of memory must be kept. For each of the three methods discussed (best-fit, first-fit, next-fit), what is the average length of the search?

7.5 Another placement algorithm for dynamic partitioning is referred to as worst-fit. In this case, the largest free block of memory is used for bringing in a process. Discuss the pros and cons of this method compared to first-, next-, and best-fit. What is the average length of the search for worst-fit?

7.6 A dynamic partitioning scheme is being used, and the following is the memory configuration at a given point in time:

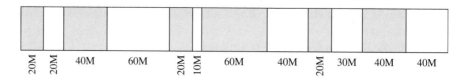

The shaded areas are allocated blocks; the white areas are free blocks. The next three memory requests are for 40M, 20M, and 10M. Indicate the starting address for each of the three blocks using the following placement algorithms:
a. First-fit
b. Best-fit
c. Next-fit. Assume the most recently added block is at the beginning of memory.
d. Worst-fit

7.7 A 1-Mbyte block of memory is allocated using the buddy system.
a. Show the results of the following sequence in a figure similar to Figure 7.6: Request 70; Request 35; Request 80; Return A; Request 60; Return B; Return D; Return C.
b. Show the binary tree representation following Return B.

7.8 Consider a buddy system in which a particular block under the current allocation has an address of 011011110000.
a. If the block is of size 4, what is the binary address of its buddy?
b. If the block is of size 16, what is the binary address of its buddy?

7.9 Let $buddy_k(x)$ = address of the buddy of the block of size 2^k whose address is x. Write a general expression for buddy $buddy_k(x)$.

7.10 The Fibonacci sequence is defined as follows:

$$F_0 = 0, \quad F_1 = 1, \quad F_{n+2} = F_{n+1} + F_n, \quad n \geq 0$$

a. Could this sequence be used to establish a buddy system?
b. What would be the advantage of this system over the binary buddy system described in this chapter?

7.11 During the course of execution of a program, the processor will increment the contents of the instruction register (program counter) by one word after each instruction fetch but will alter the contents of that register if it encounters a branch or call instruction that causes execution to continue elsewhere in the program. Now consider Figure 7.8. There are two alternatives with respect to instruction addresses:
• Maintain a relative address in the instruction register and do the dynamic address translation using the instruction register as input. When a successful branch or call is encountered, the relative address generated by that branch or call is loaded into the instruction register.

- Maintain an absolute address in the instruction register. When a successful branch or call is encountered, dynamic address translation is employed, with the results stored in the instruction register.

Which approach is preferable?

7.12 Consider a simple paging system with the following parameters: 2^{32} bytes of physical memory; page size of 2^{10} bytes; 2^{16} pages of logical address space.
   a. How many bits are in a logical address?
   b. How many bytes in a frame?
   c. How many bits in the physical address specify the frame?
   d. How many entries in the page table?
   e. How many bits in each page table entry? Assume each page table entry includes a valid/invalid bit.

7.13 A virtual address a in a paging system is equivalent to a pair (p, w), in which p is a page number and w is a byte number within the page. Let z be the number of bytes in a page. Find algebraic equations that show p and w as functions of z and a.

7.14 Consider a simple segmentation system that has the following segment table:

Starting Address	Length (bytes)
660	248
1752	422
222	198
996	604

For each of the following logical addresses, determine the physical address or indicate if a segment fault occurs:
   a. 0, 198
   b. 2, 156
   c. 1, 530
   d. 3, 444
   e. 0, 222

7.15 Consider a memory in which contiguous segments $S_1, S_2, \ldots S_n$ are placed in their order of creation from one end of the store to the other, as suggested by the following figure:

When segment S_{n+1} is being created, it is placed immediately after segment S_n even though some of the segments $S_1, S_2, \ldots S_n$ may already have been deleted. When the boundary between segments (in use or deleted) and the hole reaches the other end of the memory, the segments in use are compacted.
   a. Show that the fraction of time F spent on compacting obeys the following inequality:

$$F \geq \frac{1 - f}{1 + kf} \quad \text{where} \quad k = \frac{t}{2s} - 1$$

where

s = average length of a segment, in words
t = average lifetime of a segment, in memory references
f = fraction of the memory that is unused under equilibrium conditions

Hint: Find the average speed at which the boundary crosses the memory and assume that the copying of a single word requires at least two memory references.
   b. Find F for $f = 0.2, t = 1000$, and $s = 50$.

APPENDIX 7A LOADING AND LINKING

The first step in the creation of an active process is to load a program into main memory and create a process image (Figure 7.13). Figure 7.14 depicts a scenario typical for most systems. The application consists of a number of compiled or assembled modules in object-code form. These

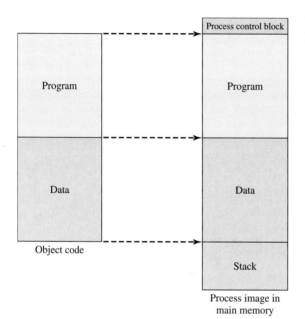

Figure 7.13   The Loading Function

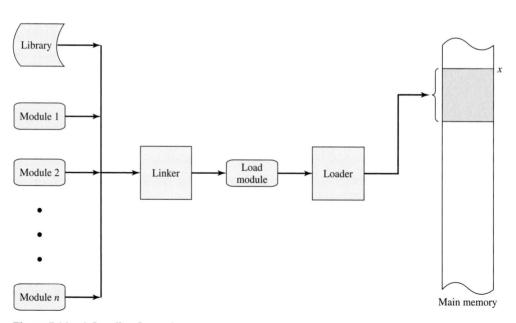

Figure 7.14   A Loading Scenario

are linked to resolve any references between modules. At the same time, references to library routines are resolved. The library routines themselves may be incorporated into the program or referenced as shared code that must be supplied by the operating system at run time. In this appendix, we summarize the key features of linkers and loaders. For clarity in the presentation, we begin with a description of the loading task when a single program module is involved; no linking is required.

Loading

In Figure 7.14, the loader places the load module in main memory starting at location x. In loading the program, the addressing requirement illustrated in Figure 7.1 must be satisfied. In general, three approaches can be taken:

- Absolute loading
- Relocatable loading
- Dynamic run-time loading

Absolute Loading An absolute loader requires that a given load module always be loaded into the same location in main memory. Thus, in the load module presented to the loader, all address references must be to specific, or absolute, main memory addresses. For example, if x in Figure 7.14 is location 1024, then the first word in a load module destined for that region of memory has address 1024.

The assignment of specific address values to memory references within a program can be done either by the programmer or at compile or assembly time (Table 7.2a). There are several disadvantages to the former approach. First, every programmer would have to know the intended assignment strategy for placing modules into main memory. Second, if any modifications are made to the program that involve insertions or deletions in the body of the module, then all of the addresses will have to be altered. Accordingly, it is preferable to allow memory references within programs to be expressed symbolically and then resolve those symbolic references at the time of compilation or assembly. This is illustrated in Figure 7.15. Every reference to an instruction or item of data is initially represented by a symbol. In preparing the module for input to an absolute loader, the assembler or compiler will convert all of these references to specific addresses (in this example, for a module to be loaded starting at location 1024), as shown in Figure 7.15b.

Relocatable Loading The disadvantage of binding memory references to specific addresses prior to loading is that the resulting load module can only be placed in one region of main memory. However, when many programs share main memory, it may not be desirable to decide ahead of time into which region of memory a particular module should be loaded. It is better to make that decision at load time. Thus we need a load module that can be located anywhere in main memory.

To satisfy this new requirement, the assembler or compiler produces not actual main memory addresses (absolute addresses) but addresses that are relative to some known point, such as the start of the program. This technique is illustrated in Figure 7.15c. The start of the load module is assigned the relative address 0, and all other memory references within the module are expressed relative to the beginning of the module.

With all memory references expressed in relative format, it becomes a simple task for the loader to place the module in the desired location. If the module is to be loaded beginning at location x, then the loader must simply add x to each memory reference as it loads the module into memory. To assist in this task, the load module must include information that tells the loader where the address references are and how they are to be interpreted (usually relative to the program origin, but also possibly relative to some other point in the program,

Table 7.2   Address Binding

(a) Loader

Binding Time	Function
Programming time	All actual physical addresses are directly specified by the programmer in the program itself.
Compile or assembly time	The program contains symbolic address references, and these are converted to actual physical addresses by the compiler or assembler.
Load time	The compiler or assembler produces relative addresses. The loader translates these to absolute addresses at the time of program loading.
Run time	The loaded program retains relative addresses. These are converted dynamically to absolute addresses by processor hardware.

(b) Linker

Linkage Time	Function
Programming time	No external program or data references are allowed. The programmer must place into the program the source code for all subprograms that are referenced.
Compile or assembly time	The assembler must fetch the source code of every subroutine that is referenced and assemble them as a unit.
Load module creation	All object modules have been assembled using relative addresses. These modules are linked together and all references are restated relative to the origin of the final load module.
Load time	External references are not resolved until the load module is to be loaded into main memory. At that time, referenced dynamic link modules are appended to the load module, and the entire package is loaded into main or virtual memory.
Run time	External references are not resolved until the external call is executed by the processor. At that time, the process is interrupted and the desired module is linked to the calling program.

such as the current location). This set of information is prepared by the compiler or assembler and is usually referred to as the relocation dictionary.

Dynamic Run–Time Loading Relocatable loaders are common and provide obvious benefits relative to absolute loaders. However, in a multiprogramming environment, even one that does not depend on virtual memory, the relocatable loading scheme is inadequate. We have referred to the need to swap process images in and out of main memory to maximize the utilization of the processor. To maximize main memory utilization, we would like to be able to swap the process image back into different locations at different times. Thus, a program, once loaded, may be swapped out to disk and then swapped back in at a different location. This would be impossible if memory references had been bound to absolute addresses at the initial load time.

The alternative is to defer the calculation of an absolute address until it is actually needed at run time. For this purpose, the load module is loaded into main memory with all memory references in relative form (Figure 7.15c). It is not until an instruction is actually

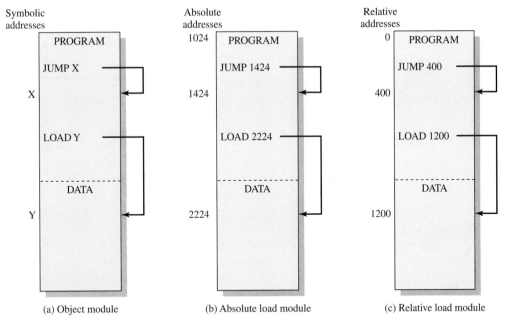

Figure 7.15 Absolute and Relocatable Load Modules

executed that the absolute address is calculated. To assure that this function does not degrade performance, it must be done by special processor hardware rather than software. This hardware is described in Section 7.2.

Dynamic address calculation provides complete flexibility. A program can be loaded into any region of main memory. Subsequently, the execution of the program can be interrupted and the program can be swapped out of main memory, to be later swapped back in at a different location.

Linking

The function of a linker is to take as input a collection of object modules and produce a load module, consisting of an integrated set of program and data modules, to be passed to the loader. In each object module, there may be address references to locations in other modules. Each such reference can only be expressed symbolically in an unlinked object module. The linker creates a single load module that is the contiguous joining of all of the object modules. Each intramodule reference must be changed from a symbolic address to a reference to a location within the overall load module. For example, module A in Figure 7.16a contains a procedure invocation of module B. When these modules are combined in the load module, this symbolic reference to module B is changed to a specific reference to the location of the entry point of B within the load module.

Linkage Editor The nature of this address linkage will depend on the type of load module to be created and when the linkage occurs (Table 7.2b). If, as is usually the case, a relocatable load module is desired, then linkage is usually done in the following fashion. Each compiled or assembled object module is created with references relative to the beginning of the object module. All of these modules are put together into a single relocatable load

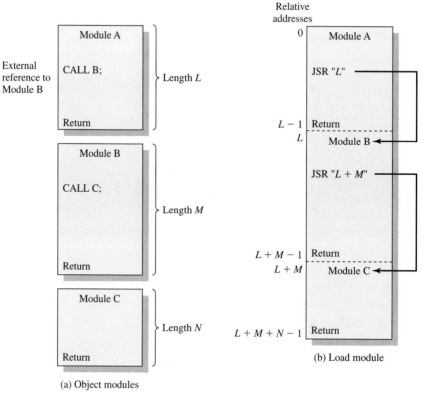

(a) Object modules

(b) Load module

Figure 7.16   The Linking Function

module with all references relative to the origin of the load module. This module can be used as input for relocatable loading or dynamic run-time loading.

A linker that produces a relocatable load module is often referred to as a linkage editor. Figure 7.16 illustrates the linkage editor function.

Dynamic Linker   As with loading, it is possible to defer some linkage functions. The term *dynamic linking* is used to refer to the practice of deferring the linkage of some external modules until after the load module has been created. Thus, the load module contains unresolved references to other programs. These references can be resolved either at load time or run time.

For **load-time dynamic linking**, the following steps occur. The load module (application module) to be loaded is read into memory. Any reference to an external module (target module) causes the loader to find the target module, load it, and alter the reference to a relative address in memory from the beginning of the application module. There are several advantages to this approach over what might be called static linking:

- It becomes easier to incorporate changed or upgraded versions of the target module, which may be an operating system utility or some other general-purpose routine. With static linking, a change to such a supporting module would require the relinking of the entire application module. Not only is this inefficient, but it may be impossible in some circumstances. For example, in the personal computer field, most commercial software is released in load module form; source and object versions are not released.

- Having target code in a dynamic link file paves the way for automatic code sharing. The operating system can recognize that more than one application is using the same target code because it loaded and linked that code. It can use that information to load a single copy of the target code and link it to both applications, rather than having to load one copy for each application.

- It becomes easier for independent software developers to extend the functionality of a widely used operating system such as Linux. A developer can come up with a new function that may be useful to a variety of applications and package it as a dynamic link module.

With **run-time dynamic linking**, some of the linking is postponed until execution time. External references to target modules remain in the loaded program. When a call is made to the absent module, the operating system locates the module, loads it, and links it to the calling module.

We have seen that dynamic loading allows an entire load module to be moved around; however, the structure of the module is static, being unchanged throughout the execution of the process and from one execution to the next. However, in some cases, it is not possible to determine prior to execution which object modules will be required. This situation is typified by transaction-processing applications, such as an airline reservation system or a banking application. The nature of the transaction dictates which program modules are required, and they are loaded as appropriate and linked with the main program. The advantage of the use of such a dynamic linker is that it is not necessary to allocate memory for program units unless those units are referenced. This capability is used in support of segmentation systems.

One additional refinement is possible: An application need not know the names of all the modules or entry points that may be called. For example, a charting program may be written to work with a variety of plotters, each of which is driven by a different driver package. The application can learn the name of the plotter that is currently installed on the system from another process or by looking it up in a configuration file. This allows the user of the application to install a new plotter that did not exist at the time the application was written.

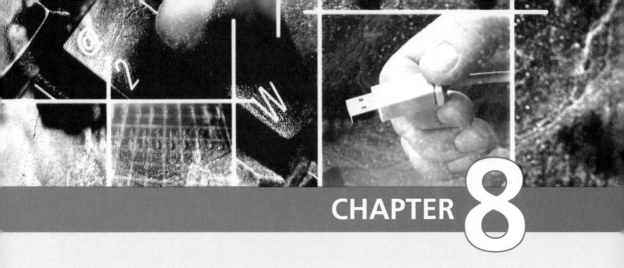

CHAPTER 8

VIRTUAL MEMORY

Chapter 7 introduced the concepts of paging and segmentation and analyzed their shortcomings. We now move to a discussion of virtual memory. An analysis of this topic is complicated by the fact that memory management is a complex interrelationship between processor hardware and operating system software. We focus first on the hardware aspect of virtual memory, looking at the use of paging, segmentation, and combined paging and segmentation. Then we look at the issues involved in the design of a virtual memory facility in operating systems.

8.1 HARDWARE AND CONTROL STRUCTURES

Comparing simple paging and simple segmentation, on the one hand, with fixed and dynamic partitioning, on the other, we see the foundation for a fundamental breakthrough in memory management. Two characteristics of paging and segmentation are the keys to this breakthrough:

1. All memory references within a process are logical addresses that are dynamically translated into physical addresses at run time. This means that a process may be swapped in and out of main memory such that it occupies different regions of main memory at different times during the course of execution.

2. A process may be broken up into a number of pieces (pages or segments) and these pieces need not be contiguously located in main memory during execution. The combination of dynamic run-time address translation and the use of a page or segment table permits this.

Now we come to the breakthrough. *If the preceding two characteristics are present, then it is not necessary that all of the pages or all of the segments of a process be in main memory during execution.* If the piece (segment or page) that holds the next instruction to be fetched and the piece that holds the next data location to be accessed are in main memory, then at least for a time execution may proceed.

Let us consider how this may be accomplished. For now, we can talk in general terms, and we will use the term *piece* to refer to either page or segment, depending on whether paging or segmentation is employed. Suppose that it is time to bring a new process into memory. The operating system begins by bringing in only one or a few pieces, to include the initial program piece and the initial data piece to which those instructions refer. The portion of a process that is actually in main memory at any time is defined to be the **resident set** of the process. As the process executes, things proceed smoothly as long as all memory references are to locations that are in the resident set. Using the segment or page table, the processor always is able to determine whether this is so. If the processor encounters a logical address that is not in main memory, it generates an interrupt indicating a memory access fault. The operating system puts the interrupted process in a blocking state and takes control. For the execution of this process to proceed later, the operating system will need to bring into main memory the piece of the process that contains the logical address that caused the access fault. For this purpose, the operating system issues a disk I/O read request. After the I/O request has been issued, the operating system can dispatch another process to run while the disk

I/O is performed. Once the desired piece has been brought into main memory, an I/O interrupt is issued, giving control back to the operating system, which places the affected process back into a Ready state.

It may immediately occur to you to question the efficiency of this maneuver, in which a process may be executing and have to be interrupted for no other reason than that you have failed to load in all of the needed pieces of the process. For now, let us defer consideration of this question with the assurance that efficiency is possible. Instead, let us ponder the implications of our new strategy. There are two implications, the second more startling than the first, and both lead to improved system utilization:

1. **More processes may be maintained in main memory.** Because we are only going to load some of the pieces of any particular process, there is room for more processes. This leads to more efficient utilization of the processor because it is more likely that at least one of the more numerous processes will be in a Ready state at any particular time.

2. **A process may be larger than all of main memory.** One of the most fundamental restrictions in programming is lifted. Without the scheme we have been discussing, a programmer must be acutely aware of how much memory is available. If the program being written is too large, the programmer must devise ways to structure the program into pieces that can be loaded separately in some sort of overlay strategy. With virtual memory based on paging or segmentation, that job is left to the operating system and the hardware. As far as the programmer is concerned, he or she is dealing with a huge memory, the size associated with disk storage. The operating system automatically loads pieces of a process into main memory as required.

Because a process executes only in main memory, that memory is referred to as **real memory**. But a programmer or user perceives a potentially much larger memory—that which is allocated on disk. This latter is referred to as **virtual memory**. Virtual memory allows for very effective multiprogramming and relieves the user of the unnecessarily tight constraints of main memory. Table 8.1 summarizes characteristics of paging and segmentation, with and without the use of virtual memory.

Locality and Virtual Memory

The benefits of virtual memory are attractive, but is the scheme practical? At one time, there was considerable debate on this point, but experience with numerous operating systems has demonstrated beyond doubt that virtual memory does work. Accordingly, virtual memory, based on either paging or paging plus segmentation, has become an essential component of contemporary operating systems.

To understand what the key issue is, and why virtual memory was a matter of much debate, let us examine again the task of the operating system with respect to virtual memory. Consider a large process, consisting of a long program plus a number of arrays of data. Over any short period of time, execution may be confined to a small section of the program (e.g., a subroutine) and access to perhaps only one or two arrays of data. If this is so, then it would clearly be wasteful to load in dozens of pieces for that process when only a few pieces will be used before the program is suspended and swapped out. We can make better use of memory by loading in just a

Table 8.1 Characteristics of Paging and Segmentation

Simple Paging	Virtual Memory Paging	Simple Segmentation	Virtual Memory Segmentation
Main memory partitioned into small fixed-size chunks called frames	Main memory partitioned into small fixed-size chunks called frames	Main memory not partitioned	Main memory not partitioned
Program broken into pages by the compiler or memory management system	Program broken into pages by the compiler or memory management system	Program segments specified by the programmer to the compiler (i.e., the decision is made by the programmer)	Program segments specified by the programmer to the compiler (i.e., the decision is made by the programmer)
Internal fragmentation within frames	Internal fragmentation within frames	No internal fragmentation	No internal fragmentation
No external fragmentation	No external fragmentation	External fragmentation	External fragmentation
Operating system must maintain a page table for each process showing which frame each page occupies	Operating system must maintain a page table for each process showing which frame each page occupies	Operating system must maintain a segment table for each process showing the load address and length of each segment	Operating system must maintain a segment table for each process showing the load address and length of each segment
Operating system must maintain a free frame list	Operating system must maintain a free frame list	Operating system must maintain a list of free holes in main memory	Operating system must maintain a list of free holes in main memory
Processor uses page number, offset to calculate absolute address	Processor uses page number, offset to calculate absolute address	Processor uses segment number, offset to calculate absolute address	Processor uses segment number, offset to calculate absolute address
All the pages of a process must be in main memory for process to run, unless overlays are used	Not all pages of a process need be in main memory frames for the process to run. Pages may be read in as needed	All the segments of a process must be in main memory for process to run, unless overlays are used	Not all segments of a process need be in main memory frames for the process to run. Segments may be read in as needed
	Reading a page into main memory may require writing a page out to disk		Reading a segment into main memory may require writing one or more segments out to disk

few pieces. Then, if the program branches to an instruction or references a data item on a piece not in main memory, a fault is triggered. This tells the operating system to bring in the desired piece.

Thus, at any one time, only a few pieces of any given process are in memory, and therefore more processes can be maintained in memory. Furthermore, time is saved because unused pieces are not swapped in and out of memory. However, the operating system must be clever about how it manages this scheme. In the steady state, practically all of main memory will be occupied with process pieces, so that the processor and operating system have direct access to as many processes as possible. Thus, when the operating system brings one piece in, it must throw another out. If it throws out a piece just before it is used, then it will just have to go get that piece again almost immediately. Too much of this leads to a condition known as **thrashing**: The system spends most of its time swapping pieces rather than executing instructions. The avoidance of thrashing was a major research area in the 1970s and led to a variety of complex but effective algorithms. In essence, the operating system tries to guess, based on recent history, which pieces are least likely to be used in the near future.

This reasoning is based on belief in the **principle of locality**, which was introduced in Chapter 1 (see especially Appendix 1A). To summarize, the principle of locality states that program and data references within a process tend to cluster. Hence, the assumption that only a few pieces of a process will be needed over a short period of time is valid. Also, it should be possible to make intelligent guesses about which pieces of a process will be needed in the near future, which avoids thrashing.

One way to confirm the principle of locality is to look at the performance of processes in a virtual memory environment. Figure 8.1 is a rather famous diagram that dramatically illustrates the principle of locality [HATF72]. Note that, during the lifetime of the process, references are confined to a subset of pages.

Thus we see that the principle of locality suggests that a virtual memory scheme may work. For virtual memory to be practical and effective, two ingredients are needed. First, there must be hardware support for the paging and/or segmentation scheme to be employed. Second, the operating system must include software for managing the movement of pages and/or segments between secondary memory and main memory. In this section, we examine the hardware aspect and look at the necessary control structures, which are created and maintained by the operating system but are used by the memory management hardware. An examination of the operating system issues is provided in the next section.

Paging

The term *virtual memory* is usually associated with systems that employ paging, although virtual memory based on segmentation is also used and is discussed next. The use of paging to achieve virtual memory was first reported for the Atlas computer [KILB62] and soon came into widespread commercial use.

In the discussion of simple paging, we indicated that each process has its own page table, and when all of its pages are loaded into main memory, the page table for a process is created and loaded into main memory. Each page table entry contains the frame number of the corresponding page in main memory. A page table is also needed for a virtual memory scheme based on paging. Again, it is typical to associate

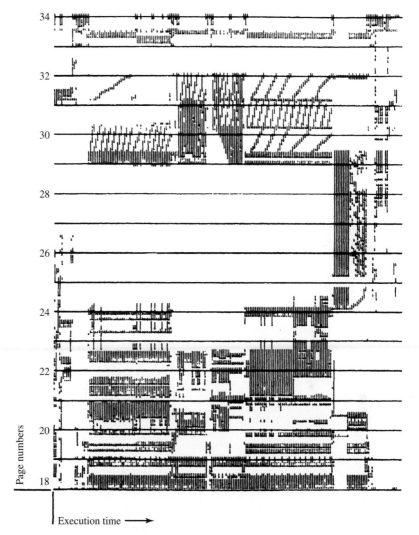

Figure 8.1 Paging Behavior

a unique page table with each process. In this case, however, the page table entries become more complex (Figure 8.2a). Because only some of the pages of a process may be in main memory, a bit is needed in each page table entry to indicate whether the corresponding page is present (P) in main memory or not. If the bit indicates that the page is in memory, then the entry also includes the frame number of that page.

The page table entry includes a modify (M) bit, indicating whether the contents of the corresponding page have been altered since the page was last loaded into main memory. If there has been no change, then it is not necessary to write the page out when it comes time to replace the page in the frame that it currently occupies. Other control bits may also be present. For example, if protection or sharing is managed at the page level, then bits for that purpose will be required.

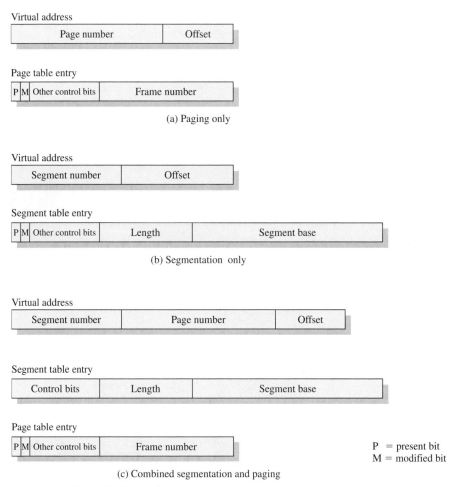

Figure 8.2 Typical Memory Management Formats

Page Table Structure The basic mechanism for reading a word from memory involves the translation of a virtual, or logical, address, consisting of page number and offset, into a physical address, consisting of frame number and offset, using a page table. Because the page table is of variable length, depending on the size of the process, we cannot expect to hold it in registers. Instead, it must be in main memory to be accessed. Figure 8.3 suggests a hardware implementation. When a particular process is running, a register holds the starting address of the page table for that process. The page number of a virtual address is used to index that table and look up the corresponding frame number. This is combined with the offset portion of the virtual address to produce the desired real address. Typically, the page number field is longer than the frame number field ($n > m$).

In most systems, there is one page table per process. But each process can occupy huge amounts of virtual memory. For example, in the VAX architecture, each process can have up to $2^{31} = 2$ Gbytes of virtual memory. Using $2^9 = 512$-byte pages, that means that as many as 2^{22} page table entries are required *per process*.

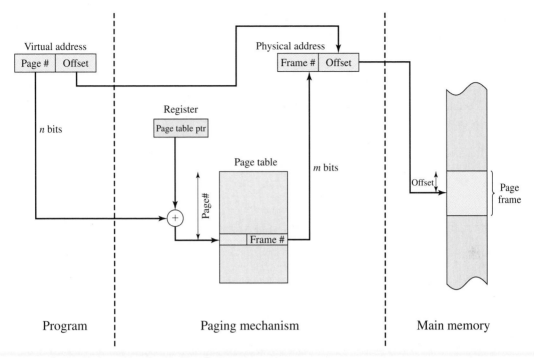

Virtual address

| Page # | Offset |

Physical address

| Frame # | Offset |

Register

| Page table ptr |

n bits

m bits

Page table

Page#

| Frame # |

Offset

Page frame

Program

Paging mechanism

Main memory

Figure 8.3   Address Translation in a Paging System

Clearly, the amount of memory devoted to page tables alone could be unacceptably high. To overcome this problem, most virtual memory schemes store page tables in virtual memory rather than real memory. This means that page tables are subject to paging just as other pages are. When a process is running, at least a part of its page table must be in main memory, including the page table entry of the currently executing page. Some processors make use of a two-level scheme to organize large page tables. In this scheme, there is a page directory, in which each entry points to a page table. Thus, if the length of the page directory is X, and if the maximum length of a page table is Y, then a process can consist of up to $X \geq Y$ pages. Typically, the maximum length of a page table is restricted to be equal to one page. For example, the Pentium processor uses this approach.

Figure 8.4 shows an example of a two-level scheme typical for use with a 32-bit address. If we assume byte-level addressing and 4-kbyte (2^{12}) pages, then the 4-Gbyte (2^{32}) virtual address space is composed of 2^{20} pages. If each of these pages is mapped by a 4-byte page table entry (PTE), we can create a user page table composed of 2^{20} PTEs requiring 4 Mbyte (2^{22}) bytes. This huge user page table, occupying 2^{10} pages, can be kept in virtual memory and mapped by a root page table with 2^{10} PTEs occupying 4 Kbyte (2^{12}) of main memory. Figure 8.5 shows the steps involved in address translation for this scheme. The root page always remains in main memory. The first 10 bits of a virtual address are used to index into the root page to find a PTE for a page of the user page table. If that page is not in main memory, a page fault occurs. If that page is in main memory, then the next 10 bits of the virtual address index into the user PTE page to find the PTE for the page that is referenced by the virtual address.

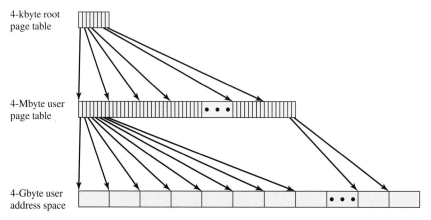

Figure 8.4 A Two-Level Hierarchical Page Table

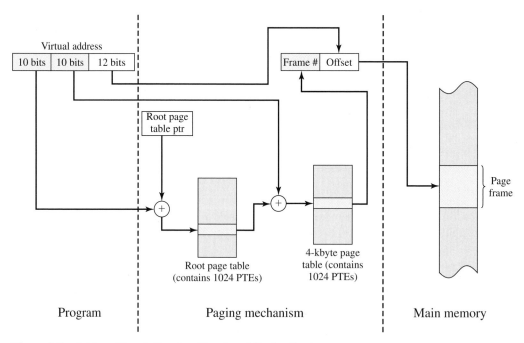

Figure 8.5 Address Translation in a Two-Level Paging System

Inverted Page Table A drawback of the type of page tables that we have been discussing is that their size is proportional to that of the virtual address space.

An alternative approach to the use of one or multiple-level page tables is the use of an **inverted page table** structure. Variations on this approach are used on the PowerPC, UltraSPARC, and the IA-64 architecture. An implementation of the Mach operating system on the RT-PC also uses this technique.

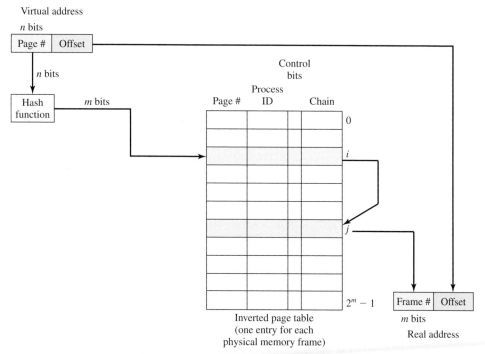

Figure 8.6   Inverted Page Table Structure

In this approach, the page number portion of a virtual address is mapped into a hash value using a simple hashing function.[1] The hash value is a pointer to the inverted page table, which contains the page table entries. There is one entry in the inverted page table for each real memory page frame rather than one per virtual page. Thus a fixed proportion of real memory is required for the tables regardless of the number of processes or virtual pages supported. Because more than one virtual address may map into the same hash table entry, a chaining technique is used for managing the overflow. The hashing technique results in chains that are typically short—between one and two entries. The page table's structure is called *inverted* because it indexes page table entries by frame number rather than by virtual page number.

Figure 8.6 shows a typical implementation of the inverted page table approach. For a physical memory size of 2^m frames, the inverted page table contains 2^m entries, so that the ith entry refers to frame i. Each entry in the page table includes the following:

- **Page number:** This is the page number portion of the virtual address.
- **Process identifier:** The process that owns this page. The combination of page number and process identifier identify a page within the virtual address space of a particular process.

---

[1]See Appendix 8A for a discussion of hashing.

- **Control bits:** This field includes flags, such as valid, referenced, and modified; and protection and locking information.
- **Chain pointer:** This field is null (perhaps indicated by a separate bit) if there are no chained entries for this entry. Otherwise, the field contains the index value (number between 0 and $2^m - 1$) of the next entry in the chain.

In this example, the virtual address includes an *n*-bit page number, with $n > m$. The hash function maps the *n*-bit page number into an *m*-bit quantity, which is used to index into the inverted page table.

Translation Lookaside Buffer   In principle, every virtual memory reference can cause two physical memory accesses: one to fetch the appropriate page table entry and one to fetch the desired data. Thus, a straightforward virtual memory scheme would have the effect of doubling the memory access time. To overcome this problem, most virtual memory schemes make use of a special high-speed cache for page table entries, usually called a **translation lookaside buffer** (TLB). This cache functions in the same way as a memory cache (see Chapter 1) and contains those page table entries that have been most recently used. The organization of the resulting paging hardware is illustrated in Figure 8.7. Given a virtual address, the processor will first examine the TLB. If the desired page table entry is present (*TLB hit*), then the frame number is retrieved and the real address is formed. If the desired page table entry is not found (*TLB miss*), then the processor uses the page number to index the process page table and examine the corresponding page table entry. If the "present bit" is set, then the

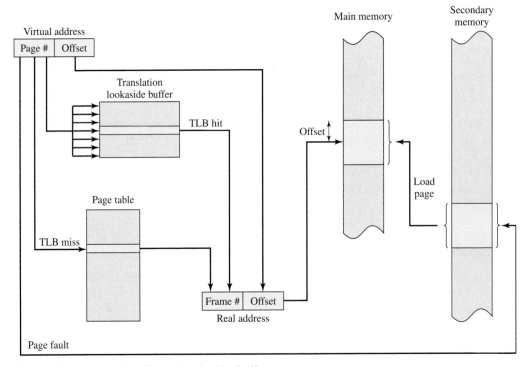

Figure 8.7   Use of a Translation Lookaside Buffer

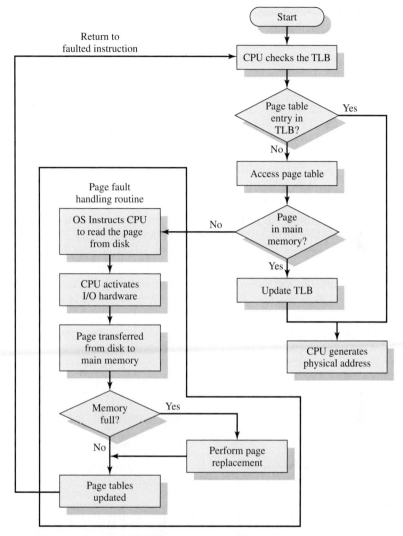

Figure 8.8 Operation of Paging and Translation Lookaside Buffer (TLB) [FURH87]

page is in main memory, and the processor can retrieve the frame number from the page table entry to form the real address. The processor also updates the TLB to include this new page table entry. Finally, if the present bit is not set, then the desired page is not in main memory and a memory access fault, called a **page fault**, is issued. At this point, we leave the realm of hardware and invoke the operating system, which loads the needed page and updates the page table.

Figure 8.8 is a flowchart that shows the use of the TLB. The flowchart shows that if the desired page is not in main memory, a page fault interrupt causes the page fault handling routine to be invoked. To keep the flowchart simple, the fact that the operating system may dispatch another process while disk I/O is underway is not shown. By the principle of locality, most virtual memory references will be to locations in recently used pages. Therefore, most references will involve page table entries in the cache. Studies of the VAX TLB have shown that this scheme can significantly improve performance [CLAR85, SATY81].

There are a number of additional details concerning the actual organization of the TLB. Because the TLB only contains some of the entries in a full page table, we cannot simply index into the TLB based on page number. Instead, each entry in the TLB must include the page number as well as the complete page table entry. The processor is equipped with hardware that allows it to interrogate simultaneously a number of TLB entries to determine if there is a match on page number. This technique is referred to as **associative mapping** and is contrasted with the direct mapping, or indexing, used for lookup in the page table in Figure 8.9. The design of the TLB also must consider the way in which entries are organized in the TLB and which entry to replace when a new entry is brought in. These issues must be considered in any hardware cache design. This topic is not pursued here; the reader may consult a treatment of cache design for further details (e.g., [STAL03]).

Finally, the virtual memory mechanism must interact with the cache system (not the TLB cache, but the main memory cache). This is illustrated in Figure 8.10. A virtual address will generally be in the form of a page number, offset. First, the memory system consults the TLB to see if the matching page table entry is present. If it is, the real (physical) address is generated by combining the frame number with the offset. If not, the entry is accessed from a page table. Once the real address is

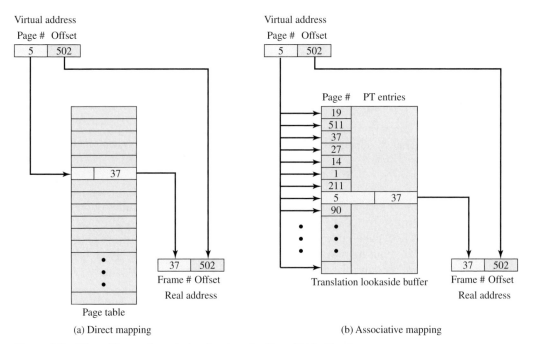

Figure 8.9 Direct Versus Associative Lookup for Page Table Entries

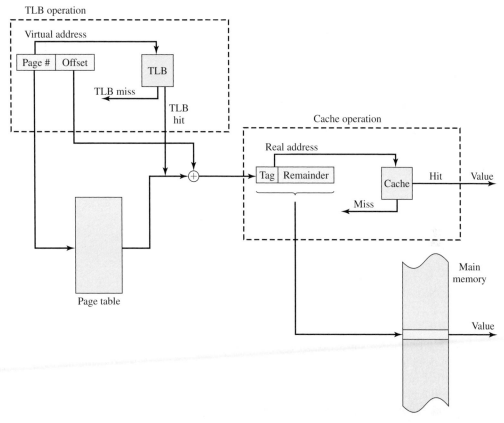

Figure 8.10   Translation Lookaside Buffer and Cache Operation

generated, which is in the form of a tag[2] and a remainder, the cache is consulted to see if the block containing that word is present. If so, it is returned to the CPU. If not, the word is retrieved from main memory.

The reader should be able to appreciate the complexity of the CPU hardware involved in a single memory reference. The virtual address is translated into a real address. This involves reference to a page table entry, which may be in the TLB, in main memory, or on disk. The referenced word may be in cache, main memory, or on disk. If the referenced word is only on disk, the page containing the word must be loaded into main memory and its block loaded into the cache. In addition, the page table entry for that page must be updated.

Page Size   An important hardware design decision is the size of page to be used. There are several factors to consider. One is internal fragmentation. Clearly, the smaller the page size, the less the amount of internal fragmentation. To optimize the use of main memory, we would like to reduce internal fragmentation. On the other hand, the smaller the page, the greater the number of pages required per process.

---

[2]See Figure 1.17. Typically, a tag is just the leftmost bits of the real address. Again, for a more detailed discussion of caches, see [STAL03].

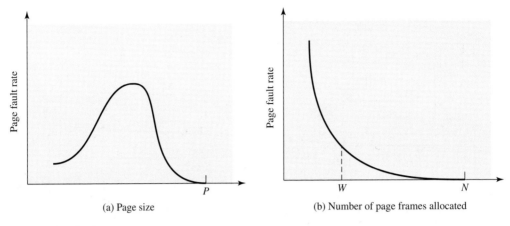

(a) Page size

(b) Number of page frames allocated

P = size of entire process
W = working set size
N = total number of pages in process

Figure 8.11 Typical Paging Behavior of a Program

More pages per process means larger page tables. For large programs in a heavily multiprogrammed environment, this may mean that some portion of the page tables of active processes must be in virtual memory, not in main memory. Thus, there may be a double page fault for a single reference to memory: first to bring in the needed portion of the page table and second to bring in the process page. Another factor is that the physical characteristics of most secondary-memory devices, which are rotational, favor a larger page size for more efficient block transfer of data.

Complicating these matters is the effect of page size on the rate at which page faults occur. This behavior, in general terms, is depicted in Figure 8.11a and is based on the principle of locality. If the page size is very small, then ordinarily a relatively large number of pages will be available in main memory for a process. After a time, the pages in memory will all contain portions of the process near recent references. Thus, the page fault rate should be low. As the size of the page is increased, each individual page will contain locations further and further from any particular recent reference. Thus the effect of the principle of locality is weakened and the page fault rate begins to rise. Eventually, however, the page fault rate will begin to fall as the size of a page approaches the size of the entire process (point P in the diagram). When a single page encompasses the entire process, there will be no page faults.

A further complication is that the page fault rate is also determined by the number of frames allocated to a process. Figure 8.11b shows that, for a fixed page size, the fault rate drops as the number of pages maintained in main memory grows.[3] Thus, a software policy (the amount of memory to allocate to each process) interacts with a hardware design decision (page size).

Table 8.2 lists the page sizes used on some machines.

Finally, the design issue of page size is related to the size of physical main memory and program size. At the same time that main memory is getting larger, the

---

[3]The parameter W represents working set size, a concept discussed in Section 8.2.

Table 8.2 Example Page Sizes

Computer	Page Size
Atlas	512 48-bit words
Honeywell-Multics	1024 36-bit word
IBM 370/XA and 370/ESA	4 Kbytes
VAX family	512 bytes
IBM AS/400	512 bytes
DEC Alpha	8 Kbytes
MIPS	4 kbyes to 16 Mbytes
UltraSPARC	8 Kbytes to 4 Mbytes
Pentium	4 Kbytes or 4 Mbytes
PowerPc	4 Kbytes
Itanium	4 Kbytes to 256 Mbytes

address space used by applications is also growing. The trend is most obvious on personal computers and workstations, where applications are becoming increasingly complex. Furthermore, contemporary programming techniques used in large programs tend to decrease the locality of references within a process [HUCK93]. For example,

- Object-oriented techniques encourage the use of many small program and data modules with references scattered over a relatively large number of objects over a relatively short period of time.
- Multithreaded applications may result in abrupt changes in the instruction stream and in scattered memory references.

For a given size of TLB, as the memory size of processes grows and as locality decreases, the hit ratio on TLB accesses declines. Under these circumstances, the TLB can become a performance bottleneck (e.g., see [CHEN92]).

One way to improve TLB performance is to use a larger TLB with more entries. However, TLB size interacts with other aspects of the hardware design, such as the main memory cache and the number of memory accesses per instruction cycle [TALL92]. The upshot is that TLB size is unlikely to grow as rapidly as main memory size. An alternative is to use larger page sizes so that each page table entry in the TLB refers to a larger block of memory. But we have just seen that the use of large page sizes can lead to performance degradation.

Accordingly, a number of designers have investigated the use of multiple page sizes [TALL92, KHAL93], and several microprocessor architectures support multiple pages sizes, including MIPS R4000, Alpha, UltraSPARC, Pentium, and IA-64. Multiple page sizes provide the flexibility needed to use a TLB effectively. For example, large contiguous regions in the address space of a process, such as program instructions, may be mapped using a small number of large pages rather than a large number of small pages, while thread stacks may be mapped using the small page size. However, most commercial operating systems still support only one page size, regardless of the capability of the underlying hardware. The reason for this is that page size affects many aspects of the operating system; thus, a change to multiple page sizes is a complex undertaking (see [GANA98] for a discussion).

Segmentation

Virtual Memory Implications Segmentation allows the programmer to view memory as consisting of multiple address spaces or segments. Segments may be of unequal, indeed dynamic, size. Memory references consist of a (segment number, offset) form of address.

This organization has a number of advantages to the programmer over a non-segmented address space:

1. It simplifies the handling of growing data structures. If the programmer does not know ahead of time how large a particular data structure will become, it is necessary to guess unless dynamic segment sizes are allowed. With segmented virtual memory, the data structure can be assigned its own segment, and the operating system will expand or shrink the segment as needed. If a segment that needs to be expanded is in main memory and there is insufficient room, the operating system may move the segment to a larger area of main memory, if available, or swap it out. In the latter case, the enlarged segment would be swapped back in at the next opportunity.

2. It allows programs to be altered and recompiled independently, without requiring the entire set of programs to be relinked and reloaded. Again, this is accomplished using multiple segments.

3. It lends itself to sharing among processes. A programmer can place a utility program or a useful table of data in a segment that can be referenced by other processes.

4. It lends itself to protection. Because a segment can be constructed to contain a well-defined set of programs or data, the programmer or system administrator can assign access privileges in a convenient fashion.

Organization In the discussion of simple segmentation, we indicated that each process has its own segment table, and when all of its segments are loaded into main memory, the segment table for a process is created and loaded into main memory. Each segment table entry contains the starting address of the corresponding segment in main memory, as well as the length of the segment. The same device, a segment table, is needed when we consider a virtual memory scheme based on segmentation. Again, it is typical to associate a unique segment table with each process. In this case, however, the segment table entries become more complex (Figure 8.2b). Because only some of the segments of a process may be in main memory, a bit is needed in each segment table entry to indicate whether the corresponding segment is present in main memory or not. If the bit indicates that the segment is in memory, then the entry also includes the starting address and length of that segment.

Another control bit in the segmentation table entry is a modify bit, indicating whether the contents of the corresponding segment have been altered since the segment was last loaded into main memory. If there has been no change, then it is not

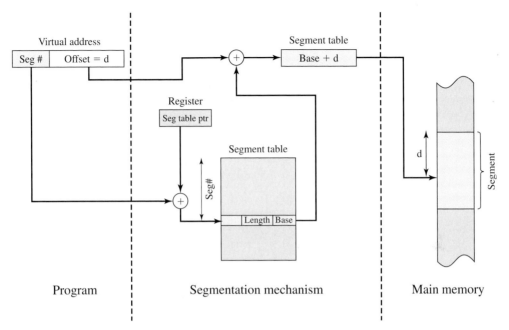

Figure 8.12   Address Translation in a Segmentation System

necessary to write the segment out when it comes time to replace the segment in the frame that it currently occupies. Other control bits may also be present. For example, if protection or sharing is managed at the segment level, then bits for that purpose will be required.

The basic mechanism for reading a word from memory involves the translation of a virtual, or logical, address, consisting of segment number and offset, into a physical address, using a segment table. Because the segment table is of variable length, depending on the size of the process, we cannot expect to hold it in registers. Instead, it must be in main memory to be accessed. Figure 8.12 suggests a hardware implementation of this scheme (note similarity to Figure 8.3). When a particular process is running, a register holds the starting address of the segment table for that process. The segment number of a virtual address is used to index that table and look up the corresponding main memory address for the start of the segment. This is added to the offset portion of the virtual address to produce the desired real address.

Combined Paging and Segmentation

Both paging and segmentation have their strengths. Paging, which is transparent to the programmer, eliminates external fragmentation and thus provides efficient use of main memory. In addition, because the pieces that are moved in and out of main memory are of fixed, equal size, it is possible to develop sophisticated memory-management algorithms that exploit the behavior of programs, as we shall see. Segmentation, which is visible to the programmer, has the strengths listed earlier, including the ability to handle growing data structures, modularity, and support for

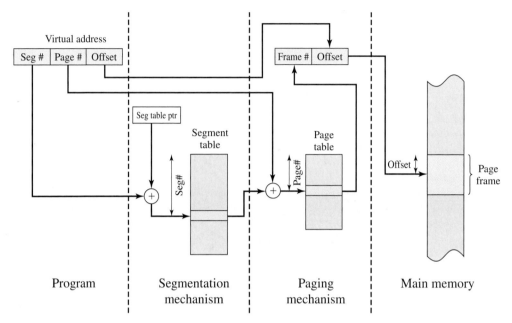

Figure 8.13 Address Translation in a Segmentation/Paging System

sharing and protection. To combine the advantages of both, some systems are equipped with processor hardware and operating system software to provide both.

In a combined paging/segmentation system, a user's address space is broken up into a number of segments, at the discretion of the programmer. Each segment is, in turn, broken up into a number of fixed-size pages, which are equal in length to a main memory frame. If a segment has length less than that of a page, the segment occupies just one page. From the programmer's point of view, a logical address still consists of a segment number and a segment offset. From the system's point of view, the segment offset is viewed as a page number and page offset for a page within the specified segment.

Figure 8.13 suggests a structure to support combined paging/segmentation (note similarity to Figure 8.5). Associated with each process is a segment table and a number of page tables, one per process segment. When a particular process is running, a register holds the starting address of the segment table for that process. Presented with a virtual address, the processor uses the segment number portion to index into the process segment table to find the page table for that segment. Then the page number portion of the virtual address is used to index the page table and look up the corresponding frame number. This is combined with the offset portion of the virtual address to produce the desired real address.

Figure 8.2c suggests the segment table entry and page table entry formats. As before, the segment table entry contains the length of the segment. It also contains a base field, which now refers to a page table. The present and modified bits are not needed because these matters are handled at the page level. Other control bits may be used, for purposes of sharing and protection. The page table entry is essentially the same as is used in a pure paging system. Each page number is mapped into a corresponding frame number if the page is present in main memory. The modified bit indicates whether this page needs to be written back out when the frame is allocated to another page. There may be other control bits dealing with protection or other aspects of memory management.

Protection and Sharing

Segmentation lends itself to the implementation of protection and sharing policies. Because each segment table entry includes a length as well as a base address, a program cannot inadvertently access a main memory location beyond the limits of a segment. To achieve sharing, it is possible for a segment to be referenced in the segment tables of more than one process. The same mechanisms are, of course, available in a paging system. However, in this case the page structure of programs and data is not visible to the programmer, making the specification of protection and sharing requirements more awkward. Figure 8.14 illustrates the types of protection relationships that can be enforced in such a system.

More sophisticated mechanisms can also be provided. A common scheme is to use a ring-protection structure, of the type we referred to in Chapter 3 (Problem 3.7). In this scheme, lower-numbered, or inner, rings enjoy greater privilege than

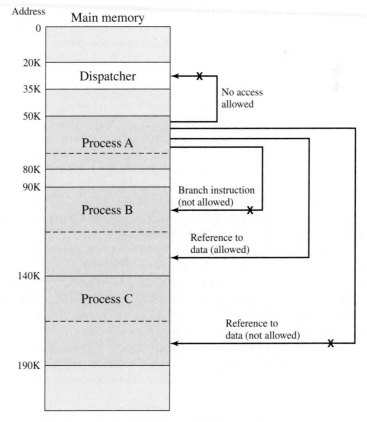

Figure 8.14   Protection Relationships between Segments

higher-numbered, or outer, rings. Typically, ring 0 is reserved for kernel functions of the operating system, with applications at a higher level. Some utilities or operating system services may occupy an intermediate ring. Basic principles of the ring system are as follows:

1. A program may access only data that reside on the same ring or a less privileged ring.
2. A program may call services residing on the same or a more privileged ring.

8.2 OPERATING SYSTEM SOFTWARE

The design of the memory-management portion of an operating system depends on three fundamental areas of choice:

- Whether or not to use virtual memory techniques
- The use of paging or segmentation or both
- The algorithms employed for various aspects of memory management

The choices made in the first two areas depend on the hardware platform available. Thus, earlier UNIX implementations did not provide virtual memory because the processors on which the system ran did not support paging or segmentation. Neither of these techniques is practical without hardware support for address translation and other basic functions.

Two additional comments about the first two items in the preceding list: First, with the exception of operating systems for some of the older personal computers, such as MS-DOS, and specialized systems, all important operating systems provide virtual memory. Second, pure segmentation systems are becoming increasingly rare. When segmentation is combined with paging, most of the memory-management issues confronting the operating system designer are in the area of paging.[4] Thus, we can concentrate in this section on the issues associated with paging.

The choices related to the third item are the domain of operating system software and are the subject of this section. Table 8.3 lists the key design elements that we examine. In each case, the key issue is one of performance: We would like to minimize the rate at which page faults occur, because page faults cause considerable software overhead. At a minimum, the overhead includes deciding which resident page or pages to replace, and the I/O of exchanging pages. Also, the operating system must schedule another process to run during the page I/O, causing a process switch. Accordingly, we would like to arrange matters so that, during the time that a process is executing, the probability of referencing a word on a missing page is minimized. In all of the areas referred to in Table 8.3, there is no definitive policy that works best. As we shall see, the task of memory management in a paging environment is fiendishly complex. Furthermore, the performance of any

---

[4]Protection and sharing are usually dealt with at the segment level in a combined segmentation/paging system. We will deal with these issues in later chapters.

Table 8.3 Operating System Policies for Virtual Memory

Fetch Policy	Resident Set Management
Demand	Resident set size
Prepaging	Fixed
	Variable
Placement Policy	Replacement Scope
	Global
Replacement Policy	Local
Basic Algorithms	
Optimal	**Cleaning Policy**
Least recently used (LRU)	Demand
First-in-first-out (FIFO)	Precleaning
Clock	
Page buffering	**Load Control**
	Degree of multiprogramming

particular set of policies depends on main memory size, the relative speed of main and secondary memory, the size and number of processes competing for resources, and the execution behavior of individual programs. This latter characteristic depends on the nature of the application, the programming language and compiler employed, the style of the programmer who wrote it, and, for an interactive program, the dynamic behavior of the user. Thus, the reader must expect no final answers here or anywhere. For smaller systems, the operating system designer should attempt to choose a set of policies that seems "good" over a wide range of conditions, based on the current state of knowledge. For larger systems, particularly mainframes, the operating system should be equipped with monitoring and control tools that allow the site manager to tune the operating system to get "good" results based on site conditions.

Fetch Policy

The fetch policy determines when a page should be brought into main memory. The two common alternatives are demand paging and prepaging. With **demand paging**, a page is brought into main memory only when a reference is made to a location on that page. If the other elements of memory-management policy are good, the following should happen. When a process is first started, there will be a flurry of page faults. As more and more pages are brought in, the principle of locality suggests that most future references will be to pages that have recently been brought in. Thus, after a time, matters should settle down and the number of page faults should drop to a very low level.

With **prepaging**, pages other than the one demanded by a page fault are brought in. Prepaging exploits the characteristics of most secondary memory devices, such as disks, which have seek times and rotational latency. If the pages of a process are stored contiguously in secondary memory, then it is more efficient to bring in a number of contiguous pages at one time rather than bringing them in one at a time over an extended period. Of course, this policy is ineffective if most of the extra pages that are brought in are not referenced.

The prepaging policy could be employed either when a process first starts up, in which case the programmer would somehow have to designate desired pages, or every time a page fault occurs. This latter course would seem preferable because it is invisible to the programmer. However, the utility of prepaging has not been established [MAEK87].

Prepaging should not be confused with swapping. When a process is swapped out of memory and put in a suspended state, all of its resident pages are moved out. When the process is resumed, all of the pages that were previously in main memory are returned to main memory.

Placement Policy

The placement policy determines where in real memory a process piece is to reside. In a pure segmentation system, the placement policy is an important design issue; policies such as best-fit, first-fit, and so on, which were discussed in Chapter 7, are possible alternatives. However, for a system that uses either pure paging or paging combined with segmentation, placement is usually irrelevant because the address translation hardware and the main memory access hardware can perform their functions for any page-frame combination with equal efficiency.

There is one area in which placement does become a concern, and this is a subject of research and development. On a so-called nonuniform memory access (NUMA) multiprocessor, the distributed, shared memory of the machine can be referenced by any processor on the machine, but the time for accessing a particular physical location varies with the distance between the processor and the memory module. Thus, performance depends heavily on the extent to which data reside close to the processors that use them [LARO92, BOLO89, COX89]. For NUMA systems, an automatic placement strategy is desirable to assign pages to the memory module that provides the best performance.

Replacement Policy

In most operating system texts, the treatment of memory management includes a section entitled "replacement policy," which deals with the selection of a page in main memory to be replaced when a new page must be brought in. This topic is sometimes difficult to explain because several interrelated concepts are involved:

- How many page frames are to be allocated to each active process
- Whether the set of pages to be considered for replacement should be limited to those of the process that caused the page fault or encompass all the page frames in main memory
- Among the set of pages considered, which particular page should be selected for replacement

We shall refer to the first two concepts as *resident set management*, which is dealt with in the next subsection, and reserve the term *replacement policy* for the third concept, which is discussed in this subsection.

The area of replacement policy is probably the most studied of any area of memory management. When all of the frames in main memory are occupied and it is necessary to bring in a new page to satisfy a page fault, the replacement policy determines which page currently in memory is to be replaced. All of the policies have as their objective that the page that is removed should be the page least likely to be referenced in the near future. Because of the principle of locality, there is often a high correlation between recent referencing history and near-future referencing patterns. Thus, most policies try to predict future behavior on the basis of past behavior. One tradeoff that must be considered is that the more elaborate and sophisticated the replacement policy, the greater the hardware and software overhead to implement it.

Frame Locking One restriction on replacement policy needs to be mentioned before looking at various algorithms: Some of the frames in main memory may be locked. When a frame is locked, the page currently stored in that frame may not be replaced. Much of the kernel of the operating system is held on locked frames, as well as key control structures. In addition, I/O buffers and other time-critical areas may be locked into main memory frames. Locking is achieved by associating a lock bit with each frame. This bit may be kept in a frame table as well as being included in the current page table.

Basic Algorithms Regardless of the resident set management strategy (discussed in the next subsection), there are certain basic algorithms that are used for the selection of a page to replace. Replacement algorithms that have been discussed in the literature include

- Optimal
- Least recently used (LRU)
- First-in-first-out (FIFO)
- Clock

The **optimal** policy selects for replacement that page for which the time to the next reference is the longest. It can be shown that this policy results in the fewest number of page faults [BELA66]. Clearly, this policy is impossible to implement, because it would require the operating system to have perfect knowledge of future events. However, it does serve as a standard against which to judge real-world algorithms.

Figure 8.15 gives an example of the optimal policy. The example assumes a fixed frame allocation (fixed resident set size) for this process of three frames. The execution of the process requires reference to five distinct pages. The page address stream formed by executing the program is

$$2\ 3\ 2\ 1\ 5\ 2\ 4\ 5\ 3\ 2\ 5\ 2$$

which means that the first page referenced is 2, the second page referenced is 3, and so on. The optimal policy produces three page faults after the frame allocation has been filled.

The **least recently used** (LRU) policy replaces the page in memory that has not been referenced for the longest time. By the principle of locality, this should be the page least likely to be referenced in the near future. And, in fact, the LRU policy does nearly as well as the optimal policy. The problem with this approach is the difficulty in implementation. One approach would be to tag each page with the time

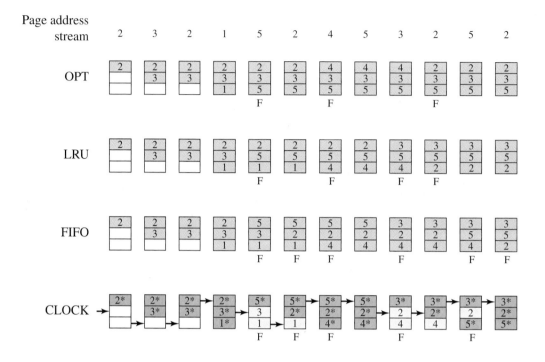

F = page fault occurring after the frame allocation is initially filled

Figure 8.15 Behavior of Four Page Replacement Algorithms

of its last reference; this would have to be done at each memory reference, both instruction and data. Even if the hardware would support such a scheme, the overhead would be tremendous. Alternatively, one could maintain a stack of page references, again an expensive prospect.

Figure 8.15 shows an example of the behavior of LRU, using the same page address stream as for the optimal policy example. In this example, there are four page faults.

The **first-in-first-out** (FIFO) policy treats the page frames allocated to a process as a circular buffer, and pages are removed in round-robin style. All that is required is a pointer that circles through the page frames of the process. This is therefore one of the simplest page replacement policies to implement. The logic behind this choice, other than its simplicity, is that one is replacing the page that has been in memory the longest: A page fetched into memory a long time ago may have now fallen out of use. This reasoning will often be wrong, because there will often be regions of program or data that are heavily used throughout the life of a program. Those pages will be repeatedly paged in and out by the FIFO algorithm.

Continuing our example in Figure 8.15, the FIFO policy results in six page faults. Note that LRU recognizes that pages 2 and 5 are referenced more frequently than other pages, whereas FIFO does not.

Whereas the LRU policy does nearly as well as an optimal policy, it is difficult to implement and imposes significant overhead. On the other hand, the FIFO policy is very simple to implement but performs relatively poorly. Over the years, operating system designers have tried a number of other algorithms to approximate the performance of LRU while imposing little overhead. Many of these algorithms are variants of a scheme referred to as the **clock policy**.

The simplest form of clock policy requires the association of an additional bit with each frame, referred to as the use bit. When a page is first loaded into a frame in memory, the use bit for that frame is set to 1. Whenever the page is subsequently referenced (after the reference that generated the page fault), its use bit is set to 1. For the page replacement algorithm, the set of frames that are candidates for replacement (this process: local scope; all of main memory: global scope[5]) is considered to be a circular buffer, with which a pointer is associated. When a page is replaced, the pointer is set to indicate the next frame in the buffer after the frame just updated. When it comes time to replace a page, the operating system scans the buffer to find a frame with a use bit set to zero. Each time it encounters a frame with a use bit of 1, it resets that bit to zero and continues on. If any of the frames in the buffer have a use bit of zero at the beginning of this process, the first such frame encountered is chosen for replacement. If all of the frames have a use bit of 1, then the pointer will make one complete cycle through the buffer, setting all the use bits to zero, and stop at its original position, replacing the page in that frame. We can see that this policy is similar to FIFO, except that, in the clock policy, any frame with a use bit of 1 is passed over by the algorithm. The policy is referred to as a clock policy because we can visualize the page frames as laid out in a circle. A number of operating systems have employed some variation of this simple clock policy (for example, Multics [CORB68]).

Figure 8.16 provides an example of the simple clock policy mechanism. A circular buffer of n main memory frames is available for page replacement. Just prior to the replacement of a page from the buffer with incoming page 727, the next frame pointer points at frame 2, which contains page 45. The clock policy is now executed. Because the use bit for page 45 in frame 2 is equal to 1, this page is not replaced. Instead, the use bit is set to zero and the pointer advances. Similarly, page 191 in frame 3 is not replaced; its use bit is set to zero and the pointer advances. In the next frame, frame 4, the use bit is set to 0. Therefore, page 556 is replaced with page 727. The use bit is set to 1 for this frame and the pointer advances to frame 5, completing the page replacement procedure.

The behavior of the clock policy is illustrated in Figure 8.15. The presence of an asterisk indicates that the corresponding use bit is equal to 1, and the arrow indicates the current position of the pointer. Note that the clock policy is adept at protecting frames 2 and 5 from replacement.

Figure 8.17 shows the results of an experiment reported in [BAER80], which compares the four algorithms that we have been discussing; it is assumed that the number of page frames assigned to a process is fixed. The results are based on the execution of 0.25×10^6 references in a FORTRAN program, using a page size of 256 words. Baer ran the experiment with frame allocations of 6, 8, 10, 12, and 14 frames. The differences among the four policies are most striking at small allocations, with FIFO being

---

[5]The concept of scope is discussed in the subsection "Replacement Scope," subsequently.

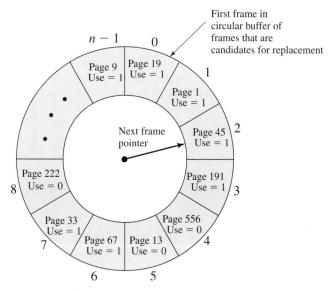

First frame in
circular buffer of
frames that are
candidates for replacement

(a) State of buffer just prior to a page replacement

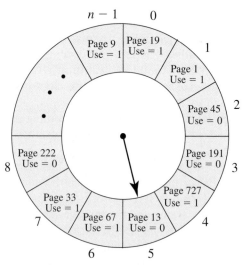

(b) State of buffer just after the next page replacement

Figure 8.16   Example of Clock Policy Operation

over a factor of 2 worse than optimal. All four curves have the same shape as the idealized behavior shown in Figure 8.11b. In order to run efficiently, we would like to be to the right of the knee of the curve (with a small page fault rate) while at the same time keeping a small frame allocation (to the left of the knee of the curve). These two constraints indicate that a desirable mode of operation would be at the knee of the curve.

Almost identical results have been reported in [FINK88], again showing a maximum spread of about a factor of 2. Finkel's approach was to simulate the

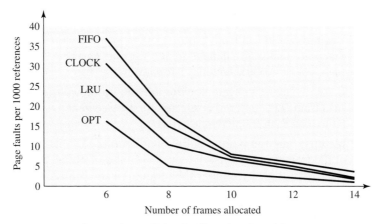

Figure 8.17   Comparison of Fixed-Allocation, Local Page Replacement Algorithms

effects of various policies on a synthesized page-reference string of 10,000 references selected from a virtual space of 100 pages. To approximate the effects of the principle of locality, an exponential distribution for the probability of referencing a particular page was imposed. Finkel observes that some might be led to conclude that there is little point in elaborate page replacement algorithms when only a factor of 2 is at stake. But he notes that this difference will have a noticeable effect either on main memory requirements (to avoid degrading operating system performance) or operating system performance (to avoid enlarging main memory).

The clock algorithm has also been compared to these other algorithms when a variable allocation and either global or local replacement scope (see the following discussion of replacement policy) is used [CARR81, CARR84]. The clock algorithm was found to approximate closely the performance of LRU.

The clock algorithm can be made more powerful by increasing the number of bits that it employs.[6] In all processors that support paging, a modify bit is associated with every page in main memory and hence with every frame of main memory. This bit is needed so that, when a page has been modified, it is not replaced until it has been written back into secondary memory. We can exploit this bit in the clock algorithm in the following way. If we take the use and modify bits into account, each frame falls into one of four categories:

- Not accessed recently, not modified ($u = 0; m = 0$)
- Accessed recently, not modified ($u = 1; m = 0$)
- Not accessed recently, modified ($u = 0; m = 1$)
- Accessed recently, modified ($u = 1; m = 1$)

---

[6]On the other hand, if we reduce the number of bits employed to zero, the clock algorithm degenerates to FIFO.

With this classification, the clock algorithm performs as follows:

1. Beginning at the current position of the pointer, scan the frame buffer. During this scan, make no changes to the use bit. The first frame encountered with $(u = 0; m = 0)$ is selected for replacement.

2. If step 1 fails, scan again, looking for the frame with $(u = 0; m = 1)$. The first such frame encountered is selected for replacement. During this scan, set the use bit to 0 on each frame that is bypassed.

3. If step 2 fails, the pointer should have returned to its original position and all of the frames in the set will have a use bit of 0. Repeat step 1 and, if necessary, step 2. This time, a frame will be found for the replacement.

In summary, the page replacement algorithm cycles through all of the pages in the buffer looking for one that has not been modified since being brought in and has not been accessed recently. Such a page is a good bet for replacement and has the advantage that, because it is unmodified, it does not need to be written back out to secondary memory. If no candidate page is found in the first sweep, the algorithm cycles through the buffer again, looking for a modified page that has not been accessed recently. Even though such a page must be written out to be replaced, because of the principle of locality, it may not be needed again anytime soon. If this second pass fails, all of the frames in the buffer are marked as having not been accessed recently and a third sweep is performed.

This strategy was used on an older version of the Macintosh virtual memory scheme [GOLD89], illustrated in Figure 8.18. The advantage of this algorithm over the simple clock algorithm is that pages that are unchanged are given preference for replacement. Because a page that has been modified must be written out before being replaced, there is an immediate saving of time.

Page Buffering Although LRU and the clock policies are superior to FIFO, they both involve complexity and overhead not suffered with FIFO. In addition, there is the related issue that the cost of replacing a page that has been modified is greater than for one that has not, because the former must be written back out to secondary memory.

An interesting strategy that can improve paging performance and allow the use of a simpler page replacement policy is page buffering. The VAX VMS approach is representative. The page replacement algorithm is simple FIFO. To improve performance, a replaced page is not lost but rather is assigned to one of two lists: the free page list if the page has not been modified, or the modified page list if it has. Note that the page is not physically moved about in main memory; instead, the entry in the page table for this page is removed and placed in either the free or modified page list.

The free page list is a list of page frames available for reading in pages. VMS tries to keep some small number of frames free at all times. When a page is to be read in, the page frame at the head of the list is used, destroying the page that was there. When an unmodified page is to be replaced, it remains in memory and its page frame is added to the tail of the free page list. Similarly, when a modified page is to be written out and replaced, its page frame is added to the tail of the modified page list.

The important aspect of these maneuvers is that the page to be replaced remains in memory. Thus if the process references that page, it is returned to the resident set of that process at little cost. In effect, the free and modified page lists

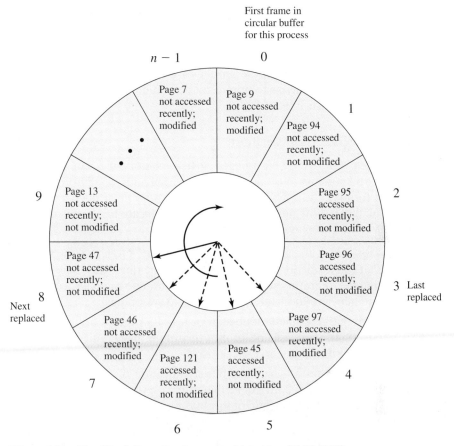

Figure 8.18 The Clock Page-Replacement Algorithm [GOLD89]

act as a cache of pages. The modified page list serves another useful function: Modified pages are written out in clusters rather than one at a time. This significantly reduces the number of I/O operations and therefore the amount of disk access time.

A simpler version of page buffering is implemented in the Mach operating system [RASH88]. In this case, no distinction is made between modified and unmodified pages.

Replacement Policy and Cache Size As was discussed earlier, main memory size is getting larger and the locality of applications is decreasing. In compensation, cache sizes have been increasing. Large cache sizes, even multimegabyte ones, are now feasible design alternatives [BORG90]. With a large cache, the replacement of virtual memory pages can have a performance impact. If the page frame selected for replacement is in the cache, then that cache block is lost as well as the page that it holds.

In systems that use some form of page buffering, it is possible to improve cache performance by supplementing the page replacement policy with a policy for page placement in the page buffer. Most operating systems place pages by selecting an arbitrary page frame from the page buffer; typically a first-in-first-out discipline is used. A study reported in [KESS92] shows that a careful page placement strategy can result in 10 to 20% fewer cache misses than naive placement.

Several page placement algorithms are examined in [KESS92]. The details are beyond the scope of this book, as they depend on the details of cache structure and policies. The essence of these strategies is to bring consecutive pages into main memory in such a way as to minimize the number of page frames that are mapped into the same cache slots.

Resident Set Management

Resident Set Size With paged virtual memory, it is not necessary and indeed may not be possible to bring all of the pages of a process into main memory to prepare it for execution. Thus, the operating system must decide how many pages to bring in, that is, how much main memory to allocate to a particular process. Several factors come into play:

- The smaller the amount of memory allocated to a process, the more processes that can reside in main memory at any one time. This increases the probability that the operating system will find at least one ready process at any given time and hence reduces the time lost due to swapping.

- If a relatively small number of pages of a process are in main memory, then, despite the principle of locality, the rate of page faults will be rather high (see Figure 8.11b).

- Beyond a certain size, additional allocation of main memory to a particular process will have no noticeable effect on the page fault rate for that process because of the principle of locality.

With these factors in mind, two sorts of policies are to be found in contemporary operating systems. A **fixed-allocation** policy gives a process a fixed number of frames in main memory within which to execute. That number is decided at initial load time (process creation time) and may be determined based on the type of process (interactive, batch, type of application) or may be based on guidance from the programmer or system manager. With a fixed-allocation policy, whenever a page fault occurs in the execution of a process, one of the pages of that process must be replaced by the needed page.

A **variable-allocation** policy allows the number of page frames allocated to a process to be varied over the lifetime of the process. Ideally, a process that is suffering persistently high levels of page faults, indicating that the principle of locality only holds in a weak form for that process, will be given additional page frames to reduce the page fault rate; whereas a process with an exceptionally low page fault rate, indicating that the process is quite well behaved from a locality point of view, will be given a reduced allocation, with the hope that this will not noticeably increase the page fault rate. The use of a variable-allocation policy relates to the concept of replacement scope, as explained in the next subsection.

The variable-allocation policy would appear to be the more powerful one. However, the difficulty with this approach is that it requires the operating system to assess the behavior of active processes. This inevitably requires software overhead in the operating system and is dependent on hardware mechanisms provided by the processor platform.

Replacement Scope The scope of a replacement strategy can be categorized as global or local. Both types of policies are activated by a page fault when there are no free page frames. A **local replacement policy** chooses only among the resident pages of the process that generated the page fault in selecting a page to replace. A **global replacement policy** considers all unlocked pages in main memory as candidates for replacement, regardless of which process owns a particular page. While it happens that local policies are easier to analyze, there is no convincing evidence that they perform better than global policies, which are attractive because of their simplicity of implementation and minimal overhead [CARR84, MAEK87].

There is a correlation between replacement scope and resident set size (Table 8.4). A fixed resident set implies a local replacement policy: To hold the size of a resident set fixed, a page that is removed from main memory must be replaced by another page from the same process. A variable-allocation policy can clearly employ a global replacement policy: The replacement of a page from one process in main memory with that of another causes the allocation of one process to grow by one page and that of the other to shrink by one page. We shall also see that variable allocation and local replacement is a valid combination. We now examine these three combinations.

Fixed Allocation, Local Scope For this case, we have a process that is running in main memory with a fixed number of frames. When a page fault occurs, the operating system must choose which page from among the currently resident pages for this process is to be replaced. Replacement algorithms such as those discussed in the preceding subsection can be used.

With a fixed-allocation policy, it is necessary to decide ahead of time the amount of allocation to give to a process. This could be decided on the basis of the

Table 8.4 Resident Set Management

	Local Replacement	**Global Replacement**
Fixed Allocation	• Number of frames allocated to process is fixed. • Page to be replaced is chosen from among the frames allocated to that process.	• Not possible.
Variable Allocation	• The number of frames allocated to a process may be changed from time to time, to maintain the working set of the process. • Page to be replaced is chosen from among the frames allocated to that process.	• Page to be replaced is chosen from all available frames in main memory; this causes the size of the resident set of processes to vary.

type of application and the amount requested by the program. The drawback to this approach is twofold: If allocations tend to be too small, then there will be a high page fault rate, causing the entire multiprogramming system to run slowly. If allocations tend to be unnecessarily large, then there will be too few programs in main memory and there will either be considerable processor idle time or considerable time spent in swapping.

Variable Allocation, Global Scope This combination is perhaps the easiest to implement and has been adopted in a number of operating systems. At any given time, there are a number of processes in main memory, each with a certain number of frames allocated to it. Typically, the operating system also maintains a list of free frames. When a page fault occurs, a free frame is added to the resident set of a process and the page is brought in. Thus, a process experiencing page faults will gradually grow in size, which should help reduce overall page faults in the system.

The difficulty with this approach is in the replacement choice. When there are no free frames available, the operating system must choose a page currently in memory to replace. The selection is made from among all of the frames in memory, except for locked frames such as those of the kernel. Using any of the policies discussed in the preceding subsection, the page selected for replacement can belong to any of the resident processes; there is no discipline to determine which process should lose a page from its resident set. Therefore, the process that suffers the reduction in resident set size may not be optimum.

One way to counter the potential performance problems of a variable-allocation, global-scope policy is to use page buffering. In this way, the choice of which page to replace becomes less significant, because the page may be reclaimed if it is referenced before the next time that a block of pages are overwritten.

Variable Allocation, Local Scope The variable-allocation, local-scope strategy attempts to overcome the problems with a global-scope strategy. It can be summarized as follows:

1. When a new process is loaded into main memory, allocate to it a certain number of page frames as its resident set, based on application type, program request, or other criteria. Use either prepaging or demand paging to fill up the allocation.

2. When a page fault occurs, select the page to replace from among the resident set of the process that suffers the fault.

3. From time to time, reevaluate the allocation provided to the process, and increase or decrease it to improve overall performance.

With this strategy, the decision to increase or decrease a resident set size is a deliberate one and is based on an assessment of the likely future demands of active processes. Because of this evaluation, such a strategy is more complex than a simple global replacement policy. However, it may yield better performance.

The key elements of the variable-allocation, local-scope strategy are the criteria used to determine resident set size and the timing of changes. One specific strategy that has received much attention in the literature is known as the **working set strategy**. Although a true working set strategy would be difficult to implement, it is useful to examine it as a baseline for comparison.

The working set is a concept introduced and popularized by Denning [DENN68, DENN70, DENN80b]; it has had a profound impact on virtual memory-management design. The working set with parameter Δ for a process at virtual time t, $W(t, \Delta)$, is the set of pages of that process that have been referenced in the last Δ virtual time units.

Virtual time is defined as follows. Consider a sequence of memory references, $r(1), r(2), \ldots$, in which $r(i)$ is the page that contains the ith virtual address generated by a given process. Time is measured in memory references; thus $t = 1, 2, 3, \ldots$ measures the process's internal virtual time.

Let us consider each of the two variables of W. The variable Δ is a window of virtual time over which the process is observed. The working set size will be a non-decreasing function of the window size. The result is illustrated in Figure 8.19 (based on [BACH86]), which shows a sequence of page references for a process. The dots indicate time units in which the working set does not change. Note that the larger the window size, the larger the working set. This can be expressed in the following relationship:

$$W(t, \Delta + 1) \supseteq W(t, \Delta)$$

Sequence of page references	Window size, Δ			
	2	3	4	5
24	24	24	24	24
15	24 15	24 15	24 15	24 15
18	15 18	24 15 18	24 15 18	24 15 18
23	18 23	15 18 23	24 15 18 23	24 15 18 23
24	23 24	18 23 24	.	.
17	24 17	23 24 17	18 23 24 17	15 18 23 24 17
18	17 18	24 17 18	.	18 23 24 17
24	18 24	.	24 17 18	.
18	.	18 24	.	24 17 18
17	18 17	24 18 17	.	.
17	17	18 17	.	.
15	17 15	17 15	18 17 15	24 18 17 15
24	15 24	17 15 24	17 15 24	.
17	24 17	.	.	17 15 24
24	.	24 17	.	.
18	24 18	17 24 18	17 24 18	15 17 24 18

Figure 8.19   Working Set of Process as Defined by Window Size

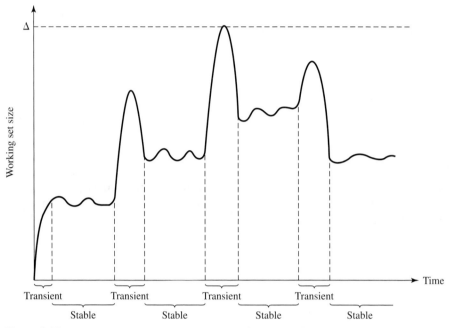

Figure 8.20 Typical Graph of Working Set Size [MAEK87]

The working set is also a function of time. If a process executes over Δ time units, ending at time t, and uses only a single page, then $|W(t, \Delta)| = 1$. A working set can also grow as large as the number of pages N of the process if many different pages are rapidly addressed and if the window size allows. Thus,

$$1 \leq |W(t, \Delta)| \leq \min(\Delta, N)$$

Figure 8.20 indicates the way in which the working set size can vary over time for a fixed value of Δ. For many programs, periods of relatively stable working set sizes alternate with periods of rapid change. When a process first begins executing, it gradually builds up to a working set as it references new pages. Eventually, by the principle of locality, the process should stabilize on a certain set of pages. Subsequent transient periods reflect a shift of the program to a new locality. During the transition phase, some of the pages from the old locality remain within the window, Δ, causing a surge in the size of the working set as new pages are referenced. As the window slides past these page references, the working set size declines until it contains only those pages from the new locality.

This concept of a working set can be used to guide a strategy for resident set size:

1. Monitor the working set of each process.

2. Periodically remove from the resident set of a process those pages that are not in its working set. This is essentially an LRU policy.

3. A process may execute only if its working set is in main memory (i.e., if its resident set includes its working set).

This strategy is appealing because it takes an accepted principle, the principle of locality, and exploits it to achieve a memory-management strategy that should minimize page faults. Unfortunately, there are a number of problems with the working set strategy:

1. The past does not always predict the future. Both the size and the membership of the working set will change over time (e.g., see Figure 8.20).

2. A true measurement of working set for each process is impractical. It would be necessary to time-stamp every page reference for every process using the virtual time of that process and then maintain a time-ordered queue of pages for each process.

3. The optimal value of Δ is unknown and in any case would vary.

Nevertheless, the spirit of this strategy is valid, and a number of operating systems attempt to approximate a working set strategy. One way to do this is to focus not on the exact page references but on the page fault rate of a process. As Figure 8.11b illustrates, the page fault rate falls as we increase the resident set size of a process. The working set size should fall at a point on this curve such as indicated by W in the figure. Therefore, rather than monitor the working set size directly, we can achieve comparable results by monitoring the page fault rate. The line of reasoning is as follows: If the page fault rate for a process is below some minimum threshold, the system as a whole can benefit by assigning a smaller resident set size to this process (because more page frames are available for other processes) without harming the process (by causing it to incur increased page faults). If the page fault rate for a process is above some maximum threshold, the process can benefit from an increased resident set size (by incurring fewer faults) without degrading the system.

An algorithm that follows this strategy is the **page fault frequency** (PFF) algorithm [CHU72, GUPT78]. The algorithm requires a use bit to be associated with each page in memory. The bit is set to 1 when that page is accessed. When a page fault occurs, the operating system notes the virtual time since the last page fault for that process; this could be done by maintaining a counter of page references. A threshold F is defined. If the amount of time since the last page fault is less than F, then a page is added to the resident set of the process. Otherwise, discard all pages with a use bit of zero, and shrink the resident set accordingly. At the same time, reset the use bit on the remaining pages of the process to zero. The strategy can be refined by using two thresholds: an upper threshold that is used to trigger a growth in the resident set size, and a lower threshold that is used to trigger a contraction in the resident set size.

The time between page faults is the reciprocal of the page fault rate. Although it would seem to be better to maintain a running average of the page fault rate, the use of a single time measurement is a reasonable compromise that allows decisions about resident set size to be based on the page fault rate. If such a strategy is supplemented with page buffering, the resulting performance should be quite good.

Nevertheless, there is a major flaw in the PFF approach, which is that it does not perform well during the transient periods when there is a shift to a new locality. With PFF, no page ever drops out of the resident set before F virtual time units have elapsed since it was last referenced. During interlocality transitions, the rapid succession of page faults causes the resident set of a process to swell before the pages of the old locality are expelled; the sudden peaks of memory demand may produce unnecessary process deactivations and reactivations, with the corresponding undesirable switching and swapping overheads.

An approach that attempts to deal with the phenomenon of interlocality transition with a similar relatively low overhead to that of PFF is the **variable-interval sampled working set** (VSWS) policy [FERR83]. The VSWS policy evaluates the working set of a process at sampling instances based on elapsed virtual time. At the beginning of a sampling interval, the use bits of all the resident pages for the process are reset; at the end, only the pages that have been referenced during the interval will have their use bit set; these pages are retained in the resident set of the process throughout the next interval, while the others are discarded. Thus the resident set size can only decrease at the end of an interval. During each interval, any faulted pages are added to the resident set; thus the resident set remains fixed or grows during the interval.

The VSWS policy is driven by three parameters:

M: The minimum duration of the sampling interval

L: The maximum duration of the sampling interval

Q: The number of page faults that are allowed to occur between sampling instances

The VSWS policy is as follows:

1. If the virtual time since the last sampling instance reaches L, then suspend the process and scan the use bits.
2. If, prior to an elapsed virtual time of L, Q page faults occur,
   (a) If the virtual time since the last sampling instance is less than M, then wait until the elapsed virtual time reaches M to suspend the process and scan the use bits.
   (b) If the virtual time since the last sampling instance is greater than or equal to M, suspend the process and scan the use bits.

The parameter values are to be selected so that the sampling will normally be triggered by the occurrence of the Qth page fault after the last scan (case 2b). The other two parameters (M and L) provide boundary protection for exceptional conditions. The VSWS policy tries to reduce the peak memory demands caused by abrupt interlocality transitions by increasing the sampling frequency, and hence the rate at which unused pages drop out of the resident set, when the page fault rate increases. Experience with this technique in the Bull mainframe operating system, GCOS 8, indicates that this approach is as simple to implement as PFF and more effective [PIZZ89].

Cleaning Policy

A cleaning policy is the opposite of a fetch policy; it is concerned with determining when a modified page should be written out to secondary memory. Two common alternatives are demand cleaning and precleaning. With **demand cleaning**, a page is written out to secondary memory only when it has been selected for replacement. A **precleaning** policy writes modified pages before their page frames are needed so that pages can be written out in batches.

There is a danger in following either policy to the full. With precleaning, a page is written out but remains in main memory until the page replacement algorithm dictates that it be removed. Precleaning allows the writing of pages in batches, but it makes little sense to write out hundreds or thousands of pages only to find that the majority of them have been modified again before they are replaced. The transfer capacity of secondary memory is limited and should not be wasted with unnecessary cleaning operations.

On the other hand, with demand cleaning, the writing of a dirty page is coupled to, and precedes, the reading in of a new page. This technique may minimize page writes, but it means that a process that suffers a page fault may have to wait for two page transfers before it can be unblocked. This may decrease processor utilization.

A better approach incorporates page buffering. This allows the adoption of the following policy: Clean only pages that are replaceable, but decouple the cleaning and replacement operations. With page buffering, replaced pages can be placed on two lists: modified and unmodified. The pages on the modified list can periodically be written out in batches and moved to the unmodified list. A page on the unmodified list is either reclaimed if it is referenced, or lost when its frame is assigned to another page.

Load Control

Load control is concerned with determining the number of processes that will be resident in main memory, which has been referred to as the multiprogramming level. The load control policy is critical in effective memory management. If too few processes are resident at any one time, then there will be many occasions when all processes are blocked, and much time will be spent in swapping. On the other hand, if too many processes are resident, then, on average, the size of the resident set of each process will be inadequate and frequent faulting will occur. The result is thrashing.

Multiprogramming Level Thrashing is illustrated in Figure 8.21. As the multiprogramming level increases from a small value, one would expect to see processor utilization rise, because there is less chance that all resident processes are blocked.

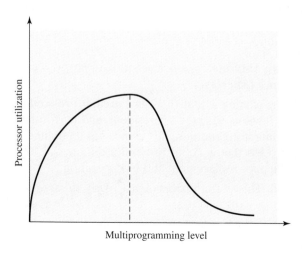

Figure 8.21 Multiprogramming Effects

However, a point is reached at which the average resident set is inadequate. At this point, the number of page faults rises dramatically, and processor utilization collapses.

There are a number of ways to approach this problem. A working set or page fault frequency algorithm implicitly incorporates load control. Only those processes whose resident set is sufficiently large are allowed to execute. In providing the required resident set size for each active process, the policy automatically and dynamically determines the number of active programs.

Another approach, suggested by Denning and his colleagues [DENN80b], is known as the $L = S$ criterion, which adjusts the multiprogramming level so that the mean time between faults equals the mean time required to process a page fault. Performance studies indicate that this is the point at which processor utilization attained a maximum. A policy with a similar effect, proposed in [LERO76], is the *50% criterion*, which attempts to keep utilization of the paging device at approximately 50%. Again, performance studies indicate that this is a point of maximum processor utilization.

Another approach is to adapt the clock page replacement algorithm described earlier (Figure 8.16). [CARR84] describes a technique, using a global scope, that involves monitoring the rate at which the pointer scans the circular buffer of frames. If the rate is below a given lower threshold, this indicates one or both of two circumstances:

1. Few page faults are occurring, resulting in few requests to advance the pointer.
2. For each request, the average number of frames scanned by the pointer is small, indicating that there are many resident pages not being referenced and are readily replaceable.

In both cases, the multiprogramming level can safely be increased. On the other hand, if the pointer scan rate exceeds an upper threshold, this indicates either a high fault rate or difficulty in locating replaceable pages, which implies that the multiprogramming level is too high.

Process Suspension If the degree of multiprogramming is to be reduced, one or more of the currently resident processes must be suspended (swapped out). [CARR84] lists six possibilities:

- **Lowest-priority process:** This implements a scheduling policy decision and is unrelated to performance issues.
- **Faulting process:** The reasoning is that there is a greater probability that the faulting task does not have its working set resident, and performance would suffer least by suspending it. In addition, this choice has an immediate payoff because it blocks a process that is about to be blocked anyway and it eliminates the overhead of a page replacement and I/O operation.
- **Last process activated:** This is the process least likely to have its working set resident.
- **Process with the smallest resident set:** This will require the least future effort to reload. However, it penalizes programs with strong locality.

- **Largest process:** This obtains the most free frames in an overcommitted memory, making additional deactivations unlikely soon.

- **Process with the largest remaining execution window:** In most process scheduling schemes, a process may only run for a certain quantum of time before being interrupted and placed at the end of the Ready queue. This approximates a shortest-processing-time-first scheduling discipline.

As in so many other areas of operating system design, which policy to choose is a matter of judgment and depends on many other design factors in the operating system as well as the characteristics of the programs being executed.

8.3 UNIX AND SOLARIS MEMORY MANAGEMENT

Because UNIX is intended to be machine independent, its memory-management scheme will vary from one system to the next. Earlier versions of UNIX simply used variable partitioning with no virtual memory scheme. Current implementations of UNIX and Solaris make use of paged virtual memory.

In SVR4 and Solaris, there are actually two separate memory-management schemes. The **paging system** provides a virtual memory capability that allocates page frames in main memory to processes and also allocates page frames to disk block buffers. Although this is an effective memory-management scheme for user processes and disk I/O, a paged virtual memory scheme is less suited to managing the memory allocation for the kernel. For this latter purpose, a **kernel memory allocator** is used. We examine these two mechanisms in turn.

Paging System

Data Structures For paged virtual memory, UNIX makes use of a number of data structures that, with minor adjustment, are machine independent (Figure 8.22 and Table 8.5):

- **Page table:** Typically, there will be one page table per process, with one entry for each page in virtual memory for that process.

- **Disk block descriptor:** Associated with each page of a process is an entry in this table that describes the disk copy of the virtual page.

- **Page frame data table:** Describes each frame of real memory and is indexed by frame number. This table is used by the replacement algorithm.

- **Swap-use table:** There is one swap-use table for each swap device, with one entry for each page on the device.

Most of the fields defined in Table 8.5 are self-explanatory. A few warrant further comment. The Age field in the page table entry is an indication of how long it has been since a program referenced this frame. However, the number of bits and the frequency of update of this field are implementation dependent. Therefore, there is no universal UNIX use of this field for page replacement policy.

The Type of Storage field in the disk block descriptor is needed for the following reason: When an executable file is first used to create a new process, only a

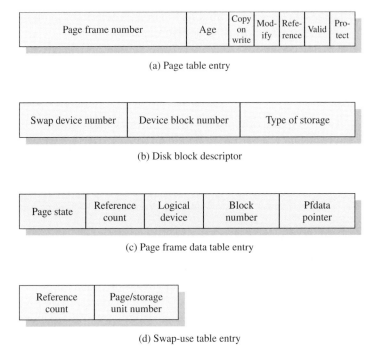

(a) Page table entry

(b) Disk block descriptor

(c) Page frame data table entry

(d) Swap-use table entry

Figure 8.22   UNIX SVR4 Memory-Management Formats

portion of the program and data for that file may be loaded into real memory. Later, as page faults occur, new portions of the program and data are loaded. It is only at the time of first loading that virtual memory pages are created and assigned to locations on one of the devices to be used for swapping. At that time, the operating system is told whether it needs to clear (set to 0) the locations in the page frame before the first loading of a block of the program or data.

Page Replacement   The page frame data table is used for page replacement. Several pointers are used to create lists within this table. All of the available frames are linked together in a list of free frames available for bringing in pages. When the number of available frames drops below a certain threshold, the kernel will steal a number of frames to compensate.

The page replacement algorithm used in SVR4 is a refinement of the clock policy algorithm (Figure 8.16) known as the two-handed clock algorithm (Figure 8.23). The algorithm uses the reference bit in the page table entry for each page in memory that is eligible (not locked) to be swapped out. This bit is set to 0 when the page is first brought in and set to 1 when the page is referenced for a read or write. One hand in the clock algorithm, the fronthand, sweeps through the pages on the list of eligible pages and sets the reference bit to 0 on each page. Sometime later, the backhand sweeps through the same list and checks the reference bit. If the bit is set to 1, then that page has been referenced since the fronthand swept by; these frames are ignored. If the bit is still set to 0, then the page has not been referenced in the time interval between the visit by fronthand and backhand; these pages are placed on a list to be paged out.

Table 8.5   UNIX SVR4 Memory Management Parameters

Page Table Entry

Page frame number
Refers to frame in real memory.

Age
Indicates how long the page has been in memory without being referenced. The length and contents of this field are processor dependent.

Copy on write
Set when more than one process shares a page. If one of the processes writes into the page, a separate copy of the page must first be made for all other processes that share the page. This feature allows the copy operation to be deferred until necessary and avoided in cases where it turns out not to be necessary.

Modify
Indicates page has been modified.

Reference
Indicates page has been referenced. This bit is set to zero when the page is first loaded and may be periodically reset by the page replacement algorithm.

Valid
Indicates page is in main memory.

Protect
Indicates whether write operation is allowed.

Disk Block Descriptor

Swap device number
Logical device number of the secondary device that holds the corresponding page. This allows more than one device to be used for swapping.

Device block number
Block location of page on swap device.

Type of storage
Storage may be swap unit or executable file. In the latter case, there is an indication as to whether the virtual memory to be allocated should be cleared first.

Page Frame Data Table Entry

Page State
Indicates whether this frame is available or has an associated page. In the latter case, the status of the page is specified: on swap device, in executable file, or DMA in progress.

Reference count
Number of processes that reference the page.

Logical device
Logical device that contains a copy of the page.

Block number
Block location of the page copy on the logical device.

Pfdata pointer
Pointer to other pfdata table entries on a list of free pages and on a hash queue of pages.

Swap-use Table Entry

Reference count
Number of page table entries that point to a page on the swap device.

Page/storage unit number
Page identifier on storage unit.

End of
page list

Beginning
of page list

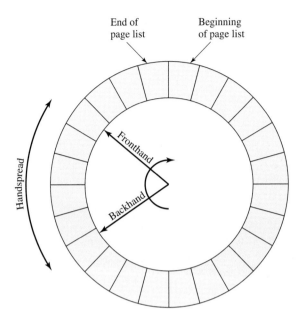

Handspread

Fronthand

Backhand

Figure 8.23 Two-Handed
Clock Page Replacement
Algorithm

Two parameters determine the operation of the algorithm:

- **Scanrate:** The rate at which the two hands scan through the page list, in pages per second
- **Handspread:** The gap between fronthand and backhand

These two parameters have default values set at boot time based on the amount of physical memory. The scanrate parameter can be altered to meet changing conditions. The parameter varies linearly between the values slowscan and fastscan (set at configuration time) as the amount of free memory varies between the values *lotsfree* and *minfree*. In other words, as the amount of free memory shrinks, the clock hands move more rapidly to free up more pages. The handspread parameter determines the gap between the fronthand and the backhand and therefore, together with scanrate, determines the window of opportunity to use a page before it is swapped out due to lack of use.

Kernel Memory Allocator

The kernel generates and destroys small tables and buffers frequently during the course of execution, each of which requires dynamic memory allocation. [VAHA96] lists the following examples:

- The pathname translation routing may allocate a buffer to copy a pathname from user space.
- The `allocb()` routine allocates STREAMS buffers of arbitrary size.
- Many UNIX implementations allocate zombie structures to retain exit status and resource usage information about deceased processes.

- In SVR4 and Solaris, the kernel allocates many objects (such as proc structures, vnodes, and file descriptor blocks) dynamically when needed.

Most of these blocks are significantly smaller than the typical machine page size, and therefore the paging mechanism would be inefficient for dynamic kernel memory allocation. For SVR4, a modification of the buddy system, described in Section 7.2, is used.

In buddy systems, the cost to allocate and free a block of memory is low compared to that of best-fit or first-fit policies [KNUT97]. However, in the case of kernel memory management, the allocation and free operations must be made as fast as possible. The drawback of the buddy system is the time required to fragment and coalesce blocks.

Barkley and Lee at AT&T proposed a variation known as a lazy buddy system [BARK89], and this is the technique adopted for SVR4. The authors observed that UNIX often exhibits steady-state behavior in kernel memory demand; that is, the amount of demand for blocks of a particular size varies slowly in time. Therefore, if a block of size 2^i is released and is immediately coalesced with its buddy into a block of size 2^{i+1}, the kernel may next request a block of size 2^i, which may necessitate splitting the larger block again. To avoid this unnecessary coalescing and splitting, the lazy buddy system defers coalescing until it seems likely that it is needed, and then coalesces as many blocks as possible.

The lazy buddy system uses the following parameters:

N_i = current number of blocks of size 2^i.

A_i = current number of blocks of size 2^i that are allocated (occupied).

G_i = current number of blocks of size 2^i that are globally free; these are blocks that are eligible for coalescing; if the buddy of such a block becomes globally free, then the two blocks will be coalesced into a globally free block of size 2^{i+1}. All free blocks (holes) in the standard buddy system could be considered globally free.

L_i = current number of blocks of size 2^i that are locally free; these are blocks that are not eligible for coalescing. Even if the buddy of such a block becomes free, the two blocks are not coalesced. Rather, the locally free blocks are retained in anticipation of future demand for a block of that size.

The following relationship holds:

$$N_i = A_i + G_i + L_i$$

In general, the lazy buddy system tries to maintain a pool of locally free blocks and only invokes coalescing if the number of locally free blocks exceeds a threshold. If there are too many locally free blocks, then there is a chance that there will be a lack of free blocks at the next level to satisfy demand. Most of the time, when a block is freed, coalescing does not occur, so there is minimal bookkeeping and operational costs. When a block is to be allocated, no

Initial value of D_i is 0
After an operation, the value of D_i is updated as follows

(I) if the next operation is a block allocate request:
    if there is any free block, select one to allocate
        if the selected block is locally free
            then $D_i := D_i + 2$
            else $D_i := D_i + 1$
    otherwise
        first get two blocks by splitting a larger one into two (recursive operation)
        allocate one and mark the other locally free
        D_i remains unchanged (but D may change for other block sizes because of the
                recursive call)

(II) if the next operation is a block free request
    Case $D_i \geq 2$
        mark it locally free and free it locally
        $D_i := D_i - 2$
    Case $D_i = 1$
        mark it globally free and free it globally; coalesce if possible
        $D_i := 0$
    Case $D_i = 0$
        mark it globally free and free it globally; coalesce if possible
        select one locally free block of size 2i and free it globally; coalesce if possible
        $D_i := 0$

Figure 8.24   Lazy Buddy System Algorithm

distinction is made between locally and globally free blocks; again, this minimizes bookkeeping.

The criterion used for coalescing is that the number of locally free blocks of a given size should not exceed the number of allocated blocks of that size (i.e., we must have $L_i \geq A_i$). This is a reasonable guideline for restricting the growth of locally free blocks, and experiments in [BARK89] confirm that this scheme results in noticeable savings.

To implement the scheme, the authors define a delay variable as follows:

$$D_i = A_i - L_i = N_i - 2L_i - G_i$$

Figure 8.24 shows the algorithm.

8.4 LINUX MEMORY MANAGEMENT

Linux shares many of the characteristics of the memory management schemes of other UNIX implementations but has its own unique features. Overall, the Linux memory-management scheme is quite complex [DUBE98]. In this section, we give a brief overview of the two main aspects of Linux memory management: process virtual memory and kernel memory allocation.

Linux Virtual Memory

Virtual Memory Addressing Linux makes use of a three-level page table structure, consisting of the following types of tables (each individual table is the size of one page):

- **Page directory:** An active process has a single page directory that is the size of one page. Each entry in the page directory points to one page of the page middle directory. The page directory must be in main memory for an active process.
- **Page middle directory:** The page middle directory may span multiple pages. Each entry in the page middle directory points to one page in the page table.
- **Page table:** The page table may also span multiple pages. Each page table entry refers to one virtual page of the process.

To use this three-level page table structure, a virtual address in Linux is viewed as consisting of four fields (Figure 8.25). The leftmost (most significant) field is used as an index into the page directory. The next field serves as an index into the page middle directory. The third field serves as an index into the page table. The fourth field gives the offset within the selected page of memory.

The Linux page table structure is platform independent and was designed to accommodate the 64-bit Alpha processor, which provides hardware support for three levels of paging. With 64-bit addresses, the use of only two levels of pages on the Alpha would result in very large page tables and directories. The 32-bit Pentium/x86 architecture has a two-level hardware paging mechanism. The Linux software accommodates the two-level scheme by defining the size of the page middle directory as one. Note that all references to an extra level of indirection are optimized away at compile time, not at run time. Therefore, there is no performance

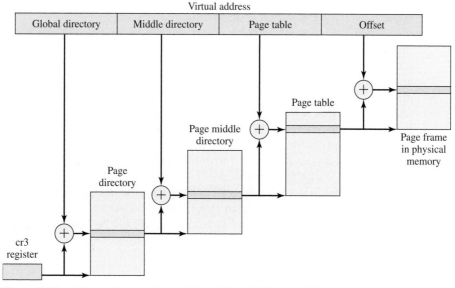

Figure 8.25   Address Translation in Linux Virtual Memory Scheme

overhead for using generic three-level design on platforms which support only two levels in hardware.

Page Allocation To enhance the efficiency of reading in and writing out pages to and from main memory, Linux defines a mechanism for dealing with contiguous blocks of pages mapped into contiguous blocks of page frames. For this purpose, the buddy system is used. The kernel maintains a list of contiguous page frame groups of fixed size; a group may consist of 1, 2, 4, 8, 16, or 32 page frames. As pages are allocated and deallocated in main memory, the available groups are split and merged using the buddy algorithm.

Page Replacement Algorithm The Linux page replacement algorithm is based on the clock algorithm described in Section 8.2 (see Figure 8.16). In the simple clock algorithm, a use bit and a modify bit are associated with each page in main memory. In the Linux scheme, the use bit is replaced with an 8-bit age variable. Each time that a page is accessed, the age variable is incremented. In the background, Linux periodically sweeps through the global page pool and decrements the age variable for each page as it rotates through all the pages in main memory. A page with an age of 0 is an "old" page that has not been referenced in some time and is the best candidate for replacement. The larger the value of age, the more frequently a page has been used in recent times and the less eligible it is for replacement. Thus, the Linux algorithm is a form of least frequently used policy.

Kernel Memory Allocation

The Linux kernel memory capability manages physical main memory page frames. Its primary function is to allocate and deallocate frames for particular uses. Possible owners of a frame include user-space processes (i.e., the frame is part of the virtual memory of a process that is currently resident in real memory), dynamically allocated kernel data, static kernel code, and the page cache.[7]

The foundation of kernel memory allocation for Linux is the page allocation mechanism used for user virtual memory management. As in the virtual memory scheme, a buddy algorithm is used so that memory for the kernel can be allocated and deallocated in units of one or more pages. Because the minimum amount of memory that can be allocated in this fashion is one page, the page allocator alone would be inefficient because the kernel requires small short-term memory chunks in odd sizes. To accommodate these small chunks, Linux uses a scheme known as *slab allocation* [BONW94] within an allocated page. On a Pentium/x86 machine, the page size is 4 Kbytes, and chunks within a page may be allocated of sizes 32, 64, 128, 252, 508, 2040, and 4080 bytes.

The slab allocator is relatively complex and is not examined in detail here; a good description can be found in [VAHA96]. In essence, Linux maintains a set of linked lists, one for each size of chunk. Chunks may be split and aggregated in a manner similar to the buddy algorithm, and moved between lists accordingly.

---

[7]The page cache has properties similar to a disk buffer, described in this chapter, as well as a disk cache, described in Chapter 11. We defer a discussion of the Linux page cache to Chapter 11.

8.5 WINDOWS MEMORY MANAGEMENT

The Windows virtual memory manager controls how memory is allocated and how paging is performed. The memory manager is designed to operate over a variety of platforms and use page sizes ranging from 4 Kbytes to 64 Kbytes. Intel, PowerPC, and MIPS platforms have 4096 bytes per page and DEC Alpha platforms have 8192 bytes per page.

Windows Virtual Address Map

Each Windows user process sees a separate 32-bit address space, allowing 4 Gbytes of memory per process. By default, a portion of this memory is reserved for the operating system, so each user actually has 2 Gbyte of available virtual address space and all processes share the same 2 Gbytes of system space. There an option that allows user space to be increased to 3 Gbytes, leaving 1 Gbyte for system space. The Windows documentation indicates that this feature is intended to support large memory intensive applications on servers with multiple gigabytes of RAM, and that the use of the larger address space can dramatically improve performance for applications such as decision support or data mining.

Figure 8.26 shows the default virtual address space seen by a user process. It consists of four regions:

- 0x00000000 to 0x0000FFFF: Set aside to help programmers catch NULL-pointer assignments.
- 0x00010000 to 0x7FFEFFFF: Available user address space. This space is divided into pages that may be loaded into main memory.
- 0x7FFF0000 to 0x7FFFFFFF: A guard page inaccessible to the user. This page makes it easier for the operating system to check on out-of-bounds pointer references.
- 0x80000000 to 0xFFFFFFFF: System address space. This 2-Gbyte process is used for the Windows Executive, microkernel, and device drivers.

Windows Paging

When a process is created, it can in principle make use of the entire user space of 2 Gbytes (minus 128 Kbytes). This space is divided into fixed-size pages, any of which can be brought into main memory. In practice, to simplify the accounting, a page can be in one of three states:

- **Available:** Pages not currently used by this process.
- **Reserved:** A set of contiguous pages that the virtual memory manager sets aside for a process but does not count against the process's memory quota until used. When a process needs to write to memory, some of the reserved memory is committed to the process.
- **Committed:** Pages for which the virtual memory manager has set aside space in its paging file (e.g., the disk file to which it writes pages when removing them from main memory).

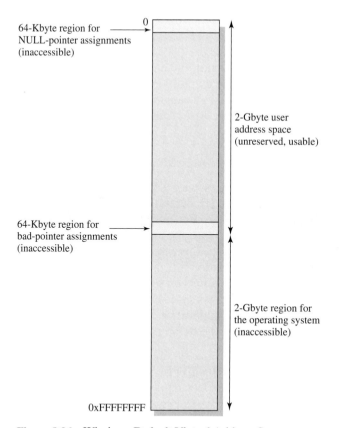

64-Kbyte region for
NULL-pointer assignments
(inaccessible)

0

2-Gbyte user
address space
(unreserved, usable)

64-Kbyte region for
bad-pointer assignments
(inaccessible)

2-Gbyte region for
the operating system
(inaccessible)

0xFFFFFFFF

Figure 8.26 Windows Default Virtual Address Space

The distinction between reserved and committed memory is useful because it (1) minimizes the amount of disk space set aside for a particular process, keeping that disk space free for other processes; and (2) enables a thread or process to declare an amount of memory that can be quickly allocated as needed.

The resident set management scheme used by Windows is variable allocation, local scope (see Table 8.4). When a process is first activated, it is assigned a certain number of page frames of main memory as its working set. When a process references a page not in memory, one of the resident pages of that process is swapped out and the new page is brought in. Working sets of active processes are adjusted using the following general conventions:

- When main memory is plentiful, the virtual memory manager allows the resident sets of active processes to grow. To do this, when a page fault occurs, a new page is brought into memory but no older page is swapped out, resulting in an increase of the resident set of that process by one page.

- When memory becomes scarce, the virtual memory manager recovers memory for the system by moving less recently used pages out of the working sets of active processes, reducing the size of those resident sets.

8.6 SUMMARY

To use the processor and the I/O facilities efficiently, it is desirable to maintain as many processes in main memory as possible. In addition, it is desirable to free programmers from size restrictions in program development.

The way to address both of these concerns is virtual memory. With virtual memory, all address references are logical references that are translated at run time to real addresses. This allows a process to be located anywhere in main memory and for that location to change over time. Virtual memory also allows a process to be broken up into pieces. These pieces need not be contiguously located in main memory during execution and, indeed, it is not even necessary for all of the pieces of the process to be in main memory during execution.

Two basic approaches to providing virtual memory are paging and segmentation. With paging, each process is divided into relatively small, fixed-size pages. Segmentation provides for the use of pieces of varying size. It is also possible to combine segmentation and paging in a single memory-management scheme.

A virtual memory-management scheme requires both hardware and software support. The hardware support is provided by the processor. The support includes dynamic translation of virtual addresses to physical addresses and the generation of an interrupt when a referenced page or segment is not in main memory. Such an interrupt triggers the memory-management software in the operating system.

A number of design issues relate to operating system support for memory management:

- **Fetch policy:** Process pages can be brought in on demand, or a prepaging policy can be used, which clusters the input activity by bringing in a number of pages at once.
- **Placement policy:** With a pure segmentation system, an incoming segment must be fit into an available space in memory.
- **Replacement policy:** When memory is full, a decision must be made as to which page or pages are to be replaced.
- **Resident set management:** The operating system must decide how much main memory to allocate to a particular process when that process is swapped in. This can be a static allocation made at process creation time, or it can change dynamically.
- **Cleaning policy:** Modified process pages can be written out at the time of replacement, or a precleaning policy can be used, which clusters the output activity by writing out a number of pages at once.
- **Load control:** Load control is concerned with determining the number of processes that will be resident in main memory at any given time.

8.7 RECOMMENDED READINGS AND WEB SITES

As might be expected, virtual memory receives good coverage in most books on operating systems. [MILE92] provides a good summary of various research areas. [CARR84] provides an excellent in-depth examination of performance issues. The classic paper, [DENN70], is still well worth a read. [DOWD93] provides an instructive performance analysis of various page replacement algorithms. [JACO98a] is a good survey of issues in virtual memory design; it includes a discussion of inverted page tables. [JACO98b] looks at virtual memory hardware organizations in various microprocessors.

It is a sobering experience to read [IBM86], which gives a detailed account of the tools and options available to a site manager in optimizing the virtual memory policies of MVS. The document illustrates the complexity of the problem.

[VAHA96] is one of the best treatments of the memory-management schemes used in the various flavors of UNIX. [GORM04] is a thorough treatment of Linux memory management.

CARR84   Carr, R. *Virtual Memory Management.* Ann Arbor, MI: UMI Research Press, 1984.

DENN70   Denning, P. "Virtual Memory." *Computing Surveys*, September 1970.

DOWD93   Dowdy, L., and Lowery, C. *P.S. to Operating Systems.* Upper Saddle River, NJ: Prentice Hall, 1993.

GORM04   Gorman, M. *Understanding the Linux Virtual Memory Manager.* Upper Saddle River, NJ: Prentice Hall, 2004.

IBM86   IBM National Technical Support, Large Systems. *Multiple Virtual Storage (MVS) Virtual Storage Tuning Cookbook.* Dallas Systems Center Technical Bulletin G320-0597, June 1986.

JACO98a   Jacob, B., and Mudge, T. "Virtual Memory: Issues of Implementation." *Computer*, June 1998.

JACO98b   Jacob, B., and Mudge, T. "Virtual Memory in Contemporary Microprocessors." *IEEE Micro*, August 1998.

MILE92   Milenkovic, M. *Operating Systems: Concepts and Design.* New York: McGraw-Hill, 1992.

VAHA96   Vahalia, U. *UNIX Internals: The New Frontiers.* Upper Saddle River, NJ: Prentice Hall, 1996.

Recommended Web Sites:

- **The Memory Management Reference:** A good source of documents and links on all aspects of memory management.

8.8 KEY TERMS, REVIEW QUESTIONS, AND PROBLEMS

Key Terms

associative mapping	page	resident set management
demand paging	page fault	segment
external fragmentation	page placement policy	segment table
fetch policy	page replacement policy	segmentation
frame	page table	slab allocation
hash table	paging	thrashing
hashing	prepaging	translation lookaside buffer
internal fragmentation	real memory	virtual memory
locality	resident set	working set

Review Questions

8.1 What is the difference between simple paging and virtual memory paging?

8.2 Explain thrashing.

8.3 Why is the principle of locality crucial to the use of virtual memory?

8.4 What elements are typically found in a page table entry? Briefly define each element.

8.5 What is the purpose of a translation lookaside buffer?

8.6 Briefly define the alternative page fetch policies.

8.7 What is the difference between resident set management and page replacement policy?

8.8 What is the relationship between FIFO and clock page replacement algorithms?

8.9 What is accomplished by page buffering?

8.10 Why is it not possible to combine a global replacement policy and a fixed allocation policy?

8.11 What is the difference between a resident set and a working set?

8.12 What is the difference between demand cleaning and precleaning?

Problems

8.1 Suppose the page table for the process currently executing on the processor looks like the following. All numbers are decimal, everything is numbered starting from zero, and all addresses are memory byte addresses. The page size is 1024 bytes.

Virtual page number	Valid bit	Reference bit	Modify bit	Page frame number
0	1	1	0	4
1	1	1	1	7
2	0	0	0	—
3	1	0	0	2
4	0	0	0	—
5	1	0	1	0

a. Describe exactly how, in general, a virtual address generated by the CPU is translated into a physical main memory address.

b. What physical address, if any, would each of the following virtual addresses correspond to? (Do not try to handle any page faults, if any.)
(i) 1052
(ii) 2221
(iii) 5499

8.2 Consider a paged virtual memory system with 32-bit virtual addresses and 1K-byte pages. Each page table entry requires 32 bits. It is desired to limit the page table size to one page.

a. How many levels of page tables are required?

b. What is the size of the page table at each level? *Hint:* One page table size is smaller.

c. The smaller page size could be used at the top level or the bottom level of the page table hierarchy. Which strategy consumes the least number of pages?

8.3 a. How much memory space is needed for the user page table of Figure 8.4?

b. Assume you want to implement a hashed inverted page table for the same addressing scheme as depicted in Figure 8.4, using a hash function that maps the 20-bit page number into a 6-bit hash value. The table entry contains the page number, the frame number, and a chain pointer. If the page table allocates space for up to 3 overflow entries per hashed entry, how much memory space does the hashed inverted page table take?

8.4 A process has four page frames allocated to it. (All the following numbers are decimal, and everything is numbered starting from zero). The time of the last loading of a page into each page frame, the time of last access to the page in each page frame, the virtual page number in each page frame, and the referenced (R) and modified (M) bits for each page frame are as shown (the times are in clock ticks from the process start at time 0 to the event—not the number of ticks since the event to the present).

Virtual page number	Page frame	Time loaded	Time referenced	R bit	M bit
2	0	60	161	0	1
1	1	130	160	1	0
0	2	26	162	1	0
3	3	20	163	1	1

A page fault to virtual page 4 has occurred at time 164. Which page frame will have its contents replaced for each of the following memory management policies? Explain why in each case.
a. FIFO (first-in-first-out)
b. LRU (least recently used)
c. Clock
d. Optimal (Use the following reference string.)
e. Given the aforementioned state of memory just before the page fault, consider the following virtual page reference string:

$$4, 0, 0, 0, 2, 4, 2, 1, 0, 3, 2$$

How many page faults would occur if the working set policy with LRU were used with a window size of 4 instead of a fixed allocation? Show clearly when each page fault would occur.

8.5 A process references five pages, A, B, C, D, and E, in the following order:

$$A; B; C; D; A; B; E; A; B; C; D; E$$

Assume that the replacement algorithm is first-in-first-out and find the number of page transfers during this sequence of references starting with an empty main memory with three page frames. Repeat for four page frames.

8.6 A process contains eight virtual pages on disk and is assigned a fixed allocation of four page frames in main memory. The following page trace occurs:

$$1, 0, 2, 2, 1, 7, 6, 7, 0, 1, 2, 0, 3, 0, 4, 5, 1, 5, 2, 4, 5, 6, 7, 6, 7, 2, 4, 2, 7, 3, 3, 2, 3$$

a. Show the successive pages residing in the four frames using the LRU replacement policy. Compute the hit ratio in main memory. Assume that the frames are initially empty.
b. Repeat part (a) for the FIFO replacement policy.
c. Compare the two hit ratios and comment on the effectiveness of using FIFO to approximate LRU with respect to this particular trace.

8.7 In the VAX, user page tables are located at virtual addresses in the system space. What is the advantage of having user page tables in virtual rather than main memory? What is the disadvantage?

8.8 Suppose the program statement

for $(i = 1; i <= n; i++)$
    $a[i] = b[i] + c[i];$

is executed in a memory with page size of 1000 words. Let $n = 1000$. Using a machine that has a full range of register-to-register instructions and employs index registers, write a hypothetical program to implement the foregoing statement. Then show the sequence of page references during execution.

8.9   The IBM System/370 architecture uses a two-level memory structure and refers to the two levels as segments and pages, although the segmentation approach lacks many of the features described earlier in this chapter. For the basic 370 architecture, the page size may be either 2 Kbytes or 4 Kbytes, and the segment size is fixed at either 64 Kbytes or 1 Mbyte. For the 370/XA and 370/ESA architectures, the page size is 4 Kbytes and the segment size is 1 Mbyte. Which advantages of segmentation does this scheme lack? What is the benefit of segmentation for the 370?

8.10 Assuming a page size of 4 Kbytes and that a page table entry takes 4 bytes, how many levels of page tables would be required to map a 64-bit address space if the top-level page table fits into a single page?

8.11 Consider a system with memory mapping done on a page basis and using a single-level page table. Assume that the necessary page table is always in memory.
   a. If a memory reference takes 200 ns, how long does a paged memory reference take?
   b. Now we add an MMU that imposes an overhead of 20 ns on a hit or a miss. If we assume that 85% of all memory references hit in the MMU TLB, what is the Effective Memory Access Time (EMAT)?
   c. Explain how the TLB hit rate affects the EMAT.

8.12 Consider a page reference string for a process with a working set of M frames, initially all empty. The page reference string is of length P with N distinct page numbers in it. For any page replacement algorithm,
   a. What is a lower bound on the number of page faults?
   b. What is an upper bound on the number of page faults?

8.13 In discussing a page replacement algorithm, one author makes an analogy with a snowplow moving around a circular track. Snow is falling uniformly on the track and a lone snowplow continually circles the track at constant speed. The snow that is plowed off the track disappears from the system.
   a. For which of the page replacement algorithms discussed in Section 8.2 is this a useful analogy?
   b. What does this analogy suggest about the behavior of the page replacement algorithm in question?

8.14 In the S/370 architecture, a storage key is a control field associated with each page-sized frame of real memory. Two bits of that key that are relevant for page replacement are the reference bit and the change bit. The reference bit is set to 1 when any address within the frame is accessed for read or write and is set to 0 when a new page is loaded into the frame. The change bit is set to 1 when a write operation is performed on any location within the frame. Suggest an approach for determining which page frames are least recently used, making use of only the reference bit.

8.15 Consider the following sequence of page references (each element in the sequence represents a page number):

$$1\ 2\ 3\ 4\ 5\ 2\ 1\ 3\ 3\ 2\ 3\ 4\ 5\ 4\ 5\ 1\ 1\ 3\ 2\ 5$$

Define the *mean working set size* after the kth reference as $s_k(\Delta) = \dfrac{1}{k} \sum_{t=1}^{k} W(t, \Delta)$ and

define the *missing page probability* after the kth reference as $m_k(\Delta) = \dfrac{1}{k} \sum_{t=1}^{k} F(t, \Delta)$,

where $F(t, \Delta) = 1$ if a page fault occurs at virtual time t and 0 otherwise.

   a. Draw a diagram similar to that of Figure 8.19 for the reference sequence just defined for the values $\Delta = 1, 2, 3, 4, 5, 6$.
   b. Plot $s_{20}(\Delta)$ as a function of Δ.
   c. Plot $m_{20}(\Delta)$ as a function of Δ.

8.16 A key to the performance of the VSWS resident set management policy is the value of Q. Experience has shown that, with a fixed value of Q for a process, there are considerable differences in page fault frequencies at various stages of execution. Furthermore, if a single value of Q is used for different processes, dramatically different frequencies of page faults occur. These differences strongly indicate that a mechanism that would dynamically adjust the value of Q during the lifetime of a process would improve the behavior of the algorithm. Suggest a simple mechanism for this purpose.

8.17 Assume that a task is divided into four equal-sized segments and that the system builds an eight-entry page descriptor table for each segment. Thus, the system has a combination of segmentation and paging. Assume also that the page size is 2 Kbytes.
   a. What is the maximum size of each segment?
   b. What is the maximum logical address space for the task?
   c. Assume that an element in physical location 00021ABC is accessed by this task. What is the format of the logical address that the task generates for it? What is the maximum physical address space for the system?

8.18 Consider a paged logical address space (composed of 32 pages of 2 Kbytes each) mapped into a 1-Mbyte physical memory space.
   a. What is the format of the processor's logical address?
   b. What is the length and width of the page table (disregarding the "access rights" bits)?
   c. What is the effect on the page table if the physical memory space is reduced by half?

8.19 The UNIX kernel will dynamically grow a process's stack in virtual memory as needed, but it will never try to shrink it. Consider the case in which a program calls a C subroutine that allocates a local array on the stack that consumes 10K. The kernel will expand the stack segment to accommodate it. When the subroutine returns, the stack pointer is adjusted and this space could be released by the kernel, but it is not released. Explain why it would be possible to shrink the stack at this point and why the UNIX kernel does not shrink it.

APPENDIX 8A HASH TABLES

Consider the following problem. A set of N items is to be stored in a table. Each item consists of a label plus some additional information, which we can refer to as the value of the item. We would like to be able to perform a number of ordinary operations on the table, such as insertion, deletion, and searching for a given item by label.

If the labels of the items are numeric, in the range 0 to $M - 1$, then a simple solution would be to use a table of length M. An item with label i would be inserted into the table at location i. As long as items are of fixed length, table lookup is trivial and involves indexing into the table based on the numeric label of the item. Furthermore, it is not necessary to store the label of an item in the table, because this is implied by the position of the item. Such a table is known as a **direct access table**.

If the labels are nonnumeric, then it is still possible to use a direct access approach. Let us refer to the items as A[1], ... A[N]. Each item A[i] consists of a label, or key, k_i, and a value v_i. Let us define a mapping function I(k) such that I(k) takes a value between 1 and M for all keys and $I(k_i) \neq I(k_j)$ for any i and j. In this case, a direct access table can also be used, with the length of the table equal to M.

The one difficulty with these schemes occurs if M is much greater than N. In this case, the proportion of unused entries in the table is large, and this is an inefficient use of memory. An alternative would be to use a table of length N and store the N items (label plus value) in the N table entries. In this scheme, the amount of memory is minimized but there is now a processing burden to do table lookup. Possibilities include the following:

Table 8.6 Average Search Length for one of N items in a Table of Length M

Technique	Search Length
Direct	1
Sequential	$\dfrac{M + 1}{2}$
Binary	$\log_2 M$
Linear hashing	$\dfrac{2 - N/M}{2 - 2N/M}$
Hash (overflow with chaining)	$1 + \dfrac{N - 1}{2M}$

- **Sequential search:** This brute-force approach is time consuming for large tables.
- **Associative search:** With the proper hardware, all of the elements in a table can be searched simultaneously. This approach is not general purpose and cannot be applied to any and all tables of interest.
- **Binary search:** If the labels or the numeric mapping of the labels are arranged in ascending order in the table, then a binary search is much quicker than sequential (Table 8.6) and requires no special hardware.

The binary search looks promising for table lookup. The major drawback with this method is that adding new items is not usually a simple process and will require reordering of the entries. Therefore, binary search is usually used only for reasonably static tables that are seldom changed.

We would like to avoid the memory penalties of a simple direct access approach and the processing penalties of the alternatives listed previously. The most frequently used method to achieve this compromise is **hashing**. Hashing, which was developed in the 1950s, is simple to implement and has two advantages. First, it can find most items with a single seek, as in direct accessing, and second, insertions and deletions can be handled without added complexity.

The hashing function can be defined as follows. Assume that up to N items are to be stored in a **hash table** of length M, with $M \geq N$, but not much larger than N. To insert an item in the table,

I1. Convert the label of the item to a near-random number n between 0 and $M - 1$. For example, if the label is numeric, a popular mapping function is to divide the label by M and take the remainder as the value of n.

I2. Use n as the index into the hash table.

    a. If the corresponding entry in the table is empty, store the item (label and value) in that entry.

    b. If the entry is already occupied, then store the item in an overflow area, as discussed subsequently.

To perform table lookup of an item whose label is known,

L1. Convert the label of the item to a near-random number n between 0 and $M - 1$, using the same mapping function as for insertion.

L2. Use n as the index into the hash table.

    a. If the corresponding entry in the table is empty, then the item has not previously been stored in the table.

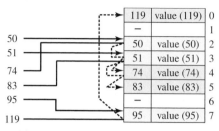

(a) Linear rehashing

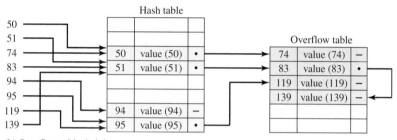

(b) Overflow with chaining

Figure 8.27   Hashing

b. If the entry is already occupied and the labels match, then the value can be retrieved.

c. If the entry is already occupied and the labels do not match, then continue the search in the overflow area.

Hashing schemes differ in the way in which the overflow is handled. One common technique is referred to as the **linear hashing** technique and is commonly used in compilers. In this approach, rule I2.b becomes

I2.b. If the entry is already occupied, set $n = n + 1 \pmod M$ and go back to step I2.a.

Rule L2.c is modified accordingly.

Figure 8.27a is an example. In this case, the labels of the items to be stored are numeric, and the hash table has eight positions ($M = 8$). The mapping function is to take the remainder upon division by 8. The figure assumes that the items were inserted in ascending numerical order, although this is not necessary. Thus, items 50 and 51 map into positions 2 and 3, respectively, and as these are empty, they are inserted there. Item 74 also maps into position 2, but as it is not empty, position 3 is tried. This is also occupied, so the position 4 is ultimately used.

It is not easy to determine the average length of the search for an item in an open hash table because of the clustering effect. An approximate formula was obtained by Schay and Spruth [SCHA62]:

$$\text{Average search length} = \frac{2 - r}{2 - 2r}$$

where $r = N/M$. Note that the result is independent of table size and depends only on how full the table is. The surprising result is that with the table 80% full, the average length of the search is still around 3.

Even so, a search length of 3 may be considered long, and the linear hashing table has the additional problem that it is not easy to delete items. A more attractive approach, which provides shorter search lengths (Table 8.6) and allows deletions as well as additions, is **overflow with chaining**. This technique is illustrated in Figure 8.27b. In this case, there is a separate table into which overflow entries are inserted. This table includes pointers passing down the chain of entries associated with any position in the hash table. In this case, the average search length, assuming randomly distributed data, is

$$\text{Average search length} = 1 + \frac{N - 1}{2M}$$

For large values of N and M, this value approaches 1.5 for $N = M$. Thus, this technique provides for compact storage with rapid lookup.

PART FOUR

Scheduling

An operating system must allocate computer resources among the potentially competing requirements of multiple processes. In the case of the processor, the resource to be allocated is execution time on the processor and the means of allocation is scheduling. The scheduling function must be designed to satisfy a number of objectives, including fairness, lack of starvation of any particular process, efficient use of processor time, and low overhead. In addition, the scheduling function may need to take into account different levels of priority or real-time deadlines for the start or completion of certain processes.

Over the years, scheduling has been the focus of intensive research, and many different algorithms have been implemented. Today, the emphasis in scheduling research is on exploiting multiprocessor systems, particularly for multithreaded applications, and real-time scheduling.

Chapter 9 Uniprocessor Scheduling

Chapter 9 concerns scheduling on a system with a single processor. In this limited context, it is possible to define and clarify many design issues related to scheduling. Chapter 9 begins with an examination of the three types of processor scheduling: long term, medium term, and short term. The bulk of the chapter focuses on short-term scheduling issues. The various algorithms that have been tried are examined and compared.

Chapter 10 Multiprocessor and Real–Time Scheduling

Chapter 10 looks at two areas that are the focus of contemporary scheduling research. The presence of multiple processors complicates the scheduling decision and opens up new opportunities. In particular, with multiple processors it is possible simultaneously to schedule for execution multiple threads within the same process. The first part of Chapter 10 provides a survey of multiprocessor and multithreaded scheduling. The remainder of the chapter deals with real-time scheduling. Real-time requirements are the most demanding for a scheduler to meet, because requirements go beyond fairness or priority by specifying time limits for the start or finish of given tasks or processes.

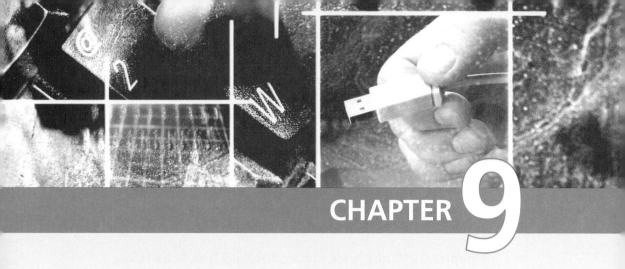

CHAPTER 9

UNIPROCESSOR SCHEDULING

In a multiprogramming system, multiple processes exist concurrently in main memory. Each process alternates between using a processor and waiting for some event to occur, such as the completion of an I/O operation. The processor or processors are kept busy by executing one process while the others wait.

The key to multiprogramming is scheduling. In fact, four types of scheduling are typically involved (Table 9.1). One of these, I/O scheduling, is more conveniently addressed in Chapter 11, where I/O is discussed. The remaining three types of scheduling, which are types of processor scheduling, are addressed in this chapter and the next.

This chapter begins with an examination of the three types of processor scheduling, showing how they are related. We see that long-term scheduling and medium-term scheduling are driven primarily by performance concerns related to the degree of multiprogramming. These issues are dealt with to some extent in Chapter 3 and in more detail in Chapters 7 and 8. Thus, the remainder of this chapter concentrates on short-term scheduling and is limited to a consideration of scheduling on a uniprocessor system. Because the use of multiple processors adds additional complexity, it is best to focus on the uniprocessor case first, so that the differences among scheduling algorithms can be clearly seen.

Section 9.2 looks at the various algorithms that may be used to make short-term scheduling decisions.

9.1 TYPES OF PROCESSOR SCHEDULING

The aim of processor scheduling is to assign processes to be executed by the processor or processors over time, in a way that meets system objectives, such as response time, throughput, and processor efficiency. In many systems, this scheduling activity is broken down into three separate functions: long-, medium-, and short-term scheduling. The names suggest the relative time scales with which these functions are performed.

Figure 9.1 relates the scheduling functions to the process state transition diagram (first shown in Figure 3.9b). Long-term scheduling is performed when a new process is created. This is a decision whether to add a new process to the set of processes that are currently active. Medium-term scheduling is a part of the swapping function. This is a decision whether to add a process to those that are at least partially in main memory and therefore available for execution. Short-term scheduling is the

Table 9.1 Types of Scheduling

Long-term scheduling	The decision to add to the pool of processes to be executed
Medium-term scheduling	The decision to add to the number of processes that are partially or fully in main memory
Short-term scheduling	The decision as to which available process will be executed by the processor
I/O scheduling	The decision as to which process's pending I/O request shall be handled by an available I/O device

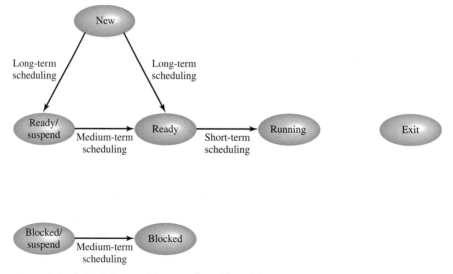

Figure 9.1 Scheduling and Process State Transitions

actual decision of which ready process to execute next. Figure 9.2 reorganizes the state transition diagram of Figure 3.9b to suggest the nesting of scheduling functions.

Scheduling affects the performance of the system because it determines which processes will wait and which will progress. This point of view is presented in Figure 9.3, which shows the queues involved in the state transitions of a process.[1] Fundamentally, scheduling is a matter of managing queues to minimize queuing delay and to optimize performance in a queuing environment.

Long-Term Scheduling

The long-term scheduler determines which programs are admitted to the system for processing. Thus, it controls the degree of multiprogramming. Once admitted, a job or user program becomes a process and is added to the queue for the short-term scheduler. In some systems, a newly created process begins in a swapped-out condition, in which case it is added to a queue for the medium-term scheduler.

In a batch system, or for the batch portion of a general-purpose operating system, newly submitted jobs are routed to disk and held in a batch queue. The long-term scheduler creates processes from the queue when it can. There are two decisions involved here. First, the scheduler must decide when the operating system can take on one or more additional processes. Second, the scheduler must decide which job or jobs to accept and turn into processes. Let us briefly consider these two decisions.

The decision as to when to create a new process is generally driven by the desired degree of multiprogramming. The more processes that are created, the smaller is the percentage of time that each process can be executed (i.e., more processes

---

[1]For simplicity, Figure 9.3 shows new processes going directly to the Ready state, whereas Figures 9.1 and 9.2 show the option of either the Ready state or the Ready/Suspend state.

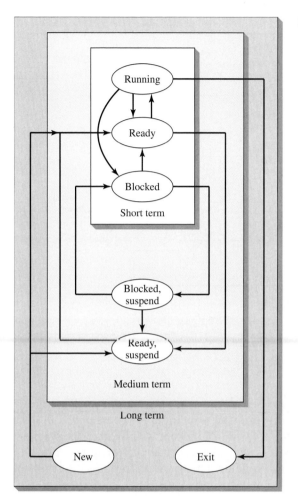

Figure 9.2   Levels of Scheduling

are competing for the same amount of processor time). Thus, the long-term scheduler may limit the degree of multiprogramming to provide satisfactory service to the current set of processes. Each time a job terminates, the scheduler may decide to add one or more new jobs. Additionally, if the fraction of time that the processor is idle exceeds a certain threshold, the long-term scheduler may be invoked.

The decision as to which job to admit next can be on a simple first-come-first-served basis, or it can be a tool to manage system performance. The criteria used may include priority, expected execution time, and I/O requirements. For example, if the information is available, the scheduler may attempt to keep a mix of processor-bound and I/O-bound processes.[2] Also, the decision may be made depending on which I/O resources are to be requested, in an attempt to balance I/O usage.

---

[2]A process is regarded as *processor bound* if it mainly performs computational work and occasionally uses I/O devices. A process is regarded as *I/O bound if* it spends more time using I/O devices than using the processor.

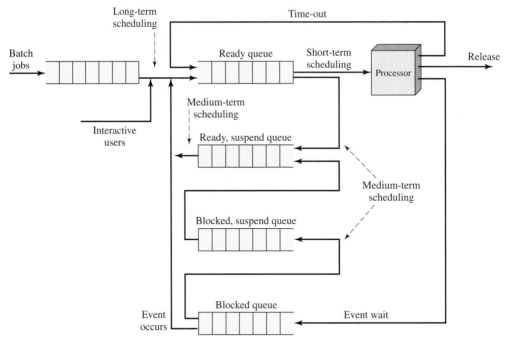

Figure 9.3 Queuing Diagram for Scheduling

For interactive programs in a time-sharing system, a process creation request can be generated by the act of a user attempting to connect to the system. Time-sharing users are not simply queued up and kept waiting until the system can accept them. Rather, the operating system will accept all authorized comers until the system is saturated, using some predefined measure of saturation. At that point, a connection request is met with a message indicating that the system is full and the user should try again later.

Medium–Term Scheduling

Medium-term scheduling is part of the swapping function. The issues involved are discussed in Chapters 3, 7, and 8. Typically, the swapping-in decision is based on the need to manage the degree of multiprogramming. On a system that does not use virtual memory, memory management is also an issue. Thus, the swapping-in decision will consider the memory requirements of the swapped-out processes.

Short-Term Scheduling

In terms of frequency of execution, the long-term scheduler executes relatively infrequently and makes the coarse-grained decision of whether or not to take on a new process and which one to take. The medium-term scheduler is executed somewhat more frequently to make a swapping decision. The short-term scheduler, also known as the dispatcher, executes most frequently and makes the fine-grained decision of which process to execute next.

The short-term scheduler is invoked whenever an event occurs that may lead to the blocking of the current process or that may provide an opportunity to preempt a currently running process in favor of another. Examples of such events include

- Clock interrupts
- I/O interrupts
- Operating system calls
- Signals (e.g., semaphores)

9.2 SCHEDULING ALGORITHMS

Short-Term Scheduling Criteria

The main objective of short-term scheduling is to allocate processor time in such a way as to optimize one or more aspects of system behavior. Generally, a set of criteria is established against which various scheduling policies may be evaluated.

The commonly used criteria can be categorized along two dimensions. First, we can make a distinction between user-oriented and system-oriented criteria. User-oriented criteria relate to the behavior of the system as perceived by the individual user or process. An example is response time in an interactive system. Response time is the elapsed time between the submission of a request until the response begins to appear as output. This quantity is visible to the user and is naturally of interest to the user. We would like a scheduling policy that provides "good" service to various users. In the case of response time, a threshold may be defined, say 2 seconds. Then a goal of the scheduling mechanism should be to maximize the number of users who experience an average response time of 2 seconds or less.

Other criteria are system oriented. That is, the focus is on effective and efficient utilization of the processor. An example is throughput, which is the rate at which processes are completed. This is certainly a worthwhile measure of system performance and one that we would like to maximize. However, it focuses on system performance rather than service provided to the user. Thus, throughput is of concern to a system administrator but not to the user population.

Whereas user-oriented criteria are important on virtually all systems, system-oriented criteria are generally of minor importance on single-user systems. On a single-user system, it probably is not important to achieve high processor utilization or high throughput as long as the responsiveness of the system to user applications is acceptable.

Another dimension along which criteria can be classified is those that are performance related and those that are not directly performance related. Performance-related criteria are quantitative and generally can be readily measured. Examples include response time and throughput. Criteria that are not performance related are either qualitative in nature or do not lend themselves readily to measurement and analysis. An example of such a criterion is predictability. We would like for the service provided to users to exhibit the same characteristics over time,

Table 9.2 Scheduling Criteria

User Oriented, Performance Related

Turnaround time This is the interval of time between the submission of a process and its completion. Includes actual execution time plus time spent waiting for resources, including the processor. This is an appropriate measure for a batch job.

Response time For an interactive process, this is the time from the submission of a request until the response begins to be received. Often a process can begin producing some output to the user while continuing to process the request. Thus, this is a better measure than turnaround time from the user's point of view. The scheduling discipline should attempt to achieve low response time and to maximize the number of interactive users receiving acceptable response time.

Deadlines When process completion deadlines can be specified, the scheduling discipline should subordinate other goals to that of maximizing the percentage of deadlines met.

User Oriented, Other

Predictability A given job should run in about the same amount of time and at about the same cost regardless of the load on the system. A wide variation in response time or turnaround time is distracting to users. It may signal a wide swing in system workloads or the need for system tuning to cure instabilities.

System Oriented, Performance Related

Throughput The scheduling policy should attempt to maximize the number of processes completed per unit of time. This is a measure of how much work is being performed. This clearly depends on the average length of a process but is also influenced by the scheduling policy, which may affect utilization.

Processor utilization This is the percentage of time that the processor is busy. For an expensive shared system, this is a significant criterion. In single-user systems and in some other systems, such as real-time systems, this criterion is less important than some of the others.

System Oriented, Other

Fairness In the absence of guidance from the user or other system-supplied guidance, processes should be treated the same, and no process should suffer starvation.

Enforcing priorities When processes are assigned priorities, the scheduling policy should favor higher-priority processes.

Balancing resources The scheduling policy should keep the resources of the system busy. Processes that will underutilize stressed resources should be favored. This criterion also involves medium-term and long-term scheduling.

independent of other work being performed by the system. To some extent, this criterion can be measured, by calculating variances as a function of workload. However, this is not nearly as straightforward as measuring throughput or response time as a function of workload.

Table 9.2 summarizes key scheduling criteria. These are interdependent, and it is impossible to optimize all of them simultaneously. For example, providing good response time may require a scheduling algorithm that switches between processes frequently. This increases the overhead of the system, reducing throughput. Thus, the design of a scheduling policy involves compromising among competing requirements; the relative weights given the various requirements will depend on the nature and intended use of the system.

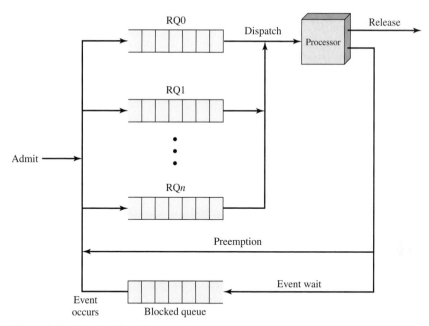

Figure 9.4   Priority Queuing

In most interactive operating systems, whether single user or time shared, adequate response time is the critical requirement. Because of the importance of this requirement, and because the definition of adequacy will vary from one application to another, the topic is explored further in an appendix to this chapter.

The Use of Priorities

In many systems, each process is assigned a priority and the scheduler will always choose a process of higher priority over one of lower priority. Figure 9.4 illustrates the use of priorities. For clarity, the queuing diagram is simplified, ignoring the existence of multiple blocked queues and of suspended states (compare Figure 3.8a). Instead of a single ready queue, we provide a set of queues, in descending order of priority: RQ0, RQ1, ... RQn, with priority[RQi] > priority[RQj] for $i < j$.[3] When a scheduling selection is to be made, the scheduler will start at the highest-priority ready queue (RQ0). If there are one or more processes in the queue, a process is selected using some scheduling policy. If RQ0 is empty, then RQ1 is examined, and so on.

One problem with a pure priority scheduling scheme is that lower-priority processes may suffer starvation. This will happen if there is always a steady supply of higher-priority ready processes. If this behavior is not desirable, the priority of a process can change with its age or execution history. We will give one example of this subsequently.

---

[3]In UNIX and many other systems, larger priority values represent lower priority processes; unless otherwise stated we follow that convention. Some systems, such as Windows, use the opposite convention: A higher number means a higher priority.

Alternative Scheduling Policies

Table 9.3 presents some summary information about the various scheduling policies that are examined in this subsection. The **selection function** determines which process, among ready processes, is selected next for execution. The function may be based on priority, resource requirements, or the execution characteristics of the process. In the latter case, three quantities are significant:

w = time spent in system so far, waiting and executing

e = time spent in execution so far

s = total service time required by the process, including e; generally, this quantity must be estimated or supplied by the user

For example, the selection function $\max[w]$ indicates a first-come-first-served (FCFS) discipline.

The **decision mode** specifies the instants in time at which the selection function is exercised. There are two general categories:

- **Nonpreemptive:** In this case, once a process is in the Running state, it continues to execute until (a) it terminates or (b) it blocks itself to wait for I/O or to request some operating system service.

- **Preemptive:** The currently running process may be interrupted and moved to the Ready state by the operating system. The decision to preempt may be performed when a new process arrives; when an interrupt occurs that places a blocked process in the Ready state; or periodically, based on a clock interrupt.

Preemptive policies incur greater overhead than nonpreemptive ones but may provide better service to the total population of processes, because they prevent any one process from monopolizing the processor for very long. In addition, the cost of preemption may be kept relatively low by using efficient process-switching mechanisms (as much help from hardware as possible) and by providing a large main memory to keep a high percentage of programs in main memory.

As we describe the various scheduling policies, we will use the set of processes in Table 9.4 as a running example. We can think of these as batch jobs, with the service time being the total execution time required. Alternatively, we can consider these to be ongoing processes that require alternate use of the processor and I/O in a repetitive fashion. In this latter case, the service times represent the processor time required in one cycle. In either case, in terms of a queuing model, this quantity corresponds to the service time.[4]

For the example of Table 9.4, Figure 9.5 shows the execution pattern for each policy for one cycle, and Table 9.5 summarizes some key results. First, the finish time of each process is determined. From this, we can determine the turnaround time. In terms of the queuing model, **turnaround time** (TAT) is the residence time T_r, or total time that the item spends in the system (waiting time plus service time). A more useful figure is the normalized turnaround time, which is the ratio of turnaround time to service time. This value indicates the relative delay experienced by a process. Typically, the longer the process execution time, the greater the absolute amount of

---

[4]See Appendix 9B for a summary of queuing model terminology.

Table 9.3   Characteristics of Various Scheduling Policies

	Selection Function	Decision Mode	Throughput	Response Time	Overhead	Effect on Processes	Starvation
FCFS	$\max[w]$	Nonpreemptive	Not emphasized	May be high, especially if there is a large variance in process execution times	Minimum	Penalizes short processes; penalizes I/O bound processes	No
Round Robin	constant	Preemptive (at time quantum)	May be low if quantum is too small	Provides good response time for short processes	Minimum	Fair treatment	No
SPN	$\min[s]$	Nonpreemptive	High	Provides good response time for short processes	Can be high	Penalizes long processes	Possible
SRT	$\min[s - e]$	Preemptive (at arrival)	High	Provides good response time	Can be high	Penalizes long processes	Possible
HRRN	$\max\left(\dfrac{w + s}{s}\right)$	Nonpreemptive	High	Provides good response time	Can be high	Good balance	No
Feedback	(see text)	Preemptive (at time quantum)	Not emphasized	Not emphasized	Can be high	May favor I/O bound processes	Possible

w = time spent waiting

e = time spent in execution so far

s = total service time required by the process, including e

Table 9.4 Process Scheduling Example

Process	Arrival Time	Service Time
A	0	3
B	2	6
C	4	4
D	6	5
E	8	2

delay that can be tolerated. The minimum possible value for this ratio is 1.0; increasing values correspond to a decreasing level of service.

First–Come–First–Served The simplest scheduling policy is first-come-first-served (FCFS), also known as first-in-first-out (FIFO) or a strict queuing scheme. As each process becomes ready, it joins the ready queue. When the currently running process ceases to execute, the process that has been in the ready queue the longest is selected for running.

FCFS performs much better for long processes than short ones. Consider the following example, based on one in [FINK88]:

Process	Arrival Time	Service Time (T_s)	Start Time	Finish Time	Turnaround Time (T_r)	T_r/T_s
W	0	1	0	1	1	1
X	1	100	1	101	100	1
Y	2	1	101	102	100	100
Z	3	100	102	202	199	1.99
Mean					100	26

The normalized turnaround time for process Y is way out of line compared to the other processes: The total time that it is in the system is 100 times the required processing time. This will happen whenever a short process arrives just after a long process. On the other hand, even in this extreme example, long processes do not fare poorly. Process Z has a turnaround time that is almost double that of Y, but its normalized residence time is under 2.0.

Another difficulty with FCFS is that it tends to favor processor-bound processes over I/O-bound processes. Consider that there is a collection of processes, one of which mostly uses the processor (processor bound) and a number of which favor I/O (I/O bound). When a processor-bound process is running, all of the I/O bound processes must wait. Some of these may be in I/O queues (blocked state) but may move back to the ready queue while the processor-bound process is executing. At this point, most or all of the I/O devices may be idle, even though there is potentially work for them to do. When the currently running process leaves the Running state, the ready I/O-bound processes quickly move through the Running state and become blocked on I/O events. If the processor-bound process is also blocked, the processor becomes idle. Thus, FCFS may result in inefficient use of both the processor and the I/O devices.

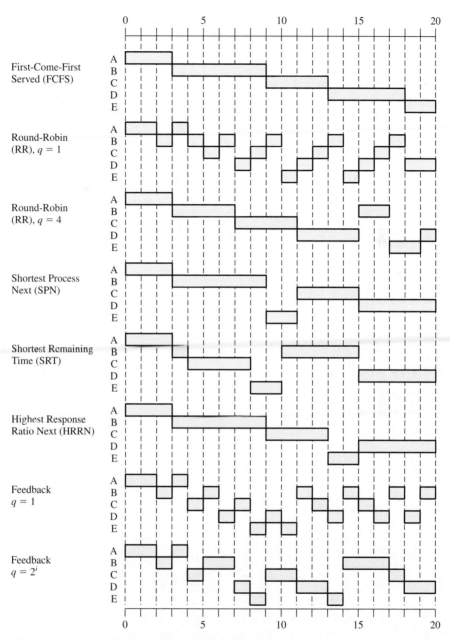

Figure 9.5   A Comparison of Scheduling Policies

FCFS is not an attractive alternative on its own for a uniprocessor system. However, it is often combined with a priority scheme to provide an effective scheduler. Thus, the scheduler may maintain a number of queues, one for each priority level, and dispatch within each queue on a first-come-first-served basis. We see one example of such a system later, in our discussion of feedback scheduling.

Table 9.5 A Comparison of Scheduling Policies

	Process	A	B	C	D	E	Mean
	Arrival Time	0	2	4	6	8	
	Service Time (T_s)	3	6	4	5	2	
FCFS	Finish Time	3	9	13	18	20	
	Turnaround Time (T_r)	3	7	9	12	12	8.60
	T_r/T_s	1.00	1.17	2.25	2.40	6.00	2.56
RR $q = 1$	Finish Time	4	18	17	20	15	
	Turnaround Time (T_r)	4	16	13	14	7	10.80
	T_r/T_s	1.33	2.67	3.25	2.80	3.50	2.71
RR $q = 4$	Finish Time	3	17	11	20	19	
	Turnaround Time (T_r)	3	15	7	14	11	10.00
	T_r/T_s	1.00	2.5	1.75	2.80	5.50	2.71
SPN	Finish Time	3	9	15	20	11	
	Turnaround Time (T_r)	3	7	11	14	3	7.60
	T_r/T_s	1.00	1.17	2.75	2.80	1.50	1.84
SRT	Finish Time	3	15	8	20	10	
	Turnaround Time (T_r)	3	13	4	14	2	7.20
	T_r/T_s	1.00	2.17	1.00	2.80	1.00	1.59
HRRN	Finish Time	3	9	13	20	15	
	Turnaround Time (T_r)	3	7	9	14	7	8.00
	T_r/T_s	1.00	1.17	2.25	2.80	3.5	2.14
FB $q = 1$	Finish Time	4	20	16	19	11	
	Turnaround Time (T_r)	4	18	12	13	3	10.00
	T_r/T_s	1.33	3.00	3.00	2.60	1.5	2.29
FB $q = 2^i$	Finish Time	4	17	18	20	14	
	Turnaround Time (T_r)	4	15	14	14	6	10.60
	T_r/T_s	1.33	2.50	3.50	2.80	3.00	2.63

Round Robin A straightforward way to reduce the penalty that short jobs suffer with FCFS is to use preemption based on a clock. The simplest such policy is round robin. A clock interrupt is generated at periodic intervals. When the interrupt occurs, the currently running process is placed in the ready queue, and the next ready job is selected on a FCFS basis. This technique is also known as **time slicing**, because each process is given a slice of time before being preempted.

With round robin, the principal design issue is the length of the time quantum, or slice, to be used. If the quantum is very short, then short processes will move through the system relatively quickly. On the other hand, there is processing over-head involved in handling the clock interrupt and performing the scheduling and dispatching function. Thus, very short time quanta should be avoided. One useful guide is that the time quantum should be slightly greater than the time required for a typical interaction or process function. If it is less, then most processes will require at least two time quanta. Figure 9.6 illustrates the effect this has on response time.

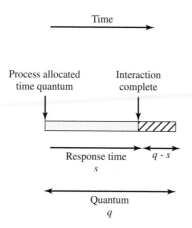

(a) Time quantum greater than typical interaction

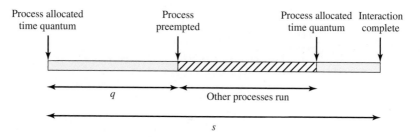

(b) Time quantum less than typical interaction

Figure 9.6   Effect of Size of Preemption Time Quantum

Note that in the limiting case of a time quantum that is longer than the longest-running process, round robin degenerates to FCFS.

Figure 9.5 and Table 9.5 show the results for our example using time quanta q of 1 and 4 time units. Note that process E, which is the shortest job, enjoys significant improvement for a time quantum of 1.

Round robin is particularly effective in a general-purpose time-sharing system or transaction processing system. One drawback to round robin is its relative treatment of processor-bound and I/O-bound processes. Generally, an I/O-bound process has a shorter processor burst (amount of time spent executing between I/O operations) than a processor-bound process. If there is a mix of processor-bound and I/O-bound processes, then the following will happen: An I/O-bound process uses a processor for a short period and then is blocked for I/O; it waits for the I/O operation to complete and then joins the ready queue. On the other hand, a processor-bound process generally uses a complete time quantum while executing and immediately returns to the ready queue. Thus, processor-bound processes tend to receive an unfair portion of processor time, which results in poor performance for I/O-bound processes, inefficient use of I/O devices, and an increase in the variance of response time.

[HALD91] suggests a refinement to round robin that he refers to as a virtual round robin (VRR) and that avoids this unfairness. Figure 9.7 illustrates the scheme. New processes arrive and join the ready queue, which is managed on an

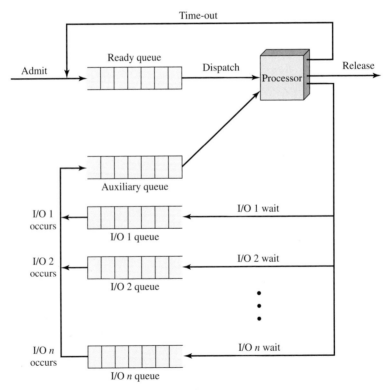

Figure 9.7 Queuing Diagram for Virtual Round-Robin Scheduler

FCFS basis. When a running process times out, it is returned to the ready queue. When a process is blocked for I/O, it joins an I/O queue. So far, this is as usual. The new feature is an FCFS auxiliary queue to which processes are moved after being released from an I/O block. When a dispatching decision is to be made, processes in the auxiliary queue get preference over those in the main ready queue. When a process is dispatched from the auxiliary queue, it runs no longer than a time equal to the basic time quantum minus the total time spent running since it was last selected from the main ready queue. Performance studies by the authors indicate that this approach is indeed superior to round robin in terms of fairness.

Shortest Process Next Another approach to reducing the bias in favor of long processes inherent in FCFS is the Shortest Process Next (SPN) policy. This is a nonpreemptive policy in which the process with the shortest expected processing time is selected next. Thus a short process will jump to the head of the queue past longer jobs.

Figure 9.5 and Table 9.5 show the results for our example. Note that process E receives service much earlier than under FCFS. Overall performance is also significantly improved in terms of response time. However, the variability of response times is increased, especially for longer processes, and thus predictability is reduced.

One difficulty with the SPN policy is the need to know or at least estimate the required processing time of each process. For batch jobs, the system may require the programmer to estimate the value and supply it to the operating system. If the programmer's estimate is substantially under the actual running time, the system may abort the job. In a production environment, the same jobs run frequently, and statistics may be gathered. For interactive processes, the operating system may keep a running average of each "burst" for each process. The simplest calculation would be the following:

$$S_{n+1} = \frac{1}{n}\sum_{i=1}^{n} T_i \tag{9.1}$$

where

T_i = processor execution time for the ith instance of this process (total execution time for batch job; processor burst time for interactive job)

S_i = predicted value for the ith instance

S_1 = predicted value for first instance; not calculated

To avoid recalculating the entire summation each time, we can rewrite Equation (9.1) as

$$S_{n+1} = \frac{1}{n}T_n + \frac{n-1}{n}S_n \tag{9.2}$$

Note that this formulation gives equal weight to each instance. Typically, we would like to give greater weight to more recent instances, because these are more likely to reflect future behavior. A common technique for predicting a future value on the basis of a time series of past values is **exponential averaging**:

$$S_{n+1} = \alpha T_n + (1 - \alpha)S_n \tag{9.3}$$

where α is a constant weighting factor $(0 < \alpha < 1)$ that determines the relative weight given to more recent observations relative to older observations. Compare with Equation (9.2). By using a constant value of α, independent of the number of past observations, we have a circumstance in which all past values are considered, but the more distant ones have less weight. To see this more clearly, consider the following expansion of Equation (9.3):

$$S_{n+1} = \alpha T_n + (1 - \alpha)\alpha T_{n-1} + \cdots + (1 - \alpha)^i \alpha T_{n-i} + \cdots + (1 - \alpha)^n S_1 \tag{9.4}$$

Because both α and $(1 - \alpha)$ are less than 1, each successive term in the preceding equation is smaller. For example, for $\alpha = 0.8$, Equation (9.4) becomes

$$S_{n+1} = 0.8T_n + 0.16T_{n-1} + 0.032T_{n-2} + 0.0064T_{n-3} + \cdots$$

The older the observation, the less it is counted in to the average.

The size of the coefficient as a function of its position in the expansion is shown in Figure 9.8. The larger the value of α, the greater the weight given to the more recent observations. For $\alpha = 0.8$, virtually all of the weight is given to the four most recent observations, whereas for $\alpha = 0.2$, the averaging is effectively spread out over the eight or so most recent observations. The advantage of using a value of α close to 1 is that the average will quickly reflect a rapid change in the observed quantity. The disadvantage is that if there is a brief surge in the value of the observed quantity and it then settles back to some average value, the use of a large value of α will result in jerky changes in the average.

Figure 9.9 compares simple averaging with exponential averaging (for two different values of α). In Figure 9.9a, the observed value begins at 1, grows gradually to a value of 10, and then stays there. In Figure 9.9b, the observed value begins at 20,

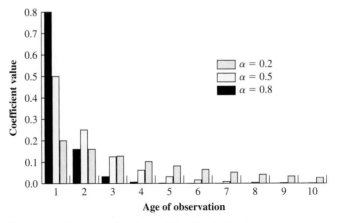

Figure 9.8 Exponential Smoothing Coefficients

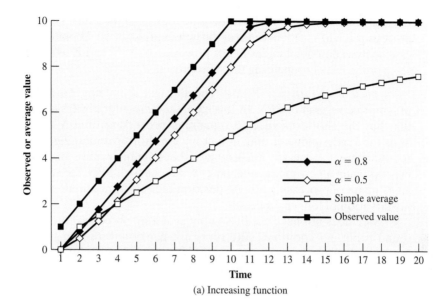

(a) Increasing function

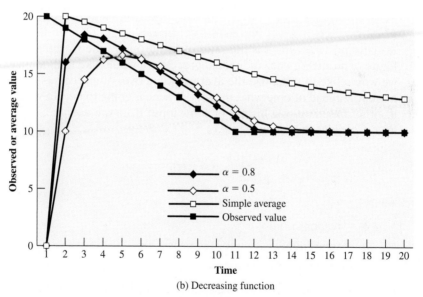

(b) Decreasing function

Figure 9.9 Use of Exponential Averaging

declines gradually to 10, and then stays there. In both cases, we start out with an estimate of $S_1 = 0$. This gives greater priority to new processes. Note that exponential averaging tracks changes in process behavior faster than does simple averaging and that the larger value of α results in a more rapid reaction to the change in the observed value.

A risk with SPN is the possibility of starvation for longer processes, as long as there is a steady supply of shorter processes. On the other hand, although SPN reduces the bias in favor of longer jobs, it still is not desirable for a time-sharing or transaction processing environment because of the lack of preemption. Looking back at our worst-case analysis described under FCFS, processes W, X, Y, and Z will still execute in the same order, heavily penalizing the short process Y.

Shortest Remaining Time The shortest remaining time (SRT) policy is a preemptive version of SPN. In this case, the scheduler always chooses the process that has the shortest expected remaining processing time. When a new process joins the ready queue, it may in fact have a shorter remaining time than the currently running process. Accordingly, the scheduler may preempt the current process when a new process becomes ready. As with SPN, the scheduler must have an estimate of processing time to perform the selection function, and there is a risk of starvation of longer processes.

SRT does not have the bias in favor of long processes found in FCFS. Unlike round robin, no additional interrupts are generated, reducing overhead. On the other hand, elapsed service times must be recorded, contributing to overhead. SRT should also give superior turnaround time performance to SPN, because a short job is given immediate preference to a running longer job.

Note that in our example (Table 9.5), the three shortest processes all receive immediate service, yielding a normalized turnaround time for each of 1.0.

Highest Response Ratio Next In Table 9.5, we have used the normalized turnaround time, which is the ratio of turnaround time to actual service time, as a figure of merit. For each individual process, we would like to minimize this ratio, and we would like to minimize the average value over all processes. In general, we cannot know ahead of time what the service time is going to be, but we can approximate it, either based on past history or some input from the user or a configuration manager. Consider the following ratio:

$$R = \frac{w + s}{s}$$

where

   R = response ratio

   w = time spent waiting for the processor

   s = expected service time

If the process with this value is dispatched immediately, R is equal to the normalized turnaround time. Note that the minimum value of R is 1.0, which occurs when a process first enters the system.

Thus, our scheduling rule becomes as follows: When the current process completes or is blocked, choose the ready process with the greatest value of R. This approach is attractive because it accounts for the age of the process. While shorter jobs are favored (a smaller denominator yields a larger ratio), aging without service increases the ratio so that a longer process will eventually get past competing shorter jobs.

As with SRT and SPN, the expected service time must be estimated to use highest response ratio next (HRRN).

Feedback If we have no indication of the relative length of various processes, then none of SPN, SRT, and HRRN can be used. Another way of establishing a preference for shorter jobs is to penalize jobs that have been running longer. In other words, if we cannot focus on the time remaining to execute, let us focus on the time spent in execution so far.

The way to do this is as follows. Scheduling is done on a preemptive (at time quantum) basis, and a dynamic priority mechanism is used. When a process first enters the system, it is placed in RQ0 (see Figure 9.4). After its first preemption, when it returns to the Ready state, it is placed in RQ1. Each subsequent time that it is preempted, it is demoted to the next lower-priority queue. A short process will complete quickly, without migrating very far down the hierarchy of ready queues. A longer process will gradually drift downward. Thus, newer, shorter processes are favored over older, longer processes. Within each queue, except the lowest-priority queue, a simple FCFS mechanism is used. Once in the lowest-priority queue, a process cannot go lower, but is returned to this queue repeatedly until it completes execution. Thus, this queue is treated in round robin fashion.

Figure 9.10 illustrates the feedback scheduling mechanism by showing the path that a process will follow through the various queues.[5] This approach is known as **multilevel feedback**, meaning that the operating system allocates the processor to a process and, when the process blocks or is preempted, feeds it back into one of several priority queues.

There are a number of variations on this scheme. A simple version is to perform preemption in the same fashion as for round robin: at periodic intervals. Our example shows this (Figure 9.5 and Table 9.5) for a quantum of one time unit. Note that in this case, the behavior is similar to round robin with a time quantum of 1.

One problem with the simple scheme just outlined is that the turnaround time of longer processes can stretch out alarmingly. Indeed, it is possible for starvation to occur if new jobs are entering the system frequently. To compensate for this, we can vary the preemption times according to the queue: A process scheduled from RQ0 is allowed to execute for one time unit and then is preempted; a process scheduled from RQ1 is allowed to execute two time units, and so on. In general, a process scheduled from RQi is allowed to execute 2^i time units before preemption. This scheme is illustrated for our example in Figure 9.5 and Table 9.5.

Even with the allowance for greater time allocation at lower priority, a longer process may still suffer starvation. A possible remedy is to promote a process to a higher-priority queue after it spends a certain amount of time waiting for service in its current queue.

Performance Comparison

Clearly, the performance of various scheduling policies is a critical factor in the choice of a scheduling policy. However, it is impossible to make definitive comparisons because relative performance will depend on a variety of factors, including the probability distribution of service times of the various processes, the efficiency of

---

[5]Dotted lines are used to emphasize that this is a time sequence diagram rather than a static depiction of possible transitions, such as Figure 9.4.

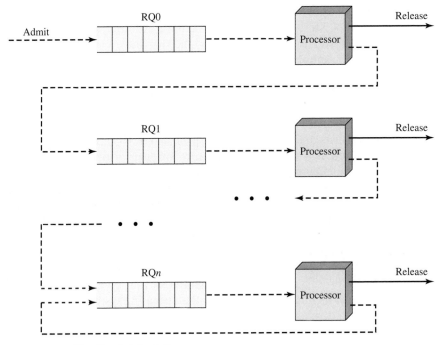

Figure 9.10   Feedback Scheduling

the scheduling and context switching mechanisms, and the nature of the I/O demand and the performance of the I/O subsystem. Nevertheless, we attempt in what follows to draw some general conclusions.

Queuing Analysis   In this section, we make use of basic queuing formulas, with the common assumptions of Poisson arrivals and exponential service times.[6]

First, we make the observation that any such scheduling discipline that chooses the next item to be served independent of service time obeys the following relationship:

$$\frac{T_r}{T_s} = \frac{1}{1 - \rho}$$

where

T_r = turnaround time or residence time; total time in system, waiting plus execution

T_s = average service time; average time spent in Running state

ρ = processor utilization

In particular, a priority-based scheduler, in which the priority of each process is assigned independent of expected service time, provides the same average turnaround

---

[6]The queuing terminology used in this chapter is summarized in Appendix 9B. A basic refresher on queuing analysis can be found at the Computer Science Student Support Site at WilliamStallings.com/StudentSupport.html.

Table 9.6 Formulas for Single-Server Queues with Two Priority Categories

Assumptions:	
1.	Poisson arrival rate.
2.	Priority 1 items are serviced before priority 2 items.
3.	First-come-first-served dispatching for items of equal priority.
4.	No item is interrupted while being served.
5.	No items leave the queue (lost calls delayed).

(a) General Formulas

$$\lambda = \lambda_1 + \lambda_2$$

$$\rho_1 = \lambda_1 T_{s1}; \rho_2 = \lambda_2 T_{s2}$$

$$\rho = \rho_1 + \rho_2$$

$$T_s = \frac{\lambda_1}{\lambda} T_{s1} + \frac{\lambda_2}{\lambda} T_{s2}$$

$$T_r = \frac{\lambda_1}{\lambda} T_{r1} + \frac{\lambda_2}{\lambda} T_{r2}$$

(b) No interrupts; exponential service times	**(c) Preemptive-resume queuing discipline; exponential service times**
$$T_{r1} = T_{s1} + \frac{\rho_1 T_{s1} + \rho_2 T_{s2}}{1 - \rho_1}$$ $$T_{r2} = T_{s2} + \frac{T_{r1} - T_{s1}}{1 - \rho}$$	$$T_{r1} = T_{s1} + \frac{\rho_1 T_{s1}}{1 - \rho_1}$$ $$T_{r2} = T_{s2} + \frac{1}{1 - \rho_1}\left(\rho_1 T_{s2} + \frac{\rho T_s}{1 - \rho}\right)$$

time and average normalized turnaround time as a simple FCFS discipline. Furthermore, the presence or absence of preemption makes no differences in these averages.

With the exception of round robin and FCFS, the various scheduling disciplines considered so far do make selections on the basis of expected service time. Unfortunately, it turns out to be quite difficult to develop closed analytic models of these disciplines. However, we can get an idea of the relative performance of such scheduling algorithms, compared to FCFS, by considering priority scheduling in which priority is based on service time.

If scheduling is done on the basis of priority and if processes are assigned to a priority class on the basis of service time, then differences do emerge. Table 9.6 shows the formulas that result when we assume two priority classes, with different service times for each class. In the table, λ refers to the arrival rate. These results can be generalized to any number of priority classes. Note that the formulas differ for nonpreemptive versus preemptive scheduling. In the latter case, it is assumed that a lower-priority process is immediately interrupted when a higher-priority process becomes ready.

As an example, let us consider the case of two priority classes, with an equal number of process arrivals in each class and with the average service time for the lower-priority class being 5 times that of the upper priority class. Thus, we wish to give preference to shorter processes. Figure 9.11 shows the overall result. By giving preference to shorter jobs, the average normalized turnaround time is improved at higher levels of utilization. As might be expected, the improvement is greatest with the use of preemption. Notice, however, that overall performance is not much affected.

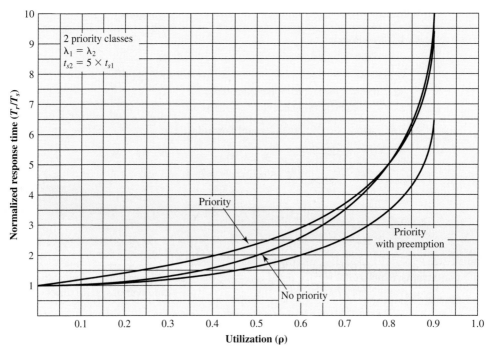

Figure 9.11 Overall Normalized Response Time

However, significant differences emerge when we consider the two priority classes separately. Figure 9.12 shows the results for the higher-priority, shorter processes. For comparison, the upper line on the graph assumes that priorities are not used but that we are simply looking at the relative performance of that half of all processes that have the shorter processing time. The other two lines assume that these processes are assigned a higher priority. When the system is run using priority scheduling without preemption, the improvements are significant. They are even more significant when preemption is used.

Figure 9.13 shows the same analysis for the lower-priority, longer processes. As expected, such processes suffer a performance degradation under priority scheduling.

Simulation Modeling Some of the difficulties of analytic modeling are overcome by using discrete-event simulation, which allows a wide range of policies to be modeled. The disadvantage of simulation is that the results for a given "run" only apply to that particular collection of processes under that particular set of assumptions. Nevertheless, useful insights can be gained.

The results of one such study are reported in [FINK88]. The simulation involved 50,000 processes with an arrival rate of $\lambda = 0.8$ and an average service time of $T_s = 1$. Thus, the assumption is that the processor utilization is $\rho = \lambda T_s = 0.8$. Note, therefore, that we are only measuring one utilization point.

To present the results, processes are grouped into service-time percentiles, each of which has 500 processes. Thus, the 500 processes with the shortest service time are in the first percentile; with these eliminated, the 500 remaining processes with the

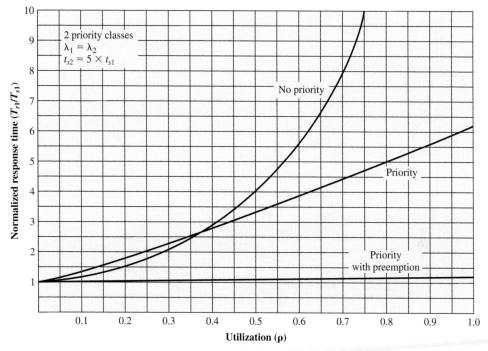

Figure 9.12   Normalized Response Time for Shorter Processes

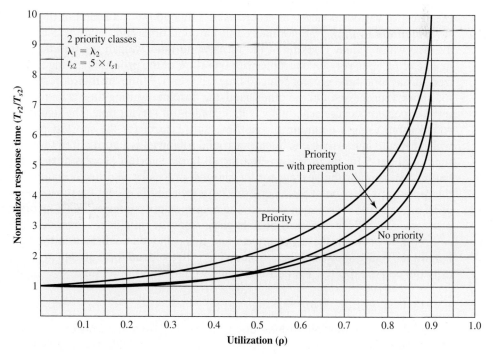

Figure 9.13   Normalized Response Time for Longer Processes

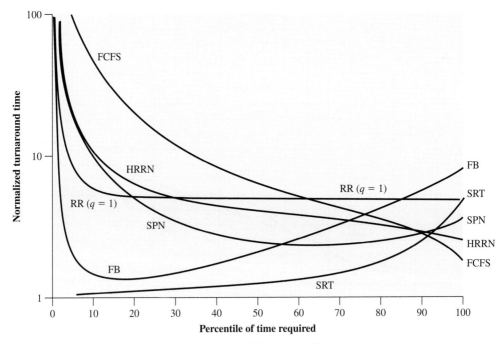

Figure 9.14 Simulation Results for Normalized Turnaround Time

shortest service time are in the second percentile; and so on. This allows us to view the effect of various policies on processes as a function of the length of the process.

Figure 9.14 shows the normalized turnaround time, and Figure 9.15 shows the average waiting time. Looking at the turnaround time, we can see that the performance of FCFS is very unfavorable, with one-third of the processes having a normalized turnaround time greater than 10 times the service time; furthermore, these are the shortest processes. On the other hand, the absolute waiting time is uniform, as is to be expected because scheduling is independent of service time. The figures show round robin using a quantum of one time unit. Except for the shortest processes, which execute in less than one quantum, round robin yields a normalized turnaround time of about 5 for all processes, treating all fairly. Shortest process next performs better than round robin, except for the shortest processes. Shortest remaining time, the preemptive version of SPN, performs better than SPN except for the longest 7% of all processes. We have seen that, among nonpreemptive policies, FCFS favors long processes and SPN favors short ones. Highest response ratio next is intended to be a compromise between these two effects, and this is indeed confirmed in the figures. Finally, the figure shows feedback scheduling with fixed, uniform quanta in each priority queue. As expected, FB performs quite well for short processes.

Fair-Share Scheduling

All of the scheduling algorithms discussed so far treat the collection of ready processes as a single pool of processes from which to select the next running process. This pool may be broken down by priority but is otherwise homogeneous.

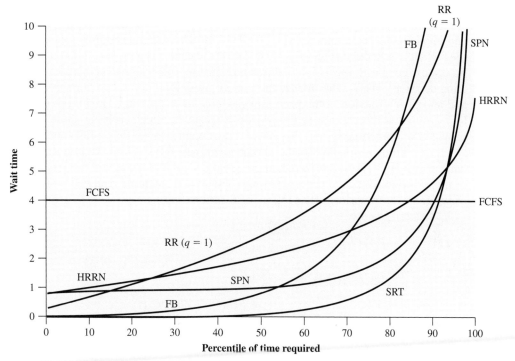

Figure 9.15   Simulation Results for Waiting Time

However, in a multiuser system, if individual user applications or jobs may be organized as multiple processes (or threads), then there is a structure to the collection of processes that is not recognized by a traditional scheduler. From the user's point of view, the concern is not how a particular process performs but rather how his or her set of processes, which constitute a single application, performs. Thus, it would be attractive to make scheduling decisions on the basis of these process sets. This approach is generally known as fair-share scheduling. Further, the concept can be extended to groups of users, even if each user is represented by a single process. For example, in a time-sharing system, we might wish to consider all of the users from a given department to be members of the same group. Scheduling decisions could then be made that attempt to give each group similar service. Thus, if a large number of people from one department log onto the system, we would like to see response time degradation primarily affect members of that department rather than users from other departments.

The term *fair share* indicates the philosophy behind such a scheduler. Each user is assigned a weighting of some sort that defines that user's share of system resources as a fraction of the total usage of those resources. In particular, each user is assigned a share of the processor. Such a scheme should operate in a more or less linear fashion, so that if user A has twice the weighting of user B, then in the long run, user A should be able to do twice as much work as user B. The objective of a fair-share scheduler is to monitor usage to give fewer resources to users who have had more than their fair share and more to those who have had less than their fair share.

A number of proposals have been made for fair-share schedulers [HENR84, KAY88, WOOD86]. In this section, we describe the scheme proposed in [HENR84] and implemented on a number of UNIX systems. The scheme is simply referred to as the fair-share scheduler (FSS). FSS considers the execution history of a related group of processes, along with the individual execution history of each process in making scheduling decisions. The system divides the user community into a set of fair-share groups and allocates a fraction of the processor resource to each group. Thus, there might be four groups, each with 25% of the processor usage. In effect, each fair-share group is provided with a virtual system that runs proportionally slower than a full system.

Scheduling is done on the basis of priority, which takes into account the underlying priority of the process, its recent processor usage, and the recent processor usage of the group to which the process belongs. The higher the numerical value of the priority, the lower the priority. The following formulas apply for process j in group k:

$$CPU_j(i) = \frac{CPU_j(i-1)}{2}$$

$$GCPU_k(i) = \frac{GCPU_k(i-1)}{2}$$

$$P_j(i) = Base_j + \frac{CPU_j(i)}{2} + \frac{GCPU_k(i)}{4 \times W_k}$$

where

$CPU_j(i)$ = Measure of processor utilization by process j through interval i

$GCPU_k(i)$ = Measure of processor utilization of group k through interval i

$P_j(i)$ = Priority of process j at beginning of interval i; lower values equal higher priorities

$Base_j$ = Base priority of process j

W_k = Weighting assigned to group k, with the constraint that
$$0 < W_k \le 1 \text{ and } \sum_k W_k = 1$$

Each process is assigned a base priority. The priority of a process drops as the process uses the processor and as the group to which the process belongs uses the processor. In the case of the group utilization, the average is normalized by dividing by the weight of that group. The greater the weight assigned to the group, the less its utilization will affect its priority.

Figure 9.16 is an example in which process A is in one group and process B and process C are in a second group, with each group having a weighting of 0.5. Assume that all processes are processor bound and are usually ready to run. All processes have a base priority of 60. Processor utilization is measured as follows: The processor is interrupted 60 times per second; during each interrupt, the processor usage field of the currently running process is incremented, as is the corresponding group processor field. Once per second, priorities are recalculated.

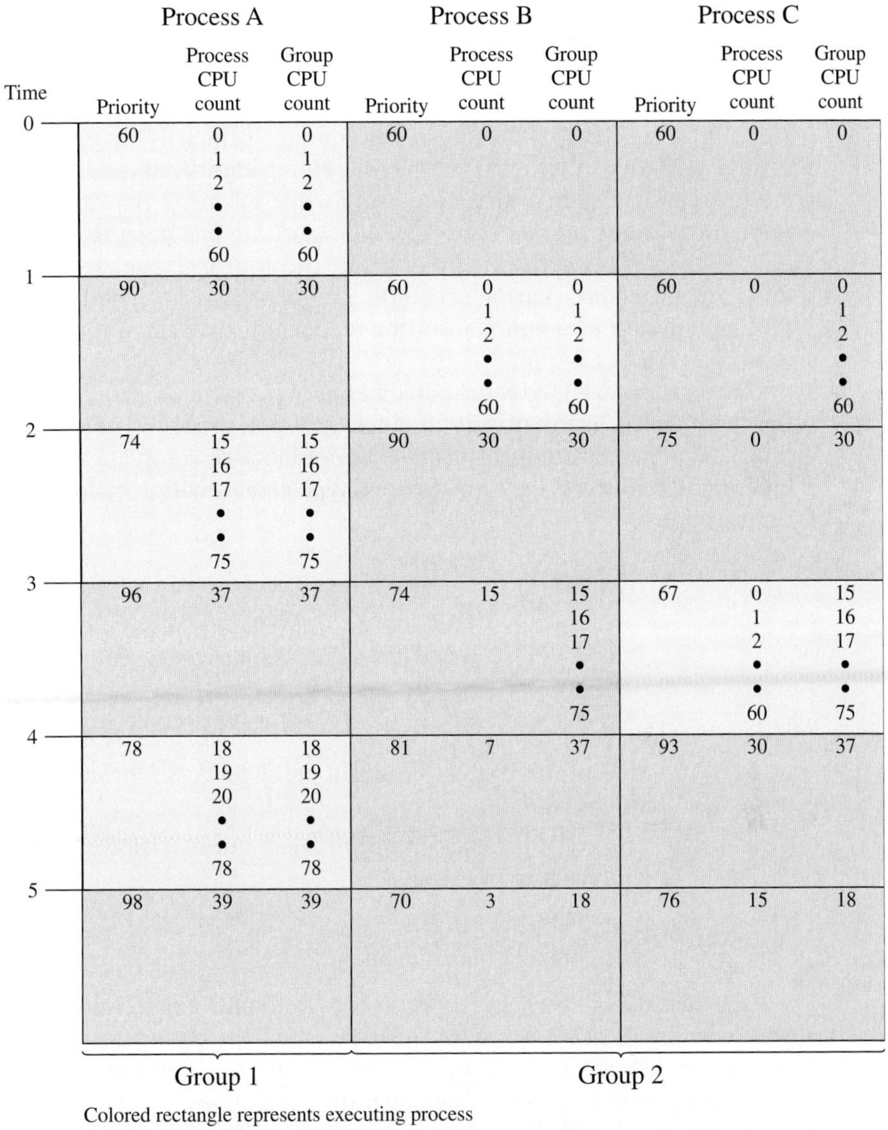

	Process A			Process B			Process C		
Time	Priority	Process CPU count	Group CPU count	Priority	Process CPU count	Group CPU count	Priority	Process CPU count	Group CPU count
0	60	0 1 2 • • 60	0 1 2 • • 60	60	0	0	60	0	0
1	90	30	30	60	0 1 2 • • 60	0 1 2 • • 60	60	0	0 1 2 • • 60
2	74	15 16 17 • • 75	15 16 17 • • 75	90	30	30	75	0	30
3	96	37	37	74	15 16 17 • • 75	15 16 17 • • 75	67	0 1 2 • • 60	15 16 17 • • 75
4	78	18 19 20 • • 78	18 19 20 • • 78	81	7	37	93	30	37
5	98	39	39	70	3	18	76	15	18

Group 1   Group 2

Colored rectangle represents executing process

Figure 9.16 Example of Fair Share Scheduler—Three Processes, Two Groups

In the figure, process A is scheduled first. At the end of one second, it is preempted. Processes B and C now have the higher priority, and process B is scheduled. At the end of the second time unit, process A has the highest priority. Note that the pattern repeats: The kernel schedules the processes in order: A, B, A, C, A, B, and so on. Thus, 50% of the processor is allocated to process A, which constitutes one group, and 50% to processes B and C, which constitute another group.

9.3 TRADITIONAL UNIX SCHEDULING

In this section we examine traditional UNIX scheduling, which is used in both SVR3 and 4.3 BSD UNIX. These systems are primarily targeted at the time-sharing interactive environment. The scheduling algorithm is designed to provide good response time for interactive users while ensuring that low-priority background jobs do not starve. Although this algorithm has been replaced in modern UNIX systems, it is worthwhile to examine the approach because it is representative of practical time-sharing scheduling algorithms. The scheduling scheme for SVR4 includes an accommodation for real-time requirements, and so its discussion is deferred to Chapter 10.

The traditional UNIX scheduler employs multilevel feedback using round robin within each of the priority queues. The system makes use of 1-second preemption. That is, if a running process does not block or complete within 1 second, it is preempted. Priority is based on process type and execution history. The following formulas apply:

$$CPU_j(i) = \frac{CPU_j(i-1)}{2}$$

$$P_j(i) = \text{Base}_j + \frac{CPU_j(i)}{2} + \text{nice}_j$$

where

$CPU_j(i)$ = Measure of processor utilization by process j through interval i

$P_j(i)$ = Priority of process j at beginning of interval i; lower values equal higher priorities

Base_j = Base priority of process j

nice_j = user-controllable adjustment factor

The priority of each process is recomputed once per second, at which time a new scheduling decision is made. The purpose of the base priority is to divide all processes into fixed bands of priority levels. The *CPU* and *nice* components are restricted to prevent a process from migrating out of its assigned band (assigned by the base priority level). These bands are used to optimize access to block devices (e.g., disk) and to allow the operating system to respond quickly to system calls. In decreasing order of priority, the bands are

- Swapper
- Block I/O device control
- File manipulation
- Character I/O device control
- User processes

This hierarchy should provide the most efficient use of the I/O devices. Within the user process band, the use of execution history tends to penalize

Time	Process A		Process B		Process C	
	Priority	CPU Count	Priority	CPU Count	Priority	CPU Count
0	60	0 1 2 • • 60	60	0	60	0
1	75	30	60	0 1 2 • • 60	60	0
2	67	15	75	30	60	0 1 2 • • 60
3	63	7 8 9 • • 67	67	15	75	30
4	76	33	63	7 8 9 • • 67	67	15
5	68	16	76	33	63	7

Colored rectangle represents executing process

Figure 9.17 Example of Traditional UNIX Process Scheduling

processor-bound processes at the expense of I/O-bound processes. Again, this should improve efficiency. Coupled with the round-robin preemption scheme, the scheduling strategy is well equipped to satisfy the requirements for general-purpose time sharing.

An example of process scheduling is shown in Figure 9.17. Processes A, B, and C are created at the same time with base priorities of 60 (we will ignore the nice value). The clock interrupts the system 60 times per second and increments a counter for the running process. The example assumes that none of the processes block themselves and that no other processes are ready to run. Compare this with Figure 9.16.

9.4 SUMMARY

The operating system must make three types of scheduling decisions with respect to the execution of processes. Long-term scheduling determines when new processes are admitted to the system. Medium-term scheduling is part of the swapping function and determines when a program is brought partially or fully into main memory so that it may be executed. Short-term scheduling determines which ready process will be executed next by the processor. This chapter focuses on the issues relating to short-term scheduling.

A variety of criteria are used in designing the short-term scheduler. Some of these criteria relate to the behavior of the system as perceived by the individual user (user oriented), while others view the total effectiveness of the system in meeting the needs of all users (system oriented). Some of the criteria relate specifically to quantitative measures of performance, while others are more qualitative in nature. From a user's point of view, response time is generally the most important characteristic of a system, while from a system point of view, throughput or processor utilization is important.

A variety of algorithms have been developed for making the short-term scheduling decision among all ready processes:

- **First-come-first-served:** Select the process that has been waiting the longest for service.
- **Round robin:** Use time-slicing to limit any running process to a short burst of processor time, and rotate among all ready processes.
- **Shortest process next:** Select the process with the shortest expected processing time, and do not preempt the process.
- **Shortest remaining time:** Select the process with the shortest expected remaining process time. A process may be preempted when another process becomes ready.
- **Highest response ratio next:** Base the scheduling decision on an estimate of normalized turnaround time.
- **Feedback:** Establish a set of scheduling queues and allocate processes to queues based on execution history and other criteria.

The choice of scheduling algorithm will depend on expected performance and on implementation complexity.

9.5 RECOMMENDED READINGS

Virtually every textbook on operating systems covers scheduling. Rigorous queuing analyses of various scheduling policies are presented in [KLEI04] and [CONW67]. [DOWD93] provides an instructive performance analysis of various scheduling algorithms.

CONW67 Conway, R.; Maxwell, W.; and Miller, L. *Theory of Scheduling.* Reading, MA: Addison-Wesley, 1967. Reprinted by Dover Publications, 2003.

DOWD93 Dowdy, L., and Lowery, C. *P.S. to Operating Systems.* Upper Saddle River, NJ: Prentice Hall, 1993.

KLEI04 Kleinrock, L. *Queuing Systems, Volume Three: Computer Applications.* New York: Wiley, 2004.

9.6   KEY TERMS, REVIEW QUESTIONS, AND PROBLEMS

Key Terms

arrival rate	medium-term scheduler	short-term scheduler
dispatcher	multilevel feedback	throughput
exponential averaging	predictability	time slicing
fair share scheduling	residence time	turnaround time (TAT)
fairness	response time	utilization
first-come-first-served (FCFS)	round robin	waiting time
first-in-first-out (FIFO)	scheduling priority	
long-term scheduler	service time	

Review Questions

9.1   Briefly describe the three types of processor scheduling.

9.2   What is usually the critical performance requirement in an interactive operating system?

9.3   What is the difference between turnaround time and response time?

9.4   For process scheduling, does a low-priority value represent a low priority or a high priority?

9.5   What is the difference between preemptive and nonpreemptive scheduling?

9.6   Briefly define FCFS scheduling.

9.7   Briefly define round-robin scheduling.

9.8   Briefly define shortest-process-next scheduling.

9.9   Briefly define shortest-remaining-time scheduling.

9.10 Briefly define highest-response-ratio-next scheduling.

9.11 Briefly define feedback scheduling.

Problems

9.1   Consider the following set of processes:

Process Name	Arrival Time	Processing Time
A	0	3
B	1	5
C	3	2
D	9	5
E	12	5

Perform the same analysis as depicted in Table 9.5 and Figure 9.5 for this set.

9.2   Repeat Problem 9.1 for the following set:

Process Name	Arrival Time	Processing Time
A	0	1
B	1	9
C	2	1
D	3	9

9.3 Prove that, among nonpreemptive scheduling algorithms, SPN provides the minimum average waiting time for a batch of jobs that arrive at the same time. Assume that the scheduler must always execute a task if one is available.

9.4 Assume the following burst-time pattern for a process: 6, 4, 6, 4, 13, 13, 13, and assume that the initial guess is 10. Produce a plot similar to those of Figure 9.9.

9.5 Consider the following pair of equations as an alternative to Equation (9.3):

$$S_{n+1} = \alpha T_n + (1 - \alpha)S_n$$
$$X_{n+1} = \min[Ubound, \max[Lbound, (\beta S_{n+1})]]$$

where *Ubound* and *Lbound* are prechosen upper and lower bounds on the estimated value of *T*. The value of X_{n+1} is used in the shortest-process-next algorithm, instead of the value of S_{n+1}. What functions do α and β perform, and what is the effect of higher and lower values on each?

9.6 In the bottom example in Figure 9.5, process A runs for 2 time units before control is passed to process B. Another plausible scenario would be that A runs for 3 time units before control is passed to process B. What policy differences in the feedback scheduling algorithm would account for the two different scenarios?

9.7 In a nonpreemptive uniprocessor system, the ready queue contains three jobs at time t immediately after the completion of a job. These jobs arrived at times $t_1, t_2,$ and t_3 with estimated execution times of $r_1, r_2,$ and r_3, respectively. Figure 9.18 shows the linear increase of their response ratios over time. Use this example to find a variant of response ratio scheduling, known as minimax response ratio scheduling, that minimizes the maximum response ratio for a given batch of jobs ignoring further arrivals. (*Hint:* Decide first which job to schedule as the last one.)

9.8 Prove that the minimax response ratio algorithm of the preceding problem minimizes the maximum response ratio for a given batch of jobs. (*Hint:* Focus attention on the job that will achieve the highest response ratio and all jobs executed before it. Consider the same subset of jobs scheduled in any other order and observe the response ratio of the job that is executed as the last one among them. Notice that this subset may now be mixed with other jobs from the total set.)

9.9 Define residence time T_r as the average total time a process spends waiting and being served. Show that for FIFO, with mean service time T_s, we have $T_r = T_s/(1 - \rho)$, where ρ is utilization.

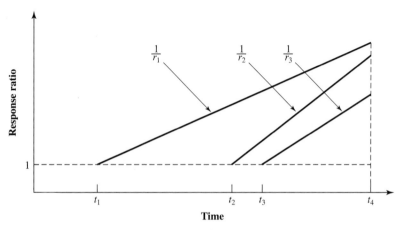

Figure 9.18 Response Ratio as a Function of Time

9.10 A processor is multiplexed at infinite speed among all processes present in a ready queue with no overhead. (This is an idealized model of round-robin scheduling among ready processes using time slices that are very small compared to the mean service time.) Show that for Poisson input from an infinite source with exponential service times, the mean response time R_x of a process with service time x is given by $R_x = x/(1 - \rho)$. (*Hint:* Review the basic queuing equations in the Queuing Analysis document at **WilliamStallings.com/StudentSupport.html**. Then consider the number of items waiting, w, in the system upon arrival of the given process.)

9.11 Most round-robin schedulers use a fixed size quantum. Give an argument in favor of a small quantum. Now give an argument in favor of a large quantum. Compare and contrast the types of systems and jobs to which the arguments apply. Are there any for which both are reasonable?

9.12 In a queuing system, new jobs must wait for a while before being served. While a job waits, its priority increases linearly with time from zero at a rate α. A job waits until its priority reaches the priority of the jobs in service; then it begins to share the processor equally with other jobs in service using round robin while its priority continues to increase at a slower rate β. The algorithm is referred to as selfish round robin, because the jobs in service try (in vain) to monopolize the processor by increasing their priority continuously. Use Figure 9.19 to show that the mean response time R_x for a job of service time x is given by

$$R_x = \frac{s}{1 - \rho} + \frac{x - s}{1 - \rho'}$$

where

$$\rho = \lambda s \qquad \rho' = \rho\left(1 - \frac{\beta}{\alpha}\right) \qquad 0 \le \beta < \alpha$$

assuming that arrival and service times are exponentially distributed with means $1/\lambda$ and s, respectively. (*Hint:* Consider the total system and the two subsystems separately.)

9.13 An interactive system using round-robin scheduling and swapping tries to give guaranteed response to trivial requests as follows: After completing a round-robin cycle

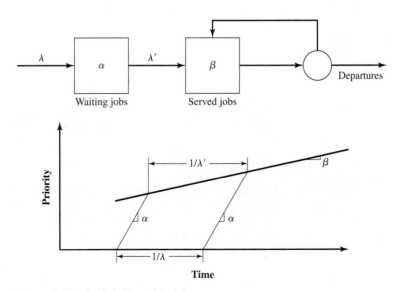

Figure 9.19   Selfish Round Robin

among all ready processes, the system determines the time slice to allocate to each ready process for the next cycle by dividing a maximum response time by the number of processes requiring service. Is this a reasonable policy?

9.14 Which type of process is generally favored by a multilevel feedback queuing scheduler—a processor-bound process or an I/O-bound process? Briefly explain why.

9.15 In priority-based process scheduling, the scheduler only gives control to a particular process if no other process of higher priority is currently in the ready state. Assume that no other information is used in making the process scheduling decision. Also assume that process priorities are established at process creation time and do not change. In a system operating with such assumptions, why would using Dekker's solution (see Section A.1) to the mutual exclusion problem be "dangerous"? Explain this by telling what undesired event could occur and how it could occur.

9.16 Five batch jobs, A through E, arrive at a computer center at essentially the same time. They have an estimated running time of 15, 9, 3, 6, and 12 minutes, respectively. Their (externally defined) priorities are 6, 3, 7, 9, and 4 respectively, with a lower value corresponding to a higher priority. For each of the following scheduling algorithms, determine the turnaround time for each process and the average turnaround for all jobs. Ignore process switching overhead. Explain how you arrived at your answers. In the last three cases, assume that only one job at a time runs until it finishes and that all jobs are completely processor bound.
a. round robin with a time quantum of 1 minute
b. priority scheduling
c. FCFS (run in order 15, 9, 3, 6, and 12)
d. shortest job first

APPENDIX 9A RESPONSE TIME

Response time is the time it takes a system to react to a given input. In an interactive transaction, it may be defined as the time between the last keystroke by the user and the beginning of the display of a result by the computer. For different types of applications, a slightly different definition is needed. In general, it is the time it takes for the system to respond to a request to perform a particular task.

Ideally, one would like the response time for any application to be short. However, it is almost invariably the case that shorter response time imposes greater cost. This cost comes from two sources:

- **Computer processing power:** The faster the processor, the shorter the response time. Of course, increased processing power means increased cost.

- **Competing requirements:** Providing rapid response time to some processes may penalize other processes.

Thus the value of a given level of response time must be assessed versus the cost of achieving that response time.

Table 9.7, based on [MART88], lists six general ranges of response times. Design difficulties are faced when a response time of less than 1 second is required. A requirement for a subsecond response time is generated by a system that controls or in some other way interacts with an ongoing external activity, such as an assembly line. Here the requirement is straightforward. When we consider human-computer interaction, such as in a data entry application, then we are in the realm of conversational response time. In this case, there is still a requirement for a short response time, but the acceptable length of time may be difficult to assess.

Table 9.7   Response Time Ranges

Greater than 15 seconds

This rules out conversational interaction. For certain types of applications, certain types of users may be content to sit at a terminal for more than 15 seconds waiting for the answer to a single simple inquiry. However, for a busy person, captivity for more than 15 seconds seems intolerable. If such delays will occur, the system should be designed so that the user can turn to other activities and request the response at some later time.

Greater than 4 seconds

These are generally too long for a conversation requiring the operator to retain information in short-term memory (the operator's memory, not the computer's!). Such delays would be very inhibiting in problem-solving activity and frustrating in data entry activity. However, after a major closure, such as the end of a transaction, delays from 4 to 15 seconds can be tolerated.

2 to 4 seconds

A delay longer than 2 seconds can be inhibiting to terminal operations demanding a high level of concentration. A wait of 2 to 4 seconds at a terminal can seem surprisingly long when the user is absorbed and emotionally committed to complete what he or she is doing. Again, a delay in this range may be acceptable after a minor closure has occurred.

Less than 2 seconds

When the terminal user has to remember information throughout several responses, the response time must be short. The more detailed the information remembered, the greater the need for responses of less than 2 seconds. For elaborate terminal activities, 2 seconds represents an important response-time limit.

Subsecond response time

Certain types of thought-intensive work, especially with graphics applications, require very short response times to maintain the user's interest and attention for long periods of time.

Decisecond response time

A response to pressing a key and seeing the character displayed on the screen or clicking a screen object with a mouse needs to be almost instantaneous—less than 0.1 second after the action. Interaction with a mouse requires extremely fast interaction if the designer is to avoid the use of alien syntax (one with commands, mnemonics, punctuation, etc.).

That rapid response time is the key to productivity in interactive applications has been confirmed in a number of studies [SHNE84; THAD81; GUYN88]. These studies show that when a computer and a user interact at a pace that ensures that neither has to wait on the other, productivity increases significantly, the cost of the work done on the computer therefore drops, and quality tends to improve. It used to be widely accepted that a relatively slow response, up to 2 seconds, was acceptable for most interactive applications because the person was thinking about the next task. However, it now appears that productivity increases as rapid response times are achieved.

The results reported on response time are based on an analysis of online transactions. A transaction consists of a user command from a terminal and the system's reply. It is the fundamental unit of work for online system users. It can be divided into two time sequences:

- **User response time:** The time span between the moment a user receives a complete reply to one command and enters the next command. People often refer to this as think time.

- **System response time:** The time span between the moment the user enters a command and the moment a complete response is displayed on the terminal.

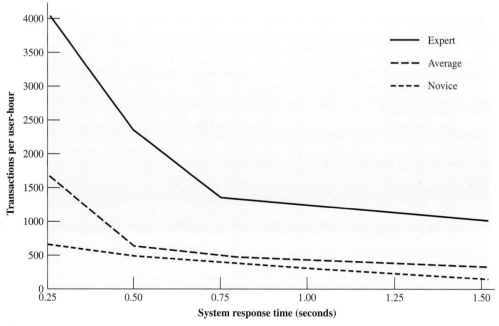

Figure 9.20   Response Time Results for High-Function Graphics

As an example of the effect of reduced system response time, Figure 9.20 shows the results of a study carried out on engineers using a computer-aided design graphics program for the design of integrated circuit chips and boards [SMIT83]. Each transaction consists of a command by the engineer that alters in some way the graphic image being displayed on the screen. The results show that the rate of transactions increases as system response time falls and rises dramatically once system response time falls below 1 second. What is happening is that as the system response time falls, so does the user response time. This has to do with the effects of short-term memory and human attention span.

Another area where response time has become critical is the use of the World Wide Web, either over the Internet or over a corporate intranet. The time it takes for a typical Web page to come up on the user's screen varies greatly. Response times can be gauged based on the level of user involvement in the session; in particular, systems with vary fast response times tend to command more user attention. As Figure 9.21 indicates [SEVC96], Web systems with a 3-second or better response time maintain a high level of user attention. With a response time of between 3 and 10 seconds, some user concentration is lost, and response times above 10 seconds discourage the user, who may simply abort the session.

APPENDIX 9B QUEUING SYSTEMS

In this chapter, and several subsequent chapters, results from queuing theory are used. In this appendix we present a brief definition of queuing systems and define key terms. For the reader not familiar with queuing analysis, a basic refresher can be found at the Computer Science Student Resource Site at WilliamStallings.com/StudentSupport.html.

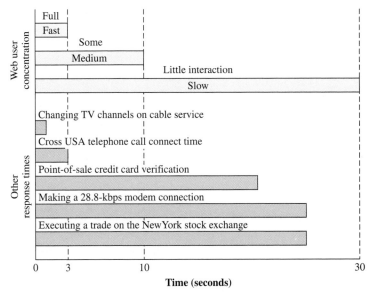

Figure 9.21 Response Time Requirements

Why Queuing Analysis?

It is often necessary to make projections of performance on the basis of existing load information or on the basis of estimated load for a new environment. A number of approaches are possible:

1. Do an after-the-fact analysis based on actual values.
2. Make a simple projection by scaling up from existing experience to the expected future environment.
3. Develop an analytic model based on queuing theory.
4. Program and run a simulation model.

Option 1 is no option at all: We will wait and see what happens. This leads to unhappy users and to unwise purchases. Option 2 sounds more promising. The analyst may take the position that it is impossible to project future demand with any degree of certainty. Therefore, it is pointless to attempt some exact modeling procedure. Rather, a rough-and-ready projection will provide ballpark estimates. The problem with this approach is that the behavior of most systems under a changing load is not what one would intuitively expect. If there is an environment in which there is a shared facility (e.g., a network, a transmission line, a time-sharing system), then the performance of that system typically responds in an exponential way to increases in demand.

Figure 9.22 is a representative example. The upper line shows what typically happens to user response time on a shared facility as the load on that facility increases. The load is expressed as a fraction of capacity. Thus, if we are dealing with a router that is capable of processing and forwarding 1000 packets per second, then a load of 0.5 represents an arrival rate of 500 packets per second, and the response time is the amount of time it takes to retransmit any incoming packet. The lower line is a simple projection[7] based on a knowledge of the behavior of the system up to a load of 0.5. Note that while things appear rosy when the simple projection is made, performance on the system will in fact collapse beyond a load of about 0.8 to 0.9.

---

[7] The lower line is based on fitting a third-order polynomial to the data available up to a load of 0.5.

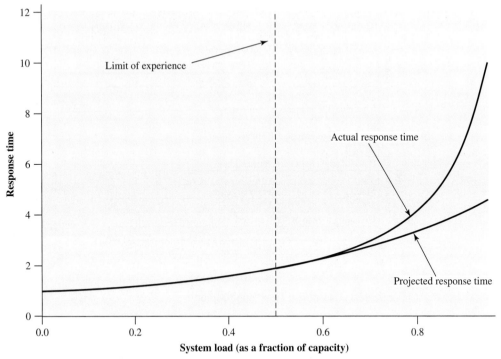

Figure 9.22 Projected versus Actual Response Time

Thus, a more exact prediction tool is needed. Option 3 is to make use of an analytic model, which is one that can be expressed as a set of equations that can be solved to yield the desired parameters (response time, throughput, etc.). For computer, operating system, and networking problems, and indeed for many practical real-world problems, analytic models based on queuing theory provide a reasonably good fit to reality. The disadvantage of queuing theory is that a number of simplifying assumptions must be made to derive equations for the parameters of interest.

The final approach is a simulation model. Here, given a sufficiently powerful and flexible simulation programming language, the analyst can model reality in great detail and avoid making many of the assumptions required of queuing theory. However, in most cases, a simulation model is not needed or at least is not advisable as a first step in the analysis. For one thing, both existing measurements and projections of future load carry with them a certain margin of error. Thus, no matter how good the simulation model, the value of the results is limited by the quality of the input. For another, despite the many assumptions required of queuing theory, the results that are produced often come quite close to those that would be produced by a more careful simulation analysis. Furthermore, a queuing analysis can literally be accomplished in a matter of minutes for a well-defined problem, whereas simulation exercises can take days, weeks, or longer to program and run.

Accordingly, it behooves the analyst to master the basics of queuing theory.

The Single-Server Queue

The simplest queuing system is depicted in Figure 9.23. The central element of the system is a server, which provides some service to items. Items from some population of items arrive at the system to be served. If the server is idle, an item is served immediately. Otherwise, an arriving item

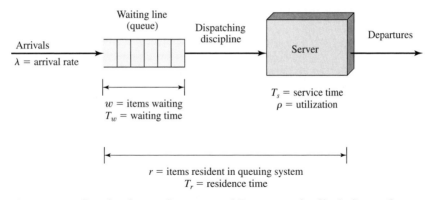

Figure 9.23 Queuing System Structure and Parameters for Single-Server Queue

Table 9.8 Notation for Queuing Systems

λ = arrival rate; mean number of arrivals per second

T_s = mean service time for each arrival; amount of time being served, not counting time waiting in the queue

ρ = utilization; fraction of time facility (server or servers) is busy

w = mean number of items waiting to be served

T_w = mean waiting time (including items that have to wait and items with waiting time = 0)

r = mean number of items resident in system (waiting and being served)

T_r = mean residence time; time an item spends in system (waiting and being served)

joins a waiting line.[8] When the server has completed serving an item, the item departs. If there are items waiting in the queue, one is immediately dispatched to the server. The server in this model can represent anything that performs some function or service for a collection of items. Examples: A processor provides service to processes; a transmission line provides a transmission service to packets or frames of data; an I/O device provides a read or write service for I/O requests.

Table 9.8 summarizes some important parameters associated with a queuing model. Items arrive at the facility at some average rate (items arriving per second) λ. At any given time, a certain number of items will be waiting in the queue (zero or more); the average number waiting is w, and the mean time that an item must wait is T_w. T_w is averaged over all incoming items, including those that do not wait at all. The server handles incoming items with an average service time T_s; this is the time interval between the dispatching of an item to the server and the departure of that item from the server. Utilization, ρ, is the fraction of time that the server is busy, measured over some interval of time. Finally, two parameters apply to the system as a whole. The average number of items resident in the system, including the item being served (if any) and the items waiting (if any), is r; and the average time that an item spends in the system, waiting and being served, is T_r; we refer to this as the mean residence time.[9]

---

[8]The waiting line is referred to as a queue in some treatments in the literature; it is also common to refer to the entire system as a queue. Unless otherwise noted, we use the term *queue* to mean waiting line.

[9]Again, in some of the literature, this is referred to as the mean queuing time, while other treatments use mean queuing time to mean the average time spent waiting in the queue (before being served).

If we assume that the capacity of the queue is infinite, then no items are ever lost from the system; they are just delayed until they can be served. Under these circumstances, the departure rate equals the arrival rate. As the arrival rate increases, the utilization increases and with it, congestion. The queue becomes longer, increasing waiting time. At $\rho = 1$, the server becomes saturated, working 100% of the time. Thus, the theoretical maximum input rate that can be handled by the system is

$$\lambda_{max} = \frac{1}{T_s}$$

However, queues become very large near system saturation, growing without bound when $\rho = 1$. Practical considerations, such as response time requirements or buffer sizes, usually limit the input rate for a single server to between 70 and 90% of the theoretical maximum.

The following assumptions are typically made:

- **Item population:** Typically, we assume an infinite population. This means that the arrival rate is not altered by the loss of population. If the population is finite, then the population available for arrival is reduced by the number of items currently in the system; this would typically reduce the arrival rate proportionally.

- **Queue size:** Typically, we assume an infinite queue size. Thus, the waiting line can grow without bound. With a finite queue, it is possible for items to be lost from the system. In practice, any queue is finite. In many cases, this will make no substantive difference to the analysis.

- **Dispatching discipline:** When the server becomes free, and if there is more than one item waiting, a decision must be made as to which item to dispatch next. The simplest approach is first-in-first-out; this discipline is what is normally implied when the term *queue* is used. Another possibility is last-in-first-out. One that you might encounter in practice is a dispatching discipline based on service time. For example, a packet-switching node may choose to dispatch packets on the basis of shortest first (to generate the most outgoing packets) or longest first (to minimize processing time relative to transmission time). Unfortunately, a discipline based on service time is very difficult to model analytically.

The Multiserver Queue

Figure 9.24 shows a generalization of the simple model we have been discussing for multiple servers, all sharing a common queue. If an item arrives and at least one server is available, then the item is immediately dispatched to that server. It is assumed that all servers are identical; thus, if more than one server is available, it makes no difference which server is chosen for the item. If all servers are busy, a queue begins to form. As soon as one server becomes free, an item is dispatched from the queue using the dispatching discipline in force.

With the exception of utilization, all of the parameters illustrated in Figure 9.23 carry over to the multiserver case with the same interpretation. If we have N identical servers, then ρ is the utilization of each server, and we can consider $N\rho$ to be the utilization of the entire system; this latter term is often referred to as the traffic intensity, u. Thus, the theoretical maximum utilization is $N \times 100\%$, and the theoretical maximum input rate is

$$\lambda_{max} = \frac{N}{T_s}$$

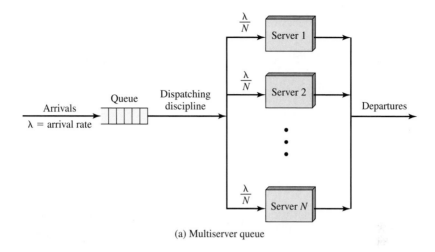

(a) Multiserver queue

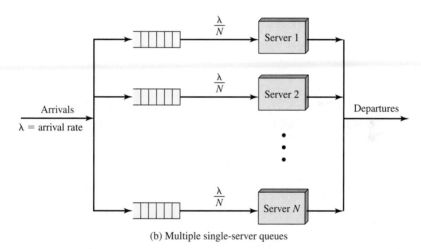

(b) Multiple single-server queues

Figure 9.24 Multiserver versus Multiple Single-Server Queues

The key characteristics typically chosen for the multiserver queue correspond to those for the single-server queue. That is, we assume an infinite population and an infinite queue size, with a single infinite queue shared among all servers. Unless otherwise stated, the dispatching discipline is FIFO. For the multiserver case, if all servers are assumed identical, the selection of a particular server for a waiting item has no effect on service time.

By way of contrast, Figure 9.24b shows the structure of multiple single-server queues.

Programming Project Two: The Host Dispatcher Shell

The Hypothetical Operating System Testbed (HOST) is a multiprogramming system with a four level priority process dispatcher operating within the constraints of finite available resources.

Four-Level Priority Dispatcher

The dispatcher operates at four priority levels:

1. Real-Time processes that must be run immediately on a First Come First Served (FCFS) basis, pre-empting any other processes running with lower priority. These processes are run till completion.

2. Normal user processes are run on a three level feedback dispatcher (Figure P2.1). The basic timing quantum of the dispatcher is 1 second. This is also the value for the time quantum of the feedback scheduler.

The dispatcher needs to maintain two submission queues - Real-Time and User priority - fed from the job dispatch list. The dispatch list is examined at every dispatcher tick and jobs that "have arrived" are transferred to the appropriate submission queue. The submission queues are then examined; any Real-Time jobs are run to completion, pre-empting any other jobs currently running.

The Real-Time priority job queue must be empty before the lower priority feedback dispatcher is reactivated. Any User priority jobs in the User job queue that can run within available resources (memory and i/o devices)

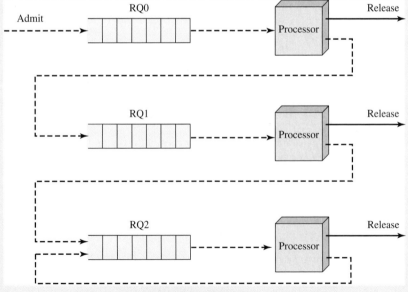

Figure P2.1　Three-Level Feedback Scheduling

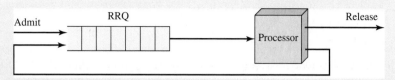

Figure P2.2   Round-Robin Dispatcher

are transferred to the appropriate priority queue. Normal operation of a feedback queue will accept all jobs at the highest priority level and degrade the priority after each completed time quantum. However, this dispatcher has the ability to accept jobs at a lower priority, inserting them in the appropriate queue. This enables the dispatcher to emulate a simple Round Robin dispatcher (Figure P2.2) if all jobs are accepted at the lowest priority.

When all "ready" higher priority jobs have been completed, the feedback dispatcher resumes by starting or resuming the process at the head of the highest priority non-empty queue. At the next tick the current job is suspended (or terminated and its resources released) if there are any other jobs "ready" of an equal or higher priority.

The logic flow should be as shown in Figure P2.3 (and as discussed in the exercises):

Resource Constraints

The HOST has the following resources:

- 2 Printers
- 1 Scanner
- 1 Modem
- 2 CD Drives
- 1024 Mbyte Memory available for processes

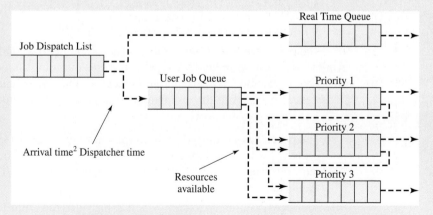

Figure P2.3   Dispatcher Logic Flow

Low priority processes can use any or all of these resources, but the HOST dispatcher is notified of which resources the process will use when the process is submitted. The dispatcher ensures that each requested resource is solely available to that process throughout its lifetime in the "ready-to-run" dispatch queues: from the initial transfer from the job queue to the Priority 1-3 queues through to process completion, including intervening idle time quanta.

Real-Time processes will not need any I/O resources (Printer / Scanner / Modem / CD), but will obviously require memory allocation - this memory requirement will always be 64 Mbytes or less for Real-Time jobs.

Memory Allocation

Memory allocation must be as a **contiguous** block of memory for each process that remains assigned to the process for the lifetime of that process.

Enough contiguous spare memory must be left so that the Real Time processes are not blocked from execution - 64 Mbytes for a running Real-Time job leaving 960 Mbytes to be shared amongst "active" User jobs.

The HOST hardware MMU cannot support virtual memory so no swapping of memory to disk is possible. Neither is it a paged system.

Within these constraints, any suitable variable partition memory allocation scheme (First Fit, Next Fit, Best Fit, Worst Fit, Buddy, etc) may be used.

Processes

Processes on HOST are simulated by the dispatcher creating a new process for each dispatched process. This process is a generic process (supplied as **process** - source: **sigtrap.c**) that can be used for any priority process. It actually runs itself at very low priority, sleeping for one-second periods and displaying:

1. A message displaying the process ID when the process starts;
2. A regular message every second the process is executed; and
3. A message when the process is Suspended, Continued, or Terminated.

The process will terminate of its own accord after 20 seconds if it is not terminated by your dispatcher. The process prints out using a randomly generated color scheme for each unique process, so that individual "slices" of processes can be easily distinguishable. Use this process rather than your own.

The life cycle of a process is:

1. The process is submitted to the dispatcher input queues via an initial process list that designates the arrival time, priority, processor time required (in seconds), memory block size and other resources requested.
2. A process is "ready-to-run" when it has "arrived" and all required resources are available.

3. Any pending Real-Time jobs are submitted for execution on a First Come First Served basis.

4. If enough resources and memory are available for a lower priority User process, the process is transferred to the appropriate priority queue within the feedback dispatcher unit, and the remaining resource indicators (memory list and i/o devices) updated.

5. When a job is started (`fork` and `exec("process", . . .)`), the dispatcher will display the job parameters (Process ID, priority, processor time remaining (in seconds), memory location and block size, and resources requested) before performing the `exec`.

6. A Real-Time process is allowed to run until its time has expired when the dispatcher kills it by sending a `SIGINT` signal to it.

7. A low priority User job is allowed to run for one dispatcher tick (one second) before it is suspended (`SIGTSTP`) or terminated (`SIGINT`) if its time has expired. If suspended, its priority level is lowered (if possible) and it is re-queued on the appropriate priority queue as shown in Figures P2.1 and P2.3. To retain synchronization of output between your dispatcher and the child process, your dispatcher should wait for the process to respond to a `SIGTSTP` or `SIGINT` signal before continuing (`waitpid(p->pid, &status, WUNTRACED)`). To match the performance sequence indicated in the comparison of scheduling policies (see Figure 9.5) the User job should not be suspended and moved to a lower priority level unless another process is waiting to be (re)started.

8. Provided no higher priority Real Time jobs are pending in the submission queue, the highest priority pending process in the feedback queues is started or restarted (`SIGCONT`).

9. When a process is terminated, the resources it used are returned to the dispatcher for reallocation to further processes.

10. When there are no more processes in the dispatch list, the input queues and the feedback queues, the dispatcher exits.

Dispatch List

The Dispatch List is the list of processes to be processed by the dispatcher. The list is contained in a text file that is specified on the command line. i.e.

>hostd dispatchlist

Each line of the list describes one process with the following data as a "*comma-space*" delimited list:

<arrival time>, <priority>, <processor time>, <Mbytes>, <#printers>, <#scanners>, <#modems>, <#CDs>

Thus,

$$12, 0, 1, 64, 0, 0, 0, 0$$
$$12, 1, 2, 128, 1, 0, 0, 1$$
$$13, 3, 6, 128, 1, 0, 1, 2$$

would indicate:

1st Job: Arrival at time 12, priority 0 (Real-Time), requiring 1 second of processor time and 64 Mbytes memory - no I/O resources required.

2nd Job: Arrival at time 12, priority 1 (high priority User job), requiring 2 seconds of processor. time, 128 Mbytes of memory, 1 printer and 1 CD drive.

3rd Job: Arrival at time 13, priority 3 (lowest priority User job), requiring 6 seconds of processor., 128 Mbytes of memory, 1 printer, 1 modem, and 2 CD drives.

The submission text file can be of any length, containing up to 1000 jobs. It will be terminated with an end-of-line followed by an end-of-file marker.

Dispatcher input lists to test the operation of the individual features of the dispatcher are described in the exercises. It should be noted that these lists will almost certainly form the basis of tests that will be applied to your dispatcher during marking. Operation as described in the exercises will be expected.

Obviously, your submitted dispatcher will be tested with more complex combinations as well!

A fully functional working example of the dispatcher will be presented during the course. If in any doubt as to the manner of operation or format of output, you should refer to this program to observe how your dispatcher is expected to operate.

Project Requirements

1. Design a dispatcher that satisfies the above criteria. In a formal design document:

   (a) Describe and discuss what memory allocation algorithms you could have used and justify your final design choice.

   (b) Describe and discuss the structures used by the dispatcher for queuing, dispatching and allocating memory and other resources.

   (c) Describe and justify the overall structure of your program, describing the various modules and major functions (descriptions of the function 'interfaces' are expected).

   (d) Discuss why such a multilevel dispatching scheme would be used, comparing it with schemes used by "real" operating systems. Outline shortcomings in such a scheme, suggesting possible improvements. Include the memory and resource allocation schemes in your discussions.

The formal design document is expected to have in-depth discussions, descriptions and arguments. The design document is to be submitted separately as a physical paper document. The design document should NOT include any source code.

2. Implement the dispatcher using the C language.

3. The source code MUST be extensively commented and appropriately structured to allow your peers to understand and easily maintain the code. Properly commented and laid out code is much easier to interpret and it is in your interests to ensure that the person marking your project is able to understand your coding without having to perform mental gymnastics!

4. Details of submission procedures will be supplied well before the deadline.

5. The submission should contain only source code file(s), include file(s), and a `makefile`. No executable program should be included. The marker will be automatically rebuilding your program from the source code provided. If the submitted code does not compile it cannot be marked!

6. The makefile should generate the binary executable file hostd (all lower case please). A sample makefile would be:

```
# Joe Citizen, s1234567 - Operating Systems Project 2
# CompLab1/01 tutor: Fred Bloggs
hostd: hostd.c utility.c hostd.h
gcc hostd.c utility.c -o hostd
```

The program hostd is then generated by typing make at the command line prompt. Note: the fourth line in the above **makefile MUST** begin with a **tab**

Deliverables

1. Source code file(s), include file(s), and a **makefile**.

2. The design document as outlined in Project Requirements section 1 above.

Submission of code

A **makefile** is required. All files will be copied to the same directory; therefore *do not include any paths in your makefile*. The **makefile** should include all dependencies that build your program. If a library is included, your **makefile** should also build the library.

To make this clear: *do not submit any binary or object code files*. All that is required is your source code and a `makefile`. Test your project by copying the source code only into an *empty* directory and then compile it with your `makefile`.

The marker will be using a shell script that copies your files to a test directory, performs a `make`, and then exercises your dispatcher with a standard set of test files. If this sequence fails due to wrong names, wrong case for names, wrong version of source code that fails to compile, non-existence of files etc. then the marking sequence will also stop. In this instance, the only further marks that can be awarded will be for the source code and design document.

CHAPTER 10

MULTIPROCESSOR AND REAL-TIME SCHEDULING

This chapter continues our survey of process and thread scheduling. We begin with an examination of issues raised by the availability of more than one processor. A number of design issues are explored. This is followed by a look at the scheduling of processes on a multiprocessor system. Then the somewhat different design considerations for multiprocessor thread scheduling are examined. The second section of this chapter covers real-time scheduling. The section begins with a discussion of the characteristics of real-time processes and then looks at the nature of the scheduling process. Two approaches to real-time scheduling, deadline scheduling and rate monotonic scheduling, are examined.

10.1 MULTIPROCESSOR SCHEDULING

When a computer system contains more than a single processor, several new issues are introduced into the design of the scheduling function. We begin with a brief overview of multiprocessors and then look at the rather different considerations when scheduling is done at the process level and the thread level.

We can classify multiprocessor systems as follows:

- **Loosely coupled or distributed multiprocessor, or cluster:** Consists of a collection of relatively autonomous systems, each processor having its own main memory and I/O channels. We address this type of configuration in Chapter 14.
- **Functionally specialized processors:** An example is an I/O processor. In this case, there is a master, general-purpose processor; specialized processors are controlled by the master processor and provide services to it. Issues relating to I/O processors are addressed in Chapter 11.
- **Tightly coupled multiprocessing:** Consists of a set of processors that share a common main memory and are under the integrated control of an operating system.

Our concern in this section is with the last category, and specifically with issues relating to scheduling.

Granularity

A good way of characterizing multiprocessors and placing them in context with other architectures is to consider the synchronization granularity, or frequency of synchronization, between processes in a system. We can distinguish five categories of parallelism that differ in the degree of granularity. These are summarized in Table 10.1, which is adapted from [GEHR87] and [WOOD89].

Independent Parallelism With independent parallelism, there is no explicit synchronization among processes. Each represents a separate, independent application or job. A typical use of this type of parallelism is in a time-sharing system. Each user is performing a particular application, such as word processing or using a spreadsheet. The multiprocessor provides the same service as a multiprogrammed uniprocessor. Because more than one processor is available, average response time to the users will be less.

It is possible to achieve a similar performance gain by providing each user with a personal computer or workstation. If any files or information are to be shared,

Table 10.1   Synchronization Granularity and Processes

Grain Size	Description	Synchronization Interval (Instructions)
Fine	Parallelism inherent in a single instruction stream.	<20
Medium	Parallel processing or multitasking within a single application	20–200
Coarse	Multiprocessing of concurrent processes in a multiprogramming environment	200–2000
Very Coarse	Distributed processing across network nodes to form a single computing environment	2000–1M
Independent	Multiple unrelated processes	(N/A)

then the individual systems must be hooked together into a distributed system supported by a network. This approach is examined in Chapter 14. On the other hand, a single, multiprocessor shared system in many instances is more cost-effective than a distributed system, allowing economies of scale in disks and other peripherals.

Coarse and Very Coarse-Grained Parallelism   With coarse and very coarse-grained parallelism, there is synchronization among processes, but at a very gross level. This kind of situation is easily handled as a set of concurrent processes running on a multiprogrammed uniprocessor and can be supported on a multiprocessor with little or no change to user software.

A simple example of an application that can exploit the existence of a multiprocessor is given in [WOOD89]. The authors have developed a program that takes a specification of files needing recompilation to rebuild a piece of software and determines which of these compiles (usually all of them) can be run simultaneously. The program then spawns one process for each parallel compile. The authors report that the speedup on a multiprocessor actually exceeds what would be expected by simply adding up the number of processors in use, due to synergies in the disk buffer caches (a topic explored in Chapter 11) and sharing of compiler code, which is loaded into memory only once.

In general, any collection of concurrent processes that need to communicate or synchronize can benefit from the use of a multiprocessor architecture. In the case of very infrequent interaction among processes, a distributed system can provide good support. However, if the interaction is somewhat more frequent, then the overhead of communication across the network may negate some of the potential speedup. In that case, the multiprocessor organization provides the most effective support.

Medium-Grained Parallelism   We saw in Chapter 4 that a single application can be effectively implemented as a collection of threads within a single process. In this case, the potential parallelism of an application must be explicitly specified by the programmer. Typically, there will need to be rather a high degree of coordination and interaction among the threads of an application, leading to a medium-grain level of synchronization.

Whereas independent, very coarse, and coarse-grain parallelism can be supported on either a multiprogrammed uniprocessor or a multiprocessor with little or no impact on the scheduling function, we need to reexamine scheduling when dealing with the scheduling of threads. Because the various threads of an application interact so frequently, scheduling decisions concerning one thread may affect the performance of the entire application. We return to this issue later in this section.

Fine-Grained Parallelism Fine-grained parallelism represents a much more complex use of parallelism than is found in the use of threads. Although much work has been done on highly parallel applications, this is so far a specialized and fragmented area, with many different approaches.

Design Issues

Scheduling on a multiprocessor involves three interrelated issues:

- The assignment of processes to processors
- The use of multiprogramming on individual processors
- The actual dispatching of a process

In looking at these three issues, it is important to keep in mind that the approach taken will depend, in general, on the degree of granularity of the applications and on the number of processors available.

Assignment of Processes to Processors If we assume that the architecture of the multiprocessor is uniform, in the sense that no processor has a particular physical advantage with respect to access to main memory or to I/O devices, then the simplest scheduling approach is to treat the processors as a pooled resource and assign processes to processors on demand. The question then arises as to whether the assignment should be static or dynamic.

If a process is permanently assigned to one processor from activation until its completion, then a dedicated short-term queue is maintained for each processor. An advantage of this approach is that there may be less overhead in the scheduling function, because the processor assignment is made once and for all. Also, the use of dedicated processors allows a strategy known as group or gang scheduling, as discussed later.

A disadvantage of static assignment is that one processor can be idle, with an empty queue, while another processor has a backlog. To prevent this situation, a common queue can be used. All processes go into one global queue and are scheduled to any available processor. Thus, over the life of a process, the process may be executed on different processors at different times. In a tightly coupled shared-memory architecture, the context information for all processes will be available to all processors, and therefore the cost of scheduling a process will be independent of the identity of the processor on which it is scheduled. Yet another option is dynamic load balancing, in which threads are moved for a queue for one processor to a queue for another processor; Linux uses this approach.

Regardless of whether processes are dedicated to processors, some means is needed to assign processes to processors. Two approaches have been used: master/slave and peer. With a master/slave architecture, key kernel functions of the operating system always run on a particular processor. The other processors may only execute user programs. The master is responsible for scheduling jobs. Once a process is active, if the slave needs service (e.g., an I/O call), it must send a request to the master and wait for the service to be performed. This approach is quite simple and requires little enhancement to a uniprocessor multiprogramming operating system. Conflict resolution is simplified because one processor has control of all memory and I/O resources. There are two disadvantages to this approach: (1) A failure of the master brings down the whole system, and (2) the master can become a performance bottleneck.

In a peer architecture, the kernel can execute on any processor, and each processor does self-scheduling from the pool of available processes. This approach complicates the operating system. The operating system must ensure that two processors do not choose the same process and that the processes are not somehow lost from the queue. Techniques must be employed to resolve and synchronize competing claims to resources.

There is, of course, a spectrum of approaches between these two extremes. One approach is to provide a subset of processors dedicated to kernel processing instead of just one. Another approach is simply to manage the difference between the needs of kernel processes and other processes on the basis of priority and execution history.

The Use of Multiprogramming on Individual Processors When each process is statically assigned to a processor for the duration of its lifetime, a new question arises: Should that processor be multiprogrammed? The reader's first reaction may be to wonder why the question needs to be asked; it would appear particularly wasteful to tie up a processor with a single process when that process may frequently be blocked waiting for I/O or because of concurrency/synchronization considerations.

In the traditional multiprocessor, which is dealing with coarse-grained or independent synchronization granularity (see Table 10.1), it is clear that each individual processor should be able to switch among a number of processes to achieve high utilization and therefore better performance. However, for medium-grained applications running on a multiprocessor with many processors, the situation is less clear. When many processors are available, it is no longer paramount that every single processor be busy as much as possible. Rather, we are concerned to provide the best performance, on average, for the applications. An application that consists of a number of threads may run poorly unless all of its threads are available to run simultaneously.

Process Dispatching The final design issue related to multiprocessor scheduling is the actual selection of a process to run. We have seen that, on a multiprogrammed uniprocessor, the use of priorities or of sophisticated scheduling algorithms based on past usage may improve performance over a simple-minded first-come-first-served strategy. When we consider multiprocessors, these complexities may be unnecessary or even counterproductive, and a simpler approach may be more effective with less overhead. In the case of thread scheduling, new issues come into play that may be more important than priorities or execution histories. We address each of these topics in turn.

Process Scheduling

In most traditional multiprocessor systems, processes are not dedicated to processors. Rather there is a single queue for all processors, or if some sort of priority scheme is used, there are multiple queues based on priority, all feeding into the common pool of processors. In any case, we can view the system as being a multiserver queuing architecture.

Consider the case of a dual-processor system in which each processor of the dual-processor system has half the processing rate of a processor in the single-processor system. [SAUE81] reports a queuing analysis that compares FCFS scheduling to round robin and to shortest remaining time. The study is concerned with process service time, which measures the amount of processor time a process needs, either for a total job or the amount of time needed each time the process is ready to use the processor. In the case of round robin, it is assumed that the time quantum is large compared to context-switching overhead and small compared to mean service time. The results depend on the variability that is seen in service times. A common measure of variability is the coefficient of variation, C_s.[1] A value of $C_s = 0$ corresponds to the case where there is no variability: The service times of all processes are equal. Increasing values of C_s correspond to increasing variability among the service times. That is, the larger the value of C_s, the more widely do the values of the services times vary. Values of C_s of 5 or more are not unusual for processor service time distributions

Figure 10.1a compares round-robin throughput to FCFS throughput as a function of C_s. Note that the difference in scheduling algorithms is much smaller in the dual-processor case. With two processors, a single process with long service time is much less disruptive in the FCFS case; other processes can use the other processor. Similar results are shown in Figure 10.1b.

The study in [SAUE81] repeated this analysis under a number of assumptions about degree of multiprogramming, mix of I/O-bound versus CPU-bound processes, and the use of priorities. The general conclusion is that the specific scheduling discipline is much less important with two processors than with one. It should be evident that this conclusion is even stronger as the number of processors increases. Thus, a simple FCFS discipline or the use of FCFS within a static priority scheme may suffice for a multiple-processor system.

Thread Scheduling

As we have seen, with threads, the concept of execution is separated from the rest of the definition of a process. An application can be implemented as a set of threads, which cooperate and execute concurrently in the same address space.

On a uniprocessor, threads can be used as a program structuring aid and to overlap I/O with processing. Because of the minimal penalty in doing a thread switch compared to a process switch, these benefits are realized with little cost.

---

[1]The value of C_s is calculated as σ_s/T_s, where σ_s is the standard deviation of service time and T_s is the mean service time. For a further explanation of C_s, see the discussion in the Queuing Analysis document at **WilliamStallings.com/StudentSupport.html.**

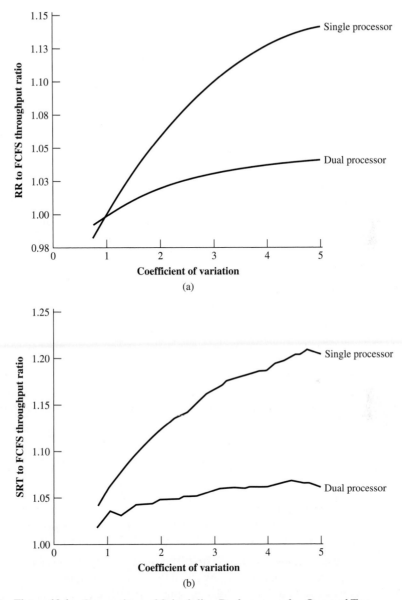

Figure 10.1   Comparison of Scheduling Performance for One and Two Processors

However, the full power of threads becomes evident in a multiprocessor system. In this environment, threads can be used to exploit true parallelism in an application. If the various threads of an application are simultaneously run on separate processors, dramatic gains in performance are possible. However, it can be shown that for applications that require significant interaction among threads (medium-grain parallelism), small differences in thread management and scheduling can have a significant performance impact [ANDE89].

Among the many proposals for multiprocessor thread scheduling and processor assignment, four general approaches stand out:

- **Load sharing:** Processes are not assigned to a particular processor. A global queue of ready threads is maintained, and each processor, when idle, selects a thread from the queue. The term **load sharing** is used to distinguish this strategy from load-balancing schemes in which work is allocated on a more permanent basis (e.g., see [FEIT90a]).[2]

- **Gang scheduling:** A set of related threads is scheduled to run on a set of processors at the same time, on a one-to-one basis.

- **Dedicated processor assignment:** This is the opposite of the load-sharing approach and provides implicit scheduling defined by the assignment of threads to processors. Each program is allocated a number of processors equal to the number of threads in the program, for the duration of the program execution. When the program terminates, the processors return to the general pool for possible allocation to another program.

- **Dynamic scheduling:** The number of threads in a process can be altered during the course of execution.

Load Sharing Load sharing is perhaps the simplest approach and the one that carries over most directly from a uniprocessor environment. It has several advantages:

- The load is distributed evenly across the processors, assuring that no processor is idle while work is available to do.

- No centralized scheduler is required; when a processor is available, the scheduling routine of the operating system is run on that processor to select the next thread.

- The global queue can be organized and accessed using any of the schemes discussed in Chapter 9, including priority-based schemes and schemes that consider execution history or anticipated processing demands,

[LEUT90] analyzes three different versions of load sharing:

- **First come first served (FCFS):** When a job arrives, each of its threads is placed consecutively at the end of the shared queue. When a processor becomes idle, it picks the next ready thread, which it executes until completion or blocking.

- **Smallest number of threads first:** The shared ready queue is organized as a priority queue, with highest priority given to threads from jobs with the smallest number of unscheduled threads. Jobs of equal priority are ordered according to which job arrives first. As with FCFS, a scheduled thread is run to completion or blocking.

- **Preemptive smallest number of threads first:** Highest priority is given to jobs with the smallest number of unscheduled threads. An arriving job with a smaller number of threads than an executing job will preempt threads belonging to the scheduled job.

---

[2]Some of the literature on this topic refers to this approach as *self-scheduling*, because each processor schedules itself without regard to other processors. However, this term is also used in the literature to refer to programs written in a language that allows the programmer to specify the scheduling (e.g., see [FOST91]).

Using simulation models, the authors report that, over a wide range of job charac-teristics, FCFS is superior to the other two policies in the preceding list. Further, the authors find that some form of gang scheduling, discussed in the next subsection, is generally superior to load sharing.

There are several disadvantages of load sharing:

- The central queue occupies a region of memory that must be accessed in a manner that enforces mutual exclusion. Thus, it may become a bottleneck if many processors look for work at the same time. When there is only a small number of processors, this is unlikely to be a noticeable problem. However, when the multiprocessor consists of dozens or even hundreds of processors, the potential for bottleneck is real.
- Preempted threads are unlikely to resume execution on the same processor. If each processor is equipped with a local cache, caching becomes less efficient.
- If all threads are treated as a common pool of threads, it is unlikely that all of the threads of a program will gain access to processors at the same time. If a high degree of coordination is required between the threads of a program, the process switches involved may seriously compromise performance.

Despite the potential disadvantages, this is one of the most commonly used schemes in current multiprocessors.

A refinement of the load-sharing technique is used in the Mach operating sys-tem [BLAC90, WEND89]. The operating system maintains a local run queue for each processor and a shared global run queue. The local run queue is used by threads that have been temporarily bound to a specific processor. A processor examines the local run queue first to give bound threads absolute preference over unbound threads. As an example of the use of bound threads, one or more proces-sors could be dedicated to running processes that are part of the operating system. Another example is that the threads of a particular application could be distributed among a number of processors; with the proper additional software, this provides support for gang scheduling, discussed next.

Gang Scheduling The concept of scheduling a set of processes simultaneously on a set of processors predates the use of threads. [JONE80] refers to the concept as group scheduling and cites the following benefits:

- If closely related processes execute in parallel, synchronization blocking may be reduced, less process switching may be necessary, and performance will increase.
- Scheduling overhead may be reduced because a single decision affects a num-ber of processors and processes at one time.

On the Cm^* multiprocessor, the term *coscheduling* is used [GEHR87]. Cosched-uling is based on the concept of scheduling a related set of tasks, called a task force. The individual elements of a task force tend to be quite small and are hence close to the idea of a thread.

The term *gang scheduling* has been applied to the simultaneous scheduling of the threads that make up a single process [FEIT90b]. Gang scheduling is for medi-um-grain to fine-grain parallel applications whose performance severely degrades when any part of the application is not running while other parts are ready to run. It is also beneficial for any parallel application, even one that is not quite so performance sensitive. The need for gang scheduling is widely recognized, and implementations exist on a variety of multiprocessor operating systems.

One obvious way in which gang scheduling improves the performance of a single application is that process switches are minimized. Suppose one thread of a process is executing and reaches a point at which it must synchronize with another thread of the same process. If that other thread is not running, but is in a ready queue, the first thread is hung up until a process switch can be done on some other processor to bring in the needed thread. In an application with tight coordination among threads, such switches will dramatically reduce performance. The simultaneous scheduling of cooperating threads can also save time in resource allocation. For example, multiple gang-scheduled threads can access a file without the additional overhead of locking during a seek, read/write operation.

The use of gang scheduling creates a requirement for processor allocation. One possibility is the following. Suppose that we have N processors and M applications, each of which has N or fewer threads. Then each application could be given $1/M$ of the available time on the N processors, using time slicing. [FEIT90a] notes that this strategy can be inefficient. Consider an example in which there are two applications, one with four threads and one with one thread. Using uniform time allocation wastes 37.5% of the processing resource, because when the single-thread application runs, three processors are left idle (see Figure 10.2). If there are several one-thread applications, these could all be fit together to increase processor utilization. If that option is not available, an alternative to uniform scheduling is scheduling that is weighted by the number of threads. Thus, the four-thread application could be given 4/5 of the time and the one-thread application given only one-fifth of the time, reducing the processor waste to 15%.

Dedicated Processor Assignment   An extreme form of gang scheduling, suggested in [TUCK89], is to dedicate a group of processors to an application for the duration of the application. That is, when an application is scheduled, each of its threads is assigned a processor that remains dedicated to that thread until the application runs to completion.

This approach would appear to be extremely wasteful of processor time. If a thread of an application is blocked waiting for I/O or for synchronization with another

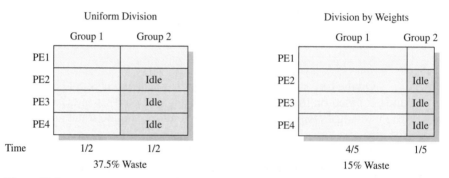

Figure 10.2   Example of Scheduling Groups with Four and One Threads [FEIT90b]

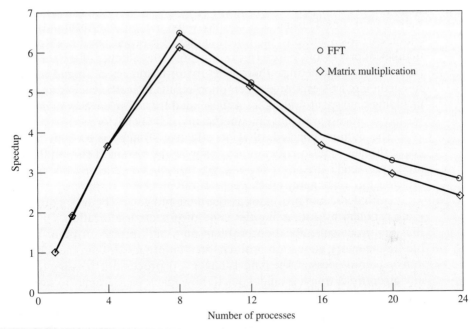

Figure 10.3 Application Speedup as a Function of Number of Processes [TUCK89]

thread, then that thread's processor remains idle: There is no multiprogramming of processors. Two observations can be made in defense of this strategy:

1. In a highly parallel system, with tens or hundreds of processors, each of which represents a small fraction of the cost of the system, processor utilization is no longer so important as a metric for effectiveness or performance.

2. The total avoidance of process switching during the lifetime of a program should result in a substantial speedup of that program.

Both [TUCK89] and [ZAHO90] report analyses that support statement 2. Figure 10.3 shows the results of one experiment [TUCK89]. The authors ran two applications, a matrix multiplication and a fast Fourier transform (FFT) calculation, on a system with 16 processors. Each application breaks its problem into a number of tasks, which are mapped onto the threads executing that application. The programs are written in such a way as to allow the number of threads to be used to vary. In essence, a number of tasks are defined and queued by an application. Tasks are taken from the queue and mapped onto the available threads by the application. If there are fewer threads than tasks, then leftover tasks remain queued and are picked up by threads as they complete their assigned tasks. Clearly, not all applications can be structured in this way, but many numerical problems and some other applications can be dealt with in this fashion.

Figure 10.3 shows the speedup for the applications as the number of threads executing the tasks in each application is varied from 1 to 24. For example, we see that when both applications are started simultaneously with 24 threads each, the speedup obtained, compared to using a single thread for each application, is 2.8 for matrix multiplication and 2.4 for FFT. The figure shows that the performance of both applications worsens considerably when the number of threads in each application exceeds 8 and thus the total number of processes in the system exceeds the number of processors. Furthermore, the larger the number of threads the worse the performance gets, because there is a greater frequency of thread preemption and rescheduling. This excessive preemption results in inefficiency from many sources, including time spent waiting for a suspended thread to leave a critical section, time wasted in process switching, and inefficient cache behavior.

The authors conclude that an effective strategy is to limit the number of active threads to the number of processors in the system. If most of the applications are either single thread or can use the task-queue structure, this will provide an effective and reasonably efficient use of the processor resources.

Both dedicated processor assignment and gang scheduling attack the scheduling problem by addressing the issue of processor allocation. One can observe that the processor allocation problem on a multiprocessor more closely resembles the memory allocation problem on a uniprocessor than the scheduling problem on a uniprocessor. The issue is how many processors to assign to a program at any given time, which is analogous to how many page frames to assign to a given process at any time. [GEHR87] proposes the term *activity working set*, analogous to a virtual memory working set, as the minimum number of activities (threads) that must be scheduled simultaneously on processors for the application to make acceptable progress. As with memory-management schemes, the failure to schedule all of the elements of an activity working set can lead to processor thrashing. This occurs when the scheduling of threads whose services are required induces the descheduling of other threads whose services will soon be needed. Similarly, processor fragmentation refers to a situation in which some processors are left over when others are allocated, and the leftover processors are either insufficient in number or unsuitably organized to support the requirements of waiting applications. Gang scheduling and dedicated processor allocation are meant to avoid these problems.

Dynamic Scheduling For some applications, it is possible to provide language and system tools that permit the number of threads in the process to be altered dynamically. This would allow the operating system to adjust the load to improve utilization.

[ZAHO90] proposes an approach in which both the operating system and the application are involved in making scheduling decisions. The operating system is responsible for partitioning the processors among the jobs. Each job uses the processors currently in its partition to execute some subset of its runnable tasks by mapping these tasks to threads. An appropriate decision about which subset to run, as well as which thread to suspend when a process is preempted, is left to the individual applications (perhaps through a set of run-time library routines). This approach may not be suitable for all applications. However, some applications could default to a single thread while others could be programmed to take advantage of this particular feature of the operating system.

In this approach, the scheduling responsibility of the operating system is primarily limited to processor allocation and proceeds according to the following policy.

When a job requests one or more processors (either when the job arrives for the first time or because its requirements change),

1. If there are idle processors, use them to satisfy the request.

2. Otherwise, if the job making the request is a new arrival, allocate it a single processor by taking one away from any job currently allocated more than one processor.

3. If any portion of the request cannot be satisfied, it remains outstanding until either a processor becomes available for it or the job rescinds the request (e.g., if there is no longer a need for the extra processors).

Upon release of one or more processors (including job departure),

4. Scan the current queue of unsatisfied requests for processors. Assign a single processor to each job in the list that currently has no processors (i.e., to all waiting new arrivals). Then scan the list again, allocating the rest of the processors on an FCFS basis.

Analyses reported in [ZAHO90] and [MAJU88] suggest that for applications that can take advantage of dynamic scheduling, this approach is superior to gang scheduling or dedicated processor assignment. However, the overhead of this approach may negate this apparent performance advantage. Experience with actual systems is needed to prove the worth of dynamic scheduling.

10.2 REAL-TIME SCHEDULING

Background

Real-time computing is becoming an increasingly important discipline. The operating system, and in particular the scheduler, is perhaps the most important component of a real-time system. Examples of current applications of real-time systems include control of laboratory experiments, process control in industrial plants, robotics, air traffic control, telecommunications, and military command and control systems. Next-generation systems will include the autonomous land rover, controllers of robots with elastic joints, systems found in intelligent manufacturing, the space station, and undersea exploration.

Real-time computing may be defined as that type of computing in which the correctness of the system depends not only on the logical result of the computation but also on the time at which the results are produced. We can define a real-time system by defining what is meant by a real-time process, or task.[3] In general, in a real-time system, some of the tasks are real-time tasks, and these have a certain degree of urgency to them. Such tasks are attempting to control or react to events that take

---

[3]As usual, terminology poses a problem, because various words are used in the literature with varying meanings. It is common for a particular process to operate under real-time constraints of a repetitive nature. That is, the process lasts for a long time and, during that time, performs some repetitive function in response to real-time events. Let us, for this section, refer to an individual function as a task. Thus, the process can be viewed as progressing through a sequence of tasks. At any given time, the process is engaged in a single task, and it is the process/task that must be scheduled.

place in the outside world. Because these events occur in "real time," a real-time task must be able to keep up with the events with which it is concerned. Thus, it is usually possible to associate a deadline with a particular task, where the deadline specifies either a start time or a completion time. Such a task may be classified as hard or soft. A **hard real-time task** is one that must meet its deadline; otherwise it will cause unacceptable damage or a fatal error to the system. A **soft real-time task** has an associated deadline that is desirable but not mandatory; it still makes sense to schedule and complete the task even if it has passed its deadline.

Another characteristic of real-time tasks is whether they are periodic or aperiodic. An **aperiodic task** has a deadline by which it must finish or start, or it may have a constraint on both start and finish time. In the case of a **periodic task**, the requirement may be stated as "once per period T" or "exactly T units apart."

Characteristics of Real-Time Operating Systems

Real-time operating systems can be characterized as having unique requirements in five general areas [MORG92]:

- Determinism
- Responsiveness
- User control
- Reliability
- Fail-soft operation

An operating system is **deterministic** to the extent that it performs operations at fixed, predetermined times or within predetermined time intervals. When multiple processes are competing for resources and processor time, no system will be fully deterministic. In a real-time operating system, process requests for service are dictated by external events and timings. The extent to which an operating system can deterministically satisfy requests depends first on the speed with which it can respond to interrupts and, second, on whether the system has sufficient capacity to handle all requests within the required time.

One useful measure of the ability of an operating system to function deterministically is the maximum delay from the arrival of a high-priority device interrupt to when servicing begins. In non-real-time operating systems, this delay may be in the range of tens to hundreds of milliseconds, while in real-time operating systems that delay may have an upper bound of anywhere from a few microseconds to a millisecond.

A related but distinct characteristic is **responsiveness**. Determinism is concerned with how long an operating system delays before acknowledging an interrupt. Responsiveness is concerned with how long, after acknowledgment, it takes an operating system to service the interrupt. Aspects of responsiveness include the following:

1. The amount of time required to initially handle the interrupt and begin execution of the interrupt service routine (ISR). If execution of the ISR requires a process switch, then the delay will be longer than if the ISR can be executed within the context of the current process.

2. The amount of time required to perform the ISR. This generally is dependent on the hardware platform.

3. The effect of interrupt nesting. If an ISR can be interrupted by the arrival of another interrupt, then the service will be delayed.

Determinism and responsiveness together make up the response time to external events. Response time requirements are critical for real-time systems, because such systems must meet timing requirements imposed by individuals, devices, and data flows external to the system.

User control is generally much broader in a real-time operating system than in ordinary operating systems. In a typical non-real-time operating system, the user either has no control over the scheduling function of the operating system or can only provide broad guidance, such as grouping users into more than one priority class. In a real-time system, however, it is essential to allow the user fine-grained control over task priority. The user should be able to distinguish between hard and soft tasks and to specify relative priorities within each class. A real-time system may also allow the user to specify such characteristics as the use of paging or process swapping, what processes must always be resident in main memory, what disk transfer algorithms are to be used, what rights the processes in various priority bands have, and so on.

Reliability is typically far more important for real-time systems than non-real-time systems. A transient failure in a non-real-time system may be solved by simply rebooting the system. A processor failure in a multiprocessor non-real-time system may result in a reduced level of service until the failed processor is repaired or replaced. But a real-time system is responding to and controlling events in real time. Loss or degradation of performance may have catastrophic consequences, ranging from financial loss to major equipment damage and even loss of life.

As in other areas the difference between a real-time and a non-real-time operating system is one of degree. Even a real-time system must be designed to respond to various failure modes. **Fail-soft operation** is a characteristic that refers to the ability of a system to fail in such a way as to preserve as much capability and data as possible. For example, a typical traditional UNIX system, when it detects a corruption of data within the kernel, issues a failure message on the system console, dumps the memory contents to disk for later failure analysis, and terminates execution of the system. In contrast, a real-time system will attempt either to correct the problem or minimize its effects while continuing to run. Typically, the system notifies a user or user process that it should attempt corrective action and then continues operation perhaps at a reduced level of service. In the event a shutdown is necessary, an attempt is made to maintain file and data consistency.

An important aspect of fail-soft operation is referred to as stability. A real-time system is stable if, in cases where it is impossible to meet all task deadlines, the system will meet the deadlines of its most critical, highest-priority tasks, even if some less critical task deadlines are not always met.

To meet the foregoing requirements, real-time operating systems typically include the following features [STAN89]:

- Fast process or thread switch
- Small size (with its associated minimal functionality)

- Ability to respond to external interrupts quickly
- Multitasking with interprocess communication tools such as semaphores, signals, and events
- Use of special sequential files that can accumulate data at a fast rate
- Preemptive scheduling based on priority
- Minimization of intervals during which interrupts are disabled
- Primitives to delay tasks for a fixed amount of time and to pause/resume tasks
- Special alarms and time-outs

The heart of a real-time system is the short-term task scheduler. In designing such a scheduler, fairness and minimizing average response time are not paramount. What is important is that all hard real-time tasks complete (or start) by their deadline and that as many as possible soft real-time tasks also complete (or start) by their deadline.

Most contemporary real-time operating systems are unable to deal directly with deadlines. Instead, they are designed to be as responsive as possible to real-time tasks so that, when a deadline approaches, a task can be quickly scheduled. From this point of view, real-time applications typically require deterministic response times in the several-millisecond to submillisecond span under a broad set of conditions; leading-edge applications—in simulators for military aircraft, for example—often have constraints in the range of 10 to 100 μs [ATLA89].

Figure 10.4 illustrates a spectrum of possibilities. In a preemptive scheduler that uses simple round-robin scheduling, a real-time task would be added to the ready queue to await its next time slice, as illustrated in Figure 10.4a. In this case, the scheduling time will generally be unacceptable for real-time applications. Alternatively, in a nonpreemptive scheduler, we could use a priority scheduling mechanism, giving real-time tasks higher priority. In this case, a real-time task that is ready would be scheduled as soon as the current process blocks or runs to completion (Figure 10.4b). This could lead to a delay of several seconds if a slow, low-priority task were executing at a critical time. Again, this approach is not acceptable. A more promising approach is to combine priorities with clock-based interrupts. Preemption points occur at regular intervals. When a preemption point occurs, the currently running task is preempted if a higher-priority task is waiting. This would include the preemption of tasks that are part of the operating system kernel. Such a delay may be on the order of several milliseconds (Figure 10.4c). While this last approach may be adequate for some real-time applications, it will not suffice for more demanding applications. In those cases, the approach that has been taken is sometimes referred to as immediate preemption. In this case, the operating system responds to an interrupt almost immediately, unless the system is in a critical-code lock-out section. Scheduling delays for a real-time task can then be reduced to 100 μs or less.

Real-Time Scheduling

Real-time scheduling is one of the most active areas of research in computer science. In this subsection, we provide an overview of the various approaches to real-time scheduling and look at two popular classes of scheduling algorithms.

In a survey of real-time scheduling algorithms, [RAMA94] observes that the various scheduling approaches depend on (1) whether a system performs schedulability

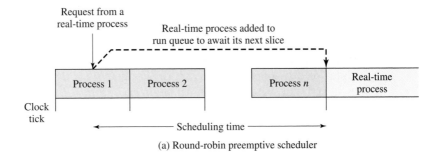

(a) Round-robin preemptive scheduler

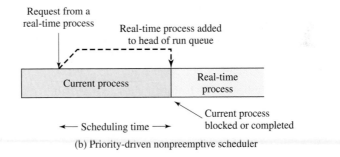

(b) Priority-driven nonpreemptive scheduler

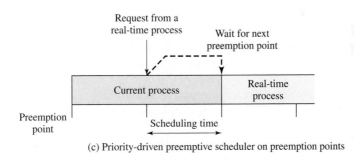

(c) Priority-driven preemptive scheduler on preemption points

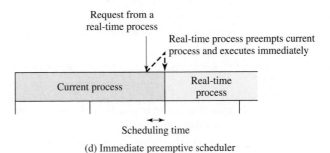

(d) Immediate preemptive scheduler

Figure 10.4   Scheduling of Real-Time Process

analysis; (2) if it does, whether it is done statically or dynamically; and (3) whether the result of the analysis itself produces a schedule or plan according to which tasks are dispatched at run time. Based on these considerations, the authors identify the following classes of algorithms:

- **Static table-driven approaches:** These perform a static analysis of feasible schedules of dispatching. The result of the analysis is a schedule that determines, at run time, when a task must begin execution.

- **Static priority-driven preemptive approaches:** Again, a static analysis is performed, but no schedule is drawn up. Rather, the analysis is used to assign priorities to tasks, so that a traditional priority-driven preemptive scheduler can be used.

- **Dynamic planning-based approaches:** Feasibility is determined at run time (dynamically) rather than offline prior to the start of execution (statically). An arriving task is accepted for execution only if it is feasible to meet its time constraints. One of the results of the feasibility analysis is a schedule or plan that is used to decide when to dispatch this task.

- **Dynamic best effort approaches:** No feasibility analysis is performed. The system tries to meet all deadlines and aborts any started process whose deadline is missed.

Static table-driven scheduling is applicable to tasks that are periodic. Input to the analysis consists of the periodic arrival time, execution time, periodic ending deadline, and relative priority of each task. The scheduler attempts to develop a schedule that enables it to meet the requirements of all periodic tasks. This is a predictable approach but one that is inflexible, because any change to any task requirements requires that the schedule be redone. Earliest-deadline-first or other periodic deadline techniques (discussed subsequently) are typical of this category of scheduling algorithms.

Static priority-driven preemptive scheduling makes use of the priority-driven preemptive scheduling mechanism common to most non-real-time multiprogramming systems. In a non-real-time system, a variety of factors might be used to determine priority. For example, in a time-sharing system, the priority of a process changes depending on whether it is processor bound or I/O bound. In a real-time system, priority assignment is related to the time constraints associated with each task. One example of this approach is the rate monotonic algorithm (discussed subsequently), which assigns static priorities to tasks based on the length of their periods.

With **dynamic planning-based scheduling**, after a task arrives, but before its execution begins, an attempt is made to create a schedule that contains the previously scheduled tasks as well as the new arrival. If the new arrival can be scheduled in such a way that its deadlines are satisfied and that no currently scheduled task misses a deadline, then the schedule is revised to accommodate the new task.

Dynamic best effort scheduling is the approach used by many real-time systems that are currently commercially available. When a task arrives, the system assigns a priority based on the characteristics of the task. Some form of deadline scheduling, such as earliest-deadline scheduling, is typically used. Typically, the tasks are aperiodic and so no static scheduling analysis is possible. With this type of scheduling, until a deadline arrives or until the task completes, we do not know whether a timing constraint will be met. This is the major disadvantage of this form of scheduling. Its advantage is that it is easy to implement.

Deadline Scheduling

Most contemporary real-time operating systems are designed with the objective of starting real-time tasks as rapidly as possible, and hence emphasize rapid interrupt handling and task dispatching. In fact, this is not a particularly useful metric in evaluating real-time operating systems. Real-time applications are generally not concerned with sheer speed but rather with completing (or starting) tasks at the most valuable times, neither too early nor too late, despite dynamic resource demands and conflicts, processing overloads, and hardware or software faults. It follows that priorities provide a crude tool and do not capture the requirement of completion (or initiation) at the most valuable time.

There have been a number of proposals for more powerful and appropriate approaches to real-time task scheduling. All of these are based on having additional information about each task. In its most general form, the following information about each task might be used:

- **Ready time:** Time at which task becomes ready for execution. In the case of a repetitive or periodic task, this is actually a sequence of times that is known in advance. In the case of an aperiodic task, this time may be known in advance, or the operating system may only be aware when the task is actually ready.
- **Starting deadline:** Time by which a task must begin.
- **Completion deadline:** Time by which task must be completed. The typical real-time application will either have starting deadlines or completion deadlines, but not both.
- **Processing time:** Time required to execute the task to completion. In some cases, this is supplied. In others, the operating system measures an exponential average (as defined in Chapter 9). For still other scheduling systems, this information is not used.
- **Resource requirements:** Set of resources (other than the processor) required by the task while it is executing.
- **Priority:** Measures relative importance of the task. Hard real-time tasks may have an "absolute" priority, with the system failing if a deadline is missed. If the system is to continue to run no matter what, then both hard and soft real-time tasks may be assigned relative priorities as a guide to the scheduler.
- **Subtask structure:** A task may be decomposed into a mandatory subtask and an optional subtask. Only the mandatory subtask possesses a hard deadline.

There are several dimensions to the real-time scheduling function when deadlines are taken into account: which task to schedule next, and what sort of preemption is allowed. It can be shown, for a given preemption strategy and using either starting or completion deadlines, that a policy of scheduling the task with the earliest deadline minimizes the fraction of tasks that miss their deadlines [BUTT99, HONG89, PANW88]. This conclusion holds both for single-processor and multiprocessor configurations.

The other critical design issue is that of preemption. When starting deadlines are specified, then a nonpreemptive scheduler makes sense. In this case, it would be the responsibility of the real-time task to block itself after completing the mandatory or critical portion of its execution, allowing other real-time starting deadlines to be satisfied. This fits the pattern of Figure 10.4b. For a system with completion deadlines, a preemptive strategy (Figure 10.4c or d) is most appropriate. For example, if task X is running and task Y is ready, there may be circumstances in which the only way to allow both X and Y to meet their completion deadlines is to preempt X, execute Y to completion, and then resume X to completion.

As an example of scheduling periodic tasks with completion deadlines, consider a system that collects and processes data from two sensors, A and B. The deadline for collecting data from sensor A must be met every 20 ms, and that for B every 50 ms. It takes 10 ms, including operating system overhead, to process each sample of data from A and 25 ms to process each sample of data from B. Table 10.2 summarizes the execution profile of the two tasks. Figure 10.5 compares three scheduling techniques using the execution profile of Table 10.2. The first row of Figure 10.5 repeats the information in Table 10.2; the remaining three rows illustrate three scheduling techniques.

The computer is capable of making a scheduling decision every 10 ms. Suppose that, under these circumstances, we attempted to use a priority scheduling scheme. The first two timing diagrams in Figure 10.5 show the result. If A has higher priority, the first instance of task B is only given 20 ms of processing time, in two 10-ms chunks, by the time its deadline is reached, and thus fails. If B is given higher priority, then A will miss its first deadline. The final timing diagram shows the use of earliest-deadline scheduling. At time $t = 0$, both A1 and B1 arrive. Because A1 has the earliest deadline, it is scheduled first. When A1 completes, B1 is given the processor.

Table 10.2 Execution Profile of Two Periodic Tasks

Process	Arrival Time	Execution Time	Ending Deadline
A(1)	0	10	20
A(2)	20	10	40
A(3)	40	10	60
A(4)	60	10	80
A(5)	80	10	100
•	•	•	•
•	•	•	•
•	•	•	•
B(1)	0	25	50
B(2)	50	25	100
•	•	•	•
•	•	•	•
•	•	•	•

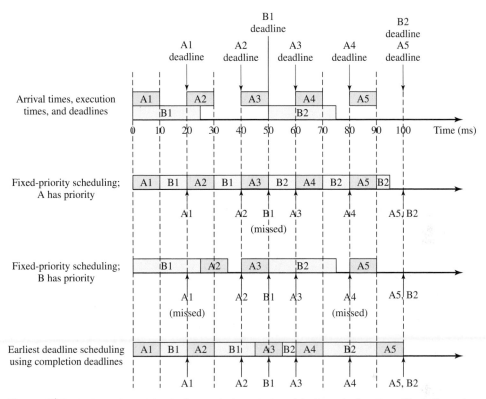

Figure 10.5   Scheduling of Periodic Real-time Tasks with Completion Deadlines (based on Table 10.2)

At $t = 20$, A2 arrives. Because A2 has an earlier deadline than B1, B1 is interrupted so that A2 can execute to completion. Then B1 is resumed at $t = 30$. At $t = 40$, A3 arrives. However, B1 has an earlier ending deadline and is allowed to execute to completion at $t = 45$. A3 is then given the processor and finishes at $t = 55$.

In this example, by scheduling to give priority at any preemption point to the task with the nearest deadline, all system requirements can be met. Because the tasks are periodic and predictable, a static table-driven scheduling approach is used.

Now consider a scheme for dealing with aperiodic tasks with starting deadlines. The top part of Figure 10.6 shows the arrival times and starting deadlines for an example consisting of five tasks each of which has an execution time of 20 ms. Table 10.3 summarizes the execution profile of the five tasks.

A straightforward scheme is to always schedule the ready task with the earliest deadline and let that task run to completion. When this approach is used in the example of Figure 10.6, note that although task B requires immediate service, the service is denied. This is the risk in dealing with aperiodic tasks, especially with starting deadlines. A refinement of the policy will improve performance if deadlines can be known in advance of the time that a task is ready. This policy, referred to as earliest deadline with unforced idle times, operates as follows: Always schedule the eligible task with the earliest deadline and let that task run to completion.

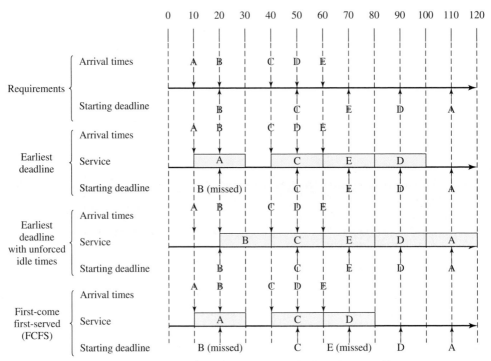

Figure 10.6 Scheduling of Aperiodic Real-Time Tasks with Starting Deadlines

Table 10.3 Execution Profile of Five Aperiodic Tasks

Process	Arrival Time	Execution Time	Starting Deadline
A	10	20	110
B	20	20	20
C	40	20	50
D	50	20	90
E	60	20	70

An eligible task may not be ready, and this may result in the processor remaining idle even though there are ready tasks. Note that in our example the system refrains from scheduling task A even though that is the only ready task. The result is that, even though the processor is not used to maximum efficiency, all scheduling requirements are met. Finally, for comparison, the FCFS policy is shown. In this case, tasks B and E do not meet their deadlines.

Rate Monotonic Scheduling

One of the more promising methods of resolving multitask scheduling conflicts for periodic tasks is rate monotonic scheduling (RMS). The scheme was first proposed

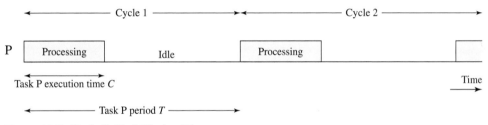

Figure 10.7 Periodic Task Timing Diagram

in [LIU73] but has only recently gained popularity [BRIA99, SHA94]. RMS assigns priorities to tasks on the basis of their periods.

Figure 10.7 illustrates the relevant parameters for periodic tasks. The task's period, T, is the amount of time between the arrival of one instance of the task and the arrival of the next instance of the task. A task's rate (in Hertz) is simply the inverse of its period (in seconds). For example, a task with a period of 50 ms occurs at a rate of 20 Hz. Typically, the end of a task's period is also the task's hard deadline, although some tasks may have earlier deadlines. The execution (or computation) time, C, is the amount of processing time required for each occurrence of the task. It should be clear that in a uniprocessor system, the execution time must be no greater than the period (must have $C \leq T$). If a periodic task is always run to completion, that is, if no instance of the task is ever denied service because of insufficient resources, then the utilization of the processor by this task is $U = C/T$. For example, if a task has a period of 80 ms and an execution time of 55 ms, its processor utilization is 55/80 = 0.6875.

For RMS, the highest-priority task is the one with the shortest period, the second highest-priority task is the one with the second shortest period, and so on. When more than one task is available for execution, the one with the shortest period is serviced first. If we plot the priority of tasks as a function of their rate, the result is a monotonically increasing function (Figure 10.8); hence the name, rate monotonic scheduling.

One measure of the effectiveness of a periodic scheduling algorithm is whether or not it guarantees that all hard deadlines are met. Suppose that we have n tasks, each with a fixed period and execution time. Then for it to be possible to meet all deadlines, the following inequality must hold:

$$\frac{C_1}{T_1} + \frac{C_2}{T_2} + \cdots + \frac{C_n}{T_n} \leq 1 \tag{10.1}$$

The sum of the processor utilizations of the individual tasks cannot exceed a value of 1, which corresponds to total utilization of the processor. Equation (10.1) provides a bound on the number of tasks that a perfect scheduling algorithm can successfully schedule. For any particular algorithm, the bound may be lower. For RMS, it can be shown that the following inequality holds:

$$\frac{C_1}{T_1} + \frac{C_2}{T_2} + \cdots + \frac{C_n}{T_n} \leq n(2^{1/n} - 1) \tag{10.2}$$

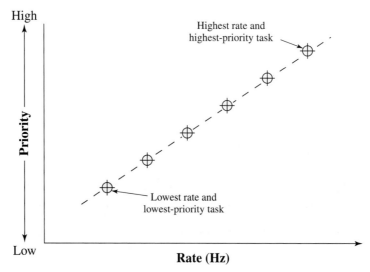

Figure 10.8   A Task Set with RMS [WARR91]

Table 10.4   Value of the RMS Upper Bound

n	$n(2^{1/n} - 1)$
1	1.0
2	0.828
3	0.779
4	0.756
5	0.743
6	0.734
•	•
•	•
•	•
∞	$\ln 2 \approx 0.693$

Table 10.4 gives some values for this upper bound. As the number of tasks increases, the scheduling bound converges to $\ln 2 \approx 0.693$.

As an example, consider the case of three periodic tasks, where $U_i = C_i/T_i$:

- Task P_1: $C_1 = 20$; $T_1 = 100$; $U_1 = 0.2$
- Task P_2: $C_2 = 40$; $T_2 = 150$; $U_2 = 0.267$
- Task P_3: $C_3 = 100$; $T_3 = 350$; $U_3 = 0.286$

The total utilization of these three tasks is $0.2 + 0.267 + 0.286 = 0.753$. The upper bound for the schedulability of these three tasks using RMS is

$$\frac{C_1}{T_1} + \frac{C_2}{T_2} + \frac{C_3}{T_3} \leq 3(2^{1/3} - 1) = 0.779$$

Because the total utilization required for the three tasks is less than the upper bound for RMS (0.753 < 0.779), we know that if RMS is used, all tasks will be successfully scheduled.

It can also be shown that the upper bound of Equation (10.1) holds for earliest deadline scheduling. Thus, it is possible to achieve greater overall processor utilization and therefore accommodate more periodic tasks with earliest deadline scheduling. Nevertheless, RMS has been widely adopted for use in industrial applications. [SHA91] offers the following explanation:

1. The performance difference is small in practice. The upper bound of Equation (10.2) is a conservative one and, in practice, utilization as high as 90% is often achieved.

2. Most hard real-time systems also have soft real-time components, such as certain noncritical displays and built-in self-tests that can execute at lower priority levels to absorb the processor time that is not used with RMS scheduling of hard real-time tasks.

3. Stability is easier to achieve with RMS. When a system cannot meet all deadlines because of overload or transient errors, the deadlines of essential tasks need to be guaranteed provided that this subset of tasks is schedulable. In a static priority assignment approach, one only needs to ensure that essential tasks have relatively high priorities. This can be done in RMS by structuring essential tasks to have short periods or by modifying the RMS priorities to account for essential tasks. With earliest deadline scheduling, a periodic task's priority changes from one period to another. This makes it more difficult to ensure that essential tasks meet their deadlines.

Priority Inversion

Priority inversion is a phenomenon that can occur in any priority-based preemptive scheduling scheme but is particularly relevant in the context of real-time scheduling. The best-known instance of priority inversion involved the Mars Pathfinder mission. This rover robot landed on Mars on July 4, 1997 and began gathering and transmitting voluminous data back to Earth. But a few days into the mission, the lander software began experiencing total system resets, each resulting in losses of data. After much effort by the Jet Propulsion Laboratory (JPL) team that built the Pathfinder, the problem was traced to priority inversion [JONE97].

In any priority scheduling scheme, the system should always be executing the task with the highest priority. **Priority inversion** occurs when circumstances within the system force a higher-priority task to wait for a lower-priority task. A simple example of priority inversion occurs if a lower-priority task has locked a resource (such as a device or a binary semaphore) and a higher-priority task attempts to lock that same resource. The higher-priority task will be put in a blocked state until the resource is available. If the lower-priority task soon finishes with the resource and releases it, the higher-priority task may quickly resume and it is possible that no real-time constraints are violated.

A more serious condition is referred to as an **unbounded priority inversion**, in which the duration of a priority inversion depends not only on the time required to handle a shared resource but also on the unpredictable actions of other unrelated tasks as well. The priority inversion experienced in the Pathfinder software was unbounded and serves as a good example of the phenomenon. Our discussion follows that of [TIME02]. The Pathfinder software included the following three tasks, in decreasing order of priority:

T_1: Periodically checks the health of the spacecraft systems and software

T_2: Processes image data

T_3: Performs an occasional test on equipment status

After T_1 executes, it reinitializes a timer to its maximum value. If this timer ever expires, it is assumed that the integrity of the lander software has somehow been compromised. The processor is halted, all devices are reset, the software is completely reloaded, the spacecraft systems are tested, and the system starts over. This recovery sequence does not complete until the next day. T_1 and T_3 share a common data structure, protected by a binary semaphore **s**. Figure 10.9a shows the sequence that caused the priority inversion:

t_1: T_3 begins executing.

t_2: T_3 locks semaphore **s** and enters its critical section.

t_3: T_1, which has a higher priority than T_3, preempts T_3 and begins executing.

t_4: T_1 attempts to enter its critical section but is blocked because the semaphore is locked by T_3; T_3 resumes execution in its critical section.

t_5: T_2, which has a higher priority than T_3, preempts T_3 and begins executing.

t_6: T_2 is suspended for some reason unrelated to T_1 and T_2, and T_3 resumes.

t_7: T_3 leaves its critical section and unlocks the semaphore. T_1 preempts T_3, locks the semaphore, and enters its critical section.

In this set of circumstances, T_1 must wait for both T_3 and T_2 to complete and fails to reset the timer before it expires.

In practical systems, two alternative approaches are used to avoid unbounded priority inversion: priority inheritance protocol and priority ceiling protocol.

The basic idea of **priority inheritance** is that a lower-priority task inherits the priority of any higher-priority task pending on a resource they share. This priority change takes place as soon as the higher-priority task blocks on the resource; it should end when the resource is released by the lower-priority task. Figure 10.9b shows that priority inheritance resolves the problem of unbounded priority inversion illustrated in Figure 10.9a. The relevant sequence of events is as follows:

t_1: T_3 begins executing.

t_2: T_3 locks semaphore **s** and enters its critical section.

t_3: T_1, which has a higher priority than T_3, preempts T_3 and begins executing.

t_4: T_1 attempts to enter its critical section but is blocked because the semaphore is locked by T_3. T_3 is immediately and temporarily assigned the same priority as T_1. T_3 resumes execution in its critical section.

t_5: T_2 is ready to execute but, because T_3 now has a higher priority, T_2 is unable to preempt T_3.

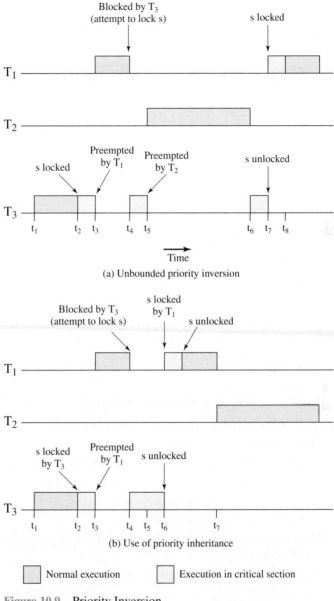

Figure 10.9   Priority Inversion

t_6: T_3 leaves its critical section and unlocks the semaphore: Its priority level is downgraded to its previous default level. T_1 preempts T_3, locks the semaphore, and enters its critical section.

t_7: T_1 is suspended for some reason unrelated to T_2, and T_2 begins executing.

In the **priority ceiling** approach, a priority is associated with each resource. The priority assigned to a resource is one level higher than the priority of its highest-priority user. The scheduler then dynamically assigns this priority to any task that accesses the resource. Once the task finishes with the resource, its priority returns to normal.

10.3 LINUX SCHEDULING

For Linux 2.4 and earlier, Linux provided a real-time scheduling capability coupled with a scheduler for non-real-time processes that made use of the traditional UNIX scheduling algorithm described in Section 9.3. Linux 2.6 includes essentially the same real-time scheduling capability as previous releases and a substantially revised scheduler for non-real-time processes. We examine these two areas in turn.

Real–Time Scheduling

The three Linux scheduling classes are as follows:

- **SCHED_FIFO:** First-in-first-out real-time threads
- **SCHED_RR:** Round-robin real-time threads
- **SCHED_OTHER:** Other, non-real-time threads

Within each class, multiple priorities may be used, with priorities in the real-time classes higher than the priorities for the SCHED_OTHER class. The default values are as follows: Real-time priority classes range from 0 to 99 inclusively, and SCHED_OTHER classes range from 100 to 139. A lower number equals a higher priority.

For FIFO threads, the following rules apply:

1. The system will not interrupt an executing FIFO thread except in the following cases:
   (a) Another FIFO thread of higher priority becomes ready.
   (b) The executing FIFO thread becomes blocked waiting for an event, such as I/O.
   (c) The executing FIFO thread voluntarily gives up the processor following a call to the primitive sched_yield.
2. When an executing FIFO thread is interrupted, it is placed in the queue associated with its priority.
3. When a FIFO thread becomes ready and if that thread has a higher priority than the currently executing thread, then the currently executing thread is preempted and the highest-priority ready FIFO thread is executed. If more than one thread has that highest priority, the thread that has been waiting the longest is chosen.

The SCHED_RR policy is similar to the SCHED_FIFO policy, except for the addition of a timeslice associated with each thread. When a SCHED_RR thread has executed for its timeslice, it is suspended and a real-time thread of equal or higher priority is selected for running.

Figure 10.10 is an example that illustrates the distinction between FIFO and RR scheduling. Assume a process has four threads with three relative priorities

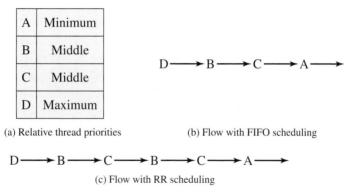

(a) Relative thread priorities   (b) Flow with FIFO scheduling

(c) Flow with RR scheduling

Figure 10.10   Example of Linux Real-Time Scheduling

assigned as shown in Figure 10.10a. Assume that all waiting threads are ready to execute when the current thread waits or terminates and that no higher-priority thread is awakened while a thread is executing. Figure 10.10b shows a flow in which all of the threads are in the SCHED_FIFO class. Thread D executes until it waits or terminates. Next, although threads B and C have the same priority, thread B starts because it has been waiting longer than thread C. Thread B executes until it waits or terminates; then thread C executes until it waits or terminates. Finally, thread A executes.

Figure 10.10c shows a sample flow if all of the threads are in the SCHED_RR class. Thread D executes until it waits or terminates. Next, threads B and C are time sliced, because they both have the same priority. Finally, thread A executes.

The final scheduling class is SCHED_OTHER. A thread in this class can only execute if there are no real-time threads ready to execute.

Non–Real-Time Scheduling

The Linux 2.4 scheduler for the SCHED_OTHER class did not scale well with increasing number of processors and increasing number of processes. To address this problem, Linux 2.6 uses a completely new scheduler known as the O(1) scheduler.[4] The scheduler is designed so that the time to select the appropriate process and assign it to a processor is constant, regardless of the load on the system or the number of processors.

The kernel maintains two scheduling data structure for each processor in the system, of the following form (Figure 10.11):

```
struct prio_array {
    int              nr_active;             /* number of tasks in this array */
    unsigned long    bitmap[BITMAP_SIZE];   /* priority bitmap */
    struct list_head queue[MAX_PRIO];       /* priority queues */
```

---

[4]The term O(1) is an example of the "big-O" notation, used for characterizing the time complexity of algorithms. An explanation of this notation is contained in a supporting document at this book's Web site.

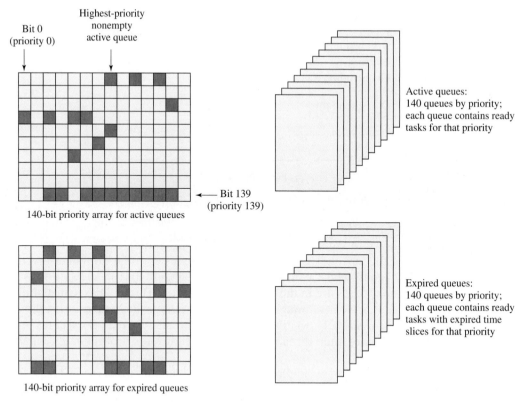

Figure 10.11   Linux Scheduling Data Structures for Each Processor

A separate queue is maintained for each priority level. The total number of queues in the structure is **MAX_PRIO**, which has a default value of 140. The structure also includes a bitmap array of sufficient size to provide one bit per priority level. Thus, with 140 priority levels and 32-bit words, **BITMAP_SIZE** has a value of 5. This creates a bitmap of 160 bits, of which 20 bits are ignored. The bitmap indicates which queues are not empty. Finally, **nr_active** indicates the total number of tasks present on all queues. Two structures are maintained: an active queues structure and an expired queues structure.

Initially, both bitmaps are set to all zeroes and all queues are empty. As a process becomes ready, it is assigned to the appropriate priority queue in the active queues structure and is assigned the appropriate timeslice. If a task is preempted before it completes its timeslice, it is returned to an active queue. When a task completes its timeslice, it goes into the appropriate queue in the expired queues structure and is assigned a new timeslice. All scheduling is done from among tasks in the active queues structure. When the active queues structure is empty, a simple pointer assignment results in a switch of the active and expired queues, and scheduling continues.

Scheduling is simple and efficient. On a given processor, the scheduler picks the highest-priority nonempty queue. If multiple tasks are in that queue, the tasks are scheduled in round-robin fashion.

Linux also includes a mechanism for moving a tasks from the queue lists of one processor to that of another. Periodically, the scheduler checks to see if there is a substantial imbalance among the number of tasks assigned to each processor. To balance the load, the schedule can transfer some tasks. The highest-priority active tasks are selected for transfer, because it is more important to distribute high-priority tasks fairly.

Calculating Priorities and Timeslices Each non-real-time task is assigned an initial priority in the range of 100 to 139, with a default of 120. This is the task's static priority and is specified by the user. As the task executes, a dynamic priority is calculated as a function of the task's static priority and its execution behavior. The Linux scheduler is designed to favor I/O-bound tasks over processor-bound tasks. This preference tends to provide good interactive response. The technique used by Linux to determine the dynamic priority is to keep a running tab on how much time a process sleeps (waiting for an event) versus how much time the process runs. In essence, a task that spends most of its time sleeping is given a higher priority.

Timeslices are assigned in the range of 10 ms to 200 ms. In general, higher-priority tasks are assigned larger timeslices.

Relationship to Real-Time Tasks Real-time tasks are handled in a different manner from non-real-time tasks in the priority queues. The following considerations apply:

1. All real-time tasks have only a static priority; no dynamic priority changes are made.
2. SCHED_FIFO tasks do not have assigned timeslices. Such tasks are scheduled in FIFO discipline. If a SHED_FIFO task is blocked, it returns to the same priority queue in the active queue list when it becomes unblocked.
3. Although SCHED_RR tasks do have assigned timeslices, they also are never moved to the expired queue list. When a SCHED_RR task exhaust its timeslice, it is returned to its priority queue with the same timeslice value. Timeslice values are never changed.

The effect of these rules is that the switch between the active queue list and the expired queue list only happens when there are no ready real-time tasks waiting to execute.

10.4 UNIX SVR4 SCHEDULING

The scheduling algorithm used in UNIX SVR4 is a complete overhaul of the scheduling algorithm used in earlier UNIX systems (described in Section 9.3). The new algorithm is designed to give highest preference to real-time processes, next-highest preference to kernel-mode processes, and lowest preference to other user-mode processes, referred to as time-shared processes.

The two major modifications implemented in SVR4 are as follows:

1. The addition of a preemptable static priority scheduler and the introduction of a set of 160 priority levels divided into three priority classes.

2. The insertion of preemption points. Because the basic kernel is not preemptive, it can only be split into processing steps that must run to completion without interruption. In between the processing steps, safe places known as preemption points have been identified where the kernel can safely interrupt processing and schedule a new process. A safe place is defined as a region of code where all kernel data structures are either updated and consistent or locked via a semaphore.

Figure 10.12 illustrates the 160 priority levels defined in SVR4. Each process is defined to belong to one of three priority classes and is assigned a priority level within that class. The classes are as follows:

- **Real time (159–100):** Processes at these priority levels are guaranteed to be selected to run before any kernel or time-sharing process. In addition, real-time processes can make use of preemption points to preempt kernel processes and user processes.

- **Kernel (99–60):** Processes at these priority levels are guaranteed to be selected to run before any time-sharing process but must defer to real-time processes.

- **Time-shared (59–0):** The lowest-priority processes, intended for user applications other than real-time applications.

Figure 10.13 indicates how scheduling is implemented in SVR4. A dispatch queue is associated with each priority level, and processes at a given priority level are executed in round-robin fashion. A bit-map vector, **dqactmap**, contains one bit for each priority level; the bit is set to one for any priority level with a nonempty queue. Whenever a running process leaves the Running state, due to a block, timeslice expiration, or preemption, the dispatcher checks **dqactmap** and dispatches a ready process from the highest-priority nonempty queue. In addition, whenever a defined

Priority Class	Global Value	Scheduling Sequence
	159	First
Real time	•	
	•	
	•	
	100	
p Kernel	99	
	•	
	•	
	60	
Time shared	59	
	•	
	•	
	•	
	•	
	0	Last

Figure 10.12 SVR4 Priority Classes

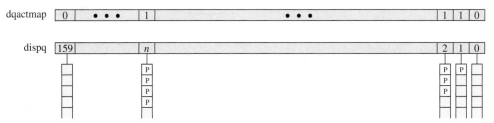

Figure 10.13 SVR4 Dispatch Queues

preemption point is reached, the kernel checks a flag called **kprunrun**. If set, this indicates that at least one real-time process is in the Ready state, and the kernel preempts the current process if it is of lower priority than the highest-priority real-time ready process.

Within the time-sharing class, the priority of a process is variable. The scheduler reduces the priority of a process each time it uses up a time quantum, and it raises its priority if it blocks on an event or resource. The time quantum allocated to a time-sharing process depends on its priority, ranging from 100 ms for priority 0 to 10 ms for priority 59. Each real-time process has a fixed priority and a fixed time quantum.

10.5 WINDOWS SCHEDULING

Windows is designed to be as responsive as possible to the needs of a single user in a highly interactive environment or in the role of a server. Windows implements a preemptive scheduler with a flexible system of priority levels that includes round-robin scheduling within each level and, for some levels, dynamic priority variation on the basis of their current thread activity.

Process and Thread Priorities

Priorities in Windows are organized into two bands, or classes: real time and variable. Each of these bands consists of 16 priority levels. Threads requiring immediate attention are in the real-time class, which includes functions such as communications and real-time tasks.

Overall, because Windows makes use of a priority-driven preemptive scheduler, threads with real-time priorities have precedence over other threads. On a uniprocessor, when a thread becomes ready whose priority is higher than the currently executing thread, the lower-priority thread is preempted and the processor given to the higher-priority thread.

Priorities are handled somewhat differently in the two classes (Figure 10.14). In the real-time priority class, all threads have a fixed priority that never changes. All of the active threads at a given priority level are in a round-robin queue. In the variable priority class, a thread's priority begins at some initial assigned value and then may change, up or down, during the thread's lifetime. Thus, there is a FIFO queue at each priority level, but a process may migrate to one of the other queues

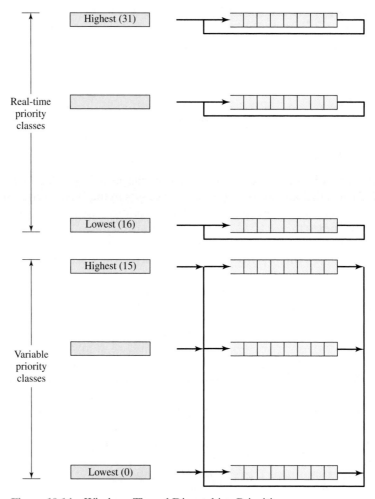

Figure 10.14 Windows Thread Dispatching Priorities

within the variable priority class. However, a thread at priority level 15 cannot be promoted to level 16 or any other level in the real-time class.

The initial priority of a thread in the variable priority class is determined by two quantities: process base priority and thread base priority. One of the attributes of a process object is process base priority, which can take on any value from 0 through 15. Each thread object associated with a process object has a thread base priority attribute that indicates the thread's base priority relative to that of the process. The thread's base priority can be equal to that of its process or within two levels above or below that of the process. So, for example, if a process has a base priority of 4 and one of its threads has a base priority of −1, then the initial priority of that thread is 3.

Once a thread in the variable priority class has been activated, its actual priority, referred to as the thread's dynamic priority, may fluctuate within given

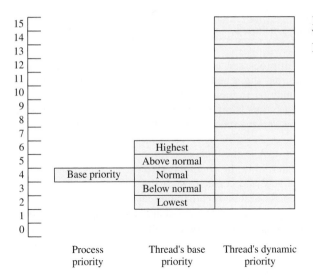

Figure 10.15 Example of Windows Priority Relationship

boundaries. The dynamic priority may never fall below the lower range of the thread's base priority and it may never exceed 15. Figure 10.15 gives an example. The process object has a base priority attribute of 4. Each thread object associated with this process object must have an initial priority of between 2 and 6. The dynamic priority for each thread may fluctuate in the range from 2 through 15. If a thread is interrupted because it has used up its current time quantum, the Windows executive lowers its priority. If a thread is interrupted to wait on an I/O event, the Windows executive raises its priority. Thus, processor-bound threads tend toward lower priorities and I/O-bound threads tend toward higher priorities. In the case of I/O-bound threads, the executive raises the priority more for interactive waits (e.g., wait on keyboard or display) than for other types of I/O (e.g., disk I/O). Thus, interactive threads tend to have the highest priorities within the variable priority class.

Multiprocessor Scheduling

When Windows is run on a single processor, the highest-priority thread is always active unless it is waiting on an event. If there is more than one thread that has the highest priority, then the processor is shared, round robin, among all the threads at that priority level. In a multiprocessor system with N processors, the $(N - 1)$ highest priority threads are always active, running exclusively on the $(N - 1)$ extra processors. The remaining, lower-priority, threads share the single remaining processor. For example, if there are three processors, the two highest-priority threads run on two processors, while all remaining threads run on the remaining processor.

The foregoing discipline is affected by the processor affinity attribute of a thread. If a thread is ready to execute but the only available processors are not in its processor affinity set, then that thread is forced to wait, and the executive schedules the next available thread.

10.6 SUMMARY

With a tightly coupled multiprocessor, multiple processors have access to the same main memory. In this configuration, the scheduling structure is somewhat more complex. For example, a given process may be assigned to the same processor for its entire life or dispatched to any processor each time it enters the Running state. Performance studies suggest that the differences among various scheduling algorithms are less significant in a multiprocessor system.

A real-time process or task is one that is executed in connection with some process or function or set of events external to the computer system and that must meet one or more deadlines to interact effectively and correctly with the external environment. A real-time operating system is one that is capable of managing real-time processes. In this context, the traditional criteria for a scheduling algorithm do not apply. Rather, the key factor is the meeting of deadlines. Algorithms that rely heavily on preemption and on reacting to relative deadlines are appropriate in this context.

10.7 RECOMMENDED READINGS

[WEND89] is an interesting discussion of approaches to multiprocessor scheduling. A good treatment of real-time scheduling is contained in [LIU00]. The following collections of papers all contain important articles on real-time operating systems and scheduling: [KRIS94], [STAN93], [LEE93], and [TILB91]. [SHA90] provides a good explanation of priority inversion, priority inheritance, and priority ceiling. [ZEAD97] analyzes the performance of the SVR4 real-time scheduler. [LIND04] provides an overview of the Linux 2.6 scheduler; [LOVE04] contains a more detailed discussion.

KRIS94   Krishna, C., and Lee, Y., eds. "Special Issue on Real-Time Systems." *Proceedings of the IEEE*, January 1994.

LEE93   Lee, Y., and Krishna, C., eds. *Readings in Real-Time Systems.* Los Alamitos, CA: IEEE Computer Society Press, 1993.

LIND04   Lindsley, R. "What's New in the 2.6 Scheduler." *Linux Journal*, March 2004.

LIU00   Liu, J. *Real-Time Systems.* Upper Saddle River, NJ: Prentice Hall, 2000.

LOVE04   Love, R. *Linux Kernel Development.* Indianapolis, IN: Sams Publishing, 2004.

SHA90   Sha, L.; Rajkumar, R.; and Lehoczky, J. "Priority Inheritance Protocols: An Approach to Real-Time Synchronization." *IEEE Transactions on Computers*, September 1990.

STAN93   Stankovic, J., and Ramamritham, K., eds. *Advances in Real-Time Systems.* Los Alamitos, CA: IEEE Computer Society Press, 1993.

TILB91   Tilborg, A., and Koob, G.. eds. *Foundations of Real-Time Computing: Scheduling and Resource Management.* Boston: Kluwer Academic Publishers, 1991.

WEND89   Wendorf, J.; Wendorf, R.; and Tokuda, H. "Scheduling Operating System Processing on Small-Scale Microprocessors." *Proceedings, 22nd Annual Hawaii International Conference on System Science*, January 1989.

ZEAD97   Zeadally, S. "An Evaluation of the Real-Time Performance of SVR4.0 and SVR4.2." *Operating Systems Review*, January 1977.

10.8 KEY TERMS, REVIEW QUESTIONS, AND PROBLEMS

Key Terms

aperiodic task	hard real-time task	real-time scheduling
deadline scheduling	load sharing	responsiveness
deterministic operating system	periodic task	soft real-time task
fail-soft operation	priority inversion	thread scheduling
gang scheduling	rate monotonic scheduling	unbounded priority inversion
granularity	real-time operating system	

Review Questions

10.1 List and briefly define five different categories of synchronization granularity.

10.2 List and briefly define four techniques for thread scheduling.

10.3 List and briefly define three versions of load sharing.

10.4 What is the difference between hard and soft real-time tasks?

10.5 What is the difference between periodic and aperiodic real-time tasks?

10.6 List and briefly define five general areas of requirements for a real-time operating system.

10.7 List and briefly define four classes of real-time scheduling algorithms.

10.8 What items of information about a task might be useful in real-time scheduling?

Problems

10.1 Consider a set of three periodic tasks with the execution profiles of Table 10.5. Develop scheduling diagrams similar to those of Figure 10.5 for this set of tasks.

10.2 Consider a set of five aperiodic tasks with the execution profiles of Table 10.6. Develop scheduling diagrams similar to those of Figure 10.6 for this set of tasks.

10.3 This problem demonstrates that, although Equation (10.2) for rate monotonic scheduling is a sufficient condition for successful scheduling, it is not a necessary condition [that is, sometimes successful scheduling is possible even if Equation (10.2) is not satisfied].

    a. Consider a task set with the following independent periodic tasks:

- Task P_1: $C_1 = 20$; $T_1 = 100$
- Task P_2: $C_2 = 30$; $T_2 = 145$

Can these tasks be successfully scheduled using rate monotonic scheduling?

    b. Now add the following task to the set:

- Task P_3: $C_3 = 68$; $T_3 = 150$

Is Equation (10.2) satisfied?

    c. Suppose that the first instance of the preceding three tasks arrives at time $t = 0$. Assume that the first deadline for each task is the following:

$$D_1 = 100; \quad D_2 = 145; \quad D_3 = 150$$

Using rate monotonic scheduling, will all three deadlines be met? What about deadlines for future repetitions of each task?

10.4 Draw a diagram similar to that of Figure 10.9b that shows the sequence events for this same example using priority ceiling.

Table 10.5 Execution Profile for Problem 10.1

Process	Arrival Time	Execution Time	Ending Deadline
A(1)	0	10	20
A(2)	20	10	40
•	•	•	•
•	•	•	•
•	•	•	•
B(1)	0	10	50
B(2)	50	10	100
•	•	•	•
•	•	•	•
•	•	•	•
C(1)	0	15	50
C(2)	50	15	100
•	•	•	•
•	•	•	•
•	•	•	•

Table 10.6   Execution Profile for Problem 10.2

Process	Arrival Time	Execution Time	Starting Deadline
A	10	20	100
B	20	20	30
C	40	20	60
D	50	20	80
E	60	20	70

PART FIVE

Input/Output and Files

Perhaps the messiest parts of the design of an operating system deal with the I/O facility and the file management system. With respect to I/O, the key issue is performance. The I/O facility is truly the performance battleground. Looking at the internal operation of a computer system, we see that processor speed continues to increase and, if a single processor is still not fast enough, SMP configurations provide multiple processors to speed the work. Internal memory access speeds are also increasing, though not at as fast a rate as processor speed. Nevertheless, with the clever use of one, two, or even more levels of internal cache, main memory access time is managing to keep up with processor speed. But I/O remains a significant performance challenge, particularly in the case of disk storage.

With file systems, performance is also an issue. Other design requirements, such as reliability and security, also come into play. From a user's point of view, the file system is perhaps the most important aspect of the operating system: The user wants rapid access to files but also guarantees that the files will not be corrupted and that they are secure from unauthorized access.

ROAD MAP FOR PART FIVE

Chapter 11 I/O Management and Disk Scheduling

Chapter 11 begins with an overview of I/O storage devices and the organization of the I/O function within the operating system. This is followed by discussion of various buffering strategies to improve performance. The remainder of the chapter is devoted to disk I/O. We look at the way in which multiple disk requests can be scheduled to take advantage of the physical characteristics of disk access to improve response time. Then we examine the use of a disk array to improve performance and reliability. Finally, we discuss the disk cache.

Chapter 12 File Management

Chapter 12 provides a survey of various types of file organizations and examines operating system issues related to file management and file access. It discusses physical and logical organization of data. It examines the services relating to file management that a typical operating system provides for users. It then looks at the specific mechanisms and data structures that are part of a file management system.

CHAPTER 11

I/O MANAGEMENT AND DISK SCHEDULING

481

Perhaps the messiest aspect of operating system design is input/output. Because there is such a wide variety of devices and applications of those devices, it is difficult to develop a general, consistent solution.

We begin this chapter with a brief discussion of I/O devices and the organization of the I/O functions. These topics, which generally come within the scope of computer architecture, set the stage for an examination of I/O from the point of view of the operating system.

The next section examines operating system design issues, including design objectives, and the way in which the I/O function can be structured. Then I/O buffering is examined; one of the basic I/O services provided by the operating system is a buffering function, which improves overall performance.

The next sections of the chapter are devoted to magnetic disk I/O. In contemporary systems, this form of I/O is the most important and is key to the performance as perceived by the user. We begin by developing a model of disk I/O performance and then examine several techniques that can be used to enhance performance.

An appendix to this chapter summarizes characteristics of secondary storage devices, including magnetic disk and optical memory.

11.1 I/O DEVICES

As was mentioned in Chapter 1, external devices that engage in I/O with computer systems can be roughly grouped into three categories:

- **Human readable:** Suitable for communicating with the computer user. Examples include printers and video display terminals, the latter consisting of display, keyboard, and perhaps other devices such as a mouse.
- **Machine readable:** Suitable for communicating with electronic equipment. Examples are disk and tape drives, sensors, controllers, and actuators.
- **Communication:** Suitable for communicating with remote devices. Examples are digital line drivers and modems.

There are great differences across classes and even substantial differences within each class. The following are among the key differences:

- **Data rate:** There may be differences of several orders of magnitude between the data transfer rates. Figure 11.1 gives some examples.
- **Application:** The use to which a device is put has an influence on the software and policies in the operating system and supporting utilities. For example, a disk used for files requires the support of file management software. A disk used as a backing store for pages in a virtual memory scheme depends on the use of virtual memory hardware and software. Furthermore, these applications have an impact on disk scheduling algorithms (discussed later in this chapter). As another example, a terminal may be used by an ordinary user or a system administrator. These uses imply different privilege levels and perhaps different priorities in the operating system.

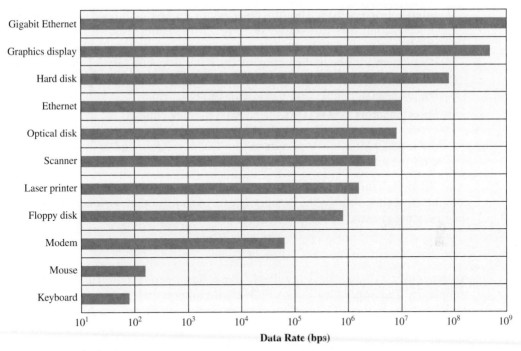

Figure 11.1   Typical I/O Device Data Rates

- **Complexity of control:** A printer requires a relatively simple control interface. A disk is much more complex. The effect of these differences on the operating system is filtered to some extent by the complexity of the I/O module that controls the device, as discussed in the next section.
- **Unit of transfer:** Data may be transferred as a stream of bytes or characters (e.g., terminal I/O) or in larger blocks (e.g., disk I/O).
- **Data representation:** Different data encoding schemes are used by different devices, including differences in character code and parity conventions.
- **Error conditions:** The nature of errors, the way in which they are reported, their consequences, and the available range of responses differ widely from one device to another.

This diversity makes a uniform and consistent approach to I/O, both from the point of view of the operating system and from the point of view of user processes, difficult to achieve.

11.2 ORGANIZATION OF THE I/O FUNCTION

Section 1.7 summarized three techniques for performing I/O:

- **Programmed I/O:** The processor issues an I/O command, on behalf of a process, to an I/O module; that process then busy waits for the operation to be completed before proceeding.

- **Interrupt-driven I/O:** The processor issues an I/O command on behalf of a process, continues to execute subsequent instructions, and is interrupted by the I/O module when the latter has completed its work. The subsequent instructions may be in the same process, if it is not necessary for that process to wait for the completion of the I/O. Otherwise, the process is suspended pending the interrupt and other work is performed.

- **Direct memory access (DMA):** A DMA module controls the exchange of data between main memory and an I/O module. The processor sends a request for the transfer of a block of data to the DMA module and is interrupted only after the entire block has been transferred.

Table 11.1 indicates the relationship among these three techniques. In most computer systems, DMA is the dominant form of transfer that must be supported by the operating system.

The Evolution of the I/O Function

As computer systems have evolved, there has been a pattern of increasing complexity and sophistication of individual components. Nowhere is this more evident than in the I/O function. The evolutionary steps can be summarized as follows:

1. The processor directly controls a peripheral device. This is seen in simple microprocessor-controlled devices.

2. A controller or I/O module is added. The processor uses programmed I/O without interrupts. With this step, the processor becomes somewhat divorced from the specific details of external device interfaces.

3. The same configuration as step 2 is used, but now interrupts are employed. The processor need not spend time waiting for an I/O operation to be performed, thus increasing efficiency.

4. The I/O module is given direct control of memory via DMA. It can now move a block of data to or from memory without involving the processor, except at the beginning and end of the transfer.

5. The I/O module is enhanced to become a separate processor, with a specialized instruction set tailored for I/O. The central processing unit (CPU) directs the I/O processor to execute an I/O program in main memory. The I/O processor fetches and executes these instructions without processor intervention. This allows the

Table 11.1 I/O Techniques

	No Interrupts	**Use of Interrupts**
I/O-to-memory transfer through processor	Programmed I/O	Interrupt-driven I/O
Direct I/O-to-memory transfer		Direct memory access (DMA)

processor to specify a sequence of I/O activities and to be interrupted only when the entire sequence has been performed.

6. The I/O module has a local memory of its own and is, in fact, a computer in its own right. With this architecture, a large set of I/O devices can be controlled, with minimal processor involvement. A common use for such an architecture has been to control communications with interactive terminals. The I/O processor takes care of most of the tasks involved in controlling the terminals.

As one proceeds along this evolutionary path, more and more of the I/O function is performed without processor involvement. The central processor is increasingly relieved of I/O-related tasks, improving performance. With the last two steps (5 and 6), a major change occurs with the introduction of the concept of an I/O module capable of executing a program.

A note about terminology: For all of the modules described in steps 4 through 6, the term *direct memory access* (DMA) is appropriate, because all of these types involve direct control of main memory by the I/O module. Also, the I/O module in step 5 is often referred to as an **I/O channel**, and that in step 6 as an **I/O processor**; however, each term is, on occasion, applied to both situations. In the latter part of this section, we will use the term *I/O channel* to refer to both types of I/O modules.

Direct Memory Access

Figure 11.2 indicates, in general terms, the DMA logic. The DMA unit is capable of mimicking the processor and, indeed, of taking over control of the system bus just like a processor. It needs to do this to transfer data to and from memory over the system bus.

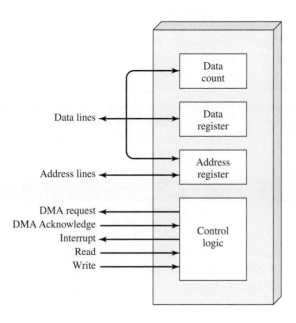

Figure 11.2   Typical DMA Block Diagram

The DMA technique works as follows. When the processor wishes to read or write a block of data, it issues a command to the DMA module by sending to the DMA module the following information:

- Whether a read or write is requested, using the read or write control line between the processor and the DMA module
- The address of the I/O device involved, communicated on the data lines
- The starting location in memory to read from or write to, communicated on the data lines and stored by the DMA module in its address register
- The number of words to be read or written, again communicated via the data lines and stored in the data count register

The processor then continues with other work. It has delegated this I/O operation to the DMA module. The DMA module transfers the entire block of data, one word at a time, directly to or from memory, without going through the processor. When the transfer is complete, the DMA module sends an interrupt signal to the processor. Thus, the processor is involved only at the beginning and end of the transfer (Figure 1.19c).

The DMA mechanism can be configured in a variety of ways. Some possibilities are shown in Figure 11.3. In the first example, all modules share the same system bus. The DMA module, acting as a surrogate processor, uses programmed I/O to exchange data between memory and an I/.O module through the DMA module. This configuration, while it may be inexpensive, is clearly inefficient: As with processor-controlled programmed I/O, each transfer of a word consumes two bus cycles (transfer request followed by transfer).

The number of required bus cycles can be cut substantially by integrating the DMA and I/O functions. As Figure 11.3b indicates, this means that there is a path between the DMA module and one or more I/O modules that does not include the system bus. The DMA logic may actually be a part of an I/O module, or it may be a separate module that controls one or more I/O modules. This concept can be taken one step further by connecting I/O modules to the DMA module using an I/O bus (Figure 11.3c). This reduces the number of I/O interfaces in the DMA module to one and provides for an easily expandable configuration. In all of these cases (Figure 11.3b and c), the system bus that the DMA module shares with the processor and main memory is used by the DMA module only to exchange data with memory and to exchange control signals with the processor. The exchange of data between the DMA and I/O modules takes place off the system bus.

11.3 OPERATING SYSTEM DESIGN ISSUES

Design Objectives

Two objectives are paramount in designing the I/O facility: efficiency and generality. **Efficiency** is important because I/O operations often form a bottleneck in a computing system. Looking again at Figure 11.1, we see that most I/O devices are extremely slow compared with main memory and the processor. One way to tackle

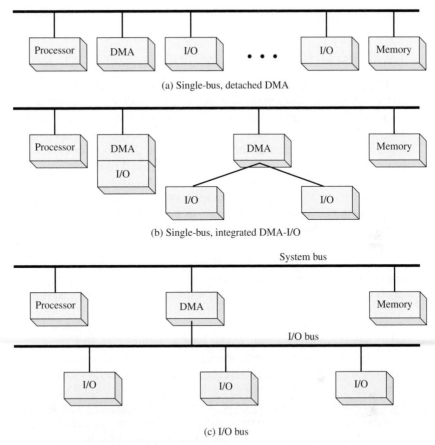

(a) Single-bus, detached DMA

(b) Single-bus, integrated DMA-I/O

(c) I/O bus

Figure 11.3   Alternative DMA Configurations

this problem is multiprogramming, which, as we have seen, allows some processes to be waiting on I/O operations while another process is executing. However, even with the vast size of main memory in today's machines, it will still often be the case that I/O is not keeping up with the activities of the processor. Swapping is used to bring in additional ready processes to keep the processor busy, but this in itself is an I/O operation. Thus, a major effort in I/O design has been schemes for improving the efficiency of the I/O. The area that has received the most attention, because of its importance, is disk I/O, and much of this chapter will be devoted to a study of disk I/O efficiency.

The other major objective is **generality**. In the interests of simplicity and freedom from error, it is desirable to handle all devices in a uniform manner. This statement applies both to the way in which processes view I/O devices and the way in which the operating system manages I/O devices and operations. Because of the diversity of device characteristics, it is difficult in practice to achieve true generality. What can be done is to use a hierarchical, modular approach to the design of the I/O function. This approach hides most of the details of device I/O in lower-level routines so that user processes and upper levels of the operating system see devices in terms of general functions, such as read, write, open, close, lock, unlock. We turn now to a discussion of this approach.

Logical Structure of the I/O Function

In Chapter 2, in the discussion of system structure, we emphasized the hierarchical nature of modern operating systems. The hierarchical philosophy is that the functions of the operating system should be separated according to their complexity, their characteristic time scale, and their level of abstraction. Following this approach leads to an organization of the operating system into a series of layers. Each layer performs a related subset of the functions required of the operating system. It relies on the next lower layer to perform more primitive functions and to conceal the details of those functions. It provides services to the next higher layer. Ideally, the layers should be defined so that changes in one layer do not require changes in other layers. Thus we have decomposed one problem into a number of more manageable subproblems.

In general, lower layers deal with a far shorter time scale. Some parts of the operating system must interact directly with the computer hardware, where events can have a time scale as brief as a few billionths of a second. At the other end of the spectrum, parts of the operating system communicate with the user, who issues commands at a much more leisurely pace, perhaps one every few seconds. The use of a set of layers conforms nicely to this environment.

Applying this philosophy specifically to the I/O facility leads to the type of organization suggested by Figure 11.4 (compare with Table 2.4). The details of the organization will depend on the type of device and the application. The three most important logical structures are presented in the figure. Of course, a particular operating system may not conform exactly to these structures. However, the general principles are valid, and most operating systems approach I/O in approximately this way.

Let us consider the simplest case first, that of a local peripheral device that communicates in a simple fashion, such as a stream of bytes or records (Figure 11.4a). The following layers are involved:

- **Logical I/O:** The logical I/O module deals with the device as a logical resource and is not concerned with the details of actually controlling the device. The logical I/O module is concerned with managing general I/O functions on behalf of user processes, allowing them to deal with the device in terms of a device identifier and simple commands such as open, close, read, write.

- **Device I/O:** The requested operations and data (buffered characters, records, etc.) are converted into appropriate sequences of I/O instructions, channel commands, and controller orders. Buffering techniques may be used to improve utilization.

- **Scheduling and control:** The actual queuing and scheduling of I/O operations occurs at this layer, as well as the control of the operations. Thus, interrupts are handled at this layer and I/O status is collected and reported. This is the layer of software that actually interacts with the I/O module and hence the device hardware.

For a communications device, the I/O structure (Figure 11.4b) looks much the same as that just described. The principal difference is that the logical I/O module is

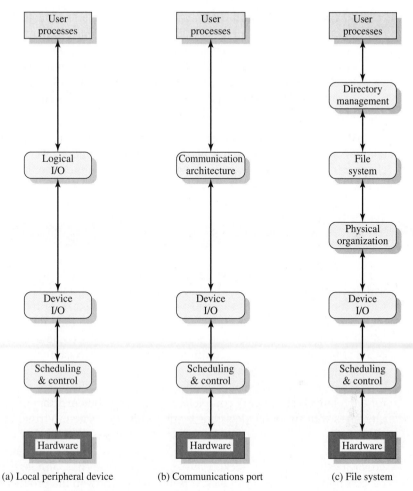

Figure 11.4   A Model of I/O Organization

replaced by a communications architecture, which may itself consist of a number of layers. An example is TCP/IP, which is discussed in Chapter 13.

Figure 11.4c shows a representative structure for managing I/O on a secondary storage device that supports a file system. The three layers not previously discussed are as follows:

- **Directory management:** At this layer, symbolic file names are converted to identifiers that either reference the file directly or indirectly through a file descriptor or index table. This layer is also concerned with user operations that affect the directory of files, such as add, delete, reorganize.
- **File system:** This layer deals with the logical structure of files and with the operations that can be specified by users, such as open, close, read, write. Access rights are also managed at this layer.

- **Physical organization:** Just as virtual memory addresses must be converted into physical main memory addresses, taking into account the segmentation and paging structure, logical references to files and records must be converted to physical secondary storage addresses, taking into account the physical track and sector structure of the secondary storage device. Allocation of secondary storage space and main storage buffers is generally treated at this layer as well.

Because of the importance of the file system, we will spend some time, in this chapter and the next, looking at its various components. The discussion in this chapter focuses on the lower three layers, while the upper two layers are examined in Chapter 12.

11.4 I/O BUFFERING

Suppose that a user process wishes to read blocks of data from a tape one at a time, with each block having a length of 512 bytes. The data are to be read into a data area within the address space of the user process at virtual location 1000 to 1511 The simplest way would be to execute an I/O command (something like Read_Block[1000, tape]) to the tape unit and then wait for the data to become available. The waiting could either be busy waiting (continuously test the device status) or, more practically, process suspension on an interrupt.

There are two problems with this approach. First, the program is hung up waiting for the relatively slow I/O to complete. The second problem is that this approach to I/O interferes with swapping decisions by the operating system. Virtual locations 1000 to 1511 must remain in main memory during the course of the block transfer. Otherwise, some of the data may be lost. If paging is being used, at least the page containing the target locations must be locked into main memory. Thus, although portions of the process may be paged out to disk, it is impossible to swap the process out completely, even if this is desired by the operating system. Notice also that there is a risk of single-process deadlock. If a process issues an I/O command, is suspended awaiting the result, and then is swapped out prior to the beginning of the operation, the process is blocked waiting on the I/O event, and the I/O operation is blocked waiting for the process to be swapped in. To avoid this deadlock, the user memory involved in the I/O operation must be locked in main memory immediately before the I/O request is issued, even though the I/O operation is queued and may not be executed for some time.

The same considerations apply to an output operation. If a block is being transferred from a user process area directly to an I/O module, then the process is blocked during the transfer and the process may not be swapped out.

To avoid these overheads and inefficiencies, it is sometimes convenient to perform input transfers in advance of requests being made and to perform output transfers some time after the request is made. This technique is known as buffering. In this section, we look at some of the buffering schemes that are supported by operating systems to improve the performance of the system.

In discussing the various approaches to buffering, it is sometimes important to make a distinction between two types of I/O devices: block oriented and

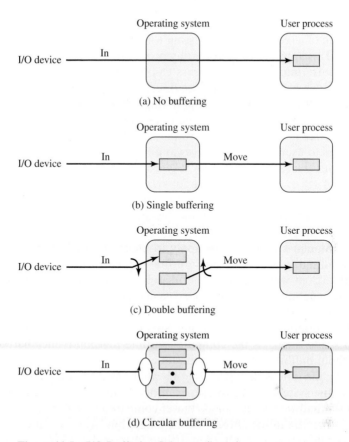

Figure 11.5   I/O Buffering Schemes (input)

stream oriented. A **block-oriented** device stores information in blocks that are usually of fixed size, and transfers are made one block at a time. Generally, it is possible to reference data by its block number. Disks and tapes are examples of block-oriented devices. A **stream-oriented** device transfers data in and out as a stream of bytes, with no block structure. Terminals, printers, communications ports, mouse and other pointing devices, and most other devices that are not secondary storage are stream oriented.

Single Buffer

The simplest type of support that the operating system can provide is single buffering (Figure 11.5b). When a user process issues an I/O request, the operating system assigns a buffer in the system portion of main memory to the operation.

For block-oriented devices, the single buffering scheme can be described as follows: Input transfers are made to the system buffer. When the transfer is complete, the process moves the block into user space and immediately requests another block. This is called reading ahead, or anticipated input; it is done in the expectation that the block will eventually be needed. For many types of computation, this is a reasonable assumption most of the time because data are usually accessed sequentially. Only at the end of a sequence of processing will a block be read in unnecessarily.

This approach will generally provide a speedup compared to the lack of system buffering. The user process can be processing one block of data while the next block is being read in. The operating system is able to swap the process out because the input operation is taking place in system memory rather than user process memory. This technique does, however, complicate the logic in the operating system. The operating system must keep track of the assignment of system buffers to user processes. The swapping logic is also affected: If the I/O operation involves the same disk that is used for swapping, it hardly makes sense to queue disk writes to the same device for swapping the process out. This attempt to swap the process and release main memory will itself not begin until after the I/O operation finishes, at which time swapping the process to disk may no longer be appropriate.

Similar considerations apply to block-oriented output. When data are being transmitted to a device, they are first copied from the user space into the system buffer, from which they will ultimately be written. The requesting process is now free to continue or to be swapped as necessary.

[KNUT97] suggests a crude but informative performance comparison between single buffering and no buffering. Suppose that T is the time required to input one block and that C is the computation time that intervenes between input requests. Without buffering, the execution time per block is essentially $T + C$. With a single buffer, the time is max $[C, T] + M$, where M is the time required to move the data from the system buffer to user memory. In most cases, execution time per block is substantially less with a single buffer compared to no buffer.

For stream-oriented I/O, the single buffering scheme can be used in a line-at-a-time fashion or a byte-at-a-time fashion. Line-at-a-time operation is appropriate for scroll-mode terminals (sometimes called dumb terminals). With this form of terminal, user input is one line at a time, with a carriage return signaling the end of a line, and output to the terminal is similarly one line at a time. A line printer is another example of such a device. Byte-at-a-time operation is used on forms-mode terminals, when each keystroke is significant, and for many other peripherals, such as sensors and controllers.

In the case of line-at-a-time I/O, the buffer can be used to hold a single line. The user process is suspended during input, awaiting the arrival of the entire line. For output, the user process can place a line of output in the buffer and continue processing. It need not be suspended unless it has a second line of output to send before the buffer is emptied from the first output operation. In the case of byte-at-a-time I/O, the interaction between the operating system and the user process follows the producer/consumer model discussed in Chapter 5.

Double Buffer

An improvement over single buffering can be had by assigning two system buffers to the operation (Figure 11.5c). A process now transfers data to (or from) one buffer while the operating system empties (or fills) the other. This technique is known as **double buffering** or **buffer swapping**.

For block-oriented transfer, we can roughly estimate the execution time as max [*C, T*]. It is therefore possible to keep the block-oriented device going at full speed if $C \leq T$. On the other hand, if $C > T$, double buffering ensures that the process will not have to wait on I/O. In either case, an improvement over single buffering is achieved. Again, this improvement comes at the cost of increased complexity.

For stream-oriented input, we again are faced with the two alternative modes of operation. For line-at-a-time I/O, the user process need not be suspended for input or output, unless the process runs ahead of the double buffers. For byte-at-a-time operation, the double buffer offers no particular advantage over a single buffer of twice the length. In both cases, the producer/consumer model is followed.

Circular Buffer

A double-buffer scheme should smooth out the flow of data between an I/O device and a process. If the performance of a particular process is the focus of our concern, then we would like for the I/O operation to be able to keep up with the process. Double buffering may be inadequate if the process performs rapid bursts of I/O. In this case, the problem can often be alleviated by using more than two buffers.

When more than two buffers are used, the collection of buffers is itself referred to as a circular buffer (Figure 11.5d), with each individual buffer being one unit in the circular buffer. This is simply the bounded-buffer producer/consumer model studied in Chapter 5.

The Utility of Buffering

Buffering is a technique that smooths out peaks in I/O demand. However, no amount of buffering will allow an I/O device to keep pace with a process indefinitely when the average demand of the process is greater than the I/O device can service. Even with multiple buffers, all of the buffers will eventually fill up and the process will have to wait after processing each chunk of data. However, in a multiprogramming environment, when there is a variety of I/O activity and a variety of process activity to service, buffering is one tool that can increase the efficiency of the operating system and the performance of individual processes.

11.5 DISK SCHEDULING

Over the last 40 years, the increase in the speed of processors and main memory has far outstripped that for disk access, with processor and main memory speeds increasing by about two orders of magnitude compared to one order of magnitude for disk. The result is that disks are currently at least four orders of magnitude slower than main memory. This gap is expected to continue into the foreseeable future. Thus, the performance of disk storage subsystem is of vital concern, and much research has gone into schemes for improving that performance. In this section, we highlight some of the key issues and look at the most important approaches. Because the performance of the disk system is tied closely to file system design issues, the discussion continues in Chapter 12.

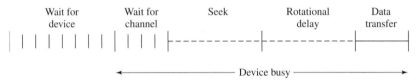

Figure 11.6   Timing of a Disk I/O Transfer

Disk Performance Parameters

The actual details of disk I/O operation depend on the computer system, the operating system, and the nature of the I/O channel and disk controller hardware. A general timing diagram of disk I/O transfer is shown in Figure 11.6.

When the disk drive is operating, the disk is rotating at constant speed. To read or write, the head must be positioned at the desired track and at the beginning of the desired sector on that track.[1] Track selection involves moving the head in a movable-head system or electronically selecting one head on a fixed-head system. On a movable-head system, the time it takes to position the head at the track is known as **seek time**. In either case, once the track is selected, the disk controller waits until the appropriate sector rotates to line up with the head. The time it takes for the beginning of the sector to reach the head is known as **rotational delay**, or rotational latency. The sum of the seek time, if any, and the rotational delay equals the **access time**, which is the time it takes to get into position to read or write. Once the head is in position, the read or write operation is then performed as the sector moves under the head; this is the data transfer portion of the operation; the time required for the transfer is the **transfer time**.

In addition to the access time and transfer time, there are several queuing delays normally associated with a disk I/O operation. When a process issues an I/O request, it must first wait in a queue for the device to be available. At that time, the device is assigned to the process. If the device shares a single I/O channel or a set of I/O channels with other disk drives, then there may be an additional wait for the channel to be available. At that point, the seek is performed to begin disk access.

In some mainframe systems, a technique known as rotational positional sensing (RPS) is used. This works as follows: When the seek command has been issued, the channel is released to handle other I/O operations. When the seek is completed, the device determines when the data will rotate under the head. As that sector approaches the head, the device tries to reestablish the communication path back to the host. If either the control unit or the channel is busy with another I/O, then the reconnection attempt fails and the device must rotate one whole revolution before it can attempt to reconnect, which is called an RPS miss. This is an extra delay element that must be added to the time line of Figure 11.6.

Seek Time   Seek time is the time required to move the disk arm to the required track. It turns out that this is a difficult quantity to pin down. The seek time consists of two key components: the initial startup time and the time taken to traverse the tracks that have to be crossed once the access arm is up to speed. Unfortunately, the traversal

---

[1]See Appendix 11A for a discussion of disk organization and formatting.

time is not a linear function of the number of tracks but includes a settling time (time after positioning the head over the target track until track identification is confirmed).

Much improvement comes from smaller and lighter disk components. Some years ago, a typical disk was 14 inches (36 cm) in diameter, whereas the most common size today is 3.5 inches (8.9 cm), reducing the distance that the arm has to travel. A typical average seek time on contemporary hard disks is under 10 ms.

Rotational Delay Disks, other than floppy disks, rotate at speeds ranging from 3600 rpm (for handheld devices such as digital cameras) up to, as of this writing, 15,000 rpm; at this latter speed, there is one revolution per 4 ms. Thus, on the average, the rotational delay will be 2 ms. Floppy disks typically rotate at between 300 and 600 rpm. Thus the average delay will be between 100 and 50 ms.

Transfer Time The transfer time to or from the disk depends on the rotation speed of the disk in the following fashion:

$$T = \frac{b}{rN}$$

where

$$T = \text{transfer time}$$
$$b = \text{number of bytes to be transferred}$$
$$N = \text{number of bytes on a track}$$
$$r = \text{rotation speed, in revolutions per second}$$

Thus the total average access time can be expressed as

$$T_a = T_s + \frac{1}{2r} + \frac{b}{rN}$$

where T_s is the average seek time.

A Timing Comparison With the foregoing parameters defined, let us look at two different I/O operations that illustrate the danger of relying on average values. Consider a disk with an advertised average seek time of 4 ms, rotation speed of 15,000 rpm, and 512-byte sectors with 500 sectors per track. Suppose that we wish to read a file consisting of 2500 sectors for a total of 1.28 Mbytes. We would like to estimate the total time for the transfer.

First, let us assume that the file is stored as compactly as possible on the disk. That is, the file occupies all of the sectors on 5 adjacent tracks (5 tracks × 500 sectors/track = 2500 sectors). This is known as *sequential organization*. The time to read the first track is as follows:

Average seek	4	ms
Rotational delay	4	ms
Read 500 sectors	8	ms
	16	ms

Suppose that the remaining tracks can now be read with essentially no seek time. That is, the I/O operation can keep up with the flow from the disk. Then, at most, we need to deal with rotational delay for each succeeding track. Thus each successive track is read in $4 + 8 = 12$ ms. To read the entire file,

$$\text{Total time} = 16 + 4 \times 12 = 64 \text{ ms} = 0.064 \text{ seconds}$$

Now let us calculate the time required to read the same data using random access rather than sequential access; that is, accesses to the sectors are distributed randomly over the disk. For each sector, we have

Average seek	4	ms
Rotational delay	4	ms
Read 1 sectors	0.016	ms
	8.016	ms

$$\text{Total time} = 500 \times 8.016 = 4008 \text{ ms} = 4.008 \text{ seconds}$$

It is clear that the order in which sectors are read from the disk has a tremendous effect on I/O performance. In the case of file access in which multiple sectors are read or written, we have some control over the way in which sectors of data are deployed, and we shall have something to say on this subject in the next chapter. However, even in the case of a file access, in a multiprogramming environment, there will be I/O requests competing for the same disk. Thus, it is worthwhile to examine ways in which the performance of disk I/O can be improved over that achieved with purely random access to the disk.

Disk Scheduling Policies

In the example just described, the reason for the difference in performance can be traced to seek time. If sector access requests involve selection of tracks at random, then the performance of the disk I/O system will be as poor as possible. To improve matters, we need to reduce the average time spent on seeks.

Consider the typical situation in a multiprogramming environment, in which the operating system maintains a queue of requests for each I/O device. So, for a single disk, there will be a number of I/O requests (reads and writes) from various processes in the queue. If we selected items from the queue in random order, then we can expect that the tracks to be visited will occur randomly, giving poor performance. This **random scheduling** is useful as a benchmark against which to evaluate other techniques.

Figure 11.7 compares the performance of various scheduling algorithms for an example sequence of I/O requests. The vertical axis corresponds to the tracks on the disk. The horizontal access corresponds to time or, equivalently, the number of tracks traversed. For this figure, we assume that the disk head is initially located at track 100. In this example, we assume a disk with 200 tracks and that the disk request queue has random requests in it. The requested tracks, in the order received by the disk scheduler, are 55, 58, 39, 18, 90, 160, 150, 38, 184. Table 11.2a tabulates the results.

First-In-First-Out The simplest form of scheduling is first-in-first-out (FIFO) scheduling, which processes items from the queue in sequential order. This strategy has

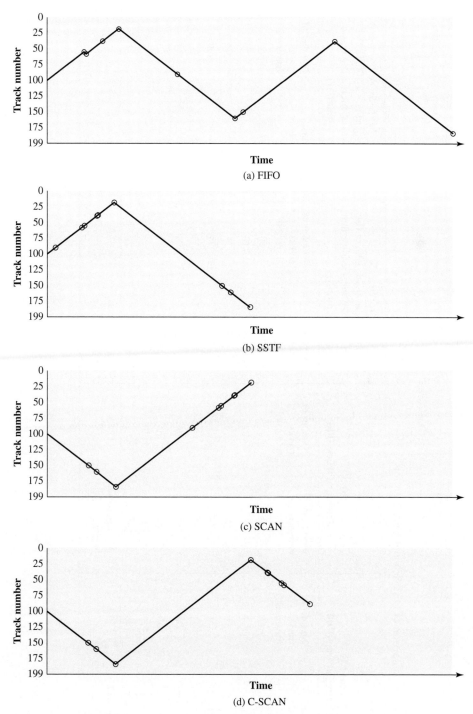

Figure 11.7 Comparison of Disk Scheduling Algorithms (see Table 11.3)

Table 11.2 Comparison of Disk Scheduling Algorithms

(a) FIFO (starting at track 100)		(b) SSTF (starting at track 100)		(c) SCAN (starting at track 100, in the direction of increasing track number)		(d) C-SCAN (starting at track 100, in the direction of increasing track number)	
Next track accessed	Number of tracks traversed	Next track accessed	Number of tracks traversed	Next track accessed	Number of tracks traversed	Next track accessed	Number of tracks traversed
55	45	90	10	150	50	150	50
58	3	58	32	160	10	160	10
39	19	55	3	184	24	184	24
18	21	39	16	90	94	18	166
90	72	38	1	58	32	38	20
160	70	18	20	55	3	39	1
150	10	150	132	39	16	55	16
38	112	160	10	38	1	58	3
184	146	184	24	18	20	90	32
Average seek length	55.3	Average seek length	27.5	Average seek length	27.8	Average seek length	35.8

Table 11.3   Disk Scheduling Algorithms

Name	Description	Remarks
	Selection according to requestor	
RSS	Random scheduling	For analysis and simulation
FIFO	First in first out	Fairest of them all
PRI	Priority by process	Control outside of disk queue management
LIFO	Last in first out	Maximize locality and resource utilization
	Selection according to requested item	
SSTF	Shortest service time first	High utilization, small queues
SCAN	Back and forth over disk	Better service distribution
C-SCAN	One way with fast return	Lower service variability
N-step-SCAN	SCAN of N records at a time	Service guarantee
FSCAN	N-step-SCAN with N = queue size at beginning of SCAN cycle	Load sensitive

the advantage of being fair, because every request is honored and the requests are honored in the order received. Figure 11.7a illustrates the disk arm movement with FIFO.

With FIFO, if there are only a few processes that require access and if many of the requests are to clustered file sectors, then we can hope for good performance. However, this technique will often approximate random scheduling in performance, if there are many processes competing for the disk. Thus, it may be profitable to consider a more sophisticated scheduling policy. A number of these are listed in Table 11.3 and will now be considered.

Priority With a system based on priority (PRI), the control of the scheduling is outside the control of disk management software. Such an approach is not intended to optimize disk utilization but to meet other objectives within the operating system. Often short batch jobs and interactive jobs are given higher priority than longer jobs that require longer computation. This allows a lot of short jobs to be flushed through the system quickly and may provide good interactive response time. However, longer jobs may have to wait excessively long times. Furthermore, such a policy could lead to countermeasures on the part of users, who split their jobs into smaller pieces to beat the system. This type of policy tends to be poor for database systems.

Last In First Out Surprisingly, a policy of always taking the most recent request has some merit. In transaction processing systems, giving the device to the most recent user should result in little or no arm movement for moving through a sequential file. Taking advantage of this locality improves throughput and reduces queue lengths. As long as a job can actively use the file system, it is processed as fast as possible. However, if the disk is kept busy because of a large workload, there is the distinct possibility of starvation. Once a job has entered an I/O request in the queue and fallen back from the head of the line, the job can never regain the head of the line unless the queue in front of it empties.

FIFO, priority, and LIFO (last in first out) scheduling are based solely on attributes of the queue or the requester. If the current track position is known to the scheduler, then scheduling based on the requested item can be employed. We examine these policies next.

Shortest Service Time First The SSTF policy is to select the disk I/O request that requires the least movement of the disk arm from its current position. Thus, we always choose to incur the minimum seek time. Of course, always choosing the minimum seek time does not guarantee that the average seek time over a number of arm movements will be minimum. However, this should provide better performance than FIFO. Because the arm can move in two directions, a random tie-breaking algorithm may be used to resolve cases of equal distances.

Figure 11.7b and Table 11.2b show the performance of SSTF on the same example as was used for FIFO.

Scan With the exception of FIFO, all of the policies described so far can leave some request unfulfilled until the entire queue is emptied. That is, there may always be new requests arriving that will be chosen before an existing request. A simple alternative that prevents this sort of starvation is the SCAN algorithm, also known as the elevator algorithm because it operates much the way an elevator does.

With SCAN, the arm is required to move in one direction only, satisfying all outstanding requests en route, until it reaches the last track in that direction or until there are no more requests in that direction. This latter refinement is sometimes referred to as the LOOK policy. The service direction is then reversed and the scan proceeds in the opposite direction, again picking up all requests in order.

Figure 11.7c and Table 11.2c illustrate the SCAN policy. As can be seen, the SCAN policy behaves almost identically with the SSTF policy. Indeed, if we had assumed that the arm was moving in the direction of lower track numbers at the beginning of the example, then the scheduling pattern would have been identical for SSTF and SCAN. However, this is a static example in which no new items are added to the queue. Even when the queue is dynamically changing, SCAN will be similar to SSTF unless the request pattern is unusual.

Note that the SCAN policy is biased against the area most recently traversed. Thus it does not exploit locality as well as SSTF or even LIFO.

It is not difficult to see that the SCAN policy favors jobs whose requests are for tracks nearest to both innermost and outermost tracks and favors the latest-arriving jobs. The first problem can be avoided via the C-SCAN policy, while the second problem is addressed by the N-step-SCAN policy.

C-Scan The C-SCAN (circular SCAN) policy restricts scanning to one direction only. Thus, when the last track has been visited in one direction, the arm is returned to the opposite end of the disk and the scan begins again. This reduces the maximum delay experienced by new requests. With SCAN, if the expected time for a scan from inner track to outer track is t, then the expected service interval for sectors at the periphery is $2t$. With C-SCAN, the interval is on the order of $t + s_{max}$, where s_{max} is the maximum seek time.

Figure 11.7d and Table 11.2d illustrate C-SCAN behavior.

N-step-SCAN and FSCAN With SSTF, SCAN, and C-SCAN, it is possible that the arm may not move for a considerable period of time. For example, if one or a few processes have high access rates to one track, they can monopolize the entire device by repeated requests to that track. High-density multisurface disks are more likely to be affected by this characteristic than lower-density disks and/or disks with only one or two surfaces. To avoid this "arm stickiness," the disk request queue can be segmented, with one segment at a time being processed completely. Two examples of this approach are N-step-SCAN and FSCAN.

The N-step-SCAN policy segments the disk request queue into subqueues of length N. Subqueues are processed one at a time, using SCAN. While a queue is being processed, new requests must be added to some other queue. If fewer than N requests are available at the end of a scan, then all of them are processed with the next scan. With large values of N, the performance of N-step-SCAN approaches that of SCAN; with a value of $N = 1$, the FIFO policy is adopted.

FSCAN is a policy that uses two subqueues. When a scan begins, all of the requests are in one of the queues, with the other empty. During the scan, all new requests are put into the other queue. Thus, service of new requests is deferred until all of the old requests have been processed.

11.6 RAID

As discussed earlier, the rate in improvement in secondary storage performance has been considerably less than the rate for processors and main memory. This mismatch has made the disk storage system perhaps the main focus of concern in improving overall computer system performance.

As in other areas of computer performance, disk storage designers recognize that if one component can only be pushed so far, additional gains in performance are to be had by using multiple parallel components. In the case of disk storage, this leads to the development of arrays of disks that operate independently and in parallel. With multiple disks, separate I/O requests can be handled in parallel, as long as the data required reside on separate disks. Further, a single I/O request can be executed in parallel if the block of data to be accessed is distributed across multiple disks.

With the use of multiple disks, there is a wide variety of ways in which the data can be organized and in which redundancy can be added to improve reliability. This could make it difficult to develop database schemes that are usable on a number of platforms and operating systems. Fortunately, industry has agreed on a standardized scheme for multiple-disk database design, known as RAID (Redundant Array of Independent Disks). The RAID scheme consists of seven levels,[2] zero through six. These levels do not imply a hierarchical relationship but designate different design architectures that share three common characteristics:

1. RAID is a set of physical disk drives viewed by the operating system as a single logical drive.

2. Data are distributed across the physical drives of an array.

---

[2]Additional levels have been defined by some researchers and some companies, but the seven levels described in this section are the ones universally agreed on.

3. Redundant disk capacity is used to store parity information, which guarantees data recoverability in case of a disk failure.

The details of the second and third characteristics differ for the different RAID levels. RAID 0 and RAID 1 do not support the third characteristic.

The term *RAID* was originally coined in a paper by a group of researchers at the University of California at Berkeley [PATT88].[3] The paper outlined various RAID configurations and applications and introduced the definitions of the RAID levels that are still used. The RAID strategy replaces large-capacity disk drives with multiple smaller-capacity drives and distributes data in such a way as to enable simultaneous access to data from multiple drives, thereby improving I/O performance and allowing easier incremental increases in capacity.

The unique contribution of the RAID proposal is to address effectively the need for redundancy. Although allowing multiple heads and actuators to operate simultaneously achieves higher I/O and transfer rates, the use of multiple devices increases the probability of failure. To compensate for this decreased reliability, RAID makes use of stored parity information that enables the recovery of data lost due to a disk failure.

We now examine each of the RAID levels. Table 11.4, from [MASS97], provides a rough guide to the seven levels. In the table, I/O performance is shown both in terms of data transfer capacity, or ability to move data, and I/O request rate, or ability to satisfy I/O requests, since these RAID levels inherently perform differently relative to these two metrics. Each RAID level's strong point is highlighted in color. Figure 11.8 is an example that illustrates the use of the seven RAID schemes to support a data capacity requiring four disks with no redundancy. The figure highlights the layout of user data and redundant data and indicates the relative storage requirements of the various levels. We refer to this figure throughout the following discussion.

RAID Level 0

RAID level 0 is not a true member of the RAID family, because it does not include redundancy to improve performance. However, there are a few applications, such as some on supercomputers, in which performance and capacity are primary concerns and low cost is more important than improved reliability.

For RAID 0, the user and system data are distributed across all of the disks in the array. This has a notable advantage over the use of a single large disk: If two different I/O requests are pending for two different blocks of data, then there is a good chance that the requested blocks are on different disks. Thus, the two requests can be issued in parallel, reducing the I/O queuing time.

But RAID 0, as with all of the RAID levels, goes further than simply distributing the data across a disk array: The data are *striped* across the available disks. This

---

[3]In that paper, the acronym RAID stood for Redundant Array of Inexpensive Disks. The term *inexpensive* was used to contrast the small relatively inexpensive disks in the RAID array to the alternative, a single large expensive disk (SLED). The SLED is essentially a thing of the past, with similar disk technology being used for both RAID and non-RAID configurations. Accordingly, the industry has adopted the term *independent* to emphasize that the RAID array creates significant performance and reliability gains.

Table 11.4 RAID Levels

Category	Level	Description	Disks Required	Data Availability	Large I/O Data Transfer Capacity	Small I/O Request Rate
Striping	0	Nonredundant	N	Lower than single disk	Very high	Very high for both read and write
Mirroring	1	Mirrored	$2N, 3N,$ etc	Higher than RAID 2, 3, 4, or 5; lower than RAID 6	Higher than single disk for read; similar to single disk for write	Up to twice that of a single disk for read; similar to single disk for write
Parallel access	2	Redundant via Hamming code	$N + m$	Much higher than single disk; higher than RAID 3, 4, or 5	Highest of all listed alternatives	Approximately twice that of a single disk
	3	Bit-interleaved parity	$N + 1$	Much higher than single disk; comparable to RAID 2, 4, or 5	Highest of all listed alternatives	Approximately twice that of a single disk
	4	Block-interleaved parity	$N + 1$	Much higher than single disk; comparable to RAID 2, 3, or 5	Similar to RAID 0 for read; significantly lower than single disk for write	Similar to RAID 0 for read; significantly lower than single disk for write
Independent access	5	Block-interleaved distributed parity	$N + 1$	Much higher than single disk; comparable to RAID 2, 3, or 4	Similar to RAID 0 for read; lower than single disk for write	Similar to RAID 0 for read; generally lower than single disk for write
	6	Block-interleaved dual distributed parity	$N + 2$	Highest of all listed alternatives	Similar to RAID 0 for read; lower than RAID 5 for write	Similar to RAID 0 for read; significantly lower than RAID 5 for write

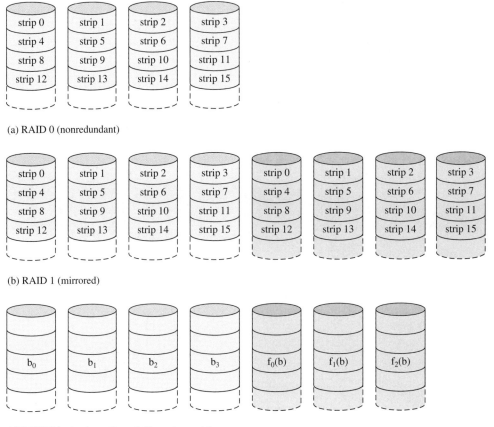

(a) RAID 0 (nonredundant)

(b) RAID 1 (mirrored)

(c) RAID 2 (redundancy through Hamming code)

Figure 11.8 RAID Levels (page 1 of 2)

is best understood by considering Figure 11.8. All user and system data are viewed as being stored on a logical disk. The logical disk is divided into strips; these strips may be physical blocks, sectors, or some other unit. The strips are mapped round robin to consecutive physical disks in the RAID array. A set of logically consecutive strips that maps exactly one strip to each array member is referred to as a *stripe*. In an *n*-disk array, the first *n* logical strips are physically stored as the first strip on each of the *n* disks, forming the first stripe; the second *n* strips are distributed as the second strips on each disk; and so on. The advantage of this layout is that if a single I/O request consists of multiple logically contiguous strips, then up to *n* strips for that request can be handled in parallel, greatly reducing the I/O transfer time.

RAID 0 for High Data Transfer Capacity The performance of any of the RAID levels depends critically on the request patterns of the host system and on the layout of the data. These issues can be most clearly addressed in RAID 0, where the impact of redundancy does not interfere with the analysis. First, let us consider the use of RAID 0 to achieve a high data transfer rate. For applications to experience a high transfer rate, two requirements must be met. First, a high transfer capacity

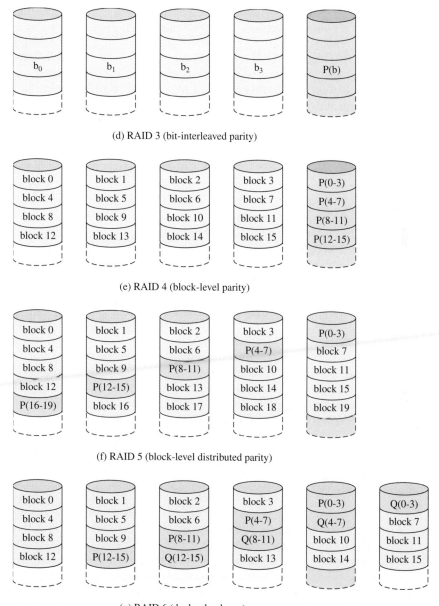

(d) RAID 3 (bit-interleaved parity)

(e) RAID 4 (block-level parity)

(f) RAID 5 (block-level distributed parity)

(g) RAID 6 (dual redundancy)

Figure 11.8 RAID Levels (page 2 of 2)

must exist along the entire path between host memory and the individual disk drives. This includes internal controller buses, host system I/O buses, I/O adapters, and host memory buses.

The second requirement is that the application must make I/O requests that drive the disk array efficiently. This requirement is met if the typical request is for large amounts of logically contiguous data, compared to the size of a strip. In this case, a single I/O request involves the parallel transfer of data from multiple disks, increasing the effective transfer rate compared to a single-disk transfer.

RAID 0 for High I/O Request Rate In a transaction-oriented environment, the user is typically more concerned with response time than with transfer rate. For an individual I/O request for a small amount of data, the I/O time is dominated by the motion of the disk heads (seek time) and the movement of the disk (rotational latency).

In a transaction environment, there may be hundreds of I/O requests per second. A disk array can provide high I/O execution rates by balancing the I/O load across multiple disks. Effective load balancing is achieved only if there are typically multiple I/O requests outstanding. This, in turn, implies that there are multiple independent applications or a single transaction-oriented application that is capable of multiple asynchronous I/O requests. The performance will also be influenced by the strip size. If the strip size is relatively large, so that a single I/O request only involves a single disk access, then multiple waiting I/O requests can be handled in parallel, reducing the queuing time for each request.

RAID Level 1

RAID 1 differs from RAID levels 2 through 6 in the way in which redundancy is achieved. In these other RAID schemes, some form of parity calculation is used to introduce redundancy, whereas in RAID 1, redundancy is achieved by the simple expedient of duplicating all the data. Figure 11.8b shows data striping being used, as in RAID 0. But in this case, each logical strip is mapped to two separate physical disks so that every disk in the array has a mirror disk that contains the same data. RAID 1 can also be implemented without data striping, though this is less common.

There are a number of positive aspects to the RAID 1 organization:

1. A read request can be serviced by either of the two disks that contains the requested data, whichever one involves the minimum seek time plus rotational latency.

2. A write request requires that both corresponding strips be updated, but this can be done in parallel. Thus, the write performance is dictated by the slower of the two writes (i.e., the one that involves the larger seek time plus rotational latency). However, there is no "write penalty" with RAID 1. RAID levels 2 through 6 involve the use of parity bits. Therefore, when a single strip is updated, the array management software must first compute and update the parity bits as well as updating the actual strip in question.

3. Recovery from a failure is simple. When a drive fails, the data may still be accessed from the second drive.

The principal disadvantage of RAID 1 is the cost; it requires twice the disk space of the logical disk that it supports. Because of that, a RAID 1 configuration is likely to be limited to drives that store system software and data and other highly critical files. In these cases, RAID 1 provides real-time backup of all data so that in the event of a disk failure, all of the critical data is still immediately available.

In a transaction-oriented environment, RAID 1 can achieve high I/O request rates if the bulk of the requests are reads. In this situation, the performance of

RAID 1 can approach double of that of RAID 0. However, if a substantial fraction of the I/O requests are write requests, then there may be no significant performance gain over RAID 0. RAID 1 may also provide improved performance over RAID 0 for data transfer intensive applications with a high percentage of reads. Improvement occurs if the application can split each read request so that both disk members participate.

RAID Level 2

RAID levels 2 and 3 make use of a parallel access technique. In a parallel access array, all member disks participate in the execution of every I/O request. Typically, the spindles of the individual drives are synchronized so that each disk head is in the same position on each disk at any given time.

As in the other RAID schemes, data striping is used. In the case of RAID 2 and 3, the strips are very small, often as small as a single byte or word. With RAID 2, an error-correcting code is calculated across corresponding bits on each data disk, and the bits of the code are stored in the corresponding bit positions on multiple parity disks. Typically, a Hamming code is used, which is able to correct single-bit errors and detect double-bit errors.

Although RAID 2 requires fewer disks than RAID 1, it is still rather costly. The number of redundant disks is proportional to the log of the number of data disks. On a single read, all disks are simultaneously accessed. The requested data and the associated error-correcting code are delivered to the array controller. If there is a single-bit error, the controller can recognize and correct the error instantly, so that the read access time is not slowed. On a single write, all data disks and parity disks must be accessed for the write operation.

RAID 2 would only be an effective choice in an environment in which many disk errors occur. Given the high reliability of individual disks and disk drives, RAID 2 is overkill and is not implemented.

RAID Level 3

RAID 3 is organized in a similar fashion to RAID 2. The difference is that RAID 3 requires only a single redundant disk, no matter how large the disk array. RAID 3 employs parallel access, with data distributed in small strips. Instead of an error-correcting code, a simple parity bit is computed for the set of individual bits in the same position on all of the data disks.

Redundancy In the event of a drive failure, the parity drive is accessed and data is reconstructed from the remaining devices. Once the failed drive is replaced, the missing data can be restored on the new drive and operation resumed.

Data reconstruction is simple. Consider an array of five drives in which X0 through X3 contain data and X4 is the parity disk. The parity for the ith bit is calculated as follows:

$$X4(i) = X3(i) \oplus X2(i) \oplus X1(i) \oplus X0(i)$$

where $\oplus$ is exclusive-OR function.

Suppose that drive X1 has failed. If we add $X4(i) \oplus X1(i)$ to both sides of the preceding equation, we get

$$X1(i) = X4(i) \oplus X3(i) \oplus X2(i) \oplus X\,0(i)$$

Thus, the contents of each strip of data on X1 can be regenerated from the contents of the corresponding strips on the remaining disks in the array. This principle is true for RAID levels 3 through 6.

In the event of a disk failure, all of the data are still available in what is referred to as reduced mode. In this mode, for reads, the missing data are regenerated on the fly using the exclusive-OR calculation. When data are written to a reduced RAID 3 array, consistency of the parity must be maintained for later regeneration. Return to full operation requires that the failed disk be replaced and the entire contents of the failed disk be regenerated on the new disk.

Performance   Because data are striped in very small strips, RAID 3 can achieve very high data transfer rates. Any I/O request will involve the parallel transfer of data from all of the data disks. For large transfers, the performance improvement is especially noticeable. On the other hand, only one I/O request can be executed at a time. Thus, in a transaction-oriented environment, performance suffers.

RAID Level 4

RAID levels 4 through 6 make use of an independent access technique. In an independent access array, each member disk operates independently, so that separate I/O requests can be satisfied in parallel. Because of this, independent access arrays are more suitable for applications that require high I/O request rates and are relatively less suited for applications that require high data transfer rates.

As in the other RAID schemes, data striping is used. In the case of RAID 4 through 6, the strips are relatively large. With RAID 4, a bit-by-bit parity strip is calculated across corresponding strips on each data disk, and the parity bits are stored in the corresponding strip on the parity disk.

RAID 4 involves a write penalty when an I/O write request of small size is performed. Each time that a write occurs, the array management software must update not only the user data but also the corresponding parity bits. Consider an array of five drives in which X0 through X3 contain data and X4 is the parity disk. Suppose that a write is performed that only involves a strip on disk X1. Initially, for each bit i, we have the following relationship:

$$X4(i) = X3(i) \oplus X2(i) \oplus X1(i) \oplus X0(i) \tag{11.1}$$

After the update, with potentially altered bits indicated by a prime symbol:

$$
\begin{aligned}
X4'(i) &= X3(i) \oplus X2(i) \oplus X1'(i) \oplus X0(i) \\
&= X3(i) \oplus X2(i) \oplus X1'(i) \oplus X0(i) \oplus X1(i) \oplus X1(i) \\
&= X3(i) \oplus X2(i) \oplus X1(i) \oplus X0(i) \oplus X1(i) \oplus X1'(i) \\
&= X4(i) \oplus X1(i) \oplus X1'(i)
\end{aligned}
$$

The preceding set of equations is derived as follows. The first line shows that a change in X1 will also affect the parity disk X4. In the second line, we add the terms $[\oplus X1(i) \oplus X1(i)]$. Because the XOR of any quantity with itself is 0, this does not affect the equation. However, it is a convenience that is used to create the third line, by reordering. Finally, Equation (11.1) is used to replace the first four terms by X4(i).

To calculate the new parity, the array management software must read the old user strip and the old parity strip. Then it can update these two strips with the new data and the newly calculated parity. Thus, each strip write involves two reads and two writes.

In the case of a larger size I/O write that involves strips on all disk drives, parity is easily computed by calculation using only the new data bits. Thus, the parity drive can be updated in parallel with the data drives and there are no extra reads or writes.

In any case, every write operation must involve the parity disk, which therefore can become a bottleneck.

RAID Level 5

RAID 5 is organized in a similar fashion to RAID 4. The difference is that RAID 5 distributes the parity strips across all disks. A typical allocation is a round-robin scheme, as illustrated in Figure 11.8f. For an n-disk array, the parity strip is on a different disk for the first n stripes, and the pattern then repeats.

The distribution of parity strips across all drives avoids the potential I/O bottleneck of a single parity disk found in RAID 4.

RAID Level 6

RAID 6 was introduced in a subsequent paper by the Berkeley researchers [KATZ89]. In the RAID 6 scheme, two different parity calculations are carried out and stored in separate blocks on different disks. Thus, a RAID 6 array whose user data require N disks consists of $N + 2$ disks.

Figure 11.8g illustrates the scheme. P and Q are two different data check algorithms. One of the two is the exclusive-OR calculation used in RAID 4 and 5. But the other is an independent data check algorithm. This makes it possible to regenerate data even if two disks containing user data fail.

The advantage of RAID 6 is that it provides extremely high data availability. Three disks would have to fail within the MTTR (mean time to repair) interval to cause data to be lost. On the other hand, RAID 6 incurs a substantial write penalty, because each write affects two parity blocks.

11.7 DISK CACHE

In Section 1.6 and Appendix 1A, we summarized the principles of cache memory. The term *cache memory* is usually used to apply to a memory that is smaller and faster than main memory and that is interposed between main memory and the processor. Such a cache memory reduces average memory access time by exploiting the principle of locality.

The same principle can be applied to disk memory. Specifically, a disk cache is a buffer in main memory for disk sectors. The cache contains a copy of some of the sectors on the disk. When an I/O request is made for a particular sector, a check is made to determine if the sector is in the disk cache. If so, the request is satisfied via the cache. If not, the requested sector is read into the disk cache from the disk. Because of the phenomenon of locality of reference, when a block of data is fetched into the cache to satisfy a single I/O request, it is likely that there will be future references to that same block.

Design Considerations

Several design issues are of interest. First, when an I/O request is satisfied from the disk cache, the data in the disk cache must be delivered to the requesting process. This can be done either by transferring the block of data within main memory from the disk cache to memory assigned to the user process, or simply by using a shared memory capability and passing a pointer to the appropriate slot in the disk cache. The latter approach saves the time of a memory-to-memory transfer and also allows shared access by other processes using the readers/writers model described in Chapter 5.

A second design issue has to do with the replacement strategy. When a new sector is brought into the disk cache, one of the existing blocks must be replaced. This is the identical problem presented in Chapter 8; there the requirement was for a page replacement algorithm. A number of algorithms have been tried. The most commonly used algorithm is least recently used (LRU): Replace that block that has been in the cache longest with no reference to it. Logically, the cache consists of a stack of blocks, with the most recently referenced block on the top of the stack. When a block in the cache is referenced, it is moved from its existing position on the stack to the top of the stack. When a block is brought in from secondary memory, remove the block that is on the bottom of the stack and push the incoming block onto the top of the stack. Naturally, it is not necessary actually to move these blocks around in main memory; a stack of pointers can be associated with the cache.

Another possibility is **least frequently used (LFU)**: Replace that block in the set that has experienced the fewest references. LFU could be implemented by associating a counter with each block. When a block is brought in, it is assigned a count of 1; with each reference to the block, its count is incremented by 1. When replacement is required, the block with the smallest count is selected. Intuitively, it might seem that LFU is more appropriate than LRU because LFU makes use of more pertinent information about each block in the selection process.

A simple LFU algorithm has the following problem. It may be that certain blocks are referenced relatively infrequently overall, but when they are referenced, there are short intervals of repeated references due to locality, thus building up high reference counts. After such an interval is over, the reference count may be misleading and not reflect the probability that the block will soon be referenced again. Thus, the effect of locality may actually cause the LFU algorithm to make poor replacement choices.

To overcome this difficulty with LFU, a technique known as frequency-based replacement is proposed in [ROBI90]. For clarity, let us first consider a simplified version, illustrated in Figure 11.9a. The blocks are logically organized in a stack, as with the LRU algorithm. A certain portion of the top part of the stack is set aside as a new section. When there is a cache hit, the referenced block is moved to the top of

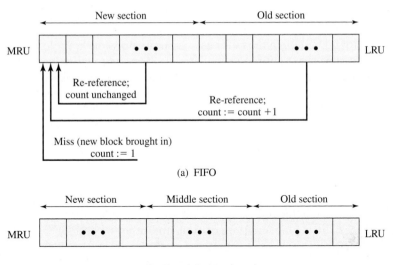

Figure 11.9 Frequency-Based Replacement

the stack. If the block was already in the new section, its reference count is not incremented; otherwise it is incremented by 1. Given a sufficiently large new section, this results in the reference counts for blocks that are repeatedly re-referenced within a short interval remaining unchanged. On a miss, the block with the smallest reference count that is not in the new section is chosen for replacement; the least recently used such block is chosen in the event of a tie.

The authors report that this strategy achieved only slight improvement over LRU. The problem is the following:

1. On a cache miss, a new block is brought into the new section, with a count of 1.
2. The count remains at 1 as long as the block remains in the new section.
3. Eventually the block ages out of the new section, with its count still at 1.
4. If the block is not now re-referenced fairly quickly it is very likely to be replaced because it necessarily has the smallest reference count of those blocks that are not in the new section. In other words, there does not seem to be a sufficiently long interval for blocks aging out of the new section to build up their reference counts even if they were relatively frequently referenced.

A further refinement addresses this problem: divide the stack into three sections: new, middle, and old (Figure 11.9b). As before, reference counts are not incremented on blocks in the new section. However, only blocks in the old section are eligible for replacement. Assuming a sufficiently large middle section, this allows relatively frequently referenced blocks a chance to build up their reference counts before becoming eligible for replacement. Simulation studies by the authors indicate that this refined policy is significantly better than simple LRU or LFU.

Regardless of the particular replacement strategy, the replacement can take place on demand or preplanned. In the former case, a sector is replaced only when the slot is needed. In the latter case, a number of slots are released at a time. The reason for this latter approach is related to the need to write back sectors. If a sector is brought into the cache and only read, then when it is replaced, it is not necessary to write it back out to the disk. However, if the sector has been updated, then it is necessary to write it back out before replacing it. In this latter case, it makes sense to cluster the writing and to order the writing to minimize seek time.

Performance Considerations

The same performance considerations discussed in Appendix 1A apply here. The issue of cache performance reduces itself to a question of whether a given miss ratio can be achieved. This will depend on the locality behavior of the disk references, the replacement algorithm, and other design factors. Principally, however, the miss ratio is a function of the size of the disk cache. Figure 11.10 summarizes results from several studies using LRU, one for a UNIX system running on a VAX [OUST85] and one for IBM mainframe operating systems [SMIT85]. Figure 11.11 shows results for simulation studies of the frequency-based replacement algorithm. A comparison of the two figures points out one of the risks of this sort of performance assessment. The figures appear to show that LRU outperforms the frequency-based replacement algorithm. However, when identical reference patterns using the same cache structure are compared, the

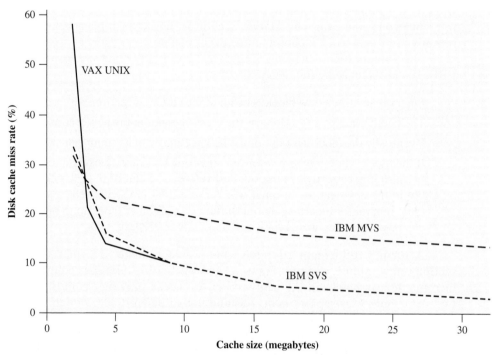

Figure 11.10 Some Disk Cache Performance Results Using LRU

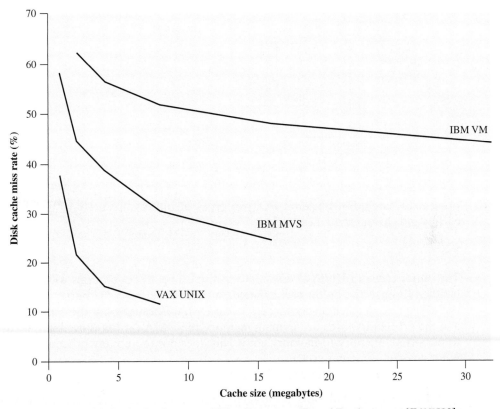

Figure 11.11   Disk Cache Performance Using Frequency-Based Replacement [ROBI90]

frequency-based replacement algorithm is superior. Thus, the exact sequence of reference patterns, plus related design issues such as block size, will have a profound influence on the performance achieved.

11.8 UNIX SVR4 I/O

In UNIX, each individual I/O device is associated with a special file. These are managed by the file system and are read and written in the same manner as user data files. This provides a clean, uniform interface to users and processes. To read from or write to a device, read and write requests are made for the special file associated with the device.

Figure 11.12 illustrates the logical structure of the I/O facility. The file subsystem manages files on secondary storage devices. In addition, it serves as the process interface to devices, because these are treated as files.

There are two types of I/O in UNIX: buffered and unbuffered. Buffered I/O passes through system buffers, whereas unbuffered I/O typically involves the DMA facility, with the transfer taking place directly between the I/O module and the

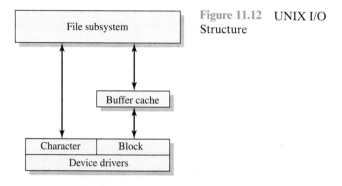

Figure 11.12   UNIX I/O Structure

process I/O area. For buffered I/O, two types of buffers are used: system buffer caches and character queues.

Buffer Cache

The buffer cache in UNIX is essentially a disk cache. I/O operations with disk are handled through the buffer cache. The data transfer between the buffer cache and the user process space always occurs using DMA. Because both the buffer cache and the process I/O area are in main memory, the DMA facility is used in this case to perform a memory-to-memory copy. This does not use up any processor cycles, but it does consume bus cycles.

To manage the buffer cache, three lists are maintained:

- **Free list:** List of all slots in the cache (a slot is referred to as a buffer in UNIX; each slot holds one disk sector) that are available for allocation
- **Device list:** List of all buffers currently associated with each disk
- **Driver I/O queue:** List of buffers that are actually undergoing or waiting for I/O on a particular device

All buffers should be on the free list or on the driver I/O queue list. A buffer, once associated with a device, remains associated with the device even if it is on the free list, until is actually reused and becomes associated with another device. These lists are maintained as pointers associated with each buffer rather than physically separate lists.

When a reference is made to a physical block number on a particular device, the operating system first checks to see if the block is in the buffer cache. To minimize the search time, the device list is organized as a hash table, using a technique similar to the overflow with chaining technique discussed in Appendix 8A (Figure 8.27b). Figure 11.13 depicts the general organization of the buffer cache. There is a hash table of fixed length that contains pointers into the buffer cache. Each reference to a (device#, block#) maps into a particular entry in the hash table. The pointer in that entry points to the first buffer in the chain. A hash pointer associated with each buffer points to the next buffer in the chain for that hash table entry. Thus, for all (device#, block#) references that map into the same hash table entry, if the corresponding block is in the buffer cache, then that buffer will be in the chain for that hash table entry. Thus, the length of the search of the

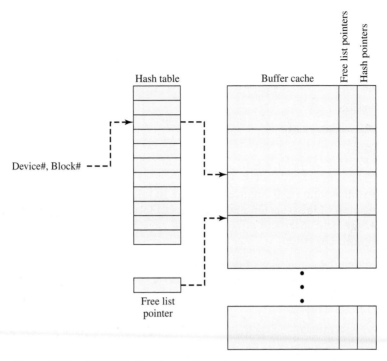

Figure 11.13   UNIX Buffer Cache Organization

buffer cache is reduced by a factor of on the order of N, where N is the length of the hash table.

For block replacement, a least-recently-used algorithm is used: After a buffer has been allocated to a disk block, it cannot be used for another block until all other buffers have been used more recently. The free list preserves this least-recently-used order.

Character Queue

Block-oriented devices, such as disk and tape, can be effectively served by the buffer cache. A different form of buffering is appropriate for character-oriented devices, such as terminals and printers. A character queue is either written by the I/O device and read by the process or written by the process and read by the device. In both cases, the producer/consumer model introduced in Chapter 5 is used. Thus, character queues may only be read once; as each character is read, it is effectively destroyed. This is in contrast to the buffer cache, which may be read multiple times and hence follows the readers/writers model (also discussed in Chapter 5).

Unbuffered I/O

Unbuffered I/O, which is simply DMA between device and process space, is always the fastest method for a process to perform I/O. A process that is performing unbuffered I/O is locked in main memory and cannot be swapped out. This reduces the opportunities for swapping by tying up part of main memory, thus reducing the

Table 11.5   Device I/O in UNIX

	Unbuffered I/O	**Buffer Cache**	**Character Queue**
Disk drive	X	X	
Tape drive	X	X	
Terminals			X
Communication lines			X
Printers	X		X

overall system performance. Also, the I/O device is tied up with the process for the duration of the transfer, making it unavailable for other processes.

UNIX Devices

Among the categories of devices recognized by UNIX are the following:

- Disk drives
- Tape drives
- Terminals
- Communication lines
- Printers

Table 11.5 shows the types of I/O suited to each type of device. Disk drives are heavily used in UNIX, are block oriented, and have the potential for reasonable high throughput. Thus, I/O for these devices tends to be unbuffered or via buffer cache. Tape drives are functionally similar to disk drives and use similar I/O schemes.

Because terminals involve relatively slow exchange of characters, terminal I/O typically makes use of the character queue. Similarly, communication lines require serial processing of bytes of data for input or output and are best handled by character queues. Finally, the type of I/O used for a printer will generally depend on its speed. Slow printers will normally use the character queue, while a fast printer might employ unbuffered I/O. A buffer cache could be used for a fast printer. However, because data going to a printer are never reused, the overhead of the buffer cache is unnecessary.

11.9 LINUX I/O

In general terms, the Linux I/O kernel facility is very similar to that of other UNIX implementation, such as SVR4. The Linux kernel associates a special file with each I/O device driver. Block, character, and network devices are recognized. In this section, we look at several features of the Linux I/O facility.

Disk Scheduling

The default disk scheduler in Linux 2.4 is known as the Linus Elevator, which is a variation on the LOOK algorithm discussed in Section 11.3. For Linux 2.6, the Elevator algorithm has been augmented by two additional algorithms: the deadline I/O scheduler and the anticipatory I/O scheduler [LOVE04b]. We examine each of these in turn.

The Elevator Scheduler The elevator scheduler maintains a single queue for disk read and write requests and performs both sorting and merging functions on the queue. In general terms, the elevator scheduler keeps the list of requests sorted by block number. Thus, as the disk requests are handled, the drive moves in a single direction, satisfying each request as it is encountered. This general strategy is refined in the following manner. When a new request is added to the queue, four operations are considered in order:

1. If the request is to the same on-disk sector or an immediately adjacent sector to a pending request in the queue, then the existing request and the new request are merged into one request.
2. If a request in the queue is sufficiently old, the new request is inserted at the tail of the queue.
3. If there is a suitable location, the new request is inserted in sorted order.
4. If there is no suitable location, the new request is placed at the tail of the queue.

Deadline Scheduler Operation 2 in the preceding list is intended to prevent starvation of a request, but is not very effective [LOVE04a]. It does not attempt to service requests in a given time frame but merely stops insertion-sorting requests after a suitable delay. Two problems manifest themselves with the elevator scheme. The first problem is that a distant block request can be delayed for a substantial time because the queue is dynamically updated. For example, consider the following stream of requests for disk blocks: 20, 30, 700, 25. The elevator scheduler reorders these so that the requests are placed in the queue as 20, 25, 30, 700, with 20 being the head of the queue. If a continuous sequence of low-numbered block requests arrive, then the request for 700 continues to be delayed.

An even more serious problem concerns the distinction between read and write requests. Typically, a write request is issued asynchronously. That is, once a process issues the write request, it need not wait for the request to actually be satisfied. When an application issues a write, the kernel copies the data into an appropriate buffer, to be written out as time permits. Once the data are captured in the kernel's buffer, the application can proceed. However, for many read operations, the process must wait until the requested data are delivered to the application before proceeding. Thus, a stream of write requests (for example, to place a large file on the disk) can block a read request for a considerable time and thus block a process.

To overcome these problems, the deadline I/O scheduler makes use of three queues (Figure 11.14). Each incoming request is placed in the sorted elevator queue, as before. In addition, the same request is placed at the tail of a read FIFO queue for a read request or a write FIFO queue for a write request. Thus, the read and write queues maintain a list of requests in the sequence in which the requests were made. Associated with each request is an expiration time, with a default value of 0.5 seconds for a read request and 5 seconds for a write request. Ordinarily, the scheduler dispatches from the sorted queue. When a request is satisfied, it is removed from the head of the sorted queue and also from the appropriate FIFO queue. However,

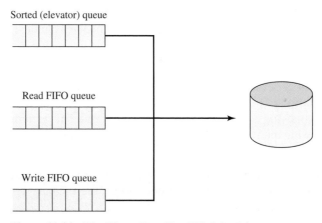

Figure 11.14   The Linux Deadline I/O Scheduler

when the item at the head of one of the FIFO queues becomes older than its expiration time, then the scheduler next dispatches from that FIFO queue, taking the expired request, plus the next few requests from the queue. As each request is dispatched, it is also removed from the sorted queue.

The deadline I/O scheduler scheme overcomes the starvation problem and also the read versus write problem.

Anticipatory I/O Scheduler The original elevator scheduler and the deadline scheduler both are designed to dispatch a new request as soon as the existing request is satisfied, thus keeping the disk as busy as possible. This same policy applies to all of the scheduling algorithms discussed in Section 11.5. However, such a policy can be counterproductive if there are numerous synchronous read requests. Typically, an application will wait until a read request is satisfied and the data available before issuing the next request. The small delay between receiving the data for the last read and issuing the next read enables the scheduler to turn elsewhere for a pending request and dispatch that request.

Because of the principle of locality, it is likely that successive reads from the same process will be to disk blocks that are near one another. If the scheduler were to delay a short period of time after satisfying a read request, to see if a new nearby read request is made, the overall performance of the system could be enhanced. This is the philosophy behind the anticipatory scheduler, proposed in [IYER01], and implemented in Linux 2.6.

In Linux, the anticipatory scheduler is superimposed on the deadline scheduler. When a read request is dispatched, the anticipatory scheduler causes the scheduling system to delay for up to 6 milliseconds, depending on the configuration. During this small delay, there is a good chance that the application that issued the last read request will issue another read request to the same region of the disk. If so, that request will be serviced immediately. If no such read request occurs, the scheduler resumes using the deadline scheduling algorithm.

[LOVE04b] reports on two tests of the Linux scheduling algorithms. The first test involved the reading of a 200 MB file while doing a long streaming write in the background. The second test involved doing a read of a large file in the background while reading every file in the kernel source tree. The results are listed in the following table:

I/O Scheduler and Kernel	Test 1	Test 2
Linus elevator on 2.4	45 seconds	30 minutes, 28 seconds
Deadline I/O scheduler on 2.6	40 seconds	3 minutes, 30 seconds
Anticipatory I/O scheduler on 2.6	4.6 seconds	15 seconds

As can be seen, the performance improvement depends on the nature of the workload. But in both cases, the anticipatory scheduler provides a dramatic improvement.

Linux Page Cache

In Linux 2.2 and earlier releases, the kernel maintained a page cache for reads and writes from regular filesystem files and for virtual memory pages, and a separate buffer cache for block I/O. For Linux 2.4 and later, there is a single unified page cache that is involved in all traffic between disk and main memory.

The page cache confers two benefits. First, when it is time to write back dirty pages to disk, a collection of them can be ordered properly and written out efficiently. Second, because of the principle of temporal locality, pages in the page cache are likely to be referenced again before they are flushed from the cache, thus saving a disk I/O operation.

Dirty pages are written back to disk in two situations:

- When free memory falls below a specified threshold, the kernel reduces the size of the page cache to release memory to be added to the free memory pool.

- When dirty pages grow older than a specified threshold, a number of dirty pages are written back to disk.

11.10 WINDOWS I/O

Figure 11.15 shows the Windows I/O manager. The I/O manager is responsible for all I/O for the operating system and provides a uniform interface that all types of drivers can call.

Basic I/O Modules

The I/O manager consists of four modules:

- **Cache manager:** The cache manager handles caching for the entire I/O subsystem. The cache manager provides a caching service in main memory to all file systems and network components. It can dynamically increase and decrease

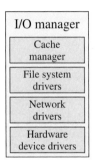

Figure 11.15 Windows I/O Manager

the size of the cache devoted to a particular activity as the amount of available physical memory varies. Cache manager includes two services to improve overall performance:

— **Lazy write:** The system records updates in the cache only and not on disk. Later, when demand on the processor is low, the cache manager writes the changes to disk. If a particular cache block is updated in the meantime, there is a net savings.

— **Lazy commit:** This is similar to lazy write for transaction processing. Instead of immediately marking a transaction as successfully completed, the system caches the committed information and later writes it to the file system log by a background process.

- **File system drivers:** The I/O manager treats a file system driver as just another device driver and routes message for certain volumes to the appropriate software driver for that device adapter.

- **Network drivers:** Windows includes integrated networking capabilities and support for distributed applications.

- **Hardware device drivers:** These drivers access the hardware registers of the peripheral devices through entry points in Windows Executive dynamic link libraries. A set of these routines exists for every platform that Windows supports; because the routine names are the same for all platforms, the source code of Windows device drivers is portable across different processor types.

Asynchronous and Synchronous I/O

Windows offers two modes of I/O operation: asynchronous and synchronous. The asynchronous mode is used whenever possible to optimize application performance. With asynchronous I/O, an application initiates an I/O operation and then can continue processing while the I/O request is fulfilled. With synchronous I/O, the application is blocked until the I/O operation completes.

Asynchronous I/O is more efficient, from the point of view of the calling thread, because it allows the thread to continue execution while the I/O operation is queued by the I/O manager and subsequently performed. However, the application that invoked the asynchronous I/O operation needs some way to determine when the operation is complete. Windows provides four different techniques for signaling I/O completion:

- **Signaling a device kernel object:** With this approach, an indicator associated with a device object is set when an operation on that object is complete. The thread that invoked the I/O operation can continue to execute until it reaches a point where it must stop until the I/O operation is complete. At that point, the thread can wait until the operation is complete and then continue. This technique is simple and easy to use but is not appropriate for handling multiple I/O requests. For example, if a thread needs to perform multiple simultaneous actions on a single file, such as reading from one portion and writing to another portion of the file, with this technique, the thread could not distinguish between the completion of the read and the completion of the write. It would simply know that some requested I/O operation on this file was complete.

- **Signaling an event kernel object:** This technique allows multiple simultaneous I/O requests against a single device or file. The thread creates an event for each request. Later, the thread can wait on a single one of these requests or on the entire collection of requests.

- **Alertable I/O:** This technique makes use of a queue associated with a thread, known as the asynchronous procedure call (APC) queue. In this case, the thread makes I/O requests, and the I/O manager places the results of these requests in the calling thread's APC queue.

- **I/O completion ports:** This technique is used on a Windows server to optimize the use of threads. In essence, a pool of threads is available for use so that it is not necessary to create a new thread to handle a new request.

Software RAID

Windows supports two sorts of RAID configurations, defined in [MS96] as follows:

- **Hardware RAID:** Separate physical disks combined into one or more logical disks by the disk controller or disk storage cabinet hardware.

- **Software RAID:** Noncontiguous disk space combined into one or more logical partitions by the fault-tolerant software disk driver, FTDISK.

In hardware RAID, the controller interface handles the creation and regeneration of redundant information. The software RAID, available on Windows Server, implements the RAID functionality as part of the operating system and can be used with any set of multiple disks. The software RAID facility implements RAID 1 and RAID 5. In the case of RAID 1 (disk mirroring), the two disks containing the primary and mirrored partitions may be on the same disk controller or different disk controllers. The latter configuration is referred to as *disk duplexing*.

11.11 SUMMARY

The computer system's interface to the outside world is its I/O architecture. This architecture is designed to provide a systematic means of controlling interaction with the outside world and to provide the operating system with the information it needs to manage I/O activity effectively.

The I/O function is generally broken up into a number of layers, with lower layers dealing with details that are closer to the physical functions to be performed and higher layers dealing with I/O in a logical and generic fashion. The result is that changes in hardware parameters need not affect most of the I/O software.

A key aspect of I/O is the use of buffers that are controlled by I/O utilities rather than by application processes. Buffering smooths out the differences between the internal speeds of the computer system and the speeds of I/O devices. The use of buffers also decouples the actual I/O transfer from the address space of the application process. This allows the operating system more flexibility in performing its memory-management function.

The aspect of I/O that has the greatest impact on overall system performance is disk I/O. Accordingly, there has been greater research and design effort in this area than in any other kind of I/O. Two of the most widely used approaches to improve disk I/O performance are disk scheduling and the disk cache.

At any time, there may be a queue of requests for I/O on the same disk. It is the object of disk scheduling to satisfy these requests in a way that minimizes the mechanical seek time of the disk and hence improves performance. The physical layout of pending requests plus considerations of locality come into play.

A disk cache is a buffer, usually kept in main memory, that functions as a cache of disk blocks between disk memory and the rest of main memory. Because of the principle of locality, the use of a disk cache should substantially reduce the number of block I/O transfers between main memory and disk.

11.12 RECOMMENDED READINGS AND WEB SITES

General discussions of computer I/O can be found in most books on computer architecture, such as [STAL03] and [PATT98]. [MEE96a] provides a good survey of the underlying recording technology of disk and tape systems. [MEE96b] focuses on the data storage techniques for disk and tape systems. [WIED87] contains an excellent discussion of disk performance issues, including those relating to disk scheduling. [NG98] looks at disk hardware performance issues. [CAO96] analyzes disk caching and disk scheduling. Good surveys of disk scheduling algorithms, with a performance analysis, are [WORT94] and [SELT90].

[ROSC03] provides a comprehensive overview of all types of external memory systems, with a modest amount of technical detail on each. Another good survey, with more emphasis on the I/O interface and less on the devices themselves, is [SCHW96]. [PAI00] is an instructive description of an integrated operating-system scheme for I/O buffering and caching.

[DELL00] provides a detailed discussion of Windows NT device drivers plus a good overview of the entire Windows I/O architecture.

An excellent survey of RAID technology, written by the inventors of the RAID concept, is [CHEN94]. A more detailed discussion is from the RAID Advisory Board, an association of suppliers and consumers of RAID-related products [MASS97]. [CHEN96] analyzes RAID performance. Another good paper is [FRIE96]. [DALT96] describes the Windows NT software RAID facility in detail.

CAO96 Cao, P.; Felten, E.; Karlin, A.; and Li, K. "Implementation and Performance of Integrated Application-Controlled File Caching, Prefetching, and Disk Scheduling." *ACM Transactions on Computer Systems*, November 1996.

CHEN94 Chen, P.; Lee, E.; Gibson, G.; Katz, R.; and Patterson, D. "RAID: High-Performance, Reliable Secondary Storage." *ACM Computing Surveys*, June 1994.

CHEN96 Chen, S., and Towsley, D. "A Performance Evaluation of RAID Architectures." *IEEE Transactions on Computers*, October 1996.

DALT96 Dalton, W., et al. *Windows NT Server 4: Security, Troubleshooting, and Optimization.* Indianapolis, IN: New Riders Publishing, 1996.

DELL00 Dekker, E., and Newcomer, J. *Developing Windows NT Device Drivers: A Programmer's Handbook.* Reading, MA: Addison Wesley, 2000.

FRIE96 Friedman, M. "RAID Keeps Going and Going and ..." *IEEE Spectrum*, April 1996.

MASS97 Massiglia, P. (editor). *The RAID Book: A Storage System Technology Handbook.* St. Peter, MN: The Raid Advisory Board, 1997.

MEE96A Mee, C., and Daniel, E. eds. *Magnetic Recording Technology.* New York: McGraw-Hill, 1996.

MEE96B Mee, C., and Daniel, E. eds. *Magnetic Storage Handbook.* New York: McGraw-Hill, 1996.

NG98 Ng, S. "Advances in Disk Technology: Performance Issues." *Computer*, May 1989.

PAI00 Pai, V.; Druschel, P.; and Zwaenepoel, W. "IO-Lite: A Unified I/O Buffering and Caching System." *ACM Transactions on Computer Systems*, February 2000.

PATT98 Patterson, D., and Hennessy, J. *Computer Organization and Design: The Hardware/Software Interface.* San Mateo, CA: Morgan Kaufmann, 1998.

ROSC03 Rosch, W. *The Winn L. Rosch Hardware Bible.* Indianapolis, IN: Sams, 2003.

SCHW96 Schwaderer, W., and Wilson, A. *Understanding I/O Subsystems.* Milpitas, CA: Adaptec Press, 1996.

SELT90 Seltzer, M.; Chen, P.; and Ousterhout, J. "Disk Scheduling Revisited." *Proceedings, USENIX Winter Technical Conference*, January 1990.

STAL03 Stallings, W. *Computer Organization and Architecture,* 5th ed. Upper Saddle River, NJ: Prentice Hall, 2000.

WIED87 Wiederhold, G. *File Organization for Database Design.* New York: McGraw-Hill, 1987.

WORT94 Worthington, B.; Ganger, G.; and Patt, Y. "Scheduling Algorithms for Modern Disk Drives." *ACM SiGMETRICS*, May 1994.

Recommended Web Sites:

- **I/O Characterization and Optimization:** A facility dedicated to education and research in the area of I/O design and performance. Useful tools and tutorials. Operated by the University of Illinois.

11.13 KEY TERMS, REVIEW QUESTIONS, AND PROBLEMS

Key Terms

block	fixed-head disk	programmed I/O
block-oriented device	floppy disk	read/write head
circular buffer	gap	redundant array of indepen-
CD-R	hard disk	dent disks (RAID)
CD-ROM	interrupt-driven I/O	removable disk
CD-RW	input/output (I/O)	rotational delay
cylinder	I/O buffer	sector
device I/O	I/O channel	seek time
digital versatile disk (DVD)	I/O processor	stream-oriented device
direct memory access (DMA)	logical I/O	track
disk access time	magnetic disk	transfer time
disk cache	movable-head disk	
disk pack	nonremovable disk	

Review Questions

11.1 List and briefly define three techniques for performing I/O.

11.2 What is the difference between logical I/O and device I/O?

11.3 What is the difference between block-oriented devices and stream-oriented devices? Give a few examples of each.

11.4 Why would you expect improved performance using a double buffer rather than a single buffer for I/O?

11.5 What delay elements are involved in a disk read or write?

11.6 Briefly define the disk scheduling policies illustrated in Figure 11.7.

11.7 Briefly define the seven RAID levels.

11.8 What is the typical disk sector size?

Problems

11.1 Consider a program that accesses a single I/O device and compare unbuffered I/O to the use of a buffer. Show that the use of the buffer can reduce the running time by at most a factor of two.

11.2 Generalize the result of Problem 11.1 to the case in which a program refers to n devices.

11.3 Perform the same type of analysis as that of Table 11.2 for the following sequence of disk track requests: 27, 129, 110, 186, 147, 41, 10, 64, 120. Assume that the disk head is initially positioned over track 100 and is moving in the direction of decreasing track number. Do the same analysis, but now assume that the disk head is moving in the direction of increasing track number.

11.4 Consider a disk with N tracks numbered from 0 to $(N - 1)$ and assume that requested sectors are distributed randomly and evenly over the disk. We want to calculate the average number of tracks traversed by a seek.

    a. First, calculate the probability of a seek of length j when the head is currently positioned over track t. *Hint:* This is a matter of determining the total number of combinations, recognizing that all track positions for the destination of the seek are equally likely.

b. Next, calculate the probability of a seek of length K. *Hint:* This involves the summing over all possible combinations of movements of K tracks.

c. Calculate the average number of tracks traversed by a seek, using the formula for expected value

$$E[x] = \sum_{i=0}^{N-1} i \sum \Pr[x = i]$$

d. Show that for large values of N, the average number of tracks traversed by a seek approaches $N/3$.

11.5 The following equation was suggested both for cache memory and disk cache memory:

$$T_S = T_C + M \times T_D$$

Generalize this equation to a memory hierarchy with N levels instead of just 2.

11.6 For the frequency based replacement algorithm (Figure 11.11), define F_{new}, F_{middle}, and F_{old} as the fraction of the cache that comprises the new, middle, and old sections, respectively. Clearly, $F_{new} + F_{middle} + F_{old} = 1$. Characterize the policy when

a. $F_{old} = 1 - F_{new}$
b. $F_{old} = 1/(\text{cache size})$

11.7 What is the transfer rate of a nine-track magnetic tape unit whose tape speed is 120 inches per second and whose tape density is 1,600 linear bits per inch?

11.8 Assume a 2400-foot tape reel; an interrecord gap of 0.6 inch, where the tape stops midway between reads; a linear rate of tape speed increase/decrease during gaps; and other characteristics of the tape the same as in Problem 11.7. Data on the tape are organized in physical records, with each physical record containing a fixed number of user-defined units, called logical records.

a. How long will it take to read a full tape of 120-byte logical records blocked 10/physical record?

b. Same as in part (a), blocked 30?

c. How many logical records will the tape hold with each of the aforementioned blocking factors?

d. What is the effective overall transfer rate for each of the two aforementioned blocking factors?

e. What is the capacity of the tape?

11.9 Calculate how much disk space (in sectors, tracks, and surfaces) will be required to store the logical records read in Problem 11.8b if the disk is fixed-sector with 512 bytes/sector, with 96 sectors/track, 110 tracks per surface, and 8 usable surfaces. Ignore any file header record(s) and track indexes, and assume that records cannot span two sectors.

11.10 Consider the disk system described in Problem 11.9, and assume that the disk rotates at 360 rpm. A processor reads one sector from the disk using interrupt-driven I/O, with one interrupt per byte. If it takes 2.5 μs to process each interrupt, what percentage of the time will the processor spend handling I/O (disregard seek time)?

11.11 Repeat Problem 11.10 using DMA, and assume one interrupt per sector.

11.12 A 32-bit computer has two selector channels and one multiplexor channel. Each selector channel supports two magnetic disk and two magnetic tape units. The multiplexor channel has two line printers, two card readers, and ten VDT terminals connected to it. Assume the following transfer rates:

Disk drive	800 Kbytes/s
Magnetic tape drive	200 Kbytes/s
Line printer	6.6 Kbytes/s
Card reader	1.2 Kbytes/s
VDT	1 Kbytes/s

Estimate the maximum aggregate I/O transfer rate in this system.

11.13   It should be clear that disk striping can improve the data transfer rate when the strip size is small compared to the I/O request size. It should also be clear that RAID 0 provides improved performance relative to a single large disk, because multiple I/O requests can be handled in parallel. However, in this latter case, is disk striping necessary? That is, does disk striping improve I/O request rate performance compared to a comparable disk array without striping?

APPENDIX 11A DISK STORAGE DEVICES

Magnetic Disk

A disk is a circular platter constructed of metal or of plastic coated with a magnetizable material. Data are recorded on and later retrieved from the disk via a conducting coil named the **head**. During a read or write operation, the head is stationary while the platter rotates beneath it.

The write mechanism is based on the fact that electricity flowing through a coil produces a magnetic field. Pulses are sent to the head, and magnetic patterns are recorded on the surface below, with different patterns for positive and negative currents. The read mechanism is based on the fact that a magnetic field moving relative to a coil produces an electrical current in the coil. When the surface of the disk passes under the head, it generates a current of the same polarity as the one already recorded.

Data Organization and Formatting The head is a relatively small device capable of reading from or writing to a portion of the platter rotating beneath it. This gives rise to the organization of data on the platter in a concentric set of rings, called **tracks**. Each track is the same width as the head. There are thousands of tracks per surface.

Figure 11.16 depicts this data layout. Adjacent tracks are separated by **gaps**. This prevents, or at least minimizes, errors due to misalignment of the head or simply interference of magnetic fields.

Data are transferred to and from the disk in **sectors** (Figure 11.16). There are typically hundreds of sectors per track, and these may be of either fixed or variable length. In most contemporary systems, fixed-length sectors are used, with 512 bytes being the nearly universal sector size. To avoid imposing unreasonable precision requirements on the system, adjacent sectors are separated by intratrack (intersector) gaps.

A bit near the center of a rotating disk travels past a fixed point (such as a read-write head) slower than a bit on the outside. Therefore, some way must be found to compensate for the variation in speed so that the head can read all the bits at the same rate. This can be done by increasing the spacing between bits of information recorded in segments of the disk. The information can then be scanned at the same rate by rotating the disk at a fixed speed, known as the **constant angular velocity (CAV)**. Figure 11.17a shows the layout of a disk using CAV. The disk is divided into a number of pie-shaped sectors and into a series of concentric tracks. The advantage of using CAV is that individual blocks of data can be directly addressed by track and sector. To move the head from its current location to a specific address, it only takes a short movement of the head to a specific track and a short wait for the proper sector to spin under the head. The disadvantage of CAV is that the amount of data that can be stored on the long outer tracks is the same as what can be stored on the short inner tracks.

Because the **density**, in bits per linear inch, increases in moving from the outermost track to the innermost track, disk storage capacity in a straightforward CAV system is limited by the maximum recording density that can be achieved on the innermost track. To

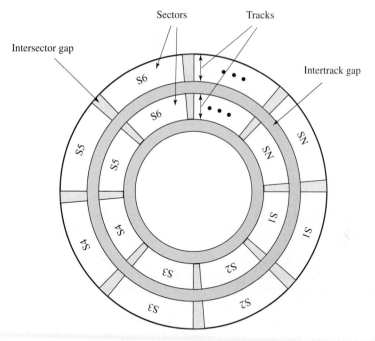

Figure 11.16   Disk Data Layout

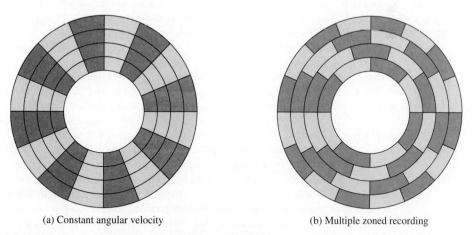

(a) Constant angular velocity

(b) Multiple zoned recording

Figure 11.17   Comparison of Disk Layout Methods

increase density, modern hard disk systems use a technique known as **multiple zone recording**, in which the surface is divided into a number of concentric zones (16 is typical). Within
a zone, the number of bits per track is constant. Zones farther from the center contain more
bits (more sectors) than zones closer to the center. This allows for greater overall storage
capacity at the expense of somewhat more complex circuitry. As the disk head moves from
one zone to another, the length (along the track) of individual bits changes, causing a change

Table 11.6   Physical Characteristics of Disk Systems

Head Motion	**Platters**
Fixed head (one per track)	Single platter
Movable head (one per surface)	Multiple platter
Disk Portability	**Head Mechanism**
Nonremovable disk	Contact (floppy)
Removable disk	Fixed gap
	Aerodynamic gap (Winchester)
Sides	
Single sided	
Double sided	

in the timing for reads and writes. Figure 11.17b suggests the nature of multiple zone recording; in this illustration, each zone is only a single track wide.

Some means is needed to locate sector positions within a track. Clearly, there must be some starting point on the track and a way of identifying the start and end of each sector. These requirements are handled by means of control data recorded on the disk. Thus, the disk is formatted with some extra data used only by the disk drive and not accessible to the user.

Physical Characteristics   Table 11.6 lists the major characteristics that differentiate among the various types of magnetic disks. First, the head may either be fixed or movable with respect to the radial direction of the platter. In a **fixed-head disk**, there is one read/write head per track. All of the heads are mounted on a rigid arm that extends across all tracks. In a **movable-head disk**, there is only one read/write head. Again, the head is mounted on an arm. Because the head must be able to be positioned above any track, the arm can be extended or retracted for this purpose.

The disk itself is mounted in a disk drive, which consists of the arm, a spindle that rotates the disk, and the electronics needed for input and output of binary data. A **nonremovable disk** is permanently mounted in the disk drive; the hard disk in a personal computer is a nonremovable disk. A **removable disk** can be removed and replaced with another disk. The advantage of the latter type is that unlimited amounts of data are available with a limited number of disk systems. Furthermore, such a disk may be moved from one computer system to another. Floppy disks and ZIP cartridge disks are examples of removable disks.

For most disks, the magnetizable coating is applied to both sides of the platter, which is then referred to as **double sided**. Some less expensive disk systems use **single-sided** disks.

Some disk drives accommodate **multiple platters** stacked vertically a fraction of an inch apart. Multiple arms are provided (Figure 11.18). Multiple-platter disks employ a movable head, with one read-write head per platter surface. All of the heads are mechanically fixed so that all are at the same distance from the center of the disk and move together. Thus, at any time, all of the heads are positioned over tracks that are of equal distance from the center of the disk. The set of all the tracks in the same relative position on the platter is referred to as a **cylinder**. For example, all of the shaded tracks in Figure 11.19 are part of one cylinder.

Finally, the head mechanism provides a classification of disks into three types. Traditionally, the read/write head has been positioned at a fixed distance above the platter, allowing an air gap. At the other extreme is a head mechanism that actually comes into physical contact with the medium during a read or write operation. This mechanism is used with the **floppy disk**, which is a small, flexible platter and the least expensive type of disk.

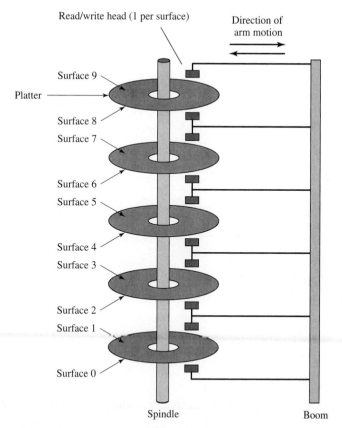

Figure 11.18   Components of a Disk Drive

To understand the third type of disk, we need to comment on the relationship between data density and the size of the air gap. The head must generate or sense an electromagnetic field of sufficient magnitude to write and read properly. The narrower the head is, the closer it must be to the platter surface to function. A narrower head means narrower tracks and therefore greater data density, which is desirable. However, the closer the head is to the disk, the greater the risk of error from impurities or imperfections. To push the technology further, the **Winchester disk** was developed. Winchester heads are used in sealed drive assemblies that are almost free of contaminants. They are designed to operate closer to the disk's surface than conventional rigid disk heads, thus allowing greater data density. The head is actually an aerodynamic foil that rests lightly on the platter's surface when the disk is motionless. The air pressure generated by a spinning disk is enough to make the foil rise above the surface. The resulting noncontact system can be engineered to use narrower heads that operate closer to the platter's surface than conventional rigid disk heads.[4]

---

[4]As a matter of historical interest, the term *Winchester* was originally used by IBM as a code name for the 3340 disk model prior to its announcement. The 3340 was a removable disk pack with the heads sealed within the pack. The term is now applied to any sealed-unit disk drive with aerodynamic head design. The Winchester disk is commonly found built into personal computers and workstations, where it is referred to as a **hard disk**.

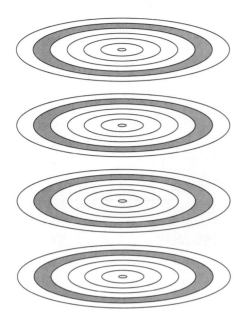

Figure 11.19 Tracks and Cylinders

Table 11.7 gives disk parameters for typical contemporary high-performance movable-head disks.

Optical Memory

In 1983, one of the most successful consumer products of all time was introduced: the compact disk (CD) digital audio system. The CD is a nonerasable disk that can store more than 60 minutes of audio information on one side. The huge commercial success of the CD enabled the development of low-cost optical-disk storage technology that has revolutionized computer data storage. A variety of optical-disk systems have been introduced (Table 11.8). We briefly review each of these.

CD-ROM Both the audio CD and the CD-ROM (compact disk read-only memory) share a similar technology. The main difference is that CD-ROM players are more rugged and have error-correction devices to ensure that data are properly transferred from disk to computer. Both types of disk are made the same way. The disk is formed from a resin, such as polycarbonate. Digitally recorded information (either music or computer data) is imprinted as a series of microscopic pits on the surface of the polycarbonate. This is done, first of all, with a finely focused, high-intensity laser to create a master disk. The master is used, in turn, to make a die to stamp out copies onto polycarbonate. The pitted surface is then coated with a highly reflective surface, usually aluminum or gold. This shiny surface is protected against dust and scratches by a top coat of clear acrylic. Finally, a label can be silkscreened onto the acrylic.

Information is retrieved from a CD or CD-ROM by a low-powered laser housed in an optical-disk player, or drive unit. The laser shines through the clear protective coating while a motor spins the disk past it. The intensity of the reflected light of the laser changes as it encounters a pit. This change is detected by a photosensor and converted into a digital signal.

Recall that on a magnetic disk, information is recorded in concentric tracks. With the simplest constant angular velocity (CAV) system, the number of bits per track is

Table 11.7 Typical Hard Disk Drive Parameters

Characteristics	Seagate Barracuda 180	Seagate Cheetah X15-36LP	Seagate Barracuda 36ES	Toshiba HDD1242	IBM Microdrive
Application	High-capacity server	High-performance server	Entry-level desktop	Portable	Handheld devices
Capacity	181.6 GB	36.7 GB	18.4 GB	5 GB	1 GB
Minimum track-to-track seek time	0.8 ms	0.3 ms	1.0 ms	—	1.0 ms
Average seek time	7.4 ms	3.6 ms	9.5 ms	15 ms	12 ms
Spindle speed	7200 rpm	15K rpm	7200	4200 rpm	3600 rpm
Average rotational delay	4.17 ms	2 ms	4.17 ms	7.14 ms	8.33 ms
Maximum transfer rate	160 MB/s	522 to 709 MB/s	25 MB/s	66 MB/s	13.3 MB/s
Bytes per sector	512	512	512	512	512
Sectors per track	793	485	600	63	—
Tracks per cylinder (number of platter surfaces)	24	8	2	2	2
Cylinders (number of tracks on one side of platter)	24,247	18,479	29,851	10,350	—

Table 11.8   Optical Disk Products

CD

Compact Disk. A nonerasable disk that stores digitized audio information. The standard system uses 12-cm disks and can record more than 60 minutes of uninterrupted playing time.

CD-ROM

Compact Disk Read-Only Memory. A nonerasable disk used for storing computer data. The standard system uses 12-cm disks and can hold more than 650 Mbytes.

CD-R

CD Recordable. Similar to a CD-ROM. The user can write to the disk only once.

CD-RW

CD Rewritable. Similar to a CD-ROM. The user can erase and rewrite to the disk multiple times.

DVD

Digital Versatile Disk. A technology for producing digitized, compressed representation of video information, as well as large volumes of other digital data. Both 8 and 12 cm diameters are used, with a double-sided capacity of up to 17 Gbytes. The basic DVD is read-only (DVD-ROM).

DVD-R

DVD Recordable. Similar to a DVD-ROM. The user can write to the disk only once. Only one-sided disks can be used.

DVD-RW

DVD Rewritable. Similar to a DVD-ROM. The user can erase and rewrite to the disk multiple times. Only one-sided disks can be used.

---

constant. An increase in density is achieved with multiple zoned recording, in which the surface is divided into a number of zones, with zones farther from the center containing more bits than zones closer to the center. Although this technique increases capacity, it is still not optimal.

To achieve greater capacity, CDs and CD-ROMs do not organize information on concentric tracks. Instead, the disk contains a single spiral track, beginning near the center and spiraling out to the outer edge of the disk. Sectors near the outside of the disk are the same length as those near the inside. Thus, information is packed evenly across the disk in segments of the same size and these are scanned at the same rate by rotating the disk at a variable speed. The pits are then read by the laser at a **constant linear velocity (CLV)**. The disk rotates more slowly for accesses near the outer edge than for those near the center. Thus, the capacity of a track and the rotational delay both increase for positions nearer the outer edge of the disk. The data capacity for a CD-ROM is about 680 MB.

CD-ROM is appropriate for the distribution of large amounts of data to a large number of users. Because of the expense of the initial writing process, it is not appropriate for individualized applications. Compared with traditional magnetic disks, the CD-ROM has three major advantages:

- The information-storage capacity is much greater on the optical disk.
- The optical disk together with the information stored on it can be mass replicated inexpensively—unlike a magnetic disk. The database on a magnetic disk has to be reproduced by copying one disk at a time using two disk drives.

- The optical disk is removable, allowing the disk itself to be used for archival storage. Most magnetic disks are nonremovable. The information on nonremovable magnetic disks must first be copied to tape before the disk drive/disk can be used to store new information.

The disadvantages of CD-ROM are as follows:

- It is read-only and cannot be updated.
- It has an access time much longer than that of a magnetic disk drive, as much as half a second.

CD Recordable To accommodate applications in which only one or a small number of copies of a set of data is needed, the write-once read-many CD, known as the CD recordable (CD-R), has been developed. For CD-R, a disk is prepared in such a way that it can be subsequently written once with a laser beam of modest intensity. Thus, with a somewhat more expensive disk controller than for CD-ROM, the customer can write once as well as read the disk.

The CD-R medium is similar to but not identical to that of a CD or CD-ROM. For CDs and CD-ROMs, information is recorded by the pitting of the surface of the medium, which changes reflectivity. For a CD-R, the medium includes a dye layer. The dye is used to change reflectivity and is activated by a high-intensity laser. The resulting disk can be read on a CD-R drive or a CD-ROM drive.

The CD-R optical disk is attractive for archival storage of documents and files. It provides a permanent record of large volumes of user data.

CD Rewritable The CD-RW optical disk can be repeatedly written and overwritten, as with a magnetic disk. Although a number of approaches have been tried, the only pure optical approach (as opposed to magneto-optical, discussed subsequently) that has proved attractive is called phase change. The phase change disk uses a material that has two significantly different reflectivities in two different phase states. There is an amorphous state, in which the molecules exhibit a random orientation that reflects light poorly; and a crystalline state, which has a smooth surface that reflects light well. A beam of laser light can change the material from one phase to the other. The primary disadvantage of phase change optical disks is that the material eventually and permanently loses its desirable properties. Current materials can be used for between 500,000 and 1,000,000 erase cycles.

The CD-RW has the obvious advantage over CD-ROM and CD-R that it can be rewritten and thus used as a true secondary storage. As such, it competes with magnetic disk. A key advantage of the optical disk is that the engineering tolerances for optical disks are much less severe than for high-capacity magnetic disks. Thus, they exhibit higher reliability and longer life.

Digital Versatile Disk With the capacious digital versatile disk (DVD), the electronics industry has at last found an acceptable replacement for the analog VHS video tape. The DVD will replace the video tape used in video cassette recorders (VCRs) and, more important for this discussion, replace the CD-ROM in personal computers and servers. The DVD takes video into the digital age. It delivers movies with impressive picture quality, and it can be randomly accessed like audio CDs, which DVD machines can also play. Vast volumes of data can be crammed onto the disk, currently seven times as much as a CD-ROM. With DVD's huge storage capacity and vivid quality, PC games will become more realistic and educational software will incorporate more video. Following in the wake of these developments will be a new crest of traffic over the Internet and corporate intranets, as this material is incorporated into Web sites. The DVD's greater capacity is due to three differences from CDs:

1. Bits are packed more closely on a DVD. The spacing between loops of a spiral on a CD is 1.6 μm and the minimum distance between pits along the spiral is 0.834 μm. The DVD uses a laser with shorter wavelength and achieves a loop spacing of 0.74 μm and

a minimum distance between pits of 0.4 μm. The result of these two improvements is about a sevenfold increase in capacity, to about 4.7 GB.

2. The DVD employs a second layer of pits and lands on top of the first layer A dual-layer DVD has a semireflective layer on top of the reflective layer, and by adjusting focus, the lasers in DVD drives can read each layer separately. This technique almost doubles the capacity of the disk, to about 8.5 GB. The lower reflectivity of the second layer limits its storage capacity so that a full doubling is not achieved.

3. The DVD-ROM can be two sided, whereas data are recorded on only one side of a CD. This brings total capacity up to 17 GB.

As with the CD, DVDs come in writeable as well as read-only versions (Table 11.8).

FILE MANAGEMENT

In most applications, the file is the central element. With the exception of real-time applications and some other specialized applications, the input to the application is by means of a file, and in virtually all applications, output is saved in a file for long-term storage and for later access by the user and by other programs.

Files have a life outside of any individual application that uses them for input and/or output. Users wish to be able to access files, save them, and maintain the integrity of their contents. To aid in these objectives, virtually all operating systems provide file management systems. Typically, a file management system consists of system utility programs that run as privileged applications. However, at the very least, a file management system needs special services from the operating system; at the most, the entire file management system is considered part of the operating system. Thus, it is appropriate to consider the basic elements of file management in this book.

We begin with an overview, followed by a look at various file organization schemes. Although file organization is generally beyond the scope of the operating system, it is essential to have a general understanding of the common alternatives to appreciate some of the design tradeoffs involved in file management. The remainder of this chapter looks at other topics in file management.

12.1 OVERVIEW

Files and File Systems

From the user's point of view, one of the most important parts of an operating system is the file system. The file system provides the resource abstractions typically associated with secondary storage. The file system permits users to create data collections, called files, with desirable properties, such as the following:

- **Long-term existence:** Files are stored on disk or other secondary storage and do not disappear when a user logs off.
- **Sharable between processes:** Files have names and can have associated access permissions that permit controlled sharing.
- **Structure:** Depending on the file system, a file can have an internal structure that is convenient for particular applications. In addition, files can be organized into hierarchical or more complex structure to reflect the relationships among files.

Any file system provides not only a means to store data organized as files, but a collection of functions that can be performed on files. Typical operations include the following:

- **Create:** A new file is defined and positioned within the structure of files.
- **Delete:** A file is removed from the file structure and destroyed.
- **Open:** An existing file is declared to be "opened" by a process, allowing the process to perform functions on the file.
- **Close:** The file is closed with respect to a process, so that the process no longer may perform functions on the file, until the process opens the file again.
- **Read:** A process reads all or a portion of the data in a file.

- **Write:** A process updates a file, either by adding new data that expands the size of the file or by changing the values of existing data items in the file.

Typically, a file system maintains a set of attributes associated with the file. These include owner, creation time, time last modified, access privileges, and so on.

File Structure

Four terms are in common use when discussing files:

- Field
- Record
- File
- Database

A **field** is the basic element of data. An individual field contains a single value, such as an employee's last name, a date, or the value of a sensor reading. It is characterized by its length and data type (e.g., ASCII string, decimal). Depending on the file design, fields may be fixed length or variable length. In the latter case, the field often consists of two or three subfields: the actual value to be stored, the name of the field, and, in some cases, the length of the field. In other cases of variable-length fields, the length of the field is indicated by the use of special demarcation symbols between fields.

A **record** is a collection of related fields that can be treated as a unit by some application program. For example, an employee record would contain such fields as name, social security number, job classification, date of hire, and so on. Again, depending on design, records may be of fixed length or variable length. A record will be of variable length if some of its fields are of variable length or if the number of fields may vary. In the latter case, each field is usually accompanied by a field name. In either case, the entire record usually includes a length field.

A **file** is a collection of similar records. The file is treated as a single entity by users and applications and may be referenced by name. Files have file names and may be created and deleted. Access control restrictions usually apply at the file level. That is, in a shared system, users and programs are granted or denied access to entire files. In some more sophisticated systems, such controls are enforced at the record or even the field level.

A **database** is a collection of related data. The essential aspects of a database are that the relationships that exist among elements of data are explicit and that the database is designed for use by a number of different applications. A database may contain all of the information related to an organization or project, such as a business or a scientific study. The database itself consists of one or more types of files. Usually, there is a separate database management system that is independent of the operating system, although that system may make use of some file management programs.

Users and applications wish to make use of files. Typical operations that must be supported include the following:

- **Retrieve_All:** Retrieve all the records of a file. This will be required for an application that must process all of the information in the file at one time. For example, an application that produces a summary of the information in the file would need to retrieve all records. This operation is often equated with the term *sequential processing*, because all of the records are accessed in sequence.

- **Retrieve_One:** This requires the retrieval of just a single record. Interactive, transaction-oriented applications need this operation.
- **Retrieve_Next:** This requires the retrieval of the record that is "next" in some logical sequence to the most recently retrieved record. Some interactive applications, such as filling in forms, may require such an operation. A program that is performing a search may also use this operation.
- **Retrieve_Previous:** Similar to Retrieve_Next, but in this case the record that is "previous" to the currently accessed record is retrieved.
- **Insert_One:** Insert a new record into the file. It may be necessary that the new record fit into a particular position to preserve a sequencing of the file.
- **Delete_One:** Delete an existing record. Certain linkages or other data structures may need to be updated to preserve the sequencing of the file.
- **Update_One:** Retrieve a record, update one or more of its fields, and rewrite the updated record back into the file. Again, it may be necessary to preserve sequencing with this operation. If the length of the record has changed, the update operation is generally more difficult than if the length is preserved.
- **Retrieve_Few:** Retrieve a number of records. For example, an application or user may wish to retrieve all records that satisfy a certain set of criteria.

The nature of the operations that are most commonly performed on a file will influence the way the file is organized, as discussed in Section 12.2.

It should be noted that not all file systems exhibit the sort of structure discussed in this subsection. On UNIX and UNIX-like systems, the basic file structure is just a stream of bytes. For example, a C program is stored as a file but does not have physical fields, records, and so on.

File Management Systems

A file management system is that set of system software that provides services to users and applications in the use of files. Typically, the only way that a user or application may access files is through the file management system. This relieves the user or programmer of the necessity of developing special-purpose software for each application and provides the system with a consistent, well-defined means of controlling its most important asset. [GROS86] suggests the following objectives for a file management system:

- To meet the data management needs and requirements of the user, which include storage of data and the ability to perform the aforementioned operations
- To guarantee, to the extent possible, that the data in the file are valid
- To optimize performance, both from the system point of view in terms of overall throughput and from the user's point of view in terms of response time
- To provide I/O support for a variety of storage device types

- To minimize or eliminate the potential for lost or destroyed data
- To provide a standardized set of I/O interface routines to use processes
- To provide I/O support for multiple users, in the case of multiple-user systems

With respect to the first point, meeting user requirements, the extent of such requirements depends on the variety of applications and the environment in which the computer system will be used. For an interactive, general-purpose system, the following constitute a minimal set of requirements:

1. Each user should be able to create, delete, read, write, and modify files.
2. Each user may have controlled access to other users' files.
3. Each user may control what types of accesses are allowed to the user's files.
4. Each user should be able to restructure the user's files in a form appropriate to the problem.
5. Each user should be able to move data between files.
6. Each user should be able to back up and recover the user's files in case of damage.
7. Each user should be able to access the user's files by using symbolic names.

These objectives and requirements should be kept in mind throughout our discussion of file management systems.

File System Architecture One way of getting a feel for the scope of file management is to look at a depiction of a typical software organization, as suggested in Figure 12.1. Of course, different systems will be organized differently, but this organization is reasonably representative. At the lowest level, **device drivers** communicate directly with peripheral devices or their controllers or channels. A device driver is responsible for starting I/O operations on a device and processing the completion of an I/O request. For file operations, the typical devices controlled are disk and tape drives. Device drivers are usually considered to be part of the operating system.

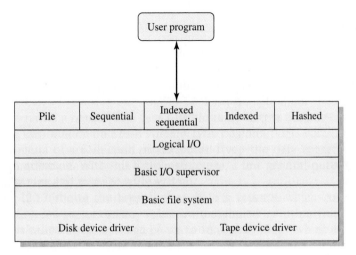

Figure 12.1 File System Software Architecture

The next level is referred to as the **basic file system**, or the **physical I/O** level. This is the primary interface with the environment outside of the computer system. It deals with blocks of data that are exchanged with disk or tape systems. Thus, it is concerned with the placement of those blocks on the secondary storage device and on the buffering of those blocks in main memory. It does not understand the content of the data or the structure of the files involved. The basic file system is often considered part of the operating system.

The **basic I/O supervisor** is responsible for all file I/O initiation and termination. At this level, control structures are maintained that deal with device I/O, scheduling, and file status. The basic I/O supervisor selects the device on which file I/O is to be performed, based on the particular file selected. It is also concerned with scheduling disk and tape accesses to optimize performance. I/O buffers are assigned and secondary memory is allocated at this level. The basic I/O supervisor is part of the operating system.

Logical I/O enables users and applications to access records. Thus, whereas the basic file system deals with blocks of data, the logical I/O module deals with file records. Logical I/O provides a general-purpose record I/O capability and maintains basic data about files.

The level of the file system closest to the user is often termed the **access method**. It provides a standard interface between applications and the file systems and devices that hold the data. Different access methods reflect different file structures and different ways of accessing and processing the data. Some of the most common access methods are shown in Figure 12.1, and these are briefly described in Section 12.2.

File Management Functions Another way of viewing the functions of a file system is shown in Figure 12.2. Let us follow this diagram from left to right. Users and application programs interact with the file system by means of commands for creating and deleting files and for performing operations on files. Before performing any operation, the file system must identify and locate the selected file. This requires the use of some sort of directory that serves to describe the location of all files, plus their attributes. In addition, most shared systems enforce user access control: Only authorized users are allowed to access particular files in particular ways. The basic operations that a user or application may perform on a file are performed at the record level. The user or application views the file as having some structure that organizes the records, such as a sequential structure (e.g., personnel records are stored alphabetically by last name). Thus, to translate user commands into specific file manipulation commands, the access method appropriate to this file structure must be employed.

Whereas users and applications are concerned with records, I/O is done on a block basis. Thus, the records of a file must be blocked for output and unblocked after input. To support block I/O of files, several functions are needed. The secondary storage must be managed. This involves allocating files to free blocks on secondary storage and managing free storage so as to know what blocks are available for new files and growth in existing files. In addition, individual block I/O requests must be scheduled; this issue was dealt with in Chapter 11. Both disk scheduling and file allocation are concerned with optimizing performance. As might be expected, these functions therefore need to be considered together. Furthermore, the optimization will depend on the structure of the files and the

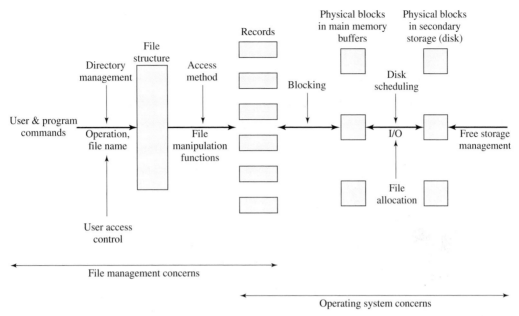

Figure 12.2   Elements of File Management

access patterns. Accordingly, developing an optimum file management system from the point of view of performance is an exceedingly complicated task.

Figure 12.2 suggests a division between what might be considered the concerns of the file management system as a separate system utility and the concerns of the operating system, with the point of intersection being record processing. This division is arbitrary; various approaches are taken in various systems.

In the remainder of this chapter, we look at some of the design issues suggested in Figure 12.2. We begin with a discussion of file organizations and access methods. Although this topic is beyond the scope of what is usually considered the concerns of the operating system, it is impossible to assess the other file-related design issues without an appreciation of file organization and access. Next, we look at the concept of file directories. These are often managed by the operating system on behalf of the file management system. The remaining topics deal with the physical I/O aspects of file management and are properly treated as aspects of operating system design. One such issue is the way in which logical records are organized into physical blocks. Finally, there are the related issues of file allocation on secondary storage and the management of free secondary storage.

12.2 FILE ORGANIZATION AND ACCESS

In this section, we use the term *file organization* to refer to the logical structuring of the records as determined by the way in which they are accessed. The physical organization of the file on secondary storage depends on the blocking strategy and the file allocation strategy, issues dealt with later in this chapter.

In choosing a file organization, several criteria are important:

- Short access time
- Ease of update
- Economy of storage
- Simple maintenance
- Reliability

The relative priority of these criteria will depend on the applications that will use the file. For example, if a file is only to be processed in batch mode, with all of the records accessed every time, then rapid access for retrieval of a single record is of minimal concern. A file stored on CD-ROM will never be updated, and so ease of update is not an issue.

These criteria may conflict. For example, for economy of storage, there should be minimum redundancy in the data. On the other hand, redundancy is a primary means of increasing the speed of access to data. An example of this is the use of indexes.

The number of alternative file organizations that have been implemented or just proposed is unmanageably large, even for a book devoted to file systems. In this brief survey, we will outline five fundamental organizations. Most structures used in actual systems either fall into one of these categories or can be implemented with a combination of these organizations. The five organizations, the first four of which are depicted in Figure 12.3, are

- The pile
- The sequential file
- The indexed sequential file
- The indexed file
- The direct, or hashed, file

Table 12.1 summarizes relative performance aspects of these five organizations.[1]

The Pile

The least-complicated form of file organization may be termed the *pile*. Data are collected in the order in which they arrive. Each record consists of one burst of data. The purpose of the pile is simply to accumulate the mass of data and save it. Records may have different fields, or similar fields in different orders. Thus, each field should be self-describing, including a field name as well as a value. The length of each field must be implicitly indicated by delimiters, explicitly included as a subfield, or known as default for that field type.

Because there is no structure to the pile file, record access is by exhaustive search. That is, if we wish to find a record that contains a particular field with a particular value, it is necessary to examine each record in the pile until the desired record is found or the

---

[1]The table employs the "big-O" notation, used for characterizing the time complexity of algorithms. An explanation of this notation is contained in a supporting document at this book's Web site.

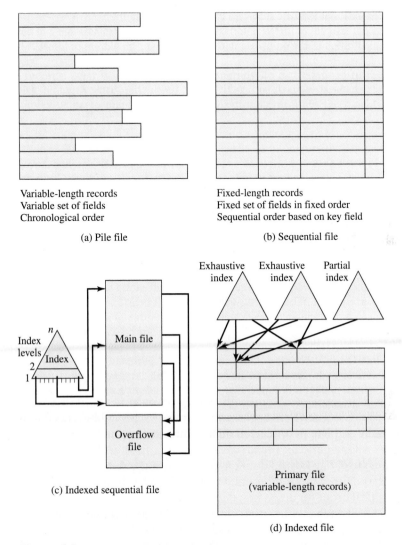

Figure 12.3 describes the following parts:

Variable-length records
Variable set of fields
Chronological order

(a) Pile file

Fixed-length records
Fixed set of fields in fixed order
Sequential order based on key field

(b) Sequential file

Index
levels

(c) Indexed sequential file

Exhaustive
index   Exhaustive
             index   Partial
                          index

Primary file
(variable-length records)

(d) Indexed file

Figure 12.3   Common File Organizations

entire file has been searched. If we wish to find all records that contain a particular field or contain that field with a particular value, then the entire file must be searched.

Pile files are encountered when data are collected and stored prior to processing or when data are not easy to organize. This type of file uses space well when the stored data vary in size and structure, is perfectly adequate for exhaustive searches, and is easy to update. However, beyond these limited uses, this type of file is unsuitable for most applications.

The Sequential File

The most common form of file structure is the sequential file. In this type of file, a fixed format is used for records. All records are of the same length, consisting of the

Table 12.1   Grades of Performance for Five Basic File Organizations [WIED87]

File Method	Space		Update		Retrieval		
	Attributes		Record Size				
	Variable	Fixed	Equal	Greater	Single record	Subset	Exhaustive
Pile	A	B	A	E	E	D	B
Sequential	F	A	D	F	F	D	A
Indexed sequential	F	B	B	D	B	D	B
Indexed	B	C	C	C	A	B	D
Hashed	F	B	B	F	B	F	E

A = Excellent, well suited to this purpose $\approx O(r)$
B = Good $\approx O(o \times r)$
C = Adequate $\approx O(r \log n)$
D = Requires some extra effort $\approx O(n)$
E = Possible with extreme effort $\approx O(r \times n)$
F = Not reasonable for this purpose $\approx O(n^{>1})$
where

    r = size of the result
    o = number of records that overflow
    n = number of records in file

same number of fixed-length fields in a particular order. Because the length and position of each field are known, only the values of fields need to be stored; the field name and length for each field are attributes of the file structure.

One particular field, usually the first field in each record, is referred to as the **key field**. The key field uniquely identifies the record; thus key values for different records are always different. Further, the records are stored in key sequence: alphabetical order for a text key, and numerical order for a numerical key.

Sequential files are typically used in batch applications and are generally optimum for such applications if they involve the processing of all the records (e.g., a billing or payroll application). The sequential file organization is the only one that is easily stored on tape as well as disk.

For interactive applications that involve queries and/or updates of individual records, the sequential file provides poor performance. Access requires the sequential search of the file for a key match. If the entire file, or a large portion of the file, can be brought into main memory at one time, more efficient search techniques are possible. Nevertheless, considerable processing and delay are encountered to access a record in a large sequential file. Additions to the file also present problems. Typically, a sequential file is stored in simple sequential ordering of the records within blocks. That is, the physical organization of the file on tape or disk directly matches the logical organization of the file. In this case, the usual procedure is to place new records in a separate pile file, called a log file or transaction file. Periodically, a batch update is performed that merges the log file with the master file to produce a new file in correct key sequence.

An alternative is to organize the sequential file physically as a linked list. One or more records are stored in each physical block. Each block on disk contains a pointer to the next block. The insertion of new records involves pointer manipulation but does not require that the new records occupy a particular physical block position. Thus, some added convenience is obtained at the cost of additional processing and overhead.

The Indexed Sequential File

A popular approach to overcoming the disadvantages of the sequential file is the indexed sequential file. The indexed sequential file maintains the key characteristic of the sequential file: Records are organized in sequence based on a key field. Two features are added: an index to the file to support random access, and an overflow file. The index provides a lookup capability to reach quickly the vicinity of a desired record. The overflow file is similar to the log file used with a sequential file but is integrated so that a record in the overflow file is located by following a pointer from its predecessor record.

In the simplest indexed sequential structure, a single level of indexing is used. The index in this case is a simple sequential file. Each record in the index file consists of two fields: a key field, which is the same as the key field in the main file, and a pointer into the main file. To find a specific field, the index is searched to find the highest key value that is equal to or precedes the desired key value. The search continues in the main file at the location indicated by the pointer.

To see the effectiveness of this approach, consider a sequential file with 1 million records. To search for a particular key value will require on average one-half million record accesses. Now suppose that an index containing 1000 entries is constructed, with the keys in the index more or less evenly distributed over the main file. Now it will take on average 500 accesses to the index file followed by 500 accesses to the main file to find the record. The average search length is reduced from 500,000 to 1000.

Additions to the file are handled in the following manner: Each record in the main file contains an additional field not visible to the application, which is a pointer to the overflow file. When a new record is to be inserted into the file, it is added to the overflow file. The record in the main file that immediately precedes the new record in logical sequence is updated to contain a pointer to the new record in the overflow file. If the immediately preceding record is itself in the overflow file, then the pointer in that record is updated. As with the sequential file, the indexed sequential file is occasionally merged with the overflow file in batch mode.

The indexed sequential file greatly reduces the time required to access a single record, without sacrificing the sequential nature of the file. To process the entire file sequentially, the records of the main file are processed in sequence until a pointer to the overflow is found; then accessing continues in the overflow file until a null pointer is encountered, at which time accessing of the main file is resumed where it left off.

To provide even greater efficiency in access, multiple levels of indexing can be used. Thus the lowest level of index file is treated as a sequential file and a higher-level index file is created for that file. Consider again a file with 1 million records. A lower-level index with 10,000 entries is constructed. A higher-level index into the lower level index of 100 entries can then be constructed. The search begins at the higher-level index (average length = 50 accesses) to find an entry point into the lower-level index. This index is then searched (average length = 50) to find an entry point into the main file, which is then searched (average length = 50). Thus the average length of search has been reduced from 500,000 to 1000 to 150.

The Indexed File

The indexed sequential file retains one limitation of the sequential file: Effective processing is limited to that which is based on a single field of the file. When it is necessary to search for a record on the basis of some other attribute than the key field, both forms of sequential file are inadequate. In some applications, this flexibility is desirable.

To achieve this flexibility, a structure is needed that employs multiple indexes, one for each type of field that may be the subject of a search. In the general indexed file, the concept of sequentiality and a single key are abandoned. Records are accessed only through their indexes. The result is that there is now no restriction on the placement of records as long as a pointer in at least one index refers to that record. Furthermore, variable-length records can be employed.

Two types of indexes are used. An exhaustive index contains one entry for every record in the main file. The index itself is organized as a sequential file for ease of searching. A partial index contains entries to records where the field of interest exists. With variable-length records, some records will not contain all fields. When a new record is added to the main file, all of the index files must be updated.

Indexed files are used mostly in applications where timeliness of information is critical and where data are rarely processed exhaustively. Examples are airline reservation systems and inventory control systems.

The Direct or Hashed File

The direct, or hashed, file exploits the capability found on disks to access directly any block of a known address. As with sequential and indexed sequential files, a key field is required in each record. However, there is no concept of sequential ordering here.

The direct file makes use of hashing on the key value. This function was explained in Appendix 8A. Figure 8.27b shows the type of hashing organization with an overflow file that is typically used in a hash file.

Direct files are often used where very rapid access is required, where fixed-length records are used, and where records are always accessed one at a time. Examples are directories, pricing tables, schedules, and name lists.

12.3 FILE DIRECTORIES

Contents

Associated with any file management system and collection of files is a file directory. The directory contains information about the files, including attributes, location, and ownership. Much of this information, especially that concerned with storage, is managed by the operating system. The directory is itself a file, accessible by various file management routines. Although some of the information in directories is available to users and applications, this is generally provided indirectly by system routines.

Table 12.2 suggests the information typically stored in the directory for each file in the system. From the user's point of view, the directory provides a mapping between file names, known to users and applications, and the files themselves. Thus, each file entry includes the name of the file. Virtually all systems deal with different types of files and different file organizations, and this information is also provided. An important category of information about each file concerns its storage, including its location and size. In shared systems, it is also important to provide information that is used to control access to the file. Typically, one user is the owner of the file and may grant certain access privileges to other users. Finally, usage information is needed to manage the current use of the file and to record the history of its usage.

Structure

The way in which the information of Table 12.2 is stored differs widely among various systems. Some of the information may be stored in a header record associated

Table 12.2   Information Elements of a File Directory

Basic Information	
File Name	Name as chosen by creator (user or program). Must be unique within a specific directory.
File Type	For example: text, binary, load module, etc.
File Organization	For systems that support different organizations
Address Information	
Volume	Indicates device on which file is stored
Starting Address	Starting physical address on secondary storage (e.g., cylinder, track, and block number on disk)
Size Used	Current size of the file in bytes, words, or blocks
Size Allocated	The maximum size of the file
Access Control Information	
Owner	User who is assigned control of this file. The owner may be able to grant/deny access to other users and to change these privileges.
Access Information	A simple version of this element would include the user's name and password for each authorized user.
Permitted Actions	Controls reading, writing, executing, transmitting over a network
Usage Information	
Date Created	When file was first placed in directory
Identity of Creator	Usually but not necessarily the current owner
Date Last Read Access	Date of the last time a record was read
Identity of Last Reader	User who did the reading
Date Last Modified	Date of the last update, insertion, or deletion
Identity of Last Modifier	User who did the modifying
Date of Last Backup	Date of the last time the file was backed up on another storage medium
Current Usage	Information about current activity on the file, such as process or processes that have the file open, whether it is locked by a process, and whether the file has been updated in main memory but not yet on disk

with the file; this reduces the amount of storage required for the directory, making it easier to keep all or much of the directory in main memory to improve speed.

The simplest form of structure for a directory is that of a list of entries, one for each file. This structure could be represented by a simple sequential file, with the name of the file serving as the key. In some earlier single-user systems, this technique has been used. However, it is inadequate when multiple users share a system and even for single users with many files.

To understand the requirements for a file structure, it is helpful to consider the types of operations that may be performed on the directory:

- **Search:** When a user or application references a file, the directory must be searched to find the entry corresponding to that file.
- **Create file:** When a new file is created, an entry must be added to the directory.
- **Delete file:** When a file is deleted, an entry must be removed from the directory.
- **List directory:** All or a portion of the directory may be requested. Generally, this request is made by a user and results in a listing of all files owned by that user, plus some of the attributes of each file (e.g., type, access control information, usage information).
- **Update directory:** Because some file attributes are stored in the directory, a change in one of these attributes requires a change in the corresponding directory entry.

The simple list is not suited to supporting these operations. Consider the needs of a single user. The user may have many types of files, including word-processing text files, graphic files, spreadsheets, and so on. The user may like to have these organized by project, by type, or in some other convenient way. If the directory is a simple sequential list, it provides no help in organizing the files and forces the user to be careful not to use the same name for two different types of files. The problem is much worse in a shared system. Unique naming becomes a serious problem. Furthermore, it is difficult to conceal portions of the overall directory from users when there is no inherent structure in the directory.

A start in solving these problems would be to go to a two-level scheme. In this case, there is one directory for each user, and a master directory. The master directory has an entry for each user directory, providing address and access control information. Each user directory is a simple list of the files of that user. This arrangement means that names must be unique only within the collection of files of a single user and that the file system can easily enforce access restriction on directories. However, it still provides users with no help in structuring collections of files.

A more powerful and flexible approach, and one that is almost universally adopted, is the hierarchical, or tree-structure, approach (Figure 12.4). As before, there is a master directory, which has under it a number of user directories. Each of these user directories, in turn, may have subdirectories and files as entries. This is true at any level: That is, at any level, a directory may consist of entries for subdirectories and/or entries for files.

It remains to say how each directory and subdirectory is organized. The simplest approach, of course, is to store each directory as a sequential file. When

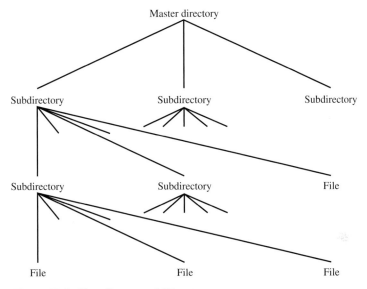

Figure 12.4   Tree-Structured Directory

directories may contain a very large number of entries, such an organization may lead to unnecessarily long search times. In that case, a hashed structure is to be preferred.

Naming

Users need to be able to refer to a file by a symbolic name. Clearly, each file in the system must have a unique name in order that file references be unambiguous. On the other hand, it is an unacceptable burden on users to require that they provide unique names, especially in a shared system.

The use of a tree-structured directory minimizes the difficulty in assigning unique names. Any file in the system can be located by following a path from the root or master directory down various branches until the file is reached. The series of directory names, culminating in the file name itself, constitutes a **pathname** for the file. As an example, the file in the lower left-hand corner of Figure 12.5 has the pathname/ User_B/Word/Unit_A/ABC. The slash is used to delimit names in the sequence. The name of the master directory is implicit, because all paths start at that directory. Note that it is perfectly acceptable to have several files with the same file name, as long as they have unique pathnames, which is equivalent to saying that the same file name may be used in different directories. In our example, there is another file in the system with the file name ABC, but that has the pathname /User_B/Draw/ABC.

Although the pathname facilitates the selection of file names, it would be awkward for a user to have to spell out the entire pathname every time a reference is made to a file. Typically, an interactive user or a process has associated with it a current directory, often referred to as the **working directory**. Files are then referenced relative to the working directory. For example, if the working directory for user B is "Word," then the pathname UnitA/ABC is sufficient to identify the file in the lower left-hand corner of Figure 12.5. When an interactive user logs on, or when a process

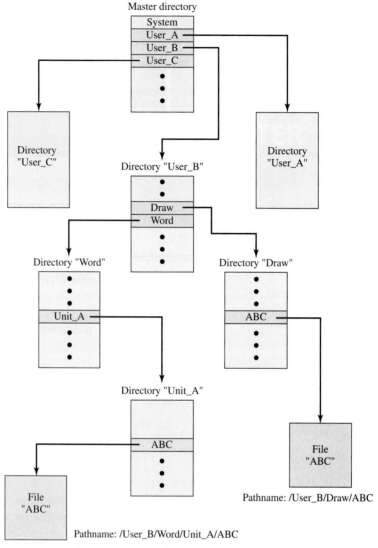

Figure 12.5 Example of Tree-Structured Directory

is created, the default for the working directory is the user home directory. During execution, the user can navigate up or down in the tree to change to a different working directory.

12.4 FILE SHARING

In a multiuser system, there is almost always a requirement for allowing files to be shared among a number of users. Two issues arise: access rights and the management of simultaneous access.

Access Rights

The file system should provide a flexible tool for allowing extensive file sharing among users. The file system should provide a number of options so that the way in which a particular file is accessed can be controlled. Typically, users or groups of users are granted certain access rights to a file. A wide range of access rights has been used. The following list is representative of access rights that can be assigned to a particular user for a particular file:

- **None:** The user may not even learn of the existence of the file, much less access it. To enforce this restriction, the user would not be allowed to read the user directory that includes this file.
- **Knowledge:** The user can determine that the file exists and who its owner is. The user is then able to petition the owner for additional access rights.
- **Execution:** The user can load and execute a program but cannot copy it. Proprietary programs are often made accessible with this restriction.
- **Reading:** The user can read the file for any purpose, including copying and execution. Some systems are able to enforce a distinction between viewing and copying. In the former case, the contents of the file can be displayed to the user, but the user has no means for making a copy.
- **Appending:** The user can add data to the file, often only at the end, but cannot modify or delete any of the file's contents. This right is useful in collecting data from a number of sources.
- **Updating:** The user can modify, delete, and add to the file's data. This normally includes writing the file initially, rewriting it completely or in part, and removing all or a portion of the data. Some systems distinguish among different degrees of updating.
- **Changing protection:** The user can change the access rights granted to other users. Typically, this right is held only by the owner of the file. In some systems, the owner can extend this right to others. To prevent abuse of this mechanism, the file owner will typically be able to specify which rights can be changed by the holder of this right.
- **Deletion:** The user can delete the file from the file system.

These rights can be considered to constitute a hierarchy, with each right implying those that precede it. Thus, if a particular user is granted the updating right for a particular file, then that user is also granted the following rights: knowledge, execution, reading, and appending.

One user is designated as owner of a given file, usually the person who initially created a file. The owner has all of the access rights listed previously and may grant rights to others. Access can be provided to different classes of users:

- **Specific user:** Individual users who are designated by user ID.
- **User groups:** A set of users who are not individually defined. The system must have some way of keeping track of the membership of user groups.
- **All:** All users who have access to this system. These are public files.

Simultaneous Access

When access is granted to append or update a file to more than one user, the operating system or file management system must enforce discipline. A brute-force approach is to allow a user to lock the entire file when it is to be updated. A finer grain of control is to lock individual records during update. Essentially, this is the readers/writers problem discussed in Chapter 5. Issues of mutual exclusion and deadlock must be addressed in designing the shared access capability.

12.5 RECORD BLOCKING

As indicated in Figure 12.2, records are the logical unit of access of a structured file,[2] whereas blocks are the unit of I/O with secondary storage. For I/O to be performed, records must be organized as blocks.

There are several issues to consider. First, should blocks be of fixed or variable length? On most systems, blocks are of fixed length. This simplifies I/O, buffer allocation in main memory, and the organization of blocks on secondary storage. Next, what should the relative size of a block be compared to the average record size? The tradeoff is this: The larger the block, the more records that are passed in one I/O operation. If a file is being processed or searched sequentially, this is an advantage, because the number of I/O operations is reduced by using larger blocks, thus speeding up processing. On the other hand, if records are being accessed randomly and no particular locality of reference is observed, then larger blocks result in the unnecessary transfer of unused records. However, combining the frequency of sequential operations with the potential for locality of reference, we can say that the I/O transfer time is reduced by using larger blocks. The competing concern is that larger blocks require larger I/O buffers, making buffer management more difficult.

Given the size of a block, there are three methods of blocking that can be used:

- **Fixed blocking:** Fixed-length records are used, and an integral number of records is stored in a block. There may be unused space at the end of each block. This is referred to as internal fragmentation.

- **Variable-length spanned blocking:** Variable-length records are used and are packed into blocks with no unused space. Thus, some records must span two blocks, with the continuation indicated by a pointer to the successor block.

- **Variable-length unspanned blocking:** Variable-length records are used, but spanning is not employed. There is wasted space in most blocks because of the inability to use the remainder of a block if the next record is larger than the remaining unused space.

Figure 12.6 illustrates these methods assuming that a file is stored in sequential blocks on a disk. The effect would not be changed if some other file allocation scheme were used (see Section 12.6).

---

[2]As opposed to a file that is treated only as a stream of bytes, such as in the UNIX file system.

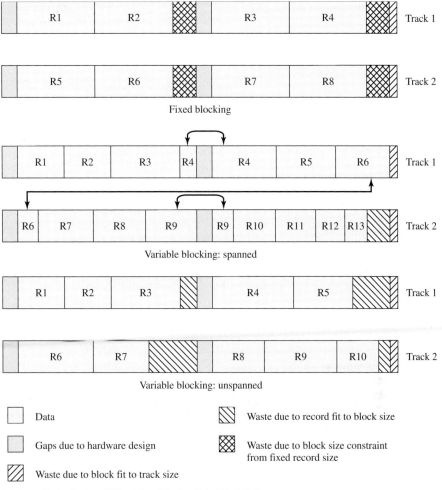

Figure 12.6   Record Blocking Methods [WIED87]

Fixed blocking is the common mode for sequential files with fixed-length records. Variable-length spanned blocking is efficient of storage and does not limit the size of records. However, this technique is difficult to implement. Records that span two blocks require two I/O operations, and files are difficult to update, regardless of the organization. Variable-length unspanned blocking results in wasted space and limits record size to the size of a block.

The record-blocking technique may interact with the virtual memory hardware, if such is employed. In a virtual memory environment, it is desirable to make the page the basic unit of transfer. Pages are generally quite small, so that it is impractical to treat a page as a block for unspanned blocking. Accordingly, some systems combine multiple pages to create a larger block for file I/O purposes. This approach is used for VSAM files on IBM mainframes.

12.6 SECONDARY STORAGE MANAGEMENT

On secondary storage, a file consists of a collection of blocks. The operating system or file management system is responsible for allocating blocks to files. This raises two management issues. First, space on secondary storage must be allocated to files, and second, it is necessary to keep track of the space available for allocation. We will see that these two tasks are related; that is, the approach taken for file allocation may influence the approach taken for free space management. Further, we will see that there is an interaction between file structure and allocation policy.

We begin this section by looking at alternatives for file allocation on a single disk. Then we look at the issue of free space management, and finally we discuss reliability.

File Allocation

Several issues are involved in file allocation:

1. When a new file is created, is the maximum space required for the file allocated at once?
2. Space is allocated to a file as one or more contiguous units, which we shall refer to as portions. The size of a portion can range from a single block to the entire file. What size of portion should be used for file allocation?
3. What sort of data structure or table is used to keep track of the portions assigned to a file? An example of such a structure is a **file allocation table** (FAT), found on DOS and some other systems.

Let us examine these issues in turn.

Preallocation versus Dynamic Allocation A preallocation policy requires that the maximum size of a file be declared at the time of the file creation request. In a number of cases, such as program compilations, the production of summary data files, or the transfer of a file from another system over a communications network, this value can be reliably estimated. However, for many applications, it is difficult if not impossible to estimate reliably the maximum potential size of the file. In those cases, users and application programmers would tend to overestimate file size so as not to run out of space. This clearly is wasteful from the point of view of secondary storage allocation. Thus, there are advantages to the use of dynamic allocation, which allocates space to a file in portions as needed.

Portion Size The second issue listed is that of the size of the portion allocated to a file. At one extreme, a portion large enough to hold the entire file is allocated. At the other extreme, space on the disk is allocated one block at a time. In choosing a portion size, there is a tradeoff between efficiency from the point of view of a single file versus overall system efficiency. [WIED87] lists four items to be considered in the tradeoff:

1. Contiguity of space increases performance, especially for Retrieve_Next operations, and greatly for transactions running in a transaction-oriented operating system.

2. Having a large number of small portions increases the size of tables needed to manage the allocation information.

3. Having fixed-size portions (for example, blocks) simplifies the reallocation of space.

4. Having variable-size or small fixed-size portions minimizes waste of unused storage due to overallocation.

Of course, these items interact and must be considered together. The result is that there are two major alternatives:

- **Variable, large contiguous portions:** This will provide better performance. The variable size avoids waste, and the file allocation tables are small. However, space is hard to reuse.

- **Blocks:** Small fixed portions provide greater flexibility. They may require large tables or complex structures for their allocation. Contiguity has been abandoned as a primary goal; blocks are allocated as needed.

Either option is compatible with preallocation or dynamic allocation. In the case of variable, large contiguous portions, a file is preallocated one contiguous group of blocks. This eliminates the need for a file allocation table; all that is required is a pointer to the first block and the number of blocks allocated. In the case of blocks, all of the portions required are allocated at one time. This means that the file allocation table for the file will remain of fixed size.

With variable-size portions, we need to be concerned with the fragmentation of free space. This issue was faced when we considered partitioned main memory in Chapter 7. The following are possible alternative strategies:

- **First fit:** Choose the first unused contiguous group of blocks of sufficient size from a free block list.

- **Best fit:** Choose the smallest unused group that is of sufficient size.

- **Nearest fit:** Choose the unused group of sufficient size that is closest to the previous allocation for the file to increase locality.

It is not clear which strategy is best. The difficulty in modeling alternative strategies is that so many factors interact, including types of files, pattern of file access, degree of multiprogramming, other performance factors in the system, disk caching, disk scheduling, and so on.

File Allocation Methods Having looked at the issues of preallocation versus dynamic allocation and portion size, we are in a position to consider specific file allocation methods. Three methods are in common use: contiguous, chained, and indexed. Table 12.3 summarizes some of the characteristics of each method.

With **contiguous allocation**, a single contiguous set of blocks is allocated to a file at the time of file creation (Figure 12.7). Thus, this is a preallocation strategy, using variable-size portions. The file allocation table needs just a single entry for each file, showing the starting block and the length of the file. Contiguous allocation is the best from the point of view of the individual sequential file. Multiple blocks can be read in at a time to improve I/O performance for sequential processing. It is

Table 12.3   File Allocation Methods

	Contiguous	**Chained**	**Indexed**	
Preallocation?	Necessary	Possible	Possible	
Fixed or variable size portions?	Variable	Fixed blocks	Fixed blocks	Variable
Portion size	Large	Small	Small	Medium
Allocation frequency	Once	Low to high	High	Low
Time to allocate	Medium	Long	Short	Medium
File allocation table size	One entry	One entry	Large	Medium

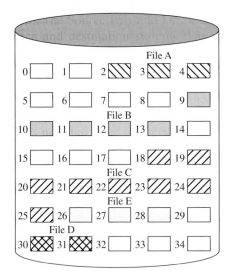

File Allocation Table

File Name	Start Block	Length
File A	2	3
File B	9	5
File C	18	8
File D	30	2
File E	26	3

Figure 12.7   Contiguous File Allocation

also easy to retrieve a single block. For example, if a file starts at block b, and the ith block of the file is wanted, its location on secondary storage is simply $b + i - 1$. Contiguous allocation presents some problems. External fragmentation will occur, making it difficult to find contiguous blocks of space of sufficient length. From time to time, it will be necessary to perform a compaction algorithm to free up additional space on the disk (Figure 12.8). Also, with preallocation, it is necessary to declare the size of the file at the time of creation, with the problems mentioned earlier.

At the opposite extreme from contiguous allocation is **chained allocation** (Figure 12.9). Typically, allocation is on an individual block basis. Each block contains a pointer to the next block in the chain. Again, the file allocation table needs just a single entry for each file, showing the starting block and the length of the file. Although preallocation is possible, it is more common simply to allocate blocks as needed. The selection of blocks is now a simple matter: Any free block can be added to a chain. There is no external fragmentation to worry about because only one

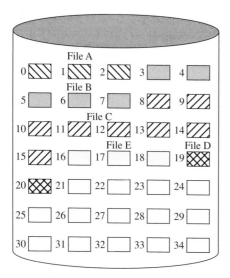

File Allocation Table		
File Name	Start Block	Length
File A	0	3
File B	3	5
File C	8	8
File D	19	2
File E	16	3

Figure 12.8   Contiguous File Allocation (After Compaction)

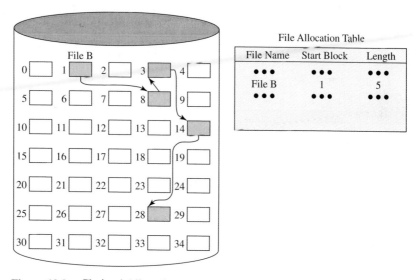

File Allocation Table		
File Name	Start Block	Length
•••	•••	•••
File B	1	5
•••	•••	•••

Figure 12.9   Chained Allocation

block at a time is needed. This type of physical organization is best suited to sequential files that are to be processed sequentially. To select an individual block of a file requires tracing through the chain to the desired block.

One consequence of chaining, as described so far, is that there is no accommodation of the principle of locality. Thus, if it is necessary to bring in several blocks of a file at a time, as in sequential processing, then a series of accesses to different parts of the disk are required. This is perhaps a more significant effect on a single-user system but may also be of concern on a shared system. To overcome this problem, some systems periodically consolidate files (Figure 12.10).

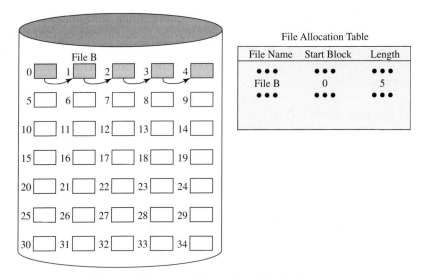

Figure 12.10 Chained Allocation (After Consolidation)

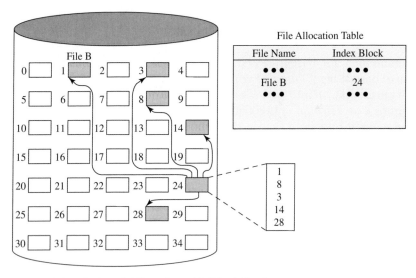

Figure 12.11 Indexed Allocation with Block Portions

Indexed allocation addresses many of the problems of contiguous and chained allocation. In this case, the file allocation table contains a separate one-level index for each file; the index has one entry for each portion allocated to the file. Typically, the file indexes are not physically stored as part of the file allocation table. Rather, the file index for a file is kept in a separate block, and the entry for the file in the file allocation table points to that block. Allocation may be on the basis of either fixed-size blocks (Figure 12.11) or variable-size portions (Figure 12.12). Allocation by blocks eliminates external fragmentation, whereas allocation by variable-size portions improves locality. In either case, file consolidation may be

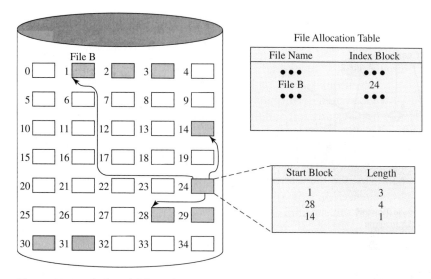

Figure 12.12   Indexed Allocation with Variable-Length Portions

done from time to time. File consolidation reduces the size of the index in the case of variable-size portions, but not in the case of block allocation. Indexed allocation supports both sequential and direct access to the file and thus is the most popular form of file allocation.

Free Space Management

Just as the space that is allocated to files must be managed, so the space that is not currently allocated to any file must be managed. To perform any of the file allocation techniques described previously, it is necessary to know what blocks on the disk are available. Thus we need a **disk allocation table** in addition to a file allocation table. We discuss here a number of techniques that have been implemented.

Bit Tables This method uses a vector containing one bit for each block on the disk. Each entry of a 0 corresponds to a free block, and each 1 corresponds to a block in use. For example, for the disk layout of Figure 12.7, a vector of length 35 is needed and would have the following value:

00111000011111000011111111111011000

A bit table has the advantage that it relatively easy to find one or a contiguous group of free blocks. Thus, a bit table works well with any of the file allocation methods outlined. Another advantage is that it is as small as possible. However, it can still be sizable. The amount of memory (in bytes) required for a block bitmap is

$$\frac{\text{disk size in bytes}}{8 \times \text{file system block size}}$$

Thus, for a 16-Gbyte disk with 512-bit blocks, the bit table occupies about 4 Mbytes. Can we spare 4 Mbytes of main memory for the bit table? If so, then the bit table can be searched without the need for disk access. But even with today's memory sizes, 4 Mbytes is a hefty chunk of main memory to devote to a single function. The alternative is to put the bit table on disk. But a 4-Mbyte bit table would require about 8000 disk blocks. We can't afford to search that amount of disk space every time a block is needed, so a bit table resident in memory is indicated.

Even when the bit table is in main memory, an exhaustive search of the table can slow file system performance to an unacceptable degree. This is especially true when the disk is nearly full and there are few free blocks remaining. Accordingly, most file systems that use bit tables maintain auxiliary data structures that summarize the contents of subranges of the bit table. For example, the table could be divided logically into a number of equal-size subranges. A summary table could include, for each subrange, the number of free blocks and the maximum-sized contiguous number of free blocks. When the file system needs a number of contiguous blocks, it can scan the summary table to find an appropriate subrange and then search that subrange.

Chained Free Portions   The free portions may be chained together by using a pointer and length value in each free portion. This method has negligible space overhead because there is no need for a disk allocation table, merely for a pointer to the beginning of the chain and the length of the first portion. This method is suited to all of the file allocation methods. If allocation is a block at a time, simply choose the free block at the head of the chain and adjust the first pointer or length value. If allocation is by variable-length portion, a first-fit algorithm may be used: The headers from the portions are fetched one at a time to determine the next suitable free portion in the chain. Again, pointer and length values are adjusted.

This method has its own problems. After some use, the disk will become quite fragmented and many portions will be a single block long. Also note that every time you allocate a block, you need to read the block first to recover the pointer to the new first free block before writing data to that block. If many individual blocks need to be allocated at one time for a file operation, this greatly slows file creation. Similarly, deleting highly fragmented files is very time consuming.

Indexing   The indexing approach treats free space as a file and uses an index table as described under file allocation. For efficiency, the index should be on the basis of variable-size portions rather than blocks. Thus, there is one entry in the table for every free portion on the disk. This approach provides efficient support for all of the file allocation methods.

Free Block List   In this method, each block is assigned a number sequentially and the list of the numbers of all free blocks is maintained in a reserved portion of the disk. Depending on the size of the disk, either 24 or 32 bits will be needed to store a single block number, so the size of the free block list is 24 or 32 times the size of the corresponding bit table and thus must be stored on disk rather than in main memory. However, this is a satisfactory method. Consider the following points:

1. The space on disk devoted the free block list is less than 1% of the total disk space. If a 32-bit block number is used, then the space penalty is 4 bytes for every 512-byte block.

2. Although the free block list is too large to store in main memory, there are two effective techniques for storing a small part of the list in main memory.

(a) The list can be treated as a push-down stack (Appendix 1B) with the first few thousand elements of the stack kept in main memory. When a new block is allocated, it is popped from the top of the stack, which is in main memory. Similarly, when a block is deallocated, it is pushed onto the stack. There only has to be a transfer between disk and main memory when the in-memory portion of the stack becomes either full or empty. Thus, this technique gives almost zero-time access most of the time.

(b) The list can be treated as a FIFO queue, with a few thousand entries from the both the head and the tail of the queue in main memory. A block is allocated by taking the first entry from the head of the queue and deallocated by adding it to the end of the tail of the queue. There only has to be a transfer between disk and main memory when either the in-memory portion of the head of the queue becomes empty or the in-memory portion of the tail of the queue becomes full.

In either of the strategies listed in the preceding point (stack or FIFO queue), a background thread can slowly sort the in-memory list or lists to facilitate contiguous allocation.

Reliability

Consider the following scenario:

1. User A requests a file allocation to add to an existing file.
2. The request is granted and the disk and file allocation tables are updated in main memory but not yet on disk.
3. The system crashes and subsequently restarts.
4. User B requests a file allocation and is allocated space on disk that overlaps the last allocation to user A.
5. User A accesses the overlapped portion via a reference that is stored inside A's file.

This difficulty arose because the system maintained a copy of the disk allocation table and file allocation table in main memory for efficiency. To prevent this type of error, the following steps could be performed when a file allocation is requested:

1. Lock the disk allocation table on disk. This prevents another user from causing alterations to the table until this allocation is completed.
2. Search the disk allocation table for available space. This assumes that a copy of the disk allocation table is always kept in main memory. If not, it must first be read in.
3. Allocate space, update the disk allocation table, and update the disk. Updating the disk involves writing the disk allocation table back onto disk. For chained disk allocation, it also involves updating some pointers on disk.
4. Update the file allocation table and update the disk.
5. Unlock the disk allocation table.

This technique will prevent errors. However, when small portions are allocated frequently, the impact on performance will be substantial. To reduce this overhead, a batch storage allocation scheme could be used. In this case, a batch of free portions on the disk is obtained for allocation. The corresponding portions on disk are marked "in use." Allocation using this batch may proceed in main memory. When the batch is exhausted, the disk allocation table is updated on disk and a new batch may be acquired. If a system crash occurs, portions on the disk marked "in use" must be cleaned up in some fashion before they can be reallocated. The technique for cleanup will depend on the file system's particular characteristics.

12.7 UNIX FILE MANAGEMENT

In the UNIX file system, six types of files are distinguished:

- **Regular or ordinary:** Contains arbitrary data in zero or more data blocks. Regular files contain information entered in them by a user, an application program, or a system utility program. The file system does not impose any internal structure to a regular file but treats it as a stream of bytes.
- **Directory:** Contains a list of file names plus pointers to associated inodes (index nodes), described later. Directories are hierarchically organized (Figure 12.4). Directory files are actually ordinary files with special write protection privileges so that only the file system can write into them, while read access is available to user programs.
- **Special:** Contains no data, but provides a mechanism to map physical devices to file names. The file names are used to access peripheral devices, such as terminals and printers. Each I/O device is associated with a special file, as discussed in Section 11.8.
- **Named pipes:** As discussed in Section 6.7, a pipe is an interprocess communications facility. A pipe file buffers data received in its input so that a process that reads from the pipe's output receives the data on a first-in-first-out basis.
- **Links:** In essence, a link is an alternative file name for an existing file.
- **Symbolic links:** This is a data file that contains the name of the file it is linked to.

In this section, we are concerned with the handling of ordinary files, which correspond to what most systems treat as files.

Inodes

All types of UNIX files are administered by the operating system by means of inodes. An inode (index node) is a control structure that contains the key information needed by the operating system for a particular file. Several file names may be associated with a single inode, but an active inode is associated with exactly one file, and each file is controlled by exactly one inode.

Table 12.4 Information in a UNIX Disk-Resident Inode

File Mode	16-bit flag that stores access and execution permissions associated with the file.	
	12–14	File type (regular, directory, character or block special, FIFO pipe
	9–11	Execution flags
	8	Owner read permission
	7	Owner write permission
	6	Owner execute permission
	5	Group read permission
	4	Group write permission
	3	Group execute permission
	2	Other read permission
	1	Other write permission
	0	Other execute permission
Link Count	Number of directory references to this inode	
Owner ID	Individual owner of file	
Group ID	Group owner associated with this file	
File Size	Number of bytes in file	
File Addresses	39 bytes of address information	
Last Accessed	Time of last file access	
Last Modified	Time of last file modification	
Inode Modified	Time of last inode modification	

The attributes of the file as well as its permissions and other control information are stored in the inode. Table 12.4 lists the file attributes stored in the inode of a typical UNIX implementation.

On the disk, there is an inode table, or inode list, that contains the inodes of all the files in the file system. When a file is opened, its inode is brought into main memory and stored in a memory-resident inode table.

File Allocation

File allocation is done on a block basis. Allocation is dynamic, as needed, rather than using preallocation. Hence, the blocks of a file on disk are not necessarily contiguous. An indexed method is used to keep track of each file, with part of the index stored in the inode for the file. The inode includes 39 bytes of address information that is organized as thirteen 3-byte addresses, or pointers. The first 10 addresses point to the first 10 data blocks of the file. If the file is longer than 10 blocks long, then one or more levels of indirection is used as follows:

- The eleventh address in the inode points to a block on disk that contains the next portion of the index. This is referred to as the single indirect block. This block contains the pointers to succeeding blocks in the file.
- If the file contains more blocks, the twelfth address in the inode points to a double indirect block. This block contains a list of addresses of additional single indirect blocks. Each of single indirect blocks, in turn, contains pointers to file blocks.

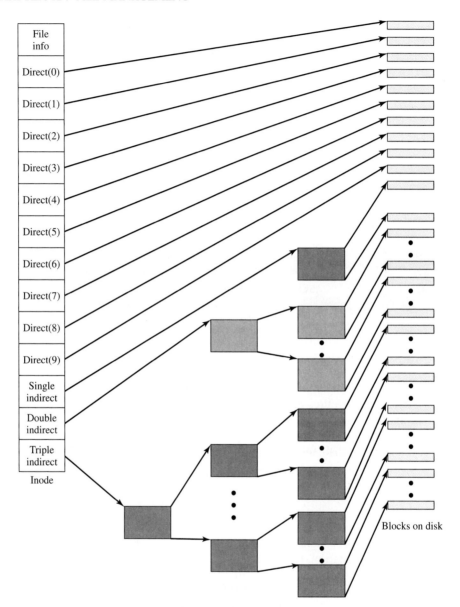

Figure 12.13   Layout of a UNIX File on Disk

- If the file contains still more blocks, the thirteenth address in the inode points to a triple indirect block that is a third level of indexing. This block points to additional double indirect blocks.

All of this is illustrated in Figure 12.13. The first entry in the inode contains information about this file or directory (Table 12.4). The remaining entries are the addresses just described. The total number of data blocks in a file depends on the capacity of the fixed-size blocks in the system. In UNIX System V, the length of a block is 1 Kbyte, and each block can hold a total of 256 block

Table 12.5 Capacity of a UNIX File

Level	Number of Blocks	Number of Bytes
Direct	10	10K
Single Indirect	256	256K
Double Indirect	$256 \times 256 = 65K$	65M
Triple Indirect	$256 \times 65K = 16M$	16G

addresses. Thus, the maximum size of a file with this scheme is over 16 Gbytes (Table 12.5).

This scheme has several advantages:

1. The inode is of fixed size and relatively small and hence may be kept in main memory for long periods.
2. Smaller files may be accessed with little or no indirection, reducing processing and disk access time.
3. The theoretical maximum size of a file is large enough to satisfy virtually all applications.

Directories

Directories are structured in a hierarchical tree. Each directory can contain files and/or other directories. A directory that is inside another directory is referred to as a subdirectory. As was mentioned, a directory is simply a file that contains a list of file names plus pointers to associated inodes. Figure 12.14 shows the overall structure. Each directory entry (dentry) contains a name for the associated file or subdirectory plus an integer called the i-number (index number). When the file or directory is accessed, its i-number is used as an index into the inode table.

Volume Structure

A UNIX file system resides on a single logical disk or disk partition and is laid out with the following elements:

- **Boot block:** Contains code required to boot the operating system
- **Superblock:** Contains attributes and information about the file system, such as partition size and inode table size
- **Inode table:** The collection of inodes for each file
- **Data blocks:** Storage space available for data files and subdirectories

12.8 LINUX VIRTUAL FILE SYSTEM

Linux includes a versatile and powerful file handling facility, designed to support a wide variety of file management systems and file structures. The approach taken in Linux is to make use of a **virtual file system (VFS)**, which presents a single, uniform

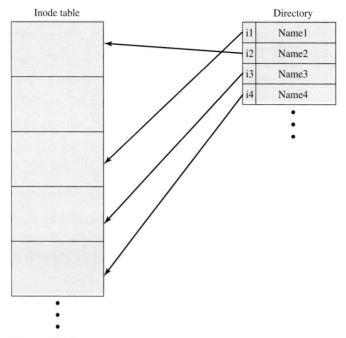

Figure 12.14   UNIX Directories and Inodes

file system interface to user processes. The VFS defines a common file model that is capable of representing any conceivable file system's general feature and behavior. The VFS assumes that files are objects in a computer's mass storage memory that share basic properties regardless of the target file system or the underlying processor hardware. Files have symbolic names that allow them to be uniquely identified within a specific directory within the file system. A file has an owner, protection against unauthorized access or modification, and a variety of other properties. A file may be created, read from, written to, or deleted. For any specific file system, a mapping module is needed to transform the characteristics of the real file system to the characteristics expected by the virtual file system.

Figure 12.15 indicates the key ingredients of the Linux file system strategy. A user process issues a file system call (e.g., read) using the VFS file scheme. The VFS converts this into an internal (to the kernel) file system call that is passed to a mapping function for a specific file system [e.g., IBM's Journaling File System (JFS)]. In most cases, the mapping function is simply a mapping of file system functional calls from one scheme to another. In some cases, the mapping function is more complex. For example, some file systems use a file allocation table (FAT), which stores the position of each file in the directory tree. In these file systems, directories are not files. For such file systems, the mapping function for such a file system must be able to construct dynamically, and when needed, the files corresponding to the directories. In any case, the original user file system call is translated into a call that is native to the target file system. The target file system software is then invoked to perform the requested function on a file or directory under its control and secondary storage. The results of the operation are then communicated back to the user in a similar fashion.

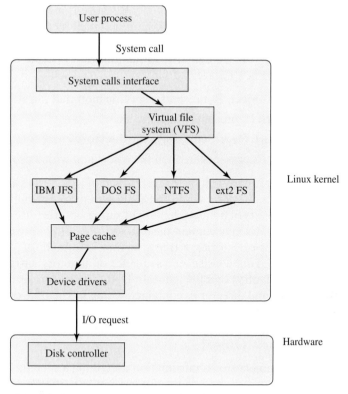

Figure 12.15   Linux Virtual File System Context

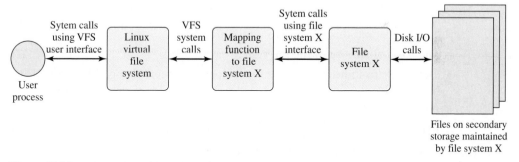

Figure 12.16   Linux Virtual File System Concept

Figure 12.16 indicates the role that VFS plays within the Linux kernel. When a process initiates a file-oriented system call (e.g., read), the kernel calls a function in the VFS. This function handles the file-system-independent manipulations and initiates a call to a function in the target file system code. This call passes through a mapping function that converts the call from the VFS into a call to the target file system. The VFS is independent of any file system, so the implementation of a mapping function must be part of the implementation of a file system on Linux. The target file system converts the file system request into device-oriented instructions that are passed to a device driver by means of page cache functions.

VFS is an object-oriented scheme. Because it is written in C, rather than a language that supports object programming (such as C++ or Java), VFS objects are implemented simply as C data structures. Each object contains both data and pointers to file-system-implemented functions that operate on data. The four primary object types in VFS are as follows:

- **Superblock object:** Represents a specific mounted file system
- **Inode object:** Represents a specific file
- **Dentry object:** Represents a specific directory entry
- **File object:** Represents an open file associated with a process

This scheme is based on the concepts used in UNIX file systems, as described in Section 12.7. The key concepts of UNIX file system to remember are the following. A file system consists of a hierarchal organization of directories. A directory is analogous to a folder and may contain files and/or other directories. Because a directory may contain other directories, a tree structure is formed. A path through the tree structure from the root consists of a sequence of directory entries, ending in either a directory entry (dentry) or a file name. In UNIX, a directory is implemented as a file that lists the files and directories contained within it. Thus, file operations can be performed on either files or directories.

The Superblock Object

The superblock object stores information describing a specific file system. Typically, the superblock corresponds to the file system superblock or file system control block, which is stored in a special sector on disk.

The superblock object consists a number of data items. Examples include the following:

- The device that this file system is mounted on
- The basic block size of the file system
- Dirty flag, to indicate that the superblock has been changed but not written back to disk
- File type
- Flags, such as a read-only flag
- Pointer to the root of the file system directory
- List of open files
- Semaphore for controlling access to the file system
- List of superblock operations

The last item on the preceding list refers to an operations object contained within the superblock object. The operation object defines the object methods (functions) that the kernel can invoke against the superblock object. The methods defined for the superblock object include the following:

- * **read_inode:** Read a specified inode from a mounted file system.
- * **write_inode:** Write given inode to disk.

- * **put_inode:** Release inode.
- * **delete_inode:** Delete inode from disk.
- * **notify_change:** Called when inode attributes are changed.
- * **put_super:** Called by the VFS on unmount to release the given superblock.
- * **write_super:** Called when the VFS decides that the superblock needs to be written to disk.
- * **statfs:** Obtain file system statistics.
- * **remount_fs:** Called by the VFS when the file system is remounted with new mount options.
- * **clear_inode:** Release inode and clear any pages containing related data.

The Inode Object

An inode is associated with each file. The inode object holds all the information about a named file except its name and the actual data contents of the file. Items contained in an inode object include owner, group, permissions, access times for a file, size of data it holds, and number of links.

The inode object also includes an inode operations object that describes the file system's implemented functions that the VFS can invoke on an inode. The methods defined for the inode object include the following:

- **create:** Create a new inode for a regular file associated with a dentry object in some directory.
- **lookup:** Searches a directory for an inode corresponding to a file name.
- **mkdir:** Creates a new inode for a directory associated with a dentry object in some directory.

The Dentry Object

A dentry (directory entry) is a specific component in a path. The component may be either a directory name or a file name. Dentry objects facilitate access to files and directories and are used in a dentry cache for that purpose.

The File Object

The file object is used to represent a file opened by a process. The object is created in response to the open() system call and destroyed in response to the close() system call. The file object consists of a number of items, including the following:

- dentry object associated with the file
- file system containing the file
- file objects usage counter
- user's user ID
- user's group ID
- file pointer, which is the current position in the file from which the next operation will take place

The file object also includes an inode operations object that describes the file system's implemented functions that the VFS can invoke on a file object. The methods defined for the file object include read, write, open, release, and lock.

12.9 WINDOWS FILE SYSTEM

Windows supports a number of file systems, including the file allocation table (FAT) that runs on Windows 95, MS-DOS, and OS/2. But the developers of Windows also designed a new file system, the Windows File System (NTFS), that is intended to meet high-end requirements for workstations and servers. Examples of high-end applications include the following:

- Client/server applications such as file servers, compute servers, and database servers
- Resource-intensive engineering and scientific applications
- Network applications for large corporate systems

This section provides an overview of NTFS.

Key Features of NTFS

NTFS is a flexible and powerful file system built, as which shall see, on an elegantly simple file system model. The most noteworthy features of NTFS include the following:

- **Recoverability:** High on the list of requirements for the new Windows file system was the ability to recover from system crashes and disk failures. In the event of such failures, NTFS is able to reconstruct disk volumes and return them to a consistent state. It does this by using a transaction processing model for changes to the file system; each significant change is treated as an atomic action that is either entirely performed or not performed at all. Each transaction that was in process at the time of a failure is subsequently backed out or brought to completion. In addition, NTFS uses redundant storage for critical file system data, so that failure of a disk sector does not cause the loss of data describing the structure and status of the file system.
- **Security:** NTFS uses the Windows object model to enforce security. An open file is implemented as a file object with a security descriptor that defines its security attributes.
- **Large disks and large files:** NTFS supports very large disks and very large files more efficiently than most other file systems, including FAT.
- **Multiple data streams:** The actual contents of a file are treated as a stream of bytes. In NTFS it is possible to define multiple data streams for a single file. An example of the utility of this feature is that it allows Windows to be used by remote Macintosh systems to store and retrieve files. On Macintosh, each file has two components: the file data and a resource fork that contains information about the file. NTFS treats these two components as two data streams.

- **General indexing facility:** NTFS associates a collection of attributes with each file. The set of file descriptions in the file management system is organized as a relational database, so that files can be indexed by any attribute.

NTFS Volume and File Structure

NTFS makes use of the following disk storage concepts:

- **Sector:** The smallest physical storage unit on the disk. The data size in bytes is a power of 2 and is almost always 512 bytes.
- **Cluster:** One or more contiguous (next to each other on the same track) sectors. The cluster size in sectors is a power of 2.
- **Volume:** A logical partition on a disk, consisting of one or more clusters and used by a file system to allocate space. At any time, a volume consists of a file system information, a collection of files, and any additional unallocated space remaining on the volume that can be allocated to files. A volume can be all or a portion of a single disk or it can extend across multiple disks. If hardware or software RAID 5 is employed, a volume consists of stripes spanning multiple disks. The maximum volume size for NTFS is 2^{64} bytes.

The cluster is the fundamental unit of allocation in NTFS, which does not recognize sectors. For example, suppose each sector is 512 bytes and the system is configured with two sectors per cluster (one cluster = 1K bytes). If a user creates a file of 1600 bytes, two clusters are allocated to the file. Later, if the user updates the file to 3200 bytes, another two clusters are allocated. The clusters allocated to a file need not be contiguous; it is permissible to fragment a file on the disk. Currently, the maximum file size supported by NTFS is 2^{32} clusters, which is equivalent to a maximum of 2^{48} bytes. A cluster can have at most 2^{16} bytes.

The use of clusters for allocation makes NTFS independent of physical sector size. This enables NTFS to support easily nonstandard disks that do not have a 512-byte sector size and to support efficiently very large disks and very large files by using a larger cluster size. The efficiency comes from the fact that the file system must keep track of each cluster allocated to each file; with larger clusters, there are fewer items to manage.

Table 12.6 shows the default cluster sizes for NTFS. The defaults depend on the size of the volume. The cluster size that is used for a particular volume is established by NTFS when the user requests that a volume be formatted.

NTFS Volume Layout NTFS uses a remarkably simple but powerful approach to organizing information on a disk volume. Every element on a volume is a file, and every file consists of a collection of attributes. Even the data contents of a file is treated as an attribute. With this simple structure, a few general-purpose functions suffice to organize and manage a file system.

Figure 12.17 shows the layout of an NTFS volume, which consists of four regions. The first few sectors on any volume are occupied by the **partition boot sector** (although it is called a sector, it can be up to 16 sectors long), which contains information about the volume layout and the file system structures as well as boot startup information and code. This is followed by the **master file table** (MFT), which contains

Table 12.6 Windows NTFS Partition and Cluster Sizes

Volume Size	Sectors per Cluster	Cluster Size
≤512 Mbyte	1	512 bytes
512 Mbyte–1 Gbyte	2	1K
1 Gbyte–2 Gbyte	4	2K
2 Gbyte–4 Gbyte	8	4K
4 Gbyte–8 Gbyte	16	8K
8 Gbyte–16 Gbyte	32	16K
16 Gbyte–32 Gbyte	64	32K
>32 Gbyte	128	64K

| Partition boot sector | Master file table | System files | File area |

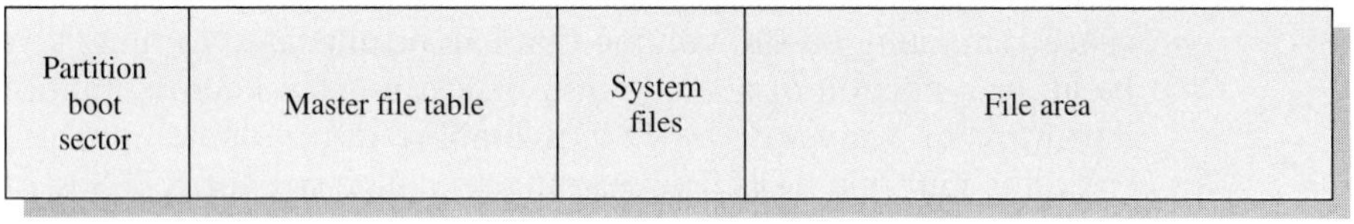

Figure 12.17 NTFS Volume Layout

information about all of the files and folders (directories) on this NTFS volume as well as information about available unallocated space. In essence, the MFT is a list of all contents on this NTFS volume, organized as a set of rows in a relational database structure.

Following the MFT is a region, typically about 1 Mbyte in length, containing **system files**. Among the files in this region are the following:

- **MFT2:** A mirror of the first three rows of the MFT, used to guarantee access to the MFT in the case of a single-sector failure
- **Log file:** A list of transaction steps used for NTFS recoverability
- **Cluster bit map:** A representation of the volume, showing which clusters are in use
- **Attribute definition table:** Defines the attribute types supported on this volume and indicates whether they can be indexed and whether they can be recovered during a system recovery operation

Master File Table The heart of the Windows file system is the MFT. The MFT is organized as a table of variable-length rows, called records. Each row describes a file or a folder on this volume, including the MFT itself, which is treated as a file. If the contents of a file are small enough, then the entire file is located in a row of the MFT. Otherwise, the row for that file contains partial information and the remainder of the file spills over into other available clusters on the volume, with pointers to those clusters in the MFT row of that file.

Each record in the MFT consists of a set of attributes that serve to define the file (or folder) characteristics and the file contents. Table 12.7 lists the attributes that may be found in a row, with the required attributes indicated by shading.

Table 12.7   Windows NTFS File and Directory Attribute Types

Attribute Type	Description
Standard information	Includes access attributes (read-only, read/write, etc.); time stamps, including when the file was created or last modified; and how many directories point to the file (link count).
Attribute list	A list of attributes that make up the file and the file reference of the MFT file record in which each attribute is located. Used when all attributes do not fit into a single MFT file record.
File name	A file or directory must have one or more names.
Security descriptor	Specifies who owns the file and who can access it.
Data	The contents of the file. A file has one default unnamed data attribute and may have one or more named data attributes.
Index root	Used to implement folders.
Index allocation	Used to implement folders.
Volume information	Includes volume-related information, such as the version and name of the volume.
Bitmap	Provides a map representing records in use on the MFT or folder.

Note: Colored rows refer to required file attributes; the other attributes are optional.

Recoverability

NTFS makes it possible to recover the file system to a consistent state following a system crash or disk failure. The key elements that support recoverability are as follows (Figure 12.18):

- **I/O manager:** Includes the NTFS driver, which handles the basic open, close, read, write functions of NTFS. In addition, the software RAID module FT-DISK can be configured for use.

- **Log file service:** Maintains a log of disk writes. The log file is used to recover an NTFS-formatted volume in the case of a system failure.

- **Cache manager:** Responsible for caching file reads and writes to enhance performance. The cache manager optimizes disk I/O by using the lazy write and lazy commit techniques, described in Section 11.8.

- **Virtual memory manager:** The NTFS accesses cached files by mapping file references to virtual memory references and reading and writing virtual memory.

It is important to note that the recovery procedures used by NTFS are designed to recover file system data, not file contents. Thus, the user should never lose a volume or the directory/file structure of an application because of a crash. However, user data are not guaranteed by the file system. Providing full recoverability, including user data, would make for a much more elaborate and resource-consuming recovery facility.

The essence of the NTFS recovery capability is logging. Each operation that alters a file system is treated as a transaction. Each suboperation of a transaction

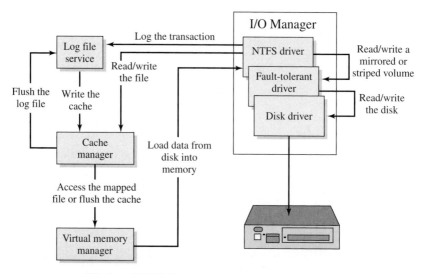

Figure 12.18 Windows NTFS Components

that alters important file system data structures is recorded in a log file before being recorded on the disk volume. Using the log, a partially completed transaction at the time of a crash can later be redone or undone when the system recovers.

In general terms, these are the steps taken to ensure recoverability, as described in [CUST94]:

1. NTFS first calls the log file system to record in the log file in the cache any transactions that will modify the volume structure.

2. NTFS modifies the volume (in the cache).

3. The cache manager calls the log file system to prompt it to flush the log file to disk.

4. Once the log file updates are safely on disk, the cache manager flushes the volume changes to disk.

12.10 SUMMARY

A file management system is a set of system software that provides services to users and applications in the use of files, including file access, directory maintenance, and access control. The file management system is typically viewed as a system service that itself is served by the operating system, rather than being part of the operating system itself. However, in any system, at least part of the file management function is performed by the operating system.

A file consists of a collection of records. The way in which these records may be accessed determines its logical organization, and to some extent its physical organization on disk. If a file is primarily to be processed as a whole, then a sequential file organization is the simplest and most appropriate. If sequential access is needed but random access to individual file is also desired, then an indexed sequential file may give the best performance. If access to the file is principally at random, then an indexed file or hashed file may be the most appropriate.

Whatever file structure is chosen, a directory service is also needed. This allows files to be organized in a hierarchical fashion. This organization is useful to the user in keeping track of files and is useful to the file management system in providing access control and other services to users.

File records, even when of fixed size, generally do not conform to the size of a physical disk block. Accordingly, some sort of blocking strategy is needed. A tradeoff among complexity, performance, and space utilization determines the blocking strategy to be used.

A key function of any file management scheme is the management of disk space. Part of this function is the strategy for allocating disk blocks to a file. A variety of methods have been employed, and a variety of data structures have been used to keep track of the allocation for each file. In addition, the space on disk that has not been allocated must be managed. This latter function primarily consists of maintaining a disk allocation table indicating which blocks are free.

12.11 RECOMMENDED READINGS

There are a number of good books on file management. The following all focus on file management systems but also address related operating system issues. Perhaps the most useful is [WIED87], which takes a quantitative approach to file management and deals with all of the issues raised in Figure 12.2, from disk scheduling to file structure. [LIVA90] emphasizes file structures, providing a good and lengthy survey with comparative performance analyses. [GROS86] provides a balanced look at issues relating to both file I/O and file access methods. It also contains general descriptions of all of the control structures needed by a file system. These provide a useful checklist in assessing a file system design. [FOLK98] emphasizes the processing of files, addressing such issues as maintenance, searching and sorting, and sharing.

The Linux file system is examined in detail in [LOVE04] and [BOVE03]. A good overview is [RUBI97].

[CUST94] provides a good overview of the NT file system. [NAGA97] covers the material in more detail.

BOVE03 Bovet, D., and Cesati, M. *Understanding the Linux Kernel*. Sebastopol, CA: O'Reilly, 2003.

CUST94 Custer, H. *Inside the Windows NT File System*. Redmond, WA: Microsoft Press, 1994.

FOLK98 Folk, M., and Zoellick, B. *File Structures: An Object-Oriented Approach with C++*. Reading, MA: Addison-Wesley, 1998.

GROS86 Grosshans, D. *File Systems: Design and Implementation*. Englewood Cliffs, NJ: Prentice Hall, 1986.

LIVA90 Livadas, P. *File Structures: Theory and Practice*. Englewood Cliffs, NJ: Prentice Hall, 1990.

LOVE04 Love, R. *Linux Kernel Development*. Indianapolis, IN: Sams Publishing, 2004.

NAGA97 Nagar, R. *Windows NT File System Internals*. Sebastopol, CA: O'Reilly, 1997.

RUBI97 Rubini, A. "The Virtual File System in Linux." *Linux Journal*, May 1997.

WIED87 Wiederhold, G. *File Organization for Database Design*. New York: McGraw-Hill, 1987.

12.12 KEY TERMS, REVIEW QUESTIONS, AND PROBLEMS

Key Terms

access method	file allocation	indexed sequential file
bit table	file allocation table	inode
block	file directory	key field
chained file allocation	file management system	pathname
contiguous file allocation	file name	pile
database	hashed file	record
disk allocation table	indexed file	sequential file
field	indexed file allocation	working directory
file		

Review Questions

12.1 What is the difference between a field and a record?

12.2 What is the difference between a file and a database?

12.3 What is a file management system?

12.4 What criteria are important in choosing a file organization?

12.5 List and briefly define five file organizations.

12.6 Why is the average search time to find a record in a file less for an indexed sequential file than for a sequential file?

12.7 What are typical operations that may be performed on a directory?

12.8 What is the relationship between a pathname and a working directory?

12.9 What are typical access rights that may be granted or denied to a particular user for a particular file?

12.10 List and briefly define three blocking methods.

12.11 List and briefly define three file allocation methods.

Problems

12.1 Define:

B = block size

R = record size

P = size of block pointer

F = blocking factor; expected number of records within a block

Give a formula for F for the three blocking methods depicted in Figure 12.6.

12.2 One scheme to avoid the problem of preallocation versus waste or lack of contiguity is to allocate portions of increasing size as the file grows. For example, begin with a portion size of one block, and double the portion size for each allocation. Consider a file of n records with a blocking factor of F, and suppose that a simple one-level index is used as a file allocation table.

a. Give an upper limit on the number of entries in the file allocation table as a function of F and n.

b. What is the maximum amount of the allocated file space that is unused at any time?

12.3   What file organization would you choose to maximize efficiency in terms of speed of access, use of storage space, and ease of updating (adding/deleting/modifying) when the data are:

  a.   updated infrequently and accessed frequently in random order?
  b.   updated frequently and accessed in its entirety relatively frequently?
  c.   updated frequently and accessed frequently in random order?

12.4   Directories can be implemented either as "special files" that can only be accessed in limited ways or as ordinary data files. What are the advantages and disadvantages of each approach?

12.5   Some operating systems have a tree-structured file system but limit the depth of the tree to some small number of levels. What effect does this limit have on users? How does this simplify file system design (if it does)?

12.6   Consider a hierarchical file system in which free disk space is kept in a free space list.

  a.   Suppose the pointer to free space is lost. Can the system reconstruct the free space list?
  b.   Suggest a scheme to ensure that the pointer is never lost as a result of a single memory failure.

12.7   Consider the organization of a UNIX file as represented by the inode (Figure 12.13). Assume that there are 12 direct block pointers and a singly, doubly, and triply indirect pointer in each inode. Further, assume that the system block size and the disk sector size are both 8K. If the disk block pointer is 32 bits, with 8 bits to identify the physical disk and 24 bits to identify the physical block, then

  a.   What is the maximum file size supported by this system?
  b.   What is the maximum file system partition supported by this system?
  c.   Assuming no information other than that the file inode is already in main memory, how many disk accesses are required to access the byte in position 13,423,956?

PART SIX

Distributed Systems and Security

Traditionally, the data processing function was organized in a centralized fashion. In a centralized data processing architecture, data processing support is provided by one or a cluster of computers, generally large computers, located in a central data processing facility. Many of the tasks performed by such a facility are initiated at the center with the results produced at the center. An example is a payroll application. Other tasks may require interactive access by personnel who are not physically located in the data processing center. For example, a data entry function, such as inventory update, may be performed by personnel at sites throughout the organization. In a centralized architecture, each person is provided with a local terminal that is connected by a communications facility to the central data processing facility.

A fully centralized data processing facility is centralized in many senses of the word:

- **Centralized computers:** One or more computers are located in a central facility. In many cases, there are one or more large mainframe computers, which require special facilities such as air conditioning and a raised floor. In a smaller organization, the central computer or computers are large minicomputers, or midrange systems. The iSeries from IBM is an example of a midrange system.

- **Centralized processing:** All applications are run on the central data processing facility. This includes applications that are clearly central or organization-wide in nature, such as payroll, as well as applications that support the needs of users in a particular organizational unit. As an example of the latter, a product design department may make use of a computer-aided design (CAD) graphics package that runs on the central facility.

- **Centralized data:** All data are stored in files and databases at the central facility and are controlled by and accessible by the central computer or computers. This includes data that are of use to many units in the organization, such as inventory figures, as well as data that support the needs of, and should be used by, only one organizational unit. As an example of the latter, the marketing organization may maintain a database with information derived from customer surveys.

Such a centralized organization has a number of attractive aspects. There may be economies of scale in the purchase and operation of equipment and software. A large central DP shop can afford to have professional programmers on staff to meet the needs of the various departments. Management can maintain control over data processing procurement, enforce standards for programming and data file structure, and design and implement a security policy.

A data processing facility may depart in varying degrees from the centralized data processing organization by implementing a distributed data processing (DDP) strategy. A distributed data processing facility is one in which computers, usually smaller computers, are dispersed throughout an organization. The objective of such dispersion is to process information in a way that is most effective based on operational, economic, and/or geographic considerations, or all three. A DDP facility may include a central facility plus satellite facilities, or it may more nearly resemble a community of peer computing facilities. In either case, some form of interconnection is usually needed; that is, the various computers in the system must be connected to one another. As may be expected, given the characterization of centralized data processing provided here, a DDP facility involves the distribution of computers, processing, and data.

The advantages of DDP include the following:

- **Responsiveness:** Local computing facilities can be managed in such a way that they can more directly satisfy the needs of local organizational management than one located in a central facility and intended to satisfy the needs of the total organization.

- **Availability:** With multiple interconnected systems, the loss of any one system should have minimal impact. Key systems and components (e.g., computers with critical applications, printers, mass storage devices) can be replicated so that a backup system can quickly take up the load after a failure.

- **Resource sharing:** Expensive hardware can be shared among users. Data files can be centrally managed and maintained, but with organization-wide access. Staff services, programs, and databases can be developed on an organization-wide basis and distributed to the dispersed facilities.

- **Incremental growth:** In a centralized facility, an increased workload or the need for a new set of applications usually involves a major equipment purchase or a major software upgrade. This involves significant expenditure.

In addition, a major change may require conversion or reprogramming of existing applications, with the risk of error and degraded performance. With a distributed system, it is possible to gradually replace applications or systems, avoiding the "all-or-nothing" approach. In addition, old equipment can be left in the facility to run a single application if the cost of moving the application to a new machine is not justified.

- **Increased user involvement and control:** With smaller, more manageable equipment physically located close to the user, the user has greater opportunity to affect system design and operation, either by direction interaction with technical personnel or through the user's immediate superior.

- **End-user productivity:** Distributed systems tend to give more rapid response time to the user, since each piece of equipment is attempting a smaller job. Also, the applications and interfaces of the facility can be optimized to the needs of the organizational unit. Unit managers are in a position to assess the effectiveness of the local portion of the facility and to make the appropriate changes.

To achieve these benefits, the operating system must provide a range of support functions for DDP. These include the software for exchanging data among machines, the capability to cluster machines to achieve high availability and high performance, and the ability to manage processes in a distributed environment.

In this age of universal electronic connectivity, of viruses and hackers, of electronic eavesdropping and electronic fraud, security has become a central issue. Two trends have come together to make the topic of this part of vital interest. First, the explosive growth in computer systems and their interconnections via networks has increased the dependence of both organizations and individuals on the information stored and communicated using these systems. This, in turn, has led to a heightened awareness of the need to protect data and resources from disclosure, to guarantee the authenticity of data and messages, and to protect systems from network-based attacks. Second, the disciplines of cryptography and computer security have matured, leading to the development of practical, readily available applications to enforce security.

Chapter 13 Networking

Data network communication and distributed applications rely on underlying communications software that is independent of applications and relieves the application of much of the burden of reliably exchanging data. This communications software is organized into a protocol architecture, the most important incarnation of which is the TCP/IP protocol suite. Chapter 13 introduces the concept of a protocol architecture and provides an overview of TCP/IP.

Chapter 14 Distributed Processing, Client/Server, and Clusters

Chapter 14 looks at the operating system support required for multiple systems to act cooperatively. The chapter looks at the increasingly important concept of client/server computing and the requirements that this architecture places on operating system. The discussion of client/server computing includes a description of two key mechanisms used to implement client/ server systems: message passing and remote procedure calls. Chapter 14 also looks at the concept of clusters.

Chapter 15 Distributed Process Management

Chapter 15 surveys key issues in developing a distributed operating system. First, we analyze the requirements and mechanisms for process migration, which enables an active process to be moved from one machine to another during the course of its lifetime, to achieve load balancing or availability goals. Then we look at the concept of a distributed global state, which is a vital element in developing a distributed operating system. Finally, we examine concurrency issues related to mutual exclusion and deadlock in a distributed environment.

Chapter 16 Security

Chapter 16 provides a survey of operating system and computer security. The chapter begins with an overview of security threats. Then computer system protection mechanisms are examined. This is followed by a discussion of ways to counter the threat of intruders: unauthorized users, or authorized users attempting to perform unauthorized actions. Viruses, one of the better-known and most damaging types of threats, are discussed next. The chapter also looks at a comprehensive approach to computer security design known as the trusted system. Then an introduction to network security is presented.

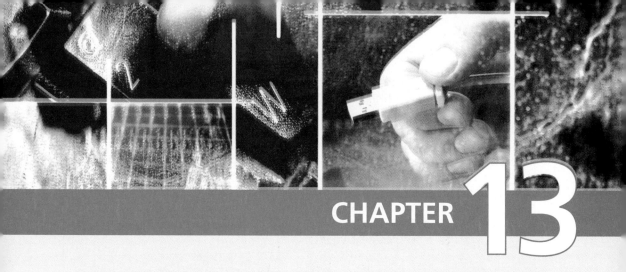

CHAPTER 13

NETWORKING

With the increasing availability of inexpensive yet powerful personal computers and servers, there has been an increasing trend toward distributed data processing (DDP), in which processors, data, and other aspects of a data processing system may be dispersed within an organization. A DDP system involves a partitioning of the computing function and may also involve a distributed organization of databases, device control, and interaction (network) control.

In many organizations, there is heavy reliance on personal computers coupled with servers. Personal computers are used to support a variety of user-friendly applications, such as word processing, spreadsheet, and presentation graphics. The servers house the corporate database plus sophisticated database management and information systems software. Linkages are needed among the personal computers and between each personal computer and the server. Various approaches are in common use, ranging from treating the personal computer as a simple terminal to a high degree of integration between personal computer applications and the server database.

These application trends have been supported by the evolution of distributed capabilities in the operating system and supporting utilities. A spectrum of distributed capabilities has been explored:

- **Communications architecture:** This is software that supports a group of networked computers. It provides support for distributed applications, such as electronic mail, file transfer, and remote terminal access. However, the computers retain a distinct identity to the user and to the applications, which must communicate with other computers by explicit reference. Each computer has its own separate operating system, and a heterogeneous mix of computers and operating systems is possible, as long as all machines support the same communications architecture. The most widely used communications architecture is the TCP/IP protocol suite, examined in this chapter.

- **Network operating system:** This is a configuration in which there is a network of application machines, usually single-user workstations and one or more "server" machines. The server machines provide networkwide services or applications, such as file storage and printer management. Each computer has its own private operating system. The network operating system is simply an adjunct to the local operating system that allows application machines to interact with server machines. The user is aware that there are multiple independent computers and must deal with them explicitly. Typically, a common communications architecture is used to support these network applications.

- **Distributed operating system:** A common operating system shared by a network of computers. It looks to its users like an ordinary centralized operating system but provides the user with transparent access to the resources of a number of machines. A distributed operating system may rely on a communications architecture for basic communications functions; more commonly, a stripped-down set of communications functions is incorporated into the operating system to provide efficiency.

The technology of the communications architecture is well developed and is supported by all vendors. Network operating systems are a more recent phenomenon, but a number of commercial products exist. The leading edge of research and development for distributed systems is in the area of distributed operating systems. Although some commercial systems have been introduced, fully functional distributed operating systems are still at the experimental stage.

In this chapter and the next two, we provide a survey of distributed processing capabilities. This chapter focuses on the underlying network protocol software.

13.1 THE NEED FOR A PROTOCOL ARCHITECTURE

When computers, terminals, and/or other data processing devices exchange data, the procedures involved can be quite complex. Consider, for example, the transfer of a file between two computers. There must be a data path between the two computers, either directly or via a communication network. But more is needed. Typical tasks to be performed include the following:

1. The source system must either activate the direct data communication path or inform the communication network of the identity of the desired destination system.

2. The source system must ascertain that the destination system is prepared to receive data.

3. The file transfer application on the source system must ascertain that the file management program on the destination system is prepared to accept and store the file for this particular user.

4. If the file formats or data representations used on the two systems are incompatible, one or the other system must perform a format translation function.

The exchange of information between computers for the purpose of cooperative action is generally referred to as *computer communications*. Similarly, when two or more computers are interconnected via a communication network, the set of computer stations is referred to as a *computer network*. Because a similar level of cooperation is required between a terminal and a computer, these terms are often used when some of the communicating entities are terminals.

In discussing computer communications and computer networks, two concepts are paramount:

- Protocols
- Computer communications architecture, or protocol architecture

A **protocol** is used for communication between entities in different systems. The terms *entity* and *system* are used in a very general sense. Examples of entities are user application programs, file transfer packages, database management systems, electronic mail facilities, and terminals. Examples of systems are computers, terminals, and remote sensors. Note that in some cases the entity and the system in which it resides are coextensive (e.g., terminals). In general, an entity is anything capable of sending or receiving information, and a system is a physically distinct object that contains one or more entities. For two entities to communicate successfully, they must "speak the same language." What is communicated, how it is communicated, and when it is communicated must conform to mutually agreed conventions between the entities involved. The conventions are referred to as a protocol, which may be defined as a set of rules governing the exchange of data between two entities. The key elements of a protocol are as follows:

- **Syntax:** Includes such things as data format and signal levels
- **Semantics:** Includes control information for coordination and error handling
- **Timing:** Includes speed matching and sequencing

Appendix 13A provides a specific example of a protocol, the Internet standard Trivial File Transfer Protocol (TFTP).

Having introduced the concept of a protocol, we can now introduce the concept of a **protocol architecture**. It is clear that there must be a high degree of cooperation between the two computer systems. Instead of implementing the logic for this as a single module, the task is broken up into subtasks, each of which is implemented separately. As an example, Figure 13.1 suggests the way in which a file transfer facility could be implemented. Three modules are used. Tasks 3 and 4 in the preceding list could be performed by a file transfer module. The two modules on the two systems exchange files and commands. However, rather than requiring the file transfer module to deal with the details of actually transferring data and commands, the file transfer modules each rely on a communications service module. This module is responsible for making sure that the file transfer commands and data are reliably exchanged between systems. The manner in which a communications service module functions is explored subsequently. Among other things, this module would perform task 2. Finally, the nature of the exchange between the two communications service modules is independent of the nature of the network that interconnects them. Therefore, rather than building details of the network interface into the communications service module, it makes sense to have a third module, a network access module, that performs task 1 by interacting with the network.

To summarize, the file transfer module contains all the logic that is unique to the file transfer application, such as transmitting passwords, file commands, and file records. These files and commands must be transmitted reliably. However, the

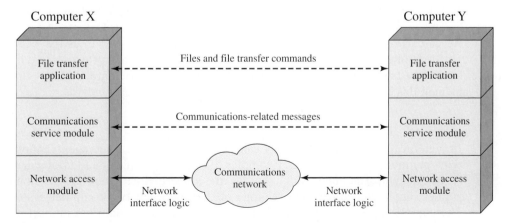

Figure 13.1   A Simplified Architecture for File Transfer

same sorts of reliability requirements are relevant to a variety of applications (e.g., electronic mail, document transfer). Therefore, these requirements are met by a separate communications service module that can be used by a variety of applications. The communications service module is concerned with assuring that the two computer systems are active and ready for data transfer and for keeping track of the data that are being exchanged to assure delivery. However, these tasks are independent of the type of network that is being used. Therefore, the logic for actually dealing with the network is put into a separate network access module. If the network to be used is changed, only the network access module is affected.

Thus, instead of a single module for performing communications, there is a structured set of modules that implements the communications function. That structure is referred to as a protocol architecture. An analogy might be useful at this point. Suppose an executive in office X wishes to send a document to an executive in office Y. The executive in X prepares the document and perhaps attaches a note. This corresponds to the actions of the file transfer application in Figure 13.1. Then the executive in X hands the document to a secretary or administrative assistant (AA). The AA in X puts the document in an envelope and puts Y's address and X's return address on the outside. Perhaps the envelope is also marked "confidential." The AA's actions correspond to the communications service module in Figure 13.1. The AA in X then gives the package to the shipping department. Someone in the shipping department decides how to send the package: mail, UPS, or express courier. The shipping department attaches the appropriate postage or shipping documents to the package and ships it out. The shipping department corresponds to the network access module of Figure 13.1. When the package arrives at Y, a similar layered set of actions occurs. The shipping department at Y receives the package and delivers it to the appropriate AA or secretary based on the name on the package. The AA opens the package and hands the enclosed document to the executive to whom it is addressed.

13.2 THE TCP/IP PROTOCOL ARCHITECTURE

TCP/IP is a result of protocol research and development conducted on the experimental packet-switched network, ARPANET, funded by the Defense Advanced Research Projects Agency (DARPA), and is generally referred to as the TCP/IP protocol suite. This protocol suite consists of a large collection of protocols that have been issued as Internet standards by the Internet Activities Board (IAB). A document at this book's Web site provides a discussion of Internet standards.

TCP/IP Layers

In general terms, communications can be said to involve three agents: applications, computers, and networks. Examples of applications include file transfer and electronic mail. The applications that we are concerned with here are distributed applications that involve the exchange of data between two computer systems. These applications, and others, execute on computers that can often support multiple simultaneous applications. Computers are connected to networks, and the data to be exchanged are transferred by the network from one computer to another. Thus, the transfer of data from one application to another involves first getting the data to the computer in which the application resides and then getting the data to the intended application within the computer.

There is no official TCP/IP protocol model. However, based on the protocol standards that have been developed, we can organize the communication task for TCP/IP into five relatively independent layers, from bottom to top:

* Physical layer
* Network access layer
* Internet layer
* Host-to-host, or transport layer
* Application layer

The **physical layer** covers the physical interface between a data transmission device (e.g., workstation, computer) and a transmission medium or network. This layer is concerned with specifying the characteristics of the transmission medium, the nature of the signals, the data rate, and related matters.

The **network access layer** is concerned with the exchange of data between an end system (server, workstation, etc.) and the network to which it is attached. The sending computer must provide the network with the address of the destination computer, so that the network may route the data to the appropriate destination. The sending computer may wish to invoke certain services, such as priority, that might be provided by the network. The specific software used at this layer depends on the type of network to be used; different standards have been developed for circuit switching, packet switching (e.g., frame relay), LANs (e.g., Ethernet), and others. Thus it makes sense to separate those functions having to do with network access into a separate layer. By doing this, the remainder of the communications software, above the network access layer, need not be concerned about the specifics of the network to be used. The same higher-layer software should function properly regardless of the particular network to which the computer is attached.

The network access layer is concerned with access to and routing data across a network for two end systems attached to the same network. In those cases where two devices are attached to different networks, procedures are needed to allow data to traverse multiple interconnected networks. This is the function of the internet layer. The **Internet Protocol (IP)** is used at this layer to provide the routing function across multiple networks. This protocol is implemented not only in the end systems but also in routers. A **router** is a processor that connects two networks and whose primary function is to relay data from one network to the other on a route from the source to the destination end system.

Regardless of the nature of the applications that are exchanging data, there is usually a requirement that data be exchanged reliably. That is, we would like to be assured that all the data arrive at the destination application and that the data arrive in the same order in which they were sent. As we shall see, the mechanisms for providing reliability are essentially independent of the nature of the applications. Thus, it makes sense to collect those mechanisms in a common layer shared by all applications; this is referred to as the host-to-host layer, or **transport layer**.

The Transmission Control Protocol (TCP) is the most commonly used protocol to provide this functionality.

Finally, the **application layer** contains the logic needed to support the various user applications. For each different type of application, such as file transfer, a separate module is needed that is peculiar to that application.

TCP and UDP

For most applications running as part of the TCP/IP protocol architecture, the transport layer protocol is TCP. TCP provides a reliable connection for the transfer of data between applications. A connection is simply a temporary logical association between two entities in different systems. For the duration of the connection each entity keeps track of segments coming and going to the other entity, in order to regulate the flow of segments and to recover from lost or damaged segments.

Figure 13.2a shows the header format for TCP, which is a minimum of 20 octets, or 160 bits. The Source Port and Destination Port fields identify the applications at the source and destination systems that are using this connection. The Sequence Number, Acknowledgment Number, and Window fields provide flow control and error control. The checksum is a 16-bit code based on the contents of the segment used to detect errors in the TCP segment.

In addition to TCP, there is one other transport-level protocol that is in common use as part of the TCP/IP protocol suite: the User Datagram Protocol (UDP). UDP does not guarantee delivery, preservation of sequence, or protection against duplication. UDP enables a process to send messages to other processes with a minimum of protocol mechanism. Some transaction-oriented applications make

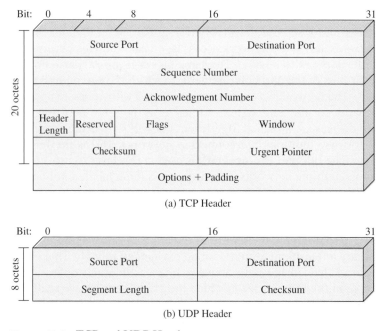

Figure 13.2 TCP and UDP Headers

use of UDP; one example is SNMP (Simple Network Management Protocol), the standard network management protocol for TCP/IP networks. Because it is connectionless, UDP has very little to do. Essentially, it adds a port addressing capability to IP. This is best seen by examining the UDP header, shown in Figure 13.2b.

IP and IPv6

For decades, the keystone of the TCP/IP protocol architecture has been IP. Figure 13.3a shows the IP header format, which is a minimum of 20 octets, or 160 bits. The header, together with the segment from the transport layer form an IP-level block referred to as an IP datagram or an IP packet. The header includes

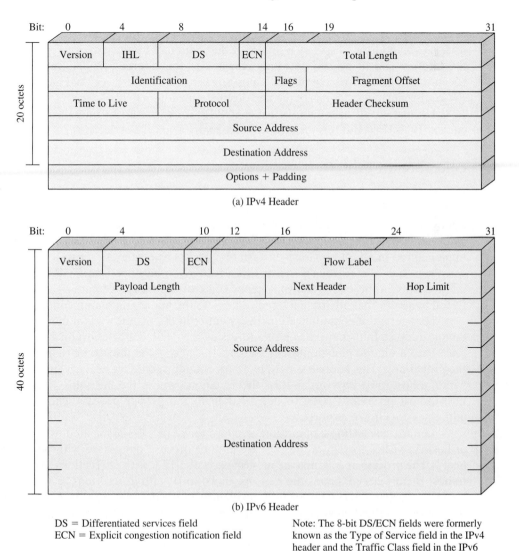

(a) IPv4 Header

(b) IPv6 Header

DS = Differentiated services field
ECN = Explicit congestion notification field

Note: The 8-bit DS/ECN fields were formerly known as the Type of Service field in the IPv4 header and the Traffic Class field in the IPv6 header.

Figure 13.3 IP Headers

32-bit source and destination addresses. The Header Checksum field is used to detect errors in the header to avoid misdelivery. The Protocol field indicates whether TCP, UDP, or some other higher-layer protocol is using IP. The ID, Flags, and Fragment Offset fields are used in the fragmentation and reassembly process, in which a single IP datagram is divided into multiple IP datagrams on transmission and then reassembled at the destination

In 1995, the Internet Engineering Task Force (IETF), which develops protocol standards for the Internet, issued a specification for a next-generation IP, known then as IPng. This specification was turned into a standard in 1996 known as IPv6. IPv6 provides a number of functional enhancements over the existing IP, designed to accommodate the higher speeds of today's networks and the mix of data streams, including graphic and video, that are becoming more prevalent. But the driving force behind the development of the new protocol was the need for more addresses. The current IP uses a 32-bit address to specify a source or destination. With the explosive growth of the Internet and of private networks attached to the Internet, this address length became insufficient to accommodate all systems needing addresses. As Figure 13.3b shows, IPv6 includes 128-bit source and destination address fields.

Ultimately, all installations using TCP/IP are expected to migrate from the current IP to IPv6, but this process will take many years, if not decades.

Operation of TCP/IP

Figure 13.4 indicates how these protocols are configured for communications. Some sort of network access protocol, such as the Ethernet logic, is used to connect a computer to a network. This protocol enables the host to send data across the network to another host or, in the case of a host on another network, to a router. IP is implemented in all end systems and routers. It acts as a relay to move a block of data from one host, through one or more routers, to another host. TCP is implemented only in the end systems; it keeps track of the blocks of data being transferred to assure that all are delivered reliably to the appropriate application.

For successful communication, every entity in the overall system must have a unique address. In fact, two levels of addressing are needed. Each host on a network must have a unique global internet address; this allows the data to be delivered to the proper host. This address is used by IP for routing and delivery. Each application within a host must have an address that is unique within the host; this allows the host-to-host protocol (TCP) to deliver data to the proper process. These latter addresses are known as ports.

Let us trace a simple operation. Suppose that a process, associated with port 3 at host A, wishes to send a message to another process, associated with port 2 at host B. The process at A hands the message down to TCP with instructions to send it to host B, port 2. TCP hands the message down to IP with instructions to send it to host B. Note that IP need not be told the identity of the destination port. All it needs to know is that the data are intended for host B. Next, IP hands the message down to the network access layer (e.g., Ethernet logic) with instructions to send it to router J (the first hop on the way to B).

To control this operation, control information as well as user data must be transmitted, as suggested in Figure 13.5. Let us say that the sending process generates

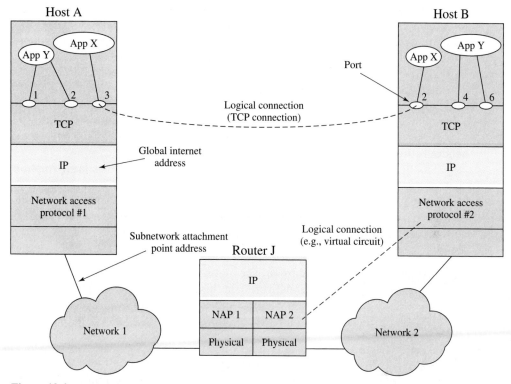

Figure 13.4   TCP/IP Concepts

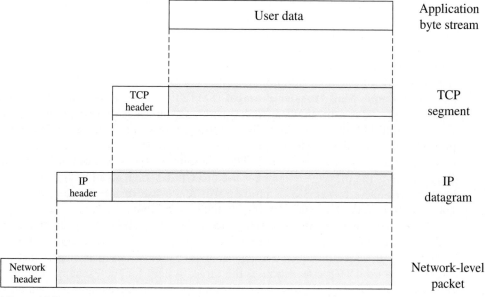

Figure 13.5   Protocol Data Units (PDUs) in the TCP/IP Architecture

a block of data and passes this to TCP. TCP may break this block into smaller pieces to make it more manageable. To each of these pieces, TCP appends control information known as the TCP header (Figure 13.2a), forming a **TCP segment**. The control information is to be used by the peer TCP protocol entity at host B.

Next, TCP hands each segment over to IP, with instructions to transmit it to B. These segments must be transmitted across one or more networks and relayed through one or more intermediate routers. This operation, too, requires the use of control information. Thus IP appends a header of control information (Figure 13.3) to each segment to form an **IP datagram**. An example of an item stored in the IP header is the destination host address (in this example, B).

Finally, each IP datagram is presented to the network access layer for transmission across the first network in its journey to the destination. The network access layer appends its own header, creating a packet, or frame. The packet is transmitted across the network to router J. The packet header contains the information that the network needs in order to transfer the data across the network. Examples of items that may be contained in this header include the following:

- **Destination network address:** The network must know to which attached device the packet is to be delivered, in this case router J.

- **Facilities requests:** The network access protocol might request the use of certain network facilities, such as priority.

At router J, the packet header is stripped off and the IP header examined. On the basis of the destination address information in the IP header, the IP module in the router directs the datagram out across network 2 to B. To do this, the datagram is again augmented with a network access header.

When the data are received at B, the reverse process occurs. At each layer, the corresponding header is removed, and the remainder is passed on to the next higher layer, until the original user data are delivered to the destination process.

TCP/IP Applications

A number of applications have been standardized to operate on top of TCP. We mention three of the most common here.

The **Simple Mail Transfer Protocol** (SMTP) provides a basic electronic mail facility. It provides a mechanism for transferring messages among separate hosts. Features of SMTP include mailing lists, return receipts, and forwarding. The SMTP protocol does not specify the way in which messages are to be created; some local editing or native electronic mail facility is required. Once a message is created, SMTP accepts the message and makes use of TCP to send it to an SMTP module on another host. The target SMTP module will make use of a local electronic mail package to store the incoming message in a user's mailbox.

The **File Transfer Protocol** (FTP) is used to send files from one system to another under user command. Both text and binary files are accommodated, and the protocol provides features for controlling user access. When a user wishes to engage in file transfer, FTP sets up a TCP connection to the target system for the exchange of control messages. This connection allows user ID and password to be transmitted and allows the user to specify the file and file actions desired. Once a file transfer is approved, a second TCP connection is set up for the data transfer. The file is transferred over the data connection, without the overhead of any headers or control information at the application level. When the transfer is complete, the control connection is used to signal the completion and to accept new file transfer commands.

TELNET provides a remote logon capability, which enables a user at a terminal or personal computer to logon to a remote computer and function as if directly connected to that computer. The protocol was designed to work with simple scroll-mode terminals. TELNET is actually implemented in two modules: User TELNET interacts with the terminal I/O module to communicate with a local terminal. It converts the characteristics of real terminals to the network standard and vice versa. Server TELNET interacts with an application, acting as a surrogate terminal handler so that remote terminals appear as local to the application. Terminal traffic between User and Server TELNET is carried on a TCP connection.

13.3 SOCKETS

The concept of sockets and sockets programming was developed in the 1980s in the UNIX environment as the Berkeley Sockets Interface. In essence, a socket enables communication between a client and server process and may be either connection-oriented or connectionless. A socket can be considered an endpoint in a communication. A client socket in one computer uses an address to call a server socket on another computer. Once the appropriate sockets are engaged, the two computers can exchange data.

Typically, computers with server sockets keep a TCP or UDP port open, ready for unscheduled incoming calls. The client typically determines the socket identification of the desired server by finding it in a Domain Name System (DNS) database. Once a connection is made, the server switches the dialogue to a different port number to free up the main port number for additional incoming calls.

Internet applications, such as TELNET and remote login (rlogin), make use of sockets, with the details hidden from the user. However, sockets can be constructed from within a program (in a language such as C or Java), enabling the programmer to easily support networking functions and applications. The sockets programming mechanism includes sufficient semantics to permit unrelated processes on different hosts to communicate.

The Berkeley Sockets Interface is the de facto standard application programming interface (API) for developing networking applications, spanning a wide range of operating systems. Windows Sockets (WinSock) is based on the Berkeley specification. The sockets API provides generic access to interprocess communications services. Thus, the sockets capability is ideally suited for students to learn the principles of protocols and distributed applications by hands-on program development.

The Socket

Recall that each TCP and UDP header includes source port and destination port fields (Figure 13.2). These **port** values identify the respective users (applications) of the two TCP entities. Also, each IPv4 and IPv6 header includes source address and destination address fields (Figure 13.3); these **IP addresses** identify the respective host systems. The concatenation of a port value and an IP address forms a **socket**, which is unique throughout the Internet. Thus, in Figure 13.4, the combination of the IP address for host B and the port number for application X uniquely identifies the socket location of application X in host B. As the figure indicates, an application may have multiple socket addresses, one for each port into the application.

The socket is used to define an **application programming interface** (API), which is a generic communication interface for writing programs that use TCP or UDP. In practice, when used as an API, a socket is identified by the triple (protocol, local-address, local-process). The local-address is an IP address and the local-process is a port number. Because port numbers are unique within a system, the port number implies the protocol (TCP or UDP). However, for clarity and ease of implementation, sockets used for an API include the protocol as well as the IP address and port number in defining a unique socket.

Corresponding to the two protocols, the Sockets API recognizes two types of sockets: stream sockets and datagram sockets. **Stream sockets** make use of TCP, which provides a connection-oriented reliable data transfer. Therefore, with stream sockets, all blocks of data sent between a pair of sockets are guaranteed for delivery and arrive in the order that they were sent. **Datagram sockets** make use of UDP, which does not provide the connection-oriented features of TCP. Therefore, with datagram sockets, delivery is not guaranteed, nor is order necessarily preserved.

There is a third type of socket provided by the Sockets API: raw sockets. **Raw sockets** allow direct access to lower layer protocols, such as IP.

Socket Interface Calls

This subsection summarizes the key system calls.

Socket Setup The first step in using Sockets is to create a new socket using the `socket()` command. This command includes three parameters; the protocol family is always `PF_INET`, for the TCP/IP protocol suite. *Type* specifies whether this is a stream or datagram socket, and *protocol* specifies either TCP or UDP. The reason that both *type* and *protocol* need to be specified is to allow additional transport-level protocols to be included in a future implementation. Thus, there might be more than one datagram-style transport protocol or more than one connection-oriented transport protocol. The `socket()` command returns an integer result that identifies this socket; it is similar to a UNIX file descriptor. The exact socket data structure depends on the implementation. It includes the source port and IP address and, if a connection is open or pending, the destination port and IP address and various options and parameters associated with the connection.

After a socket is created, it must have an address to listen to. The `bind()` function binds a socket to a socket address. The address has the structure

```
struct sockaddr_in {
    short int sin_family;              // Address family (TCP/IP)
    unsigned short int sin_port;       // Port number
```

```
        struct in_addr sin_addr;          // Internet address
        unsigned char sin_zero[8];        // Same size as struct sockaddr
    };
```

Socket Connection For a stream socket, once the socket is created, a connection must be set up to a remote socket. One side functions as a client, and requests a connection to the other side, which acts as a server.

The server side of a connection setup requires two steps. First, a server application issues a `listen()`, indicating that the given socket is ready to accept incoming connections. The parameter *backlog* is the number of connections allowed on the incoming queue. Each incoming connections is placed in this queue until a matching `accept()` is issued by the server side. Next, the `accept()` call is used to remove one request from the queue. If the queue is empty, the `accept()` blocks the process until a connection request arrives. If there is a waiting call, then `accept()` returns a new file descriptor for the connection. This creates a new socket, which has the IP address and port number of the remote party, the IP address of this system, and a new port number. The reason that a new socket with a new port number is assigned is that this enables the local application to continue to listen for more requests. As a result, an application may have multiple connections active at any time, each with a different local port number. This new port number is returned across the TCP connection to the requesting system.

A client application issues a `connect()` that specifies both a local socket and the address of a remote socket. If the connection attempt is unsuccessful `connect()` returns the value −1. If the attempt is successful, `connect()` returns a 0 and fills in the file descriptor parameter to include the IP address and port number of the local and foreign sockets. Recall that the remote port number may differ from that specified in the `foreignAddress` parameter because the port number is changed on the remote host.

Once a connection is set up, `getpeername()` can be used to find out who is on the other end of the connected stream `socket`. The function returns a value in the `sockfd` parameter.

Socket Communication For **stream communication**, the functions `send()` and `recv()` are used to send or receive data over the connection identified by the `sockfd` parameter. In the `send()` call, the `*msg` parameter points to the block of data to be sent and the `len` parameter specifies the number of bytes to be sent. The `flags` parameter contains control flags, typically set to 0. The `send()` call returns the number of bytes sent, which may be less than the number specified in the len parameter. In the `recv()` call, the `*buf` parameter points to the buffer for storing incoming data, with an upper limit on the number of bytes set by the `len` parameter.

At any time, either side can close the connection with the `close()` call, which prevents further sends and receives. The `shutdown()` call allows the caller to terminate sending or receiving or both.

Figure 13.6 shows the interaction of the clients and server sides in setting up, using, and terminating a connection.

For **datagram communication**, the functions `sendto()` and `recvfrom()` are used. The `sendto()` call includes all the parameters of the `send()` call plus a specification of the destination address (IP address and port). Similarly, the `recvfrom()` call includes an address parameter, which is filled in when data are received.

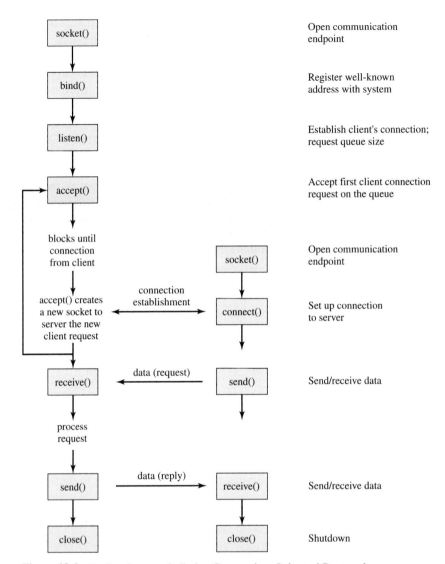

Figure 13.6 Socket System Calls for Connection-Oriented Protocol

13.4 LINUX NETWORKING

Linux supports a variety of networking architectures, in particular TCP/IP by means of Berkeley Sockets. Figure 13.7 shows the overall structure of Linux support for TCP/IP. User-level processes interact with networking devices by means of system calls to the Sockets interface. The Sockets module in turn interacts with a software package in the kernel that handles transport-layer (TCP and UDP) and IP protocol operations. This software package exchanges data with the device driver for the network interface card.

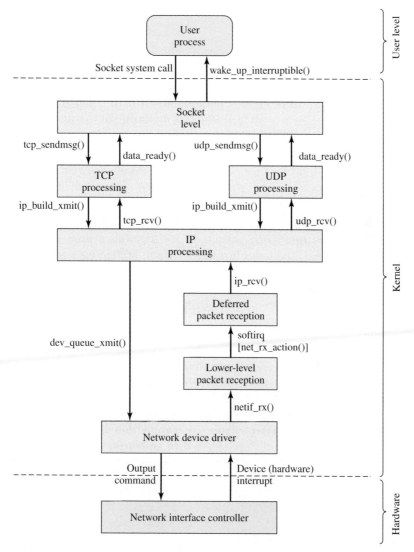

Figure 13.7   Linux Kernel Components for TCP/IP Processing

Linux implements sockets as special files. Recall from Section 12.7 that, in UNIX systems, a special file is one that contains no data but provides a mechanism to map physical devices to file names. For every new socket, the Linux kernel creates a new inode in the *sockfs* special file system.

Figure 13.7 depicts the relationships among various kernel modules involved in sending and receiving TCP/IP-based data blocks. The remainder of this section looks at the sending and receiving facilities.

Sending Data

A user process uses the sockets calls described in Section 13.3 create new sockets, set up connections to remote sockets, and send and receive data. To send data, the user process writes data to the socket with the following file system call:

$$\text{write}(sockfd, mesg, mesglen)$$

where mesglen is the length of the **mesg** buffer in bytes.

This call triggers the **write** method of the file object associated with the **sockfd** file descriptor. The file descriptor indicates whether this is a socket set up for TCP or UDP. The kernel allocates the appropriate data structures and invokes the appropriate sockets-level function to pass data to either a TCP module or a UDP module. The corresponding functions are **tcp_sendmsg()** and **udp_sendmsg()**, respectively. The transport-layer module allocates a data structure of the TCP or UPD header and performs **ip_build_xmit()** to invoke the IP-layer processing module. This module builds an IP datagram for transmission and places it in a transmission buffer for this socket. The IP-layer module then performs **dev_queue_xmit()** to queue the socket buffer for later transmission via the network device driver. When it is available, the network device driver will transmit buffered packets.

Receiving Data

Data reception is an unpredictable event and so involves the use of interrupts and deferrable functions. When an IP datagram arrives, the network interface controller issues a hardware interrupt to the corresponding network device driver. The interrupt triggers an interrupt service routine that handles the interrupt as part of the network device driver module. The driver allocates a kernel buffer for the incoming data block and transfers the data from the device controller to the buffer. The driver then performs **netif_rx()** to invoke a lower-level packet reception routine. In essence, the **netif_rx()** function places the incoming data block in a queue and then issues a soft interrupt request (**softirq**) so that the queued data will eventually be processed. The action to be performed when the **softirq** is processed is the **net_rx_action()** function.

Once a **softirq** has been queued, processing of this packet is halted until the kernel executes the **softirq** function, which is equivalent to saying until the kernel responds to this soft interrupt request and executes the function (in this case, **net_rx_action()**) associated with this soft interrupt. There are three places in the kernel, where the kernel checks to see if any **softirqs** are pending: when a hardware interrupt has been processed, when an application-level process invokes a system call, and when a new process is scheduled for execution.

When the **net_rx_action()** function is performed, it retrieves the queued packet and passes it on to the IP packet handler by means of an **ip_rcv** call. The IP packet handler processes the IP header and then uses **tcp_rcv** or **udp_rcv** to invoke the transport-layer processing module. The transport-layer module processes the transport-layer header and passes the data to the user through the sockets interface by means of a **wake_up_interruptible()** call, which awakens the receiving process.

13.5 SUMMARY

The communication functionality required for distributed applications is quite complex. This functionality is generally implemented as a structured set of modules. The modules are arranged in a vertical, layered fashion, with each layer providing a particular portion of the needed functionality and relying on the next lower layer for more primitive functions. Such a structure is referred to as a protocol architecture.

One motivation for the use of this type of structure is that it eases the task of design and implementation. It is standard practice for any large software package to break up the functions into modules that can be designed and implemented separately. After each module is designed and implemented, it can be tested. Then the modules can be combined and tested together. This motivation has led computer vendors to develop proprietary layered protocol architectures. An example of this is the Systems Network Architecture (SNA) of IBM.

A layered architecture can also be used to construct a standardized set of communication protocols. In this case, the advantages of modular design remain. But, in addition, a layered architecture is particularly well suited to the development of standards. Standards can be developed simultaneously for protocols at each layer of the architecture. This breaks down the work to make it more manageable and speeds up the standards-development process. The TCP/IP protocol architecture is the standard architecture used for this purpose. This architecture contains five layers. Each layer provides a portion of the total communications function required for distributed applications. Standards have been developed for each layer. Development work continues, particularly at the top (application) layer, where new distributed applications are still being defined.

13.6 RECOMMENDED READINGS AND WEB SITES

[STAL04] provides a detailed description of the TCP/IP model and of the standards at each layer of the model. A very useful reference work on TCP/IP is [RODR02], which covers the spectrum of TCP/IP-related protocols in a technically concise but thorough fashion.

An excellent concise introduction to using Sockets is [DONA01]; another good overview is [HALL01]. [MCKU96] and [WRIG95] provide details of Sockets implementation.

[BOVE03] provides good coverage of Linux networking. Another useful source is [INSO02a] and [INSO02b].

BOVE03   Bovet, D., and Cesati, M. *Understanding the Linux Kernel.* Sebastopol, CA: O'Reilly, 2003.

DONA01   Donahoo, M., and Clavert, K. *The Pocket Guide to TCP/IP Sockets.* San Francisco, CA: Morgan Kaufmann, 2001.

HALL01   Hall, B. *Beej's Guide to Network Programming Using Internet Sockets.* 2001. **http://www.ecst.csuchico.edu/~beej/guide/net/html/**

INSO02a   Insolvibile, G. "Inside the Linux Packet Filter." *Linux Journal,* February 2002.

INSO02b   Insolvibile, G. "Inside the Linux Packet Filter, Part II." *Linux Journal,* March 2002.

MCKU96   McKusick, M.; Bostic, K.; Karels, M.; and Quartermain, J. *The Design and Implementation of the 4.4BSD UNIX Operating System.* Reading, MA: Addison-Wesley, 1996.

RODR02   Rodriguez, A., et al. *TCP/IP Tutorial and Technical Overview.* Upper Saddle River: NJ: Prentice Hall, 2002.

STAL04   Stallings, W. *Computer Networking with Internet Protocols and Technology.* Upper Saddle River: NJ: Prentice Hall, 2004.

WRIG95   Wright, G., and Stevens, W. *TCP/IP Illustrated, Volume 2: The Implementation.* Reading, MA: Addison-Wesley, 1995.

Recommended Web Sites:

- **Networking Links:** Excellent collection of links related to TCP/IP
- **IPng:** Information about IPv6 and related topics

13.7 KEY TERMS, REVIEW QUESTIONS, AND PROBLEMS

Key Terms

application programming interface (API)	protocol	stream sockets
	protocol architecture	TELNET
datagram sockets	raw sockets	Transmission Control Protocol (TCP)
File Transfer Protocol (FTP)	Simple Mail Transfer Protocol (SMTP)	
Internet Protocol (IP)		User Datagram Protocol (UDP)
port	sockets	

Review Questions

13.1   What is the major function of the network access layer?

13.2   What tasks are performed by the transport layer?

13.3   What is a protocol?

13.4   What is a protocol architecture?

13.5   What is TCP/IP?

13.6   What is the purpose of the Sockets interface?

Problems

13.1   **a.**   The French and Chinese prime ministers need to come to an agreement by telephone, but neither speaks the other's language. Further, neither has on hand a translator that can translate to the language of the other. However, both prime ministers have English translators on their staffs. Draw a diagram similar to Figure 13.8 to depict the situation, and describe the interaction at each layer.

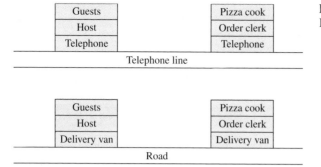

Figure 13.8 Architecture for Problem 13.1

b. Now suppose that the Chinese prime minister's translator can translate only into Japanese and that the French prime minister has a German translator available. A translator between German and Japanese is available in Germany. Draw a new diagram that reflects this arrangement and describe the hypothetical phone conversation.

13.2 List the major disadvantages of the layered approach to protocols.

13.3 A TCP segment consisting of 1500 bits of data and 160 bits of header is sent to the IP layer, which appends another 160 bits of header. This is then transmitted through two networks, each of which uses a 24-bit packet header. The destination network has a maximum packet size of 800 bits. How many bits, including headers, are delivered to the network layer protocol at the destination?

13.4 Why does the TCP header have a header length field while the UDP header does not?

13.5 The previous version of the TFTP specification, RFC 783, included the following statement:

All packets other than those used for termination are acknowledged individually unless a timeout occurs.

The new specification revises this to say

All packets other than duplicate ACKs and those used for termination are acknowledged unless a timeout occurs.

The change was made to fix a problem referred to as the "Sorcerer's Apprentice." Deduce and explain the problem.

13.6 What is the limiting factor in the time required to transfer a file using TFTP?

13.7 This chapter mentions the use of Frame Relay as a specific protocol or system used to connect to a wide area network. Each organization will have a certain collection of services available (like Frame Relay), but this is dependent upon provider provisioning, cost, and customer premises equipment. What are some of the services available to you in your area?

13.8 Ethereal is a free packet sniffer that allows you to capture traffic on a local area network. It can be used on a variety of operating systems and is available at **www.ethereal.com**. You must also install the WinPcap packet capture driver, which can be obtained from **http://winpcap.mirror.ethereal.com/**.

After starting a capture from Ethereal, start a TCP-based application like telnet, FTP or http (Web browser). Can you determine the following from your capture?
a. Source and destination layer 2 addresses (MAC)
b. Source and destination layer 3 addresses (IP)
c. Source and destination layer 4 addresses (port numbers)

13.9 Packet capture software or sniffers can be powerful management and security tools. By using the filtering capability that is built in, you can trace traffic based on several different criteria and eliminate everything else. Use the filtering capability built into Ethereal to do the following:

a. Capture only traffic coming from your computer's MAC address.
b. Capture only traffic coming from your computer's IP address.
c. Capture only UDP-based transmissions.

APPENDIX 13A THE TRIVIAL FILE TRANSFER PROTOCOL

This appendix provides an overview of the Internet standard Trivial File Transfer Protocol (TFTP). Our purpose is to give the reader some flavor for the elements of a protocol.

Introduction to TFTP

TFTP is far simpler than the Internet standard File Transfer Protocol (FTP). There are no provisions for access control or user identification, so TFTP is only suitable for public access file directories. Because of its simplicity, TFTP is easily and compactly implemented. For example, some diskless devices use TFTP to download their firmware at boot time.

TFTP runs on top of UDP. The TFTP entity that initiates the transfer does so by sending a read or write request in a UDP segment with a destination port of 69 to the target system. This port is recognized by the target UDP module as the identifier of the TFTP module. For the duration of the transfer, each side uses a transfer identifier (TID) as its port number.

TFTP Packets

TFTP entities exchange commands, responses, and file data in the form of packets, each of which is carried in the body of a UDP segment. TFTP supports five types of packets (Figure 13.9); the first two bytes contain an opcode that identifies the packet type:

- **RRQ:** The read request packet requests permission to transfer a file from the other system. The packet includes a file name, which is a sequence of ASCII[1] bytes terminated by a zero byte. The zero byte is the means by which the receiving TFTP entity knows when the file name is terminated. The packet also includes a mode field, which indicates whether the data file is to be interpreted as a string of ASCII bytes or as raw 8-bit bytes of data.

- **WRQ:** The write request packet requests permission to transfer a file to the other system.

- **Data:** The block numbers on data packets begin with one and increase by one for each new block of data. This convention enables the program to use a single number to discriminate between new packets and duplicates. The data field is from zero to 512 bytes long. If it is 512 bytes long, the block is not the last block of data; if it is from zero to 511 bytes long, it signals the end of the transfer.

- **ACK:** This packet is used to acknowledge receipt of a data packet or a WRQ packet. An ACK of a data packet contains the block number of the data packet being acknowledged. An ACK of a WRQ contains a block number of zero.

---

[1]ASCII is the American Standard Code for Information Interchange, a standard of the American National Standards Institute. It designates a unique 7-bit pattern for each letter, with an eighth bit used for parity. ASCII is equivalent to the International Reference Alphabet (IRA), defined in ITU-T Recommendation T.50. A description and table of the IRA code is contained in a supporting document at this book's Web site.

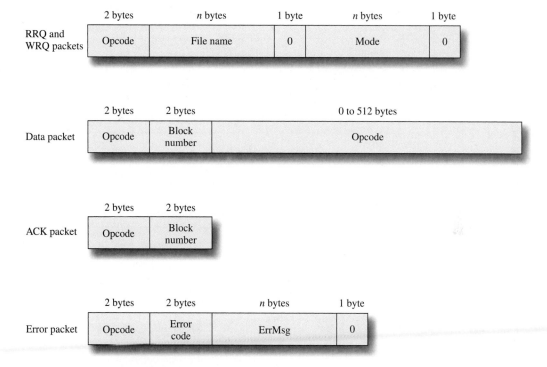

Figure 13.9   TFTP Packet Formats

Table 13.1   TFTP Error Codes

Value	Meaning
0	Not defined, see error message (if any)
1	File not found
2	Access violation
3	Disk full or allocation exceeded
4	Illegal TFTP operation
5	Unknown transfer ID
6	File already exists
7	No such user

- **Error:** An error packet can be the acknowledgment of any other type of packet. The error code is an integer indicating the nature of the error (Table 13.1). The error message is intended for human consumption and should be in ASCII. Like all other strings, it is terminated with a zero byte.

All packets other than duplicate ACKs (explained subsequently) and those used for termination are to be acknowledged. Any packet can be acknowledged by an error packet. If

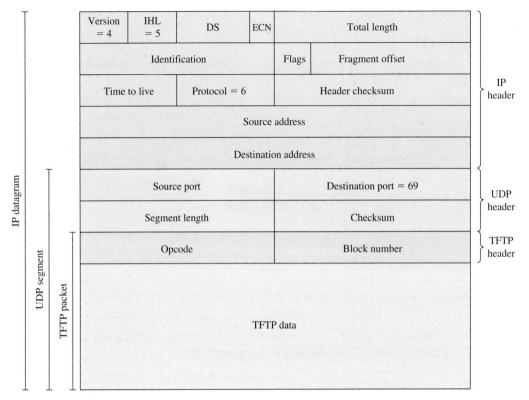

Figure 13.10   A TFTP Packet in Context

there are no errors, then the following conventions apply. A WRQ or a data packet is acknowledged by an ACK packet. When a RRQ is sent, the other side responds (in the absence of error) by beginning to transfer the file; thus, the first data block serves as an acknowledgment of the RRQ packet. Unless a file transfer is complete, each ACK packet from one side is followed by a data packet from the other, so that the data packet functions as an acknowledgment. An error packet can be acknowledged by any other kind of packet, depending on the circumstance.

Figure 13.10 shows a TFTP data packet in context. When such a packet is handed down to UDP, UDP adds a header to form a UDP segment. This is then passed to IP, which adds an IP header to form an IP datagram.

Overview of a Transfer

The example illustrated in Figure 13.11 is of a simple file transfer operation from A to B. No errors occur and the details of the option specification are not explored.

The operation begins when the TFTP module in system A sends a write request (WRQ) to the TFTP module in system B. The WRQ packet is carried as the body of a UDP segment. The write request includes the name of the file (in this case, XXX) and a mode of octet, or raw data. In the UDP header, the destination port number is 69, which alerts the receiving UDP entity that this message is intended for the TFTP application. The source port number is a TID selected by A, in this case 1511. System B is prepared to accept the file and so responds with an ACK with a block number of 0. In the UDP header, the destination port

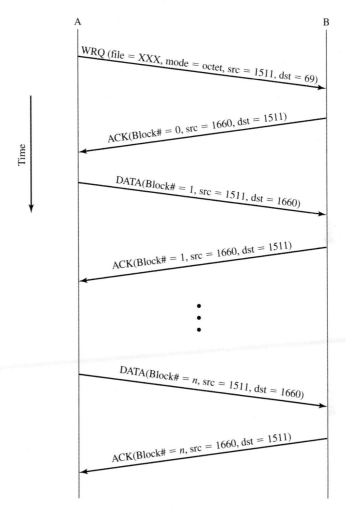

Figure 13.11   Example TFTP Operation

is 1511, which enables the UDP entity at A to route the incoming packet to the TFTP module, which can match this TID with the TID in the WRQ. The source port is a TID selected by B for this file transfer, in this case 1660.

Following this initial exchange, the file transfer proceeds. The transfer consists of one or more data packets from A, each of which is acknowledged by B. The final data packet contains less than 512 bytes of data, which signals the end of the transfer.

Errors and Delays

If TFTP operates over a network or the Internet (as opposed to a direct data link), it is possible for packets to be lost. Because TFTP operates over UDP, which does not provide a reliable delivery service, there needs to be some mechanism in TFTP to deal with lost packets. TFTP uses the common technique of a time-out mechanism. Suppose that A sends a packet to B that requires an acknowledgment (i.e., any packet other than duplicate ACKs and those used for termination). When A has transmitted the packet, it starts a timer. If the timer expires before the acknowledgment is received from B, A retransmits the same packet. If in fact the original packet was lost, then the retransmission will be the first copy of this packet received by B. If the original packet was not lost but the acknowledgment from B was lost, then B will receive two copies of the same packet from A and simply acknowledges both copies. Because of the use of block numbers, this causes no confusion. The only exception to this rule is for duplicate ACK packets. The second ACK is ignored.

Syntax, Semantics, and Timing

In Section 5.1, it was mentioned that the key features of a protocol can be classified as syntax, semantics, and timing. These categories are easily seen in TFTP. The formats of the various TFTP packets determine the **syntax** of the protocol. The **semantics** of the protocol are shown in the definitions of each of the packet types and the error codes. Finally, the sequence in which packets are exchanged, the use of block numbers, and the use of timers are all aspects of the **timing** of TFTP.

CHAPTER 14

DISTRIBUTED PROCESSING, CLIENT/SERVER, AND CLUSTERS

In this chapter, we begin with an examination of some of the key concepts in distributed software, including client/server architecture, message passing, and remote procedure calls. Then we examine the increasingly important cluster architecture.

14.1 CLIENT/SERVER COMPUTING

The concept of client/server computing and related concepts, have become increasingly important in information technology systems. This section begins with a description of the general nature of client/server computing. This is followed by a discussion of alternative ways of organizing the client/server functions. The issue of file cache consistency, raised by the use of file servers, is then examined. Finally, this section introduces the concept of middleware.

What Is Client/Server Computing?

As with other new waves in the computer field, client/server computing comes with its own set of jargon words. Table 14.1 lists some of the terms that are commonly found in descriptions of client/server products and applications.

Figure 14.1 attempts to capture the essence of the client/server concept. As the term suggests, a client/server environment is populated by clients and servers. The **client** machines are generally single-user PCs or workstations that provide a highly user-friendly interface to the end user. The client-based station generally presents the type of graphical interface that is most comfortable to users, including the use of windows and a mouse. Microsoft Windows and Macintosh OS provide examples of such interfaces. Client-based applications are tailored for ease of use and include such familiar tools as the spreadsheet.

Table 14.1 Client/Server Terminology

Applications Programming Interface (API)
    A set of function and call programs that allow clients and servers to intercommunicate

Client
    A networked information requester, usually a PC or workstation, that can query database and/or other information from a server

Middleware
    A set of drivers, APIs, or other software that improves connectivity between a client application and a server

Relational Database
    A database in which information access is limited to the selection of rows that satisfy all search criteria

Server
    A computer, usually a high-powered workstation, a minicomputer, or a mainframe, that houses information for manipulation by networked clients

Structured Query Language (SQL)
    A language developed by IBM and standardized by ANSI for addressing, creating, updating, or querying relational databases

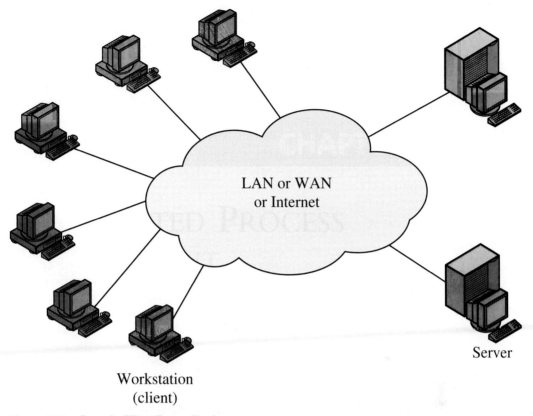

Figure 14.1   Generic Client/Server Environment

Each **server** in the client/server environment provides a set of shared services to the clients. The most common type of server currently is the database server, usually controlling a relational database. The server enables many clients to share access to the same database and enables the use of a high-performance computer system to manage the database.

In addition to clients and servers, the third essential ingredient of the client/server environment is the **network**. Client/server computing is typically distributed computing. Users, applications, and resources are distributed in response to business requirements and linked by a single LAN or WAN or by an internet of networks.

How does a client/server configuration differ from any other distributed processing solution? There are a number of characteristics that stand out and that, together, make client/server distinct from other types of distributed processing:

- There is a heavy reliance on bringing user-friendly applications to the user on his or her own system. This gives the user a great deal of control over the timing and style of computer usage and gives department-level managers the ability to be responsive to their local needs.

- Although applications are dispersed, there is an emphasis on centralizing corporate databases and many network management and utility functions. This enables corporate management to maintain overall control of the total capital investment in computing and information systems and to provide interoperability so that systems are tied together. At the same time it relieves individual departments and divisions of much of the overhead of maintaining sophisticated computer-based facilities but enables them to choose just about any type of machine and interface they need to access data and information.

- There is a commitment, both by user organizations and vendors, to open and modular systems. This means that the user has more choice in selecting products and in mixing equipment from a number of vendors.

- Networking is fundamental to the operation. Thus, network management and network security have a high priority in organizing and operating information systems.

Client/Server Applications

The key feature of a client/server architecture is the allocation of application-level tasks between clients and servers. Figure 14.2 illustrates the general case. In both client and server, of course, the basic software is an operating system running on the hardware platform. The platforms and the operating systems of client and server may differ. Indeed, there may be a number of different types of client platforms and operating systems and a number of different types of server platforms in a single environment. As long as a particular client and server share the same communications protocols and support the same applications, these lower-level differences are irrelevant.

It is the communications software that enables client and server to interoperate. The principal example of such software is TCP/IP. Of course, the point of all of this support software (communications and operating system) is to provide a base for distributed applications. Ideally, the actual functions performed by the application can be split up between client and server in a way that optimizes the use of resources. In some cases, depending on the application needs, the bulk of the applications software

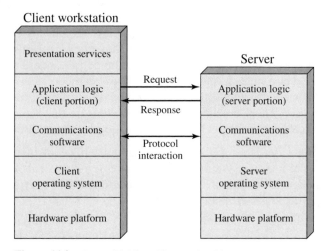

Figure 14.2   Generic Client/Server Architecture

executes at the server, while in other cases, most of the application logic is located at the client.

An essential factor in the success of a client/server environment is the way in which the user interacts with the system as a whole. Thus, the design of the user interface on the client machine is critical. In most client/server systems, there is heavy emphasis on providing a **graphical user interface (GUI)** that is easy to use, easy to learn, yet powerful and flexible. Thus, we can think of a presentation services module in the client workstation that is responsible for providing a user-friendly interface to the distributed applications available in the environment.

Database Applications As an example that illustrates the concept of splitting application logic between client and server, let us consider one of the most common families of client/server applications: those that use relational databases. In this environment, the server is essentially a database server. Interaction between client and server is in the form of transactions in which the client makes a database request and receives a database response.

Figure 14.3 illustrates, in general terms, the architecture of such a system. The server is responsible for maintaining the database, for which purpose a complex database management system software module is required. A variety of different applications that make use of the database can be housed on client machines. The "glue" that ties client and server together is software that enables the client to make requests for access to the server's database. A popular example of such logic is the structured query language (SQL).

Figure 14.3 suggests that all of the application logic—the software for "number crunching" or other types of data analysis—is on the client side, while the server is only concerned with managing the database. Whether such a configuration is appropriate depends on the style and intent of the application. For

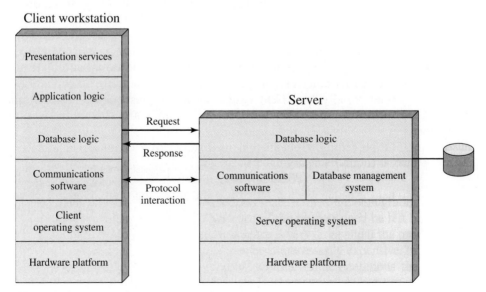

Figure 14.3 Client/Server Architecture for Database Applications

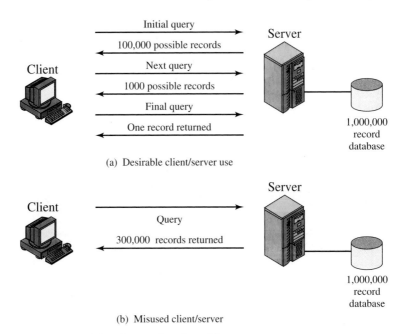

Figure 14.4 Client/Server Database Usage

example, suppose that the primary purpose is to provide online access for record lookup. Figure 14.4a suggests how this might work. Suppose that the server is maintaining a database of 1 million records (called rows in relational database terminology), and the user wants to perform a lookup that should result in zero, one, or at most a few records. The user could search for these records using a number of search criteria (e.g., records older than 1992; records referring to individuals in Ohio; records referring to a specific event or characteristic, etc.). An initial client query may yield a server response that there are 100,000 records that satisfy the search criteria. The user then adds additional qualifiers and issues a new query. This time, a response indicating that there are 1000 possible records is returned. Finally, the client issues a third request with additional qualifiers. The resulting search criteria yield a single match, and the record is returned to the client.

The preceding application is well suited to a client/server architecture for two reasons:

1. There is a massive job of sorting and searching the database. This requires a large disk or bank of disks, a high-speed CPU, and a high-speed I/O architecture. Such capacity and power is not needed and is too expensive for a single-user workstation or PC.

2. It would place too great a traffic burden on the network to move the entire 1-million-record file to the client for searching. Therefore, it is not enough for the server just to be able to retrieve records on behalf of a client; the

server needs to have database logic that enables it to perform searches on behalf of a client.

Now consider the scenario of Figure 14.4b, which has the same 1-million-record database. In this case, a single query results in the transmission of 300,000 records over the network. This might happen if, for example, the user wishes to find the grand total or mean value of some field across many records or even the entire database.

Clearly, this latter scenario is unacceptable. One solution to this problem, which maintains the client/server architecture with all of its benefits, is to move part of the application logic over to the server. That is, the server can be equipped with application logic for performing data analysis as well as data retrieval and data searching.

Classes of Client/Server Applications Within the general framework of client/server, there is a spectrum of implementations that divide the work between client and server differently. Figure 14.5 illustrates in general terms some of the major options for database applications. Other splits are possible, and the options may have a different characterization for other types of applications. In any case, it is useful to examine this figure to get a feel for the kind of tradeoffs possible.

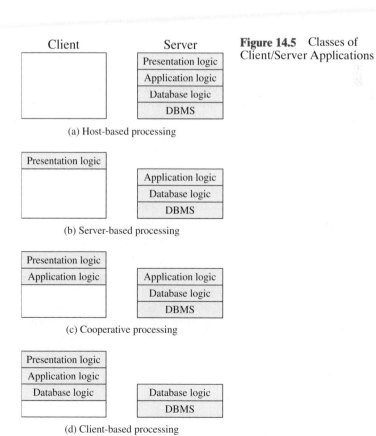

Figure 14.5 Classes of Client/Server Applications

Figure 14.5 depicts four classes:

- **Host-based processing:** Host-based processing is not true client/server computing as the term is generally used. Rather, host-based processing refers to the traditional mainframe environment in which all or virtually all of the processing is done on a central host. Often the user interface is via a dumb terminal. Even if the user is employing a microcomputer, the user's station is generally limited to the role of a terminal emulator.

- **Server-based processing:** The most basic class of client/server configuration is one in which the client is principally responsible for providing a graphical user interface, while virtually all of the processing is done on the server. This configuration is typical of early client/server efforts, especially departmental-level systems. The rationale behind such configurations is that the user workstation is best suited to providing a user-friendly interface and that databases and applications can easily be maintained on central systems. Although the user gains the advantage of a better interface, this type of configuration does not generally lend itself to any significant gains in productivity or to any fundamental changes in the actual business functions that the system supports.

- **Client-based processing:** At the other extreme, virtually all application processing may be done at the client, with the exception of data validation routines and other database logic functions that are best performed at the server. Generally, some of the more sophisticated database logic functions are housed on the client side. This architecture is perhaps the most common client/server approach in current use. It enables the user to employ applications tailored to local needs.

- **Cooperative processing:** In a cooperative processing configuration, the application processing is performed in an optimized fashion, taking advantage of the strengths of both client and server machines and of the distribution of data. Such a configuration is more complex to set up and maintain but, in the long run, this type of configuration may offer greater user productivity gains and greater network efficiency than other client/server approaches.

Figures 14.5c and d correspond to configurations in which a considerable fraction of the load is on the client. This so-called **fat client** model has been popularized by application development tools such as Sybase Inc.'s PowerBuilder and Gupta Corp.'s SQL Windows. Applications developed with these tools are typically departmental in scope, supporting between 25 and 150 users [ECKE95]. The main benefit of the fat client model is that it takes advantage of desktop power, offloading application processing from servers and making them more efficient and less likely to be bottlenecks.

There are, however, several disadvantages to the fat client strategy. The addition of more functions rapidly overloads the capacity of desktop machines, forcing companies to upgrade. If the model extends beyond the department to incorporate many users, the company must install high-capacity LANs to support the large volumes of transmission between the thin servers and the fat clients. Finally, it is difficult to maintain, upgrade, or replace applications distributed across tens or hundreds of desktops.

Figure 14.5b is representative of a **thin client** approach. This approach more nearly mimics the traditional host-centered approach and is often the migration path for evolving corporate-wide applications from the mainframe to a distributed environment.

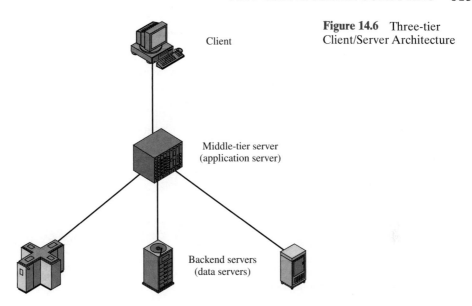

Client

Figure 14.6   Three-tier
Client/Server Architecture

Middle-tier server
(application server)

Backend servers
(data servers)

Three-Tier Client/Server Architecture   The traditional client/server architecture involves two levels, or tiers: a client tier and a server tier. A three-tier architecture is also common (Figure 14.6). In this architecture, the application software is distributed among three types of machines: a user machine, a middle-tier server, and a backend server. The user machine is the client machine we have been discussing and, in the three-tier model, is typically a thin client. The middle-tier machines are essentially gateways between the thin user clients and a variety of backend database servers. The middle-tier machines can convert protocols and map from one type of database query to another. In addition, the middle-tier machine can merge/integrate results from different data sources. Finally, the middle-tier machine can serve as a gateway between the desktop applications and the backend legacy applications by mediating between the two worlds.

The interaction between the middle-tier server and the backend server also follows the client/server model. Thus, the middle-tier system acts as both a client and a server.

File Cache Consistency   When a file server is used, performance of file I/O can be noticeably degraded relative to local file access because of the delays imposed by the network. To reduce this performance penalty, individual systems can use file caches to hold recently accessed file records. Because of the principle of locality, use of a local file cache should reduce the number of remote server accesses that must be made.

Figure 14.7 illustrates a typical distributed mechanism for caching files among a networked collection of workstations. When a process makes a file access, the request is presented first to the cache of the process's workstation ("file traffic"). If not satisfied there, the request is passed either to the local disk, if the file is stored there ("disk traffic"), or to a file server, where the file is stored ("server traffic"). At the server, the server's cache is first interrogated and, if there is a miss, then the server's disk is accessed. The dual caching approach is used to reduce communications traffic (client cache) and disk I/O (server cache).

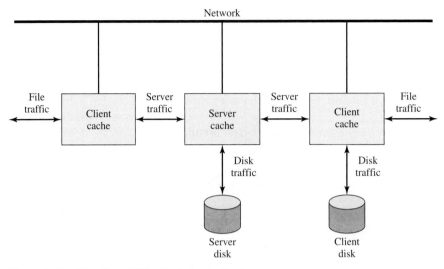

Figure 14.7   Distributed File Cacheing in Sprite

When caches always contain exact copies of remote data, we say that the caches are **consistent**. It is possible for caches to become inconsistent when the remote data are changed and the corresponding obsolete local cache copies are not discarded. This can happen if one client modifies a file that is also cached by other clients. The difficulty is actually at two levels. If a client adopts a policy of immediately writing any changes to a file back to the server, then any other client that has a cache copy of the relevant portion of the file will have obsolete data. The problem is made even worse if the client delays writing back changes to the server. In that case, the server itself has an obsolete version of the file, and new file read requests to the server may obtain obsolete data. The problem of keeping local cache copies up to date to changes in remote data is known as the **cache consistency** problem.

The simplest approach to cache consistency is to use file-locking techniques to prevent simultaneous access to a file by more than one client. This guarantees consistency at the expense of performance and flexibility. A more powerful approach is provided with the facility in Sprite [NELS88, OUST88]. Any number of remote processes may open a file for read and create their own client cache. But when an open file request to a server requests write access and other processes have the file open for read access, the server takes two actions. First, it notifies the writing process that, although it may maintain a cache, it must write back all altered blocks immediately upon update. There can be at most one such client. Second, the server notifies all reading processes that have the file open that the file is no longer cacheable.

Middleware

The development and deployment of client/server products has far outstripped efforts to standardize all aspects of distributed computing, from the physical layer up to the application layer. This lack of standards makes it difficult to implement an integrated, multivendor, enterprise-wide client/server configuration. Because much of the benefit of the client/server approach is tied up with its modularity and the ability to mix and match platforms and applications to provide a business solution, this interoperability problem must be solved.

To achieve the true benefits of the client/server approach, developers must have a set of tools that provide a uniform means and style of access to system resources across all platforms. This will enable programmers to build applications that not only look and feel the same on various PCs and workstations but that use the same method to access data regardless of the location of that data.

The most common way to meet this requirement is by the use of standard programming interfaces and protocols that sit between the application above and communications software and operating system below. Such standardized interfaces and protocols have come to be referred to as middleware. With standard programming interfaces, it is easy to implement the same application on a variety of server types and workstation types. This obviously benefits the customer, but vendors are also motivated to provide such interfaces. The reason is that customers buy applications, not servers; customers will only choose among those server products that run the applications they want. The standardized protocols are needed to link these various server interfaces back to the clients that need access to them.

There is a variety of middleware packages ranging from the very simple to the very complex. What they all have in common is the capability to hide the complexities and disparities of different network protocols and operating systems. Client and server vendors generally provide a number of the more popular middleware packages as options. Thus, a user can settle on a particular middleware strategy and then assemble equipment from various vendors that support that strategy.

Middleware Architecture   Figure 14.8 suggests the role of middleware in a client/server architecture. The exact role of the middleware component will depend

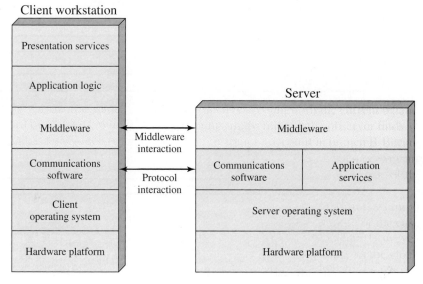

Figure 14.8   The Role of Middleware in Client/Server Architecture

on the style of client/server computing being used. Referring back to Figure 14.5, recall that there are a number of different client/server approaches, depending on the way in which application functions are split up. In any case, Figure 14.8 gives a good general idea of the architecture involved.

Note that there is both a client and server component of middleware. The basic purpose of middleware is to enable an application or user at a client to access a variety of services on servers without being concerned about differences among servers. To look at one specific application area, the structured query language (SQL) is supposed to provide a standardized means for access to a relational database by either a local or remote user or application. However, many relational database vendors, although they support SQL, have added their own proprietary extensions to SQL. This enables vendors to differentiate their products but also creates potential incompatibilities.

As an example, consider a distributed system used to support, among other things, the personnel department. The basic employee data, such as employee name and address, might be stored on a Gupta database, whereas salary information might be contained on an Oracle database. When a user in the personnel department requires access to particular records, that user does not want to be concerned with which vendor's database contains the records needed. Middleware provides a layer of software that enables uniform access to these differing systems.

It is instructive to look at the role of middleware from a logical, rather than an implementation, point of view. This viewpoint is illustrated in Figure 14.9. Middleware enables the realization of the promise of distributed client/server computing. The entire distributed system can be viewed as a set of applications and resources available to users. Users need not be concerned with the location

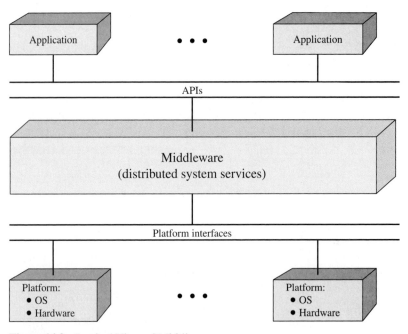

Figure 14.9   Logical View of Middleware

of data or indeed the location of applications. All applications operate over a uniform applications programming interface (API). The middleware, which cuts across all client and server platforms, is responsible for routing client requests to the appropriate server.

Although there is a wide variety of middleware products, these products are typically based on one of two underlying mechanisms: message passing or remote procedure calls. These two methods are examined in the next two sections.

14.2 DISTRIBUTED MESSAGE PASSING

It is usually the case in a distributed processing systems that the computers do not share main memory; each is an isolated computer system. Thus, interprocessor communication techniques that rely on shared memory, such as semaphores, cannot be used. Instead, techniques that rely on message passing are used. In this section and the next, we look at the two most common approaches. The first is the straightforward application of messages as they are used in a single system. The second is a separate technique that relies on message passing as a basic function: the remote procedure call.

Figure 14.10a shows the use of message passing to implement client/server functionality. A client process requires some service (e.g., read a file, print) and sends a message containing a request for service to a server process. The server process honors the request and sends a message containing a reply. In its simplest form, only two functions are needed: Send and Receive. The Send function specifies a destination and includes the message content. The Receive function tells from whom a message is desired (including "all") and provides a buffer where the incoming message is to be stored.

Figure 14.11 suggests an implementation for message passing. Processes make use of the services of a message-passing module. Service requests can be expressed in terms of primitives and parameters. A primitive specifies the function to be performed, and the parameters are used to pass data and control information. The actual form of a primitive depends on the message-passing software. It may be a procedure call or it may itself be a message to a process that is part of the operating system.

The Send primitive is used by the process that desires to send the message. Its parameters are the identifier of the destination process and the contents of the message. The message-passing module constructs a data unit that includes these two elements. This data unit is sent to the machine that hosts the destination process, using some sort of communications facility, such as TCP/IP. When the data unit is received in the target system, it is routed by the communications facility to the message-passing module. This module examines the process ID field and stores the message in the buffer for that process.

In this scenario, the receiving process must announce its willingness to receive messages by designating a buffer area and informing the message-passing module by a Receive primitive. An alternative approach does not require such an announcement. Instead, when the message-passing module receives a message, it signals the destination process with some sort of Receive signal and then makes the received message available in a shared buffer.

Several design issues are associated with distributed message passing, and these are addressed in the remainder of this section.

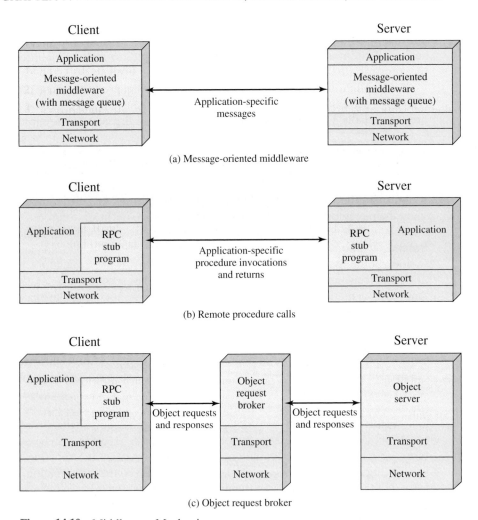

Figure 14.10   Middleware Mechanisms

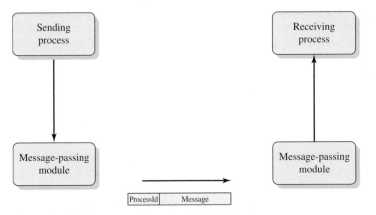

Figure 14.11   Basic Message-Passing Primitives

Reliability versus Unreliability

A reliable message-passing facility is one that guarantees delivery if possible. Such a facility makes use of a reliable transport protocol or similar logic and performs error checking, acknowledgment, retransmission, and reordering of misordered messages. Because delivery is guaranteed, it is not necessary to let the sending process know that the message was delivered. However, it might be useful to provide an acknowledgment back to the sending process so that it knows that delivery has already taken place. In either case, if the facility fails to achieve delivery (e.g., persistent network failure, crash of destination system), the sending process is notified of the failure.

At the other extreme, the message-passing facility may simply send the message out into the communications network but will report neither success nor failure. This alternative greatly reduces the complexity and processing and communications overhead of the message-passing facility. For those applications that require confirmation that a message has been delivered, the applications themselves may use request and reply messages to satisfy the requirement.

Blocking versus Nonblocking

With nonblocking, or asynchronous, primitives, a process is not suspended as a result of issuing a Send or Receive. Thus, when a process issues a Send primitive, the operating system returns control to the process as soon as the message has been queued for transmission or a copy has been made. If no copy is made, any changes made to the message by the sending process before or even while it is being transmitted are made at the risk of the process. When the message has been transmitted or copied to a safe place for subsequent transmission, the sending process is interrupted to be informed that the message buffer may be reused. Similarly, a nonblocking Receive is issued by a process that then proceeds to run. When a message arrives, the process is informed by interrupt, or it can poll for status periodically.

Nonblocking primitives provide for efficient, flexible use of the message-passing facility by processes. The disadvantage of this approach is that it is difficult to test and debug programs that use these primitives. Irreproducible, timing-dependent sequences can create subtle and difficult problems.

The alternative is to use blocking, or synchronous, primitives. A blocking Send does not return control to the sending process until the message has been transmitted (unreliable service) or until the message has been sent and an acknowledgment received (reliable service). A blocking Receive does not return control until a message has been placed in the allocated buffer.

14.3 REMOTE PROCEDURE CALLS

A variation on the basic message-passing model is the remote procedure call. This is now a widely accepted and common method for encapsulating communication in a distributed system. The essence of the technique is to allow programs on different machines to interact using simple procedure call/return semantics, just as if the two programs were on the same machine. That is, the procedure call is used for access to remote services. The popularity of this approach is due to the following advantages.

1. The procedure call is a widely accepted, used, and understood abstraction.

2. The use of remote procedure calls enables remote interfaces to be specified as a set of named operations with designated types. Thus, the interface can be clearly documented and distributed programs can be statically checked for type errors.

3. Because a standardized and precisely defined interface is specified, the communication code for an application can be generated automatically.

4. Because a standardized and precisely defined interface is specified, developers can write client and server modules that can be moved among computers and operating systems with little modification and recoding.

The remote procedure call mechanism can be viewed as a refinement of reliable, blocking message passing. Figure 14.10b illustrates the general architecture, and Figure 14.12 provides a more detailed look. The calling program makes a normal procedure call with parameters on its machine. For example,

$$\text{CALL } P(X, Y)$$

where

P = procedure name

X = passed arguments

Y = returned values

It may or may not be transparent to the user that the intention is to invoke a remote procedure on some other machine. A dummy or stub procedure P must be included

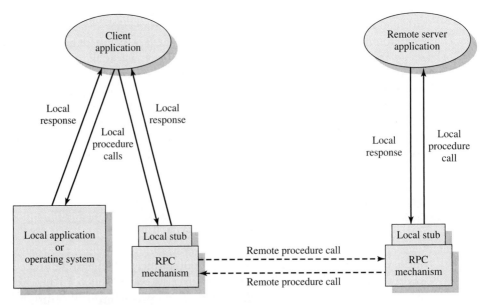

Figure 14.12   Remote Procedure Call Mechanism

in the caller's address space or be dynamically linked to it at call time. This procedure creates a message that identifies the procedure being called and includes the parameters. It then sends this message to a remote system and waits for a reply. When a reply is received, the stub procedure returns to the calling program, providing the returned values.

At the remote machine, another stub program is associated with the called procedure. When a message comes in, it is examined and a local CALL $P(X, Y)$ is generated. This remote procedure is thus called locally, so its normal assumptions about where to find parameters, the state of the stack, and so on are identical to the case of a purely local procedure call.

Several design issues are associated with remote procedure calls, and these are addressed in the remainder of this section.

Parameter Passing

Most programming languages allow parameters to be passed as values (call by value) or as pointers to a location that contains the value (call by reference). Call by value is simple for a remote procedure call: The parameters are simply copied into the message and sent to the remote system. It is more difficult to implement call by reference. A unique, systemwide pointer is needed for each object. The overhead for this capability may not be worth the effort.

Parameter Representation

Another issue is how to represent parameters and results in messages. If the called and calling programs are in identical programming languages on the same type of machines with the same operating system, then the representation requirement may present no problems. If there are differences in these areas, then there will probably be differences in the ways in which numbers and even text are represented. If a full-blown communications architecture is used, then this issue is handled by the presentation layer. However, the overhead of such an architecture has led to the design of remote procedure call facilities that bypass most of the communications architecture and provide their own basic communications facility. In that case, the conversion responsibility falls on the remote procedure call facility (e.g., see [GIBB87]).

The best approach to this problem is to provide a standardized format for common objects, such as integers, floating-point numbers, characters, and character strings. Then the native parameters on any machine can be converted to and from the standardized representation.

Client/Server Binding

Binding specifies how the relationship between a remote procedure and the calling program will be established. A binding is formed when two applications have made a logical connection and are prepared to exchange commands and data.

Nonpersistent binding means that a logical connection is established between the two processes at the time of the remote procedure call and that as soon as the values are returned, the connection is dismantled. Because a connection requires the maintenance of state information on both ends, it consumes resources. The nonpersistent style is used to conserve those resources. On the other hand, the overhead involved in establishing connections makes nonpersistent binding inappropriate for remote procedures that are called frequently by the same caller.

With **persistent binding**, a connection that is set up for a remote procedure call is sustained after the procedure return. The connection can then be used for future remote procedure calls. If a specified period of time passes with no activity on the connection, then the connection is terminated. For applications that make many repeated calls to remote procedures, persistent binding maintains the logical connection and allows a sequence of calls and returns to use the same connection.

Synchronous versus Asynchronous

The concepts of synchronous and asynchronous remote procedure calls are analogous to the concepts of blocking and nonblocking messages. The traditional remote procedure call (RPC) is synchronous, which requires that the calling process wait until the called process returns a value. Thus, the **synchronous RPC** behaves much like a subroutine call.

The synchronous RPC is easy to understand and program because its behavior is predictable. However, it fails to exploit fully the parallelism inherent in distributed applications. This limits the kind of interaction the distributed application can have, resulting in lower performance.

To provide greater flexibility, various **asynchronous RPC** facilities have been implemented to achieve a greater degree of parallelism while retaining the familiarity and simplicity of the RPC [ANAN92]. Asynchronous RPCs do not block the caller; the replies can be received as and when they are needed, thus allowing client execution to proceed locally in parallel with the server invocation.

A typical asynchronous RPC use is to enable a client to invoke a server repeatedly so that the client has a number of requests in the pipeline at one time, each with its own set of data. Synchronization of client and server can be achieved in one of two ways:

1. A higher-layer application in the client and server can initiate the exchange and then check at the end that all requested actions have been performed.

2. A client can issue a string of asynchronous RPCs followed by a final synchronous RPC. The server will respond to the synchronous RPC only after completing all of the work requested in the preceding asynchronous RPCs.

In some schemes, asynchronous RPCs require no reply from the server and the server cannot send a reply message. Other schemes either require or allow a reply, but the caller does not wait for the reply.

Object-Oriented Mechanisms

As object-oriented technology becomes more prevalent in operating system design, client/server designers have begun to embrace this approach. In this approach, clients and servers ship messages back and forth between objects. Object communications may rely on an underlying message or RPC structure or be developed directly on top of object-oriented capabilities in the operating system.

A client that needs a service sends a request to an object request broker, which acts as a directory of all the remote service available on the network (Figure 14.10c). The broker calls the appropriate object and passes along any relevant data. Then the remote object services the request and replies to the broker, which returns the response to the client.

The success of the object-oriented approach depends on standardization of the object mechanism. Unfortunately, there are several competing designs in this area. One is Microsoft's Component Object Model (COM), the basis for Object Linking and Embedding (OLE). A competing approach, developed by the Object Management Group, is the Common Object Request Broker Architecture (CORBA), which has wide industry support. IBM, Apple, Sun, and many other vendors support the CORBA approach.

14.4 CLUSTERS

An important and relatively recent development computer system design is clustering. Clustering is an alternative to symmetric multiprocessing (SMP) as an approach to providing high performance and high availability and is particularly attractive for server applications. We can define a cluster as a group of interconnected, whole computers working together as a unified computing resource that can create the illusion of being one machine. The term *whole computer* means a system that can run on its own, apart from the cluster; in the literature, each computer in a cluster is typically referred to as a *node*.

[BREW97] lists four benefits that can be achieved with clustering. These can also be thought of as objectives or design requirements:

- **Absolute scalability:** It is possible to create large clusters that far surpass the power of even the largest standalone machines. A cluster can have dozens or even hundreds of machines, each of which is a multiprocessor.

- **Incremental scalability:** A cluster is configured in such a way that it is possible to add new systems to the cluster in small increments. Thus, a user can start out with a modest system and expand it as needs grow, without having to go through a major upgrade in which an existing small system is replaced with a larger system.

- **High availability:** Because each node in a cluster is a standalone computer, the failure of one node does not mean loss of service. In many products, fault tolerance is handled automatically in software.

- **Superior price/performance:** By using commodity building blocks, it is possible to put together a cluster with equal or greater computing power than a single large machine, at much lower cost.

Cluster Configurations

In the literature, clusters are classified in a number of different ways. Perhaps the simplest classification is based on whether the computers in a cluster share access

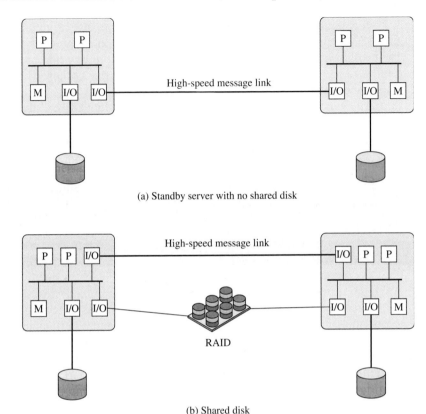

(a) Standby server with no shared disk

(b) Shared disk

Figure 14.13 Cluster Configurations

to the same disks. Figure 14.13a shows a two-node cluster in which the only inter-connection is by means of a high-speed link that can be used for message exchange to coordinate cluster activity. The link can be a LAN that is shared with other computers that are not part of the cluster or the link can be a dedicated interconnection facility. In the latter case, one or more of the computers in the cluster will have a link to a LAN or WAN so that there is a connection between the server cluster and remote client systems. Note that in the figure, each computer is depicted as being a multiprocessor. This is not necessary but does enhance both performance and availability.

In the simple classification depicted in Figure 14.13, the other alternative is a shared-disk cluster. In this case, there generally is still a message link between nodes. In addition, there is a disk subsystem that is directly linked to multiple computers within the cluster. In Figure 14.13b, the common disk subsystem is a RAID system. The use of RAID or some similar redundant disk technology is common in clusters so that the high availability achieved by the presence of multiple computers is not compromised by a shared disk that is a single point of failure.

A clearer picture of the range of clustering approaches can be gained by looking at functional alternatives. A white paper from Hewlett Packard [HP96] provides a useful classification along functional lines (Table 14.2), which we now discuss.

Table 14.2 Clustering Methods: Benefits and Limitations

Clustering Method	Description	Benefits	Limitations
Passive Standby	A secondary server takes over in case of primary server failure.	Easy to implement.	High cost because the secondary server is unavailable for other processing tasks.
Active Secondary	The secondary server is also used for processing tasks.	Reduced cost because secondary servers can be used for processing.	Increased complexity.
Separate Servers	Separate servers have their own disks. Data is continuously copied from primary to secondary server.	High availability.	High network and server overhead due to copying operations.
Servers Connected to Disks	Servers are cabled to the same disks, but each server owns its disks. If one server fails, its disks are taken over by the other server.	Reduced network and server overhead due to elimination of copying operations.	Usually requires disk mirroring or RAID technology to compensate for risk of disk failure.
Servers Share Disks	Multiple servers simultaneously share access to disks.	Low network and server overhead. Reduced risk of downtime caused by disk failure.	Requires lock manager software. Usually used with disk mirroring or RAID technology.

A common, older method, known as **passive standby**, is simply to have one computer handle all of the processing load while the other computer remains inactive, standing by to take over in the event of a failure of the primary. To coordinate the machines, the active, or primary, system periodically sends a "heartbeat" message to the standby machine. Should these messages stop arriving, the standby assumes that the primary server has failed and puts itself into operation. This approach increases availability but does not improve performance. Further, if the only information that is exchanged between the two systems is a heartbeat message, and if the two systems do not share common disks, then the standby provides a functional backup but has no access to the databases managed by the primary.

The passive standby is generally not referred to as a cluster. The term *cluster* generally refers to the use of multiple interconnected computers that are all actively doing processing while maintaining the image of a single system to the outside world. The term **active secondary** is often used in referring to this configuration. Three methods of clustering can be identified: separate servers, shared nothing, and shared memory.

In one approach to clustering, each computer is a **separate server** with its own disks and there are no disks shared between systems (Figure 14.13a). This arrangement provides high performance as well as high availability. In this case, some type of management or scheduling software is needed to assign incoming client requests to servers so that the load is balanced and high utilization is achieved. It is desirable to have a failover capability, which means that if a computer fails while executing an application, another computer in the cluster can pick up and complete the application. For this to happen, data must constantly be copied among systems so that each system has access to the current data of the other systems. The overhead of this data exchange ensures high availability at the cost of a performance penalty.

To reduce the communications overhead, most clusters now consist of servers connected to common disks (Figure 14.13b). One variation of this approach is simply called **shared nothing**. In this approach, the common disks are partitioned into volumes, and each volume is owned by a single computer. If that computer fails, the cluster must be reconfigured so that some other computer has ownership of the volumes of the failed computer.

It is also possible to have multiple computers share the same disks at the same time (called the **shared disk** approach), so that each computer has access to all of the volumes on all of the disks. This approach requires the use of some type of locking facility to ensure that data can only be accessed by one computer at a time.

Operating System Design Issues

Full exploitation of a cluster hardware configuration requires some enhancements to a single-system operating system.

Failure Management How failures are managed by a cluster depends on the clustering method used (Table 14.2). In general, two approaches can be taken to dealing with failures: highly available clusters and fault-tolerant clusters. A highly available cluster offers a high probability that all resources will be in service. If a failure does occur, such as a node goes down or a disk volume is lost, then the queries in progress are lost. Any lost query, if retried, will be serviced by a different computer in the cluster. However, the cluster operating system makes no guarantee about the state of partially executed transactions. This would need to be handled at the application level.

A fault-tolerant cluster ensures that all resources are always available. This is achieved by the use of redundant shared disks and mechanisms for backing out uncommitted transactions and committing completed transactions.

The function of switching an application and data resources over from a failed system to an alternative system in the cluster is referred to as **failover**. A related function is the restoration of applications and data resources to the original system once it has been fixed; this is referred to as **failback**. Failback can be automated, but this is desirable only if the problem is truly fixed and unlikely to recur. If not, automatic failback can cause subsequently failed resources to bounce back and forth between computers, resulting in performance and recovery problems.

Load Balancing A cluster requires an effective capability for balancing the load among available computers. This includes the requirement that the cluster be incrementally scalable. When a new computer is added to the cluster, the load-balancing facility should automatically include this computer in scheduling applications. Middleware mechanisms need to recognize that services can appear on different members of the cluster and may migrate from one member to another.

Parallelizing Computation In some cases, effective use of a cluster requires executing software from a single application in parallel. [KAPP00] lists three general approaches to the problem:

- **Parallelizing compiler:** A parallelizing compiler determines, at compile time, which parts of an application can be executed in parallel. These are then split off to be assigned to different computers in the cluster. Performance depends on the nature of the problem and how well the compiler is designed.

- **Parallelized application:** In this approach, the programmer writes the application from the outset to run on a cluster and uses message passing to move data, as required, between cluster nodes. This places a high burden on the programmer but may be the best approach for exploiting clusters for some applications.

- **Parametric computing:** This approach can be used if the essence of the application is an algorithm or program that must be executed a large number of times, each time with a different set of starting conditions or parameters. A good example is a simulation model, which will run a large number of different scenarios and then develop statistical summaries of the results. For this approach to be effective, parametric processing tools are needed to organize, run, and manage the jobs in an orderly manner.

Cluster Computer Architecture

Figure 14.14 shows a typical cluster architecture. The individual computers are connected by some high-speed LAN or switch hardware. Each computer is capable of operating independently. In addition, a middleware layer of software is installed in each computer to enable cluster operation. The cluster middleware provides a unified system image to the user, known as a **single-system image**. The middleware may also be responsible for providing high availability, by means of load balancing and

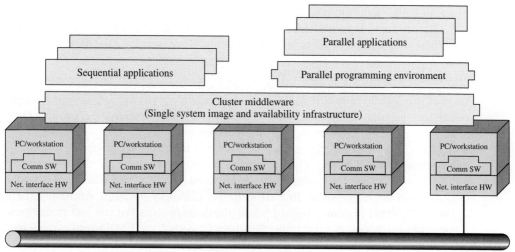

Figure 14.14 Cluster Computer Architecture [BUYY99a]

responding to failures in individual components. [HWAN99] lists the following as desirable cluster middleware services and functions:

- **Single entry point:** A user logs onto the cluster rather than to an individual computer.
- **Single file hierarchy:** The user sees a single hierarchy of file directories under the same root directory.
- **Single control point:** There is a default node used for cluster management and control.
- **Single virtual networking:** Any node can access any other point in the cluster, even though the actual cluster configuration may consist of multiple interconnected networks. There is a single virtual network operation.
- **Single memory space:** Distributed shared memory enables programs to share variables.
- **Single job-management system:** Under a cluster job scheduler, a user can submit a job without specifying the host computer to execute the job.
- **Single user interface:** A common graphic interface supports all users, regardless of the workstation from which they enter the cluster.
- **Single I/O space:** Any node can remotely access any I/O peripheral or disk device without knowledge of its physical location.
- **Single process space:** A uniform process-identification scheme is used. A process on any node can create or communicate with any other process on a remote node.
- **Checkpointing:** This function periodically saves the process state and intermediate computing results, to allow rollback recovery after a failure.
- **Process migration:** This function enables load balancing.

The last four items on the preceding list enhance the availability of the cluster. The remaining items are concerned with providing a single system image.

Returning to Figure 14.14, a cluster will also include software tools for enabling the efficient execution of programs that are capable of parallel execution.

Clusters Compared to SMP

Both clusters and symmetric multiprocessors provide a configuration with multiple processors to support high-demand applications. Both solutions are commercially available, although SMP has been around far longer.

The main strength of the SMP approach is that an SMP is easier to manage and configure than a cluster. The SMP is much closer to the original single-processor model for which nearly all applications are written. The principal change required in going from a uniprocessor to an SMP is to the scheduler function. Another benefit of the SMP is that it usually takes up less physical space and draws less power than a comparable cluster. A final important benefit is that the SMP products are well established and stable.

Over the long run, however, the advantages of the cluster approach are likely to result in clusters dominating the high-performance server market. Clusters are far superior to SMPs in terms of incremental and absolute scalability. Clusters are also superior in terms of availability, because all components of the system can readily be made highly redundant.

14.5 WINDOWS CLUSTER SERVER

Windows Cluster Server (formerly code named Wolfpack) is a shared-nothing cluster, in which each disk volume and other resources are owned by a single system at a time. The Windows Cluster Server design makes use of the following concepts:

- **Cluster Service:** The collection of software on each node that manages all cluster-specific activity.
- **Resource:** An item managed by the cluster service. All resources are objects representing actual resources in the system, including hardware devices such as disk drives and network cards and logical items such as logical disk volumes, TCP/IP addresses, entire applications, and databases.
- **Online:** A resource is said to be online at a node when it is providing service on that specific node.
- **Group:** A collection of resources managed as a single unit. Usually, a group contains all of the elements needed to run a specific application and for client systems to connect to the service provided by that application.

The concept of group is of particular importance. A group combines resources into larger units that are easily managed, both for failover and load balancing. Operations performed on a group, such as transferring the group to another node, automatically affect all of the resources in that group. Resources are implemented as dynamically linked libraries (DLLs) and managed by a resource monitor. The resource monitor interacts with the cluster service via remote procedure calls and responds to cluster service commands to configure and move resource groups.

Figure 14.15 depicts the Windows Cluster Server components and their relationships in a single system of a cluster. The **node manager** is responsible for maintaining this node's membership in the cluster. Periodically, it sends heartbeat messages to the node managers on other nodes in the cluster. In the event that one node manager detects a loss of heartbeat messages from another cluster node, it broadcasts a message to the entire cluster, causing all members to exchange messages to verify their view of current cluster membership. If a node manager does not respond, it is removed from the cluster and its active groups are transferred to one or more other active nodes in the cluster.

The **configuration database manager** maintains the cluster configuration database. The database contains information about resources and groups and node ownership of groups. The database managers on each of the cluster nodes cooperate to maintain a consistent picture of configuration information. Fault-tolerant transaction software is used to assure that changes in the overall cluster configuration are performed consistently and correctly.

The **resource manager/failover manager** makes all decisions regarding resource groups and initiates appropriate actions such as startup, reset, and failover. When

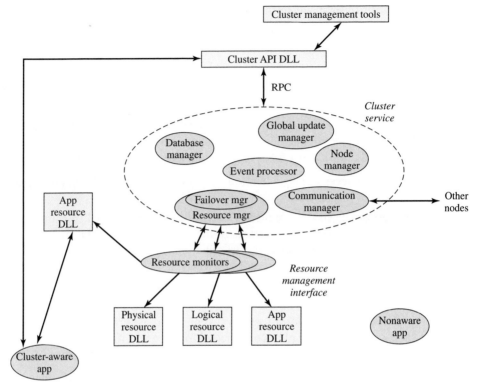

Figure 14.15   Windows Cluster Server Block Diagram [SHOR97]

failover is required, the failover managers on the active node cooperate to negotiate a distribution of resource groups from the failed system to the remaining active systems. When a system restarts after a failure, the failover manager can decide to move some groups back to this system. In particular, any group may be configured with a preferred owner. If that owner fails and then restarts, the group is moved back to the node in a rollback operation.

The **event processor** connects all of the components of the cluster service, handles common operations, and controls cluster service initialization. The communications manager manages message exchange with all other nodes of the cluster. The global update manager provides a service used by other components within the cluster service.

14.6 SUN CLUSTER

Sun Cluster is a distributed operating system built as a set of extensions to the base Solaris UNIX system. It provides cluster with a single-system image; that is, the cluster appears to the user and applications as a single computer running the Solaris operating system.

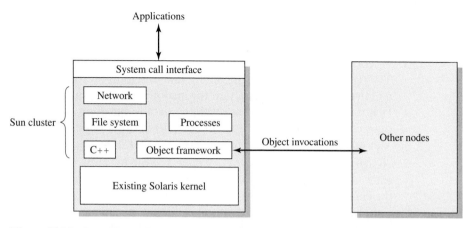

Figure 14.16   Sun Cluster Structure

Figure 14.16 shows the overall architecture of Sun Cluster. The major components are

- Object and communication support
- Process management
- Networking
- Global distributed file system

Object and Communication Support

The Sun Cluster implementation is object oriented. The CORBA object model (see Appendix B) is used to define objects and the remote procedure call (RPC) mechanism implemented in Sun Cluster. The CORBA Interface Definition Language (IDL) is used to specify interfaces between MC components in different nodes. The elements of MC are implemented in the object-oriented language C++. The use of a uniform object model and IDL provides a mechanism for internode and intranode interprocess communication. All of this is built on top of the Solaris kernel with virtually no changes required to the kernel.

Process Management

Global process management extends process operations so that the location of a process is transparent to the user. Sun Cluster maintains a global view of processes so that there is a unique identifier for each process in the cluster and so that each node can learn the location and status of each process. Process migration (described in Chapter 15) is possible: A process can move from one node to another during its lifetime, to achieve load balancing or for failover. However, the threads of a single process must be on the same node.

Networking

The designers of Sun Cluster considered three approaches for handling network traffic:

1. Perform all network protocol processing on a single node. In particular, for a TCP/IP-based application, incoming (and outgoing) traffic would go through a network-connection node that for incoming traffic would analyze TCP and IP headers and route the encapsulated data to the appropriate node; and for outgoing traffic would encapsulate data from other nodes in TCP/IP headers. This approach is not scalable to a large number of nodes and so was rejected.

2. Assign a unique IP address to each node and run the network protocols over the external network directly to each node. One difficulty with this approach is that the cluster configuration is no longer transparent to the outside world. Another complication is the difficulty of failover when a running application moves to another node with a different underlying network address.

3. Use a packet filter to route packets to the proper node and perform protocol processing on that node. Externally, the cluster appears as a single server with a single IP address. Incoming connections (client requests) are load balanced among the available nodes of the cluster. This is the approach adopted in Sun Cluster.

The Sun Cluster networking subsystem has three key elements:

1. Incoming packets are first received on the node that has the network adapter physically attached to it; the receiving node filters the packet and delivers it to the correct target node over the cluster interconnect.

2. All outgoing packets are routed over the cluster interconnect to the node (or one of multiple alternative nodes) that has an external network physical connection. All protocol processing for outgoing packets is done by the originating node.

3. A global network configuration database is maintained to keep track of network traffic to each node.

Global File System

The most important element of Sun Cluster is the global file system, depicted in Figure 14.17, which contrasts MC file management with the basic Solaris scheme. Both are built on the use of vnode and virtual file system concepts.

In Solaris, the virtual node (vnode) structure is used to provide a powerful, general-purpose interface to all types of file systems. A vnode is used to map pages of memory into the address space of a process and to permit access to a file system. While an inode is used to map processes to UNIX files, a vnode can map a process to an object in any file system type. In this way, a system call need not understand the actual object being manipulated, only how to make the proper object-oriented type call using the vnode interface. The vnode interface accepts general-purpose file manipulation commands, such as read and write, and translates them into actions appropriate for the subject file system. Just as vnodes are used to describe individual file system objects, the virtual file system (vfs) structures are used to describe entire file systems. The vfs interface accepts general-purpose commands that operate on entire files and translates them into actions appropriate for the subject file system.

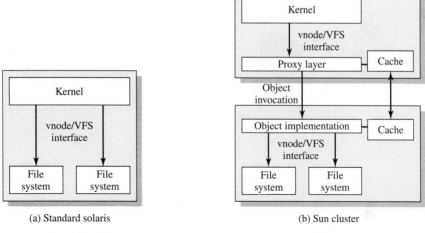

Figure 14.17   Sun Cluster File System Extensions

In Sun Cluster, the global file system provides a uniform interface to files distributed over the cluster. A process can open a file located anywhere in the cluster, and processes on all nodes use the same pathname to locate a file. To implement global file access, MC includes a proxy file system built on top of the existing Solaris file system at the vnode interface. The vfs/vnode operations are converted by a proxy layer into object invocations (see Figure 14.17b). The invoked object may reside on any node in the system. The invoked object performs a local vnode/vfs operation on the underlying file system. Neither the kernel nor the existing file systems have to be modified to support this global file environment.

To reduce the number of remote object invocations, caching is used. Sun Cluster supports caching of file contents, directory information, and file attributes.

14.7 BEOWULF AND LINUX CLUSTERS

In 1994, the Beowulf project was initiated under the sponsorship of the NASA High Performance Computing and Communications (HPCC) project. Its goal was to investigate the potential of clustered PCs for performing important computation tasks beyond the capabilities of contemporary workstations at minimum cost. Today, the Beowulf approach is widely implemented and is perhaps the most important cluster technology available.

Beowulf Features

Key features of Beowulf include the following [RIDG97]:

- Mass market commodity components
- Dedicated processors (rather than scavenging cycles from idle workstations)

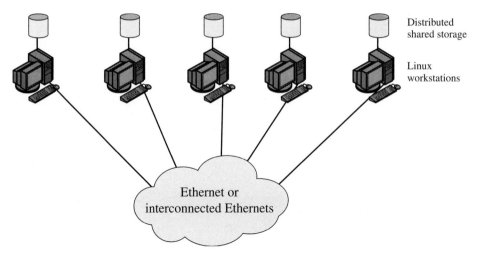

Distributed
shared storage

Linux
workstations

Ethernet or
interconnected Ethernets

Figure 14.18   Generic Beowulf Configuration

- A dedicated, private network (LAN or WAN or internetted combination)
- No custom components
- Easy replication from multiple vendors
- Scalable I/O
- A freely available software base
- Use of freely available distribution computing tools with minimal changes
- Return of the design and improvements to the community

Although elements of Beowulf software have been implemented on a number of different platforms, the most obvious choice for a base is Linux, and most Beowulf implementations use a cluster of Linux workstations and/or PCs. Figure 14.18 depicts a representative configuration. The cluster consists of a number of workstations, perhaps of differing hardware platforms, all running the Linux operating system. Secondary storage at each workstation may be made available for distributed access (for distributed file sharing, distributed virtual memory, or other uses). The cluster nodes (the Linux systems) are interconnected with a commodity networking approach, typically Ethernet. The Ethernet support may be in the form of a single Ethernet switch or an interconnected set of switches. Commodity Ethernet products at the standard data rates (10 Mbps, 100 Mbps, 1 Gbps) are used.

Beowulf Software

The Beowulf software environment is implemented as an add-on to commercially available, royalty-free base Linux distributions. The principal source of open-source Beowulf software is the Beowulf site at **www.beowulf.org**, but numerous other organizations also offer free Beowulf tools and utilities.

Each node in the Beowulf cluster runs its own copy of the Linux kernel and can function as an autonomous Linux system. To support the Beowulf cluster concept, extensions are made to the Linux kernel to allow the individual nodes to participate in a number of global namespaces. Examples of Beowulf system software are as follows:

- **Beowulf distributed process space (BPROC):** This package allows a process ID space to span multiple nodes in a cluster environment and also provides mechanisms for starting processes on other nodes. The goal of this package is to provide key elements needed for a single system image on Beowulf cluster. BPROC provides a mechanism to start processes on remote nodes without ever logging into another node and by making all the remote processes visible in the process table of the cluster's front-end node.

- **Beowulf Ethernet Channel Bonding:** This is a mechanism that joins multiple low-cost networks into a single logical network with higher bandwidth. The only additional work over using single network interface is the computationally simple task of distributing the packets over the available device transmit queues. This approach allows load balancing over multiple Ethernets connected to Linux workstations.

- **Pvmsync:** This is a programming environment that provides synchronization mechanisms and shared data objects for processes in a Beowulf cluster.

- **EnFuzion:** EnFuzion consists of a set of tools for doing parametric computing, as described in Section 14.4. Parametric computing involves the execution of a program as a large number of jobs, each with different parameters or starting conditions. EnFusion emulates a set of robot users on a single root node machine, each of which will log into one of the many clients that form a cluster. Each job is set up to run with a unique, programmed scenario, with an appropriate set of starting conditions [KAPP00].

14.8 SUMMARY

Client/server computing is the key to realizing the potential of information systems and networks to improve productivity significantly in organizations. With client/server computing applications are distributed to users on single-user workstations and personal computers. At the same time resources that can and should be shared are maintained on server systems that are available to all clients. Thus, the client/server architecture is a blend of decentralized and centralized computing.

Typically, the client system provides a graphical user interface (GUI) that enables a user to exploit a variety of applications with minimal training and relative ease. Servers support shared utilities, such as database management systems. The actual application is divided between client and server in a way intended to optimize ease of use and performance.

The key mechanism required in any distributed system is interprocess communication. Two techniques are in common use. A message-passing facility generalizes the use of messages within a single system. The same sorts of conventions and synchronization rules apply. Another approach is the use of the remote procedure call. This is a technique by which two programs on different machines interact using procedure call/return syntax and semantics. Both the called and calling program behave as if the partner program were running on the same machine.

A cluster is a group of interconnected, whole computers working together as a unified computing resource that can create the illusion of being one machine. The term *whole computer* means a system that can run on its own, apart from the cluster.

14.9 RECOMMENDED READINGS AND WEB SITES

[SING99] provides good coverage of the topics in this chapter. [BERS96] provides a good technical discussion of the design issues involved in allocating applications to client and server and in middleware approaches; the book also discusses products and standardization efforts. A good overview of middleware technology and products is [BRIT04]. [REAG00a] and [REAG00b] provide a thorough treatment of client/server computing and network design approaches for supporting client/server computing.

[TANE85] is a survey of distributed operating systems that covers both distributed process communication and distributed process management. [CHAN90] provides an overview of distributed message passing operating systems. [TAY90] is a survey of the approach taken by various operating systems in implementing remote procedure calls.

[PFIS98] is essential reading for anyone interested in clusters; the book covers the hardware and software design issues and contrasts clusters with SMP. A thorough treatment of clusters can be found in [BUYY99a] and [BUYY99b]. The former has a good treatment of Beowulf, which is also nicely covered in [RIDG97]. A more detailed treatment of Beowulf is [STER99]. Windows Cluster Server is described in [SHOR97]; [RAJA00] provides a more detailed treatment. Sun Cluster is described in [SUN99] and [KHAL96].

BERS96 Berson, A. *Client/Server Architecture.* New York: McGraw-Hill, 1996.

BRIT04 Britton, C. *IT Architectures and Middleware.* Reading, MA: Addison-Wesley, 2004.

BUYY99a Buyya, R. *High Performance Cluster Computing: Architectures and Systems.* Upper Saddle River, NJ: Prentice Hall, 1999.

BUYY99b Buyya, R. *High Performance Cluster Computing: Programming and Applications.* Upper Saddle River, NJ: Prentice Hall, 1999.

CHAN90 Chandras, R. "Distributed Message Passing Operating Systems." *Operating Systems Review*, January 1990.

KHAL96 Khalidi, Y., et al. "Solaris MC: A Multicomputer OS." Proceedings, 1996 USENIX Conference, January 1996.

PFIS98 Pfister, G. *In Search of Clusters.* Upper Saddle River, NJ: Prentice Hall, 1998.

RAJA00 Rajagopal, R. *Introduction to Microsoft Windows NT Cluster Server.* Boca Raton, FL: CRC Press, 2000.

REAG00a Reagan, P. *Client/Server Computing.* Upper Saddle River, NJ: Prentice Hall, 2000.

REAG00b Reagan, P. *Client/Server Network: Design, Operation and Management.* Upper Saddle River, NJ: Prentice Hall, 2000.

RIDG97 Ridge, D., et al. "Beowulf: Harnessing the Power of Parallelism in a Pile-of-PCs." *Proceedings, IEEE Aerospace*, 1997.

SHOR97 Short, R.; Gamache, R.; Vert, J.; and Massa, M. "Windows NT Clusters for Availability and Scalability." *Proceedings, COMPCON Spring 97*, February 1997.

SING99 Singh, H. *Progressing to Distributed Multiprocessing.* Upper Saddle River, NJ: Prentice Hall, 1999.

STER99   Sterling, T., et al. *How to Build a Beowulf.* Cambridge, MA: MIT Press, 1999.

SUN99   Sun Microsystems. "Sun Cluster Architecture: A White Paper." *Proceedings, IEEE Computer Society International Workshop on Cluster Computing*, December 1999.

TANE85   Tanenbaum, A., and Renesse, R. "Distributed Operating Systems." *Computing Surveys*, December 1985.

TAY90   Tay, B., and Ananda, A. "A Survey of Remote Procedure Calls." *Operating Systems Review*, July 1990.

Recommended Web Sites:

- **SQL Standards:** A central source of information about the SQL standards process and its current documents
- **IEEE Computer Society Task Force on Cluster Computing:** An international forum to promote cluster computing research and education
- **Beowulf:** An international forum to promote cluster computing research and education

14.10 KEY TERMS, REVIEW QUESTIONS, AND PROBLEMS

Key Terms

applications programming interface (API)	distributed message passing	message
	failback	middleware
Beowulf	failover	remote procedure call (RPC)
client	fat client	server
client/server	file cache consistency	thin client
cluster	graphical user interface (GUI)	

Review Questions

14.1   What is client/server computing?

14.2   What distinguishes client/server computing from any other form of distributed data processing?

14.3   What is the role of a communications architecture such as TCP/IP in a client/server environment?

14.4   Discuss the rationale for locating applications on the client, the server, or split between client and server.

14.5   What are fat clients and thin clients, and what are the differences in philosophy of the two approaches?

14.6   Suggest pros and cons for fat client and thin client strategies.

14.7   Explain the rationale behind the three-tier client/server architecture.

14.8   What is middleware?

14.9   Because we have standards such as TCP/IP, why is middleware needed?

14.10   List some benefits and disadvantages of blocking and nonblocking primitives for message passing.

14.11   List some benefits and disadvantages of nonpersistent and persistent binding for RPCs.

14.12   List some benefits and disadvantages of synchronous and asynchronous RPCs.

14.13   List and briefly define four different clustering methods.

Problems

14.1   Let α be the percentage of program code that can be executed simultaneously by n computers in a cluster, each computer using a different set of parameters or initial conditions. Assume that the remaining code must be executed sequentially by a single processor. Each processor has an execution rate of x MIPS.
   a. Derive an expression for the effective MIPS rate when using the system for exclusive execution of this program, in terms of n, α, and x.
   b. If $n = 16$ and $x = 4$ MIPS, determine the value of α that will yield a system performance of 40 MIPS.

14.2   An application program is executed on a 9-computer cluster. A benchmark program takes time T on this cluster. Further, 25% of T is time in which the application is running simultaneously on all 9 computers. The remaining time, the application has to run on a single computer.
   a. Calculate the effective speedup under the aforementioned condition as compared to executing the program on a single computer. Also calculate α, the percentage of code that has been parallelized (programmed or compiled so as to use the cluster mode) in the preceding program.
   b. Suppose that we are able to effectively use 18 computers rather than 9 computers on the parallelized portion of the code. Calculate the effective speedup that is achieved.

14.3   The following FORTRAN program is to be executed on a computer, and a parallel version is to be executed on a 32-computer cluster.

```
L1:            DO 10 I = 1, 1024
L2:                SUM(I) = 0
L3:                DO 20 J = 1, I
L4:      20            SUM(I) = SUM(I) + I
L5:      10        CONTINUE
```

Suppose lines 2 and 4 each take two machine cycle times, including all processor and memory-access activities. Ignore the overhead caused by the software loop control statements (lines 1, 3, 5) and all other system overhead and resource conflicts.
   a. What is the total execution time (in machine cycle times) of the program on a single computer?
   b. Divide the I-loop iterations among the 32 computers as follows: Computer 1 executes the first 32 iterations (I = 1 to 32), processor 2 executes the next 32 iterations, and so on. What are the execution time and speedup factor compared with part (a)? (Note that the computational workload, dictated by the J-loop, is unbalanced among the computers.)
   c. Explain how to modify the parallelizing to facilitate a balanced parallel execution of all the computational workload over 32 computers. By a balanced load is meant an equal number of additions assigned to each computer with respect to both loops.
   d. What is the minimum execution time resulting from the parallel execution on 32 computers? What is the resulting speedup over a single computer?

DISTRIBUTED PROCESS MANAGEMENT

This chapter examines key mechanisms used in distributed operating systems. First we look at process migration, which is the movement of an active process from one machine to another. Next, we examine the question of how processes on different systems can coordinate their activities when each is governed by a local clock and when there is a delay in the exchange of information. Finally, we explore two key issues in distributed process management: mutual exclusion and deadlock.

15.1 PROCESS MIGRATION

Process migration is the transfer of a sufficient amount of the state of a process from one computer to another for the process to execute on the target machine. Interest in this concept grew out of research into methods of load balancing across multiple networked systems, although the application of the concept now extends beyond that one area.

In the past, only a few of the many papers on load distribution were based on true implementations of process migration, which includes the ability to preempt a process on one machine and reactivate it later on another machine. Experience showed that preemptive process migration is possible, although with higher overhead and complexity than originally anticipated [ARTS89a]. This cost led some observers to conclude that process migration was not practical. Such assessments have proved too pessimistic. New implementations, including those in commercial products, have fueled a continuing interest and new developments in this area. This section provides an overview.

Motivation

Process migration is desirable in distributed systems for a number of reasons [SMIT88, JUL88], including the following:

- **Load sharing:** By moving processes from heavily loaded to lightly loaded systems, the load can be balanced to improve overall performance. Empirical data suggest that significant performance improvements are possible [LELA86, CABR86]. However, care must be taken in the design of load-balancing algorithms. [EAGE86] points out that the more communication necessary for the distributed system to perform the balancing, the worse the performance becomes. A discussion of this issue, with references to other studies, can be found in [ESKI90].

- **Communications performance:** Processes that interact intensively can be moved to the same node to reduce communications cost for the duration of their interaction. Also, when a process is performing data analysis on some file or set of files larger than the process's size, it may be advantageous to move the process to the data rather than vice versa.

- **Availability:** Long-running processes may need to move to survive in the face of faults for which advance notice is possible or in advance of scheduled down-time. If the operating system provides such notification, a process that wants to continue can either migrate to another system or ensure that it can be restarted on the current system at some later time.

- **Utilizing special capabilities:** A process can move to take advantage of unique hardware or software capabilities on a particular node.

Process Migration Mechanisms

A number of issues need to be addressed in designing a process migration facility. Among these are the following:

- Who initiates the migration?
- What portion of the process is migrated?
- What happens to outstanding messages and signals?

Initiation of Migration Who initiates migration will depend on the goal of the migration facility. If the goal is load balancing, then some module in the operating system that is monitoring system load will generally be responsible for deciding when migration should take place. The module will be responsible for preempting or signaling a process to be migrated. To determine where to migrate, the module will need to be in communication with peer modules in other systems so that the load patterns on other systems can be monitored. If the goal is to reach particular resources, then a process may migrate itself as the need arises. In this latter case, the process must be aware of the existence of a distributed system. In the former case, the entire migration function, and indeed the existence of multiple systems, may be transparent to the process.

What Is Migrated? When a process is migrated, it is necessary to destroy the process on the source system and create it on the target system. This is a movement of a process, not a replication. Thus, the process image, consisting of at least the process control block, must be moved. In addition, any links between this process and other processes, such as for passing messages and signals, must be updated. Figure 15.1 illustrates these considerations. Process 3 has migrated out of machine S to become Process 4 in machine D. All link identifiers held by processes (denoted in lowercase letters) remain the same as before. It is the responsibility of the operating system to move the process control block and to update link mappings. The transfer of the process of one machine to another is invisible to both the migrated process and its communication partners.

The movement of the process control block is straightforward. The difficulty, from a performance point of view, concerns the process address space and any open files assigned to the process. Consider first the process address space and let us assume that a virtual memory scheme (paging or paging/segmentation) is being used. The following strategies have been considered [MILO00]:

- **Eager (all):** Transfer the entire address space at the time of migration. This is certainly the cleanest approach. No trace of the process need be left behind at the old system. However, if the address space is very large and if the process is likely not to need most of it, then this may be unnecessarily expensive. Initial costs of migration may be on the order of minutes. Implementations that provide a checkpoint/restart facility are likely to use this approach, because it is simpler to do the checkpointing and restarting if all of the address space is localized.

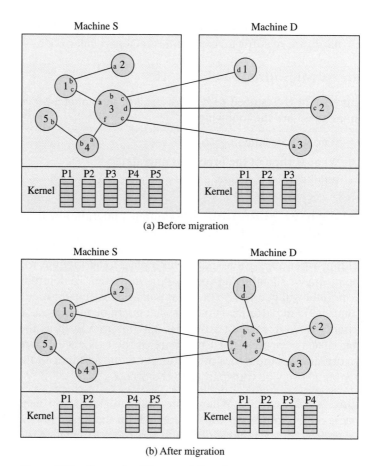

(a) Before migration

(b) After migration

Figure 15.1 Example of Process Migration

- **Precopy:** The process continues to execute on the source node while the address space is copied to the target node. Pages modified on the source during the precopy operation have to be copied a second time. This strategy reduces the time that a process is frozen and cannot execute during migration.
- **Eager (dirty):** Transfer only those pages of the address space that are in main memory and have been modified. Any additional blocks of the virtual address space will be transferred on demand only. This minimizes the amount of data that are transferred. It does require, however, that the source machine continue to be involved in the life of the process by maintaining page and/or segment table entries and it requires remote paging support.
- **Copy-on-reference:** This is a variation of eager (dirty) in which pages are only brought over when referenced. This has the lowest initial cost of process migration, ranging from a few tens to a few hundreds of microseconds.
- **Flushing:** The pages of the process are cleared from the main memory of the source by flushing dirty pages to disk. Then pages are accessed as needed from disk instead of from memory on the source node. This strategy relieves the

source of the need to hold any pages of the migrated process in main memory, immediately freeing a block of memory to be used for other processes.

If it is likely that the process will not use much of its address space while on the target machine (for example, the process is only temporarily going to another machine to work on a file and will soon return), then one of the last three strategies makes sense. On the other hand, if much of the address space will be eventually be accessed while on the target machine, then the piecemeal transfer of blocks of the address space may be less efficient than simply transferring all of the address space at the time of migration, using one of the first two strategies.

In many cases, it may not be possible to know in advance whether or not much of the nonresident address space will be needed. However, if processes are structured as threads, and if the basic unit of migration is the thread rather than the process, then a strategy based on remote paging would seem to be the best. Indeed, such a strategy is almost mandated, because the remaining threads of the process are left behind and also need access to the address space of the process. Thread migration is implemented in the Emerald operating system [JUL89].

Similar considerations apply to the movement of open files. If the file is initially on the same system as the process to be migrated and if the file is locked for exclusive access by that process, then it may make sense to transfer the file with the process. The danger here is that the process may only be gone temporarily and may not need the file until its return. Therefore, it may make sense to transfer the entire file only after an access request is made by the migrated process. If a file is shared by multiple distributed processes, then distributed access to the file should be maintained without moving the file.

If caching is permitted, as in the Sprite system (Figure 14.7), then an additional complexity is introduced. For example, if a process has a file open for writing and it forks and migrates a child, the file would then be open for writing on two different hosts; Sprite's cache consistency algorithm dictates that the file be made noncacheable on the machines on which the two processes are executing [DOUG89, DOUG91].

Messages and Signals The final issue listed previously, the fate of messages and signals, is addressed by providing a mechanism for temporarily storing outstanding messages and signals during the migration activity and then directing them to the new destination. It may be necessary to maintain forwarding information at the initial site for some time to assure that all outstanding messages and signals get through.

A Migration Scenario As a representative example of self-migration, let us consider the facility available on IBM's AIX operating system [WALK89], which is a distributed UNIX operating system. A similar facility is available on the LOCUS operating system [POPE85], and in fact the AIX system is based on the LOCUS development. This facility has also been ported to the OSF/1 AD operating system, under the name TNC [ZAJC93].

The following sequence of events occurs:

1. When a process decides to migrate itself, it selects a target machine and sends a remote tasking message. The message carries a part of the process image and open file information.

2. At the receiving site, a kernel server process forks a child, giving it this information.

3. The new process pulls over data, environment, arguments, or stack information as needed to complete its operation. Program text is copied over if it is dirty or demand paged from the global file system if it is clean.

4. The originating process is signaled on the completion of the migration. This process sends a final done message to the new process and destroys itself.

A similar sequence would be followed when another process initiates the migration. The principal difference is that the process to be migrated must be suspended so that it can be migrated in a nonrunning state. This procedure is followed in Sprite, for example [DOUG89].

In the foregoing scenario, migration is a dynamic activity involving a number of steps for moving the process image over. When migration is initiated by another process, rather than self-migration, another approach is to copy the process image and its entire address space into a file, destroy the process, copy the file to another machine using a file transfer facility, and then re-create the process from the file on the target machine. [SMIT89] describes such an approach.

Negotiation of Migration

Another aspect of process migration relates to the decision about migration. In some cases, the decision is made by a single entity. For example, if load balancing is the goal, a load-balancing module monitors the relative load on various machines and performs migration as necessary to maintain a load balance. If self-migration is used to allow a process access to special facilities or to large remote files, then the process itself may make the decision. However, some systems allow the designated target system to participate in the decision. One reason for this could be to preserve response time for users. A user at a workstation, for example, might suffer noticeable response time degradation if processes migrate to the user's system, even if such migration served to provide better overall balance.

An example of a negotiation mechanism is that found in Charlotte [FINK89, ARTS89b]. Migration policy (when to migrate which process to what destination) is the responsibility of the Starter utility, which is a process that is also responsible for long-term scheduling and memory allocation. The Starter can therefore coordinate policy in these three areas. Each Starter process may control a cluster of machines. The Starter receives timely and fairly elaborate load statistics from the kernel of each of its machines.

The decision to migrate must be reached jointly by two Starter processes (one on the source node and one on the destination node), as illustrated in Figure 15.2. The following steps occur:

1. The Starter that controls the source system (S) decides that a process P should be migrated to a particular destination system (D). It sends a message to D's Starter, requesting the transfer.

2. If D's Starter is prepared to receive the process, it sends back a positive acknowledgment.

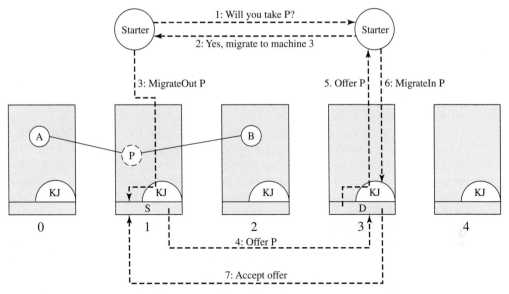

Figure 15.2 Negotiation of Process Migration

3. S's Starter communicates this decision to S's kernel via service call (if the starter runs on S) or a message to the KernJob (KJ) of machine S (if the starter runs on another machine). KJ is a process used to convert messages from remote processes into service calls.

4. The kernel on S then offers to send the process to D. The offer includes statistics about P, such as its age and processor and communication loads.

5. If D is short of resources, it may reject the offer. Otherwise, the kernel on D relays the offer to its controlling Starter. The relay includes the same information as the offer from S.

6. The Starter's policy decision is communicated to D by a MigrateIn call.

7. D reserves necessary resources to avoid deadlock and flow-control problems and then sends an acceptance to S.

Figure 15.2 also shows two other processes, A and B, that have links open to P. Following the foregoing steps, machine 1, where S resides, must send a link update message to both machines 0 and 2 to preserve the links from A and B to P. Link update messages tell the new address of each link held by P and are acknowledged by the notified kernels for synchronization purposes. After this point a message sent to P on any of its links will be sent directly to D. These messages can be exchanged concurrently with the steps just described. Finally, after step 7 and after all links have been updated, S collects all of P's context into a single message and sends it to D.

Machine 4 is also running Charlotte but is not involved in this migration and therefore has no communication with the other systems in this episode.

Eviction

The negotiation mechanism allows a destination system to refuse to accept the migration of a process to itself. In addition, it might also be useful to allow a system to evict a process that has been migrated to it. For example, if a workstation is idle, one or more processes may be migrated to it. Once the user of that workstation becomes active, it may be necessary to evict the migrated processes to provide adequate response time.

An example of an eviction capability is that found in Sprite [DOUG89]. In Sprite, which is a workstation operating system, each process appears to run on a single host throughout its lifetime. This host is known as the home node of the process. If a process is migrated, it becomes a foreign process on the destination machine. At any time the destination machine may evict the foreign process, which is then forced to migrate back to its home node.

The elements of the Sprite eviction mechanism are as follows:

1. A monitor process at each node keeps track of current load to determine when to accept new foreign processes. If the monitor detects activity at the workstation's console, it initiates an eviction procedure on each foreign process.

2. If a process is evicted, it is migrated back to its home node. The process may be migrated again if another node is available.

3. Although it may take some time to evict all processes, all processes marked for eviction are immediately suspended. Permitting an evicted process to execute while it is waiting for eviction would reduce the time during which the process is frozen but also reduce the processing power available to the host while evictions are underway.

4. The entire address space of an evicted process is transferred to the home node. The time to evict a process and migrate it back to its home node may be reduced substantially by retrieving the memory image of a evicted process from its previous foreign host as referenced. However, this compels the foreign host to dedicate resources and honor service requests from the evicted process for a longer period of time than necessary.

Preemptive versus Nonpreemptive Transfers

The discussion in this section has dealt with preemptive process migration, which involves transferring a partially executed process, or at least a process whose creation has been completed. A simpler function is nonpreemptive process transfer, which involves only processes that have not begun execution and hence do not require transferring the state of the process. In both types of transfer, information about the environment in which the process will execute must be transferred to the remote node. This may include the user's current working directory, the privileges inherited by the process, and inherited resources such as file descriptions.

Nonpreemptive process migration can be useful in load balancing (e.g., see [SHIV92]). It has the advantage that it avoids the overhead of full-blown process migration. The disadvantage is that such a scheme does not react well to sudden changes in load distribution.

Global States and Distributed Snapshots

All of the concurrency issues that are faced in a tightly coupled system, such as mutual exclusion, deadlock, and starvation, are also faced in a distributed system. Design strategies in these areas are complicated by the fact that there is no global state to the system. That is, it is not possible for the operating system, or any process, to know the current state of all processes in the distributed system. A process can only know the current state of all the processes on the local system, by access to process control blocks in memory. For remote processes, a process can only know state information that is received via messages, which represent the state of the remote process sometime in the past. This is analogous to the situation in astronomy: Our knowledge of a distant star or galaxy consists of light and other electromagnetic waves arriving from the distant object, and these waves provide a picture of the object sometime in the past. For example, our knowledge of an object at a distance of five light-years is five years old.

The time lags imposed by the nature of distributed systems complicate all issues relating to concurrency. To illustrate this, we present an example taken from [ANDR90]. We will use process/event graphs (Figures 15.3 and 15.4) to illustrate the problem. In these graphs, there is a horizontal line for each process representing the time axis. A point on the line corresponds to an event (e.g., internal process event, message send, message receive). A box surrounding a point represents a snapshot of the local process state taken at that point. An arrow represents a message between two processes.

In our example, an individual has a bank account distributed over two branches of a bank. To determine the total amount in the customer's account, the bank must determine the amount in each branch. Suppose that the determination is to be made at exactly 3:00 P.M. Figure 15.3a shows an instance in which a balance of $100.00 in the combined account is found. But the situation in Figure 15.3b is also possible. Here, the balance from branch A is in transit to branch B at the time of observation; the result is a false reading of $0.00. This particular problem can be solved by examining all messages in transit at the time of observation. Branch A will keep a record of all transfers out of the account, together with the identity of the destination of the transfer. Therefore, we will include in the "state" of a branch A account both the current balance and a record of transfers. When the two accounts are examined, the observer finds a transfer that has left branch A destined for the customer's account in branch B. Because the amount has not yet arrived at branch B, it is added into the total balance. Any amount that has been both transferred and received is counted only once, as part of the balance at the receiving account.

This strategy is not foolproof, as shown in Figure 15.3c. In this example, the clocks at the two branches are not perfectly synchronized. The state of the customer account at branch A at 3:00 P.M. indicates a balance of $100.00. However, this amount is subsequently transferred to branch B at 3:01 according to the clock at A but arrives at B at 2:59 according to B's clock. Therefore, the amount is counted twice for a 3:00 observation.

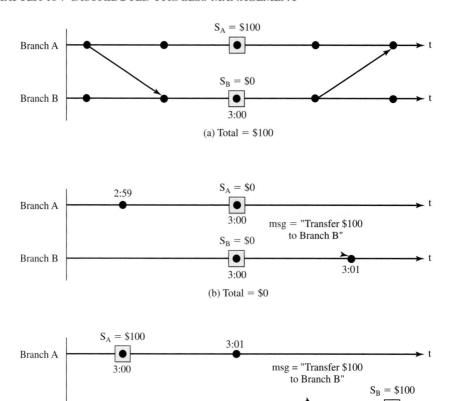

Figure 15.3   Example of Determining Global States

To understand the difficulty we face and to formulate a solution, let us define the following terms:

- **Channel:** A channel exists between two processes if they exchange messages. We can think of the channel as the path or means by which the messages are transferred. For convenience, channels are viewed as unidirectional. Thus, if two processes exchange messages, two channels are required, one for each direction of message transfer.
- **State:** The state of a process is the sequence of messages that have been sent and received along channels incident with the process.
- **Snapshot:** A snapshot records the state of a process. Each snapshot includes a record of all messages sent and received on all channels since the last snapshot.
- **Global state:** The combined state of all processes.
- **Distributed snapshot:** A collection of snapshots, one for each process.

The problem is that a true global state cannot be determined because of the time lapse associated with message transfer. We can attempt to define a global state by

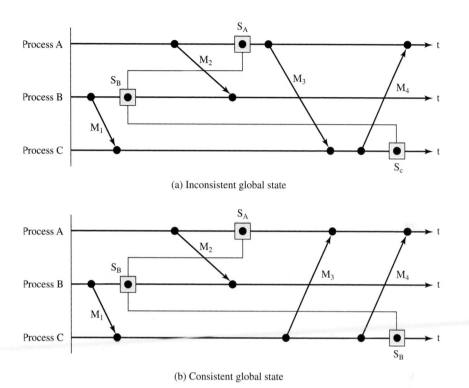

(a) Inconsistent global state

(b) Consistent global state

Figure 15.4 Inconsistent and Consistent Global States

collecting snapshots from all processes. For example, the global state of Figure 15.4a at the time of the taking of snapshots shows a message in transit on the <A,B> channel, one in transit on the <A,C> channel, and one in transit on the <C,A> channel. Messages 2 and 4 are represented appropriately, but message 3 is not. The distributed snapshot indicates that this message has been received but not yet sent.

We desire that the distributed snapshot record a consistent global state. A global state is consistent if for every process state that records the receipt of a message, the sending of that message is recorded in the process state of the process that sent the message. Figure 15.4b gives an example. An inconsistent global state arises if a process has recorded the receipt of a message but the corresponding sending process has not recorded that the message has been sent (Figure 15.4a).

The Distributed Snapshot Algorithm

A distributed snapshot algorithm that records a consistent global state has been described in [CHAN85]. The algorithm assumes that messages are delivered in the order that they are sent and that no messages are lost. A reliable transport protocol (e.g., TCP) satisfies these requirements. The algorithm makes use of a special control message, called a **marker**.

Some process initiates the algorithm by recording its state and sending a marker on all outgoing channels before any more messages are sent. Each process p

then proceeds as follows. Upon the first receipt of the marker (say from process q), receiving process p performs the following:

1. p records its local state S_p.
2. p records the state of the incoming channel from q to p as empty.
3. p propagates the marker to all of its neighbors along all outgoing channels.

These steps must be performed atomically; that is, no messages can be sent or received by p until all 3 steps are performed.

At any time after recording its state, when p receives a marker from another incoming channel (say from process r), it performs the following:

1. p records the state of the channel from r to p as the sequence of messages p has received from r from the time p recorded its local state S_p to the time it received the marker from r.

The algorithm terminates at a process once the marker has been received along every incoming channel.

[ANDR90] makes the following observations about the algorithm:

1. Any process may start the algorithm by sending out a marker. In fact, several nodes could independently decide to record the state and the algorithm would still succeed.
2. The algorithm will terminate in finite time if every message (including marker messages) is delivered in finite time.
3. This is a distributed algorithm: Each process is responsible for recording its own state and the state of all incoming channels.
4. Once all of the states have been recorded (the algorithm has terminated at all processes), the consistent global state obtained by the algorithm can be assembled at every process by having every process send the state data that it has recorded along every outgoing channel and having every process forward the state data that it receives along every outgoing channel. Alternatively, the initiating process could poll all processes to acquire the global state.
5. The algorithm does not affect and is not affected by any other distributed algorithm that the processes are participating in.

As an example of the use of the algorithm (taken from [BEN90]), consider the set of processes illustrated in Figure 15.5. Each process is represented by a node, and

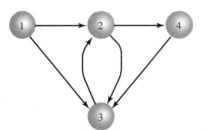

Figure 15.5 Process and Channel Graph

Process 1	Process 3
Outgoing channels	Outgoing channels
2 sent 1, 2, 3, 4, 5, 6	2 sent 1, 2, 3, 4, 5, 6, 7, 8
3 sent 1, 2, 3, 4, 5, 6	Incoming channels
Incoming channels	1 received 1, 2, 3 stored 4, 5, 6
	2 received 1, 2, 3 stored 4
	4 received 1, 2, 3

	Process 2 Process 4
Outgoing channels	Outgoing channels
3 sent 1, 2, 3, 4	3 sent 1, 2, 3
4 sent 1, 2, 3, 4	Incoming channels
Incoming channels	2 received 1, 2 stored 3, 4
1 received 1, 2, 3, 4 stored 5, 6	
3 received 1, 2, 3, 4, 5, 6, 7, 8	

Figure 15.6   An Example of a Snapshot

each unidirectional channel is represented by a line between two nodes, with the direction indicated by an arrowhead. Suppose that the snapshot algorithm is run, with nine messages being sent along each of its outgoing channels by each process. Process 1 decides to record the global state after sending six messages and process 4 independently decides to record the global state after sending three messages. Upon termination, the snapshots are collected from each process; the results are shown in Figure 15.6. Process 2 sent four messages on each of the two outgoing channels to processes 3 and 4 prior to the recording of the state. It received four messages from process 1 before recording its state, leaving messages 5 and 6 to be associated with the channel. The reader should check the snapshot for consistency: Each message sent was either received at the destination process or recorded as being in transit in the channel.

The distributed snapshot algorithm is a powerful and flexible tool. It can be used to adapt any centralized algorithm to a distributed environment, because the basis of any centralized algorithm is knowledge of the global state. Specific examples include detection of deadlock and detection of process termination (e.g., see [BEN90], [LYNC96]). It can also be used to provide a checkpoint of a distributed algorithm to allow rollback and recovery if a failure is detected.

15.3 DISTRIBUTED MUTUAL EXCLUSION

Recall that in Chapters 5 and 6 we addressed issues relating to the execution of concurrent processes. Two key problems that arose were those of mutual exclusion and deadlock. Chapters 5 and 6 focused on solutions to this problem in the context of a single system, with one or more processors but with a common main memory. In dealing with a distributed operating system and a collection of processors that do not share common main memory or clock, new difficulties arise and new solutions are called for. Algorithms for mutual exclusion and deadlock must depend on the exchange of messages and cannot depend on access to common memory. In this section and the next, we examine mutual exclusion and deadlock in the context of a distributed operating system.

Distributed Mutual Exclusion Concepts

When two or more processes compete for the use of system resources, there is a need for a mechanism to enforce mutual exclusion. Suppose that two or more processes require access to a single nonsharable resource, such as a printer. During the course of execution, each process will be sending commands to the I/O device, receiving status information, sending data, and/or receiving data. We will refer to such a resource as a critical resource, and the portion of the program that uses it as a critical section of the program. It is important that only one program at a time be allowed in its critical section. We cannot simply rely on the operating system to understand and enforce this restriction, because the detailed requirement may not be obvious. In the case of the printer, for example, we wish any individual process to have control of the printer while it prints an entire file. Otherwise, lines from competing processes will be interleaved.

The successful use of concurrency among processes requires the ability to define critical sections and enforce mutual exclusion. This is fundamental for any concurrent processing scheme. Any facility or capability that is to provide support for mutual exclusion should meet the following requirements:

1. Mutual exclusion must be enforced: Only one process at a time is allowed into its critical section, among all processes that have critical sections for the same resource or shared object.

2. A process that halts in its noncritical section must do so without interfering with other processes.

3. It must not be possible for a process requiring access to a critical section to be delayed indefinitely: no deadlock or starvation.

4. When no process is in a critical section, any process that requests entry to its critical section must be permitted to enter without delay.

5. No assumptions are made about relative process speeds or number of processors.

6. A process remains inside its critical section for a finite time only.

Figure 15.7 shows a model that we can use for examining approaches to mutual exclusion in a distributed context. We assume some number of systems interconnected by some type of networking facility. Within each system, we assume that some function or process within the operating system is responsible for resource allocation. Each such process controls a number of resources and serves a number of user processes. The task is to devise an algorithm by which these processes may cooperate in enforcing mutual exclusion.

Algorithms for mutual exclusion may be either centralized or distributed. In a fully **centralized algorithm**, one node is designated as the control node and controls access to all shared objects. When any process requires access to a critical resource, it issues a Request to its local resource-controlling process. This process, in turn, sends a Request message to the control node, which returns a Reply (permission) message when the shared object becomes available. When a process has finished

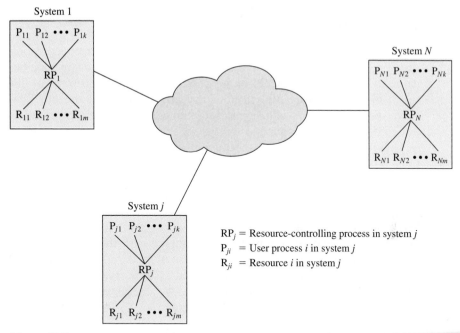

Figure 15.7 Model for Mutual Exclusion Problem in Distributed Process Management

with a resource, a Release message is sent to the control node. Such a centralized algorithm has two key properties:

1. Only the control node makes resource-allocation decisions.
2. All necessary information is concentrated in the control node, including the identity and location of all resources and the allocation status of each resource.

The centralized approach is straightforward, and it is easy to see how mutual exclusion is enforced: The control node will not satisfy a request for a resource until that resource has been released. However, such a scheme suffer several drawbacks. If the control node fails, then the mutual exclusion mechanism breaks down, at least temporarily. Furthermore, every resource allocation and deallocation requires an exchange of messages with the control node. Thus, the control node may become a bottleneck.

Because of the problems with centralized algorithms, there has been more interest in the development of distributed algorithms. A fully **distributed algorithm** is characterized by the following properties [MAEK87]:

1. All nodes have an equal amount of information, on average.
2. Each node has only a partial picture of the total system and must make decisions based on this information.
3. All nodes bear equal responsibility for the final decision.
4. All nodes expend equal effort, on average, in effecting a final decision.
5. Failure of a node, in general, does not result in a total system collapse.

6. There exists no systemwide common clock with which to regulate the timing of events.

Points 2 and 6 may require some elaboration. With respect to point 2, some distributed algorithms require that all information known to any node be communicated to all other nodes. Even in this case, at any given time, some of that information will be in transit and will not have arrived at all of the other nodes. Thus, because of time delays in message communication, a node's information is usually not completely up to date and is in that sense only partial information.

With respect to point 6, because of the delay in communication among systems, it is impossible to maintain a systemwide clock that is instantly available to all systems. Furthermore, it is also technically impractical to maintain one central clock and to keep all local clocks synchronized precisely to that central clock; over a period of time, there will be some drift among the various local clocks that will cause a loss of synchronization.

It is the delay in communication, coupled with the lack of a common clock, that makes it much more difficult to develop mutual exclusion mechanisms in a distributed system compared to a centralized system. Before looking at some algorithms for distributed mutual exclusion, we examine a common approach to overcoming the clock inconsistency problem.

Ordering of Events in a Distributed System

Fundamental to the operation of most distributed algorithms for mutual exclusion and deadlock is the temporal ordering of events. The lack of a common clock or a means of synchronizing local clocks is thus a major constraint. The problem can be expressed in the following manner. We would like to be able to say that an event a at system i occurred before (or after) event b at system j, and we would like to be able to arrive consistently at this conclusion at all systems in the network. Unfortunately, this statement is not precise for two reasons. First, there may be a delay between the actual occurrence of an event and the time that it is observed on some other system. Second, the lack of synchronization leads to a variance in clock readings on different systems.

To overcome these difficulties, a method referred to as timestamping has been proposed by Lamport [LAMP78], which orders events in a distributed system without using physical clocks. This technique is so efficient and effective that it is used in the great majority of algorithms for distributed mutual exclusion and deadlock.

To begin, we need to decide on a definition of the term *event*. Ultimately, we are concerned with actions that occur at a local system, such as a process entering or leaving its critical section. However, in a distributed system, the way in which processes interact is by means of messages. Therefore, it makes sense to associate events with messages. A local event can be bound to a message very simply, for example, a process can send a message when it desires to enter its critical section or when it is leaving its critical section. To avoid ambiguity, we associate events with the sending of messages only, not with the receipt of messages. Thus, each time that a process transmits a message, an event is defined that corresponds to the time that the message leaves the process.

The timestamping scheme is intended to order events consisting of the transmission of messages. Each system i in the network maintains a local counter, C_i, which functions as a clock. Each time a system transmits a message, it first increments its clock by 1. The message is sent in the form

$$(m, T_i, i)$$

where

$$m = \text{contents of the message}$$
$$T_i = \text{timestamp for this message, set to equal } C_i$$
$$i = \text{numerical identifier of this site}$$

When a message is received, the receiving system j sets its clock to one more than the maximum of its current value and the incoming timestamp:

$$C_j \leftarrow 1 + \max[C_j, T_i]$$

At each site, the ordering of events is determined by the following rules. For a message x from site i and a message y from site j, x is said to precede y if one of the following conditions holds:

1. If $T_i < T_j$, or
2. If $T_i = T_j$ and $i < j$.

The time associated with each message is the timestamp accompanying the message, and the ordering of these times is determined by the two foregoing rules. That is, two messages with the same timestamp are ordered by the numbers of their sites. Because the application of these rules is independent of site, this approach avoids any problems of drift among the various clocks of the communicating processes.

An example of the operation of this algorithm is shown in Figure 15.8. There are three sites, each of which is represented by a process that controls the

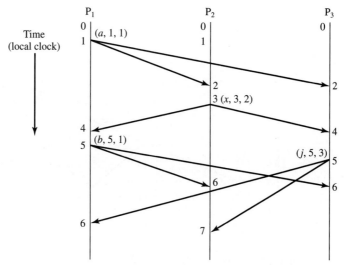

Figure 15.8 Example of Operation of Timestamping Algorithm

timestamping algorithm. Process P_1 begins with a clock value of 0. To transmit message a, it increments its clock by 1 and transmits $(a, 1, 1)$, where the first numerical value is the timestamp and the second is the identity of the site. This message is received by processes at sites 2 and 3. In both cases, the local clock has a value of zero and is set to a value of $2 = 1 + \max[0, 1]$. P_2 issues the next message, first incrementing its clock to 3. Upon receipt of this message, P_1 and P_3 increment their clocks to 4. Then P_1 issues message b and P_3 issues message j at about the same time and with the same timestamp. Because of the ordering principle outlined previously, this causes no confusion. After all of these events have taken place, the ordering of messages is the same at all sites, namely $\{a, x, b, j\}$.

The algorithm works in spite of differences in transmission times between pairs of systems, as illustrated in Figure 15.9. Here, P_1 and P_4 issue messages with the same timestamp. The message from P_1 arrives earlier than that of P_4 at site 2 but later than that of P_4 at site 3. Nevertheless, after all messages have been received at all sites, the ordering of messages is the same at all sites: $\{a, q\}$.

Note that the ordering imposed by this scheme does not necessarily correspond to the actual time sequence. For the algorithms based on this timestamping scheme, it is not important which event actually happened first. It is only important that all processes that implement the algorithm agree on the ordering that is imposed on the events.

In the two examples just discussed, each message is sent from one process to all other processes. If some messages are not sent this way, some sites do not receive all of the messages in the system and it is therefore impossible that all sites have the same ordering of messages. In such a case, a collection of partial orderings exist. However, we are primarily concerned with the use of timestamps in distributed algorithm for mutual exclusion and deadlock detection. In such algorithms, a process usually sends a message (with its timestamp) to every other process, and the timestamps are used to determine how the messages are processed.

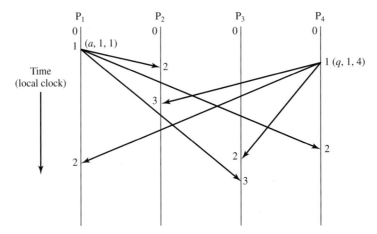

Figure 15.9   Another Example of Operation of Timestamping Algorithm

Distributed Queue

First Version One of the earliest proposed approaches to providing distributed mutual exclusion is based on the concept of a distributed queue [LAMP78]. The algorithm is based on the following assumptions:

1. A distributed system consists of N nodes, uniquely numbered from 1 to N. Each node contains one process that makes requests for mutually exclusive access to resources on behalf of other processes; this process also serves as an arbitrator to resolve incoming requests from other nodes that overlap in time.

2. Messages sent from one process to another are received in the same order in which they are sent.

3. Every message is correctly delivered to its destination in a finite amount of time.

4. The network is fully connected; this means that every process can send messages directly to every other process, without requiring an intermediate process to forward the message.

Assumptions 2 and 3 can be realized by the use of a reliable transport protocol, such as TCP (Chapter 13).

For simplicity, we describe the algorithm for the case in which each site only controls a single resource. The generalization to multiple resources is trivial.

The algorithm attempts to generalize an algorithm that would work in a straightforward manner in a centralized system. If a single central process managed the resource, it could queue incoming requests and grant requests in a first-in-first-out manner. To achieve this same algorithm in a distributed system, all of the sites must have a copy of the same queue. Timestamping can be used to assure that all sites agree on the order in which resource requests are to be granted. One complication arises: Because it takes some finite amount of time for messages to transit a network, there is a danger that two different sites will not agree on which process is at the head of the queue. Consider Figure 15.9. There is a point at which message a has arrived at P_2, and message q has arrived at P_3, but both messages are still in transit to other processes. Thus, there is a period of time in which P_1 and P_2 consider message a to be the head of the queue and in which P_3 and P_4 consider message q to be the head of the queue. This could lead to a violation of the mutual exclusion requirement. To avoid this, the following rule is imposed: For a process to make an allocation decision based on its own queue, it needs to have received a message from each of the other sites such that the process is guaranteed that no message earlier than its own head of queue is still in transit. This rule is explained in part 3b of the algorithm described subsequently.

At each site, a data structure is maintained that keeps a record of the most recent message received from each site (including the most recent message generated at this site). Lamport refers to this structure as a queue; actually it is an array with one entry for each site. At any instant, entry $q[j]$ in the local array contains a message from P_j. The array is initialized as follows:

$$q[j] = (\text{Release}, 0, j) \qquad j = 1, \ldots, N$$

Three types of messages are used in this algorithm:

- (Request, T_i, i): A request for access to a resource is made by P_i.
- (Reply, T_j, j): P_j grants access to a resource under its control.
- (Release, T_k, k): P_k releases a resource previously allocated to it.

The algorithm is as follows:

1. When P_i requires access to a resource, it issues a request (Request, T_i, i), time-stamped with the current local clock value. It puts this message in its own array at $q[i]$ and sends the message to all other processes.

2. When P_j receives (Request, T_i, i), it puts this message in its own array at $q[i]$. If $q[j]$ does not contain a request message, then P_j transmits (Reply, T_j, j) to P_i. It is this action that implements the rule described previously, which assures that no earlier Request message is in transit at the time of a decision.

3. P_i can access a resource (enter its critical section) when both of these conditions hold:

    (a) P_i's own Request message in array q is the earliest Request message in the array; because messages are consistently ordered at all sites, this rule permits one and only one process to access the resource at any instant.

    (b) All other messages in the local array are later than the message in $q[i]$; this rule guarantees that P_i has learned about all requests that preceded its current request.

4. P_i releases a resource by issuing a release (Release, T_i, i), which it puts in its own array and transmits to all other processes.

5. When P_i receives (Release, T_j, j), it replaces the current contents of $q[j]$ with this message.

6. When P_i receives (Reply, T_j, j), it replaces the current contents of $q[j]$ with this message.

It is easily shown that this algorithm enforces mutual exclusion, is fair, avoids deadlock, and avoids starvation:

- **Mutual exclusion:** Requests for entry into the critical section are handled according to the ordering of messages imposed by the timestamping mechanism. Once P_i decides to enter its critical section, there can be no other Request message in the system that was transmitted before its own. This is true because P_i has by then necessarily received a message from all other sites and these messages from other sites date from later than its own Request message. We can be sure of this because of the Reply message mechanism; remember that messages between two sites cannot arrive out of order.

- **Fair:** Requests are granted strictly on the basis of timestamp ordering. Therefore, all processes have equal opportunity.

- **Deadlock free:** Because the timestamp ordering is consistently maintained at all sites, deadlock cannot occur.

- **Starvation free:** Once P_i has completed its critical section, it transmits the Release message. This has the effect of deleting P_i's Request message at all other sites, allowing some other process to enter its critical section.

As a measure of efficiency of this algorithm, note that to guarantee exclusion, $3 \times (N - 1)$ messages are required: $(N - 1)$ Request messages, $(N - 1)$ Reply messages, and $(N - 1)$ Release messages.

Second Version A refinement of the Lamport algorithm was proposed in [RICA81]. It seeks to optimize the original algorithm by eliminating Release messages. The same assumptions as before are in force, except that it is not necessary that messages sent from one process to another are received in the same order in which they are sent.

As before, each site includes one process that controls resource allocation. This process maintains an array q and obeys the following rules:

1. When P_i requires access to a resource, it issues a request (Request, T_i, i), time-stamped with the current local clock value. It puts this message in its own array at $q[i]$ and sends the message to all other processes.
2. When P_j receives (Request, T_i, i), it obeys the following rules:
   (a) If P_j is currently in its critical section, it defers sending a Reply message (see Rule 4, which follows).
   (b) If P_j is not waiting to enter its critical section (has not issued a Request that is still outstanding), it transmits (Reply, T_j, j) to P_i.
   (c) If P_j is waiting to enter its critical section and if the incoming message follows P_j's request, then it puts this message in its own array at $q[i]$ and defers sending a Reply message.
   (d) If P_j is waiting to enter its critical section and if the incoming message precedes P_j's request, then it puts this message in its own array at $q[i]$ and transmits (Reply, T_j, j) to P_i.
3. P_i can access a resource (enter its critical section) when it has received a Reply message from all other processes.
4. When P_i leaves its critical section, it releases the resource by sending a Reply message to each pending Request.

The state transition diagram for each process is shown in Figure 15.10.

To summarize, when a process wishes to enter its critical section, it sends a timestamped Request message to all other processes. When it receives a Reply from all other processes, it may enter its critical section. When a process receives a Request from another process, it must eventually send a matching Reply. If a process does not wish to enter its critical section, it sends a Reply at once. If it wants to enter its critical section, it compares the timestamp of its Request with that of the last Request received, and if the latter is more recent, it defers its Reply; otherwise Reply is sent at once.

With this method, $2 \times (N - 1)$ messages are required: $(N - 1)$ Request messages to indicate P_i's intention of entering its critical section, and $(N - 1)$ Reply messages to allow the access it has requested.

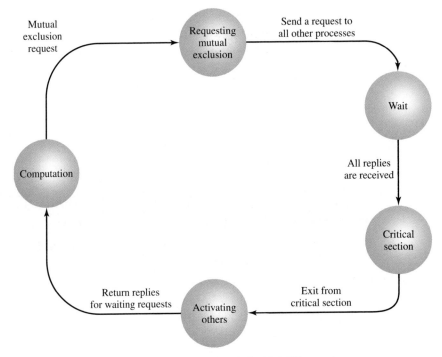

Figure 15.10 State Diagram for Algorithm in [RICA81]

The use of timestamping in this algorithm enforces mutual exclusion. It also avoids deadlock. To prove the latter, assume the opposite: that it is possible that, when there are no more messages in transit, we have a situation in which each process has transmitted a Request and has not received the necessary Reply. This situation cannot arise, because a decision to defer a Reply is based on a relation that orders Requests. There is therefore one Request that has the earliest time-stamp and that will receive all the necessary Replies. Deadlock is therefore impossible.

Starvation is also avoided because Requests are ordered. Because Requests are served in that order, every Request will at some stage become the oldest and will then be served.

A Token-Passing Approach

A number of investigators have proposed a quite different approach to mutual exclusion, which involves passing a token among the participating processes. The token is an entity that at any time is held by one process. The process holding the token may enter its critical section without asking permission. When a process leaves its critical section, it passes the token to another process.

In this subsection, we look at one of the most efficient of these schemes. It was first proposed in [SUZU82]; a logically equivalent proposal also appeared in [RICA83]. For this algorithm, two data structures are needed. The token, which is passed from process to process, is actually an array, token, whose kth element records timestamp of the last time that the token visited process P_k. In addition, each process maintains an array, request, whose jth element records the timestamp of the last Request received from P_j.

The procedure is as follows. Initially, the token is assigned arbitrarily to one of the processes. When a process wishes to use its critical section, it may do so if it currently possesses the token; otherwise it broadcasts a timestamped request message to all other processes and waits until it receives the token. When process P_j leaves its critical section, it must transmit the token to some other process. It chooses the next process to receive the token by searching the request array in the order $j + 1, j + 2, \ldots, 1, 2, \ldots, j - 1$ for the first entry request $[k]$ such that the timestamp for P_k's last request for the token is greater than the value recorded in the token for P_k's last holding of the token; i.e., request $[k]$ > token $[k]$.

Figure 15.11 depicts the algorithm, which is in two parts. The first part deals with the use of the critical section and consists of a prelude, followed by the critical section, followed by a postlude. The second part concerns the action to be taken upon receipt of a request. The variable clock is the local counter used for the timestamp function. The operation wait (access, token) causes the process to wait until a message of the type "access" is received, which is then put into the variable array token.

The algorithm requires either of the following:

- N messages ($N - 1$ to broadcast the request and 1 to transfer the token) when the requesting process does not hold the token
- No messages, if the process already holds the token

15.4 DISTRIBUTED DEADLOCK

In Chapter 6, we defined deadlock as the permanent blocking of a set of processes that either compete for system resources or communicate with one another. This definition is valid for a single system as well as for a distributed system. As with mutual exclusion, deadlock presents more complex problems in a distributed system, compared with a shared memory system. Deadlock handling is complicated in a distributed system because no node has accurate knowledge of the current state of the overall system and because every message transfer between processes involves an unpredictable delay.

Two types of distributed deadlock have received attention in the literature: those that arise in the allocation of resources, and those that arise with the communication of messages. In resource deadlocks, processes attempt to access resources, such as data objects in a database or I/O resources on a server; deadlock occurs if each process in a set of processes requests a resource held by another process in the set. In communications deadlocks, messages are the resources for which processes wait; deadlock occurs if each process in a set is waiting for a message from another process in the set and no process in the set ever sends a message.

```
if  (!token_present)
{
      clock++;                                    /* Prelude */
      broadcast (Request, clock, i);
      wait (access, token);
      token_present = true;
}
token_held = true;
<critical section>;
token[i] = clock;                                 /* Postlude */
token_held = false;
for  (int j = i + 1; j < n; j++)
{
      if  (request(j) > token[j] && token_present)
      {
            token_present = false;
            send (access, token[j]);
      }
}
for  (j = 1; j <= i-1; j++)
{
      if  (request(j) > token[j] && token_present)
      {
            token_present = false;
            send(access, token[j]);
      }
}
```

(a) First Part

```
if  (received (Request, k, j))
{
      request (j) = max(request(j), k);
      if  (token_present && !token_held)
            <text of postlude>;
}
```

(b) Second Part

Notation
send (j, access, token)	end message of type access, with token, by process j
broadcast (request, clock, i)	send message from process i of type request, with time-stamp clock, to all other processes
received (request, t, j)	receive message from process j of type request, with time-stamp t

Figure 15.11   Token-Passing Algorithm (for process P_i)

Deadlock in Resource Allocation

Recall from Chapter 6 that a deadlock in resource allocation exists only if all of the following conditions are met:

- **Mutual exclusion:** Only one process may use a resource at a time. No process may access a resource unit that has been allocated to another process.

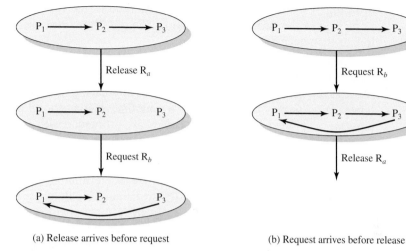

(a) Release arrives before request   (b) Request arrives before release

Figure 15.12   Phantom Deadlock

- **Hold and wait:** A process may hold allocated resources while awaiting assignment of others.
- **No preemption:** No resource can be forcibly removed from a process holding it.
- **Circular wait:** A closed chain of processes exists, such that each process holds at least one resource needed by the next process in the chain.

The aim of an algorithm that deals with deadlock is either to prevent the formation of a circular wait or to detect its actual or potential occurrence. In a distributed system, the resources are distributed over various sites and access to them is regulated by control processes that do not have complete, up-to-date knowledge of the global state of the system and must therefore make their decisions on the basis of local information. Thus, new deadlock algorithms are required.

One example of the difficulty faced in distributed deadlock management is the phenomenon of phantom deadlock. An example of phantom deadlock is illustrated in Figure 15.12. The notation $P_1 \rightarrow P_2 \rightarrow P_3$ means that P_1 is halted waiting for a resource held by P_2, and P_2 is halted waiting for a resource held by P_3. Let us say that at the beginning of the example, P_3 owns resource R_a and P_1 owns resource R_b. Suppose now that P_3 issues first a message releasing R_a and then a message requesting R_b. If the first message reaches a cycle-detecting process before the second, the sequence of Figure 15.12a results, which properly reflects resource requirements. If, however, the second message arrives before the first message, a deadlock is registered (Figure 15.12b). This is a false detection, not a real deadlock, due to the lack of a global state, such as would exist in a centralized system.

Deadlock Prevention   Two of the deadlock prevention techniques discussed in Chapter 6 can be used in a distributed environment.

1. The circular-wait condition can be prevented by defining a linear ordering of resource types. If a process has been allocated resources of type R, then it may subsequently request only those resources of types following R in the

ordering. A major disadvantage of this method is that resources may not be requested in the order in which they are used; thus resources may be held longer than necessary.

2. The hold-and-wait condition can be prevented by requiring that a process request all of its required resources at one time and blocking the process until all requests can be granted simultaneously. This approach is inefficient in two ways. First, a process may be held up for a long time waiting for all of its resource requests to be filled, when in fact it could have proceeded with only some of the resources. Second, resources allocated to a process may remain unused for a considerable period, during which time they are denied to other processes.

Both of these methods require that a process determine its resource requirements in advance. This is not always the case; an example is a database application in which new items can be added dynamically. As an example of an approach that does not require this foreknowledge, we consider two algorithms proposed in [ROSE78]. These were developed in the context of database work, so we shall speak of transactions rather than processes.

The proposed methods make use of timestamps. Each transaction carries throughout its lifetime the timestamp of its creation. This establishes a strict ordering of the transactions. If a resource R already being used by transaction T1 is requested by another transaction T2, the conflict is resolved by comparing their timestamps. This comparison is used to prevent the formation of a circular wait condition. Two variations of this basic method are proposed by the authors, referred to as the "wait-die" method and the "wound-wait" method.

Let us suppose that T1 currently holds R and that T2 issues a request. For the **wait-die method**, Figure 15.13a shows the algorithm used by the resource allocator at the site of R. The timestamps of the two transactions are denoted as $e(T1)$ and $e(T2)$. If T2 is older, it is blocked until T1 releases R, either by actively issuing a release or by being "killed" when requesting another resource. If T2 is younger, then T2 is restarted but with the same timestamp as before.

Thus, in a conflict, the older transaction takes priority. Because a killed transaction is revived with its original timestamp it grows older and therefore gains increased priority. No site needs to know the state of allocation of all resources. All that are required are the timestamps of the transactions that request its resources.

The **wound-wait method** immediately grants the request of an older transaction by killing a younger transaction that is using the required resource. This is shown in Figure 15.13b. In contrast to the wait-die method, a transaction never has to wait for a resource being used by a younger transaction.

if $(e(T2) < e(T1))$
     halt_T2 ('wait');
else
     kill_T2 ('die');
	if $(e(T2) < e(T1))$
	     kill_T1 ('wound');
	else
	     halt_T2 ('wait');

(a) Wait-die method	(b) Wound-wait method

Figure 15.13   Deadlock Prevention Methods

Deadlock Avoidance Deadlock avoidance is a technique in which a decision is made dynamically whether a given resource allocation request could, if granted, lead to a deadlock. [SING94b] points out that distributed deadlock avoidance is impractical for the following reasons:

1. Every node must keep track of the global state of the system; this requires substantial storage and communications overhead.

2. The process of checking for a safe global state must be mutually exclusive. Otherwise, two nodes could each be considering the resource request of a different process and concurrently reach the conclusion that it is safe to honor the request, when in fact if both requests are honored, deadlock will result.

3. Checking for safe states involves considerable processing overhead for a distributed system with a large number of processes and resources.

Deadlock Detection With deadlock detection, processes are allowed to obtain free resources as they wish, and the existence of a deadlock is determined after the fact. If a deadlock is detected, one of the *constituent* processes is selected and required to release the resources necessary to break the deadlock.

The difficulty with distributed deadlock detection is that each site only knows about its own resources, whereas a deadlock may involve distributed resources. Several approaches are possible, depending on whether the system control is centralized, hierarchical, or distributed (Table 15.1).

With **centralized control**, one site is responsible for deadlock detection. All request and release messages are sent to the central process as well as to the process

Table 15.1 Distributed Deadlock Detection Strategies

Centralized Algorithms		Hierarchical Algorithms		Distributed Algorithms	
Strengths	Weaknesses	Strengths	Weaknesses	Strengths	Weaknesses
• Algorithms are conceptually simple and easy to implement • Central site has complete information and can optimally resolve deadlocks	• Considerable communications overhead; every node must send state information to central node • Vulnerable to failure of central node	• Not vulnerable to single point of failure • Deadlock resolution activity is limited if most potential deadlocks are relatively localized	• May be difficult to configure system so that most potential deadlocks are localized; otherwise there may actually be more overhead than in a distributed approach	• Not vulnerable to single point of failure • No node is swamped with deadlock detection activity	• Deadlock resolution is cumbersome because several sites may detect the same deadlock and may not be aware of other nodes involved in the deadlock • Algorithms are difficult to design because of timing considerations

that controls the particular resource. Because the central process has a complete picture, it is in a position to detect a deadlock. This approach requires a lot of messages and is vulnerable to a failure of the central site. In addition, phantom deadlocks may be detected.

With **hierarchical control**, the sites are organized in a tree structure, with one site serving as the root of the tree. At each node, other than leaf nodes, information about the resource allocation of all dependent nodes is collected. This permits deadlock detection to be done at lower levels than the root node. Specifically, a deadlock that involves a set of resources will be detected by the node that is the common ancestor of all sites whose resources are among the objects in conflict.

With **distributed control**, all processes cooperate in the deadlock detection function. In general, this means that considerable information must be exchanged, with timestamps; thus the overhead is significant. [RAYN88] cites a number of approaches based on distributed control, and [DATT90] provides a detailed examination of one approach.

We now give an example of a distributed deadlock detection algorithm ([DATT92], [JOHN91]). The algorithm deals with a distributed database system in which each site maintains a portion of the database and transactions may be initiated from each site. A transaction can have at most one outstanding resource request. If a transaction needs more than one data object, the second data object can be requested only after the first data object has been granted.

Associated with each data object i at a site are two parameters: a unique identifier D_i, and the variable Locked_by (D_i). This latter variable has the value nil if the data object is not locked by any transaction; otherwise its value is the identifier of the locking transaction.

Associated with each transaction j at a site are four parameters:

- A unique identifier T_j.
- The variable Held_by (T_j), which is set to nil if transaction T_j is executing or in a Ready state. Otherwise, its value is the transaction that is holding the data object required by transaction T_j.
- The variable Wait_for (T_j), which has the value nil if transaction T_i is not waiting for any other transaction. Otherwise, its value is the identifier of the transaction that is at the head of an ordered list of transactions that are blocked.
- A queue Request_ Q(T_j), which contains all outstanding requests for data objects being held by T_j. Each element in the queue is of the form (T_k, D_k), where T_k is the requesting transaction and D_k is the data object held by T_j.

For example, suppose that transaction T_2 is waiting for a data object held by T_1, which is, in turn, waiting for a data object held by T_0. Then the relevant parameters have the following values:

Transaction	Wait_for	Held_by	Request_Q
T_0	nil	nil	T_1
T_1	T_0	T_0	T_2
T_2	T_0	T_1	nil

This example highlights the difference between Wait_for (T_i) and Held_by (T_i). Neither process can proceed until T_0 releases the data object needed by T_1, which can then execute and release the data object needed by T_2.

Figure 15.14 shows the algorithm used for deadlock detection. When a transaction makes a lock request for a data object, a server process associated with that data object either grants or denies the request. If the request is not granted, the server process returns the identity of the transaction holding the data object.

When the requesting transaction receives a granted response, it locks the data object. Otherwise, the requesting transaction updates its Held_by variable to the identity of the transaction holding the data object. It adds its identity to the Request_Q of the holding transaction. It updates is Wait_for variable either to the identity of the holding transaction (if that transaction is not waiting) or to the identity of the Wait_for variable of the holding transaction. In this way, the Wait_for variable is set to the value of the transaction that ultimately is blocking execution. Finally, the requesting transaction issues an update message to all of the transactions in its own Request_Q to modify all the Wait_for variables that are affected by this change.

When a transaction receives an update message, it updates its Wait_for variable to reflect the fact that the transaction on which it had been ultimately waiting is now blocked by yet another transaction. Then it does the actual work of deadlock detection by checking to see if it is now waiting for one of the processes that is waiting for it. If not, it forwards the update message. If so, the transaction sends a clear message to the transaction holding its requested data object and allocates every data object that it holds to the first requester in its Request_Q and enqueues remaining requesters to the new transaction.

An example of the operation of the algorithm is shown in Figure 15.15. When T_0 makes a request for a data object held by T_3, a cycle is created. T_0 issues an update message that propagates from T_1 to T_2 to T_3. At this point, T_3 discovers that the intersection of its Wait_for and Request_Q variables is not empty. T_3 sends a clear message to T_2 so that T_3 is purged from Request_ $Q(T_2)$, and it releases the data objects it held, activating T_4 and T_6.

Deadlock in Message Communication

Mutual Waiting Deadlock occurs in message communication when each of a group of processes is waiting for a message from another member of the group and there are no messages in transit.

To analyze this situation in more detail, we define the dependence set (DS) of a process. For a process P_i that is halted, waiting for a message, $DS(P_i)$ consists of all processes from which P_i is expecting a message. Typically, P_i can proceed if any of the expected messages arrives. An alternative formulation is that P_i can proceed only after all of the expected messages arrive. The former situation is the more common one and is considered here.

With the preceding definition, a deadlock in a set S of processes can be defined as follows:

1. All the processes in S are halted, waiting for messages.
2. S contains the dependence set of all processes in S.
3. No messages are in transit between members of S.

```
/* Data object Dj receiving a lock_request(Ti) */
if (Locked_by(Dj) == null)
    send(granted);
else
{
    send not granted to Ti;
    send Locked_by(Dj) to Ti
}

/* Transaction Ti makes a lock request for data object Dj */
send lock_request(Ti) to Dj;
wait for granted/not granted;
if (granted)
{
    Locked_by(Dj) = Ti;
    Held_by(Ti) = _;
}
else /* suppose Dj is being used by transaction Tj */
{
    Held_by(Ti) = Tj;
    Enqueue(Ti, Request_Q(Tj));
    if (Wait_for(Tj) == null)
        Wait_for(Ti) = Tj;
    Else
        Wait_for(Ti) = Wait_for(Tj);
    update(Wait_for(Ti), Request_Q(Ti));
}

/* Transaction Tj receiving an update message */
if (Wait_for(Ti) != Wait_for(Tj))
    Wait_for(Tj) = Wait_for(Ti);
if (intersect(Wait_for(Tj), Request_Q(Tj)) = null)
    update(Wait_for(Ti), Request_Q(Tj));
else
{
    DECLARE DEADLOCK;
    /* initiate deadlock resolution as follows */
    /* Tj is chosen as the transaction to be aborted */
    /* Tj releases all the data objects it holds */
    send_clear(Tj, Held_by(Tj));
    allocate each data object Di held by Tj to the
first    requester Tk in Request_Q(Tj);
    for (every transaction Tn in Request_Q(Tj)
requesting    data object Di held by Tj)
    {
        Enqueue(Tn, Request_Q(Tk));
    }
}

/* Transaction Tk receiving a clear(Tj, Tk) message */
purge the tuple having Tj as the requesting transaction
from Request_Q(Tk);
```

Figure 15.14   A Distributed Deadlock Detection Algorithm

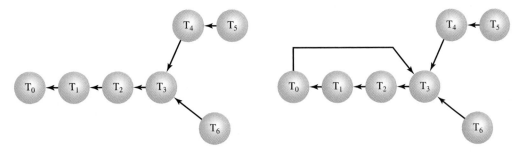

Transaction	Wait_for	Held_by	Request_Q
T_0	nil	nil	T_1
T_1	T_0	T_0	T_2
T_2	T_0	T_1	T_3
T_3	T_0	T_2	T_4, T_6
T_4	T_0	T_3	T_5
T_5	T_0	T_4	nil
T_6	T_0	T_3	nil

Transaction	Wait_for	Held_by	Request_Q
T_0	T_0	T_3	T_1
T_1	T_0	T_0	T_2
T_2	T_0	T_1	T_3
T_3	T_0	T_2	T_4, T_6, T_0
T_4	T_0	T_3	T_5
T_5	T_0	T_4	nil
T_6	T_0	T_3	nil

(a) (b)

Figure 15.15 Example of Distributed Deadlock Detection Algorithm of Figure 15.14

Any process in S is deadlocked because it can never receive a message that will release it.

In graphical terms, there is a difference between message deadlock and resource deadlock. With resource deadlock, a deadlock exists if there is a closed loop, or cycle, in the graph that depicts process dependencies. In the resource case, one process is dependent on another if the latter holds a resource that the former requires. With message deadlock, the condition for deadlock is that all successors of any member of S are themselves in S.

Figure 15.16 illustrates the point. In Figure 15.16a, P_1 is waiting for a message from either P_2 or P_5; P_5 is not waiting for any message and so can send a message to P_1, which is therefore released. As a result, the links (P_1, P_5) and (P_1, P_2) are deleted. Figure 15.16b adds a dependency: P_5 is waiting for a message from P_2, which is waiting

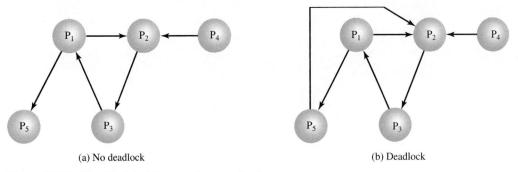

(a) No deadlock (b) Deadlock

Figure 15.16 Deadlock in Message Communication

for a message from P_3, which is waiting for a message from P_1, which is waiting for a message from P_2. Thus, deadlock exists.

As with resource deadlock, message deadlock can be attacked by either prevention or detection. [RAYN88] gives some examples.

Unavailability of Message Buffers Another way in which deadlock can occur in a message-passing system has to do with the allocation of buffers for the storage of messages in transit. This kind of deadlock is well known in packet-switching data networks. We first examine this problem in the context of a data network and then view it from the point of view of a distributed operating system.

The simplest form of deadlock in a data network is direct store-and-forward deadlock and can occur if a packet-switching node uses a common buffer pool from which buffers are assigned to packets on demand. Figure 15.17a shows a situation in which all of the buffer space in node A is occupied with packets destined for B. The reverse is true at B. Neither node can accept any more packets because their buffers are full. Thus neither node can transmit or receive on any link.

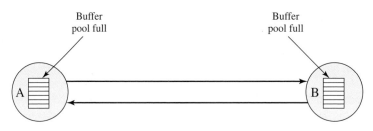

Buffer pool full   Buffer pool full

(a) Direct store-and-forward deadlock

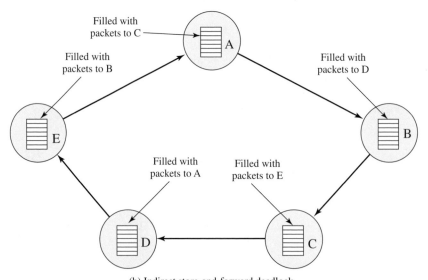

Filled with packets to C

Filled with packets to B

Filled with packets to D

Filled with packets to A

Filled with packets to E

(b) Indirect store-and-forward deadlock

Figure 15.17 Store-and-Forward Deadlock

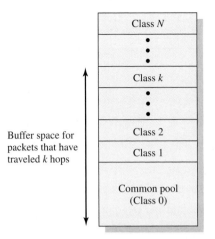

Figure 15.18 Structured Buffer Pool for Deadlock Prevention

Class N

•
•
•

Class k

•
•
•

Class 2

Class 1

Common pool (Class 0)

Buffer space for packets that have traveled k hops

Direct store-and-forward deadlock can be prevented by not allowing all buffers to end up dedicated to a single link. Using separate fixed-size buffers, one for each link, will achieve this prevention. Even if a common buffer pool is used, deadlock is avoided if no single link is allowed to acquire all of the buffer space.

A more subtle form of deadlock, indirect store-and-forward deadlock, is illustrated in Figure 15.17b. For each node, the queue to the adjacent node in one direction is full with packets destined for the next node beyond. One simple way to prevent this type of deadlock is to employ a structured buffer pool (Figure 15.18). The buffers are organized in a hierarchical fashion. The pool of memory at level 0 is unrestricted; any incoming packet can be stored there. From level 1 to level N (where N is the maximum number of hops on any network path), buffers are reserved in the following way: Buffers at level k are reserved for packets that have traveled at least k hops so far. Thus, in heavy load conditions, buffers fill up progressively from level 0 to level N. If all buffers up through level k are filled, arriving packets that have covered k or less hops are discarded. It can be shown [GOPA85] that this strategy eliminates both direct and indirect store-and-forward deadlocks.

The deadlock problem just described would be dealt with in the context of a communications architecture, typically at the network layer. The same sort of problem can arise in a distributed operating system that uses message passing for interprocess communication. Specifically, if the send operation is nonblocking, then a buffer is required to hold outgoing messages. We can think of the buffer used to hold messages to be sent from process X to process Y to be a communications channel between X and Y. If this channel has finite capacity (finite buffer size), then it is possible for the send operation to result in process suspension. That is, if the buffer is of size n and there are currently n messages in transit (not yet received by the destination process), then the execution of an additional send will block the sending process until a receive has opened up space in the buffer.

Figure 15.19 illustrates how the use of finite channels can lead to deadlock. The figure shows two channels, each with a capacity of four messages, one from process X to process Y and one from Y to X. If exactly four messages are in transit

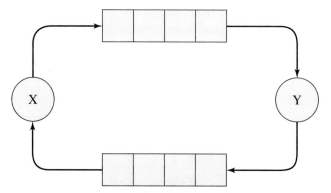

Figure 15.19 Communication Deadlock in a Distributed System

in each of the channels and both X and Y attempt a further transmission before executing a receive, then both are suspended and a deadlock arises.

If it is possible to establish upper bounds on the number of messages that will ever be in transit between each pair of processes in the system, then the obvious prevention strategy would be to allocate as many buffer slots as needed for all these channels. This might be extremely wasteful and of course requires this foreknowledge. If requirements cannot be known ahead of time, or if allocating based on upper bounds is deemed too wasteful, then some estimation technique is needed to optimize the allocation. It can be shown that this problem is unsolvable in the general case; some heuristic strategies for coping with this situation are suggested in [BARB90].

15.5 SUMMARY

A distributed operating system may support process migration. This is the transfer of a sufficient amount of the state of a process from one machine to another for the process to execute on the target machine. Process migration may be used for load balancing, to improve performance by minimizing communication activity, to increase availability, or to allow processes access to specialized remote facilities.

With a distributed system, it is often important to establish global state information, to resolve contention for resources, and to coordinate processes. Because of the variable and unpredictable time delay in message transmission, care must be taken to assure that different processes agree on the order in which events have occurred.

Process management in a distributed system includes facilities for enforcing mutual exclusion and for taking action to deal with deadlock. In both cases, the problems are more complex than those in a single system.

15.6 RECOMMENDED READINGS

[GALL00] and [TEL01] cover all of the topics in this chapter.

A broad and detailed survey of process migration mechanisms and implementations is [MILO00]. [ESKI90] and [SMIT88] are other useful surveys. [NUTT94] describes a number of

OS implementations of process migration. [FIDG96] surveys a number of approaches to ordering events in distributed systems and concludes that the general approach outlined in this chapter is preferred.

Algorithms for distributed process management (mutual exclusion, deadlock) can be found in [SINH97] and [RAYN88]. More formal treatment are contained in [RAYN90], [GARG02], and [LYNC96].

ESKI90 Eskicioglu, M. "Design Issues of Process Migration Facilities in Distributed Systems." *Newsletter of the IEEE Computer Society Technical Committee on Operating Systems and Application Environments*, Summer 1990.

FIDG96 Fidge, C. "Fundamentals of Distributed System Observation." *IEEE Software*, November 1996.

GALL00 Galli, D. *Distributed Operating Systems: Concepts and Practice.* Upper Saddle River, NJ: Prentice Hall, 2000.

GARG02 Garg, V. *Elements of Distributed Computing.* New York: Wiley, 2002.

LYNC96 Lynch, N. *Distributed Algorithms.* San Francisco, CA: Morgan Kaufmann, 1996.

MILO00 Milojicic, D.; Douglis, F.; Paindaveine, Y.; Wheeler, R.; and Zhou, S. "Process Migration." *ACM Computing Surveys*, September 2000.

NUTT94 Nuttal, M. "A Brief Survey of Systems Providing Process or Object Migration Facilities." *Operating Systems Review*, October 1994.

RAYN88 Raynal, M. *Distributed Algorithms and Protocols.* New York: Wiley, 1988.

RAYN90 Raynal, M., and Helary, J. *Synchronization and Control of Distributed Systems and Programs.* New York: Wiley, 1990.

SING94 Singhal, M., and Shivaratri, N. *Advanced Concepts in Operating Systems.* New York: McGraw-Hill, 1994.

SINH97 Sinha, P. *Distributed Operating Systems.* Piscataway, NJ: IEEE Press, 1997.

SMIT88 Smith, J. "A Survey of Process Migration Mechanisms." *Operating Systems Review*, July 1988.

TEL01 Tel, G. *Introduction to Distributed Algorithms.* Cambridge: Cambridge University Press, 2001.

15.7 KEY TERMS, REVIEW QUESTIONS, AND PROBLEMS

Key Terms

channel	eviction	preemptive transfer
distributed deadlock	global state	process migration
distributed mutual exclusion	nonpreemptive transfer	snapshot

Review Questions

15.1 Discuss some of the reasons for implementing process migration.

15.2 How is the process address space handled during process migration?

15.3 What are the motivations for preemptive and nonpreemptive process migration?

15.4   Why is it impossible to determine a true global state?

15.5   What is the difference between distributed mutual exclusion enforced by a centralized algorithm and enforced by a distributed algorithm?

15.6   Define the two types of distributed deadlock.

Problems

15.1   The flushing policy is described in the subsection on process migration strategies in Section 15.1.
    a. From the perspective of the source, which other strategy does flushing resemble?
    b. From the perspective of the target, which other strategy does flushing resemble?

15.2   For Figure 15.9, it is claimed that all four processes assign an ordering of $\{a, q\}$ to the two messages, even though q arrives before a at P_3. Work through the algorithm to demonstrate the truth of the claim.

15.3   For Lamport's algorithm, are there any circumstances under which P_i can save itself the transmission of a Reply message?

15.4   For the mutual exclusion algorithm of [RICA81],
    a. Prove that mutual exclusion is enforced.
    b. If messages do not arrive in the order that they are sent, the algorithm does not guarantee that critical sections are executed in the order of their requests. Is starvation possible?

15.5   In the token-passing mutual exclusion algorithm, is the timestamping used to reset clocks and correct drifts, as in the distributed queue algorithms? If not, what is the function of the timestamping?

15.6   For the token-passing mutual exclusion algorithm, prove that it
    a. guarantees mutual exclusion
    b. avoids deadlock
    c. is fair

15.7   In Figure 15.11b, explain why the second line cannot simply read "request $(j) = t$"

CHAPTER 16

SECURITY

The area of computer security is a broad one and encompasses physical and administrative controls as well as automated controls. In this chapter, we confine ourselves to consideration of automated security tools. Figure 16.1 suggests the scope of responsibility of these tools. We begin by examining the types of threats faced by computer-communications facilities. Then the bulk of the chapter deals with specific tools that can be used to enhance security. Section 16.2 deals with traditional approaches to computer security, which are based on the protection of various computer resources, including memory and data. Then we look at the threat posed by individuals attempting to overcome these protection mechanisms. The next section examines the threat posed by viruses and similar mechanisms. Next, we examine the concept of trusted systems. Finally, an appendix to this chapter introduces encryption, which is a basic tool used in many security applications.

16.1 SECURITY THREATS

To understand the types of threats to security that exist, we need to have a definition of security requirements. Computer and network security address four requirements:

- **Confidentiality:** Requires that the information in a computer system only be accessible for reading by authorized parties. This type of access includes printing, displaying, and other forms of disclosure, including simply revealing the existence of an object.
- **Integrity:** Requires that computer system assets can be modified only by authorized parties. Modification includes writing, changing, changing status, deleting, and creating.
- **Availability:** Requires that computer system assets are available to authorized parties.
- **Authenticity:** Requires that a computer system be able to verify the identity of a user.

Types of Threats

The types of attacks on the security of a computer system or network are best characterized by viewing the function of the computer system as providing information. In general, there is a flow of information from a source, such as a file or a region of main memory, to a destination, such as another file or a user. This normal flow is depicted in Figure 16.2a. The remaining parts of the figure show the following four general categories of attack:

- **Interruption:** An asset of the system is destroyed or becomes unavailable or unusable. This is an attack on **availability**. Examples include destruction of a piece of hardware, such as a hard disk, the cutting of a communication line, or the disabling of the file management system.
- **Interception:** An unauthorized party gains access to an asset. This is an attack on **confidentiality**. The unauthorized party could be a person, a program, or a

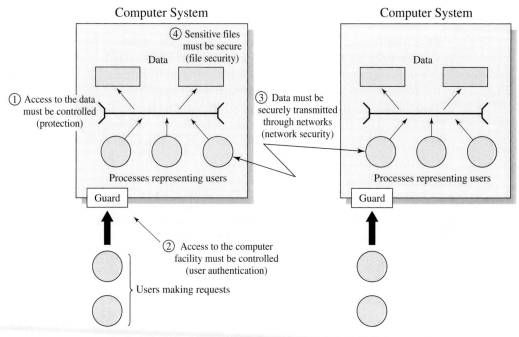

Figure 16.1   Scope of System Security [MAEK87]

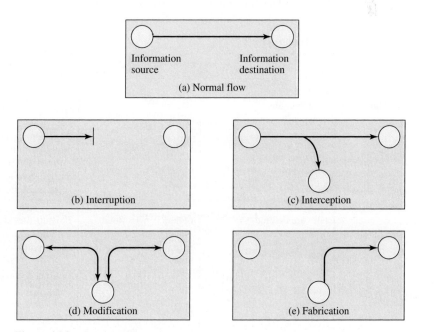

Figure 16.2   Security Threats

computer. Examples include wiretapping to capture data in a network and the illicit copying of files or programs.

- **Modification:** An unauthorized party not only gains access to but also tampers with an asset. This is an attack on **integrity**. Examples include changing values in a data file, altering a program so that it performs differently, and modifying the content of messages being transmitted in a network.

- **Fabrication:** An unauthorized party inserts counterfeit objects into the system. This is an attack on **authenticity**. Examples include the insertion of spurious messages in a network or the addition of records to a file.

Computer System Assets

The assets of a computer system can be categorized as hardware, software, data, and communication lines and networks. Table 16.1 indicates the nature of the threats faced by each category of asset. Let us consider each of these in turn.

Hardware   The main threat to computer system hardware is in the area of availability. Hardware is the most vulnerable to attack and the least amenable to automated controls. Threats include accidental and deliberate damage to equipment as well as theft. The proliferation of personal computers and workstations and the increasing use of local area networks increase the potential for losses in this area. Physical and administrative security measures are needed to deal with these threats.

Software   The operating system, utilities, and application programs are what make computer system hardware useful to businesses and individuals. Several distinct threats need to be considered.

Table 16.1   Security Threats and Assets

	Availability	**Secrecy**	**Integrity/Authenticity**
Hardware	Equipment is stolen or disabled, thus denying service.		
Software	Programs are deleted, denying access to users.	An unauthorized copy of software is made.	A working program is modified, either to cause it to fail during execution or to cause it to do some unintended task.
Data	Files are deleted, denying access to users.	An unauthorized read of data is performed. An analysis of statistical data reveals underlying data.	Existing files are modified or new files are fabricated.
Communication Lines	Messages are destroyed or deleted. Communication lines or networks are rendered unavailable.	Messages are read. The traffic pattern of messages is observed.	Messages are modified, delayed, reordered, or duplicated. False messages are fabricated.

A key threat to software is an attack on availability. Software, especially application software, is often easy to delete. Software can also be altered or damaged to render it useless. Careful software configuration management, which includes making backups of the most recent version of software, can maintain high availability. A more difficult problem to deal with is software modification that results in a program that still functions but that behaves differently than before, which is a threat to integrity/authenticity. Computer viruses and related attacks fall into this category and are treated later in this chapter. A final problem is software secrecy. Although certain countermeasures are available, by and large the problem of unauthorized copying of software has not been solved.

Data Hardware and software security are typically concerns of computing center professionals, or individual concerns of personal computer users. A much more widespread problem is data security, which involves files and other forms of data controlled by individuals, groups, and business organizations.

Security concerns with respect to data are broad, encompassing availability, secrecy, and integrity. In the case of availability, the concern is with the destruction of data files, which can occur either accidentally or maliciously.

The obvious concern with secrecy, of course, is the unauthorized reading of data files or databases, and this area has been the subject of perhaps more research and effort than any other area of computer security. A less obvious secrecy threat involves the analysis of data and manifests itself in the use of so-called statistical databases, which provide summary or aggregate information. Presumably, the existence of aggregate information does not threaten the privacy of the individuals involved. However, as the use of statistical databases grows, there is an increasing potential for disclosure of personal information. In essence, characteristics of constituent individuals may be identified through careful analysis. To take a simple-minded example, if one table records the aggregate of the incomes of respondents A, B, C, and D and another records the aggregate of the incomes of A, B, C, D, and E, the difference between the two aggregates would be the income of E. This problem is exacerbated by the increasing desire to combine data sets. In many cases, matching several sets of data for consistency at levels of aggregation appropriate to the problem requires a retreat to elemental units in the process of constructing the necessary aggregates. Thus, the elemental units, which are the subject of privacy concerns, are available at various stages in the processing of data sets.

Finally, data integrity is a major concern in most installations. Modifications to data files can have consequences ranging from minor to disastrous.

Communication Lines and Networks A useful means of classifying network security attacks is in terms of passive attacks and active attacks. A passive attack attempts to learn or make use of information from the system but does not affect system resources. An active attack attempts to alter system resources or affect their operation.

Passive attacks are in the nature of eavesdropping on, or monitoring of, transmissions. The goal of the opponent is to obtain information that is being transmitted. Two types of passive attacks are release of message contents and traffic analysis.

The **release of message contents** is easily understood (Figure 16.3a). A telephone conversation, an electronic mail message, and a transferred file may contain

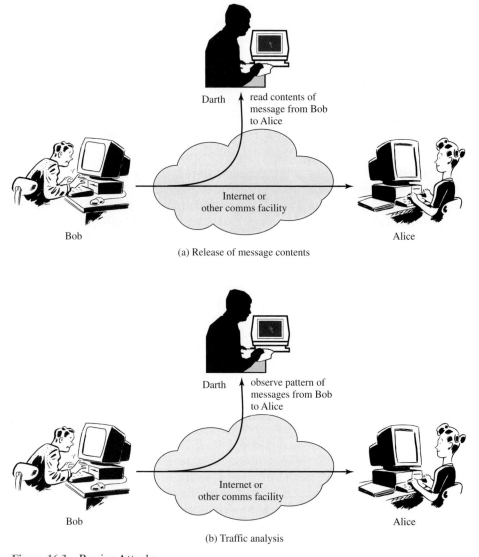

(a) Release of message contents

(b) Traffic analysis

Figure 16.3 Passive Attacks

sensitive or confidential information. We would like to prevent an opponent from learning the contents of these transmissions.

A second type of passive attack, **traffic analysis**, is subtler (Figure 16.3b). Suppose that we had a way of masking the contents of messages or other information traffic so that opponents, even if they captured the message, could not extract the information from the message. The common technique for masking contents is encryption. If we had encryption protection in place, an opponent might still be able to observe the pattern of these messages. The opponent could determine the location and identity of communicating hosts and could observe the frequency and length of messages being exchanged. This information might be useful in guessing the nature of the communication that was taking place.

Passive attacks are very difficult to detect because they do not involve any alteration of the data. Typically, the message traffic is sent and received in an apparently normal fashion and neither the sender nor receiver is aware that a third party has read the messages or observed the traffic pattern. However, it is feasible to prevent the success of these attacks, usually by means of encryption. Thus, the emphasis in dealing with passive attacks is on prevention rather than detection.

Active attacks involve some modification of the data stream or the creation of a false stream and can be subdivided into four categories: masquerade, replay, modification of messages, and denial of service.

A **masquerade** takes place when one entity pretends to be a different entity (Figure 16.4a on page 684). A masquerade attack usually includes one of the other forms of active attack. For example, authentication sequences can be captured and replayed after a valid authentication sequence has taken place, thus enabling an authorized entity with few privileges to obtain extra privileges by impersonating an entity that has those privileges.

Replay involves the passive capture of a data unit and its subsequent retransmission to produce an unauthorized effect (Figure 16.4b on page 684).

Modification of messages simply means that some portion of a legitimate message is altered, or that messages are delayed or reordered, to produce an unauthorized effect (Figure 16.4c on page 685). For example, a message meaning "Allow John Smith to read confidential file accounts" is modified to mean "Allow Fred Brown to read confidential file accounts."

The **denial of service** prevents or inhibits the normal use or management of communications facilities (Figure 16.4d on page 685). This attack may have a specific target; for example, an entity may suppress all messages directed to a particular destination (e.g., the security audit service). Another form of service denial is the disruption of an entire network, either by disabling the network or by overloading it with messages so as to degrade performance.

Active attacks present the opposite characteristics of passive attacks. Whereas passive attacks are difficult to detect, measures are available to prevent their success. On the other hand, it is quite difficult to prevent active attacks absolutely, because to do so would require physical protection of all communications facilities and paths at all times. Instead, the goal is to detect them and to recover from any disruption or delays caused by them. Because the detection has a deterrent effect, it may also contribute to prevention.

16.2 PROTECTION

The introduction of multiprogramming brought about the ability to share resources among users. This sharing involves not just the processor but also the following:

- Memory
- I/O devices, such as disks and printers

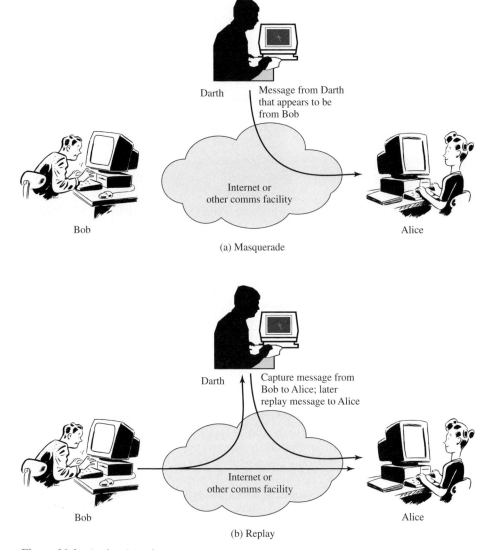

Figure 16.4 Active Attacks

- Programs
- Data

The ability to share these resources introduced the need for protection. [PFLE97] points out that an operating system may offer protection along the following spectrum:

- **No protection:** This is appropriate when sensitive procedures are being run at separate times.
- **Isolation:** This approach implies that each process operates separately from other processes, with no sharing or communication. Each process has its own address space, files, and other objects.

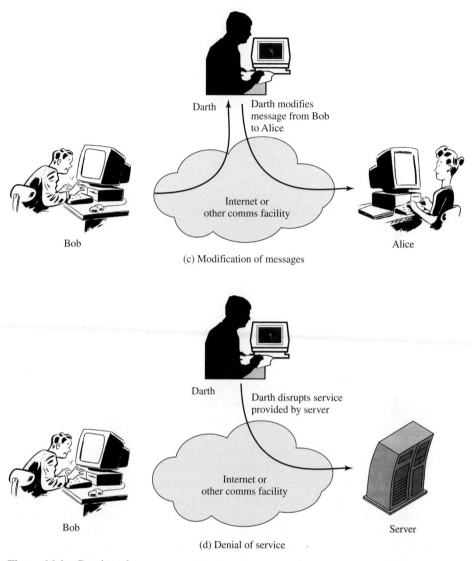

(c) Modification of messages

(d) Denial of service

Figure 16.4   Continued

- **Share all or share nothing:** The owner of an object (e.g., a file or memory segment) declares it to be public or private. In the former case, any process may access the object; in the latter, only the owner's processes may access the object.

- **Share via access limitation:** The operating system checks the permissibility of each access by a specific user to a specific object. The operating system therefore acts as a guard, or gatekeeper, between users and objects, ensuring that only authorized accesses occur.

- **Share via dynamic capabilities:** This allows dynamic creation of sharing rights for objects.

- **Limit use of an object:** This form of protection limits not just access to an object but the use to which that object may be put. For example, a user may be allowed to view a sensitive document, but not print it. Another example is that a user may be allowed access to a database to derive statistical summaries but not to determine specific data values.

The preceding items are listed roughly in increasing order of difficulty to implement, but also in increasing order of fineness of protection that they provide. A given operating system may provide different degrees of protection for different objects, users, or applications.

The operating system needs to balance the need to allow sharing, which enhances the utility of the computer system with the need to protect the resources of individual users. In this section, we consider some of the mechanisms by which operating systems have enforced protection for these objects.

Protection of Memory

In a multiprogramming environment, protection of main memory is essential. The concern here is not just security, but the correct functioning of the various processes that are active. If one process can inadvertently write into the memory space of another process, then the latter process may not execute properly.

The separation of the memory space of various processes is easily accomplished with a virtual memory scheme. Either segmentation or paging, or the two in combination, provides an effective means of managing main memory. If complete isolation is sought, then the operating system must simply assure that each segment or page is accessible only by the process to which it is assigned. This is easily accomplished by requiring that there be no duplicate entries in page and/or segment tables.

If sharing is to be allowed, then the same segment or page may appear in more than one table. This type of sharing is most easily accomplished in a system that supports segmentation or a combination of segmentation and paging. In this case, the segment structure is visible to the application, and the application can declare individual segments to be sharable or nonsharable. In a pure paging environment, it becomes more difficult to discriminate between the two types of memory, because the memory structure is transparent to the application.

An example of the hardware support that can be provided for memory protection is that of the IBM zSeries of machines, on which z/OS runs. Associated with each page frame in main memory is a 7-bit storage control key, which may be set by the operating system. Two of the bits indicate whether the page occupying this frame has been referenced and changed; these are used by the page replacement algorithm. The remaining bits are used by the protection mechanism: a 4-bit access control key and a fetch-protection bit. Processor references to memory and DMA I/O memory references must use a matching key to gain permission to access that page. The fetch protection bit indicates whether the access control key applies to writes or to both reads and writes. In the processor, there is a program status word (PSW), which contains control information relating to the process that is currently executing. Included in this word is a 4-bit PSW key. When a process attempts to access a page or to initiate a DMA operation on a page, the current PSW key is compared to the access code. A write operation is permitted only if the codes match. If the fetch bit is set, then the PSW key must match the access code for read operations.

User-Oriented Access Control

The measures taken to control access in a data processing system fall into two categories: those associated with the user and those associated with the data.

The control of access by user is, unfortunately, sometimes referred to as authentication. Because this term is now widely used in the sense of message authentication, we will refrain from applying it here. The reader is warned, however, that this usage may be encountered in the literature.

The most common technique for user access control on a shared system or server is the user log on, which requires both a user identifier (ID) and a password. The system will allow a user to logon only if that user's ID is known to the system and if the user knows the password associated by the system with that ID. This ID/password system is a notoriously unreliable method of user access control. Users can forget their passwords and accidentally or intentionally reveal their password. Hackers have become very skillful at guessing IDs for special users, such as system control and system management personnel. Finally, the ID/password file is subject to penetration attempts. We discuss countermeasures in Section 16.3.

User access control in a distributed environment can be either centralized or decentralized. In a centralized approach, the network provides a logon service, determining who is allowed to use the network and to whom the user is allowed to connect.

Decentralized user access control treats the network as a transparent communication link, and the usual logon procedure is carried out by the destination host. Of course, the security concerns for transmitting passwords over the network must still be addressed.

In many networks, two levels of access control may be used. Individual hosts may be provided with a logon facility to protect host-specific resources and application. In addition, the network as a whole may provide protection to restrict network access to authorized users. This two-level facility is desirable for the common case, currently, in which the network connects disparate hosts and simply provides a convenient means of terminal-host access. In a more uniform network of hosts, some centralized access policy could be enforced in a network control center.

Data-Oriented Access Control

Following successful logon, the user has been granted access to one or a set of hosts and applications. This is generally not sufficient for a system that includes sensitive data in its database. Through the user access control procedure, a user can be identified to the system. Associated with each user, there can be a profile that specifies permissible operations and file accesses. The operating system can then enforce rules based on the user profile. The database management system, however, must control access to specific records or even portions of records. For example, it may be permissible for anyone in administration to obtain a list of company personnel, but only selected individuals may have access to salary information. The issue is more than just one of level of detail.

Whereas the operating system may grant a user permission to access a file or use an application, following which there are no further security checks, the database management system must make a decision on each individual access attempt. That decision will depend not only on the user's identity but also on the specific parts of the data being accessed and even on the information already divulged to the user.

A general model of access control as exercised by a file or database management system is that of an **access matrix** (Figure 16.5a, based on a figure in [SAND94]). The basic elements of the model are as follows:

- **Subject:** An entity capable of accessing objects. Generally, the concept of subject equates with that of process. Any user or application actually gains access to an object by means of a process that represents that user or application.

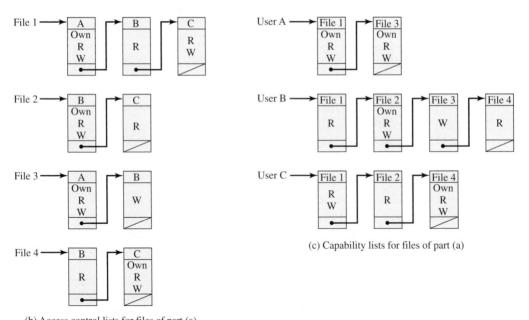

	File 1	File 2	File 3	File 4	Account 1	Account 2
User A	Own R W		Own R W		Inquiry Credit	
User B	R	Own R W	W	R	Inquiry Debit	Inquiry Credit
User C	R W	R		Own R W		Inquiry Debit

(a) Access matrix

File 1 → A Own R W → B R → C R W

File 2 → B Own R W → C R

File 3 → A Own R W → B W

File 4 → B R → C Own R W

(b) Access control lists for files of part (a)

User A → File 1 Own R W → File 3 Own R W

User B → File 1 R → File 2 Own R W → File 3 W → File 4 R

User C → File 1 R W → File 2 R → File 4 Own R W

(c) Capability lists for files of part (a)

Figure 16.5 Example of Access Control Structures

- **Object:** Anything to which access is controlled. Examples include files, portions of files, programs, segments of memory, and software objects (e.g., Java objects).
- **Access right:** The way in which an object is accessed by a subject. Examples are read, write, execute, and functions in software objects.

One dimension of the matrix consists of identified subjects that may attempt data access. Typically, this list will consist of individual users or user groups, although access could be controlled for terminals, hosts, or applications instead of or in addition to users. The other dimension lists the objects that may be accessed. At the greatest level of detail, objects may be individual data fields. More aggregate groupings, such as records, files, or even the entire database, may also be objects in the matrix. Each entry in the matrix indicates the access rights of that subject for that object.

In practice, an access matrix is usually sparse and is implemented by decomposition in one of two ways. The matrix may be decomposed by columns, yielding **access control lists** (Figure 16.5b). Thus for each object, an access control list lists users and their permitted access rights. The access control list may contain a default, or public, entry. This allows users that are not explicitly listed as having special rights to have a default set of rights. Elements of the list may include individual users as well as groups of users.

Decomposition by rows yields **capability tickets** (Figure 16.5c). A capability ticket specifies authorized objects and operations for a user. Each user has a number of tickets and may be authorized to loan or give them to others. Because tickets may be dispersed around the system, they present a greater security problem than access control lists. In particular, the ticket must be unforgeable. One way to accomplish this is to have the operating system hold all tickets on behalf of users. These tickets would have to be held in a region of memory inaccessible to users.

Network considerations for data-oriented access control parallel those for user-oriented access control. If only certain users are permitted to access certain items of data, then encryption may be needed to protect those items during transmission to authorized users. Typically, data access control is decentralized, that is, controlled by host-based database management systems. If a network database server exists on a network, then data access control becomes a network function.

16.3 INTRUDERS

One of the two most publicized threats to security is the intruder (the other is viruses), generally referred to as a hacker or cracker. In an important early study of intrusion, Anderson [ANDE80] identified three classes of intruders:

- **Masquerader:** An individual who is not authorized to use the computer and who penetrates a system's access controls to exploit a legitimate user's account
- **Misfeasor:** A legitimate user who accesses data, programs, or resources for which such access is not authorized, or who is authorized for such access but misuses his or her privileges

- **Clandestine user:** An individual who seizes supervisory control of the system and uses this control to evade auditing and access controls or to suppress audit collection

The masquerader is likely to be an outsider; the misfeasor generally is an insider; and the clandestine user can be either an outsider or an insider.

Intruder attacks range from the benign to the serious. At the benign end of the scale, there are many people who simply wish to explore internets and see what is out there. At the serious end are individuals who are attempting to read privileged data, perform unauthorized modifications to data, or disrupt the system.

Intrusion Techniques

The objective of the intruder is to gain access to a system or to increase the range of privileges accessible on a system. Generally, this requires the intruder to acquire information that should have been protected. In most cases, this information is in the form of a user password. With knowledge of some other user's password, an intruder can log in to a system and exercise all the privileges accorded to the legitimate user.

Typically, a system must maintain a file that associates a password with each authorized user. If such a file is stored with no protection, then it is an easy matter to gain access to it and learn passwords. The password file can be protected in one of two ways:

- **One-way encryption:** The system stores only an encrypted form of the user's password. When the user presents a password, the system encrypts that password and compares it with the stored value. In practice, the system usually performs a one-way transformation (not reversible) in which the password is used to generate a key for the encryption function and in which a fixed-length output is produced.

- **Access control:** Access to the password file is limited to one or a very few accounts.

If one or both of these countermeasures are in place, some effort is needed for a potential intruder to learn passwords. On the basis of a survey of the literature and interviews with a number of password crackers, [ALVA90] reports the following techniques for learning passwords:

1. Try default passwords used with standard accounts that are shipped with the system. Many administrators do not bother to change these defaults.
2. Exhaustively try all short passwords (those of one to three characters).
3. Try words in the system's online dictionary or a list of likely passwords. Examples of the latter are readily available on hacker bulletin boards and the Internet.
4. Collect information about users, such as their full names, the names of their spouse and children, pictures in their office, and books in their office that are related to hobbies.
5. Try users' phone numbers, social security numbers, and room numbers.
6. Try all legitimate license plate numbers for this state.

7. Use a Trojan horse (described in Section 16.4) to bypass restrictions on access.
8. Tap the line between a remote user and the host system.

The first six methods are various ways of guessing a password. If an intruder has to verify the guess by attempting to log in, it is a tedious and easily countered means of attack. For example, a system can simply reject any login after three password attempts, thus requiring the intruder to reconnect to the host to try again. Under these circumstances, it is not practical to try more than a handful of passwords. However, the intruder is unlikely to try such crude methods. For example, if an intruder can gain access with a low level of privileges to an encrypted password file, then the strategy would be to capture that file and then use the encryption mechanism of that particular system at leisure until a valid password that provided greater privileges was discovered.

Guessing attacks are feasible, and indeed highly effective, when a large number of guesses can be attempted automatically and each guess verified, without the guessing process being detectable. Later in this section, we have more to say about thwarting guessing attacks.

The seventh method of attack listed earlier, the Trojan horse, can be particularly difficult to counter. An example of a program that bypasses access controls was cited in [ALVA90]. A low-privilege user produced a game program and invited the system operator to use it in his or her spare time. The program did indeed play a game, but in the background it also contained code to copy the password file, which was unencrypted but access protected, into the user's file. Because the game was running under the operator's high-privilege mode, it was able to gain access to the password file.

The eighth attack listed, line tapping, is a matter of physical security. It can be countered with link encryption techniques.

We turn now to a discussion of the two principal countermeasures: prevention and detection. Prevention is a challenging security goal and an uphill battle at all times. The difficulty stems from the fact that the defender must attempt to thwart all possible attacks, whereas the attacker is free to try to find the weakest link in the defense chain and attack at that point. Detection is concerned with learning of an attack, either before or after its success.

Password Protection

The front line of defense against intruders is the password system. Virtually all multiuser systems require that a user provide not only a name or identifier (ID) but also a password. The password serves to authenticate the ID of the individual logging on to the system. In turn, the ID provides security in the following ways:

- The ID determines whether the user is authorized to gain access to a system. In some systems, only those who already have an ID filed on the system are allowed to gain access.
- The ID determines the privileges accorded to the user. A few users may have supervisory or "superuser" status that enables them to read files and perform functions that are especially protected by the operating system. Some systems have guest or anonymous accounts, and users of these accounts have more limited privileges than others.

- The ID is used in what is referred to as discretionary access control. For example, by listing the IDs of the other users, a user may grant permission to them to read files owned by that user.

The Vulnerability of Passwords To understand the nature of the attack, let us consider a scheme that is widely used on UNIX systems, in which passwords are never stored in the clear. Rather, the following procedure is employed (Figure 16.6a). Each user selects a password of up to eight printable characters in length. This is converted into a 56-bit value (using 7-bit ASCII) that serves as the key input to an encryption routine. The encryption routine, known as crypt(3), is based on the Data Encryption Standard (DES), described in Appendix 16A. The DES algorithm is modified using a 12-bit "salt" value. Typically, this value is related to the time at which

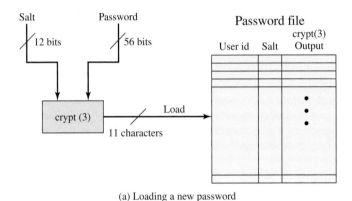

(a) Loading a new password

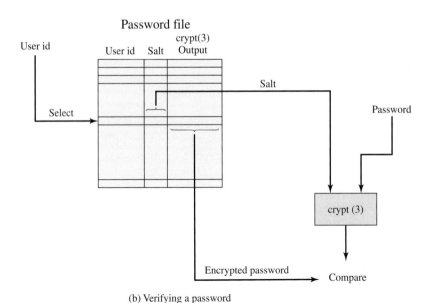

(b) Verifying a password

Figure 16.6 UNIX Password Scheme

the password is assigned to the user. The modified DES algorithm is exercised with a data input consisting of a 64-bit block of zeros. The output of the algorithm then serves as input for a second encryption. This process is repeated for a total of 25 encryptions. The resulting 64-bit output is then translated into an 11-character sequence. This ciphertext password is then stored, together with a plaintext copy of the salt, in the password file for the corresponding user ID.

The salt serves three purposes:

- It prevents duplicate passwords from being visible in the password file. Even if two users choose the same password, those passwords will be assigned at different times. Hence, the "extended" passwords of the two users will differ.

- It effectively increases the length of the password without requiring the user to remember two additional characters. Hence, the number of possible passwords is increased by a factor of 4096, increasing the difficulty of guessing a password.

- It prevents the use of a hardware implementation of DES, which would ease the difficulty of a brute-force guessing attack.

When a user attempts to log on to a UNIX system, the user provides an ID and a password. The operating system uses the ID to index into the password file and retrieve the plaintext salt and the encrypted password, which are used as input to the encryption routine. If the result matches the stored value, the password is accepted.

The encryption routine is designed to discourage guessing attacks. Software implementations of DES are slow compared to hardware versions, and the use of 25 iterations multiplies the time required by 25. However, since the original design of this algorithm, two changes have occurred. First, newer implementations of the algorithm itself have resulted in speedups. For example, the Internet worm was able to do online password guessing of a few hundred passwords in a reasonably short time by using a more efficient encryption algorithm than the standard one stored on the UNIX systems that it attacked. Second, hardware performance continues to increase, so that any software algorithm executes more quickly.

Thus, there are two threats to the UNIX password scheme. First, a user can gain access on a machine using a guest account or by some other means and then run a password-guessing program, called a password cracker, on that machine. The attacker should be able to check hundreds and perhaps thousands of possible passwords with little resource consumption. In addition, if an opponent is able to obtain a copy of the password file, then a cracker program can be run on another machine at leisure. This enables the opponent to run through many thousands of possible passwords in a reasonable period.

As an example, a password cracker was reported on the Internet in August 1993 [MADS93]. Using a Thinking Machines Corporation parallel computer, a performance of 1560 encryptions per second per vector unit was achieved. With four vector units per processing node (a standard configuration), this works out to 800,000 encryptions per second on a 128-node machine (which is a modest size) and 6.4 million encryptions per second on a 1024-node machine.

Even these stupendous guessing rates do not yet make it feasible for an attacker to use a dumb brute-force technique of trying all possible combinations of characters to discover a password. Instead, password crackers rely on the fact that some people choose easily guessable passwords.

Table 16.2   Observed Password Lengths

Length	Number	Fraction of Total
1	55	0.004
2	87	0.006
3	212	0.02
4	449	0.03
5	1,260	0.09
6	3,035	0.22
7	2,917	0.21
8	5,772	0.42
Total	13,787	1.0

Some users, when permitted to choose their own password, pick one that is absurdly short. The results of one study at Purdue University are shown in Table 16.2. The study observed password change choices on 54 machines, representing approximately 7000 user accounts. Almost 3% of the passwords were three characters or fewer in length. An attacker could begin the attack by exhaustively testing all possible passwords of length 3 or fewer. A simple remedy is for the system to reject any password choice of fewer than, say, six characters or even to require that all passwords be exactly eight characters in length. Most users would not complain about such a restriction.

Password length is only part of the problem. Many people, when permitted to choose their own password, pick a password that is guessable, such as their own name, their street name, a common dictionary word, and so forth. This makes the job of password cracking straightforward. The cracker simply has to test the password file against lists of likely passwords. Because many people use guessable passwords, such a strategy should succeed on virtually all systems.

One demonstration of the effectiveness of guessing is reported in [KLEI90]. From a variety of sources, the author collected UNIX password files, containing nearly 14,000 encrypted passwords. The result, which the author rightly characterizes as frightening, is shown in Table 16.3. In all, nearly one-fourth of the passwords were guessed. The following strategy was used:

1. Try the user's name, initials, account name, and other relevant personal information. In all, 130 different permutations for each user were tried.

2. Try words from various dictionaries. The author compiled a dictionary of over 60,000 words, including the online dictionary on the system itself, and various other lists as shown.

3. Try various permutations on the words from step 2. This included making the first letter uppercase or a control character, making the entire word uppercase, reversing the word, changing the letter "o" to the digit "zero," and so on. These permutations added another 1 million words to the list.

4. Try various capitalization permutations on the words from step 2 that were not considered in step 3. This added almost 2 million additional words to the list.

Table 16.3   Passwords Cracked from a Sample Set of 13,797 Accounts [KLEI90]

Type of Password	Search Size	Number of Matches	Percentage of Passwords Matched
User/account name	130	368	2.7%
Character sequences	866	22	0.2%
Numbers	427	9	0.1%
Chinese	392	56	0.4%
Place names	628	82	0.6%
Common names	2,239	548	4.0%
Female names	4,280	161	1.2%
Male names	2,866	140	1.0%
Uncommon names	4,955	130	0.9%
Myths and legends	1,246	66	0.5%
Shakespearean	473	11	0.1%
Sports terms	238	32	0.2%
Science fiction	691	59	0.4%
Movies and actors	99	12	0.1%
Cartoons	92	9	0.1%
Famous people	290	55	0.4%
Phrases and patterns	933	253	1.8%
Surnames	33	9	0.1%
Biology	58	1	0.0%
System dictionary	19,683	1,027	7.4%
Machine names	9,018	132	1.0%
Mnemonics	14	2	0.0%
King James bible	7,525	83	0.6%
Miscellaneous words	3,212	54	0.4%
Yiddish words	56	0	0.0%
Asteroids	2,407	19	0.1%
TOTAL	62,727	3,340	24.2%

Thus, the test involved in the neighborhood of 3 million words. Using the fastest Thinking Machines implementation listed earlier, the time to encrypt all these words for all possible salt values is under an hour. Keep in mind that such a thorough search could produce a success rate of about 25%, whereas even a single hit may be enough to gain a wide range of privileges on a system.

More recently, an approach that takes advantage of continuing increases in processing speed and storage size has been reported [PERR03]. In this approach, a large number of possible passwords with alternative salt values was precomputed and stored for a table lookup approach at password cracking. This report shows the feasibility of attacking the UNIX password scheme.

Currently, some UNIX and all Linux vendors offer more secure alternatives to the crypt(3) approach.

Access Control One way to thwart a password attack is to deny the opponent access to the password file. If the encrypted password portion of the file is accessible only by a privileged user, then the opponent cannot read it without already knowing the password of a privileged user. [SPAF92] points out several flaws in this strategy:

- Many systems, including most UNIX systems, are susceptible to unanticipated break-ins. Once an attacker has gained access by some means, he or she may wish to obtain a collection of passwords in order to use different accounts for different logon sessions to decrease the risk of detection. Or a user with an account may desire another user's account to access privileged data or to sabotage the system.
- An accident of protection might render the password file readable, thus compromising all the accounts.
- Some of the users have accounts on other machines in other protection domains, and they use the same password. Thus, if the passwords could be read by anyone on one machine, a machine in another location might be compromised.

Thus, a more effective strategy would be to force users to select passwords that are difficult to guess.

Password Selection Strategies

The lesson from the two experiments just described (Tables 16.2 and 16.3) is that, left to their own devices, many users choose a password that is too short or too easy to guess. At the other extreme, if users are assigned passwords consisting of eight randomly selected printable characters, password cracking is effectively impossible. But it would be almost as impossible for most users to remember their passwords. Fortunately, even if we limit the password universe to strings of characters that are reasonably memorable, the size of the universe is still too large to permit practical cracking. Our goal, then, is to eliminate guessable passwords while allowing the user to select a password that is memorable. Four basic techniques are in use:

- User education
- Computer-generated passwords
- Reactive password checking
- Proactive password checking

Users can be told the importance of using hard-to-guess passwords and can be provided with guidelines for selecting strong passwords. This **user education** strategy is unlikely to succeed at most installations, particularly where there is a large user population or a lot of turnover. Many users will simply ignore the guidelines. Others may not be good judges of what is a strong password. For example, many users (mistakenly) believe that reversing a word or capitalizing the last letter makes a password unguessable.

Computer-generated passwords also have problems. If the passwords are quite random in nature, users will not be able to remember them. Even if the password is pronounceable, the user may have difficulty remembering it and so be tempted to write it down. In general, computer-generated password schemes have a history of poor acceptance by users. FIPS PUB 181 defines one of the best-designed automated password generators. The standard includes not only a description of the approach but also a complete listing of the C source code of the algorithm. The algorithm generates words by forming pronounceable syllables and concatenating them to form a word. A random number generator produces a random stream of characters used to construct the syllables and words.

A **reactive password-checking** strategy is one in which the system periodically runs its own password cracker to find guessable passwords. The system cancels any passwords that are guessed and notifies the user. This tactic has a number of drawbacks. First, it is resource intensive if the job is done right. Because a determined opponent who is able to steal a password file can devote full CPU time to the task for hours or even days, an effective reactive password checker is at a distinct disadvantage. Furthermore, any existing passwords remain vulnerable until the reactive password checker finds them.

The most promising approach to improved password security is a **proactive password checker**. In this scheme, a user is allowed to select his or her password. However, at the time of selection, the system checks to see if the password is allowable and, if not, rejects it. Such checkers are based on the philosophy that, with sufficient guidance from the system, users can select memorable passwords from a fairly large password space that are not likely to be guessed in a dictionary attack.

The trick with a proactive password checker is to strike a balance between user acceptability and strength. If the system rejects too many passwords, users will complain that it is too hard to select a password. If the system uses some simple algorithm to define what is acceptable, this provides guidance to password crackers to refine their guessing technique. In the remainder of this subsection, we look at possible approaches to proactive password checking.

The first approach is a simple system for rule enforcement. For example, the following rules could be enforced:

- All passwords must be at least eight characters long.
- In the first eight characters, the passwords must include at least one each of uppercase, lowercase, numeric digits, and punctuation marks.

These rules could be coupled with advice to the user. Although this approach is superior to simply educating users, it may not be sufficient to thwart password crackers. This scheme alerts crackers as to which passwords not to try but may still make it possible to do password cracking.

Another possible procedure is simply to compile a large dictionary of possible "bad" passwords. When a user selects a password, the system checks to make sure that it is not on the disapproved list. There are two problems with this approach:

- **Space:** The dictionary must be very large to be effective. For example, the dictionary used in the Purdue study [SPAF92] occupies more than 30 megabytes of storage.
- **Time:** The time required to search a large dictionary may itself be large. In addition, to check for likely permutations of dictionary words, either those words most be included in the dictionary, making it truly huge, or each search must also involve considerable processing.

Intrusion Detection

Inevitably, the best intrusion prevention system will fail. A system's second line of defense is intrusion detection, and this has been the focus of much research in recent years. This interest is motivated by a number of considerations, including the following:

1. If an intrusion is detected quickly enough, the intruder can be identified and ejected from the system before any damage is done or any data are compromised. Even if the detection is not sufficiently timely to preempt the intruder, the sooner that the intrusion is detected, the less the amount of damage and the more quickly that recovery can be achieved.

2. An effective intrusion detection system can serve as a deterrent, so acting to prevent intrusions.

3. Intrusion detection enables the collection of information about intrusion techniques that can be used to strengthen the intrusion prevention facility.

Intrusion detection is based on the assumption that the behavior of the intruder differs from that of a legitimate user in ways that can be quantified. Of course, we cannot expect that there will be a crisp, exact distinction between an attack by an intruder and the normal use of resources by an authorized user. Rather, we must expect that there will be some overlap.

Figure 16.7 suggests, in very abstract terms, the nature of the task confronting the designer of an intrusion detection system. Although the typical behavior of an intruder differs from the typical behavior of an authorized user, there is an overlap in these behaviors. Thus, a loose interpretation of intruder behavior, which will catch more intruders, will also lead to a number of "false positives," or authorized users identified as intruders. On the other hand, an attempt to limit false positives by a tight interpretation of intruder behavior will lead to an increase in false negatives, or intruders not identified as intruders. Thus, there is an element of compromise and art in the practice of intrusion detection.

In Anderson's study [ANDE80], it was postulated that one could, with reasonable confidence, distinguish between a masquerader and a legitimate user. Patterns of legitimate user behavior can be established by observing past history, and significant deviation from such patterns can be detected. Anderson suggests that the task of detecting a misfeasor (legitimate user performing in an unauthorized fashion) is more difficult, in that the distinction between abnormal and normal behavior may be small. Anderson concluded that such violations would be undetectable solely through the search for

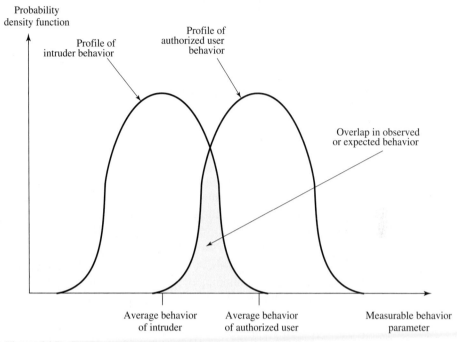

Figure 16.7 Profiles of Behavior of Intruders and Authorized Users

anomalous behavior. However, misfeasor behavior might nevertheless be detectable by intelligent definition of the class of conditions that suggest unauthorized use. Finally, the detection of the clandestine user was felt to be beyond the scope of purely automated techniques. These observations, which were made in 1980, remain true today.

[PORR92] identifies the following approaches to intrusion detection:

1. **Statistical anomaly detection:** Involves the collection of data relating to the behavior of legitimate users over a period of time. Then statistical tests are applied to observed behavior to determine with a high level of confidence whether that behavior is not legitimate user behavior.

   (a) Threshold detection: This approach involves defining thresholds, independent of user, for the frequency of various events.

   (b) Profile based: A profile of the activity of each user is developed and used to detect changes in the behavior of individual accounts.

2. **Rule-based detection:** Involves an attempt to define a set of rules that can be used to decide that a given behavior is that of an intruder.

   (a) Anomaly detection: Rules are developed to detect deviation from previous usage patterns.

   (b) Penetration identification: An expert system approach that searches for suspicious behavior.

In a nutshell, statistical approaches attempt to define normal, or expected, behavior, whereas rule-based approaches attempt to define proper behavior.

In terms of the types of attackers listed earlier, statistical anomaly detection is effective against masqueraders, who are unlikely to mimic the behavior patterns of the accounts they appropriate. On the other hand, such techniques may be unable to deal with misfeasors. For such attacks, rule-based approaches may be able to recognize events and sequences that, in context, reveal penetration. In practice, a system may exhibit a combination of both approaches to be effective against a broad range of attacks.

A fundamental tool for intrusion detection is the audit record. Some record of ongoing user activity must be maintained for input to an intrusion detection system. Basically, two plans are used:

- **Native audit records:** Virtually all multiuser operating systems include accounting software that collects information on user activity. The advantage of using this information is that no additional collection software is needed. The disadvantage is that the native audit records may not contain the needed information or may not contain it in a convenient form.

- **Detection-specific audit records:** A collection facility can be implemented that generates audit records containing only that information required by the intrusion detection system. One advantage of such an approach is that it could be made vendor independent and ported to a variety of systems. The disadvantage is the extra overhead involved in having, in effect, two accounting packages running on a machine.

A good example of detection-specific audit records is one developed by Dorothy Denning [DENN87]. Each audit record contains the following fields:

- **Subject:** Initiators of actions. A subject is typically a terminal user but might also be a process acting on behalf of users or groups of users. All activity arises through commands issued by subjects. Subjects may be grouped into different access classes, and these classes may overlap.

- **Action:** Operation performed by the subject on or with an object; for example, login, read, perform I/O, execute.

- **Object:** Receptors of actions. Examples include files, programs, messages, records, terminals, printers, and user- or program-created structures. When a subject is the recipient of an action, such as electronic mail, then that subject is considered an object. Objects may be grouped by type. Object granularity may vary by object type and by environment. For example, database actions may be audited for the database as a whole or at the record level.

- **Exception-Condition:** Denotes which, if any, exception condition is raised on return.

- **Resource-Usage:** A list of quantitative elements in which each element gives the amount used of some resource (e.g., number of lines printed or displayed, number of records read or written, processor time, I/O units used, session elapsed time).

- **Time-Stamp:** Unique time-and-date stamp identifying when the action took place.

Most user operations are made up of a number of elementary actions. For example, a file copy involves the execution of the user command, which includes doing access validation and setting up the copy, plus the read from one file, plus the write to another file. Consider the command

COPY GAME.EXE TO <Library>GAME.EXE

issued by Smith to copy an executable file GAME from the current directory to the <Library> directory. The following audit records may be generated:

| Smith | execute | <Library>COPY.EXE | 0 | CPU = 00002 | 11058721678 |

| Smith | read | <Smith>GAME.EXE | 0 | RECORDS = 0 | 11058721679 |

| Smith | execute | <Library>COPY.EXE | write-viol | RECORDS = 0 | 11058721680 |

In this case, the copy is aborted because Smith does not have write permission to `<Library>`.

The decomposition of a user operation into elementary actions has three advantages:

1. Because objects are the protectable entities in a system, the use of elementary actions enables an audit of all behavior affecting an object. Thus, the system can detect attempted subversions of access controls (by noting an anomaly in the number of exception conditions returned) and can detect successful subversions by noting an anomaly in the set of objects accessible to the subject.

2. Single-object, single-action audit records simplify the model and the implementation.

3. Because of the simple, uniform structure of the detection-specific audit records, it may be relatively easy to obtain this information or at least part of it by a straightforward mapping from existing native audit records to the detection-specific audit records.

16.4 MALICIOUS SOFTWARE

Perhaps the most sophisticated types of threats to computer systems are presented by programs that exploit vulnerabilities in computing systems. In this context, we are concerned with application programs as well as utility programs, such as editors and compilers. The generic term for such threats is malicious software, or malware. Malware is software designed to cause damage to or use up the resources of a target computer. It is frequently concealed within or masquerades as legitimate software. In some cases, it spreads itself to other computers via e-mail or infected floppy disks.

We begin this section with an overview of the spectrum of such software threats. The remainder of the section is devoted to viruses, first looking at their nature and then at countermeasures.

Malicious Programs

Figure 16.8 provides an overall taxonomy of malicious software. These threats can be divided into two categories: those that need a host program, and those that are independent. The former are essentially fragments of programs that cannot exist independently of some actual application program, utility, or system program. The latter are self-contained programs that can be scheduled and run by the operating system.

We can also differentiate between those software threats that do not replicate and those that do. The former are fragments of programs that are to be activated when the host program is invoked to perform a specific function. The latter consist of either a program fragment (virus) or an independent program (worm, zombie) that, when executed, may produce one or more copies of itself to be activated later on the same system or some other system.

Although the taxonomy of Figure 16.8 is useful in organizing the information we are discussing, it is not the whole picture. In particular, logic bombs or Trojan horses may be part of a virus or worm.

Trap Door A trap door is a secret entry point into a program that allows someone who is aware of the trap door to gain access without going through the usual security access procedures. Trap doors have been used legitimately for many years by programmers to debug and test programs. This usually is done when the programmer is developing an application that has an authentication procedure, or a long setup, requiring the user to enter many different values to run the application. To debug the program, the developer may wish to gain special privileges or to avoid all the necessary setup and authentication. The programmer may also want to ensure that there is a method of activating the program should something be wrong with the authentication procedure that is being built into the application. The trap

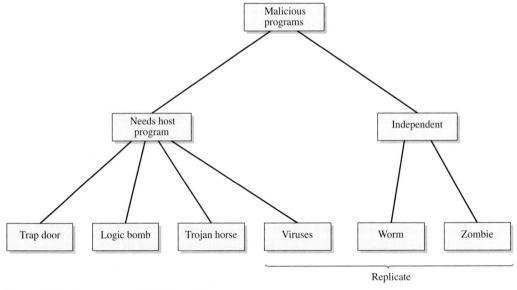

Figure 16.8 Taxonomy of Malicious Programs

door is code that recognizes some special sequence of input or is triggered by being run from a certain user ID or by an unlikely sequence of events.

Trap doors become threats when they are used by unscrupulous programmers to gain unauthorized access. The trap door was the basic idea for the vulnerability portrayed in the movie War Games [COOP89]. Another example is that during the development of Multics, penetration tests were conducted by an Air Force "tiger team" (simulating adversaries). One tactic employed was to send a bogus operating system update to a site running Multics. The update contained a Trojan horse that could be activated by a trap door and that allowed the tiger team to gain access. The threat was so well implemented that the Multics developers could not find it, even after they were informed of its presence [ENGE80].

It is difficult to implement operating system controls for trap doors. Security measures must focus on the program development and software update activities.

Logic Bomb One of the oldest types of program threat, predating viruses and worms, is the logic bomb. The logic bomb is code embedded in some legitimate program that is set to "explode" when certain conditions are met. Examples of conditions that can be used as triggers for a logic bomb are the presence or absence of certain files, a particular day of the week or date, or a particular user running the application. Once triggered, a bomb may alter or delete data or entire files, cause a machine halt, or do some other damage. A striking example of how logic bombs can be employed was the case of Tim Lloyd, who was convicted of setting a logic bomb that cost his employer, Omega Engineering, more than $10 million, derailed its corporate growth strategy, and eventually led to the layoff of 80 workers [GAUD00]. Ultimately, Lloyd was sentenced to 41 months in prison and ordered to pay $2 million in restitution.

Trojan Horse A Trojan horse is a useful, or apparently useful, program or command procedure containing hidden code that, when invoked, performs some unwanted or harmful function.

Trojan horse programs can be used to accomplish functions indirectly that an unauthorized user could not accomplish directly. For example, to gain access to the files of another user on a shared system, a user could create a Trojan horse program that, when executed, changed the invoking user's file permissions so that the files are readable by any user. The author could then induce users to run the program by placing it in a common directory and naming it such that it appears to be a useful utility. An example is a program that ostensibly produces a listing of the user's files in a desirable format. After another user has run the program, the author can then access the information in the user's files. An example of a Trojan horse program that would be difficult to detect is a compiler that has been modified to insert additional code into certain programs as they are compiled, such as a system login program [THOM84]. The code creates a trap door in the login program that permits the author to log on to the system using a special password. This Trojan horse can never be discovered by reading the source code of the login program.

Another common motivation for the Trojan horse is data destruction. The program appears to be performing a useful function (e.g., a calculator program), but it may also be quietly deleting the user's files. For example, a CBS executive was victimized by a Trojan horse that destroyed all information contained in his computer's memory [TIME90]. The Trojan horse was implanted in a graphics routine offered on an electronic bulletin board system.

Virus   A virus is a program that can "infect" other programs by modifying them; the modification includes a copy of the virus program, which can then go on to infect other programs.

Biological viruses are tiny scraps of genetic code—DNA or RNA—that can take over the machinery of a living cell and trick it into making thousands of flawless replicas of the original virus. Like its biological counterpart, a computer virus carries in its instructional code the recipe for making perfect copies of itself. Lodged in a host computer, the typical virus takes temporary control of the computer's disk operating system. Then, whenever the infected computer comes into contact with an uninfected piece of software, a fresh copy of the virus passes into the new program. Thus, the infection can be spread from computer to computer by unsuspecting users who either swap disks or send programs to one another over a network. In a network environment, the ability to access applications and system services on other computers provides a perfect culture for the spread of a virus.

Viruses are examined in greater detail later in this section.

Worms   Network worm programs use network connections to spread from system to system. Once active within a system, a network worm can behave as a computer virus, or it could implant Trojan horse programs or perform any number of disruptive or destructive actions.

To replicate itself, a network worm uses some sort of network vehicle. Examples include

- **Electronic mail facility:** A worm mails a copy of itself to other systems.
- **Remote execution capability:** A worm executes a copy of itself on another system.
- **Remote login capability:** A worm logs onto a remote system as a user and then uses commands to copy itself from one system to the other.

The new copy of the worm program is then run on the remote system where, in addition to any functions that it performs at that system, it continues to spread in the same fashion.

A network worm exhibits the same characteristics as a computer virus: a dormant phase, a propagation phase, a triggering phase, and an execution phase. The propagation phase generally performs the following functions:

1. Search for other systems to infect by examining host tables or similar repositories of remote system addresses.
2. Establish a connection with a remote system.
3. Copy itself to the remote system and cause the copy to be run.

The network worm may also attempt to determine whether a system has previously been infected before copying itself to the system. In a multiprogramming system, it may also disguise its presence by naming itself as a system process or using some other name that may not be noticed by a system operator.

As with viruses, network worms are difficult to counter. However, both network security and single-system security measures, if properly designed and implemented, minimize the threat of worms.

Zombie A zombie is a program that secretly takes over another Internet-attached computer and then uses that computer to launch attacks that are difficult to trace to the zombie's creator. Zombies are used in denial-of-service attacks, typically against targeted Web sites. The zombie is planted on hundreds of computers belonging to unsuspecting third parties, and then used to overwhelm the target Web site by launching an overwhelming onslaught of Internet traffic.

The Nature of Viruses

A virus can do anything that other programs do. The only difference is that it attaches itself to another program and executes secretly when the host program is run. Once a virus is executing, it can perform any function, such as erasing files and programs, that is allowed by the privileges of the current user.

During its lifetime, a typical virus goes through the following four stages:

- **Dormant phase:** The virus is idle. The virus will eventually be activated by some event, such as a date, the presence of another program or file, or the capacity of the disk exceeding some limit. Not all viruses have this stage.

- **Propagation phase:** The virus places an identical copy of itself into other programs or into certain system areas on the disk. Each infected program will now contain a clone of the virus, which will itself enter a propagation phase.

- **Triggering phase:** The virus is activated to perform the function for which it was intended. As with the dormant phase, the triggering phase can be caused by a variety of system events, including a count of the number of times that this copy of the virus has made copies of itself.

- **Execution phase:** The function is performed. The function may be harmless, such as a message on the screen, or damaging, such as the destruction of programs and data files.

Most viruses carry out their work in a manner that is specific to a particular operating system and, in some cases, specific to a particular hardware platform. Thus, they are designed to take advantage of the details and weaknesses of particular systems.

Types of Viruses

There has been a continuous arms race between virus writers and writers of antivirus software since viruses first appeared. As effective countermeasures have been developed for existing types of viruses, new types have been developed. [STEP93] suggests the following categories as being among the most significant types of viruses:

- **Parasitic virus:** The traditional and still most common form of virus. A parasitic virus attaches itself to executable files and replicates, when the infected program is executed, by finding other executable files to infect.

- **Memory-resident virus:** Lodges in main memory as part of a resident system program. From that point on, the virus infects every program that executes.

- **Boot sector virus:** Infects a master boot record or boot record and spreads when a system is booted from the disk containing the virus.
- **Stealth virus:** A form of virus explicitly designed to hide itself from detection by antivirus software.
- **Polymorphic virus:** A virus that mutates with every infection, making detection by the "signature" of the virus impossible.

One example of a **stealth virus** is one that uses compression so that the infected program is exactly the same length as an uninfected version. Far more sophisticated techniques are possible. For example, a virus can place intercept logic in disk I/O routines, so that when there is an attempt to read suspected portions of the disk using these routines, the virus will present back the original, uninfected program. Thus, stealth is not a term that applies to a virus as such but, rather, is a technique used by a virus to evade detection.

A **polymorphic virus** creates copies during replication that are functionally equivalent but have distinctly different bit patterns. As with a stealth virus, the purpose is to defeat programs that scan for viruses. In this case, the "signature" of the virus will vary with each copy. To achieve this variation, the virus may randomly insert superfluous instructions or interchange the order of independent instructions. A more effective approach is to use encryption. A portion of the virus, generally called a mutation engine, creates a random encryption key to encrypt the remainder of the virus. The key is stored with the virus, and the mutation engine itself is altered. When an infected program is invoked, the virus uses the stored random key to decrypt the virus. When the virus replicates, a different random key is selected.

Another weapon in the virus writers' armory is the virus-creation toolkit. Such a toolkit enables a relative novice to create quickly a number of different viruses. Although viruses created with toolkits tend to be less sophisticated than viruses designed from scratch, the sheer number of new viruses that can be generated creates a problem for antivirus schemes.

Yet another tool of the virus writer is the virus exchange bulletin board. A number of such boards have sprung up [ADAM92] in the United States and other countries. These boards offer copies of viruses that can be downloaded, as well as tips for the creation of viruses.

Macro Viruses

In recent years, the number of viruses encountered at corporate sites has risen dramatically. Much of this increase is due to the proliferation of one of the macro virus. Macro viruses are particularly threatening for a number of reasons:

1. A macro virus is platform independent. Virtually all of the macro viruses infect Microsoft Word documents. Any hardware platform and operating system that supports Word can be infected.
2. Macro viruses infect documents, not executable portions of code. Most of the information introduced onto a computer system is in the form of a document rather than a program.
3. Macro viruses are easily spread. A very common method is by electronic mail.

Macro viruses take advantage of a feature found in Word and other office applications such as Microsoft Excel, namely the macro. In essence, a macro is an executable program embedded in a word processing document or other type of file. Typically, users employ macros to automate repetitive tasks and thereby save keystrokes. The macro language is usually some form of the Basic programming language. A user might define a sequence of keystrokes in a macro and set it up so that the macro is invoked when a function key or special short combination of keys is input.

What makes it possible to create a macro virus is the autoexecuting macro. This is a macro that is automatically invoked, without explicit user input. Common autoexecute events are opening a file, closing a file, and starting an application. Once a macro is running, it can copy itself to other documents, delete files, and cause other sorts of damage to the user's system. In Microsoft Word, there are three types of autoexecuting macros:

- **Autoexecute:** If a macro named AutoExec is in the "normal.dot" template or in a global template stored in Word's startup directory, it is executed whenever Word is started.

- **Automacro:** An automacro executes when a defined event occurs, such as opening or closing a document, creating a new document, or quitting Word.

- **Command macro:** If a macro in a global macro file or a macro attached to a document has the name of an existing Word command, it is executed whenever the user invokes that command (e.g., File Save).

A common technique for spreading a macro virus is as follows. An automacro or command macro is attached to a Word document that is introduced into a system by e-mail or disk transfer. At some point after the document is opened, the macro executes. The macro copies itself to the global macro file. When the next session of Word opens, the infected global macro is active. When this macro executes, it can replicate itself and cause damage.

Successive releases of Word provide increased protection against macro viruses. For example, Microsoft offers an optional Macro Virus Protection tool that detects suspicious Word files and alerts the customer to the potential risk of opening a file with macros. Various antivirus product vendors have also developed tools to detect and correct macro viruses. As in other types of viruses, the arms race continues in the field of macro viruses.

Antivirus Approaches

The ideal solution to the threat of viruses is prevention: Do not allow a virus to get into the system in the first place. This goal is, in general, impossible to achieve, although prevention can reduce the number of successful viral attacks. The next best approach is to be able to do the following:

- **Detection:** Once the infection has occurred, determine that it has occurred and locate the virus.

- **Identification:** Once detection has been achieved, identify the specific virus that has infected a program.

- **Removal:** Once the specific virus has been identified, remove all traces of the virus from the infected program and restore it to its original state. Remove the virus from all infected systems so that the disease cannot spread further.

If detection succeeds but either identification or removal is not possible, then the alternative is to discard the infected program and reload a clean backup version.

Advances in virus and antivirus technology go hand in hand. Early viruses were relatively simple code fragments and could be identified and purged with relatively simple antivirus software packages. As the virus arms race has evolved, both viruses and, necessarily, antivirus software have grown more complex and sophisticated. Increasingly sophisticated antivirus approaches and products continue to appear. In this subsection, we highlight two of the most important.

Generic Decryption   Generic decryption (GD) technology enables the antivirus program to detect easily even the most complex polymorphic viruses while maintaining fast scanning speeds [NACH97]. Recall that when a file containing a polymorphic virus is executed, the virus must decrypt itself to activate. In order to detect such a structure, executable files are run through a GD scanner, which contains the following elements:

- **CPU emulator:** A software-based virtual computer. Instructions in an executable file are interpreted by the emulator rather than executed on the underlying processor. The emulator includes software versions of all registers and other processor hardware, so that the underlying processor is unaffected by programs interpreted on the emulator.
- **Virus signature scanner:** A module that scans the target code looking for known virus signatures.
- **Emulation control module:** Controls the execution of the target code.

At the start of each simulation, the emulator begins interpreting instructions in the target code, one at a time. Thus, if the code includes a decryption routine that decrypts and hence exposes the virus, that code is interpreted. In effect, the virus does the work for the antivirus program by exposing the virus. Periodically, the control module interrupts interpretation to scan the target code for virus signatures.

During interpretation, the target code can cause no damage to the actual personal computer environment, because it is being interpreted in a completely controlled environment.

The most difficult design issue with a GD scanner is to determine how long to run each interpretation. Typically, virus elements are activated soon after a program begins executing, but this need not be the case. The longer the scanner emulates a particular program, the more likely it is to catch any hidden viruses. However, the antivirus program can take up only a limited amount of time and resources before users complain.

Digital Immune System   The digital immune system is a comprehensive approach to virus protection developed by IBM [WHIT99, KEPH97a, KEPH97b]. The motivation for this development has been the rising threat of Internet-based virus propagation. We first say a few words about this threat and then summarize IBM's approach.

Traditionally, the virus threat was characterized by the relatively slow spread of new viruses and new mutations. Antivirus software was typically updated on a monthly basis, and this was sufficient to control the problem. Up until the late 1990s, the Internet played a comparatively small role in the spread of viruses. But as [CHES97] points out, two major trends in Internet technology have an increasing impact on the rate of virus propagation:

- **Integrated mail systems:** Systems such as Lotus Notes and Microsoft Outlook make it very simple to send anything to anyone and to work with objects that are received.
- **Mobile-program systems:** Capabilities such as Java and ActiveX allow programs to move on their own from one system to another.

In response to the threat posed by these Internet-based capabilities, IBM has developed a prototype digital immune system. This system expands on the use of program emulation discussed in the preceding subsection and provides a general-purpose emulation and virus-detection system. The objective of this system is to provide rapid response time so that viruses can be stamped out almost as soon as they are introduced. When a new virus enters an organization, the immune system automatically captures it, analyzes it, adds detection and shielding for it, removes it, and passes information about that virus to systems running IBM AntiVirus so that it can be detected before it is allowed to run elsewhere.

Figure 16.9 illustrates the typical steps in digital immune system operation:

1. A monitoring program on each PC uses a variety of heuristics based on system behavior, suspicious changes to programs, or family signature to infer that a virus may be present. The monitoring program forwards a copy of any program thought to be infected to an administrative machine within the organization.
2. The administrative machine encrypts the sample and sends it to a central virus analysis machine.
3. This machine creates an environment in which the infected program can be safely run for analysis. Techniques used for this purpose include emulation, or the creation of a protected environment within which the suspect program can be executed and monitored. The virus analysis machine then produces a prescription for identifying and removing the virus.
4. The resulting prescription is sent back to the administrative machine.
5. The administrative machine forwards the prescription to the infected client.
6. The prescription is also forwarded to other clients in the organization.
7. Subscribers around the world receive regular antivirus updates that protect them from the new virus.

The success of the digital immune system depends on the ability of the virus analysis machine to detect new and innovative virus strains. By constantly analyzing and monitoring the viruses found in the wild, it should be possible continually to update the digital immune software to keep up with the threat.

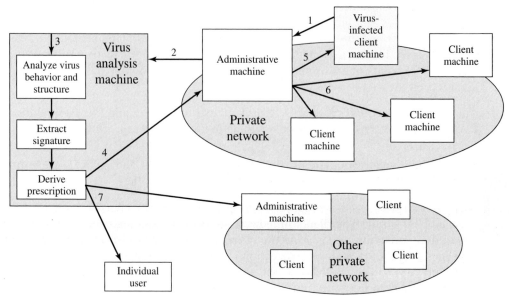

Figure 16.9   Digital Immune System

E-mail Viruses

The latest development in malicious software is the e-mail virus. The first rapidly spreading e-mail viruses, such as Melissa, made use of a Microsoft Word macro embedded in an attachment. If the recipient opens the e-mail attachment, the Word macro is activated. Then

1. The e-mail virus sends itself to everyone on the mailing list in the user's e-mail package.
2. The virus does local damage.

At the end of 1999, a more powerful version of the e-mail virus appeared. This newer version can be activated merely by opening an e-mail that contains the virus rather than opening an attachment. The virus uses the Visual Basic scripting language supported by the e-mail package.

Thus we see a new generation of malware that arrives via e-mail and uses email software features to replicate itself across the Internet. The virus propagates itself as soon as activated (either by opening an e-mail attachment of by opening the e-mail) to all of the e-mail addresses known to the infected host. As a result, whereas viruses used to take months or years to propagate, they now do so in hours. This makes it very difficult for antivirus software to respond before much damage is done. Ultimately, a greater degree of security must be built into Internet utility and application software on PCs to counter the growing threat [SCHN99].

16.5 TRUSTED SYSTEMS

Much of what we have discussed so far has been concerned with protecting a given message or item from passive or active attack by a given user. A somewhat different but widely applicable requirement is to protect data or resources on the basis of levels of security. This is commonly found in the military, where information is categorized as unclassified (U), confidential (C), secret (S), top secret (TS), or beyond. This concept is equally applicable in other areas, where information can be organized into gross categories and users can be granted clearances to access certain categories of data. For example, the highest level of security might be for strategic corporate planning documents and data, accessible by only corporate officers and their staff; next might come sensitive financial and personnel data, accessible only by administration personnel, corporate officers, and so on.

When multiple categories or levels of data are defined, the requirement is referred to as **multilevel security**. The general statement of the requirement for multilevel security is that a subject at a high level may not convey information to a subject at a lower or noncomparable level unless that flow accurately reflects the will of an authorized user. For implementation purposes, this requirement is in two parts and is simply stated. A multilevel secure system must enforce the following:

- **No read up:** A subject can only read an object of less or equal security level. This is referred to in the literature as the **simple security property**.
- **No write down:** A subject can only write into an object of greater or equal security level. This is referred to in the literature as the * property[1] (pronounced *star property*).

These two rules, if properly enforced, provide multilevel security. For a data processing system, the approach that has been taken, and has been the object of much research and development, is based on the reference monitor concept. This approach is depicted in Figure 16.10. The reference monitor is a controlling element in the hardware and operating system of a computer that regulates the access of subjects to objects on the basis of security parameters of the subject and object. The reference monitor has access to a file, known as the *security kernel database*, that lists the access privileges (security clearance) of each subject and the protection attributes (classification level) of each object. The reference monitor enforces the security rules (no read up, no write down) and has the following properties:

- **Complete mediation:** The security rules are enforced on every access, not just, for example, when a file is opened.
- **Isolation:** The reference monitor and database are protected from unauthorized modification.

---

[1]The "*" does not stand for anything. No one could think of an appropriate name for the property during the writing of the first report on the model. The asterisk was a dummy character entered in the draft so that a text editor could rapidly find and replace all instances of its use once the property was named. No name was ever devised, and so the report was published with the "*" intact.

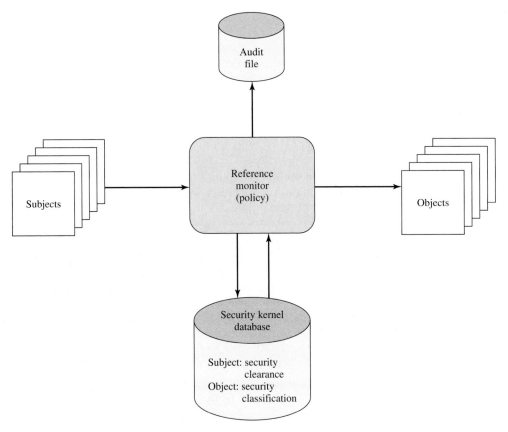

Figure 16.10 Reference Monitor Concept

- **Verifiability:** The reference monitor's correctness must be provable. That is, it must be possible to demonstrate mathematically that the reference monitor enforces the security rules and provides complete mediation and isolation.

These are stiff requirements. The requirement for complete mediation means that every access to data within main memory and on disk and tape must be mediated. Pure software implementations impose too high a performance penalty to be practical; the solution must be at least partly in hardware. The requirement for isolation means that it must not be possible for an attacker, no matter how clever, to change the logic of the reference monitor or the contents of the security kernel database. Finally, the requirement for mathematical proof is formidable for something as complex as a general-purpose computer. A system that can provide such verification is referred to as a **trusted system**.

A final element illustrated in Figure 16.10 is an audit file. Important security events, such as detected security violations and authorized changes to the security kernel database, are stored in the audit file.

In an effort to meet its own needs and as a service to the public, the U.S. Department of Defense in 1981 established the Computer Security Center within the National Security Agency (NSA) with the goal of encouraging the widespread availability of trusted computer systems. This goal is realized through the center's Commercial Product Evaluation Program. In essence, the center attempts to evaluate commercially available products as meeting the security requirements just outlined. The center classifies evaluated products according to the range of security features that they provide. These evaluations are needed for Department of Defense procurements but are published and freely available. Hence, they can serve as guidance to commercial customers for the purchase of commercially available, off-the-shelf equipment.

Trojan Horse Defense

One way to secure against Trojan horse attacks is the use of a secure, trusted operating system. Figure 16.11 illustrates an example [BOEB85]. In this case, a Trojan horse is used to get around the standard security mechanism used by most file management and operating systems: the access control list. In this example, a user named Bob interacts through a program with a data file containing the critically sensitive character string "CPE170KS." User Bob has created the file with read/write permission provided only to programs executing on his own behalf: that is, only processes that are owned by Bob may access the file.

The Trojan horse attack begins when a hostile user, named Alice, gains legitimate access to the system and installs both a Trojan horse program and a private file to be used in the attack as a "back pocket." Alice gives read/write permission to herself for this file and gives Bob write-only permission (Figure 16.11a). Alice now induces Bob to invoke the Trojan horse program, perhaps by advertising it as a useful utility. When the program detects that it is being executed by Bob, it reads the sensitive character string from Bob's file and copies it into Alice's back-pocket file (Figure 16.11b). Both the read and write operations satisfy the constraints imposed by access control lists. Alice then has only to access the back-pocket file at a later time to learn the value of the string.

Now consider the use of a secure operating system in this scenario (Figure 16.11c). Security levels are assigned to subjects at logon on the basis of criteria such as the terminal from which the computer is being accessed and the user involved, as identified by password/ID. In this example, there are two security levels, sensitive (gray) and public (white), ordered so that sensitive is higher than public. Processes owned by Bob and Bob's data file are assigned the security level sensitive. Alice's file and processes are restricted to public. If Bob invokes the Trojan horse program (Figure 16.11d), that program acquires Bob's security level. It is therefore able, under the simple security property, to observe the sensitive character string. When the program attempts to store the string in a public file (the back-pocket file), however, the *-property is violated and the attempt is disallowed by the reference monitor. Thus, the attempt to write into the back-pocket file is denied even though the access control list permits it: The security policy takes precedence over the access control list mechanism.

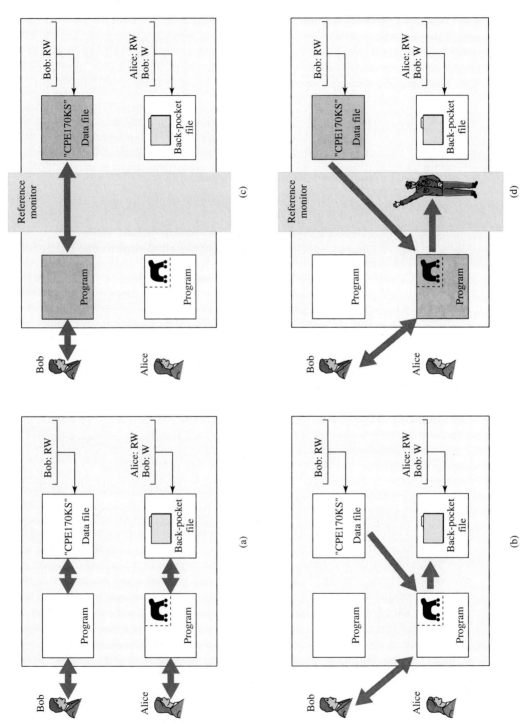

Figure 16.11 Trojan Horse and Secure Operating System

714

16.6 WINDOWS SECURITY

A good example of the access control concepts we have been discussing is the Windows access control facility, which exploits object-oriented concepts to provide a powerful and flexible access control capability.

Windows provides a uniform access control facility that applies to processes, threads, files, semaphores, windows, and other objects. Access control is governed by two entities: an access token associated with each process and a security descriptor associated with each object for which interprocess access is possible.

Access Control Scheme

When a user logs on to an Windows system, Windows uses a name/password scheme to authenticate the user. If the logon is accepted, a process is created for the user and an access token is associated with that process object. The access token, whose details are described later, include a security ID (SID), which is the identifier by which this user is known to the system for purposes of security. When any additional processes are spawned by the initial user process, the new process object inherits the same access token.

The access token serves two purposes:

1. It keeps all necessary security information together to speed access validation. When any process associated with a user attempts access, the security subsystem can make use of the token associated with that process to determine the user's access privileges.

2. It allows each process to modify its security characteristics in limited ways without affecting other processes running on behalf of the user.

The chief significance of the second point has to do with privileges that may be associated with a user. The access token indicates which privileges a user may have. Generally, the token is initialized with each of these privileges in a disabled state. Subsequently, if one of the user's processes needs to perform a privileged operation, the process may enable the appropriate privilege and attempt access. It would be undesirable to keep all of the security information for a user in one systemwide place, because in that case enabling a privilege for one process enables it for all of them.

Associated with each object for which interprocess access is possible is a security descriptor. The chief component of the security descriptor is an access control list that specifies access rights for various users and user groups for this object. When a process attempts to access this object , the SID of the process is matched against the access control list of the object to determine if access will be allowed.

When an application opens a reference to a securable object, Windows verifies that the object's security descriptor grants the application's user access. If the check succeeds, Windows caches the resulting granted access rights.

An important aspect of Windows security is the concept of impersonation, which simplifies the use of security in a client/server environment. If client and

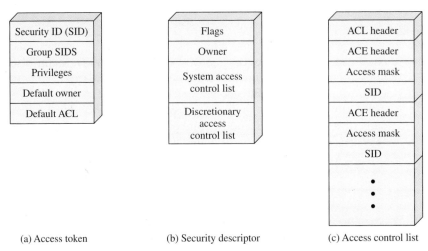

| (a) Access token | (b) Security descriptor | (c) Access control list |

Figure 16.12   Windows Security Structures

server talk through a RPC connection, the server can temporarily assume the identity of the client so that it can evaluate a request for access relative to that client's rights. After the access, the server reverts to its own identity.

Access Token

Figure 16.12a shows the general structure of an access token, which includes the following parameters:

- **Security ID:** Identifies a user uniquely across all of the machines on the network. This generally corresponds to a user's logon name.
- **Group SIDs:** A list of the groups to which this user belongs. A group is simply a set of user IDs that are identified as a group for purposes of access control. Each group has a unique group SID. Access to an object can be defined on the basis of group SIDs, individual SIDs, or a combination.
- **Privileges:** A list of security-sensitive system services that this user may call. An example is create token. Another example is the set backup privilege; users with this privilege are allowed to use a backup tool to back up files that they normally would not be able to read. Most users will have no privileges.
- **Default owner:** If this process creates another object, this field specifies who is the owner of the new object. Generally, the owner of the new process is the same as the owner of the spawning process. However, a user may specify that the default owner of any processes spawned by this process is a group SID to which this user belongs.
- **Default ACL:** This is an initial list of protections applied to the objects that the user creates. The user may subsequently alter the ACL for any object that it owns or that one of its groups owns.

Security Descriptors

Figure 16.12b shows the general structure of a security descriptor, which includes the following parameters:

- **Flags:** Defines the type and contents of a security descriptor. The flags indicate whether or not the SACL and DACL are present, whether or not they were placed on the object by a defaulting mechanism, and whether the pointers in the descriptor use absolute or relative addressing. Relative descriptors are required for objects that are transmitted over a network, such as information transmitted in a RPC.

- **Owner:** The owner of the object can generally perform any action on the security descriptor. The owner can be an individual or a group SID. The owner has the authority to change the contents of the DACL.

- **System Access Control List (SACL):** Specifies what kinds of operations on the object should generate audit messages. An application must have the corresponding privilege in its access token to read or write the SACL of any object. This is to prevent unauthorized applications from reading SACLs (thereby learning what not to do to avoid generating audits) or writing them (to generate many audits to cause an illicit operation to go unnoticed).

- **Discretionary Access Control List (DACL):** Determines which users and groups can access this object for which operations. It consists of a list of access control entries (ACEs).

When an object is created, the creating process can assign as owner its own SID or any group SID in its access token. The creating process cannot assign an owner that is not in the current access token. Subsequently, any process that has been granted the right to change the owner of an object may do so, but again with the same restriction. The reason for the restriction is to prevent a user from covering his tracks after attempting some unauthorized action.

Let us look in more detail at the structure of access control lists, because these are at the heart of the Windows access control facility (Figure 16.12c). Each list consists of an overall header and a variable number of access control entries. Each entry specifies an individual or group SID and an access mask that defines the rights to be granted to this SID. When a process attempts to access an object, the object manager in the Windows executive reads the SID and group SIDs from the access token and then scans down the object's DACL. If a match is found, that is if an ACE is found with a SID that matches one of the SIDs from the access token, then the process has the access rights specified by the access mask in that ACE.

Figure 16.13 shows the contents of the access mask. The least significant 16 bits specify access rights that apply to a particular type of object. For example, bit 0 for a file object is File_Read_Data access and bit 0 for an event object is Event_Query_Status access.

The most significant 16 bits of the mask contains bits that apply to all types of objects. Five of these are referred to as standard access types:

- **Synchronize:** Gives permission to synchronize execution with some event associated with this object. In particular, this object can be used in a wait function.

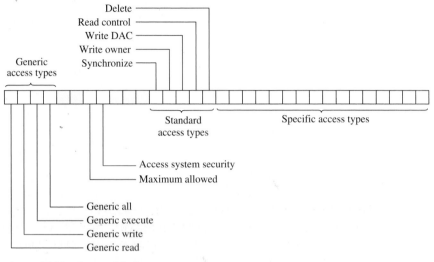

Figure 16.13 Access Mask

- **Write_owner:** Allows a program to modify the owner of the object. This is useful because the owner of an object can always change the protection on the object (the owner may not be denied Write DAC access).
- **Write_DAC:** Allows the application to modify the DACL and hence the protection on this object.
- **Read_control:** Allows the application to query the owner and DACL fields of the security descriptor of this object.
- **Delete:** Allows the application to delete this object.

The high-order half of the access mask also contains the four generic access types. These bits provide a convenient way to set specific access types in a number of different object types. For example, suppose an application wishes to create several types of objects and ensure that users have read access to the objects, even though read has a somewhat different meaning for each object type. To protect each object of each type without the generic access bits, the application would have to construct a different ACE for each type of object and be careful to pass the correct ACE when creating each object. It is more convenient to create a single ACE that expresses the generic concept allow read, simply apply this ACE to each object that is created, and have the right thing happen. That is the purpose of the generic access bits, which are

- Generic_all: Allow all access
- Generic_execute: Allow execution if executable
- Generic_write: Allow write access
- Generic_read: Allow read only access

The generic bits also affect the standard access types. For example, for a file object, the Generic_Read bit maps to the standard bits Read_Control and Synchronize and to the object-specific bits File_Read_Data, File_Read_Attributes, and File_Read_EA. Placing an ACE on a file object that grants some SID Generic_Read grants those five access rights as if they had been specified individually in the access mask.

The remaining two bits in the access mask have special meanings. The Access_System_Security bit allows modifying audit and alarm control for this object. However, not only must this bit be set in the ACE for a SID, but the access token for the process with that SID must have the corresponding privilege enabled.

Finally, the Maximum_Allowed bit is not really an access bit, but a bit that modifies Windows 's algorithm for scanning the DACL for this SID. Normally, Windows will scan through the DACL until it reaches an ACE that specifically grants (bit set) or denies (bit not set) the access requested by the requesting process or until it reaches the end of the DACL, in which latter case access is denied. The Maximum_Allowed bit allows the object's owner to define a set of access rights that is the maximum that will be allowed to a given user. With this in mind, suppose that an application does not know all of the operations that it is going to be asked to perform on an object during a session. There are three options for requesting access:

1. Attempt to open the object for all possible accesses. The disadvantage of this approach is that the access may be denied even though the application may have all of the access rights actually required for this session.

2. Only open the object when a specific access is requested, and open a new handle to the object for each different type of request. This is generally the preferred method because it will not unnecessarily deny access, nor will it allow more access than necessary. However, it imposes additional overhead.

3. Attempt to open the object for as much access as the object will allow this SID. The advantage is that the user will not be artificially denied access, but the application may have more access than it needs. This latter situation may mask bugs in the application.

An important feature of Windows security is that applications can make use of the Windows security framework for user-defined objects. For example, a database server might create it own security descriptors and attach them to portions of a database. In addition to normal read/write access constraints, the server could secure database-specific operations, such as scrolling within a result set or performing a join. It would be the server's responsibility to define the meaning of special rights and perform access checks. But the checks would occur in a standard context, using systemwide user/group accounts and audit logs. The extensible security model should prove useful to implementers of foreign files systems.

16.7 SUMMARY

The requirements for security are best assessed by examining the various security threats faced by an organization. The interruption of service is a threat to availability. The interception of information is a threat to secrecy. Finally, both the modification of legitimate information and the unauthorized fabrication of information are threats to integrity.

One key area of computer security involves the protection of memory. This is essential in any system in which multiple processes are active at one time. Virtual memory schemes are typically equipped with the appropriate mechanisms for this task.

Another important security technique is access control. The purpose of access control is to ensure that only authorized users have access to a particular system and its individual resources and that access to and modification of particular portions of data are limited to authorized individuals and programs. Strictly speaking, access control is a computer security rather than a network security issue. That is, in most cases, access control mechanisms are implemented within a single computer to control the access to that computer. However, because much of the access to a computer is by means of a networking or communications facility, access control mechanisms must be designed that can operate effectively in a distributed, networking environment.

An increasingly worrisome type of threat is that posed by viruses and similar software mechanisms. These threats exploit vulnerabilities in system software either to gain unauthorized access to information or to degrade system service.

A technology that is coming to have increasing application in military and commercial environments is the trusted system. The trusted system provides a means of regulating access to data on the basis of who is authorized to access what. The key point is that the system is designed and implemented in such a way that the users can have complete trust that the system will enforce the given security policy.

16.8 RECOMMENDED READINGS AND WEB SITES

The topics in this chapter are covered in more detail in [STAL03]. For coverage of cryptographic algorithms, [SCHN96] is an essential reference work; it contains descriptions of numerous cryptographic algorithms and protocols. Good discussions of operating system issues can be found in [PIEP03], [GOLL99], and [PFLE97]. Two useful survey articles on intrusion detection are [KENT00] and [MCHU00]. For a thorough understanding of viruses, the book to read is [HARL01]. Good overview articles on viruses and worms are [CASS01], [FORR97], [KEPH97], and [NACH97].

[COX00] and [CLER04] provide detailed coverage of Windows security; both focus on administration and management, but both discuss some features of Windows internals related to security.

CASS01 Cass, S. "Anatomy of Malice." IEEE Spectrum, November 2001.

CLER04 Clercq, J. *Windows Server 2003 Security Infrastructure: Core Security Features*. Burlington, MA: Digital Press, 2004.

COX00 Cox, P., and Sheldon, T. *Windows NT Security Handbook*. New York: Osborne McGraw-Hill, 2000.

FORR97 Forrest, S.; Hofmeyr, S.; and Somayaji, A. "Computer Immunology." Communications of the ACM, October 1997.

GOLL99 Gollmann, D. *Computer Security*. New York: Wiley, 1999.

HARL01 Harley, D.; Slade, R.; and Gattiker, U. *Viruses Revealed*. New York: Osborne/McGraw-Hill, 2001.

KENT00 Kent, S. "On the Trail of Intrusions into Information Systems." *IEEE Spectrum*, December 2000.

KEPH97 Kephart, J.; Sorkin, G.; Chess, D.; and White, S. "Fighting Computer Viruses." *Scientific American*, November 1997.

MCHU00 McHugh, J.; Christie, A.; and Allen, J. "The Role of Intrusion Detection Systems." IEEE Software, September/October 2000.

NACH97 Nachenberg, C. "Computer Virus-Antivirus Coevolution." Communications of the ACM, January 1997.

PEIP03 Pieprzyk, J.; Hardjono, T.; and Seberry, J. *Fundamentals of Computer Security*. New York: Springer, 2003.

PFLE97 Pfleeger, C. *Security in Computing*. Upper Saddle River, NJ: Prentice Hall PTR, 1997.

SCHN96 Schneier, B. *Applied Cryptography*. New York: Wiley, 1996.

STAL03 Stallings, W. *Cryptography and Network Security: Principles and Practice, 3rd edition*. Upper Saddle River, NJ: Prentice Hall, 2003.

Recommended Web Sites:

- **Computer Security Resource Center:** Maintained by the National Institute on Standards and Technology (NIST). Contains a broad range of information on security threats, technology, and standards.
- **CERT Coordination Center:** The organization that grew from the computer emergency response team formed by the Defense Advanced Research Projects Agency. Site provides good information on Internet security threats, vulnerabilities, and attack statistics.
- **Intrusion Detection Working Group:** Includes all of the documents generated by this group.
- **AntiVirus On-line:** IBM's site on virus information; one of the best.
- **Vmyths:** Dedicated to exposing virus hoaxes and dispelling misconceptions about real viruses.

16.9 KEY TERMS, REVIEW QUESTIONS, AND PROBLEMS

Key Terms

access control	encryption	replay
active threat	e-mail virus	RSA
advanced encryption standard (AES)	integrity	symmetric encryption
	intruder	trap door
authenticity	intrusion detection	triple DES (3DES)
availability	logic bomb	trojan horse
confidentiality	macro virus	trusted system
conventional encryption	malicious software (malware)	virus
data encryption standard (DES)	passive threat	worm
	password	zombie
denial of service	public-key encryption	

Review Questions

16.1   What are the fundamental requirements addressed by computer security?

16.2   What is the difference between passive and active security threats?

16.3   List and briefly define categories of passive and active security threats.

16.4   What elements are required for the most common user access control techniques?

16.5   In access control, what is the difference between a subject and an object?

16.6   Explain the purpose of the salt in Figure 16.6.

16.7   Explain the difference between statistical anomaly intrusion detection and rule-based intrusion detection.

16.8   The e-mail attachment and e-mail VBS malware developments in 1999 and 2000 (e.g., Melissa, love letter) are termed e-mail viruses in the media. Would the term e-mail worms be more accurate?

16.9   What role does encryption play in the design of viruses?

16.10   What are the two general approaches to attacking a conventional encryption scheme?

16.11   What are DES and triple DES?

16.12   How is the AES expected to be an improvement over triple DES?

16.13   What evaluation criteria will be used in assessing AES candidates?

16.14   Explain the difference between conventional encryption and public-key encryption.

16.15   What are the distinctions among the terms public key, private key, secret key?

Problems

16.1   Assume that passwords are selected from four-character combinations of 26 alphabetic characters. Assume that an adversary is able to attempt passwords at a rate of one per second.
   a.   Assuming no feedback to the adversary until each attempt has been completed, what is the expected time to discover the correct password?
   b.   Assuming feedback to the adversary flagging an error as each incorrect character is entered, what is the expected time to discover the correct password?

16.2   Assume that a source element of length k is mapped in some uniform fashion into a target element of length p. If each digit can take on one of r values, then the number of source elements is r^k and the number of target elements is the smaller number i. A particular source element x_i is mapped to a particular target element y_j.
   a.   What is the probability that the correct source element can be selected by an adversary on one try?
   b.   What is the probability that a different source element x_k ($x_i \neq x_k$) that results in the same target element, y_j, could be produced by an adversary?
   c.   What is the probability that the correct target element can be produced by an adversary on one try?

16.3   A phonetic password generator picks two segments randomly for each six-letter password. The form of each segment is CVC (consonant, vowel, consonant), where V = <a, e, i, o, u> and C = $\overline{V}$.
   a.   What is the total password population?
   b.   What is the probability of an adversary guessing a password correctly?

16.4   Assume that passwords are limited to the use of the 95 printable ASCII characters and that all passwords are 10 characters in length. Assume a password cracker with an encryption rate of 6.4 million encryptions per second. How long will it take to test exhaustively all possible passwords on a UNIX system?

16.5 Because of the known risks of the UNIX password system, the SunOS-4.0 documentation recommends that the password file be removed and replaced with a publicly readable file called /etc/publickey. An entry in the file for user A consists of a user's identifier ID_A, the user's public key, KU_a, and the corresponding private key KR_a. This private key is encrypted using DES with key derived from the user's login password P_a. When A logs in the system decrypts $E_{P_a}[KR_a]$ to obtain KR_a. We use the notation $E_x[a]$ to mean the encryption or decryption of a using key x.

   a. The system then verifies that P_a was correctly supplied. How?
   b. How can an opponent attack this system?

16.6 The encryption scheme used for UNIX passwords is one way; it is not possible to reverse it. Therefore, would it be accurate to say that this is, in fact, a hash code rather than an encryption of the password?

16.7 It was stated that the inclusion of the salt in the UNIX password scheme increases the difficulty of guessing by a factor of 4096. But the salt is stored in plaintext in the same entry as the corresponding ciphertext password. Therefore, those two characters are known to the attacker and need not be guessed. Therefore, why is it asserted that the salt increases security?

16.8 Assuming that you have successfully answered the preceding problem and understand the significance of the salt, here is another question. Wouldn't it be possible to thwart completely all password crackers by dramatically increasing the salt size to, say, 24 or 48 bits?

16.9 The question arises as to whether it is possible to develop a program that can analyze a piece of software to determine if it is a virus. Consider that we have a program D that is supposed to be able to do that. That is, for any program P, if we run D(P), the result returned is TRUE (P is a virus) or FALSE (P is not a virus). Now consider the following program:

```
Program CV :=
    { ...
    main-program :=
        {if D(CV) then goto next:
            else infect-executable;
        }
    next:
    }
```

In the preceding program, infect-executable is a module that scans memory for executable programs and replicates itself in those programs. Determine if D can correctly decide whether CV is a virus.

16.10 The necessity of the "no read up" rule for a multilevel secure system is fairly obvious. What is the importance of the "no write down" rule?

16.11 In Figure 16.11 one link of the Trojan horse copy-and-observe-later chain is broken. There are two other possible angles of attack by Alice: Alice logging on and attempting to read the string directly, and Alice assigning a security level of sensitive to the back-pocket file. Does the reference monitor prevent these attacks?

16.12 Suppose that someone suggests the following way to confirm that the two of you are both in possession of the same secret key. You create a random bit string the length of the key, XOR it with the key, and send the result over the channel. Your partner XORs the incoming block with the key (which should be the same as your key) and sends it back. You check and if what you receive is your original random string, you have verified that your partner has the same secret key, yet neither of you has ever transmitted the key. Is there a flaw in this scheme?

APPENDIX 16A ENCRYPTION

The essential technology underlying virtually all automated network and computer security applications is cryptography. Two fundamental approaches are in use: symmetric encryption, also known as conventional encryption, and public-key encryption, also known as asymmetric encryption. This appendix provides an overview of both types of encryption, together with a brief discussion of some important encryption algorithms.

Symmetric Encryption

Symmetric encryption was the only type of encryption in use prior to the introduction of public-key encryption in the late 1970s. Symmetric encryption has been used for secret communication by countless individuals and groups, from Julius Caesar to the German U-boat force to present-day diplomatic, military, and commercial users. It remains by far the more widely used of the two types of encryption.

A symmetric encryption scheme has five ingredients (Figure 16.14):

- **Plaintext:** This is the original message or data that is fed into the algorithm as input.
- **Encryption algorithm:** The encryption algorithm performs various substitutions and transformations on the plaintext.
- **Secret key:** The secret key is also input to the encryption algorithm. The exact substitutions and transformations performed by the algorithm depend on the key.
- **Ciphertext:** This is the scrambled message produced as output. It depends on the plaintext and the secret key. For a given message, two different keys will produce two different ciphertexts.
- **Decryption algorithm:** This is essentially the encryption algorithm run in reverse. It takes the ciphertext and the secret key and produces the original plaintext.

There are two requirements for secure use of symmetric encryption:

1. We need a strong encryption algorithm. At a minimum, we would like the algorithm to be such that an opponent who knows the algorithm and has access to one or more ciphertexts would be unable to decipher the ciphertext or figure out the key. This requirement is usually stated in a stronger form: The opponent should be unable to decrypt ciphertext or discover the key even if he or she is in possession of a number of ciphertexts together with the plaintext that produced each ciphertext.

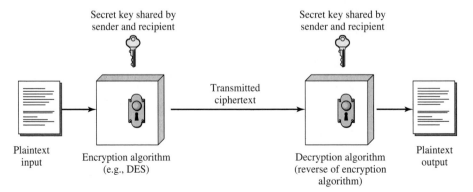

Figure 16.14   Simplified Model of Symmetric Encryption

2. Sender and receiver must have obtained copies of the secret key in a secure fashion and must keep the key secure. If someone can discover the key and knows the algorithm, all communication using this key is readable.

There are two general approaches to attacking a symmetric encryption scheme. The first attack is known as **cryptanalysis**. Cryptanalytic attacks rely on the nature of the algorithm plus perhaps some knowledge of the general characteristics of the plaintext or even some sample plaintext-ciphertext pairs. This type of attack exploits the characteristics of the algorithm to attempt to deduce a specific plaintext or to deduce the key being used. If the attack succeeds in deducing the key, the effect is catastrophic: All future and past messages encrypted with that key are compromised.

The second method, known as the **brute-force** attack, is to try every possible key on a piece of ciphertext until an intelligible translation into plaintext is obtained. On average, half of all possible keys must be tried to achieve success. Table 16.4 shows how much time is involved for various key sizes. The table shows results for each key size, assuming that it takes 1 μs to perform a single decryption, a reasonable order of magnitude for today's computers. With the use of massively parallel organizations of microprocessors, it may be possible to achieve processing rates many orders of magnitude greater. The final column of the table considers the results for a system that can process 1 million keys per microsecond. As one can see, at this performance level, a 56-bit key can no longer be considered computationally secure.

The most commonly used symmetric encryption algorithms are block ciphers. A block cipher processes the plaintext input in fixed-size blocks and produces a block of ciphertext of equal size for each plaintext block. The two most important symmetric algorithms, both of which are block ciphers, are the Data Encryption Standard (DES) and the Advanced Encryption Standard (AES).

The Data Encryption Standard (DES) DES has been the dominant encryption algorithm since its introduction in 1977. However, because DES uses only a 56-bit key, it was only a matter of time before computer processing speed made DES obsolete. In 1998, the Electronic Frontier Foundation (EFF) announced that it had broken a DES challenge using a special-purpose "DES cracker" machine that was built for less than $250,000. The attack took less than three days. The EFF has published a detailed description of the machine, enabling others to build their own cracker [EFF98]. And, of course, hardware prices continue to drop as speeds increase, making DES worthless.

The life of DES was extended by the use of triple DES (3DES), which involves repeating the basic DES algorithm three times, using either two or three unique keys, for a key size of 112 or 168 bits.

Table 16.4   Average Time Required for Exhaustive Key Search

Key Size (bits)	Number of Alternative Keys	Time required at 1 encryption/μs	Time required at 10^6 encryptions/μs
32	$2^{32} = 4.3 \times 10^9$	2^{31} μs = 35.8 minutes	2.15 milliseconds
56	$2^{56} = 7.2 \times 10^{16}$	2^{55} μs = 1142 years	10.01 hours
128	$2^{128} = 3.4 \times 10^{38}$	2^{127} μs = 5.4 $\times 10^{24}$ years	5.4 $\times 10^{18}$ years
168	$2^{168} = 3.7 \times 10^{50}$	2^{167} μs = 5.9 $\times 10^{36}$ years	5.9 $\times 10^{30}$ years
26 characters (permutation)	$26! = 4 \times 10^{26}$	2×10^{26} μs = 6.4 $\times 10^{12}$ years	6.4 $\times 10^6$ years

The principal drawback of 3DES is that the algorithm is relatively sluggish in software. A secondary drawback is that both DES and 3DES use a 64-bit block size. For reasons of both efficiency and security, a larger block size is desirable.

Advanced Encryption Standard   Because of these drawbacks, 3DES is not a reasonable candidate for long-term use. As a replacement, the National Institute of Standards and Technology (NIST) in 1997 issued a call for proposals for a new Advanced Encryption Standard (AES), which should have a security strength equal to or better than 3DES and significantly improved efficiency. In addition to these general requirements, NIST specified that AES must be a symmetric block cipher with a block length of 128 bits and support for key lengths of 128, 192, and 256 bits. Evaluation criteria include security, computational efficiency, memory requirements, hardware and software suitability, and flexibility. In 2001, NIST issued AES as a federal information processing standard (FIPS 197).

Public-Key Encryption

Public-key encryption, first publicly proposed by Diffie and Hellman in 1976, is the first truly revolutionary advance in encryption in literally thousands of years. For one thing, public-key algorithms are based on mathematical functions rather than on simple operations on bit patterns. More important, public-key cryptography is asymmetric, involving the use of two separate keys, in contrast to symmetric encryption, which uses only one key. The use of two keys has profound consequences in the areas of confidentiality, key distribution, and authentication.

Before proceeding, we should first mention several common misconceptions concerning public-key encryption. One is that public-key encryption is more secure from cryptanalysis than symmetric encryption. In fact, the security of any encryption scheme depends on the length of the key and the computational work involved in breaking a cipher. There is nothing in principle about either symmetric or public-key encryption that makes one superior to another from the point of view of resisting cryptanalysis. A second misconception is that public-key encryption is a general-purpose technique that has made symmetric encryption obsolete. On the contrary, because of the computational overhead of current public-key encryption schemes, there seems no foreseeable likelihood that symmetric encryption will be abandoned. Finally, there is a feeling that key distribution is trivial when using public-key encryption, compared to the rather cumbersome handshaking involved with key distribution centers for symmetric encryption. In fact, some form of protocol is needed, often involving a central agent, and the procedures involved are no simpler nor any more efficient than those required for symmetric encryption.

A public-key encryption scheme has six ingredients (Figure 16.15):

- **Plaintext:** This is the readable message or data that is fed into the algorithm as input.
- **Encryption algorithm:** The encryption algorithm performs various transformations on the plaintext.
- **Public and private key:** This is a pair of keys that have been selected so that if one is used for encryption, the other is used for decryption. The exact transformations performed by the encryption algorithm depend on the public or private key that is provided as input.
- **Ciphertext:** This is the scrambled message produced as output. It depends on the plaintext and the key. For a given message, two different keys will produce two different ciphertexts.
- **Decryption algorithm:** This algorithm accepts the ciphertext and the matching key and produces the original plaintext.

The process works (produces the correct plaintext on output) regardless of the order in which the pair of keys is used. As the names suggest, the public key of the pair is made public for others to use, while the private key is known only to its owner.

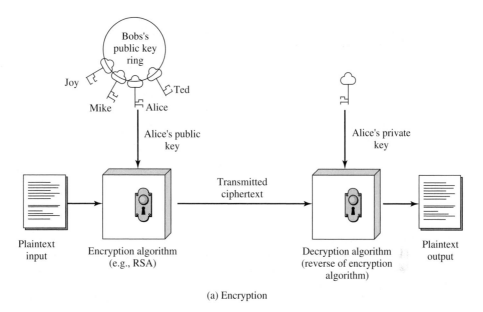

(a) Encryption

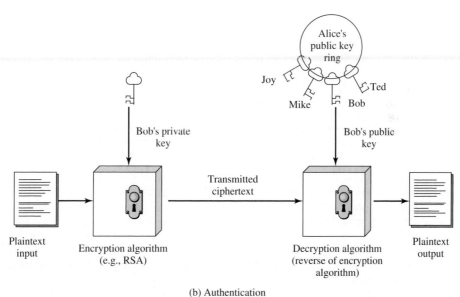

(b) Authentication

Figure 16.15   Public-Key Cryptography

Now, say that Bob wants to send a private message to Alice and suppose that he has Alice's public key and Alice has the matching private key (Figure 16.15a). Using Alice's public key, Bob encrypts the message to produce ciphertext. The ciphertext is then transmitted to Alice. When Alice gets the ciphertext, she decrypts it using her private key. Because only Alice has a copy of her private key, no one else can read the message.

Public-key encryption can be used in another way, as illustrated in Figure 16.15b. Suppose that Bob wants to send a message to Alice and, although it isn't important that the message be kept secret, he wants Alice to be certain that the message is indeed from him. In this case Bob uses his own private key to encrypt the message. When Alice receives the cipher-text, she finds that she can decrypt it with Bob's public key, thus proving that the message must have been encrypted by Bob: No one else has Bob's private key and therefore no one else could have created a ciphertext that could be decrypted with Bob's public key.

A general-purpose public-key cryptographic algorithm relies on one key for encryption and a different but related key for decryption. Furthermore, these algorithms have the following important characteristics:

- It is computationally infeasible to determine the decryption key given only knowledge of the cryptographic algorithm and the encryption key.
- Either of the two related keys can be used for encryption, with the other used for decryption.

The essential steps are the following:

1. Each user generates a pair of keys to be used for the encryption and decryption of messages.
2. Each user places one of the two keys in a public register or other accessible file. This is the public key. The companion key is kept private. As Figure 16.15a suggests, each user maintains a collection of public keys obtained from others.
3. If Bob wishes to send a private message to Alice, Bob encrypts the message using Alice's public key.
4. When Alice receives the message, she decrypts it using her private key. No other recipient can decrypt the message because only Alice knows Alice's private key.

With this approach, all participants have access to public keys, and private keys are generated locally by each participant and therefore need never be distributed. As long as a user protects his or her private key, incoming communication is secure. At any time, a user can change the private key and publish the companion public key to replace the old public key.

The key used in symmetric encryption is typically referred to as a **secret key**. The two keys used for public-key encryption are referred to as the **public key** and the **private key**. Invariably, the private key is kept secret, but it is referred to as a private key rather than a secret key to avoid confusion with symmetric encryption.

Rivest-Shamir-Adleman (RSA) Algorithm One of the first public-key schemes was developed in 1977 by Ron Rivest, Adi Shamir, and Len Adleman at MIT. The RSA scheme has since that time reigned supreme as the only widely accepted and implemented approach to public-key encryption. RSA is a cipher in which the plaintext and ciphertext are integers between 0 and $n - 1$ for some n. Encryption involves modular arithmetic. The strength of the algorithm is based on the difficulty of factoring numbers into their prime factors.

APPENDIX A

TOPICS IN CONCURRENCY

A.1 MUTUAL EXCLUSION: SOFTWARE APPROACHES

Software approaches can be implemented for concurrent processes that execute on a single processor or a multiprocessor machine with shared main memory. These approaches usually assume elementary mutual exclusion at the memory access level ([LAMP91], but see Problem A.3). That is, simultaneous accesses (reading and/or writing) to the same location in main memory are serialized by some sort of memory arbiter, although the order of access granting is not specified ahead of time. Beyond this, no support in the hardware, operating system, or programming language is assumed.

Dekker's Algorithm

Dijkstra [DIJK65] reported an algorithm for mutual exclusion for two processes, designed by the Dutch mathematician Dekker. Following Dijkstra, we develop the solution in stages. This approach has the advantage of illustrating many of the common bugs encountered in developing concurrent programs.

First Attempt As mentioned earlier, any attempt at mutual exclusion must rely on some fundamental exclusion mechanism in the hardware. The most common of these is the constraint that only one access to a memory location can be made at a time. Using this constraint, we reserve a global memory location labeled **turn**. A process (P0 or P1) wishing to execute its critical section first examines the contents of **turn**. If the value of **turn** is equal to the number of the process, then the process may proceed to its critical section. Otherwise, it is forced to wait. Our waiting process repeatedly reads the value of turn until it is allowed to enter its critical section. This procedure is known as **busy waiting**, or **spin waiting**, because the thwarted process can do nothing productive until it gets permission to enter its critical section. Instead, it must linger and periodically check the variable; thus it consumes processor time (busy) while waiting for its chance.

After a process has gained access to its critical section and after it has completed that section, it must update the value of **turn** to that of the other process.

In formal terms, there is a shared global variable:

int turn = 0;

Figure A.1a shows the program for the two processes. This solution guarantees the mutual exclusion property but has two drawbacks. First, processes must strictly alternate in their use of their critical section; therefore, the pace of execution is dictated by the slower of the two processes. If P0 uses its critical section only once per hour but P1 would like to use its critical section at a rate of 1000 times per hour, P1 is forced to adopt the pace of P0. A much more serious problem is that if one process fails, the other process is permanently blocked. This is true whether a process fails in its critical section or outside of it.

The foregoing construction is that of a **coroutine**. Coroutines are designed to be able to pass execution control back and forth between themselves (see Problem 5.1). While this is a useful structuring technique for a single process, it is inadequate to support concurrent processing.

```
/* PROCESS 0 */            /* PROCESS 1 */

•                          •
•                          •
while (turn != 0)          while (turn != 1)
     /* do nothing */;          /* do nothing */;
/* critical section*/;     /* critical section*/;
turn = 1;                  turn = 0;
•                          •
```

(a) First attempt

```
/* PROCESS 0 */            /* PROCESS 1 */

•                          •
•                          •
flag[0] = true;            flag[1] = true;
while (flag[1])            while (flag[0])
     /* do nothing */;          /* do nothing */;
/* critical section*/;     /* critical section*/;
flag[0] = false;           flag[1] = false;
•                          •
```

(c) Third attempt

```
/* PROCESS 0 */            /* PROCESS 1 */

•                          •
•                          •
while (flag[1])            while (flag[0])
     /* do nothing */;          /* do nothing */;
flag[0] = true;            flag[1] = true;
/*critical section*/;      /* critical section*/;
flag[0] = false;           flag[1] = false;
•                          •
```

(b) Second attempt

```
/* PROCESS 0 */            /* PROCESS 1 */

•                          •
•                          •
flag[0] = true;            flag[1] = true;
while (flag[1])            while (flag[0])
{                          {
   flag[0] = false;           flag[1] = false;
   /*delay */;                /*delay */;
   flag[0] = true;            flag[1] = true;
}                          }
/*critical section*/;      /* critical section*/;
flag[0] = false;           flag[1] = false;
•                          •
```

(d) Fourth attempt

Figure A.1   Mutual Exclusion Attempts

Second Attempt The problem with the first attempt is that it stores the name of the process that may enter its critical section, when in fact we need state information about both processes. In effect, each process should have its own key to the critical section so that if one fails, the other can still access its critical section. To meet this requirement a Boolean vector **flag** is defined, with **flag[0]** corresponding to P0 and **flag[1]** corresponding to P1. Each process may examine the other's flag but may not alter it. When a process wishes to enter its critical section, it periodically checks the other's flag until that flag has the value **false**, indicating that the other process is not in its critical section. The checking process immediately sets its own flag to **true** and proceeds to its critical section. When it leaves its critical section, it sets its flag to **false**.

The shared global variable[1] now is

> **enum**   boolean (false = 0; true = 1);
> **boolean**   flag[2] = {0, 0}

Figure A.1b shows the algorithm. If one process fails outside the critical section, including the flag-setting code, then the other process is not blocked. In fact, the other process can enter its critical section as often as it likes, because the flag of the other process is always false. However, if a process fails inside its critical section or after setting its flag to true just before entering its critical section, then the other process is permanently blocked.

This solution is, if anything, worse than the first attempt because it does not even guarantee mutual exclusion. Consider the following sequence:

> P0 executes the **while** statement and finds **flag[1]** set to false.
>
> P1 executes the **while** statement and finds **flag[0]** set to false.
>
> P0 sets **flag[0]** to true and enters its critical section.
>
> P1 sets **flag[1]** to true and enters its critical section.

Because both processes are now in their critical sections, the program is incorrect. The problem is that the proposed solution is not independent of relative process execution speeds.

Third Attempt Because a process can change its state after the other process has checked it but before the other process can enter its critical section, the second attempt failed. Perhaps we can fix this problem with a simple interchange of two statements, as shown in Figure A.1c.

As before, if one process fails inside its critical section, including the flag-setting code controlling the critical section, then the other process is blocked, and if a process fails outside its critical section, then the other process is not blocked.

Next, let us check that mutual exclusion is guaranteed, using the point of view of process P0. Once P0 has set **flag[0]** to true, P1 cannot enter its critical section until after P0 has entered and left its critical section. It could be that P1 is already in its critical section when P0 sets its flag. In that case, P0 will be blocked by the **while**

---

[1]The **enum** declaration is used here to declare a data type (**boolean**) and to assign its values.

statement until P1 has left its critical section. The same reasoning applies from the point of view of P1.

This guarantees mutual exclusion but creates yet another problem. If both processes set their flags to true before either has executed the `while` statement, then each will think that the other has entered its critical section, causing deadlock.

Fourth Attempt In the third attempt, a process sets its state without knowing the state of the other process. Deadlock occurs because each process can insist on its right to enter its critical section; there is no opportunity to back off from this position. We can try to fix this in a way that makes each process more deferential: Each process sets its flag to indicate its desire to enter its critical section but is prepared to reset the flag to defer to the other process, as shown in Figure A.1d.

This is close to a correct solution but is still flawed. Mutual exclusion is still guaranteed, using similar reasoning to that followed in the discussion of the third attempt. However, consider the following sequence of events:

P0 sets `flag[0]` to true.

P1 sets `flag[1]` to true.

P0 checks `flag[1]`.

P1 checks `flag[0]`.

P0 sets `flag[0]` to false.

P1 sets `flag[1]` to false.

P0 sets `flag[0]` to true.

P1 sets `flag[1]` to true.

This sequence could be extended indefinitely, and neither process could enter its critical section. Strictly speaking, this is not deadlock, because any alteration in the relative speed of the two processes will break this cycle and allow one to enter the critical section. This condition is referred to as **livelock**. Recall that deadlock occurs when a set of processes wishes to enter their critical sections but no process can succeed. With livelock, there are possible sequences of executions that succeed, but it is also possible to describe one or more execution sequences in which no process ever enters its critical section.

Although the scenario just described is not likely to be sustained for very long, it is nevertheless a possible scenario. Thus we reject the fourth attempt.

A Correct Solution We need to be able to observe the state of both processes, which is provided by the array variable `flag`. But, as the fourth attempt shows, this is not enough. We must impose an order on the activities of the two processes to avoid the problem of "mutual courtesy" that we have just observed. The variable `turn` from the first attempt can be used for this purpose; in this case the variable indicates which process has the right to insist on entering its critical region.

We can describe this solution, referred to as Dekker's algorithm, as follows. When P0 wants to enter its critical section, it sets its flag to true. It then checks the flag of P1. If that is false, P0 may immediately enter its critical section. Otherwise, P0 consults `turn`. If it finds that `turn = 0`, then it knows that it is its turn to insist and periodically checks P1's flag. P1 will at some point note that it is its turn to defer and set its to flag false, allowing P0 to proceed. After P0 has used its critical section, it sets its flag to false to free the critical section and sets turn to 1 to transfer the right to insist to P1.

Figure A.2 provides a specification of Dekker's algorithm. The construct **parbegin** (P1, P2, ... , P*n*) means the following: Suspend the execution of the main program; initiate concurrent execution of procedures P1, P2, ... , P*n*; when all of P1, P2, ... , P*n* have terminated, resume the main program. A verification of Dekker's algorithm is left as an exercise (see Problem A.1).

Peterson's Algorithm

Dekker's algorithm solves the mutual exclusion problem but with a rather complex program that is difficult to follow and whose correctness is tricky to prove. Peterson [PETE81] has provided a simple, elegant solution. As before, the global array variable `flag` indicates the position of each process with respect to mutual exclusion, and the global variable `turn` resolves simultaneity conflicts. The algorithm is presented in Figure A.3.

That mutual exclusion is preserved is easily shown. Consider process P0. Once it has set `flag[0]` to true, P1 cannot enter its critical section. If P1 already is in its critical section, then `flag[1]  = true` and P0 is blocked from entering its critical section. On the other hand, mutual blocking is prevented. Suppose that P0 is blocked in its `while` loop. This means that `flag[1]` is true and `turn = 1`. P0 can enter its critical section when either `flag[1]` becomes false or turn becomes 0. Now consider three exhaustive cases:

1. P1 has no interest in its critical section. This case is impossible, because it implies `flag[1] = false`.

2. P1 is waiting for its critical section. This case is also impossible, because if `turn = 1`, P1 is able to enter its critical section.

3. P1 is using its critical section repeatedly and therefore monopolizing access to it. This cannot happen, because P1 is obliged to give P0 an opportunity by setting turn to 0 before each attempt to enter its critical section.

Thus we have a simple solution to the mutual exclusion problem for two processes. Furthermore, Peterson's algorithm is easily generalized to the case of *n* processes [HOFR90].

A.2 RACE CONDITIONS AND SEMAPHORES

Although the definition of a race condition, provided in Section 5.1, seems straightforward, experience has shown that students usually have difficult pinpoint race conditions in their programs. The purpose of this section, which is based on [CARR01],[2] is to step through a series of examples using semaphores that should help clarify the topic of race conditions.

---

[2]I am grateful to Professor Ching-Kuang Shene of Michigan Technological University for permission to use this example.

```
boolean flag [2];
int turn;
void P0( )
{
    while (true)
    {
        flag [0] = true;
        while (flag [1])
            if (turn == 1)
            {
                flag [0] = false;
                while (turn == 1)
                    /* do nothing */;
                flag [0] = true;
            }
        /* critical section  */;
        turn = 1;
        flag [0] = false;
        /* remainder   */;
    }
}
void P1( )
{
    while (true)
    {
        flag [1] = true;
        while (flag [0])
        if (turn == 0)
            {
                flag [1] = false;
                while (turn == 0)
                    /* do nothing */;
                flag [1] = true;
            }
        /* critical section   */;
        turn = 0;
        flag [1] = false;
        /* remainder   */;
    }
}
void main ( )
{
    flag [0] = false;
    flag [1] = false;
    turn = 1;
    parbegin (P0, P1);
}
```

Figure A.2   Dekker's Algorithm

```
boolean flag [2];
int turn;
void P0()
{
    while (true)
    {
        flag [0] = true;
        turn = 1;
        while (flag [1] && turn == 1)
            /* do nothing */;
        /* critical section   */;
        flag [0] = false;
        /* remainder   */;
    }
}
void P1()
{
    while (true)
    {
        flag [1] = true;
        turn = 0;
        while (flag [0] && turn == 0)
            /* do nothing */;
        /* critical section   */;
        flag [1] = false;
        /* remainder   */
    }
}
void main()
{
    flag [0] = false;
    flag [1] = false;
    parbegin (P0, P1);
}
```

Figure A.3   Peterson's Algorithm for Two Processes

Problem Statement

Assume that there are two processes, **A** and **B**, each of which consists of a number of concurrent threads. Each thread includes an infinite loop in which a message is exchanged with a thread in the other process. Each message consists of an integer placed in a shared global buffer. There are two requirements:

1. After a thread A1 of process **A** makes a message available to some thread B1 in **B**, A1 can only proceed after it receives a message from B1. Similarly, after B1 makes a message available to A1, it can only proceed after it receives a message from A1.

2. Once a thread A1 makes a message available, it must make sure that no other thread in **A** overwrites the global buffer before the message is retrieved by a thread in **B**.

In the remainder of this section, we show four attempts to implement this scheme using semaphores, each of which can result in a race condition. Finally, we show a correct solution.

First Attempt

Consider this approach:

semaphore a = 0, b = 0; int buf_a, buf_b;	

thread_A(...)
{
    int var_a;
    . . .
    while (true) {
        . . .
        var_a = ...;
        semSignal(b);
        semWait(a);
        buf_a = var_a;
        var_a = buf_b;
        . . .;
    }
}
	thread_B(...)
	{
	    int var_b;
	    . . .
	    while (true) {
	        . . .
	        var_b = ...;
	        semSignal(a);
	        semWait(b);
	        buf_b = var_b;
	        var_b = buf_a;
	        . . .;
	    }
	}

This is a simple handshaking protocol. When a thread A1 in **A** is ready to exchange messages, it sends a signal to a thread in **B** and then waits for a thread B1 in **B** to be ready. Once a signal comes back from B1, which A perceives by performing `semWait(a)`, then A1 assumes that B1 is ready and performs the exchange. B1 behaves similarly, and the exchange happens regardless of which thread is ready first.

This attempt can lead to race conditions. For example consider the following sequence, with time going vertically down the table:

Thread A1	Thread B1
semSignal(b)	
semWait(a)	
	semSignal(a)
	semWait(b)
buf_a = var_a	
var_a = buf_b	
	buf_b = var_b

In the preceding sequence, A1 reaches `semWait(a)` and is blocked. B1 reaches semWait(b) and is not blocked, but is switched out before it can update its `buf_b`. Meanwhile, A1 executes and reads from `buf_b` before it has the intended value. At this point `buf_b` may have a value provided by previously by another thread or provided by B1 in a previous exchange. This is a race condition.

A more subtle race condition can be seen if two threads in **A** and **B** are active. Consider the following sequence:

Thread A1	Thread A2	Thread B1	Thread B2
semSignal(b)			
semWait(a)			
		semSignal(a)	
		semWait(b)	
	semSignal(b)		
	semWait(a)		
		buf_b = var_b1	
			semSignal(a)
buf_a = var_a1			
	buf_a = var_a2		

In this sequence, threads A1 and B1 attempt to exchange messages and go through the proper semaphore signaling instructions. However, immediately after the two **semWait** signals occur (in threads A1 and B1), thread A2 runs and executes **semSignal(b)** and **semWait(a)**, which causes thread B2 to execute **semSignal(a)** to release A2 from **semWait(a)**. At this point either A1 or A2 could update **buf_a** next, and we have a race condition. By changing the sequence of execution among the threads, we can readily find other race conditions.

Lesson Learned: When a variable is shared by multiple threads, race conditions are likely to occur unless proper mutual exclusion protection is used.

Second Attempt

For this attempt, we use a semaphore to protect the shared variable. The purpose is to ensure that access to **buf_a** and **buf_b** are mutually exclusive. The program is as follows:

```
semaphore a = 0, b = 0; mutex = 1;
int buf_a, buf_b;
```

```
thread_A(...)                          thread_B(...)
{                                      {
    int var_a;                             int var_b;
    ...                                    ...
    while (true)  {                        while (true)   {
        ...                                    ...
        var_a = ... ;                          var_b = ... ;
        semSignal(b);                          semSignal(a);
        semWait(a);                            semWait(b);
            semWait(mutex);                        semWait(mutex);
                buf_a = var_a;                         buf_b = var_b;
            semSignal(mutex);                      semSignal(mutex);
        semSignal(b);                          semSignal(a);
        semWait(a);                            semWait(b);
            semWait(mutex);                        semWait(mutex);
                var_a = buf_b;                         var_b = buf_a;
            semSignal(mutex);                      semSignal(mutex);
        ...;                                   ...;
    }                                      }
}                                      }
```

Before a thread can exchange a message, it follows the same handshaking protocol as in the first attempt. The semaphore **mutex** protects **buf_a** and **buf_b** in an attempt to assure that update precedes reading. But the protection is not adequate. Once both threads complete the first handshaking stage, the values of semaphores **a** and **b** are both 1. There are three possibilities that could occur:

1. Two threads, say A1 and B1, complete the first handshaking and continue with the second stage of the exchange.

2. Another pair of threads starts the first stage.

3. One of the current pair will continue and exchange a message with a newcomer in the other pair.

All of these possibilities can lead to race conditions. As an example of a race condition based on the third possibility, consider the following sequence:

Thread A1	Thread A2	Thread B1
semSignal(b)		
semWait(a)		
		semSignal(a)
		semWait(b)
buf_a = var_a1		
		buf_b = var_b1
	semSignal(b)	
	semWait(a)	
		semSignal(a)
		semWait(b)
	buf_a = var_a2	

In this example, after A1 and B1 go through the first handshake, they both update the corresponding global buffers. Then A2 initiates the first handshaking stage. Following this, B1 initiates the second handshaking stage. At this point A2 updates **buf_a** before B1 can retrieve the value placed in **buf_a** by A1. This is a race condition.

Lesson Learned: Protecting a single variable may be insufficient if the use of that variable is part of a long execution sequence. Protect the whole execution sequence.

Third Attempt

For this attempt, we want to expand the critical section to include the entire message exchange (two threads each update one of two buffers and read from the other buffer). A single semaphore is insufficient because this could lead to deadlock, with each side waiting on the other. The program is as follows:

---

semaphore aready = 1, adone = 0, bready = 1 bdone = 0;
int buf_a, buf_b;

thread_A(...)	thread_B(...)
{	{
int var_a;	**int** var_b;
...	...
while (true) {	**while** (true) {
...	...
var_a = ... ;	var_b = ... ;
semWait(aready);	semWait(bready);
buf_a = var_a;	buf_b = var_b;
semSignal(adone);	semSignal(bdone);
semWait(bdone);	semWait(adone);
var_a = buf_b;	var_b = buf_a;
semSignal(aready);	semSignal(bready);
...;	...;
}	}
}	}

The semaphore **aready** is intended to insure that no other thread in A can update **buf_a** while one thread from **A** enters its critical section. The semaphore **adone** is intended to insure that no thread from **B** will attempt to read **buf_a** until **buf_a** has been updated. The same considerations apply to **bready** and **bdone**. However, this scheme does not prevent race conditions. Consider the following sequence:

Thread A1	Thread B1
buf_a = var_a	
semSignal(adone)	
semWait(bdone)	
	buf_b = var_b
	semSignal(bdone)
	semWait(adone)
var_a = buf_b;	
semSignal(aready)	
...loop back...	
semWait(aready)	
buf_a = var_a	
	var_b = buf_a

In this sequence, both A1 and B1 enter their critical sections, deposit their messages, and reach the second wait. Then A1 copies the message from B1 and leaves its critical section. At this point, A1 could loop back in its program, generate a new message, and deposit it in **buf_a**, as shown in the preceding execution sequence. Another possibility is that at this same point another thread of **A** could generate a message and put it in **buf_a**. In either case, a message is lost and a race condition occurs.

Lesson Learned: If we have a number of cooperating thread groups, mutual exclusion guaranteed for one group may not prevent interference from threads in other groups. Further, if a critical section is repeatedly entered by one thread, then the timing of the cooperation between threads must be managed properly.

Fourth Attempt

The third attempt fails to force a thread to remain in its critical section until the other thread retrieves the message. Here is an attempt to achieve this objective:

semaphore aready = 1, adone = 0, bready = 1 bdone = 0; **int** buf_a, buf_b;	

thread_A(...)
{
    int var_a;
 	
    . . .
    while (true) {
        . . .
        var_a = ...;
        semWait(bready);
            buf_a = var_a;
            semSignal(adone);
            semWait(bdone);
            var_a = buf_b;
        semSignal(aready);
        . . . ;
    }
}
	thread_B(...)
	{
	    int var_b;
	
	    . . .
	    while (true) {
	        . . .
	        var_b = ...;
	        semWait(aready);
	            buf_b = var_b;
	            semSignal(bdone);
	            semWait(adone);
	            var_b = buf_a;
	        semSignal(bready);
	        . . . ;
	    }
	}

In this case, the first thread in **A** to enter its critical section decrements `bready` to 0. No subsequent thread from **A** can attempt a message exchange until a thread from **B** completes the message exchange and increments `bready` to 1. This approach too can lead to race conditions, such as in the following sequence:

Thread A1	**Thread A2**	**Thread B1**
semWait(bready)		
buf_a = var_a1		
semSignal(adone)		
		semWait(aready)
		buf_b = var_b1
		semSignal(bdone)
		semWait(adone)
		var_b = buf_a
		semSignal(bready)
	semWait(bready)	
	• • •	
	semWait(bdone)	
	var_a2 = buf_b	

In this sequence, threads A1 and B1 enter corresponding critical sections in order to exchange messages. Thread B1 retrieves its message and signals **bready**. This enables another thread from **A**, A2, to enter its critical section. If A2 is faster than A1, then A2 may retrieve the message that was intended for A1.

Lesson Learned: If the semaphore for mutual exclusion is not released by its owner, race conditions can occur. In this fourth attempt, a semaphore is locked by a thread in **A** and then unlocked by a thread in **B**. This is risky programming practice.

A Good Attempt

The reader may notice that the problem in this section is a variation of the bounded-buffer problem and can be approached in a manner similar to the discussion in Section 5.4. The most straightforward approach is to use two buffers one for B-to-A messages and one for A-to-B messages. The size of each buffer needs to be one. To see the reason for this, consider that there is no ordering assumption for releasing threads from a synchronization primitive. If a buffer has more than one slot, then we cannot guarantee that the messages will be properly matched. For example, B1 could receive a message from A1 and then send a message to A1. But if the buffer has multiple slots, another thread in **A** may retrieve the message from the slot intended for A1.

Using the same basic approach as was used in Section 5.4, we can develop the following program:

```
semaphore notFull_A = 1, notFull_B = 1;
semaphore notEmpty_A = 0, notEmpty_B = 0;
int buf_a, buf_b;
```

thread_A(...)	thread_B(...)
`{`	`{`
`    int var_a;`	`    int var_b;`
`    . . .`	`    . . .`
`    while (true)  {`	`    while (true)  {`
`        . . .`	`        . . .`
`        var_a = ...;`	`        var_b = ...;`
`        semWait(notFull_A);`	`        semWait(notFull_B);`
`            buf_a = var_a;`	`            buf_b = var_b;`
`            semSignal(notEmpty_A);`	`            semSignal(notEmpty_B);`
`        semWait(notEmpty_B);`	`        semWait(notEmpty_A);`
`            var_a = buf_b;`	`            var_b = buf_a;`
`            semSignal(notFull_B);`	`            semSignal(notFull_A);`
`            . . .;`	`            . . .;`
`    }`	`    }`
`}`	`}`

To verify that this solution works, we need to address three issues:

1. The message exchange section is mutually exclusive within the thread group. Because the initial value of **notFull_A** is 1, only one thread in **A** can pass

through `semWait(notFull_A)` until the exchange is complete as signaled by a thread in **B** that executes `semSignal(notFull_A)`. A similar reasoning applies to threads in **B**. Thus, this condition is satisfied.

2. Once two threads enter their critical sections, they exchange messages without interference from any other threads. No other thread in **A** can enter its critical section until the thread in **B** is completely done with the exchange, and no other thread in **B** can enter its critical section until the thread in **A** is completely done with the exchange. Thus, this condition is satisfied.

3. After one thread exits its critical section, no thread in the same group can rush in and ruin the existing message. This condition is satisfied because a one-slot buffer is used in each direction. Once a thread in **A** has executed `semWait(notFull_A)` and entered its critical section, no other thread in **A** can update `buf_a` until the corresponding thread in **B** has retrieved the value in `buf_a` and issued a `semSignal(notFull_A)`.

Lesson Learned: It is well to review the solutions to well-known problems, because a correct solution to the problem at hand may be a variation of a solution to a known problem.

A.3 A BARBERSHOP PROBLEM

As another example of the use of semaphores to implement concurrency, we consider a simple barbershop problem.[3] This example is instructive because the problems encountered when attempting to provide tailored access to barbershop resources are similar to those encountered in a real operating system.

Our barbershop has three chairs, three barbers, and a waiting area that can accommodate four customers on a sofa and that has standing room for additional customers (Figure A.4). Fire codes limit the total number of customers in the shop to 20. In this example, we assume that the barbershop will eventually process 50 customers.

A customer will not enter the shop if it is filled to capacity with other customers. Once inside, the customer takes a seat on the sofa or stands if the sofa is filled. When a barber is free, the customer that has been on the sofa the longest is served and, if there are any standing customers, the one that has been in the shop the longest takes a seat on the sofa. When a customer's haircut is finished, any barber can accept payment, but because there is only one cash register, payment is accepted for one customer at a time. The barbers divide their time among cutting hair, accepting payment, and sleeping in their chair waiting for a customer.

---

[3]I am indebted to Professor Ralph Hilzer of California State University at Chico for supplying this treatment of the problem.

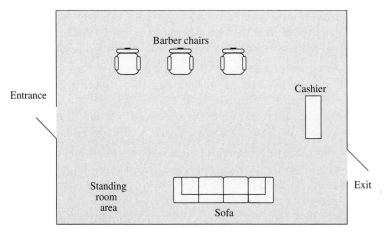

Figure A.4   The Barbershop

An Unfair Barbershop

Figure A.5 shows an implementation using semaphores; the three procedures are listed side-by-side to conserve space. We assume that all semaphore queues are handled with a first-in-first-out policy.

The main body of the program activates 50 customers, 3 barbers, and the cashier process. We now consider the purpose and positioning of the various synchronization operators:

- **Shop and sofa capacity:** The capacity of the shop and the capacity of the sofa are governed by the semaphores **max_capacity** and **sofa**, respectively. Every time a customer attempts to enter the shop, the **max_capacity** semaphore is decremented by 1; every time a customer leaves, the semaphore is incremented. If a customer finds the shop full, then that customer's process is blocked on **max_capacity** by the **semWait** function. Similarly, the **semWait** and **semSignal** operations surround the actions of sitting on and getting up from the sofa.

- **Barber chair capacity:** There are three barber chairs, and care must be taken that they are used properly. The semaphore **barber_chair** assures that no more than three customers attempt to obtain service at a time, trying to avoid the undignified occurrence of one customer sitting on the lap of another. A customer will not get up from the sofa until at least one chair is free [**semWait(barber_chair)**], and each barber signals when a customer has left its chair [**semSignal(barber_chair)**]. Fair access to the barber chairs is guaranteed by the semaphore queue organization: The first customer to be blocked is the first one allowed into an available chair. Note that, in the customer procedure, if **semWait(barber_chair)** occurred after **semSignal(sofa)**, each customer would only briefly sit on the sofa and then stand in line at the barber chairs, creating congestion and leaving the barbers with little elbow room.

```
/* program barbershop1 */
semaphore max_capacity = 20;
semaphore sofa = 4;
semaphore barber_chair = 3;
semaphore coord = 3;
semaphore cust_ready = 0, finished = 0, leave_b_chair = 0, payment= 0, receipt = 0;

void customer ()              void barber()                void cashier()
{                             {                            {
    wait(max_capacity);           while (true)                 while (true)
    enter_shop();                 {                            {   wait(payment);
    wait(sofa);                       wait(cust_ready);            wait(coord);
    sit_on_sofa();                    wait(coord);                 accept_pay();
    wait(barber_chair);               cut_hair();                  signal(coord);
    get_up_from_sofa();               signal(coord);               signal(receipt);
    signal(sofa);                     signal(finished);        }
    sit_in_barber_chair;              wait(leave_b_chair);     }
    signal(cust_ready);               signal(barber_chair);
    wait(finished);               }
    leave_barber_chair();     }
    signal(leave_b_chair);
    pay();
    signal(payment);
    wait(receipt);
    exit_shop();
    signal(max_capacity)
}

void main()
{
parbegin (customer, ... 50 times, ... customer, barber, barber, barber, cashier);
}
```

Figure A.5   An Unfair Barbershop

- **Ensuring customers are in barber chair:** The semaphore `cust_ready` provides a wakeup signal for a sleeping barber, indicating that a customer has just taken a chair. Without this semaphore, a barber would never sleep but would begin cutting hair as soon as a customer left the chair; if no new customer had grabbed the seat, the barber would be cutting air.

- **Holding customers in barber chair:** Once seated, a customer remains in the chair until the barber gives the signal that the haircut is complete, using the semaphore `finished`.

- **Limiting one customer to a barber chair:** The semaphore `barber_chair` is intended to limit the number of customers in barber chairs to three. However, by itself, barber_chair does not succeed in doing this. A customer that fails to get the processor immediately after his barber executes `semSignal(finished)` (that is, one who falls into a trance or stops to chat with a neighbor) may still be in the chair when the next customer is given the go ahead to be seated. The semaphore `leave_b_chair` is intended to correct this problem by restraining the barber from inviting a new customer into the chair until the lingering one has announced his departure from it. In the problems at the end of this chapter, we will find that even this precaution fails to stop the mettlesome customer lap sittings.

- **Paying and receiving:** Naturally, we want to be careful when dealing with money. The cashier wants to be assured that each customer pays before leaving the shop, and the customer wants verification that payment was received (a receipt). This is accomplished, in effect, by a face-to-face transfer of the money. Each customer, upon arising from a barber chair, pays, then alerts the cashier that money has been passed over [`semSignal(payment)`], and then waits for a receipt [`semWait(receipt)`]. The cashier process repeatedly takes payments: It waits for a payment to be signaled, accepts the money, and then signals acceptance of the money. Several programming errors need to be avoided here. If `semSignal(payment)` occurred just before the action `pay`, then a customer could be interrupted after so signaling; this would leave the cashier free to accept payment even though none had been offered. An even more serious error would be to reverse the positions of the `semSignal(payment)` and `semWait(receipt)` lines. This would lead to deadlock because that would cause all customers and the cashier to block at their respective `semWait` operators.

- **Coordinating barber and cashier functions:** To save money, this barbershop does not employ a separate cashier. Each barber is required to perform that task when not cutting hair. The semaphore `coord` ensures that barbers perform only one task at a time.

Table A.1 summarizes the use of each of the semaphores in the program.

The cashier process could be eliminated by merging the payment function into the barber procedure. Each barber would sequentially `cut` hair and then `accept` pay. However, with a single cash register, it is necessary to limit access to the `accept` pay function to one barber at a time. This could be done by treating that function as a critical section and guarding it with a semaphore.

A Fair Barbershop

Figure A.5 is a good effort, but some difficulties remain. One problem is solved in the remainder of this section; others are left as exercises for the reader (see Problem A.6).

There is a timing problem in Figure A.5 that could lead to unfair treatment of customers. Suppose that three customers are currently seated in the three barber chairs. In that case, the customers would most likely be blocked on semWait(finished), and due to the queue organization they would be released in the order they entered the barber chair. However, what if one of the barbers is very fast or one of the customers is quite bald? Releasing the first customer to enter the chair could result in a situation where one customer is summarily ejected from his seat and forced to pay full price for a partial haircut while another is restrained from leaving his chair even though his haircut is complete.

The problem is solved with more semaphores, as shown in Figure A.6. We assign a unique customer number to each customer; this is equivalent to having each customer take a number upon entering the shop. The semaphore `mutex1` protects access to the

Table A.1 Purpose of Semaphores in Figure A.5

Semaphore	Wait Operation	Signal Operation
`max_capacity`	Customer waits for space to enter shop.	Exiting customer signals customer waiting to enter.
`sofa`	Customer waits for seat on sofa.	Customer leaving sofa signals customer waiting for sofa.
`barber_chair`	Customer waits for empty barber chair.	Barber signals when that barber's chair is empty.
`cust_ready`	Barber waits until a customer is in the chair.	Customer signals barber that customer is in the chair.
`finished`	Customer waits until his haircut is complete.	Barber signals when done cutting hair of this customer.
`leave_b_chair`	Barber waits until customer gets up from the chair.	Customer signals barber when customer gets up from chair.
`payment`	Cashier waits for a customer to pay.	Customer signals cashier that he has paid.
`receipt`	Customer waits for a receipt for payment.	Cashier signals that payment has been accepted.
`coord`	Wait for a barber resource to be free to perform either the hair cutting or cashiering function.	Signal that a barber resource is free.

global variable `count` so that each customer receives a unique number. The semaphore `finished` is redefined to be an array of 50 semaphores. Once a customer is seated in a barber chair, he executes `semWait(finished[custnr])` to wait on his own unique semaphore; when the barber is finished with that customer, the barber executes `semSignal(finished[b_cust])` to release the correct customer.

It remains to say how a customer's number is known to the barber. A customer places his number on the queue `enqueue1` just prior to signaling the barber with the semaphore `cust_ready`. When a barber is ready to cut hair, `dequeue1(b_cust)` removes the top customer number from `queue1` and places it in the barber's local variable `b_cust`.

A.4 PROBLEMS

A.1 Demonstrate the correctness of Dekker's algorithm.
a. Show that mutual exclusion is enforced. *Hint:* Show that when Pi enters its critical section, the following expression is true:

flag[i] **and** (**not** flag[1 – i])

b. Show that a process requiring access to its critical section will not be delayed indefinitely. *Hint:* Consider the following cases: (1) A single process is attempting to enter the critical section; (2) both processes are attempting to enter the critical section, and (2a) *turn* = 0 and *flag*[0] = false, and (2b) *turn* = 0 and *flag*[0] = true.

```
/* program barbershop2 */
semaphore max_capacity = 20;
semaphore sofa = 4;
semaphore barber_chair = 3, coord = 3;
semaphore mutex1 = 1, mutex2 = 1;
semaphore cust_ready = 0, leave_b_chair = 0, payment = 0, receipt = 0;
semaphore finished [50] = {0};
int count;

void customer()                void barber()                    void cashier()
{                              {                                {
    int custnr;                    int b_cust;                      while (true)
    wait(max_capacity);            while (true)                     {
    enter_shop();                  {                                    wait(payment);
    wait(mutex1);                      wait(cust_ready);                wait(coord);
    custnr = count;                    wait(mutex2);                    accept_pay();
    count++;                           dequeue1(b_cust);                signal(coord);
    signal(mutex1);                    signal(mutex2);                  signal(receipt);
    wait(sofa);                        wait(coord);                 }
    sit_on_sofa();                     cut_hair();              }
    wait(barber_chair);                signal(coord);
    get_up_from_sofa();                signal(finished[b_cust]);
    signal(sofa);                      wait(leave_b_chair);
    sit_in_barber_chair();             signal(barber_chair);
    wait(mutex2);                  }
    enqueue1(custnr);          }
    signal(cust_ready);
    signal(mutex2);
    wait(finished[custnr]);
    leave_barber_chair();
    signal(leave_b_chair);
    pay();
    signal(payment);
    wait(receipt);
    exit_shop();
    signal(max_capacity)
}

void main()
{   count := 0;
    parbegin (customer, . . . 50 times, . . . customer, barber, barber, barber, cashier);
}
```

Figure A.6   A Fair Barbershop

A.2   Consider Dekker's algorithm, written for an arbitrary number of processes by changing the statement executed when leaving the critical section from

turn = 1 – i   /* i.e. P0 sets turn to 1 and P1 sets turn to 0 */

to

turn = (turn + 1) % n   /* n = number of processes */

Evaluate the algorithm when the number of concurrently executing processes is greater than two.

A.3   Demonstrate that the following software approaches to mutual exclusion do not depend on elementary mutual exclusion at the memory access level:

a. the bakery algorithm
b. Peterson's algorithm

A.4 Develop a solution to the problem discussed in Section A.2 in which a single one-slot buffer is used. In this case, the two threads must take turns in exchanging their messages rather than operating in parallel.

A.5 Answer the following questions relating to the fair barbershop (Figure A.6):
a. Does the code require that the barber who finishes a customer's haircut collect that customer's payment?
b. Do barbers always use the same barber chair?

A.6 A number of problems remain with the fair barbershop of Figure A.6. Modify the program to correct the following problems.
a. The cashier may accept pay from one customer and release another if two or more are waiting to pay. Fortunately, once a customer presents payment, there is no way for him to un-present it, so in the end, the right amount of money ends up in the cash register. Nevertheless, it is desirable to release the right customer as soon as his payment is taken.
b. The semaphore leave_b_chair supposedly prevents multiple access to a single barber chair. Unfortunately, this semaphore does not succeed in all cases. For example, suppose that all three barbers have finished cutting hair and are blocked at **semWait(leave_b_chair)**. Two of the customers are in an interrupted state just prior to **leave barber chair**. The third customer leaves his chair and executes **semSignal(leave_b_chair)**. Which barber is released? Because the **leave_b_chair** queue is first-in-first-out, the first barber that was blocked is released. Is that the barber that was cutting the signaling customer's hair? Maybe, but maybe not. If not, then a new customer will come along and sit on the lap of a customer that was just about to get up.
c. The program requires a customer first sits on the sofa even if a barber chair is empty. Granted, this is a rather minor problem, and fixing it makes code that is already a bit messy even messier. Nevertheless, give it a try.

APPENDIX B

OBJECT-ORIENTED DESIGN

Windows and several other contemporary operating systems rely heavily on object-oriented design principles. This appendix provides a brief overview of the main concepts of object-oriented design.

B.1 MOTIVATION

Object-oriented concepts have become quite popular in the area of computer programming, with the promise of interchangeable, reusable, easily updated, and easily interconnected software parts. More recently, database designers have begun to appreciate the advantages of an object orientation, with the result that object-oriented database management systems (OODBMS) are beginning to appear. Operating systems designers have also recognized the benefits of the object-oriented approach.

Object-oriented programming and object-oriented database management systems are in fact different things, but they share one key concept: that software or data can be "containerized." Everything goes into a box, and there can be boxes within boxes. In the simplest conventional program, one program step equates to one instruction; in an object-oriented language, each step might be a whole boxful of instructions. Similarly, with an object-oriented database, one variable, instead of equating to a single data element, may equate to a whole boxful of data.

Table B.1 introduces some of the key terms used in object-oriented design.

Table B.1   Key Object-Oriented Terms

Term	Definition
Attribute	Data variables contained within an object.
Containment	A relationship between two object instances in which the containing object includes a pointer to the contained object.
Encapsulation	The isolation of the attributes and services of an object instance from the external environment. Services may only be invoked by name and attributes may only be accessed by means of the services.
Inheritance	A relationship between two object classes in which the attributes and services of a parent class are acquired by a child class.
Interface	A description closely related to an object class. An interface contains method definitions (without implementations) and constant values. An interface cannot be instantiated as an object.
Message	The means by which objects interact.
Method	A procedure that is part of an object and that can be activated from outside the object to perform certain functions.
Object	An abstraction of a real-world entity.
Object Class	A named set of objects that share the same names, sets of attributes, and services.
Object Instance	A specific member of an object class, with values assigned to the attributes.
Polymorphism	Refers to the existence of multiple objects that use the same names for services and present the same interface to the external world but that represent different types of entities.
Service	A function that performs an operation on an object.

B.2 OBJECT-ORIENTED CONCEPTS

The central concept of object-oriented design is the object. An object is a distinct software unit that contains a collection of related variables (data) and methods (procedures). Generally, these variables and methods are not directly visible outside the object. Rather, well-defined interfaces exist that allow other software to have access to the data and the procedures.

An object represents some thing, be it a physical entity, a concept, a software module, or some dynamic entity such as a TCP connection. The values of the variables in the object express the information that is known about the thing that the object represents. The methods include procedures whose execution affect the values in the object and possibly also affect that thing being represented.

Figures B.1 and B.2 illustrate key object-oriented concepts.

Object Structure

The data and procedures contained in an object are generally referred to as variables and methods, respectively. Everything that an object "knows" can be expressed in its variables, and everything it can do is expressed in its methods.

The **variables** in an object, also called **attributes**, are typically simple scalars or tables. Each variable has a type, possibly a set of allowable values, and may either be

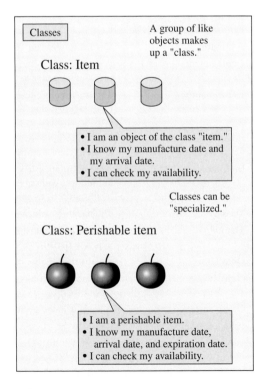

Figure B.1 Objects

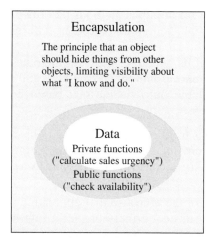

Encapsulation

The principle that an object should hide things from other objects, limiting visibility about what "I know and do."

Data

Private functions
("calculate sales urgency")
Public functions
("check availability")

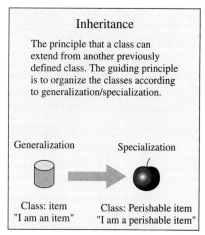

Inheritance

The principle that a class can extend from another previously defined class. The guiding principle is to organize the classes according to generalization/specialization.

Generalization   Specialization

Class: item   Class: Perishable item
"I am an item"   "I am a perishable item"

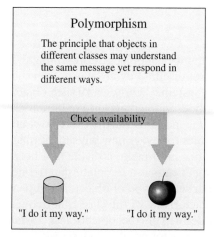

Polymorphism

The principle that objects in different classes may understand the same message yet respond in different ways.

Check availability

"I do it my way."   "I do it my way."

Figure B.2   Object Concepts

constant or variable (by convention, the term *variable* is used even for constants). Access restrictions may also be imposed on variables for certain users, classes of users, or situations.

The **methods** in an object are procedures that can be triggered from outside to perform certain functions. The method may change the state of the object, update some of its variables, or act on outside resources to which the object has access.

Objects interact by means of **messages**. A message includes the name of the sending object, the name of the receiving object, the name of a method in the receiving object, and any parameters needed to qualify the execution of the method. A message can only be used to invoke a method within an object. The only way to access the data inside an object is by means of the object's methods. Thus, a method may cause an action to be taken or for the object's variables to be accessed, or both. For local objects, passing a message to an object is the same as calling an object's method. When objects are distributed, passing a message is exactly what it sounds like.

The interface of an object is a set of public methods that the object supports. An interface says nothing about implementation; objects in different classes may have different implementations of the same interfaces.

The property of an object that its only interface with the outside world is by means of messages is referred to as **encapsulation**. The methods and variables of an object are encapsulated and available only via message-based communication. Encapsulation offers two advantages:

1. It protects an object's variables from corruption by other objects. This protection may include protection from unauthorized access and protection from the types of problems that arise from concurrent access, such as deadlock and inconsistent values.

2. It hides the internal structure of the object so that interaction with the object is relatively simple and standardized. Furthermore, if the internal structure or procedures of an object are modified without changing its external functionality, other objects are unaffected.

Object Classes

In practice, there will typically be a number of objects representing the same types of things. For example, if a process is represented by an object, then there will be one object for each process present in a system. Clearly, every such object needs its own set of variables. However, if the methods in the object are reentrant procedures, then all similar objects could share the same methods. Furthermore, it would be inefficient to redefine both methods and variables for every new but similar object.

The solution to these difficulties is to make a distinction between an object class and an object instance. An **object class** is a template that defines the methods and variables to be included in a particular type of object. An **object instance** is an actual object that includes the characteristics of the class that defines it. The object contains values for the variables defined in the object class. **Instantiation** is the process of creating a new object instance for an object class.

Inheritance   The concept of an object class is powerful because it allows for the creation of many object instances with a minimum of effort. This concept is made even more powerful by the use of the mechanism of inheritance [TAIV96].

Inheritance enables a new object class to be defined in terms of an existing class. The new (lower level) class, called the **subclass**, or the **child class**, automatically includes the methods and variable definitions in the original (higher level) class, called the **superclass**, or **parent class**. A subclass may differ from its superclass in a number of ways:

1. The subclass may include additional methods and variables not found in its superclass.

2. The subclass may override the definition of any method or variable in its superclass by using the same name with a new definition. This provides a simple and efficient way of handling special cases.

3. The subclass may restrict a method or variable inherited from its superclass in some way.

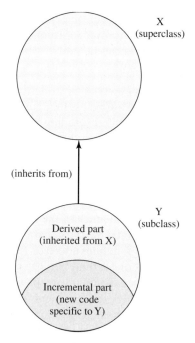

X
(superclass)

(inherits from)

Y
(subclass)

Derived part
(inherited from X)

Incremental part
(new code
specific to Y)

Figure B.3   Inheritance

Figure B.3, based on one in [KORS90], illustrates the concept.

The inheritance mechanism is recursive, allowing a subclass to become the superclass of its own subclasses. In this way, an **inheritance hierarchy** may be constructed. Conceptually, we can think of the inheritance hierarchy as defining a search technique for methods and variables. When an object receives a message to carry out a method that is not defined in its class, it automatically searches up the hierarchy until it finds the method. Similarly, if the execution of a method results in the reference to a variable not defined in that class, the object searches up the hierarchy for the variable name.

Polymorphism Polymorphism is an intriguing and powerful characteristic that makes it possible to hide different implementations behind a common interface. Two objects that are polymorphic to each other utilize the same names for methods and present the same interface to other objects. For example, there may be a number of print objects, for different output devices, such as printDotmatrix, printLaser, printScreen, and so forth, or for different types of documents, such as printText, printDrawing, printCompound. If each such object includes a method called print, then any document could be printed by sending the message print to the appropriate object, without concern for how that method is actually carried out. Typically, polymorphism is used to allow you have the same method in multiple subclasses of the same superclass, each with a different detailed implementation.

It is instructive to compare polymorphism to the usual modular programming techniques. An objective of top-down, modular design is to design lower-level modules of general utility with a fixed interface to higher-level modules. This allows the one lower-level module to be invoked by many different higher-level modules. If the internals of the lower-level module are changed without changing its interface, then none of the upper-level modules that use it are affected. By contrast, with polymorphism, we are concerned with the ability of one higher-level object to invoke many different lower-level objects using the same message format to accomplish similar functions. With polymorphism, new lower-level objects can be added with minimal changes to existing objects.

Interfaces Inheritance enables a subclass object to use functionality of a superclass. There may be cases when you wish to define a subclass that has functionality of more than one superclass. This could be accomplished by allowing a subclass to inherit from more than one superclass. C++ is one language that allows such multiple inheritance. However, for simplicity, most modern object-oriented languages, including Java, C#, and Visual Basic .NET, limit a class to inheriting from only one superclass. Instead, a feature known as *interfaces* is used to enable a class to borrow some functionality from one class and other functionality from a completely different class.

Unfortunately, the term *interface* is used in much of the literature on objects with both a general-purpose and a specific functional meaning. An interface, as we are discussing it here, specifies an application-programming interface (API) for certain functionality. It does not define any implementation for that API. The syntax for an interface definition typically looks similar to a class definition, except that there is no code defined for the methods, just the method names, the arguments passed, and the type of the value returned. An interface may be implemented by a class. This works in much the same way that inheritance works. If a class implements an interface, it must have the properties and methods of the interface defined in the class. The methods that are implemented can be coded in any fashion, so long as the name, arguments, and return type of each method from the interface are identical to the definition in the interface.

Containment

Object instances that contain other objects are called **composite objects**. Containment may be achieved by including the pointer to one object as a value in another object. The advantage of composite objects is that they permit the representation of complex structures. For example, an object contained in a composite object may itself be a composite object.

Typically, the structures built up from composite objects are limited to a tree topology; that is, no circular references are allowed and each "child" object instance may have only one "parent" object instance.

It is important to be clear about the distinction between an inheritance hierarchy of object classes and a containment hierarchy of object instances. The two are not related. The use of inheritance simply allows many different object types to be defined with a minimum of efforts. The use of containment allows the construction of complex data structures.

B.3 BENEFITS OF OBJECT-ORIENTED DESIGN

[CAST92] lists the following benefits of object-oriented design:

- **Better organization of inherent complexity:** Through the use of inheritance, related concepts, resources, and other objects can be efficiently defined. Through the use of containment, arbitrary data structures, which reflect the underlying task at hand, can be constructed. Object-oriented programming languages and data structures enable designers to describe operating system resources and functions in a way that reflects the designer's understanding of those resources and functions.

- **Reduced development effort through reuse:** Reusing object classes that have been written, tested, and maintained by others cuts development, testing, and maintenance time.

- **More extensible and maintainable systems:** Maintenance, including product enhancements and repairs, traditionally consumes about 65% of the cost of any product life cycle. Object-oriented design drives that percentage down. The use of object-based software helps limit the number of potential interactions of different parts of the software, ensuring that changes to the implementation of a class can be made with little impact on the rest of the system.

These benefits are driving operating system design in the direction of object-oriented systems. Objects enable programmers to customize an operating system to meet new requirements, without disrupting system integrity. Objects also pave the road to distributed computing. Because objects communicate by means of messages, it matters not whether two communicating objects are on the same system or on two different systems in a network. Data, functions, and threads can be dynamically assigned to workstations and servers as needed. Accordingly, the object-oriented approach to the design of operating systems is becoming increasingly evident in PC and workstation operating systems.

B.4   CORBA

As we have seen in this book, object-oriented concepts have been used to design and implement operating system kernels, bringing benefits of flexibility, manageability, and portability. The benefits of using object-oriented techniques extend with equal or greater benefit to the realm of distributed software, including distributed operating systems. The application of object-oriented techniques to the design and implementation of distributed software is referred to as distributed object computing (DOC).

The motivation for DOC is the increasing difficulty in writing distributed software: while computing and network hardware get smaller, faster, and cheaper, distributed software gets larger, slower, and more expensive to develop and maintain. [SCHM97] points out that the challenge of distributed software stems from two types of complexity:

- **Inherent:** Inherent complexities arise from fundamental problems of distribution. Chief among these are detecting and recovering from network and host failures, minimizing the impact of communication latency, and determining an optimal partitioning of service components and workload onto computers throughout a network. In addition, concurrent programming, with issues of resource locking and deadlocks, is still hard, and distributed systems are inherently concurrent.

- **Accidental:** Accidental complexities arise from limitations with tools and techniques used to build distributed software. A common source of accidental complexity is the widespread use of functional design, which results in nonextensible and non-reusable systems.

DOC is a promising approach to managing both types of complexity. The centerpiece of the DOC approach are object request brokers (ORBs), which act as intermediaries for communication between local and remote objects. ORBs eliminate some of the tedious, error-prone, and nonportable aspects of designing and implementing distributed applications. Supplementing the ORB must be a number of conventions and formats for message exchange and interface definition between applications and the object-oriented infrastructure.

There are three main competing technologies in the DOC market: the object management group (OMG) architecture, called Common Object Request Broker Architecture (CORBA); the Java remote method invocation (RMI) system; and Microsoft's distributed component object model (DCOM). CORBA is the most advanced and well established of the three. A number of industry leaders, including IBM, Sun, Netscape, and Oracle, support CORBA, and Microsoft has announced that it will link its Windows-only DCOM with CORBA. The remainder of this appendix provides a brief overview of CORBA.

Table B.2 defines some key terms used in CORBA. The main features of CORBA are (Figure B.4):

- **Clients:** Clients generate requests and access object services through a variety of mechanisms provided by the underlying ORB.
- **Object implementations:** These implementations provide the services requested by various clients in the distributed system. One benefit of the CORBA architecture is that both clients and object implementations can be written in any number of programming languages and can still provide the full range of required services.
- **ORB core:** The ORB core is responsible for communication between objects. The ORB finds an object on the network, delivers requests to the object, activates the object (if not already active), and returns any message back to the sender. The ORB core provides **access transparency** because programmers use exactly the same method with the same parameters when invoking a local method or a remote method. The ORB core also provides **location transparency**: Programmers do not need to specify the location of an object.
- **Interface:** An object's interface specifies the operations and types supported by the object and thus defines the requests that can be made on the object. CORBA interfaces are similar to classes in C++ and interfaces in Java. Unlike C++ classes, a CORBA interface specifies methods and their parameters and return values but is silent about their implementation. Two objects of the same C++ class have the same implementation of their methods.

Table B.2   Key Concepts in a Distributed CORBA System

CORBA Concept	Definition
Client application	Invokes requests for a server to perform operations on objects. A client application uses one or more interface definitions that describe the objects and operations the client can request. A client application uses object references, not objects, to make requests.
Exception	Contains information that indicates whether a request was successfully performed.
Implementation	Defines and contains one or more methods that do the work associated with an object operation. A server can have one or more implementations.
Interface	Describes how instances of an object will behave, such as what operations are valid on those objects.
Interface definition	Describes the operations that are available on a certain type of object.
Invocation	The process of sending a request.
Method	The server code that does the work associated with an operation. Methods are contained within implementations.
Object	Represents a person, place, thing, or piece of software. An object can have operations performed on it, such as the promote operation on an employee object.
Object instance	An occurrence of one particular kind of object.
Object reference	An identifier of an object instance.
OMG Interface Definition Language (IDL)	A definition language for defining interfaces in CORBA.
Operation	The action that a client can request a server to perform on an object instance.
Request	A message sent between a client and a server application.
Server application	Contains one or more implementations of objects and their operations.

- **OMG interface definition language (IDL):** IDL is the language used to define objects. An example IDL interface definition is

```
//OMG IDL
interface Factory
  { Object create ( ) ;
} ;
```

This definition specifies an interface named Factory that supports one operation, create. The create operation takes no parameters and returns an object reference of type Object. Given an object reference for an object of type Factory, a client could invoke it to create a new CORBA object. IDL is a programming-independent language and, for this reason, a client does not invoke directly any object operation. It needs a mapping to the client programming language to do that. It is possible, as well, that the server and the client are programmed in different programming languages. The use of a specification

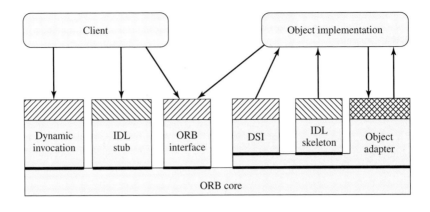

Figure B.4   Common Object Request Broker Architecture

language is a way to deal with heterogeneous processing across multiple languages and platform environments. Thus, IDL enables **platform independence**.

- **Language binding creation:** IDL compilers map one OMG IDL file to different programming languages, which may or may not be object oriented, such as Java, Smalltalk, Ada, C, C++, and COBOL. That mapping includes the definition of the language-specific data types and procedure interfaces to access service objects, the IDL client stub interface, the IDL skeleton, the object adapters, the dynamic skeleton interface, and the direct ORB interface. Usually, clients have a compile-time knowledge of the object interface and use client stubs to do a static invocation; in certain cases, clients do not have that knowledge and they must do a dynamic invocation.

- **IDL stub:** Makes calls to the ORB core on behalf of a client application. IDL stubs provide a set of mechanisms that abstract the ORB core functions into direct RPC (remote procedure call) mechanisms that can be employed by the end-client applications. These stubs make the combination of the ORB and remote object implementation appear as if they were tied to the same in-line process. In most cases, IDL compilers generate language-specific interface libraries that complete the interface between the client and object implementations.

- **IDL skeleton:** Provides the code that invokes specific server methods. Static IDL skeletons are the server-side complements to the client-side IDL stubs. They include the bindings between the ORB core and the object implementations that complete the connection between the client and object implementations.

- **Dynamic invocation:** Using the dynamic invocation interface (DII), a client application can invoke requests on any object without having compile-time knowledge of the object's interfaces. The interface details are filled in by consulting with an interface repository and/or other run-time sources. The DII allows a client to issue one-way commands (for which there is no response).

- **Dynamic skeleton interface (DSI):** Similar to the relationship between IDL stubs and static IDL skeletons, the DSI provides dynamic dispatch to objects. Equivalent to dynamic invocation on the server side.

- **Object adapter:** An object adapter is CORBA system component provided by the CORBA vendor to handle general ORB-related tasks, such as activating objects and activating implementations. The adapter takes these general tasks and ties them to particular implementations and methods in the server.

B.5 RECOMMENDED READINGS AND WEB SITES

[KORS90] is a good overview of object-oriented concepts. [STRO88] is a clear description of object-oriented programming. An interesting perspective on object-oriented concepts is provided in [SYND93]. [VINO97] is an overview of CORBA.

KORS90 Korson, T., and McGregor, J. "Understanding Object-Oriented: A Unifying Paradigm." *Communications of the ACM*, September 1990.

STRO88 Stroustrup, B. "What is Object-Oriented Programming?" *IEEE Software*, May 1988.

SNYD93 Snyder, A. "The Essence of Objects: Concepts and Terms." *IEEE Software*, January 1993.

VINO97 Vinoski, S. "CORBA: Integrating Diverse Applications Within Distributed Heterogeneous Environments." *IEEE Communications Magazine*, February 1997.

Recommended Web Sites:

- **Object Management Group:** Industry consortium that promotes CORBA and related object technologies

APPENDIX C

PROGRAMMING AND OPERATING SYSTEM PROJECTS

762

Many instructors believe that implementation or research projects are crucial to the clear understanding of operating system concepts. Without projects, it may be difficult for students to grasp some of the basic OS abstractions and interactions among components; a good example of a concept that many students find difficult to master is that of semaphores. Projects reinforce the concepts introduced in this book, give the student a greater appreciation of how the different pieces of an OS fit together, and can motivate students and give them confidence that they are capable of not only understanding but implementing the details of an OS.

In this text, I have tried to present the concepts of OS internals as clearly as possible and have provided numerous homework problems to reinforce those concepts. However, many instructors will wish to supplement this material with projects. This appendix provides some guidance in that regard and describes support material available at the instructor's Web site. Further details are provided in Appendices D and E.

C.1   PROJECTS FOR TEACHING OPERATING SYSTEMS

The instructor can choose from the following approaches.

- **Operating Systems Projects (OSP):** OSP is both an implementation of a modern operating system and a flexible environment for generating implementation projects appropriate for an introductory course in OS design. OSP is accompanied by a number of project assignments.

- **Ben-Ari Concurrent Interpreter (BACI):** BACI simulates concurrent process execution and supports binary and counting semaphores and monitors. BACI is accompanied by a number of project assignments to be used to reinforce concurrency concepts.

- **Nachos:** As with OSP, Nachos is an environment for generating implementation projects to reinforce concepts and is also accompanied by a number of project assignments.

- **Research projects:** The instructor's Web site provides a series of research assignments that assign the student to research a particular topic on the Internet and write a report.

- **Programming projects:** The instructor's Web site provides a set of small programming projects that can be assigned to reinforce concepts in the book; any language can be used. The projects cover a wide range of topics dealt with in this book.

- **Reading/report assignments:** The instructor's Web site includes a list of important papers, one or more for each chapter, that can be assigned to students to produce a short report analyzing the paper.

This appendix provides a brief discussion of these topics. Appendix D provides a more detailed introduction to OSP, with information about how to obtain the system and the programming assignments. Appendix E provides the same type of information for BACI. Nachos is well documented at its Web site and is described briefly in the next section.

C.2 NACHOS

Nachos Overview

Nachos is an instructional operating system that runs as a UNIX process, to provide students with a reproducible debugging environment, and that simulates an operating system and its underlying hardware [CHRI93]. The goal of Nachos is to provide a project environment that is realistic enough to show how real operating systems work yet simple enough that students can understand and modify it in significant ways.

A free distribution package is available via the Web that includes

- An overview paper.
- Simple baseline code for a working operating system.
- A simulator for a generic personal computer/workstation.
- Sample assignments: The assignments illustrate and explore all areas of modern operating systems, including threads and concurrency, multiprogramming, system calls, virtual memory, software-loaded TLBs, file systems, network protocols, remote procedure calls, and distributed systems.
- A C++ primer (Nachos is written in an easy-to-learn subset of C++, and the primer helps teach C programmers this subset).

Nachos has been used at hundreds of universities around the world and has been ported to numerous systems, including Linux, FreeBSD, NetBSD, DEC MIPS, DEC Alpha, Sun Solaris, SGI IRIX, HP-UX, IBM AIX, MS-DOS, and Apple Macintosh. Future plans include a port to Stanford's SimOS, a complete machine simulation of an SGI workstation.

Nachos is freely available from its Web site (there is a link to their Web site from WilliamStallings.com/OS/OS5e.html); a solution set is available to instructors by e-mail from nachos@cs.berkeley.edu. In addition, there is a mailing list for instructors and a newsgroup (alt.os.nachos).

Choosing among Nachos, OSP, and BACI

If the instructor is willing to take the time to port one of these three simulators to the local environment available to the students, then the choice among these three will depend on the instructor's objectives and personal opinion. If the focus of the projects is to be on concurrency, then BACI is the clear choice. BACI provides an excellent environment for studying the intricacies and subtleties of semaphores, monitors, and concurrent programming.

If, instead, the instructor wishes to have students explore a variety of OS mechanisms, including concurrent programming, address spaces and scheduling, virtual memory, file systems, networking, and so on, then either Nachos or OSP may be used.

I have included an appendix on OSP because I feel it is one of the best vehicles available for supporting OS projects. OSP is in use at over 100 sites and provides a great deal of support and documentation. One potential drawback is that although the system, sample assignments, and mailing-list support are free, there is a small user's manual that students are expected to purchase. However, this must be balanced against the strengths of this environment. Nachos is similarly widely used and provides support, documentation, and suggested assignments. The instructor is urged to study Appendix D and, if interested, compare it to the Nachos overview paper and other documentation available at the Nachos Web site.

C.3 RESEARCH PROJECTS

An effective way of reinforcing basic concepts from the course and for teaching students research skills is to assign a research project. Such a project could involve a literature search as well as a Web search of vendor products, research lab activities, and standardization efforts. Projects could be assigned to teams or, for smaller projects, to individuals. In any case, it is best to require some sort of project proposal early in the term, giving the instructor time to evaluate the proposal for appropriate topic and appropriate level of effort. Student handouts for research projects should include

- A format for the proposal
- A format for the final report
- A schedule with intermediate and final deadlines
- A list of possible project topics

The students can select one of the listed topics or devise their own comparable project. The instructor's Web site includes a suggested format for the proposal and final report as well as a list of possible research topics developed by Professor Tan N. Nguyen of George Mason University.

C.4 PROGRAMMING PROJECTS

An alternative to the development of portions of an OS, using OSP or Nachos, or concentrating on concurrency, using BACI, is to assign a number of programming projects that require no infrastructure. There are several advantages of programming projects versus the use of a support framework such as OSP or BACI:

1. The instructor can choose from a wide variety of OS-related concepts to assign projects, not just those that would fit in the support framework.
2. The projects can be programmed by the students on any available computer and in any appropriate language: They are platform- and language-independent.
3. The instructor need not download, install, and configure the infrastructure.

There is also flexibility in the size of projects. Larger projects give students more a sense of achievement, but students with less ability or fewer organizational skills can be left behind. Larger projects usually elicit more overall effort from the best students. Smaller projects can have a higher concepts-to-code ratio, and because more of them can be assigned, the opportunity exists to address a variety of different areas. On balance, the advantage seems to lie with smaller projects. Accordingly, the instructor's Web site contains a series of small projects, each intended to be completed in a week or so, which can be very satisfying to both student and teacher. These projects were developed by Stephen Taylor at Worcester Polytechnic Institute, who has used and refined the projects in the course of teaching operating systems a dozen times.

In addition, two more substantial programming projects are outlined in the text, after Chapters 3 and 9. A more detailed, step-by-step set of instructions for these two projects is provided at the instructor's Web site.

C.5 READING/REPORT ASSIGNMENTS

Another excellent way to reinforce concepts from the course and to give students research experience is to assign papers from the literature to be read and analyzed. The instructor's Web site includes a suggested list of papers to be assigned, organized by chapter. All of the papers are readily available either via the Internet or in any good college technical library. The instructor's Web site also includes a suggested assignment wording.

APPENDIX D

OSP: An Environment for Operating Systems Projects*

---

*By Michael Kifer and Scott A. Smolka, Department of Computer Science SUNY at Stony Brook, {kifer,sas}@cs.sunysb.edu.

D.1 OVERVIEW

OSP2 and OSP are both an implementation of a modern operating system and a flexible environment for generating implementation projects appropriate for an introductory course in operating system design [KEFE92]. It is intended to complement the use of an introductory textbook on operating systems and contains enough projects for up to three semesters. These projects expose students to many essential features of operating systems while at the same time isolating them from low-level machine-dependent concerns. Thus, even in one semester, students can learn about page replacement strategies in virtual memory management, processor scheduling strategies, disk seek time optimization, and other issues in operating system design. At the same time, both systems provide convenient environments in which to create and administer implementation projects for the students, thereby automating this routine work for the instructor. Projects can be organized in any desired order so as to progress in a manner consistent with the lecture material.

Students program their OSP 2 projects in the Java programming language. Additionally, the original OSP system, which is based on the C programming language, is still available. The new OSP 2 system can be used in both the Windows and UNIX/Linux environments; the original OSP system works under UNIX/Linux only. While the operating system model underlying OSP 2 is more modern and featurefull, some instructors prefer to have their students program in C. This need can be satisfied by the original OSP system.

Both OSP2 and OSP consist of a number of modules, each of which performs a basic operating systems service, such as device scheduling, processor scheduling, interrupt handling, file management, memory management, process management, resource management, and interprocess communication. By selectively omitting any subset of modules, the instructor can generate a project in which the students are to implement the missing parts. This process is completely automated. Projects can be organized in any desired order so as to progress in a manner consistent with the lecture material.

Each project consists of a "partial load module" of standard modules to which the students link their implementation of the assigned modules. The result is a new and complete operating system, partially implemented by the student. The projects also come with module template files, which contain declarations of requisite data structures for each of the assigned modules. These files are given as part of a project assignment in which the students are to fill in the procedure bodies. In this way, template files help eliminate much of the routine typing, both by the instructor and by the students.

At the heart of OSP 2 and OSP are simulators that give the illusion of a computer system with a dynamically evolving collection of user processes to be multiprogrammed. All the other modules of OSP2 and OSP are built to respond appropriately to the simulator-generated events that drive the operating system. The simulator "understands" its interaction with the other modules in that it can often detect an erroneous response by a module to a simulated event. In such cases, the simulator will gracefully terminate execution of the program by delivering a meaningful error message to the user, indicating where the error might be found. This facility serves both as a debugging tool for the student and as teaching tool for the instructor, as it ensures that student programs acceptable to the simulator are virtually bug free.

The difficulty of the job streams generated by the simulator can be dynamically adjusted by manipulating the simulation parameters. This yields a simple and effective way of testing the quality of student programs. There are also facilities that allow the students to debug their programs by interacting with OSP2 or OSP during simulation.

The underlying model of OSP 2 and OSP is not a clone of any specific operating system. Rather it is an abstraction of the features commonly found in several systems (although a bias toward UNIX can be seen, at times). Although OSP 2 and OSP modules were designed to hide many of the low-level concerns one encounters in operating system design and implementation, the modules still encompass the most salient aspects of their real-life counterparts in modern systems. Their implementation is well suited as the project component of an introductory course in operating systems. OSP 2 is described in the following book, which is to be published by Addison-Wesley by the end of 2004:

> *Introduction to Operating System Design and Implementation: The OSP 2 Approach,* Michael Kifer and Scott A. Smolka, Addison-Wesley.

The original OSP is documented in the following book, which is still available from the publisher:

> *OSP: An Environment for Operating System Projects,* Michael Kifer and Scott A. Smolka, Addison-Wesley, ISBN 0-201-54887-9 (1991).

Instructor's manuals are available to instructors only from the OSP Web site: http://www.cs.sunysb.edu/osp. Users must be registered with the site and be verified as instructors.

D.2 INNOVATIVE ASPECTS OF OSP

The major innovative aspects of OSP 2 and OSP are as follows:

- The modules that students write over the course of a semester are built to respond appropriately to the simulator-generated events that drive the operating system. Students can adjust the difficulty of the job streams generated by the simulator by supplying different values for the simulation parameters requested by the system. This yields a simple and effective way for students to test the quality of their programs. There are also facilities that allow students to debug their programs by interacting with OSP2 or OSP during simulation.

- OSP provides the instructor with a convenient environment, the OSP Project Generator, in which to create implementation projects. The Project Generator produces generates a "partial load module" of standard OSP modules to which the students link their implementations of the assigned modules. The result is a new and complete operating system, partially implemented by the student. OSP 2 also provides a project generator but additionally comes equipped with preassembled projects; this further lessens the effort required of the instructor in developing student projects.

   Additionally, the project generator automatically creates template files containing procedure headings and declarations of requisite data structures for each of the assigned modules. These files are given as part of a project assignment in which the students are to fill in the procedure bodies. This ensures a consistent interface to OSP and eliminates much of the routine typing, both by the instructor and by the students.

- OSP 2 and OSP also include optional project submission systems, which the instructor can use to have students submit their assignments in a convenient and "safe" fashion. The submission system will compile the student's sources and run the executable with a given parameter file.

  The sources of the student-implemented modules and the output from the compilation stage and the simulation runs are placed in a submissions directory in the course account. Students do not have access to these output files, so they cannot be tampered with.

  Students may submit their programs any number of times. Each new submission overwrites the previous one. Each submission has an associated time stamp, so the instructor can verify deadlines.

- The OSP2 and OSP simulators carefully monitor the run-time behavior of student-implemented modules and in many cases can issue a warning message when the behavior of a student module deviates from the norm. For example, if the student has written the module that handles user I/O requests, the simulator will check that an I/O Request Block (IORB) has been properly inserted on the appropriate device queue. If not, the simulator will issue a descriptive message warning the student that the I/O request has not been correctly handled.

  The careful monitoring carried out by the simulator constitutes a valuable interactive debugging aid to the student: It is almost always the case that if the execution of a student's solution proceeds without eliciting any simulator warning messages, then the student's code is functionally correct.

- OSP2 and OSP provide a comprehensive debugging interface to the simulator that allows the student to periodically view (take a snapshot of) the system -status during simulation. Information displayed during a snapshot includes the contents of the main memory frame table, device tables, PCB (Process Control Block) pool, and event queues. A snapshot also offers the user an opportunity to change the simulation parameters. One such parameter, the `snapshot_interval/`, may be set by the user to indicate how often during simulation the system status is to be displayed.

- OSP 2 and OSP are fully documented in two textbooks; they provide students with all the information they will need to complete their assignments, including detailed specifications of each of the modules, and instructions for compiling, executing, and submitting their assignments. The instructor's manual supplements these texts with information on how to install each system and with instructions on how to use the submission system.

  The OSP Web site, http://www.cs.sunysb.edu/osp/, contains a number of OSP 2 /OSP programming assignments that have been assigned by us and other instructors to our students.

- The OSP Web site provides registered users with a discussion forum. The purpose of the forum is to serve as a medium for discussions on OSP among its users and as a means of informing the OSP community of any changes to the software and documentation (e.g., bug fixes, enhancements, future versions).

D.3 COMPARISON WITH OTHER OPERATING SYSTEM COURSEWARE

Operating system courseware can be categorized into two groups: those based on a simulator (e.g., Berkeley's Toy operating system and Nachos, MPX) and those that are based on the source code of actual operating systems that run directly on a bare machine (e.g., MINIX [TANE97]), XINU [COME84], and Linux). OSP clearly falls into the first category. The two categories of courseware can be seen to fill two distinct niches in operating system education. Bare-machine software enjoys the benefit of allowing the student to become intimately familiar with the low-level details of the machine architecture and yields a sense of immediacy that may not be present in simulator-based software. Simulator-based software, on the other hand, intentionally shields the student from the bare essentials of any particular machine architecture and allows the student to focus on implementing operating system concepts discussed in class or in the course text.

Within the realm of simulator-based software, OSP2 and OSP are distinguished by the following combination of attributes:

- **Flexibility:** Instructors have complete freedom in assigning projects around their favorite topics, in any desired order. Furthermore, each project is not bound to any specific disk or processor scheduling strategy, memory management or deadlock avoidance policy, and so on.

- **Degree of realism offered by the simulator:** OSP2 and OSP are based on a faithful simulation of events that occur in a typical operating system so that the instructor is well equipped to evaluate the quality of student implementations. The simulator has a number of built-in security checks that make it difficult to forge results and thereby simplify the verification of a student's projects.

- **Ease of use:** Experience has shown that OSP2 and OSP are relatively easy to use from both the instructor and student perspectives. The instructor is spared the administrative burden of handcrafting assignments. These are generated automatically by the Project Generator and contain all the information necessary for the students to complete the assignments. The debugging interface to the simulator significantly decreases the amount of time a student need spend completing an assignment. Finally, the project submission system makes life easier for both the instructor and the student.

Note that the aforementioned OSP Web site is intended solely for use by instructors of operating systems courses that use the OSP 2 and OSP software. In particular, it is not intended for students of such courses. Therefore, each registered user must be verified as an instructor before any downloads can be seen.

APPENDIX E

BACI: THE BEN-ARI CONCURRENT PROGRAMMING SYSTEM*†

*By Bill Bynum, College of William and Mary, and Tracy Camp, Colorado School of Mines.
†This work was supported in part by National Science Foundation (NSF) Grant NCR-9702449.

E.1 INTRODUCTION

In Chapter 5, concurrency concepts are introduced (e.g., mutual exclusion and the critical section problem) and synchronization techniques are proposed (e.g., semaphores, monitors, and message passing). Deadlock and starvation issues for concurrent programs are discussed in Chapter 6. Due to the increasing emphasis on parallel and distributed computing, understanding concurrency and synchronization is more necessary than ever. To obtain a thorough understanding of these concepts, practical experience writing concurrent programs is needed.

Three options exist for this desired "hands-on" experience. First, we can write concurrent programs with an established concurrent programming language such as Concurrent Pascal, Modula, Ada, or the SR Programming Language. To experiment with a variety of synchronization techniques, however, we must learn the syntax of many concurrent programming languages. Second, we can write concurrent programs using system calls in an operating system such as UNIX. It is easy, however, to be distracted from the goal of understanding concurrent programming by the details and peculiarities of a particular operating system (e.g., details of the semaphore system calls in UNIX). Lastly, we can write concurrent programs with a language developed specifically for giving experience with concurrency concepts such as the Ben-Ari Concurrent Interpreter (BACI) [BYNU96]. Using such a language offers a variety of synchronization techniques with a syntax that is usually familiar. Languages developed specifically for giving experience with concurrency concepts are the best option to obtain the desired hands-on experience.

Section E.2 contains a brief overview of the BACI system and how to obtain the system. Section E.3 contains examples of BACI programs, and Section E.4 contains a discussion of projects for practical concurrency experience at the implementation and programming levels. Lastly, Section E.5 contains a description of changes to the BACI system that are in progress or have been planned.

E.2 BACI

System Overview

BACI is a direct descendant of Ben-Ari's modification to sequential Pascal (Pascal-S). Pascal-S is a subset of standard Pascal by Wirth, without files, except INPUT and OUTPUT, sets, pointer variables, and goto statements. Ben-Ari took the Pascal-S language and added concurrent programming constructs such as the **cobegin . . . coend** construct and the semaphore variable type with **wait** and **signal** operations [BEN82]. BACI is Ben-Ari's modification to Pascal-S with additional synchronization features (e.g., monitors) as well as encapsulation mechanisms to ensure that a user is prevented from modifying a variable inappropriately (e.g., a semaphore variable should only be modified by semaphore functions).

BACI simulates concurrent process execution and supports the following synchronization techniques: general semaphores, binary semaphores, and monitors. The BACI system is composed of two subsystems, as illustrated in Figure E.1. The first subsystem, the compiler, compiles a user's program into intermediate object code, called PCODE. There are two compilers available with the BACI system,

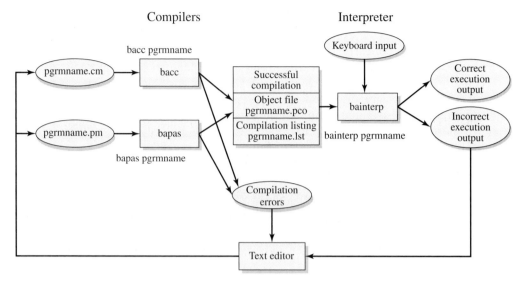

Figure E.1   Overview of the BACI System

corresponding to two popular languages taught in introductory programming courses. The syntax of one compiler is similar to standard Pascal; BACI programs that use the Pascal syntax are denoted as pgrm-name.pm. The syntax of the other compiler is similar to standard C++; these BACI programs are denoted as pgrm-name.cm. Both compilers create two files during the compilation: **pgrm-name.lst** and **pgrm-name.pco**.

The second subsystem in the BACI system, the interpreter, executes the object code created by the compiler. In other words, the interpreter executes **pgrm-name.pco**. The core of the interpreter is a preemptive scheduler; during execution, this scheduler randomly swaps between concurrent processes, thus simulating a parallel execution of the concurrent processes. The interpreter offers a number of different debug options, such as single-step execution, disassembly of PCODE instructions, and display of program storage locations.

Concurrency Constructs in BACI

In the rest of this appendix, we focus on the compiler similar to standard C++. We call this compiler C--; although the syntax is similar to C++, it does not include inheritance, encapsulation, or other object-oriented programming features. In this section, we give an overview of the BACI concurrency constructs; see the user's guides at the BACI Web site for further details of the required Pascal or C-- BACI syntax.

cobegin   A list of processes to be run concurrently is enclosed in a cobegin block. Such blocks cannot be nested and must appear in the main program.

$$\text{cobegin } \{ \text{proc1}(...); \text{proc2}(...); ... ; \text{procN}(...); \}$$

The PCODE statements created by the compiler for the above block are interleaved by the interpreter in an arbitrary, "random" order; multiple executions of the same program containing a cobegin block will appear to be nondeterministic.

Semaphores A semaphore in BACI is a nonnegative-valued **int** variable, which can only be accessed by the semaphore calls defined subsequently. A binary semaphore in BACI, one that only assumes the values 0 and 1, is supported by the **binarysem** subtype of the **semaphore** type. During compilation and execution, the compiler and interpreter enforce the restrictions that a **binarysem** variable can only have the values 0 or 1 and that semaphore type can only be nonnegative. BACI semaphore calls include

- initialsem(semaphore sem, int expression)
- p(semaphore sem): If the value of **sem** is greater than zero, then the interpreter decrements **sem** by one and returns, allowing **p's** caller to continue. If the value of **sem** is equal to zero, then the interpreter puts **p's** caller to sleep. The command **wait** is accepted as a synonym for **p**.
- **v(semaphore sem)**: If the value of **sem** is equal to zero and one or more processes are sleeping on **sem**, then wake up one of these processes. If no processes are waiting on **sem**, then increment **sem** by one. In any event, **v's** caller is allowed to continue. (BACI conforms to Dijkstra's original semaphore proposal by randomly choosing which process to wake up when a signal arrives.) The command **signal** is accepted as a synonym for **v**.

Monitors BACI supports the monitor concept, as proposed by Hoare [HOAR74], with some restrictions; the implementation is based on work done by [PRAM84]. A monitor is a C++ block, like a block defined by a procedure or function, with some additional properties (e.g., conditional variables). In BACI, a monitor must be declared at the outermost, global level and it cannot be nested with another monitor block. Three constructs are used by the procedures and functions of a monitor to control concurrency: condition variables, **waitc** (wait on a condition), and **signalc** (signal a condition). A condition never actually "has" a value; it is somewhere to wait or something to signal. A monitor process can wait for a condition to hold or signal that a given condition now holds through the **waitc** and **signalc** calls. **waitc** and **signalc** calls have the following syntax and semantics:

- **waitc(condition cond, int prio)**: The monitor process (and hence the outside process calling the monitor process) is blocked on the condition **cond** and assigned the priority **prio**.
- **waitc(condition cond)**: This call has the same semantics as the **waitc** call, but the **wait** is assigned a default priority of 10.
- **signalc(condition cond)**: Wake some process waiting on **cond** with the smallest (highest) priority; if no process is waiting on **cond**, do nothing.

BACI conforms to the immediate resumption requirement. In other words, a process waiting on a condition has priority over a process trying to enter the monitor, if the process waiting on a condition has been signaled.

Other Concurrency Constructs The C-- BACI compiler provides several low-level concurrency constructs that can be used to create new concurrency control primitives. If a function is defined as atomic, then the function is nonpreemptible. In other words, the interpreter will not interrupt an atomic function with a context switch. In BACI, the suspend function puts the calling process to sleep and the revive function revives a suspended process.

How to Obtain BACI

The BACI system, with two user guides (one for each of the two compilers) and detailed project descriptions, is available at the BACI Web site (there is a link to their Web site from WilliamStallings.com/OS/OS5e.html). The BACI system is written in C and, therefore, easily portable. Currently, the BACI system can be compiled in Linux, RS/6000 AIX, Sun OS, DOS, and CYGWIN on Windows with minimal modifications to the Makefile file. (See the README file in the distribution for installation details for a given platform.) We can be reached at bynum@cs.wm.edu or tcamp@mines.edu.

E.3   EXAMPLES OF BACI PROGRAMS

In Chapters 5 and 6, a number of the classical synchronization problems were discussed (e.g., the readers/writers problem and the dining philosophers problem). In this section, we illustrate the BACI system with three BACI programs. Our first example illustrates the nondeterminism in the execution of concurrent processes in the BACI system. Consider the following program:

```
const int m = 5;
int n;
void incr(char id)
{
    int i;
    for(i = 1; i <= m; i = i + 1)
    {
        n = n + 1;
        cout << id << " n =" << n << " i =";
        cout << i << " " << id << endl;
    }
}
main( )
{
    n = 0;
    cobegin {
        incr( 'A'); incr( 'B' ); incr('C');
    }
    cout << "The sum is " << n << endl;
}
```

Note in the preceding program that if each of the three processes created (A, B, and C) executed sequentially, the output sum would be 15. Concurrent execution of the statement **n = n + 1**;, however, can lead to different values of the output sum. After we compiled the preceding program with bacc, we executed the PCODE file with bainterp a number of times. Each execution produced output sums between 9 and 15. One sample execution produced by the BACI interpreter is the following.

```
Source file: incremen.cm Fri Aug 1 16:51:00 1997
CB n =2 i =1 C n =2
A n =2 i =1 i =1 A
CB
    n =3 i =2 C
A n =4 i =2 C n =5 i =3 C
A
B n =6C i =2 B
    n =7 i =4 C
A n =8 i =3 A
BC n =10 n =10 i =5 C
A n = i =311 i =4 A
 B
A n =12 i =B5  n =13A
   i =4 B
B n =14 i =5 B
The sum is 14
```

Special machine instructions are needed to synchronize the access of processes to a common main memory. Mutual exclusion protocols, or synchronization primitives, are then built on top of these special instructions. In BACI, the interpreter will not interrupt a function defined as atomic with a context switch. This feature allows users to implement these low-level special machine instructions. For example, the following program is a BACI implementation of the testset function defined in Section 5.2.

```
// Test and set instruction
// Stallings, Section 5.2
//
atomic int testset(int& i)
{
   if (i == 0) {
      i = 1;
      return 1;
   }
```

```
        else
            return 0;
    }
```

We can use testset to implement mutual exclusion protocols, as shown in the following program. This program is a BACI implementation of a mutual exclusion program based on the test and set instruction. The program assumes three concurrent processes; each process requests mutual exclusion 10 times.

```
int bolt = 0;
const int RepeatCount = 10;
void proc(int id)
{
    int i = 0;
    while(i < RepeatCount) {
        while (testset(bolt)); // wait
            // enter critical section
            cout << id;
        // leave critical section
        bolt = 0;
        i++;
    }
}
main( )
{
    cobegin {
        proc(0); proc(1); proc(2);
    }
}
```

The following two programs are a BACI solution to the bounded-buffer producer/consumer problem with semaphores (see Figure 5.13). In this example, we have two producers, three consumers, and a buffer size of five. We first list the program details for this problem. We then list the include file that defines the bounded buffer implementation.

```
// A solution to the bounded-buffer producer/consumer problem
// Stallings, Figure 5.13
// bring in the bounded buffer machinery
#include "boundedbuff.inc"
const int ValueRange = 20; // integers in 0..19 will be produced
semaphore to;   // for exclusive access to terminal output
```

```
semaphore s;    // mutual exclusion for the buffer
semaphore n;    // # consumable items in the buffer
semaphore e;    // # empty spaces in the buffer
int produce(char id)
{
    int tmp;
    tmp = random(ValueRange);
    wait(to);
    cout << "Producer " << id << " produces " << tmp << endl;
    signal(to);
    return tmp;
}
void consume(char id, int i)
{
    wait(to);
    cout << "Consumer " << id << " consumes " << i << endl;
    signal(to);
}
void producer(char id)
{
    int i;
    for (;;) {
        i = produce(id);
        wait(e);
        wait(s);
        append(i);
        signal(s);
        signal(n);
    }
}
void consumer(char id)
{
    int i;
    for (;;) {
        wait(n);
        wait(s);
        i = take();
        signal(s);
        signal(e);
        consume(id,i);
    }
}
```

```
main( )
{
    initialsem(s,1);
    initialsem(n,0);
    initialsem(e,SizeOfBuffer);
    initialsem(to,1);
    cobegin {
        producer('A'); producer('B');
        consumer('x'); consumer('y'); consumer('z');
    }
}
// boundedbuff.inc -- bounded buffer include file
const int SizeOfBuffer = 5;
int buffer[SizeOfBuffer];
int in = 0;      // index of buffer to use for next append
int out = 0;     // index of buffer to use for next take
void append(int v)
    // add v to the buffer
    // overrun is assumed to be taken care of
    // externally through semaphores or conditions
{
    buffer[in] = v;
    in = (in + 1) % SizeOfBuffer;
}
int take( )
    // return an item from the buffer
// underrun is assumed to be taken care of
// externally through a semaphore or condition
{
    int tmp;
    tmp = buffer[out];
    out = (out + 1) % SizeOfBuffer;
    return tmp;
}
```

One sample execution of the preceding bounded-buffer solution in BACI is the following.

```
Source file: semprodcons.cm Fri Aug 1 12:36:55 1997
Producer B produces 4
Producer A produces 13
Producer B produces 12
```

Producer A produces 4
Producer B produces 17
Consumer x consumes 4
Consumer y consumes 13
Producer A produces 16
Producer B produces 11
Consumer z consumes 12
Consumer x consumes 4
Consumer y consumes 17
Producer B produces 6

. . .

E.4 BACI PROJECTS

In this section, we discuss two general types of projects one can implement in BACI. We first discuss projects that involve the implementation of low-level operations (e.g., special machine instructions that are used to synchronize the access of processes to a common main memory). We then discuss projects that are built on top of these low-level operations (e.g. classical synchronization problems). For more information on these projects see [BYNU96] and the project descriptions included in the BACI distribution. For solutions to some of these projects, teachers should contact the authors. In addition to the projects discussed in this section, many of the problems at the end of Chapter 5 and Appendix A can be implemented in BACI.

Implementation of Synchronization Primitives

Implementation of Machine Instructions There are numerous machine instructions that one can implement in BACI. For example, one can implement the exchange instruction given in Figure 5.2 or the compare-and-swap operation given in [HERL90]. The implementation of these instructions should be based on an atomic function that returns an int value. You can test your implementation of the machine instruction by building a mutual exclusion protocol on top of your low-level operation.

Implementation of Fair Semaphores (FIFO) The semaphore operation in BACI is implemented with a random wake up order, which is how semaphores were originally defined by Dijkstra. As discussed in Section 5.3, however, the fairest policy is FIFO. We can implement semaphores with this FIFO wake up order in BACI. At least the following four procedures should be defined in the implementation:

- `CreateSemaphores()` to initialize the program code
- `InitSemaphore(int sem-index)` to initialize the semaphore represented by `sem-index`
- `FIFOP(int sem-index)`
- `FIFOV(int sem-index)`

This code needs to be written as a system implementation and, as such, should handle all possible errors. In other words, the semaphore designer is responsible for producing code that is robust in the presence of ignorant, stupid, or even malicious use by the user community.

Semaphores, Monitors, and Implementations

There are many classical concurrent programming problems: the producer/consumer problem, the dining philosophers, the reader/writer problem with different priorities, the sleeping barber problem, and the cigarette smokers problem. All of these problems can be implemented in BACI. In this section, we discuss nonstandard semaphore/monitor projects that one can implement in BACI to further aid the understanding of concurrency and synchronization concepts.

As and Bs and Semaphores For the following program outline in BACI,

```
// global semaphore declarations here
void A( )
{
    p( )'s and v( )'s ONLY
}
void B( )
{
    p( )'s and v( )'s ONLY
}
main( )
{
    // semaphore initialization here
    cobegin {
        A( ); A( ); A( ); B( ); B( );
    }
}
```

complete the program using the least number of general semaphores, such that the processes ALWAYS terminate in the order A (any copy), B (any copy), A (any copy), A, B. Use the -t option of the interpreter to display process termination. (Many variations of this project exist. For example, have four concurrent processes terminate in the order ABAA or eight concurrent processes terminate in the order AABABABB.)

Using Binary Semaphores Repeat the previous project using binary semaphores. Evaluate why assignment and IF-THEN-ELSE statements are necessary in this solution, although they were not necessary in solutions to the previous project. In other words, explain why you cannot use only Ps and Vs in this case.

Busy Waiting versus Semaphores Compare the performance of a solution to mutual exclusion that uses busy waiting (e.g. the testset instruction) to a solution that uses semaphores. For example, compare a semaphore solution and a testset solution to the ABAAB project discussed previously. In each case, use a large number of executions (say, 1000) to obtain better statistics. Discuss your results, explaining why one implementation is preferred over another.

Semaphores and Monitors In the spirit of Problem 5.17, implement a monitor using general semaphores and then implement a general semaphore using a monitor in BACI.

General and Binary Semaphores Prove that general semaphores and binary semaphores are equally powerful, by implementing one type of semaphore with the other type of semaphore and vice versa.

Time Ticks: A Monitor Project Similar to Problem 7.17 in [SILB02], write a program containing a monitor AlarmClock. The monitor must have an `int` variable `theClock` (initialized to zero) and two functions:

- `Tick()`: This function increments `theClock` each time that it is called. It can do other things, like `signalc`, if needed.
- `int Alarm(int id, int delta)`: This function blocks the caller with identifier `id` for at least `delta` ticks of `theClock`.

The main program should have two functions as well:

- `void Ticker()`: This procedure calls `Tick()` in a repeat-forever loop.
- `void Thread(int id, int myDelta)`: This function calls `Alarm` in a repeat-forever loop.

You may endow the monitor with any other variables that it needs. The monitor should be able to accommodate up to five simultaneous alarms.

A Problem of a Popular Baker Due to the recent popularity of a bakery, almost every customer needs to wait for service. To maintain service, the baker wants to install a ticket system that will ensure that customers are served in turn. Construct a BACI implementation of this ticket system.

E.5 ENHANCEMENTS TO THE BACI SYSTEM

We are enhancing the BACI System in several ways.

1. We have added a graphical user interface (GUI) for the UNIX version of BACI. This GUI allows the user to edit, compile, and interpret BACI programs all in the same system. Colored windows illustrate the execution of a BACI program. The BACI GUI is available at http://www.mines.edu/fs_home/tcamp/GUI/index.html. For an alternative GUI, see below.

2. We have created a distributed version of BACI. Similar to concurrent programs, it is difficult to prove the correctness of distributed programs without an implementation. Distributed BACI will allow distributed programs to be easily implemented. In addition to proving the correctness of a distributed program, one can use distributed BACI to test the program's performance. Distributed BACI is available at http://www.mines.edu/fs_home/tcamp/dbaci/index.html.

3. We have a PCODE disassembler that will provide the user with an annotated listing of a PCODE file, showing the mnemonics for each PCODE instruction and, if available, the corresponding program source that generated the instruction. This PCODE disassembler is included in the BACI System.

4. We have added the capability of separate compilation and external variables to both compilers. The BACI System includes an archiver and a linker that enable the creation and use of libraries of BACI PCODE. For more details, see the BACI Separate Compilation User's Guide.

5. An implementation of the BACI System in Java is currently under construction with completion expected in the summer of 2004. This version of the BACI System will run on any computer that has an installation of the Java Virtual Machine.

The BACI system has also been enhanced by others.

1. David Strite, an M.S. student who worked with Linda Null from the Pennsylvania State University, created a BACI Debugger: A GUI Debugger for the BACI System. This GUI is available at http://cs.hbg.psu.edu/~null/baci/.

2. Using BACI and the BACI GUI from Pennsylvania State University, Moti Ben-Ari from the Weizmann Institute of Science in Israel created an integrated development environment for learning concurrent programming by simulating concurrency called jBACI. jBACI is available at: http://stwww.weizmann.ac.il/g-cs/benari/jbaci/.

GLOSSARY

access method   The method that is used to find a file, a record, or a set of records.

address space   The range of addresses available to a computer program.

address translator   A functional unit that transforms virtual addresses to real addresses.

application programming interface (API)   A standardized library of programming tools used by software developers to write applications that are compatible with a specific operating system or graphic user interface.

asynchronous operation   An operation that occurs without a regular or predictable time relationship to a specified event, for example, the calling of an error diagnostic routine that may receive control at any time during the execution of a computer program.

base address   An address that is used as the origin in the calculation of addresses in the execution of a computer program.

batch processing   Pertaining to the technique of executing a set of computer programs such that each is completed before the next program of the set is started.

Beowulf   Defines a class of clustered computing that focuses on minimizing the price-to-performance ratio of the overall system without compromising its ability to perform the computation work for which it is being built. Most Beowulf systems are implemented on Linux computers.

binary semaphore   A semaphore that takes on only the values 0 and 1. A binary semaphore allows only one process or thread to have access to a shared critical resource at a time.

block   (1) A collection of contiguous records that are recorded as a unit; the units are separated by interblock gaps. (2) A group of bits that are transmitted as a unit.

busy waiting   The repeated execution of a loop of code while waiting for an event to occur.

cache memory   A memory that is smaller and faster than main memory and that is interposed between the processor and main memory. The cache acts as a buffer for recently used memory locations.

central processing unit (CPU)   That portion of a computer that fetches and executes instructions. It consists of an Arithmetic and Logic Unit (ALU), a control unit, and registers. Often simply referred to as a *processor*.

chained list   A list in which data items may be dispersed but in which each item contains an identifier for locating the next item.

client   A process that requests services by sending messages to server processes.

cluster   A group of interconnected, whole computers working together as a unified computing resource that can create the illusion of being one machine. The term *whole computer* means a system that can run on its own, apart from the cluster.

communications architecture   The hardware and software structure that implements the communications function.

compaction   A technique used when memory is divided into variable-size partitions. From time to time, the operating system shifts the partitions so that they are contiguous and so that all of the free memory is together in one block. See *external fragmentation*.

concurrent Pertaining to processes or threads that take place within a common interval of time during which they may have to alternately share common resources.

consumable resource A resource that can be created (produced) and destroyed (consumed). When a resource is acquired by a process, the resource ceases to exist. Examples of consumable resources are interrupts, signals, messages, and information in I/O buffers.

critical section In an asynchronous procedure of a computer program, a part that cannot be executed simultaneously with an associated critical section of another asynchronous procedure. See *mutual exclusion*.

database A collection of interrelated data, often with controlled redundancy, organized according to a schema to serve one or more applications; the data are stored so that they can be used by different programs without concern for the data structure or organization. A common approach is used to add new data and to modify and retrieve existing data.

deadlock (1) An impasse that occurs when multiple processes are waiting for the availability of a resource that will not become available because it is being held by another process that is in a similar wait state. (2) An impasse that occurs when multiple processes are waiting for an action by or a response from another process that is in a similar wait state.

deadlock avoidance A dynamic technique that examines each new resource request for deadlock. If the new request could lead to a deadlock, then the request is denied.

deadlock detection A technique in which requested resources are always granted when available. Periodically, the operating system tests for deadlock.

deadlock prevention A technique that guarantees that a deadlock will not occur. Prevention is achieved by assuring that one of the necessary conditions for deadlock is not met.

demand paging The transfer of a page from secondary memory to main memory storage at the moment of need. Compare *prepaging*.

device driver An operating system module (usually in the kernel) that deals directly with a device or I/O module.

direct access The capability to obtain data from a storage device or to enter data into a storage device in a sequence independent of their relative position, by means of addresses that indicate the physical location of the data.

direct memory access (DMA) A form of I/O in which a special module, called a DMA module, controls the exchange of data between main memory and an I/O device. The processor sends a request for the transfer of a block of data to the DMA module and is interrupted only after the entire block has been transferred.

disabled interrupt A condition, usually created by the operating system, during which the processor will ignore interrupt request signals of a specified class.

disk allocation table A table that indicates which blocks on secondary storage are free and available for allocation to files.

disk cache A buffer, usually kept in main memory, that functions as a cache of disk blocks between disk memory and the rest of main memory.

dispatch To allocate time on a processor to jobs or tasks that are ready for execution.

distributed operating system A common operating system shared by a network of computers. The distributed operating system provides support for interprocess communication, process migration, mutual exclusion, and the prevention or detection of deadlock.

dynamic relocation   A process that assigns new absolute addresses to a computer program during execution so that the program may be executed from a different area of main storage.

enabled interrupt   A condition, usually created by the operating system, during which the processor will respond to interrupt request signals of a specified class.

encryption   The conversion of plain text or data into unintelligible form by means of a reversible mathematical computation.

execution context   Same as *process state*.

external fragmentation   Occurs when memory is divided into variable-size partitions corresponding to the blocks of data assigned to the memory (e.g., segments in main memory). As segments are moved into and out of the memory, gaps will occur between the occupied portions of memory.

field   (1) Defined logical data that is part of a record. (2) The elementary unit of a record that may contain a data item, a data aggregate, a pointer, or a link.

file   A set of related records treated as a unit.

file allocation table (FAT)   A table that indicates the physical location on secondary storage of the space allocated to a file. There is one file allocation table for each file.

file management system   A set of system software that provides services to users and applications in the use of files, including file access, directory maintenance, and access control.

file organization   The physical order of records in a file, as determined by the access method used to store and retrieve them.

first come first served (FCFS)   Same as *FIFO*.

first in first out (FIFO)   A queuing technique in which the next item to be retrieved is the item that has been in the queue for the longest time.

frame   In paged virtual storage, a fixed length block of main memory that is used to hold one page of virtual memory.

gang scheduling   The scheduling of a set of related threads to run on a set of processors at the same time, on a one-to-one basis.

hash file   A file in which records are accessed according to the values of a key field. Hashing is used to locate a record on the basis of its key value.

hashing   The selection of a storage location for an item of data by calculating the address as a function of the contents of the data. This technique complicates the storage allocation function but results in rapid random retrieval.

hit ratio   In a two-level memory, the fraction of all memory accesses that are found in the faster memory (e.g., the cache).

indexed access   Pertaining to the organization and accessing of the records of a storage structure through a separate index to the locations of the stored records.

indexed file   A file in which records are accessed according to the value of key fields. An index is required that indicates the location of each record on the basis of each key value.

indexed sequential access   Pertaining to the organization and accessing of the records of a storage structure through an index of the keys that are stored in arbitrarily partitioned sequential files.

indexed sequential file   A file in which records are ordered according to the values of a key field. The main file is supplemented with an index file that contains a partial list of key values; the index provides a lookup capability to reach quickly reach the vicinity of a desired record.

instruction cycle The time period during which one instruction is fetched from memory and executed when a computer is given an instruction in machine language.

internal fragmentation Occurs when memory is divided into fixed-size partitions (e.g., page frames in main memory, physical blocks on disk). If a block of data is assigned to one or more partitions, then there may be wasted space in the last partition. This will occur if the last portion of data is smaller than the last partition.

interrupt A suspension of a process, such as the execution of a computer program, caused by an event external to that process and performed in such a way that the process can be resumed.

interrupt handler A routine, generally part of the operating system. When an interrupt occurs, control is transferred to the corresponding interrupt handler, which take some action in response to the condition that caused the interrupt.

job A set of computational steps packaged to run as a unit.

job control language (JCL) A problem-oriented language that is designed to express statements in a job that are used to identify the job or to describe its requirements to an operating system.

kernel A portion of the operating system that includes the most heavily used portions of software. Generally, the kernel is maintained permanently in main memory. The kernel runs in a privileged mode and responds to calls from processes and interrupts from devices.

kernel mode A privileged mode of execution reserved for the kernel of the operating system. Typically, kernel mode allows access to regions of main memory that are unavailable to processes executing in a less-privileged mode and also enables execution of certain machine instructions that are restricted to the kernel mode. Also referred to as *system mode* or *privileged mode*.

last in first out (LIFO) A queuing technique in which the next item to be retrieved is the item most recently placed in the queue.

lightweight process A thread.

livelock A condition in which two or more processes continuously change their state in response to changes in the other process(es) without doing any useful work. This is similar to deadlock in that no progress is made but differs in that neither process is blocked or waiting for anything.

locality of reference The tendency of a processor to access the same set of memory locations repetitively over a short period of time.

logical address A reference to a memory location independent of the current assignment of data to memory. A translation must be made to a physical address before the memory access can be achieved.

logical record A record independent of its physical environment; portions of one logical record may be located in different physical records or several logical records or parts of logical records may be located in one physical record.

macrokernel A large operating system core that provides a wide range of services.

mailbox A data structure shared among a number of processes that is used as a queue for messages. Messages are sent to the mailbox and retrieved from the mailbox rather than passing directly from sender to receiver.

main memory Memory that is internal to the computer system, is program addressable, and can be loaded into registers for subsequent execution or processing.

malicious software Any software designed to cause damage to or use up the resources of a target computer. Malicious software (malware) is frequently concealed within or masquerades as legitimate software. In some cases, it spreads itself to other computers via e-mail or infected floppy disks. Types of malicious software include viruses, Trojan horses, worms, and hidden software for launching denial-of-service attacks.

memory cycle time The time it takes to read one word from or write one word to memory. This is the inverse of the rate at which words can be read from or written to memory.

memory partitioning The subdividing of storage into independent sections.

message A block of information that may be exchanged between processes as a means of communication.

microkernel A small privileged operating system core that provides process scheduling, memory management, and communication services and relies on other processes to perform some of the functions traditionally associated with the operating system kernel.

mode switch A hardware operation that occurs that causes the processor to execute in a different mode (kernel or process). When the mode switches from process to kernel, the program counter, processor status word, and other registers are saved. When the mode switches from kernel to process, this information is restored.

monitor A programming language construct that encapsulates variables, access procedures and initialization code within an abstract data type. The monitor's variable may only be accessed via its access procedures and only one process may be actively accessing the monitor at any one time. The access procedures are *critical sections*. A monitor may have a queue of processes that are waiting to access it.

monolithic kernel A large kernel containing virtually the complete operating system, including scheduling, file system, device drivers, and memory management. All the functional components of the kernel have access to all of its internal data structures and routines. Typically, a monolithic kernel is implemented as a single process, with all elements sharing the same address space.

multilevel security A capability that enforces access control across multiple levels of classification of data.

multiprocessing A mode of operation that provides for parallel processing by two or more processors of a multiprocessor.

multiprocessor A computer that has two or more processors that have common access to a main storage.

multiprogramming A mode of operation that provides for the interleaved execution of two or more computer programs by a single processor. The same as multitasking, using different terminology.

multiprogramming level The number of processes that are partially or fully resident in main memory.

multitasking A mode of operation that provides for the concurrent performance or interleaved execution of two or more computer tasks. The same as multiprogramming, using different terminology.

mutex A binary semaphore.

mutual exclusion A condition in which there is a set of processes, only one of which is able to access a given resource or perform a given function at any time. See *critical section*.

nonprivileged state An execution context that does not allow sensitive hardware instructions to be executed, such as the halt instruction and I/O instructions.

nonuniform memory access (NUMA) multiprocessor A shared-memory multiprocessor in which the access time from a given processor to a word in memory varies with the location of the memory word.

object request broker An entity in an object-oriented system that acts as an intermediary for requests sent from a client to a server.

operating system   Software that controls the execution of programs and that provides services such as resource allocation, scheduling, input/output control, and data management.

page   In virtual storage, a fixed length block that has a virtual address and that is transferred as a unit between main memory and secondary memory.

page fault   Occurs when the page containing a referenced word is not in main memory. This causes an interrupt and requires that the proper page be brought into main memory.

page frame   A fixed-size contiguous block of main memory used to hold a page.

paging   The transfer of pages between main memory and secondary memory.

physical address   The absolute location of a unit of data in memory (e.g., word or byte in main memory, block on secondary memory).

pipe   A circular buffer allowing two processes to communicate on the producer-consumer model. Thus, it is a first-in-first-out queue, written by one process and read by another. In some systems, the pipe is generalized to allow any item in the queue to be selected for consumption.

preemption   Reclaiming a resource from a process before the process has finished using it.

prepaging   The retrieval of pages other than the one demanded by a page fault. The hope is that the additional pages will be needed in the near future, conserving disk I/O. Compare *demand paging*.

priority inversion   A circumstance in which the operating system forces a higher-priority task to wait for a lower-priority task.

privileged instruction   An instruction that can be executed only in a specific mode, usually by a supervisory program.

privileged mode   Same as *kernel mode*.

process   A program in execution. A process is controlled and scheduled by the operating system. Same as *task*.

process control block   The manifestation of a process in an operating system. It is a data structure containing information about the characteristics and state of the process.

process descriptor   Same as process control block.

process image   All of the ingredients of a process, including program, data, stack, and process control block.

process migration   The transfer of a sufficient amount of the state of a process from one machine to another for the process to execute on the target machine.

process spawning   The creation of a new process by another process.

process state   All of the information that the operating system needs to manage a process and that the processor needs to properly execute the process. The process state includes the contents of the various processor registers, such as the program counter and data registers; it also includes information of use to the operating system, such as the priority of the process and whether the process is waiting for the completion of a particular I/O event. Same as *execution context*.

process switch   An operation that switches the processor from one process to another, by saving all the process control block, registers, and other information for the first and replacing them with the process information for the second.

processor   In a computer, a functional unit that interprets and executes instructions. A processor consists of at least an instruction control unit and an arithmetic unit.

program counter Instruction address register.

program status word (PSW) A register or set of registers that contains condition codes, execution mode, and other status information that reflects the state of a process.

programmed I/O A form of I/O in which the CPU issues an I/O command to an I/O module and must then wait for the operation to be complete before proceeding.

race condition Situation in which multiple processes access and manipulate shared data with the outcome dependent on the relative timing of the processes.

real address A physical address in main memory.

real-time System An operating system that must schedule and manage real-time tasks.

real-time Task A task that is executed in connection with some process or function or set of events external to the computer system and that must meet one or more deadlines to interact effectively and correctly with the external environment.

record A group of data elements treated as a unit.

reentrant procedure A routine that may be entered before the completion of a prior execution of the same routine and execute correctly.

registers High-speed memory internal to the CPU. Some registers are user visible; that is, available to the programmer via the machine instruction set. Other registers are used only by the CPU, for control purposes.

relative address An address calculated as a displacement from a base address.

remote procedure call (RPC) A technique by which two programs on different machines interact using procedure call/return syntax and semantics. Both the called and calling program behave as if the partner program were running on the same machine.

rendezvous In message passing, a condition in which both the sender and receiver of a message are blocked until the message is delivered.

resident Set That portion of a process that is actually in main memory at a given time. Compare *working set*.

response time In a data system, the elapsed time between the end of transmission of an enquiry message and the beginning of the receipt of a response message, measured at the enquiry terminal.

reusable resource A resource that can be safely used by only one process at a time and is not depleted by that use. Processes obtain reusable resource units that they later release for reuse by other processes. Examples of reusable resources include processors, I/O channels, main and secondary memory, devices, and data structures such as files, databases, and semaphores.

round robin A scheduling algorithm in which processes are activated in a fixed cyclic order; that is, all processes are in a circular queue. A process that cannot proceed because it is waiting for some event (e.g., termination of a child process or an input/output operation) returns control to the scheduler.

scheduling To select jobs or tasks that are to be dispatched. In some operating systems, other units of work, such as input/output operations, may also be scheduled.

secondary memory Memory located outside the computer system itself; that is, it cannot be processed directly by the processor. It must first be copied into main memory. Examples include disk and tape.

segment In virtual memory, a block that has a virtual address. The blocks of a program may be of unequal length and may even be of dynamically varying lengths.

segmentation   The division of a program or application into segments as part of a virtual memory scheme.

semaphore   An integer value used for signaling among processes. Only three operations may be performed on a semaphore, all of which are atomic: initialize, decrement, and increment. Depending on the exact definition of the semaphore, the decrement operation may result in the blocking of a process, and the increment operation may result in the unblocking of a process. Also known as a **counting semaphore** or a **general semaphore**.

sequential access   The capability to enter data into a storage device or a data medium in the same sequence as the data are ordered, or to obtain data in the same order as they were entered.

sequential file   A file in which records are ordered according to the values of one or more key fields and processed in the same sequence from the beginning of the file.

server   (1) A process that responds to request from clients via messages. (2) In a network, a data station that provides facilities to other stations; for example, a file server, a print server, a mail server.

session   A collection of one or more processes that represents a single interactive user application or operating system function. All keyboard and mouse input is directed to the foreground session, and all output from the foreground session is directed to the display screen.

shell   The portion of the operating system that interprets interactive user commands and job control language commands. It functions as an interface between the user and the operating system.

spin lock   Mutual exclusion mechanism in which a process executes in an infinite loop waiting for the value of a lock variable to indicate availability.

spooling   The use of secondary memory as buffer storage to reduce processing delays when transferring data between peripheral equipment and the processors of a computer.

stack   An ordered list in which items are appended to and deleted from the same end of the list, known as the top. That is, the next item appended to the list is put on the top, and the next item to be removed from the list is the item that has been in the list the shortest time. This method is characterized as last-in-first-out.

starvation   A condition in which a process is indefinitely delayed because other processes are always given preference.

strong semaphore   A semaphore in which all processes waiting on the same semaphore are queued and will eventually proceed in the same order as they executed the wait (P) operations (FIFO order).

swapping   A process that interchanges the contents of an area of main storage with the contents of an area in secondary memory.

symmetric multiprocessing (SMP)   A form of multiprocessing that allows the operating system to execute on any available processor or on several available processors simultaneously.

synchronous operation   An operation that occurs regularly or predictably with respect to the occurrence of a specified event in another process, for example, the calling of an input/output routine that receives control at a precoded location in a computer program.

synchronization   Situation in which two or more processes coordinate their activities based on a condition.

system bus   A bus used to interconnect major computer components (CPU, memory, I/O).

system mode   Same as *kernel mode*.

task   Same as *process*.

thrashing A phenomenon in virtual memory schemes, in which the processor spends most of its time swapping pieces rather than executing instructions.

thread A dispatchable unit of work. It includes a processor context (which includes the program counter and stack pointer) and its own data area for a stack (to enable subroutine branching). A thread executes sequentially and is interruptible so that the processor can turn to another thread. A process may consist of multiple threads.

thread switch The act of switching processor control from one thread to another within the same process.

time sharing The concurrent use of a device by a number of users.

time slice The maximum amount of time that a process can execute before being interrupted.

time slicing A mode of operation in which two or more processes are assigned quanta of time on the same processor.

trace A sequence of instructions that are executed when a process is running.

translation lookaside buffer (TLB) A high-speed cache used to hold recently referenced page table entries as part of a paged virtual memory scheme. The TLB reduces the frequency of access to main memory to retrieve page table entries.

trap An unprogrammed conditional jump to a specified address that is automatically activated by hardware; the location from which the jump was made is recorded.

trap door Secret undocumented entry point into a program, used to grant access without normal methods of access authentication.

trojan horse Secret undocumented routine embedded within a useful program. Execution of the program results in execution of the secret routine.

trusted system A computer and operating system that can be verified to implement a given security policy.

user mode The least-privileged mode of execution. Certain regions of main memory and certain machine instructions cannot be used in this mode.

virus Secret undocumented routine embedded within a useful program. Execution of the program results in execution of the secret routine.

virtual address The address of a storage location in virtual memory.

virtual memory The storage space that may be regarded as addressable main storage by the user of a computer system in which virtual addresses are mapped into real addresses. The size of virtual storage is limited by the addressing scheme of the computer system and by the amount of secondary memory available and not by the actual number of main storage locations.

weak semaphore A semaphore in which all processes waiting on the same semaphore proceed in an unspecified order (i.e., the order is unknown or indeterminate).

word An ordered set of bytes or bits that is the normal unit in which information may be stored, transmitted, or operated on within a given computer. Typically, if a processor has a fixed-length instruction set, then the instruction length equals the word length.

working set The working set with parameter Δ for a process at virtual time t, $W(t, \Delta)$, is the set of pages of that process that have been referenced in the last Δ time units. Compare *resident set*.

worm Program that can travel from computer to computer across network connections. May contain a virus or bacteria.

REFERENCES

ABBREVIATIONS

ACM   Association for Computing Machinery
IEEE   Institute of Electrical and Electronics Engineers
IRE   Institute of Radio Engineers

ABRA87   Abrams, M., and Podell, H. *Computer and Network Security.* Los Alamitos, CA: IEEE Computer Society Press, 1987.

ADAM92   Adam, J. "Virus Threats and Countermeasures." *IEEE Spectrum*, August 1992.

AGAR89   Agarwal, A. *Analysis of Cache Performance for Operating Systems and Multiprogramming.* Boston: Kluwer Academic Publishers, 1989.

ALVA90   Alvare, A. "How Crackers Crack Passwords or What Passwords to Avoid." *Proceedings, UNIX Security Workshop II*, August 1990.

ANAN92   Ananda, A.; Tay, B.; and Koh, E. "A Survey of Asynchronous Remote Procedure Calls." *Operating Systems Review,* April 1992.

ANDE80   Anderson, J. *Computer Security Threat Monitoring and Surveillance.* Fort Washington, PA: James P. Anderson Co., April 1980.

ANDE89   Anderson, T.; Laxowska, E.; and Levy, H. "The Performance Implications of Thread Management Alternatives for Shared-Memory Multiprocessors." *IEEE Transactions on Computers*, December 1989.

ANDE97   Anderson, T.; Bershad, B.; Lazowska, E.; and Levy, H. "Thread Management for Shared-Memory Multiprocessors." in [TUCK97]

ANDR90   Andrianoff, S. "A Module on Distributed Systems for the Operating System Course." *Proceedings, Twenty-First SIGCSE Technical Symposium on Computer Science Education, SIGSCE Bulletin*, February 1990.

ARDE80   Arden, B., editor. *What Can Be Automated?* Cambridge, MA: MIT Press, 1980.

ARTS89a   Artsy, Y., ed. Special Issue on Process Migration. *Newsletter of the IEEE Computer Society Technical Committee on Operating Systems*, Winter 1989.

ARTS89b   Artsy, Y. "Designing a Process Migration Facility: The Charlotte Experience." *Computer*, September 1989.

ATLA89   Atlas, A., and Blundon, B. "Time to Reach for It All." *UNIX Review*, January 1989.

AXFO88   Axford, T. *Concurrent Programming: Fundamental Techniques for Real-Time and Parallel Software Design.* New York: Wiley, 1988.

BACH86   Bach, M. *The Design of the UNIX Operating System.* Englewood Cliffs, NJ: Prentice Hall, 1986.

BACO03   Bacon, J., and Harris, T. *Operating Systems: Concurrent and Distributed Software Design.* Reading, MA: Addison-Wesley, 1998.

BAEN97   Baentsch, M., et al. "Enhancing the Web's Infrastructure: From Caching to Replication." *Internet Computing*, March/April 1997.

BAER80   Baer, J. *Computer Systems Architecture.* Rockville, MD: Computer Science Press, 1980.

BAR00   Bar, M. *Linux Internals.* New York, McGraw-Hill, 2000.

BARB90   Barbosa, V. "Strategies for the Prevention of Communication Deadlocks in Distributed Parallel Programs." *IEEE Transactions on Software Engineering*, November 1990.

BARK89   Barkley, R., and Lee, T. "A Lazy Buddy System Bounded by Two Coalescing Delays per Class." *Proceedings of the Twelfth ACM Symposium on Operating Systems Principles*, December 1989.

BAYS77   Bays, C. "A Comparison of Next-Fit, First-Fit, and Best-Fit." *Communications of the ACM*, March 1977.

BECK90   Beck, L. *System Software.* Reading, MA: Addison-Wesley, 1990.

BELA66   Belady, L. "A Study of Replacement Algorithms for a Virtual Storage Computer." *IBM Systems Journal*, No. 2, 1966.

BEN82   Ben-Ari, M. *Principles of Concurrent Programming.* Englewood Cliffs, NJ: Prentice Hall, 1982.

BEN90   Ben-Ari, M. *Principles of Concurrent and Distributed Programming.* Englewood Cliffs, NJ: Prentice Hall, 1990.

BEN98   Ben-Ari, M., and Burns, A. "Extreme Interleavings" *IEEE Concurrency*, July-September, 1998.

BIRR89   Birrell, A. *An Introduction to Programming with Threads.* SRC Research Report 35, Compaq Systems Research Center, Palo Alto, CA, January 1989. Available at http://www.research.compaq.com/SRC.

BLAC90   Black, D. "Scheduling Support for Concurrency and Parallelism in the Mach Operating System." *Computer*, May 1990.

BOEB85   Boebert, W.; Kain, R.; and Young, W. "Secure Computing: the Secure Ada Target Approach." *Scientific Honeyweller*, July 1985. Reprinted in [ABRA87].

BOLO89   Bolosky, W.; Fitzgerald, R.; and Scott, M. "Simple But Effective Techniques for NUMA Memory Management." *Proceedings, Twelfth ACM Symposium on Operating Systems Principles*, December 1989.

BONW94   Bonwick, J. "An Object-Caching Memory Allocator." *Proceedings, USENIX Summer Technical Conference*, 1994.

BORG90   Borg, A.; Kessler, R.; and Wall, D. "Generation and Analysis of Very Long Address Traces." *Proceedings of the 17th Annual International Symposium on Computer Architecture*, May 1990.

BOSW03   Boswell, W. *Inside Windows Server 2003.* Reading, MA: Addison-Wesley, 2003.

BOVE03   Bovet, D., and Cesati, M. *Understanding the Linux Kernel.* Sebastopol, CA: O'Reilly, 2003.

BREN89   Brent, R. "Efficient Implementation of the First-Fit Strategy for Dynamic Storage Allocation." *ACM Transactions on Programming Languages and Systems*, July 1989.

BREW97   Brewer, E. "Clustering: Multiply and Conquer." *Data Communications*, July 1997.

BRIA99   Briand, L, and Roy, D. *Meeting Deadlines in Hard Real-Time Systems: The Rate Monotonic Approach.* Los Alamitos, CA: IEEE Computer Society Press, 1999.

BRIN73   Brinch Hansen, P. *Operating System Principles.* Englewood Cliffs, NJ: Prentice Hall, 1973.

BRIN01   Brinch Hansen, P. *Classic Operating Systems: From Batch Processing to Distributed Systems.* New York: Springer-Verlag, 2001.

BROW84   Brown, R.; Denning, P.; and Tichy, W. "Advanced Operating Systems." *Computer*, October 1984.

BUHR95   Buhr, P., and Fortier, M. "Monitor Classification." *ACM Computing Surveys*, March 1995.

BUTT99   Buttazzo, G. "Optimal Deadline Assignment for Scheduling Soft Aperiodic Tasks in Hard Real-Time Environments. *IEEE Transactions on Computers*, October 1999.

BUYY99a   Buyya, R. *High Performance Cluster Computing: Architectures and Systems.* Upper Saddle River, NJ: Prentice Hall, 1999.

BUYY99b   Buyya, R. *High Performance Cluster Computing: Programming and Applications.* Upper Saddle River, NJ: Prentice Hall, 1999.

BYNU96   Bynum, B., and Camp, T. "After You, Alfonse: A Mutual Exclusion Toolkit," *Proceedings of the 27th SIGCSE Technical Symposium on Computer Science Education*, February 1996.

CABR86   Cabrear, L. "The Influence of Workload on Load Balancing Strategies." *USENIX Conference Proceedings*, Summer 1986.

CAO96   Cao, P.; Felten, E.; Karlin, A.; and Li, K. "Implementation and Performance of Integrated Application-Controlled File Caching, Prefetching, and Disk Scheduling." *ACM Transactions on Computer Systems*, November 1996.

CARR81   Carr, R., and Hennessey, J. "WSClock—A Simple and Efficient Algorithm for Virtual Memory Management." *Proceedings of the Eighth Symposium on Operating System Principles.*" December 1981.

CARR84   Carr, R. *Virtual Memory Management.* Ann Arbor, MI: UMI Research Press, 1984.

CARR89   Carriero, N., and Gelernter, D. "How to Write Parallel Programs: A Guide for the Perplexed." *ACM Computing Surveys*, September 1989.

CARR01   Carr, S; Mayo, J.; and Shene, C. "Race Conditions: A Case Study." *The Journal of Computing in Small Colleges*, October 2001.

CASA94   Casavant, T., and Singhal, M. *Distributed Computing Systems.* Los Alamitos, CA: IEEE Computer Society Press, 1994.

CASS01   Cass, S. "Anatomy of Malice." *IEEE Spectrum*, November 2001.

CAST92   Castillo, C.; Flanagan, E.; and Wilkinson, N. "Object-Oriented Design and Programming." *AT&T Technical Journal*, November/December 1992.

CHAN85   Chandy, K., and Lamport, L. "Distributed Snapshots: Determining Global States of Distributed Systems." *ACM Transactions on Computer Systems*, February 1985.

CHEN92   Chen, J.; Borg, A.; and Jouppi, N. "A Simulation Based Study of TLB Performance." *Proceedings of the 19th Annual International Symposium on Computer Architecture*, May 1992.

CHEN94   Chen, P.; Lee, E.; Gibson, G.; Katz, R.; and Patterson, D. "RAID: High-Performance, Reliable Secondary Storage." *ACM Computing Surveys*, June 1994.

CHEN96   Chen, S., and Towsley, D. "A Performance Evaluation of RAID Architectures." *IEEE Transactions on Computers*, October 1996.

CHES97   Chess, D. "The Future of Viruses on the Internet." *Proceedings, Virus Bulletin International Conference*, October 1997.

CHRI93   Christopher, W.; Procter, S.; and Anderson, T. "The Nachos Instructional Operating System." *Proceedings, 1993 USENIX Winter Technical Conference*, 1993.

CHU72   Chu, W., and Opderbeck, H. "The Page Fault Frequency Replacement Algorithm." *Proceedings, Fall Joint Computer Conference*, 1972.

CLAR85   Clark, D., and Emer, J. "Performance of the VAX-11/780 Translation Buffer: Simulation and Measurement." *ACM Transactions on Computer Systems*, February 1985.

CLAR98   Clarke, D., and Merusi, D. *System Software Programming: The Way Things Work.* Upper Saddle River, NJ: Prentice Hall, 1998.

CLER04   Clercq, J. *Windows Server 2003 Security Infrastructure: Core Security Features.* Burlington, MA: Digital Press, 2004.

COFF71   Coffman, E.; Elphick, M.; and Shoshani, A. "System Deadlocks." *Computing Surveys*, June 1971.

COME84   Comer, D., and Fossum, T. *Operating System Design: The Xinu Approach.* Englewood Cliffs, NJ: Prentice Hall, 1984.

CONW63   Conway, M. "Design of a Separable Transition-Diagram Compiler." *Communications of the ACM*, July 1963.

CONW67   Conway, R.; Maxwell, W.; and Miller, L. *Theory of Scheduling.* Reading, MA: Addison-Wesley, 1967. Reprinted by Dover Publications, 2003.

COOP89   Cooper, J. *Computer and Communications Security: Strategies for the 1990s.* New York: McGraw-Hill, 1990.

CORB62   Corbato, F.; Merwin-Daggett, M.; and Dealey, R. "An Experimental Time-Sharing System." *Proceedings of the 1962 Spring Joint Computer Conference*, 1962. Reprinted in [BRIN01].

CORB68   Corbato, F. "A Paging Experiment with the Multics System." *MIT Project MAC Report MAC-M-384*, May 1968.

CORB96   Corbett, J. "Evaluating Deadlock Detection Methods for Concurrent Software." *IEEE Transactions on Software Engineering*, March 1996.

COX89   Cox, A., and Fowler, R. "The Implementation of a Coherent Memory Abstraction on a NUMA Multiprocessor: Experiences with PLATINUM." *Proceedings, Twelfth ACM Symposium on Operating Systems Principles*, December 1989.

COX00   Cox, P., and Sheldon, T. *Windows NT Security Handbook.* New York: Osborne McGraw-Hill, 2000.

CUST93   Custer, H. *Inside the Windows NT.* Redmond, WA: Microsoft Press, 1993.

CUST94   Custer, H. *Inside the Windows NT File System.* Redmond, WA: Microsoft Press, 1994.

DALE68   Daley, R, and Dennis, R. "Virtual Memory, Processes, and Sharing in MULTICS." *Communications of the ACM*, May 1968.

DALT96   Dalton, W., et al. *Windows NT Server 4: Security, Troubleshooting, and Optimization.* Indianapolis, IN: New Riders Publishing, 1996.

DASG92   Dasgupta, P.; et. al. "The Clouds Distributed Operating System." *IEEE Computer*, November 1992.

DATT90   Datta, A., and Ghosh, S. "Deadlock Detection in Distributed Systems." *Proceedings, Phoenix Conference on Computers and Communications*, March 1990.

DATT92   Datta, A.; Javagal, R.; and Ghosh, S. "An Algorithm for Resource Deadlock Detection in Distributed Systems," *Computer Systems Science and Engineering*, October 1992.

DELL00   Dekker, E., and Newcomer, J. *Developing Windows NT Device Drivers: A Programmer's Handbook.* Reading, MA: Addison-Wesley, 2000.

DENN68   Denning, P. "The Working Set Model for Program Behavior." *Communications of the ACM*, May 1968.

DENN70   Denning, P. "Virtual Memory." *Computing Surveys*, September 1970.

DENN80a   Denning, P.; Buzen, J.; Dennis, J.; Gaines, R.; Hansen, P.; Lynch, W.; and Organick, E. "Operating Systems." in [ARDE80].

DENN80b   Denning, P. "Working Sets Past and Present." *IEEE Transactions on Software Engineering*, January 1980.

DENN84   Denning, P., and Brown, R. "Operating Systems." *Scientific American*, September 1984.

DENN87   Denning, D. "An Intrusion-Detection Model." *IEEE Transactions on Software Engineering*, February 1987.

DIJK65   Dijkstra, E. *Cooperating Sequential Processes.* Technological University, Eindhoven, The Netherlands, 1965. (Reprinted in *Great Papers in Computer Science*, P. Laplante, ed., IEEE Press, New York, NY, 1996.) Also reprinted in [BRIN01].

DIJK71   Dijkstra, E. "Hierarchical Ordering of sequential Processes." *Acta informatica*, Volume 1, Number 2, 1971. Reprinted in [BRIN01].

DIMI98   Dimitoglou, G. "Deadlocks and Methods for Their Detection, Prevention, and Recovery in Modern Operating Systems." *Operating Systems Review*, July 1998.

DONA01   Donahoo, M., and Clavert, K. *The Pocket Guide to TCP/IP Sockets.* San Francisco, CA: Morgan Kaufmann, 2001.

DOUG89   Douglas, F., and Ousterhout, J. "Process Migration in Sprite: A Status Report." *Newsletter of the IEEE Computer Society Technical Committee on Operating Systems*, Winter 1989.

DOUG91   Douglas, F., and Ousterhout, J. "Transparent Process Migration: Design Alternatives and the Sprite Implementation." *Software Practice and Experience*, August 1991.

DOWD93   Dowdy, L., and Lowery, C. *P.S. to Operating Systems.* Upper Saddle River, NJ: Prentice Hall, 1993.

DUBE98   Dube, R. *A Comparison of the Memory Management Sub-Systems in FreeBSD and Linux.* Technical Report CS-TR-3929, University of Maryland, September 25, 1998.

EAGE86   Eager, D.; Lazowska, E.; and Zahnorjan, J. "Adaptive Load Sharing in Homogeneous Distributed Systems." *IEEE Transactions on Software Engineering*, May 1986.

ECKE95   Eckerson, W. "Client Server Architecture." *Network World Collaboration*, Winter 1995.

EFF98   Electronic Frontier Foundation. *Cracking DES: Secrets of Encryption Research, Wiretap Politics, and Chip Design.* Sebastopol, CA: O'Reilly, 1998

ENGE80   Enger, N., and Howerton, P. *Computer Security.* New York: Amacom, 1980.

ESKI90   Eskicioglu, M. "Design Issues of Process Migration Facilities in Distributed Systems." *Newsletter of the IEEE Computer Society Technical Committee on Operating Systems and Application Environments*, Summer 1990.

FEIT90a   Feitelson, D., and Rudolph, L. "Distributed Hierarchical Control for Parallel Processing." *Computer*, May 1990.

FEIT90b   Feitelson, D., and Rudolph, L. "Mapping and Scheduling in a Shared Parallel Environment Using Distributed Hierarchical Control." *Proceedings, 1990 International Conference on Parallel Processing*, August 1990.

FERR83   Ferrari, D., and Yih, Y. "VSWS: The Variable-Interval Sampled Working Set Policy." *IEEE Transactions on Software Engineering*, May 1983.

FIDG96   Fidge, C. "Fundamentals of Distributed System Observation." *IEEE Software*, November 1996.

FINK88   Finkel, R. *An Operating Systems Vade Mecum.* Englewood Cliffs, NJ: Prentice Hall, 1988.

FINK89   Finkel, R. "The Process Migration Mechanism of Charlotte." *Newsletter of the IEEE Computer Society Technical Committee on Operating Systems* , Winter 1989.

FINK97   Finkel, R. "What is an Operating System." In [TUCK97].

FLYN72   Flynn, M. "Computer Organizations and Their Effectiveness." *IEEE Transactions on Computers*, September 1972.

FOLK98   Folk, M., and Zoellick, B. *File Structures: An Object-Oriented Approach with C++.* Reading, MA: Addison-Wesley, 1998.

FORR97   Forrest, S.; Hofmeyr, S.; and Somayaji, A. "Computer Immunology." *Communications of the ACM*, October 1997.

FRAN97   Franz, M. "Dynamic Linking of Software Components." *Computer*, March 1997.

FRIE96   Friedman, M. "RAID Keeps Going and Going and . . . " *IEEE Spectrum*, April 1996.

GALL00   Galli, D. *Distributed Operating Systems: Concepts and Practice.* Upper Saddle River, NJ: Prentice Hall, 2000.

GANA98   Ganapathy, N., and Schimmel, C. "General Purpose Operating System Support for Multiple Page Sizes." *Proceedings, USENIX Symposium*, 1998.

GARG02   Garg, V. *Elements of Distributed Computing.* New York: Wiley, 2002.

GAUD00   Gaudin, S. "The Omega Files." *Network World*, June 26, 2000.

GEHR87   Gehringer, E.; Siewiorek, D.; and Segall, Z. *Parallel Processing: The Cm^* Experience.* Bedford, MA: Digital Press, 1987.

GIBB87   Gibbons, P. "A Stub Generator for Multilanguage RPC in Heterogeneous Environments." *IEEE Transactions on Software Engineering,* January 1987.

GING90   Gingras, A. "Dining Philosophers Revisited." *ACM SIGCSE Bulletin*, September 1990.

GOLD89   Goldman, P. "Mac VM Revealed." *Byte*, November 1989.

GOLL99   Gollmann, D. *Computer Security.* New York: Wiley, 1999.

GOOD94   Goodheart, B., and Cox, J. *The Magic Garden Explained: The Internals of UNIX System V Release 4.* Englewood Cliffs, NJ: Prentice Hall, 1994.

GOPA85   Gopal, I. "Prevention of Store-and-Forward Deadlock in Computer Networks." *IEEE Transactions on Communications*, December 1985.

GOYE99   Goyeneche, J., and Souse, E. "Loadable Kernel Modules." *IEEE Software*, January/February 1999.

GRAY97   Gray, J. *Interprocess Communications in Unix: The Nooks and Crannies.* Upper Saddle River, NJ: Prentice Hall, 1997.

GROS86   Grosshans, D. *File Systems: Design and Implementation.* Englewood Cliffs, NJ: Prentice Hall, 1986.

GUPT78   Gupta, R., and Franklin, M. "Working Set and Page Fault Frequency Replacement Algorithms: A Performance Comparison." *IEEE Transactions on Computers*, August 1978.

GUYN88   Guynes, J. "Impact of System Response Time on State Anxiety." *Communications of the ACM*, March 1988.

HALD91   Haldar, S., and Subramanian, D. "Fairness in Processor Scheduling in Time Sharing Systems" *Operating Systems Review*, January 1991.

HALL01   Hall, B. *Beej's Guide to Network Programming Using Internet Sockets.* 2001. http://www.ecst.csuchico.edu/~beej/guide/net/html/

HARL01   Harley, D.; Slade, R.; and Gattiker, U. *Viruses Revealed.* New York: Osborne/McGraw-Hill, 2001.

HART97   Hartig, H., et al. "The Performance of a μ-Kernel-Based System." *Proceedings, Sixteenth ACM Symposium on Operating Systems Principles*, December 1997.

HATF72   Hatfield, D. "Experiments on Page Size, Program Access Patterns, and Virtual Memory Performance." *IBM Journal of Research and Development*, January 1972.

HENN02   Hennessy, J., and Patterson, D. *Computer Architecture: A Quantitative Approach.* San Mateo, CA: Morgan Kaufmann, 2002.

HENR84   Henry, G. "The Fair Share Scheduler." *AT&T Bell Laboratories Technical Journal*, October 1984.

HERL90   Herlihy, M. "A Methodology for Implementing Highly Concurrent Data Structures," *Proceedings of the Second ACM SIGPLAN Symposium on Principles and Practices of Parallel Programming*, March 1990.

HOAR74   Hoare, C. "Monitors: An Operating System Structuring Concept." *Communications of the ACM*, October 1974.

HOAR85   Hoare, C. *Communicating Sequential Processes.* Englewood Cliffs, NJ: Prentice Hall, 1985.

HOFR90   Hofri, M. "Proof of a Mutual Exclusion Algorithm." *Operating Systems Review*, January 1990.

HOLT72   Holt, R. "Some Deadlock Properties of Computer Systems." *Computing Surveys*, September 1972.

HONG89   Hong, J.; Tan, X.; and Towsley, D. "A Performance Analysis of Minimum Laxity and Earliest Deadline Scheduling in a Real-Time System." *IEEE Transactions on Computers*, December 1989.

HOWA73   Howard, J. "Mixed Solutions for the Deadlock Problem." *Communications of the ACM*, July 1973.

HP96   Hewlett Packard. *White Paper on Clustering.* June 1996.

HUCK83   Huck, T. *Comparative Analysis of Computer Architectures.* Stanford University Technical Report Number 83-243, May 1983.

HUCK93   Huck, J., and Hays, J. "Architectural Support for Translation Table Management in Large Address Space Machines." *Proceedings of the 20th Annual International Symposium on Computer Architecture*, May 1993.

HWAN99   Hwang, K, et al. "Designing SSI Clusters with Hierarchical Checkpointing and Single I/O Space." *IEEE Concurrency*, January-March 1999.

HYMA66   Hyman, H. "Comments on a Problem in Concurrent Programming Control." *Communications of the ACM*, January 1966.

IBM86   IBM National Technical Support, Large Systems. *Multiple Virtual Storage (MVS) Virtual Storage Tuning Cookbook.* Dallas Systems Center Technical Bulletin G320-0597, June 1986.

INSO02a   Insolvibile, G. "Inside the Linux Packet Filter." *Linux Journal*, February, 2002.

INSO02b   Insolvibile, G. "Inside the Linux Packet Filter, Part II." *Linux Journal*, March, 2002.

ISLO80   Isloor, S., and Marsland, T. "The Deadlock Problem: An Overview." *Computer*, September 1980.

IYER01   Iyer, S., and Druschel, P. "Anticipatory Scheduling: A Disk Scheduling Framework to Overcome Deceptive Idleness in Synchronous I/O." *Proceedings, 18th ACM Symposium on Operating Systems Principles*, October 2001.

JACO98a   Jacob, B., and Mudge, T. "Virtual Memory: Issues of Implementation." *Computer*, June 1998.

JACO98b   Jacob, B., and Mudge, T. "Virtual Memory in Contemporary Microprocessors." *IEEE Micro*, August 1998.

JOHN91   Johnston, B.; Javagal, R.; Datta, A.; and Ghosh, S. "A Distributed Algorithm for Resource Deadlock Detection." *Proceedings, Tenth Annual Phoenix Conference on Computers and Communications*, March 1991.

JOHN92   Johnson, T., and Davis, T. "Space Efficient Parallel Buddy Memory Management." *Proceedings, Third International Conference on Computers and Information*, May 1992.

JONE80   Jones, S., and Schwarz, P. "Experience Using Multiprocessor Systems—A Status Report." *Computing Surveys*, June 1980.

JONE97   Jones, M. "What Really Happened on Mars?" http://research.microsoft.com/~mbj/ Mars_Pathfinder/Mars_Pathfinder.html, 1997.

JUL88   Jul, E.; Levy, H.; Hutchinson, N.; and Black, A. "Fine-Grained Mobility in the Emerald System." *ACM Transactions on Computer Systems*, February 1988.

JUL89   Jul, E. "Migration of Light-Weight Processes in Emerald." *Newsletter of the IEEE Computer Society Technical Committee on Operating Systems*, Winter 1989.

KANG98   Kang, S., and Lee, J. "Analysis and Solution of Non-Preemptive Policies for Scheduling Readers and Writers." *Operating Systems Review*, July 1998.

KAPP00   Kapp, C. "Managing Cluster Computers." *Dr. Dobb's Journal*, July 2000.

KATZ89   Katz, R.; Gibson, G.; and Patterson, D. "Disk System Architecture for High Performance Computing." *Proceedings of the IEEE*, December 1989.

KAY88   Kay, J., and Lauder, P. "A Fair Share Scheduler." *Communications of the ACM*, January 1988.

KEFE92   Kefir, M., and Smolka, S. "OSP: An Environment for Operating System Projects." *Operating Systems Review*, April 1992.

KENT00   Kent, S. "On the Trail of Intrusions into Information Systems." *IEEE Spectrum*, December 2000.

KEPH97a   Kephart, J.; Sorkin, G.; Chess, D.; and White, S. "Fighting Computer Viruses." *Scientific American*, November 1997.

KEPH97b   Kephart, J.; Sorkin, G.; Swimmer, B.; and White, S. "Blueprint for a Computer Immune System." *Proceedings, Virus Bulletin International Conference*, October 1997.

KESS92   Kessler, R., and Hill, M. "Page Placement Algorithms for Large Real-Indexed Caches." *ACM Transactions on Computer Systems*, November 1992.

KHAL93   Khalidi, Y.; Talluri, M.; Williams, D.; and Nelson, M. "Virtual Memory Support for Multiple Page Sizes." *Proceedings, Fourth Workshop on Workstation Operating Systems*, October 1993.

KIFE92   Kifer, M., and Smolka, S. "OSP: An Environment for Operating Systems Projects." *ACM Operating Systems Review*, October 1992.

KILB62   Kilburn, T.; Edwards, D.; Lanigan, M.; and Sumner, F. "One-Level Storage System." *IRE Transactions*, April 1962.

KLEI90   Klein, D. "Foiling the Cracker: A Survey of, and Improvements to, Password Security." *Proceedings, UNIX Security Workshop II*, August 1990.

KLEI95   Kleiman, S. "Interrupts as Threads." *Operating System Review*, April 1995.

KLEI96   Kleiman, S.; Shah, D.; and Smallders, B. *Programming with Threads.* Upper Saddle River, NJ: Prentice Hall, 1996.

KLEI04   Kleinrock, L. *Queuing Systems, Volume Three: Computer Applications.* New York: Wiley, 2004.

KNUT71   Knuth, D. "An Experimental Study of FORTRAN Programs." *Software Practice and Experience*, Vol. 1, 1971.

KNUT97   Knuth, D. *The Art of Computer Programming, Volume 1: Fundamental Algorithms.* Reading, MA: Addison-Wesley, 1997.

KORS90   Korson, T., and McGregor, J. "Understanding Object-Oriented: A Unifying Paradigm." *Communications of the ACM*, September 1990.

KRIS94   Krishna, C., and Lee, Y., eds. "Special Issue on Real-Time Systems." *Proceedings of the IEEE*, January 1994.

KRIS03   Krishnaprasad, S. "Concurrent/Distributed Programming Illustrated Using the Dining Philosophers Problem." *The Journal of Computing in Small Colleges*, April 2003.

KRON90   Kron, P. "A Software Developer Looks at OS/2." *Byte,* August 1990.

LAMP74   Lamport, L. "A New Solution to Dijkstra's Concurrent Programming Problem." *Communications of the ACM*, August 1974.

LAMP78   Lamport, L. "Time, Clocks, and the Ordering of Events in a Distributed System." *Communications of the ACM*, July 1978.

LAMP80   Lampson, B., and Redell D. "Experience with Processes and Monitors in Mesa." *Communications of the ACM*, February 1980.

LAMP86   Lamport, L. "The Mutual Exclusion Problem." *Journal of the ACM*, April 1986.

LAMP91   Lamport, L. "The Mutual Exclusion Problem Has Been Solved." *Communications of the ACM*, January 1991.

LARO92   LaRowe, R.; Holliday, M.; and Ellis, C. "An Analysis of Dynamic Page Placement an a NUMA Multiprocessor." Proceedings, *1992 ACM SIGMETRICS and Performance '92*, June 1992.

LEBL87   LeBlanc, T., and Mellor-Crummey, J. "Debugging Parallel Programs with Instant Replay." *IEEE Transactions on Computers*, April 1987.

LEE93   Lee, Y., and Krishna, C., eds. *Readings in Real-Time Systems.* Los Alamitos, CA: IEEE Computer Society Press, 1993.

LELA86   Leland, W., and Ott, T. "Load-Balancing Heuristics and Process Behavior." *Proceedings, ACM SigMetrics Performance 1986 Conference*, 1986.

LERO76   Leroudier, J., and Potier, D. "Principles of Optimality for Multiprogramming." *Proceedings, International Symposium on Computer Performance Modeling, Measurement, and Evaluation*, March 1976.

LETW88   Letwin, G. *Inside OS/2.* Redmond, WA: Microsoft Press, 1988.

LEUT90   Leutenegger, S., and Vernon, M. "The Performance of Multiprogrammed Multiprocessor Scheduling Policies." *Proceedings, Conference on Measurement and Modeling of Computer Systems*, May 1990.

LEVI99   Levine, J. *Linkers and Loaders.* New York: Elsevier Science and Technology, 1999.

LEVI03a   Levine, G. "Defining Deadlock." *Operating Systems Review*, January 2003.

LEVI03b   Levine, G. "Defining Deadlock with Fungible Resources." *Operating Systems Review*, July 2003.

LEWI96   Lewis, B., and Berg, D. *Threads Primer.* Upper Saddle River, NJ: Prentice Hall, 1996.

LIED95   Liedtke, J. "On μ-Kernel Construction." *Proceedings of the Fifteenth ACM Symposium on Operating Systems Principles*, December 1995.

LIED96a   Liedtke, J. "Toward Real Microkernels." *Communications of the ACM*, September 1996.

LIED96b   Liedtke, J. "Microkernels Must and Can Be Small." *Proceedings, Fifth International Workshop on Object Orientation in Operating Systems*, October 1996.

LIND04   Lindsley, R. "What's New in the 2.6 Scheduler." *Linux Journal*, March 2004.

LIST93   Lister, A., and Eager, R. *Fundamentals of Operating Systems.* New York: Springer-Verlag, 1993.

LIU73   Liu, C., and Layland, J. "Scheduling Algorithms for Multiprogramming in a Hard Real-time Environment." Journal of the ACM, February 1973.

LIU00   Liu, J. *Real-Time Systems.* Upper Saddle River, NJ: Prentice Hall, 2000.

LIVA90   Livadas, P. *File Structures: Theory and Practice.* Englewood Cliffs, NJ: Prentice Hall, 1990.

LOVE04a   Love, R. *Linux Kernel Development.* Indianapolis, IN: Sams Publishing, 2004.

LOVE04b   Love, R. "I/O Schedulers." *Linux Journal*, February 2004.

LYNC96   Lynch, N. *Distributed Algorithms.* San Francisco, CA: Morgan Kaufmann, 1996.

MADS93   Madsen, J. "World Record in Password Checking." *USENET, comp.security.misc newsgroup*, August 18, 1993.

MAEK87   Maekawa, M.; Oldehoeft, A.; and Oldehoeft, R. *Operating Systems: Advanced Concepts.* Menlo Park, CA: Benjamin Cummings, 1987.

MAJU88   Majumdar, S.; Eager, D.; and Bunt, R. "Scheduling in Multiprogrammed Parallel Systems." *Proceedings, Conference on Measurement and Modeling of Computer Systems*, May 1988.

MART88   Martin, J. *Principles of Data Communication.* Englewood Cliffs, NJ: Prentice Hall, 1988.

MASS97   Massiglia, P. (editor). *The RAID Book: A Storage System Technology Handbook.* St. Peter, MN: The Raid Advisory Board, 1997.

MAUR01   Mauro, J., and McDougall, R. *Solaris Internals: Core Kernel Architecture.* Palo Alto, CA: Sun Microsystems Press, 2001.

MCHU00   McHugh, J.; Christie, A.; and Allen, J. "The Role of Intrusion Detection Systems." *IEEE Software*, September/October 2000.

MCKU96   McKusick, M.; Bostic, K.; Karels, M.; and Quartermain, J. *The Design and Implementation of the 4.4BSD UNIX Operating System.* Reading, MA: Addison-Wesley, 1996.

MEE96a   Mee, C., and Daniel, E. eds. *Magnetic Recording Technology.* New York: McGraw-Hill, 1996.

MEE96b   Mee, C., and Daniel, E. eds. *Magnetic Storage Handbook.* New York: McGraw-Hill, 1996.

MESS96   Messer, A., and Wilkinson, T. "Components for Operating System Design." *Proceedings, Fifth International Workshop on Object Orientation in Operating Systems*, October 1996.

MILE92   Milenkovic, M. *Operating Systems: Concepts and Design.* New York: McGraw-Hill, 1992.

MILO00   Milojicic, D.; Douglis, F.; Paindaveine, Y.; Wheeler, R.; and Zhou, S. "Process Migration." *ACM Computing Surveys*, September 2000.

MORG92   Morgan, K. "The RTOS Difference." *Byte*, August 1992.

MS96   Microsoft Corp. *Microsoft Windows NT Workstation Resource Kit.* Redmond, WA: Microsoft Press, 1996.

NACH97   Nachenberg, C. "Computer Virus-Antivirus Coevolution." *Communications of the ACM*, January 1997.

NEHM75   Nehmer, J. "Dispatcher Primitives for the Construction of Operating System Kernels." *Acta Informatica*, vol 5, 1975.

NELS88   Nelson, M.; Welch, B.; and Ousterhout, J. "Caching in the Sprite Network File System." *ACM Transactions on Computer Systems*, February 1988.

NELS91	Nelson, G. *Systems Programming with Modula-3.* Englewood Cliffs, NJ: Prentice Hall, 1991.
NG98	Ng, S. "Advances in Disk Technology: Performance Issues." *Computer*, May 1989.
NUTT94	Nuttal, M. "A Brief Survey of Systems Providing Process or Object Migration Facilities." *Operating Systems Review*, October 1994.
NUTT04	Nutt, G. *Operating System.* Reading, MA: Addison-Wesley, 2004.
OUST85	Ousterhout, J., et al. "A Trace-Drive Analysis of the UNIX 4.2 BSD File System." *Proceedings, Tenth ACM Symposium on Operating System Principles*, 1985.
OUST88	Ousterhout, J., et al. "The Sprite Network Operating System." *Computer,* February 1988.
PAI00	Pai, V.; Druschel, P.; and Zwaenepoel, W. "IO-Lite: A Unified I/O Buffering and Caching System." *ACM Transactions on Computer Systems*, February 2000.
PANW88	Panwar, S.; Towsley, D.; and Wolf, J. "Optimal Scheduling Policies for a Class of Queues with Customer Deadlines in the Beginning of Service." *Journal of the ACM*, October 1988.
PATT82	Patterson, D., and Sequin, C. "A VLSI RISC." *Computer*, September 1982.
PATT85	Patterson, D. "Reduced Instruction Set Computers." *Communications of the ACM*, January 1985.
PATT88	Patterson, D.; Gibson, G.; and Katz, R. "A Case for Redundant Arrays of Inexpensive Disks (RAID)." *Proceedings, ACM SIGMOD Conference of Management of Data*, June 1988.
PATT98	Patterson, D., and Hennessy, J. *Computer Organization and Design: The Hardware/Software Interface.* San Mateo, CA: Morgan Kaufmann, 1998.
PEIP03	Pieprzyk, J.; Hardjono, T.; and Seberry, J. *Fundamentals of Computer Security.* New York: Springer, 2003.
PERR03	Perrine, T. "The End of crypt() Passwords . . . Please?" *;login*, December 2003.
PETE77	Peterson, J., and Norman, T. "Buddy Systems." *Communications of the ACM*, June 1977.
PETE81	Peterson, G. "Myths About the Mutual Exclusion Problem." *Information Processing Letters*, June 1981.
PFLE97	Pfleeger, C. *Security in Computing.* Upper Saddle River, NJ: Prentice Hall PTR, 1997.
PINK89	Pinkert, J., and Wear, L. *Operating Systems: Concepts, Policies, and Mechanisms.* Englewood Cliffs, NJ: Prentice Hall, 1989.
PIZZ89	Pizzarello, A. "Memory Management for a Large Operating System." *Proceedings, International Conference on Measurement and Modeling of Computer Systems*, May 1989.
POPE85	Popek, G., and Walker, B. *The LOCUS Distributed System Architecture*, Cambridge, MA: MIT Press, 1985.
PORR92	Porras, P. *STAT: A State Transition Analysis Tool for Intrusion Detection.* Master's Thesis, University of California at Santa Barbara, July 1992.
PRAM84	Pramanik, S., and Weinberg, B. "The Implementation Kit with Monitors," *SIGPLAN Notices*, Number 9, 1984.
PRZY88	Przybylski, S.; Horowitz, M.; and Hennessy, J. "Performance Trade-offs in Cache Design." *Proceedings, Fifteenth Annual International Symposium on Computer Architecture*, June 1988.
RAMA94	Ramamritham, K., and Stankovic, J. "Scheduling Algorithms and Operating Systems Support for Real-Time Systems." *Proceedings of the IEEE*, January 1994.
RASH88	Rashid, R., et al. "Machine-Independent Virtual Memory Management for Paged Uniprocessor and Multiprocessor Architectures." *IEEE Transactions on Computers*, August 1988.
RAYN86	Raynal, M. *Algorithms for Mutual Exclusion.* Cambridge, MA: MIT Press, 1986.

RAYN88   Raynal, M. *Distributed Algorithms and Protocols.* New York: Wiley, 1988.

RAYN90   Raynal, M., and Helary, J. *Synchronization and Control of Distributed Systems and Programs.* New York: Wiley, 1990.

RICA81   Ricart, G., and Agrawala, A. "An Optimal Algorithm for Mutual Exclusion in Computer Networks." *Communications of the ACM*, January 1981 (Corrigendum in *Communications of the ACM*, September 1981).

RICA83   Ricart, G., and Agrawala, A. "Author's Response to 'On Mutual Exclusion in Computer Networks' by Carvalho and Roucairol." *Communications of the ACM*, February 1983.

RIDG97   Ridge, D., et al. "Beowulf: Harnessing the Power of Parallelism in a Pile-of-PCs." *Proceedings, IEEE Aerospace*, 1997.

RITC74   Ritchie, D., and Thompson, K. "The UNIX Time-Sharing System." *Communications of the ACM*, July 1974.

RITC78   Ritchie, D. "UNIX Time-Sharing System: A Retrospective." *The Bell System Technical Journal*, July–August 1978.

ROBI90   Robinson, J., and Devarakonda, M. "Data Cache Management Using Frequency-Based Replacement." *Proceedings, Conference on Measurement and Modeling of Computer Systems*, May 1990.

RODR02   Rodriguez, A., et al. *TCP/IP Tutorial and Technical Overview.* Upper Saddle River: NJ: Prentice Hall, 2002.

ROSC03   Rosch, W. *The Winn L. Rosch Hardware Bible.* Indianapolis, IN: Sams, 2003.

ROSE78   Rosenkrantz, D.; Stearns, R.; and Lewis, P. "System Level Concurrency Control in Distributed Database Systems." *ACM Transactions on Database Systems*, June 1978.

RUBI97   Rubini, A. "The Virtual File System in Linux." *Linux Journal*, May 1997.

RUDO90   Rudolph, B. "Self-Assessment Procedure XXI: Concurrency." *Communications of the ACM*, May 1990.

SAND94   Sandhu, R, and Samarati, P. "Access Control: Principles and Practice." *IEEE Communications*, September 1994.

SATY81   Satyanarayanan, M. and Bhandarkar, D. "Design Trade-Offs in VAX-11 Translation Buffer Organization." *Computer*, December 1981.

SAUE81   Sauer, C, and Chandy, K. *Computer Systems Performance Modeling.* Englewood Cliffs, NJ: Prentice Hall, 1981.

SCHA62   Schay, G., and Spruth, W. "Analysis of a File Addressing Method." *Communications of the ACM*, August 1962.

SCHM97   Schmidt, D. "Distributed Object Computing." *IEEE Communications Magazine*, February 1997.

SCHN96   Schneier, B. *Applied Cryptography.* New York: Wiley, 1996.

SCHN99   Schneier, B. "The Trojan Horse Race." *Communications of the ACM*, September 1999.

SCHW96   Schwaderer, W., and Wilson, A. *Understanding I/O Subsystems.* Milpitas, CA: Adaptec Press, 1996.

SELT90   Seltzer, M.; Chen, P.; and Ousterhout, J. "Disk Scheduling Revisited." *Proceedings, USENIX Winter Technical Conference*, January 1990.

SEVC96   Sevcik, P. "Designing a High-Performance Web Site." *Business Communications Review*, March 1996.

SHA90   Sha, L.; Rajkumar, R.; and Lehoczky, J. "Priority Inheritance Protocols: An Approach to Real-Time Synchronization." *IEEE Transactions on Computers*, September 1990.

SHA91   Sha, L.; Klein, M.; and Goodenough, J. "Rate Monotonic Analysis for Real-Time Systems." in [TILB91].

SHA94   Sha, L.; Rajkumar, R.; and Sathaye, S. "Generalized Rate-Monotonic Scheduling Theory: A Framework for Developing Real-Time Systems." *Proceedings of the IEEE*, January 1994.

SHEN02   Shene, C. "Multithreaded Programming Can Strengthen an Operating Systems Course." *Computer Science Education Journal*, December 2002.

SHIV92   Shivaratri, N.; Krueger, P.; and Singhal, M. "Load Distributing for Locally Distributed Systems." *Computer*, December 1992.

SHNE84   Shneiderman, B. "Response Time and Display Rate in Human Performance with Computers." *ACM Computing Surveys*, September 1984.

SHOR75   Shore, J. "On the External Storage Fragmentation Produced by First-Fit and Best-Fit Allocation Strategies." *Communications of the ACM*, August, 1975.

SHUB03   Shub, C. "A Unified Treatment of Deadlock." *Journal of Computing in Small Colleges*, October 2003. Available through the ACM digital library.

SILB98   Silberschatz, A., and Galvin, P. *Operating System Concepts.* Reading, MA: Addison-Wesley, 1998.

SILB04   Silberschatz, A.; Galvin, P.; and Gagne, G. *Operating System Concepts with Java.* Reading, MA: Addison-Wesley, 2004.

SING94a   Singhal, M., and Shivaratri, N. *Advanced Concepts in Operating Systems.* New York: McGraw-Hill, 1994.

SING94b   Singhal, M. "Deadlock Detection in Distributed Systems." In [CASA94].

SINH97   Sinha, P. *Distributed Operating Systems.* Piscataway, NJ: IEEE Press, 1997.

SMIT82   Smith, A. "Cache Memories." *ACM Computing Surveys*, September 1982.

SMIT83   Smith, D. "Faster Is Better: A Business Case for Subsecond Response Time." *Computerworld*, April 18, 1983.

SMIT85   Smith, A. "Disk Cache—Miss Ratio Analysis and Design Considerations." *ACM Transactions on Computer Systems*, August 1985.

SMIT88   Smith, J. "A Survey of Process Migration Mechanisms." *Operating Systems Review*, July 1988.

SMIT89   Smith, J. "Implementing Remote *fork()* with Checkpoint/restart." *Newsletter of the IEEE Computer Society Technical Committee on Operating Systems,* Winter 1989.

SOLO00   Solomon, D. *Inside Microsoft Windows 2000.* Redmond, WA: Microsoft Press, 2000.

SPAF92   Spafford, E. "Observing Reusable Password Choices." *Proceedings, UNIX Security Symposium III*, September 1992.

STAL03a   Stallings, W. *Computer Organization and Architecture, 6th ed.* Upper Saddle River, NJ: Prentice Hall, 2003.

STAL03b   Stallings, W. *Cryptography and Network Security: Principles and Practice, Third Edition.* Upper Saddle River, NJ: Prentice Hall, 2003.

STAL04   Stallings, W. *Computer Networking with Internet Protocols and Technology.* Upper Saddle River: NJ: Prentice Hall, 2004.

STAN89   Stankovic, J., and Ramamrithan, K. "The Spring Kernel: A New Paradigm for Real-Time Operating Systems." *Operating Systems Review*, July 1989.

STAN93   Stankovic, J., and Ramamritham, K., eds. *Advances in Real-Time Systems.* Los Alamitos, CA: IEEE Computer Society Press, 1993.

STEP93   Stephenson, P. "Preventive Medicine." *LAN Magazine*, November 1993.

STON93   Stone, H. *High-Performance Computer Architecture.* Reading, MA: Addison-Wesley, 1993.

STRE83   Strecker, W. "Transient Behavior of Cache Memories." *ACM Transactions on Computer Systems,* November 1983.

STRO88   Stroustrup, B. "What is Object-Oriented Programming?" *IEEE Software*, May 1988.

SNYD93   Snyder, A. "The Essence of Objects: Concepts and Terms." *IEEE Software*, January 1993.

SUZU82   Suzuki, I., and Kasami, T. "An Optimality Theory for Mutual Exclusion Algorithms in Computer Networks." *Proceedings of the Third International Conference on Distributed Computing Systems,* October 1982.

TALL92   Talluri, M.; Kong, S.; Hill, M.; and Patterson, D. "Tradeoffs in Supporting Two Page Sizes." *Proceedings of the 19th Annual International Symposium on Computer Architecture*, May 1992.

TAMI83   Tamir, Y., and Sequin, C. "Strategies for Managing the Register File in RISC." *IEEE Transactions on Computers*, November 1983.

TANE78   Tanenbaum, A. "Implications of Structured Programming for Machine Architecture." *Communications of the ACM*, March 1978.

TANE97   Tanenbaum, A., and Woodhull, A. *Operating Systems: Design and Implementation.* Upper Saddle River, NJ: Prentice Hall, 1997.

TANE01   Tanenbaum, A. *Modern Operating Systems.* Upper Saddle River, NJ: Prentice Hall, 2001.

TAIV96   Taivalsaari, A. "On the Nature of Inheritance." *ACM Computing Surveys*, September 1996.

TEL01   Tel, G. *Introduction to Distributed Algorithms.* Cambridge: Cambridge University Press, 2001.

THAD81   Thadhani, A. "Interactive User Productivity." *IBM Systems Journal*, No. 1, 1981.

THOM84   Thompson, K. "Reflections on Trusting Trust (Deliberate Software Bugs)." *Communications of the ACM*, August 1984.

TILB91   Tilborg, A., and Koob, G.. eds. *Foundations of Real-Time Computing: Scheduling and Resource Management.* Boston: Kluwer Academic Publishers, 1991.

TIME90   Time, Inc. *Computer Security, Understanding Computers Series.* Alexandria, VA: Time-Life Books, 1990.

TIME02   TimeSys Corp. "Priority Inversion: Why You Care and What to Do About It" *TimeSys White Paper*, 2002. http://www.techonline.com/community/ed_resource/tech_paper/21779

TUCK89   Tucker, A., and Gupta, A. "Process Control and Scheduling Issues for Multiprogrammed Shared-Memory Multiprocessors." *Proceedings, Twelfth ACM Symposium on Operating Systems Principles*, December 1989.

VAHA96   Vahalia, U. *UNIX Internals: The New Frontiers.* Upper Saddle River, NJ: Prentice Hall, 1996.

VINO97   Vinoski, S. "CORBA: Integrating Diverse Applications Within Distributed Heterogeneous Environments." *IEEE Communications Magazine*, February 1997.

WALK89   Walker, B., and Mathews, R. "Process Migration in AIX's Transparent Computing Facility." *Newsletter of the IEEE Computer Society Technical Committee on Operating Systems*, Winter 1989.

WARD80   Ward, S. "TRIX: A Network-Oriented Operating System." *Proceedings, COMP/CON '80*, 1980.

WARR91   Warren, C. "Rate Monotonic Scheduling." *IEEE Micro*, June 1991.

WAYN94a   Wayner, P. "Small Kernels Hit it Big." *Byte*, January 1994.

WAYN94b   Wayner, P. "Objects on the March." *Byte*, January 1994.

WEIZ81   Weizer, N. "A History of Operating Systems." *Datamation*, January 1981.

WEND89   Wendorf, J.; Wendorf, R.; and Tokuda, H. "Scheduling Operating System Processing on Small-Scale Microprocessors." *Proceedings, 22nd Annual Hawaii International Conference on System Science*, January 1989.

WHIT99   White, S.; Swimmer, M.; Pring, E.; Arnold, B.; Chess, D.; and Morar, J. *Anatomy of a Commercial-Grade Immune System.* IBM White Paper, 1999. www.research.ibm.com/antivirus/SciPapers.htm.

WIED87   Wiederhold, G. *File Organization for Database Design.* New York: McGraw-Hill, 1987.

WOOD86   Woodside, C. "Controllability of Computer Performance Tradeoffs Obtained Using Controlled-Share Queue Schedulers." *IEEE Transactions on Software Engineering*, October 1986

WOOD89   Woodbury, P. et al. "Shared Memory Multiprocessors: The Right Approach to Parallel Processing." *Proceedings, COMPCON Spring '89*, March 1989.

WORT94   Worthington, B.; Ganger, G.; and Patt, Y. "Scheduling Algorithms for Modern Disk Drives." *ACM SiGMETRICS*, May 1994.

WRIG95   Wright, G., and Stevens, W. *TCP/IP Illustrated, Volume 2: The Implementation.* Reading, MA: Addison-Wesley, 1995.

YOUN87   Young, M., et. al. "The Duality of Memory and Communication in the Implementation of a Multiprocessor Operating System." *Proceedings of the Eleventh ACM Symposium on Operating Systems Principles*, December 1987.

ZAHO90   Zahorjan, J., and McCann, C. "Processor Scheduling in Shared Memory Multiprocessors." *Proceedings, Conference on Measurement and Modeling of Computer Systems*, May 1990.

ZAJC93   Zajcew, R., et al. "An OSF/1 UNIX for Massively Parallel Multicomputers." *Proceedings, Winter USENIX Conference*, January 1993.

ZEAD97   Zeadally, S. "An Evaluation of the Real-Time Performance of SVR4.0 and SVR4.2." *Operating Systems Review*, January 1977.

INDEX